FOOTB...

What do Ke... ..., ..., and Eric
Dickerson have in common?

ILLEGAL PROCEDURES

Which two players did Commissioner Peter
Rozelle suspend for the entirety of 1963 for
gambling on league games?

WORLD OF THEIR OWN

Who scored the first regular season touchdown
in the WLAF?

**Emphasizing the unusual and the significant—
never the commonly known—this tough quiz
book will keep both the trivia whiz and football fanatic on the defensive. But this is your
chance to take the challenge and score yourself
in a full-of-fun competition that's guaranteed
to make every football fan stand up and cheer!**

PLUS: PAYDIRT (The answers!)

THE ALL-NEW ULTIMATE FOOTBALL QUIZ BOOK

Warren Etheredge

A SIGNET BOOK

SIGNET
Published by the Penguin Group
Penguin Books USA Inc., 375 Hudson Street,
New York, New York 10014, U.S.A.
Penguin Books Ltd, 27 Wrights Lane,
London W8 5TZ, England
Penguin Books Australia Ltd, Ringwood,
Victoria, Australia
Penguin Books Canada Ltd, 10 Alcorn Avenue,
Toronto, Ontario, Canada M4V 3B2
Penguin Books (N.Z.) Ltd, 182–190 Wairau Road,
Auckland 10, New Zealand

Penguin Books Ltd, Registered Offices:
Harmondsworth, Middlesex, England

First published by Signet, an imprint of Dutton Signet,
a division of Penguin Books USA Inc.

First Printing, August, 1993
10 9 8 7 6 5 4 3

 REGISTERED TRADEMARK—MARCA REGISTRADA

Printed in the United States of America

Of fathers, I've forgotten one
and been fortunate to find another.
Thank you, Gerry.

ACKNOWLEDGMENTS

To the good people of REM Studio: my gratitude.
To Jennifer: my head, my heart, my hope,
and . . . oh, my thanks.

CONTENTS

THE COIN TOSS

Few people truly appreciate football. Fewer still, understand my love for the game. "You like football, Warren? You *watch* football?" Apparently, they are deceived by my appearance. I have no beer belly, nor bulging biceps. But I do love the game. To the layperson, it may appear to be a slap-dash, free-for-all wrestlefest, with the snap of the ball and the blow of the whistle merely marking endless bouts of legalized mayhem. But for those who have played and/or studied the game, it is obvious that football is an incredibly complex sport that demands an almost ascetic devotion to fully comprehend.

This book is for those who have realized the beauty of the game and have immersed themselves in every facet of it. The quizzes and puzzles are designed to challenge even diehard fans. The answers include additional information so that those who claim to know it all, may someday be right.

You have won the coin toss and elected to receive. Good luck!

THE ONE AND ONLY'S

For more than 20 years, football announcers repeatedly reminded their viewers during Dallas games that, "Tom Landry is the only coach the Cowboys have ever had." The one and only.

In 1989, all of that changed. Maverick businessman Jerry Jones purchased America's franchise and brought in his ol' Razorback buddy Jimmy Johnson to replace the legend and lead the squad. The transition was unceremonious and Landry's distinction was lost. Landry will always be remembered, but he is no longer the one and only.

Below, 25 questions pertaining to players, coaches, and teams that can brag about their unique status.

1. Which is the one and only team to go undefeated through both the regular and post-seasons?

2. Who is the only head coach of Hispanic descent in the National Football League?

3. Only one player has been selected as the Most Valuable Player of the Super Bowl on three separate occasions. Who has successfully "mined" three MVP trophies and four Super Bowl rings?

4. Only once in the 56-year history of the NFL draft, has a wide receiver not been selected in the first round. In which year were the wideouts "overthrown"?

5. Which is the one and only team never to have defeated either the Oakland or Los Angeles Raiders?

6. In only one Super Bowl has a player from the losing team been selected as the game's MVP. Who was it?

7. Who is the only graduate of the University of Puget Sound to play in the NFL?

8. Which is the only team ever to field both the league's leaders in rushing and receiving yardage in the same season?

9. The Washington Redskins, despite their many gloried seasons and countless glory boys, have retired only one jersey number in the history of their franchise. What is the number and who wore it?

10. In 1991, running back Barry Sanders played in every regular-season game but one. With only

one Lion missing from their lair, how did Detroit fare?

11. Only one player has scored more than 2,000 points in his career? Who is he?

12. Only one head coach has directed his team to Super Bowl victories with three different starting quarterbacks. Who is the sideline commander and who were his winning field generals?

13. Who is the only Kansas City Chief to ever lead the league in rushing?

14. Which was the only team to not advance to the playoffs during the 1980s?

15. Only one head coach has led three different teams to divisional titles. Name the coach and his winning trifecta.

16. In only one Super Bowl have *two* players been cited for the game's MVP honors. Name the recipients and number the Super Bowl.

17. Which was the only team not involved in a single trade during the 1987 campaign?

18. Only once has a Heisman Trophy winner been drafted by that year's Lombardi Trophy winners. Identify the collegiate all-star and the Super Bowl champions who drafted him.

19. Who is the only person to have been named Coach of the Year in the World Football League, the National Football League, the United States Football League, and the NCAA's Southwest Conference? (Hint: The leagues have been ordered in accordance with this coach's résumé.)

20. Since moving from Cleveland in 1946, the Rams have won one, and only one, NFL championship. Which team did Los Angeles defeat for the title and in what year did they do so?

21. Clem Daniels retired as the AFL's career-rushing leader, despite an inauspicious beginning with the Dallas Texans. In 1960, his rookie season, Daniels carried the ball once, only once. How many yards did he gain?

22. Only once has an NFL game that has gone into overtime been decided by a safety. Which two teams were involved and who scored the decisive 2-pointer?

23. Who is the only professional football player to have died in action during the Vietnam Conflict?

24. On the day of and the days prior to the 1992 NFL Draft, only one trade was completed that included future considerations. Which two teams and which player were involved in the deal?

25. In his rookie season in the NFL, Jimmy Johnson coached Dallas to only one victory during their excruciating 1989 campaign. Which was the only team to succumb to the Cowboys and what was the game's final score?

NICKNAMES

There have been Bullets (Bob Hayes, Bill Dudley) and Sugar Bears (Ray Hamilton, Willie Young) and a bevy of Bubbas (Baker, Smith, McDowell, etc.). All were tagged affectionately, but without much flair. For simply by its utterance, the *artful* nickname evokes the image and energy of a specific individual. Say "Crazy Legs" and Elroy Hirsch's awkward stride is immediately recalled. The mere mention of "The Hammer" summons Fred Williamson and his nail-biting tackles to mind. These nicknames are as unique as the players who inspired their colorful epithets. Joe Namath will always be "Broadway"-bound, Ed Jones, forever "Too Tall," and Joe Greene, "Mean."

Listed below, 25 players, each followed by a multiple of monikers. Match each with his appropriate alias.

1. CRAIG HEYWARD
   a. The Mallet   b. Musclehead
   c. Ironhead   d. Warhead

2. JEFF HOSTETLER
   a. Adam
   b. Hoss
   c. Little Joe
   d. Cartwright

3. "NEON" DEION SANDERS
   a. Prime Time
   b. Grandstand
   c. Box Office
   d. White Shoes

4. MICHAEL IRVIN
   a. The Rainmaker
   b. Playboy
   c. Flash
   d. The Playmaker

5. GARY CLARK, ART MONK, AND RICKY SANDERS
   a. The Hoglets
   b. The Good Hands People
   c. The Three Amigos
   d. The Posse

6. WILLIE ANDERSON
   a. Flipper
   b. Shamu
   c. Sherwood
   d. Robin Hood

7. CHRISTIAN OKOYE
   a. The Ethiopian Eclipse
   b. The Nigerian Nightmare
   c. The Cheboygan Commando
   d. The Nuclear Namibian

8. REGGIE WHITE
   a. The Pass-rushing Preacher
   b. The Sensei of Pain
   c. The Minister of Defense
   d. Rabbi Red-dog

9. DESMOND HOWARD
   a. Magic   b. Flash
   c. The Rocket   d. The Sprocket

10. RAGHIB ISMAIL
    a. The Turk   b. Call Me
    c. The Canuck   d. The Rocket

11. JAMES GEATHERS
    a. Go-To   b. Jumpy
    c. Fair Weather d. Rush

12. MARK JACKSON, VANCE JOHNSON,
    AND RICKY NATTIEL
    a. The Posse   b. The Fun Bunch
    c. The Three Amigos d. The Fly Boys

13. RED GRANGE
    a. The Galloping   b. Casper
       Ghost
    c. The Gipper   d. Dust Bowl

14. JOHN RIGGINS
    a. Hoglet   b. Jerry-rigged
    c. Pigboy   d. The Diesel

15. FRED BILETNIKOFF
    a. Blinky   b. Grumpy
    c. Specs   d. Carrots

16. HENRY WILLIAMS
    a. Stripe   b. Gizmo
    c. Gremlin   d. Beetle

17. TOM TRACY
    a. Tom Thumb   b. Tom Cat
    c. Tom the Bomb   d. Tom Terrific

18. JIM HUNT
    a. Volcano   b. Earthquake
    c. Buffalo   d. Disaster

19. CHARLES PHILYAW
    a. Godzilla   b. Jaws
    c. King Kong   d. Frankenstein

20. TOM SULLIVAN
    a. Silky   b. Smooth
    c. Moves   d. Shakes

21. CLARENCE MANDERS
    a. Pit Bull   b. Pug
    c. Boxer   d. Mutt

22. DICK BASS
    a. The String   b. The Striped
    c. The Spark Plug d. The Scooter

23. ANDY NELSON
    a. Bones   b. Scottie
    c. Doc   d. Stretcher

24. FRED EVANS
    a. Astaire   b. Rogers
    c. Dippy   d. Dancer

25. BART BUETOW
   a. The Nutty
      Professor
   c. Teach

   b. The Absentminded
      Professor
   d. The Mad Scientist

MUDDLE IN THE HUDDLE #1 (SAFETIES)

This is the first of three quizzes in which the names of 10 prominent or promising players have been encoded. Each letter below corresponds to another, for example, *w* might represent *e* and *j* might represent *b*, and so on.

As coach, it is your job to reassign the x's and o's so that the true identities of these players may be revealed. The years and teams for which each has played are included to assist you.

As there are no ladies present, safeties first!

1. YDMXM BDVBDMK
   Denver Broncos (1989–   )

2. HMEEQM HRBFMY
   Detroit Lions (1988–   )

3. CBKZ NBKKQMK
   Chicago Bears (1990–   )

4. FMKTE NSMKKP
   Kansas City Chiefs (1981–   )

5. FBXQF AORNSMK
   Cincinnati Bengals (1986–   )

6. HKMDD CBLQM
   New Orleans Saints (1985–   )

7. DQC CnFTEBRF
   St. Louis Cardinals (1987), Phoenix Cardinals
   (1988–   )

8. MKQZ CnCQRRBE
   New York Jets (1988–   )

9. RTOQY TRQXMK
   Miami Dolphins (1989–   )

10. BEFKM VBDMKY
    Philadelphia Eagles (1984–   )

FIRST AND TEN

This is the first of four chapters in which clues are provided to identify 25 players, past or present, memorable or forgettable. The clues become progressively more obscure as the chapters become progressively more difficult ("First and Ten"—the easiest, "Fourth and Long"—the toughest.) Identify all the players correctly, Coach, and your team will pick up the first down. Good luck!

1. This former Bear back broke many records, perhaps the "sweetest" being that for career rushing yardage.

2. After quarterbacks Joe Montana and Steve Young were felled by injuries in 1991, this no-name third-stringer stepped up to lead the 49ers to a 10–6 season.

3. The Indianapolis Colts have had little to brag about during the past few seasons, except for the perseverance and promise shown by their "franchise" quarterback.

4. This Buffalo Bill was the league leader in combined yardage from the line of scrimmage for the second straight season in 1991.

5. This Cleveland Brown defensive tackle is the brother of Chicago's "Fridge."

6. This defensive tackle was the first player chosen in the 1991 NFL draft. The University of Miami graduate was the recipient of the 1990 Outland Trophy.

7. This Packer wide receiver is never "dull." In 1989, he led the league with 90 receptions (for 1,423 yards).

8. This running back has not achieved the success the Jets had hoped for when they selected him with the second pick overall in the 1990 draft. Some speculate that his slow start and propensity for injury are a result of an improper recovery from a college ailment.

9. Prior to the 1992 season, New Orleans matched an offer sheet extended by Detroit to retain the services of their free-agent linebacker. The contract that kept this Saint sacker in the bag also made him the highest-paid defensive player in the NFL.

10. A Detroit Lion from 1980–1991, he was one of the league's most accurate kickers.

11. This wide receiver has played for the Seattle Seahawks since 1988, the same year his younger brother, a safety, signed with the Detroit Lions.

12. In 1992, the Cincinnati Bengals drafted this quarterback from Houston as the heir apparent to lefty Boomer Esiason.

13. This Houston Oiler wide-out led the league with 100 receptions in 1991.

14. Many would suggest that the Buccaneers blundered, rather than plundered, when they selected this player with the first pick overall in the 1987 draft.

15. This New York Giant was the oldest active running back playing in the NFL during the 1992 season.

16. The New England Patriots selected this running back in the first round of the 1991 NFL draft. The Arizona State graduate ranked fourth in the AFC in rushing yardage in his rookie season.

17. New England's other first-round selection of 1991 was also an impact player. This USC graduate, chosen with the eleventh pick overall, assumed a starting tackle position immediately with the Patriots.

18. In 1991, this kicker outscored the entire Indianapolis Colts' squad.

19. This Pittsburgh Steeler cornerback/kick returner was once a world-class hurdler.

20. This Buffalo Bill defensive end brags that Lawrence Taylor is no longer the premier defensive player in the NFL, because he is.

21. The Falcons used the first pick overall in the 1988 draft to select this linebacker from Auburn University. Unfortunately for Atlanta, he never developed into the Gritz-blitzer they had expected. After efforts to convert him into a defensive end, a defensive tackle, and even a tight end had failed, Jerry Glanville gave up and left him unprotected as a Plan B free agent following the 1991 season. Subsequently, he was signed by the Raiders.

22. Despite leading the league in completion percentage in 1991, this Seattle quarterback was designated a Plan B free agent by the Seahawks in the off-season. Thereafter, he signed with the Kansas City Chiefs.

23. This San Diego Charger was the first defensive lineman selected in the 1989 NFL draft. That year, he was the eighth player chosen overall.

24. This former Minnesota Viking safety has three brothers—Jim, Keith, and Ross—who have also played professionally.

25. Despite challenges from Bo Jackson and Roger Craig and Eric Dickerson, he remains the most consistent star in the Los Angeles Raiders' backfield.

SCRIMMAGED LINES #1 (DEFENSIVE LINEMEN)

A teammate nicknamed defensive tackle Randy White the "Manster." The alias was a reference to the former Cowboy's presumed hybrid nature: half man, half monster. White accepted the moniker. After all, defensive linemen frequently are called far worse. There is a common misconception among the public and even their pigskin peers, that members of the front four—perhaps due to their abnormal size and strength—are at least, part beast. With a few exceptions, this is rarely the case.

Below are the names of 27 of the NFL's most gentle "mansters." Kindly return each to his proper position in the blank crossword diagram on the facing page.

3-LETTER NAMES
Jeff ALM

Blenda GAY
Art MAY
Mel TOM

4-LETTER NAMES
Dave BUTZ
Mike GANN
Bill MAAS
Ken SIMS

5-LETTER NAMES
Tony McGEE
Mike PITTS
Leon SEALS
Garin VERIS
Joe YOUNG

6-LETTER NAMES
Lyle ALZADO
Doug MARTIN
Tim NEWTON
Tracy ROCKER
Daniel STUBBS

7-LETTER NAMES
Fred SMERLAS
Diron TALBERT

8-LETTER NAMES
Alphonso CARREKER
Bob LURTSEMA
Russell MARYLAND
Gerald ROBINSON

9-LETTER NAMES
Trace ARMSTRONG
Gary BALDINGER

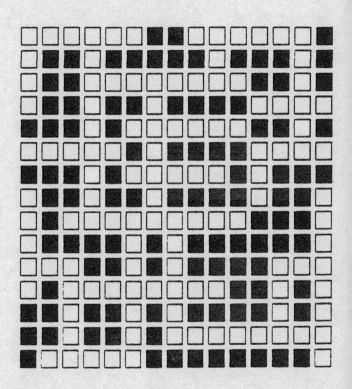

NAME FIND #1
(QUARTERBACKS)

Find the last names of the 63 quarterbacks hidden in the accompanying puzzle. (Yes, they run diagonally, too.)

Terry **BAKER**	Bobby **HEBERT**
Pete **BEATHARD**	King **HILL**
Bob **BERRY**	Don **HORN**
Steve **BONO**	John **HUARTE**
Chris **CHANDLER**	George **IZO**
Len **DAWSON**	Bert **JONES**
Benjy **DIAL**	Jeff **KEMP**
Hunter **ENIS**	Tommy **KRAMER**
Jim **EVERETT**	Dave **KRIEG**
Tom **GREENE**	Gary **LANE**
Bob **GRIESE**	Bob **LEE**
Steve **GROGAN**	Chuck **LONG**
Pat **HADEN**	Clint **LONGLEY**
John **HADL**	Dean **LOOK**
Galen **HALL**	Archie **MANNING**
James **HARRIS**	Dan **MARINO**

Dave **MAYS**
Jim **McMAHON**
Hugh **MILLEN**
Chris **MILLER**
George **MIRA**
Warren **MOON**
Earl **MORRALL**
Browning **NAGLE**
Joe **NAMATH**
Mike **NOTT**
Ken **O'BRIEN**
Mike **PAGEL**
Nick **PAPAC**
Rodney **PEETE**
Warren **RABB**
Mike **RAE**

Joe **REED**
Frank **REICH**
Timm **ROSENBACH**
Benny **RUSSELL**
Steve **SLOAN**
Butch **SONGIN**
Ken **STABLER**
Bart **STARR**
Rick **STROM**
Joe **THEISMANN**
Y. A. **TITTLE**
Johnny **UNITAS**
Billy **WADE**
Andre **WARE**
Marc **WILSON**

```
N A G L E D A W S O N I R A M
R U N E D A H A I P A P A C I
U E L T T I T R E L L I M H L
S B K R P I A E N I S A M A L
S L O A N B T L D A H O R N E
E Y G U B E L B K O O L N D N
L E A H T A M A N N I N G L E
L L L I H T A T A E O T S E E
A G L S E H Y S R G S T A R R
R N A L I A S D E E R E T B G
R O N L S R R I Z O B R I E R
O L E E M D R I M P M E K R O
M E N B A K R A M E R U H R G
R O S E N B A C H C I E R Y A
J N I G N O S O N O B R I E N
```

SCORECARD

"You can't tell the players without a scorecard!"

This enthusiastic reminder is chanted weekly by hundreds of vendors at the NFL's 14 host venues. The peanut brokers and souvenir salesmen hawk gameday programs, targeting the sport's uninitiated who need the occasional "nudge" as to which is the home team, as well as to who's wearing #12. But for those whose Sunday ritual includes either stadium-grazing or television-gazing, the program is unnecessary. The Cowboys' #12 will always be Roger the Dodger, the Jets' #12 will always be Broadway Joe, and so on.

Below, 100 players are ordered by the numbers with which their jerseys have been adorned. Following each, a few additional clues as to their identities: the position and the team(s) and the years for which they've played.

00. Center
    Oakland Raiders (1960–1974)

 1. Quarterback
    Edmonton—CFL (1978–1983), Houston Oilers
    (1984–   )

2. Punter
   Philadelphia Eagles (1984–1985), Minnesota Vikings (1986), Denver Broncos (1986–)

3. Kicker
   Kansas City Chiefs (1967–1979), Green Bay Packers (1980–1983), Minnesota Vikings (1984–1985)

4. Quarterback
   Chicago Bears (1987–)

5. Punter
   New York Giants (1985–)

6. Kicker
   Chicago Bears (1985–)

7. Kicker
   New Orleans Saints (1982–)

8. Quarterback
   Dallas Cowboys (1989–)

9. Quarterback
   Detroit Lions (1989–)

10. Kicker
    Miami Dolphins (1989–)

11. Quarterback
    Los Angeles Rams (1986–)

12. Quarterback
    Atlanta Falcons (1987–)

13. Quarterback
    Miami Dolphins (1983–)

14. Quarterback
    San Diego Chargers (1973–1987)

15. Quarterback
    St. Louis Cardinals (1981–1987), Phoenix
    Cardinals (1988–1989)

16. Quarterback
    San Francisco 49ers (1979–)

17. Quarterback
    Seattle Seahawks (1980–1991), Kansas City
    Chiefs (1992–)

18. Quarterback
    Chicago Bears (1985–1990), Green Bay Packers
    (1991), Cleveland Browns (1992–)

19. Quarterback
    Cleveland Browns (1985–)

20. Running Back
    Detroit Lions (1989–)

21. Cornerback
    Atlanta Falcons (1989–)

22. Defensive Back
    New York Jets (1988–   )

23. Running Back
    New Orleans Saints (1987–1988), Kansas City
    Chiefs (1990–   )

24. Running Back
    Detroit Lions (1967–1973)

25. Safety
    Houston Oilers (1989–   )

26. Cornerback/Kick Returner
    Pittsburgh Steelers (1987–   )

27. Safety
    Denver Broncos (1989–   )

28. Cornerback
    Washington Redskins (1983–   )

29. Cornerback
    Houston Oilers (1984–   )

30. Running Back/Kick Returner
    New York Giants (1989–   )

31. Running Back
    Green Bay Packers (1958–1966), New Orleans
    Saints (1967)

32. Fullback
    Cleveland Browns (1956–1965)

33. Safety
    Cincinnati Bengals (1986–)

34. Running Back
    Buffalo Bills (1988–)

35. Running Back
    Chicago Bears (1986–)

36. Safety
    Detroit Lions (1988–)

37. Cornerback
    Buffalo Bills (1987–)

38. Running Back
    Pittsburgh Steelers (1989–)

39. Running Back
    Los Angeles Rams (1988–)

40. Defensive Back
    Dallas Cowboys (1983–)

41. Running Back
    Philadelphia Eagles (1986–)

42. Running Back
    Cincinnati Bengals (1989–)

43. Running Back
    Washington Redskins (1969–1976)

44. Running Back
    New England Patriots (1988–   )

45. Cornerback
    New York Giants (1987–1988), Tampa Bay
    Buccaneers (1990–   )

46. Tight End
    New England Patriots (1989–   )

47. Safety
    Minnesota Vikings (1983–1991)

48. Cornerback
    St. Louis Cardinals (1983–1986), Los Angeles
    Raiders (1987–   )

49. Safety
    Denver Broncos (1981–   )

50. Linebacker
    Chicago Bears (1981–   )

51. Linebacker
    Denver Broncos (1991–   )

52. Linebacker
    New York Giants (1986–   )

53. Center
    Indianapolis Colts (1980–)

54. Linebacker
    Detroit Lions (1988–)

55. Linebacker
    Buffalo Bills (1987–)

56. Defensive End
    Minnesota Vikings (1985–)

57. Linebacker
    Pittsburgh Steelers (1982–1988), Minnesota
    Vikings (1989–)

58. Middle Linebacker
    Pittsburgh Steelers (1974–1984)

59. Linebacker
    New York Jets (1985–)

60. Guard/Tackle
    New York Giants (1988–)

61. Guard
    Miami Dolphins (1982–)

62. Tackle
    Pittsburgh Steelers (1980–)

63. Center
    Chicaog Bears (1981–)

64. Guard
Minnesota Vikings (1988–   )

65. Guard
Detroit Lions (1988–1991)

66. Middle Linebacker
Green Bay Packers (1958–1972)

67. Guard
Denver Broncos (1989–   )

68. Offensive Lineman
Washington Redskins (1981–1991)

69. Nose Tackle
Cincinnati Bengals (1983–   )

70. Tackle
Dallas Cowboys (1967–1979)

71. Defensive End
Washington Redskins (1983–   )

72. Defensive End
St. Louis Cardinals (1987), Phoenix Cardinals
(1988–   )

73. Guard
New England Patriots (1973–1985)

74. Tackle
Chicago Bears (1983–1991)

75. Tackle
Baltimore Colts (1983), Indianapolis Colts
(1984–   )

76. Guard
Los Angeles Raiders (1989–   )

77. Tackle
Green Bay Packers (1989–   )

78. Tackle
Miami Dolphins (1990–   )

79. Tackle
San Francisco 49ers (1953–1963)

80. Wide Receiver
Indianapolis Colts (1989), Atlanta Falcons
(1990–   )

81. Wide Receiver/Kick Returner
Los Angeles Raiders (1988–   )

82. Wide Receiver
San Francisco 49ers (1987–   )

83. Wide Receiver
Los Angeles Rams (1988–   )

84. Wide Receiver
Green Bay Packers (1988–   )

85. Linebacker
Boston Patriots (1962–1968), Miami Dolphins
(1969–1976)

86. Wide Receiver
   Phoenix Cardinals (1988–   )

87. Flanker/Offensive End
   Houston Oilers (1960–1966)

88. Wide Receiver
   New York Jets (1985–   )

89. Special Teams/Wide Receiver
   Houston Oilers (1985–1986), Buffalo Bills
   (1986–   )

90. Defensive End
   Kansas City Chiefs (1988–   )

91. Linebacker
   Los Angeles Rams (1985–   )

92. Defensive End
   Philadelphia Eagles (1985–   )

93. Nose Tackle
   Detroit Lions (1987–   )

94. Linebacker/Defensive End
   San Francisco 49ers (1986–1991), Dallas Cowboys (1992–   )

95. Nose Tackle
   San Francisco 49ers (1984–   )

96. Defensive Tackle
    Seattle Seahawks (1990–)

97. Defensive End
    New Orleans Saints (1990–)

98. Defensive End
    Phoenix Cardinals (1991–)

99. Defensive Tackle
    Philadelphia Eagles (1987–1991)

RUNNING MATES

A head coach selects his backfield pairing during the preseason; a political party elects its ticket tandem through the primary process. Throughout their respective campaigns, each will learn if they have chosen wisely. At first, the decision may not seem monumental, but should the President fall or the runner stumble, the "second-in-line" must be prepared to carry the ball, and not to fumble.

In the '70s, the mighty Miami Dolphins fielded three great runners: Larry Csonka, Jim Kiick, and Eugene "Mercury" Morris. Most teams are lucky to find just one. Listed below are the names of 20 superstar striders, past and present. Match them with their equally-abled running mates.

1. O. J. Simpson   a. Barry Wood

2. Red Grange   b. Brad Muster

3. William Andrews   c. Dan Reeves

4. Kevin Mack   d. Dalton Hilliard

5.	Chuck Muncie	e.	Jim Taylor
6.	Franco Harris	f.	Tom Rathman
7.	Christian Okoye	g.	Maurice Carthon
8.	Ottis Anderson	h.	Gerald Riggs
9.	Marion Butts	i.	Emerson Boozer
10.	Marcus Allen	j.	John L. Williams
11.	Craig Heyward	k.	Earnest Byner
12.	Johnny Johnson	l.	Bo Jackson
13.	Paul Hornung	m.	Bronco Nagurski
14.	Neal Anderson	n.	Stump Mitchell
15.	Ken Willard	o.	Rod Bernstine
16.	Roger Craig	p.	Jim Braxton
17.	Rodney Hampton	q.	Tony Galbreath
18.	Curt Warner	r.	John David Crow
19.	Don Perkins	s.	Anthony Thompson
20.	Matt Snell	t.	Rocky Bleier

MUDDLE IN THE HUDDLE #2 (TIGHT ENDS)

This is the second of three quizzes in which the names of 10 prominent or promising players have been encoded. Each letter below corresponds to another; for example, *e* might represent *v* and *a* might represent *c,* and so on.

As coach, it is your job to reassign the x's and o's so that the true identities of these players may be revealed. The years and teams for which each has played are included to assist you.

If you crack the code properly, there will be no loose ends, only tight ends.

1. QACR CILYYLI
   New Orleans Saints (1981–   )

2. CIBOL OAUWLX
   Cincinnati Bengals (1969–1976)

3. EBUXVY KLYYLR
   Chicago Bears (1967–1969), Buffalo Bills
   (1970–1971)

4. SLIILWW LKFBYKU
   Miami Dolphins (1988–   )

5. LIVO DILLY
   Pittsburgh Steelers (1990–   )

6. GLVXQ ZEOGUAY
   Philadelphia Eagles (1988–1991), Miami Dolphins (1992–   )

7. CILYX ZAYLU
   San Francisco 49ers (1987–   )

8. AHHVL YLPUAFL
   Cleveland Browns (1978–1990)

9. ZER YAMEOLG
   St. Louis Cardinals (1985–1987), Phoenix
   Cardinals (1988–1989), Dallas Cowboys (1990–   )

10. KAY PEILLY
    Washington Redskins (1979–1991)

SECOND AND EIGHT

A first down, off-tackle run by your fullback netted a mere 2-yard gain. Now, it is second down . . . 8 yards to go. Will you pass or keep it on the ground, Coach?

This is the second of four chapters in which clues are provided to identify 25 players, past or present, memorable or forgettable. Identify all the players correctly and you will pick up the first down.

1. Despite having missed what surely would have been the game-winning field goal in Super Bowl XXV, this Bill kicker was received as warmly by fans in Buffalo as he may have been by celebratory fans in New York following the game.

2. This defensive end holds the Chicago Bears' single-season record for quarterback traps.

3. This Detroit Lion's 25.8 yards per kickoff return led the league in 1991.

4. The Buccaneers did not make a selection in the first round of the 1992 draft because they had

traded their pick to the Indianapolis Colts for this quarterback. (Tampa Bay waived the infrequent starter and inconsequential backup on November 5, 1991.)

5. This Pittsburgh linebacker was named the team's Most Valuable Player for the 1991 season. The Steeler maintains his man-of-steel physique with biweekly tae kwon do classes and daily weight-room sessions.

6. This Raider running back was courageous/stupid enough to once claim that playing behind the Colts' offensive line "is like playing Russian roulette."

7. This offensive lineman was the Oilers' first-round draft choice in 1982. In his 10 years with Houston, he has been selected for the AFC's Pro Bowl squad seven times.

8. He was once a world-record holder in the high hurdles and a wide receiver with the San Francisco 49ers.

9. In 1991, this Miami Dolphin led the league in punting when rated according to gross yardage.

10. Ranked by gross yardage, this Phoenix Cardinal finished third in the NFL's 1991 race for the punting title. Ranked by net yardage, however, he'd be #1.

11. Remarkably, the nose tackle for the Kansas City Chiefs is more difficult to block than his name is to pronounce.

12. This TCU graduate was Dallas' final pick of the 1991 draft. Despite being the team's twelfth-round selection, he wound up a starter in the Cowboys' defensive backfield by the end of his rookie season.

13. Currently, this quarterback owns the NFL record for most consecutive passing attempts without an interception.

14. This Eagle defensive back intercepted the aforementioned quarterback (question #13) to end the streak at 308.

15. As a junior, this quarterback was the 1990 Heisman Trophy winner. He played his senior year and entered the NFL draft in 1991. Regardless of the accolades, the Brigham Young graduate was not selected until the ninth round.

16. In 1991, this New England Patriot ranked a dismal 23rd in the league in punting despite having booted one 93 yards, the season's best effort.

17. His 30.6 yard average per kickoff return is the best in the history of the NFL.

18. In his 11-year career with the Washington Redskins, he started at center, guard, and tackle.

Upon his retirement, he joined Joe Gibbs' staff as an assistant to the tight ends coach.

19. This defensive lineman died on May 14, 1992, due to complications of a rare form of brain cancer. The former Bronco, Brown, and Raider blamed his demise on steroids, which he had used to enhance his physique and career.

20. Although considered by many to be the best running back available in the 1992 draft, he was not selected until the New Orleans Saints took him with the 21st pick overall.

21. This Purdue Boilermaker was Houston's first-round draft choice in 1986 (the third pick overall). Unable to sign the quarterback, the Oilers traded him on September 18, 1986, to the Los Angeles Rams.

22. In 1991, he led all NFL tight ends in receiving.

23. Today, this retired Jets quarterback is almost as famous for his knees and his commercial pitches as he once was for his stockinged legs and Super Bowl passes.

24. The Green Bay Packers have been "singing" the praises of their first-round draft choice of 1990, a linebacker from Mississippi.

25. He was the last of an era, the last to play the game of football without wearing a face mask.

THE HOLLYWOOD
BOWL

In football, excellence is rewarded at every level of play, either by election to all-star squads or participation in all-star games. In high school, top players are considered All-Americans. In college, they are sent to the Blue-Gray Game or the Senior Bowl, to name just two. The pros vote their peers onto their respective AFC and NFC Pro Bowl squads.

For those players who graduate from football to filmdom, it is unlikely there will be any more honors, any more awards. It is unlikely that any will ever know Oscar or Emmy or Tony. So, to ease the transition of those running to the spotlight rather than daylight, I am inaugurating the Hollywood Bowl.

Listed below, the 11 Hollywood "stars" who comprise my all-star team. Match each "player" with his "part."

1. Lyle Alzado   a. The "cyclops giant" with an eye for Earthlings on TV's *Lost in Space.*

2. Brian Bosworth

b. A crime lord who's sent to the Lord by *The Divine Enforcer*.

3. Jim Brown

c. A cop who rules with an iron fist in *Steele's Law*.

4. Dick Butkus

d. A fishmonger and Sela Ward's ex-husband on TV's *Sisters*.

5. Rosey Grier

e. A gay informant keeping time with TV's *Hollywood Beat*.

6. Lamar Lundy

f. An ex-con named Bulk who "escorts" Vanity in *Neon City*.

7. Ed Marinaro

g. An unexpected, but politically correct, addition to *Force 10 from Navarone*.

8. John Matuszak

h. "Himself" visiting TV's favorite family, *The Brady Bunch*.

9. Ken Stabler

i. An undercover cop who infiltrates a motorcycle gang in *Stone Cold*.

10. Carl Weathers

j. A parolee who infil-
trates a motorcycle
gang with TV's
MacGyver.

11. Fred Williamson

k. "Himself," a spokes-
person for the
"Lungbrush," on *Sat-
urday Night Live*.

NAME FIND #2
(CENTERS)

Find the last names of the 61 centers hidden in the accompanying puzzle. (Yes, they run diagonally, too.)

Mike **ALFORD**	Blair **BUSH**
Charlie **ANE**	Mark **CANNON**
Mike **BAAB**	Jim **CLACK**
Ted **BANKER**	Rich **COADY**
Tom **BANKS**	Jim **COOPER**
Tom **BAUGH**	Eric **COYLE**
Forrest **BLUE**	Randy **CROSS**
Tom **BRAHANEY**	Dave **CROSSAN**
Pete **BROCK**	Bob **DeMARCO**

Jim **EIDSON**	Kani **KAUAHI**
Roger **ELLIS**	Alex **KROLL**
Grant **FEASEL**	Jim **LANGER**
Gerry **FEEHERY**	Chuck **LANZA**
Chris **FOOTE**	Bill **LEWIS**
Will **GRANT**	Dave **LLOYD**
Randy **GRIMES**	Ron **LOU**
Lee **GROSS**	Tommy **LYONS**
Courtney **HALL**	Don **MACEK**
Ken **HELMS**	Ken **MEDENHALL**
R. W. **HICKS**	Jon **MORRIS**
Jay **HILGENBERG**	Dan **NEAL**
Ralph **HILL**	Bart **OATES**
Fred **HOAGLIN**	Mike **ORIARD**
E. J. **HOLUB**	Jim **OTTO**
Kent **HULL**	Tom **RAFFERTY**
Ken **IMAN**	Geoff **REECE**

Bill **REID**

Chuck **THOMAS**

Dan **ROSADO**

Steve **WILSON**

Karl **RUBKE**

George **YARNO**

Bob **RUSH**

Bob **YATES**

Jesse **SAPOLU**

```
L L A H N E D E M A R C O J O
Y J E N Y E N A H A R B T A N
O D R O F L A O B O A F T H R
N M E K R O L L S U O E O O A
S A P O L U A S B D S E T A Y
K C O R B N A H A M I H N G T
N E O I Z N O S L I W E A L R
A K C A J B O E C E E R R I E
B A O R D R H U L L L Y G N F
T U Y D J Y U L A N G E R O F
H A L H H S J B C A N N O N A
O H E I I B A N K E R T S A R
M I C L E S A E F E E D S M U
A K L L O Y D A J M O R R I S
S E M I R G R E B N E G L I H
```

[67]

OUT OF BOUNDS

Officially, an NFL playing field is 120 yards long and 53⅓ yards wide. These precise borders may confine the sport; but Football, the spectacle, is a pageant that travels far outside the turf's finite realm. For across the sidelines and beyond the end zones, players roam, fans roar, and trivia rules.

Below, 20 multiple-choice questions to test your knowledge of Football . . . out of bounds!

1. As a child, Dan Fouts was a ball boy for the San Francisco 49ers?
   a. True   b. False

2. Pass-rusher extraordinaire and film buff Pat Swilling relaxes at home by watching videos on his ——— -inch home television system.
   a. 26   b. 70
   c. 96   d. 100

3. NFL players sometimes use Zylocaine during a game. Zylocaine is . . .
   a. A legal form of   b. A popular brand of
      "stickum"   chewing tobacco
   c. A sugar substitute   d. A painkiller

4. Which NFL head coach appeared on the cover of *Personal Selling Power* magazine in 1991?
   a. Sam Wyche   b. Mike Ditka
   c. Jack Pardee   d. Dennis Green

5. The Dallas Cowboys Cheerleaders have come to represent the "best" in their specialized field. For their hard work and easy good looks, each "cowgirl" received $——— for each of the 10 home games they performed at Texas Stadium during the 1991 season.
   a. $150   b. $250
   c. $15   d. $500

6. Homer Jones, formerly of the New York Giants, today is the president of Zesty Pictures, a small, New York-based film production company.
   a. True   b. False

7. Which former quarterback authored *How to Watch Pro Football on TV?*
   a. Johnny Unitas   b. Earl Morrall
   c. Rusty Hilger   d. Y. A. Tittle

8. Baseball maverick Charlie O. Finley branched out in 1991 with his reinvention of the venerable "pigskin." His version of the football has not yet been adopted by the pros, but many colleges—including Michigan—have. What does Finley's altered design feature?
   a. Day-Glo stripes   b. Hidden laces
   c. Inverted "pebbles"   d. A gyroscope

9. Joe Montana's life story has been depicted in comic book form.
   a. True   b. False

10. Which position does Katie Brown, the granddaughter of Paul Brown, currently hold in the Cincinnati Bengals' organization?
    a. Cheerleader   b. Corporate Secretary/
                                 Legal Counsel
    c. General Manager   d. Pro Personnel Director

11. Who created the ad campaign for ESPN's 1991 schedule of Sunday night games, which featured the porcine epithet, "Pig Out!"?
    a. Steve Sabol   b. Chris Berman
    c. George Lois   d. Lex Flesher

12. Philadelphia defensive end Reggie White has authored a book entitled *The Reggie White Touch Football Playbook*.
    a. True   b. False

13. He gambled on a life after football, in . . . gambling! Which former NFL player is currently the Director of Development for Bally's in Atlantic City?
    a. Art Schlicter   b. Chalmers Tschappatt
    c. Spain Musgrove   d. Joe Pagliei

14. Which of the following billed itself as "The Official Airline of the NFL" in 1991?
    a. MGM Grand Air   b. American Airlines
    c. Northwest   d. Air Jordan
       Airlines

15. The body of which late, great head coach is interred at Mount Olivet Cemetery in Middletown, New Jersey?
    a. Knute Rockne   b. Paul Brown
    c. Vince Lombardi   d. Weeb Ewbank

16. Are Chicago's Mark Anthony Carrier and Tampa Bay's John Mark Carrier related?
    a. Yes   b. No

17. Which of the following four players weighed in as the heaviest during the 1991 season?
    a. Bubba Paris   b. William Perry
    c. Kevin Gogan   d. Tootie Robbins

18. The mother of which Pittsburgh Steeler was voted "Miss Turkey" of 1950?
    a. Jack Lambert   b. Bubby Brister
    c. Tunch Ilkin   d. Merril Hoge

19. Buffalo running back Thurman Thomas was absent during the Bills' opening drive of Super Bowl XXVI because he had lost his helmet.
    a. True   b. False

20. Which of the following awards did Steven Emtman *not* receive during his collegiate career at the University of Washington?
    a. The Outland   b. The Lombardi Trophy
       Trophy
    c. The Morris Trophy d. The Lombardi Award

B(U)Y THE BOOK

Aspiring all-stars, from pee-wee to professional, are raised by the book. The playbook, that is. They are expected to scrutinize and memorize the circles and squares, the curved and squiggly lines, for they will be tested on this knowledge constantly. And creativity will not count. At night, players voraciously devour pages of scribbled scrimmages and skirmishes, which they systematically regurgitate on the practice field the following day. Thus, it is no wonder that when their careers come to an end, or at least a pause, the students of the game are eager to express themselves in their own words. They are quick to evade the guidelines of the sidelines in favor of those of an autobiography's byline.

Listed below are the autobiographies of a dozen players, who could either outrun you or easily bench-press 500 pounds. So, if one of them suggests you *buy* his book, I suggest you do. For now, all I ask, is that you match these 12 titles with their respective authors (and collaborators).

1. *Audibles—My Life in Football*

a. Roger Staubach (w/Sam Blair and Bob St. John)

2. *I Am Third*

b. Don Strock (and Harvey Frommer)

3. *They're Playing My Game*

c. Bill Walsh (with Glenn Dickey)

4. *The End of the Line*

d. Hank Stram (with Lou Sahadi)

5. *First Down, Lifetime to Go*

e. Tony Dorsett (and Harvey Frommer)

6. *Instant Replay*

f. Leonard Marshall (with Dave Klein)

7. *One Giant Leap*

g. Brian Bosworth (with Rick Reilly)

8. *Building a Champion*

h. Terry Bradshaw (with Buddy Martin)

9. *Running Tough*

i. Gale Sayers

10. *Behind the Lines*

j. Jerry Kramer

MUDDLE IN THE HUDDLE #3 (LINEBACKERS)

This is the last of three quizzes in which the names of 10 prominent or promising players have been encoded. Each letter below corresponds to another; for example, *c* might represent *k* and *g* might represent *s,* and so on.

As coach, it is your job to reassign the x's and o's so that the true identities of these players may be revealed. The years and teams for which each has played are included to assist you.

Now, pick up the "blitz" of these anagrammatized linebackers and prove once and for all that you are a proficient code-cracker.

1. RUPAFNH PWVNZ
   Detroit Lions (1983–)

2. CNJUY BZNNYN
   Los Angeles Rams (1985–)

3. DUR AFZZUX
   Green Bay Packers (1986–1991), San Francisco
   49ers (1991–   )

4. XFR ATVV
   New York Giants (1956–1963), Washington
   Redskins (1964–1967, 1969)

5. JFTBAFY SWAYXWY
   New Orleans Saints (1986–   )

6. XNDA SWQYNZ
   Philadelphia Eagles (1986–   )

7. CFZH RNPCHNYLTZB
   Denver Broncos (1983–   )

8. SWAY WVVNZKFAH
   Miami Dolphins (1986–   )

9. KFZZQH DFHHNQ
   Buffalo Bills (1983–   )

10. KNZZUPC DAWRFX
    Kansas City Chiefs (1989–   )

A WORLD
OF THEIR OWN

Much like the madmen in the movies, NFL owners have long dreamed of world domination. Of course, like their silver-screen counterparts, they claim their intentions are, and their reign would be, benevolent. Their quest: simply, to indoctrinate every member of the global community as a card-carrying football fan. (Note: That's *football*, not soccer.) Though the scheme may sound insane, almost diabolical, the NFL has already launched its first and second offensives in their campaign to build a sport-homogeneous society.

Step One has birthed the American Bowl, a series of preseason exhibition contests held annually in such football towns as Tokyo, Berlin, Montreal, and Tokyo. (Mexico City may soon be a host, as well.) Step Two, the far more insidious, has unleashed the World League of American Football. The WLAF operates a 10-week spring season with 10 teams, six from the continental United States, one from Canada, and three from Europe. Although its novelty raised some interest during its rookie season, 1991, it remains a question as to whether or not the sport can be successfully exported. Their vision all-consuming, the NFL owners support their "minor" league and fight for its expansion. They live with their heads in the clouds . . . in a world of their own.

1. The World League of American Football was comprised of 10 teams in its inaugural season, 1991. In 1992, there were still 10 teams, but one of the original franchises had folded and been replaced by another. Name both squads.

2. Who was the first player chosen in the WLAF's 1992 draft?

3. This Barcelona Dragon is believed to be the first (and only?) WLAF player with his own fan club. Who is he?

4. Who holds the WLAF record for longest kick-off return?

5. Who scored the first regular-season touchdown in the WLAF?

6. Which quarterback and receiver hooked up for the longest pass play in WLAF history?

7. Former Cowboy head coach Tom Landry is a co-owner of which WLAF franchise?

8. Who holds the WLAF record for most consecutive completed passes?

9. In 1992, the NFL "loaned" 110 players to their poorer relations in the WLAF. Of those 110, how many appeared on the league's opening-day rosters?

10. Why was the start of the May 10, 1992, contest between the San Antonio Riders and the Barcelona Dragons delayed 45 minutes?

THIRD AND THIRTEEN

Your lead-footed receiver was trapped for a 5-yard loss after you ill-advisedly called for a reverse on second down. Your team now faces a treacherous third and thirteen, Coach. What play will you call? It is an obvious passing down, isn't it? Or are you hoping that this is precisely what the defense believes, and thus, you'll opt for a delayed draw?

This is the third of four chapters in which clues are provided to identify 25 players, past or present, memorable or forgettable. Although the clues have become a little more obscure, if you can still identify all the players correctly, you will pick up the first down.

1. This tackle played a full 16-game schedule for the Cardinals in 1984, joined the USFL's Memphis Showboats for their 12-game spring season, and then rejoined the Cardinals for the entire '85 campaign.

2. The Chicago Bears and New England Patriots determined he was too small to sit in the pocket. In the CFL, however, he has stood tall. In 1991, this British Columbia Lion was honored as the league's most valuable player.

3. At 6′ 8″, he is the tallest quarterback ever to be selected in the NFL draft.

4. In 1974, he led the New England Patriots in yardage gained returning punts, returning kick-offs, rushing, and receiving.

5. This Pittsburgh Steeler cornerback played linebacker at UCLA.

6. In 1991, he became only the fourth player selected in the first round of an NFL draft by the Washington Redskins since 1968.

7. This wide receiver was a member of the U.S. 4 × 100 relay team that captured the gold medal at the 1984 Summer Olympic games in Los Angeles.

8. At these same Olympic games, this nose tackle took the silver in the shotput competition.

9. He has appeared in more Pro Bowl games than any other Philadelphia Eagle.

10. This Detroit linebacker has finished first or sec-

ond in the Lions sack totals in every season
since 1986.

11. During the 1988 preseason, this Green Bay
quarterback wore #5 on his uniform rather
than his "magic" #7.

12. This well-traveled back is the cousin of safety
Kevin Porter.

13. This Indianapolis Colt was shot and killed on
May 2, 1992.

14. This running back hoped to join the U.S. Olympic
karate team for the 1992 summer games.

15. This Seattle Seahawk quarterback led the
WLAF's London Monarchs to the league's first
championship in 1991.

16. This Alabama running back was converted to
linebacker after becoming the New Orleans
Saints' first first-round draft pick in 1967.

17. This 1983 Heisman Trophy winner from Ne-
braska played two years in the USFL before
joining the Houston Oilers and, subsequently,
the Atlanta Falcons, who claimed him off waivers during the 1990 season.

18. This Kansas City defensive back was the winner
of the 1988 Byron "Whizzer" White Humani-
tarian Award.

19. This linebacker is the son of a former heavy-weight boxing champion.

20. Once a Bengals' linebacker and member of the Charter Committee of the Cincinnati City Council, he is now General Manager of the World League's New York/New Jersey Knights.

21. This running back was the New York Giants' first-round draft pick in 1971. The West Texas State graduate never fulfilled his promise and retired in 1973 after suffering a broken vertebra.

22. He beat tremendous odds in 1983 when he be-came the youngest player to quarterback his team to the Super Bowl. In 1992, he faced even greater odds, when illness dictated a liver trans-plant for this former Dolphin.

23. He was the first player to rush for 1,000 yards or more in a season for two different teams.

24. This Houston Oiler has had a tougher time off the field than on. In 1988, he sought and began treatment for a cocaine dependency problem. With that behind him, the defensive tackle spent the 1990 season recovering from a gun-shot wound.

25. A fear of flying propelled this Minnesota Vik-ing tackle to learn how to fly.

FOOTBALL CONNECTIONS

Dick Butkus, Randy Gradishar, and Mike Croel command the respect of football's faithful. Fans will immediately acknowledge each as a terrific linebacker, but only the game's historians and the trivially obsessed will recognize the trifle that links these three, other than their terrific play.

Give up? Despite having made his name as *the* Monster of the Midway, Butkus was originally a first-round draft choice of the Denver Broncos. Only two other linebackers have been accorded this honor by the Broncos. You guessed it: Gradishar and Croel.

Below, players and teams are grouped in threes or fours. Identify the strand of insignifica that weaves each group together. (Note: The "connections" become progressively obscure.)

1. Running backs Jim Brown, Larry Csonka, Floyd Little, and Jim Nance.

2. Quarterbacks Joe Montana, Terry Bradshaw, and Bart Starr.

3. Tony Collins, Dexter Manley, and Stanley Wilson.

4. Joe Montana, Boomer Esiason, and Howie Long.

5. Deion Sanders, Brian Jordan, and D. J. Dozier.

6. Running backs Ricky Bell, Brian Piccolo, and John Cappeletti.

7. The New York Jets, the Houston Oilers, and the Denver Broncos.

8. Bill Bates, Tunch Ilkin, Hoby Brenner, and Gary Reasons.

9. Jim McMahon, Tom Landry, and Sonny Jurgenson.

10. Keith Byars, Keith Jackson, and Eric Dickerson.

GAME FILMS

A football player's lot is not an easy one. Daily, in preparation for a game, he will lift weights, work out, and scrimmage. Additionally, he will spend many hours preparing for his opponent scrutinizing films (today, videos) of his foe's previous performances. But much like the wayward student who sneaks a comic into his Chemistry textbook, I'm sure the pros occasionally sneak a peek at a full-length feature during their late-night study sessions.

Below, questions concerning 10 films that players may have slipped onto the projector, surreptitiously. Each features pro football either as a backdrop or a plot device.

Have you been doing *your* "homework"? Do you know these . . . game films?

1. In John Frankenheimer's 1977 thriller, *Black Sunday*, perennial psycho-looney Bruce Dern piloted a bomb-bearing blimp toward the Orange Bowl, an unsuspecting crowd, and an unintimidated President of the United States. Robert Shaw raced to save the day, the Prez,

and the fans from an explosive climax to which Super Bowl contest?

2. Who portrayed Elroy Hirsch in the eponymously-titled 1953 film, *Crazylegs*?

3. In which film did Billy Crystal and his buddy Bruno Kirby attend a Detroit Lions–New York Giants game at the Meadowlands? (Hint: The two unenthusiastically participated in a crowd "wave" while Crystal discussed the dissolution of his first marriage.)

4. Charlton Heston plays Ron "Cat" Catlan in Tom Gries' 1969 footbal flick, *Number One*. Catlan, an aging quarterback is besieged by marital woes and injurious blows from unbeatable foes at the helm of which NFL franchise?

5. *Paper Lion* is the true story of a writer who attended the training camp of the Detroit Lions as a "rookie" quarterback in order to gather information for an article to appear in *Sports Illustrated*. Name the author/socialite portrayed by Alan Alda in Alex March's 1968 film.

6. The road to the Super Bowl can be demanding. The length of the season and the pressure of fans and the media can be discouraging. But the competitive spirit can drive an individual to achieve the incredible. In *Heaven Can Wait*, Warren Beatty overcame the ordinary and battled the extraordinary to reach the champion-

ship game. After his "premature" cremation, the star quarterback returns from the afterlife in the bodies of first, a millionaire, and then his backup, to lead his team to the NFL title. For which professional franchise did Beatty's character compete?

7. Harry Hinkle and Willie Gingrich conspire to sue CBS, the Cleveland Browns, and Municipal Stadium after Hinkle, a television cameraman, is bowled over by a running back during a Browns–Vikings contest. Name the actors who portrayed Hinkle and Gingrich in *The Fortune Cookie*.

8. Which film features Fred Williamson as Spear-chucker Jones, a former pro player called in as a "ringer" for a wartime football skirmish?

9. James Caan is a cop, tracking drug-smuggling "newcomers" in the futuristic thriller *Alien Nation*, with Mandy Patinkin. Throughout the film, he wears a T-shirt emblazoned with the name of a current NFL franchise. Of which team was Caan apparently a diehard fan?

10. In George Roy Hill's *The World According to Garp*, based on John Irving's novel of the same name, John Lithgow portrayed a former Phila-delphia Eagle tight end (#90) who undergoes a sex-change operation and becomes a nurse/-counselor at a hospice for abused women. What was his post-op name?

SCRIMMAGED LINES #2 (DEFENSIVE BACKS)

A defensive back always swaggers, though he sometimes staggers on the field. A wide receiver's well-run route can make the most erudite and agile DB look foolish and clumsy. Yet, even if beaten for a touchdown, the defensive back must regain his composure and take the field for the next series with the conviction that he is invincible. He may be deemed cocky, but he has to be. Lack of speed may be a liability, but, in the NFL, lack of confidence is a fatal flaw.

Below are the names of 24 of the NFL's most confident: safeties and cornerbacks. Help them "shadow" the appropriate "patterns" in the blank crossword diagram on the facing page.

3-LETTER NAMES
Carl LEE

4-LETTER NAMES
Dave AMES
Ronnie LOTT
Tommy NECK
John SISK

5-LETTER NAMES
Bill BATES
Lester HAYES
Mark KELSO
Lonnie YOUNG

6-LETTER NAMES
Bennie BLADES
Jim DUNCAN
Kenny EASLEY
Terry KINARD
Jerry LAWSON
Jesse STOKES

7-LETTER NAMES
Herb ADDERLY
Steve ATWATER
Martin BAYLESS
Mark CARRIER
Chris DISHMAN
David JOHNSON
Rod WOODSON

8-LETTER NAMES
Dick ANDERSON
Reyna THOMPSON

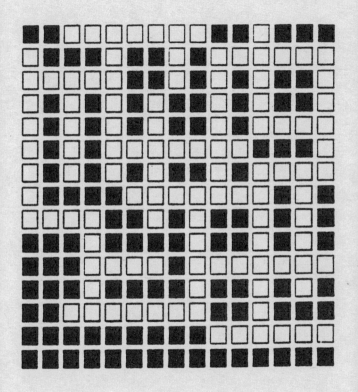

ILLEGAL PROCEDURES

In football, the most serious infractions result in the loss of 15 yards, a down, and/or ejection from the game. The consequences in real life are far more serious. Lady Justice may be blindfolded, but unlike most referees, she is not blind. And, in turn, she metes out punishment far more severely than any umpire could.

Below, 10 questions pertaining to players whose "unsportsmanlike conduct" and/or "personal fouls" have culminated and been ruled upon in . . . (il)legal procedures.

1. Litigation initiated by a single headstrong player may change the fates and fortunes of all footballers to follow. The case, heard by a Minneapolis federal district court in June 1992, may establish unrestricted free agency in the National Football League. Who filed the lawsuit?

2. Which two players did Commissioner Pete Rozelle suspend for the entirety of the 1963 season

because they had bet on the outcomes of league games?

3. In February 1992, this retired New York linebacker testified in a case brought against the Genovese crime family. Before a New Jersey State Commission of investigation, the part-owner of the Satin Dolls Lounge claimed a member of the mob "persuaded" him to pay $500 a week to "protect" his investment. Which former Giant played David in an effort to topple organized crime's Goliath?

4. Despite pleas for leniency by his former coach, Don Coryell, and teammates, this running back was sentenced to two-and-a half years in prison. Name the former Saint and Charger who was found guilty of perjury and the possession and sale of cocaine.

5. Which player sued the pay-cable station Home Box Office for "exposing" him in their post-game, locker-room coverage of the Denver Broncos–Houston Oilers 1991 AFC playoff game?

6. This defensive back received a lifetime suspension after having tested positive for a third time in a league-administered drug test. Name the Detroit Lion who was the Seattle Seahawks' first-round draft pick in 1984.

7. New Orleans' third-round draft pick in 1986, this running back missed what should have been his rookie season. In '86, the Virginia grad spent 18 weeks in jail after having been convicted on a cocaine distribution charge. Name the ex-con who began play with the Saints the following year and signed with the Chiefs as a free agent three years later.

8. True or False? The NFL fined John Elway after the Denver quarterback threw a "souvenir" ball to a wheelchair-bound fan in 1991.

9. The Dallas Cowboys' all-time leading scorer was released by America's Team a week after he had been arrested on charges of sexual misconduct with a 10-year-old girl in 1986. Name the soccer-style kicker who was as much a South-of-the-border sensation as he was a Lone Star legend.

10. During the 1987 NFL Players' Association strike, team owners fielded replacement squads to "protect the integrity of the game." The owners promised the so-called scabs all of the benefits normally accorded their unionized counterparts. Now, a class-action suit, filed in Atlanta, claims that the owners did not make good on their word. Reportedly, the owners did not allot the strike-busters severance pay upon the return of the "real" pros. Which replacement player, briefly a punter for the Atlanta Falcons, has been named the plaintiff in this lawsuit?

FOURTH AND TWO

A clutch grab by your tight end recouped 11 yards on third down, leaving you just 2 yards short of the first. A lo-o-o-ng 2 yards! Do you have the nerve to go for it, or will you trot out your unreliable kicker? Well, Coach? The fans are waiting . . .

This is the last of four chapters in which clues are provided to identify 25 players, past or present, memorable or forgettable. These clues are the most obscure, but, if you can identify all the players correctly, you will pick up the first down. (And the fans will love you, for at least one more set of downs!)

1. This graduate of the University of Florida led the Chicago Bears in rushing for six consecutive seasons.

2. He was the first Seattle Seahawk to return a kickoff for a touchdown.

3. This San Diego Charger was voted the team's Most Inspirational Player from 1988 to 1990.

4. This retired Minnesota Viking defensive lineman now is a member of Minnesota Supreme Court.

5. This offensive lineman was banned from the 1986 Citrus Bowl, which followed his senior season at USC, because he had tested positive for steroids.

6. He quarterbacked the New York Giants (1954–1959), the Dallas Cowboys (1960), and the Oakland Raiders (1962). Later, this Washington graduate served as an assistant coach with the Cowboys, Giants, Saints, Rams, Steelers, and 49ers.

7. This Buffalo Bill opened holes for "The Juice," but lost his "juice," after his agent swindled him of his football earnings. Since then, the retired lineman has worked as a high school's groundskeeper, attempted a comeback in the Arena Football League at age 40, and boxed professionally.

8. Football fanatics will remember him for his courageous contributions to the Giants as both a wide receiver and a special teams player during New York's 1986 Super Bowl season. Actress Kim Basinger cherishes another memory of him. She once remarked that the midshipman had the best butt in the NFL.

9. This offensive lineman had his number retired by the San Diego Chargers when he retired in

1969. The number was put back into circulation, however, when he returned to pro football with the Raiders in '71.

10. As a student at Woodlawn High School in Louisiana, this quarterback proved to be as proficient tossing javelins as he was tossing footballs. He set an American high school record with one such effort, which traveled 244 feet, 11 inches.

11. During halftime of the Buccaneers' December 6, 1987, encounter with the New Orleans Saints, then Tampa Bay head coach Ray Perkins punched this offensive lineman for uttering the word "quit" in his presence.

12. This defensive tackle won the 1963 Outland Trophy. The Texas Longhorn played for the Houston Oilers (1964–1966) and the San Diego Chargers (1967–1968).

13. Along with Kevin Murphy, a linebacker with the USFL's Birmingham Stallions from 1985 to 1987, this former Buffalo Bill running back founded N.E. Wear, a sportswear company, in 1991.

14. This San Diego Charger missed most of the 1990 season, having suffered severe head injuries in an assault outside a local restaurant.

15. When this Green Bay Packer rushed for 1,052 yards in 1949, he became only the third back in league history to do so.

16. This defensive lineman legally changed his name in 1977. In 1976, he played for the Jets as Larry Faulk.

17. This Philadelphia defenseman appeared on teammate Randall Cunningham's television show regularly during the 1991 season. Once, he wrestled a bull in anticipation of an impending clash with the Cowboys. Another time, he crawled around a *real* dog pound before the Eagles made their trip to Cleveland's "Dawg Pound."

18. This Redskin walked out of training camp and *announced* his retirement in 1988 in hopes of returning to his native Canada to pursue a career as a carpenter.

19. This Miami Dolphin is the grandson of Tony "The Tuna" Accardo, the reputed Chicago crime boss.

20. The Chicago Bears won the 1963 NFL Championship, defeating the New York Giants, 14–10, in the title game. The Bears' hopes for consecutive crowns were demolished, however, when they lost these two offensive stars in a tragic auto accident prior to the '64 season.

21. This tight end was the winner of the 1992 National Cutting Horse Association–NFL Super Cutting event.

22. The Buffalo brain-trust probably considered heritage as well as talent when making their eighth-round draft pick in 1990. After all, this Bill plays the same position his mother had in a professional women's league during the 1970s— linebacker.

23. He was the first NFL player to publicly declare himself a homosexual.

24. This Tampa Bay safety intercepted a pass in each of his first two regular season games and recovered a fumble in his third.

25. This Detroit dynamo was a double threat as a quarterback on the Lions' replacement team during the 1987 NFLPA strike and a pitcher in the Tiger's farm system.

NAME FIND #3
(WIDE RECEIVERS)

Find the last names of the 70 wide receivers hidden in the accompanying puzzle. (Yes, they run diagonally, too.)

Pete **ATHAS**
Stephen **BAKER**
Sanjay **BEACH**
Ken **BELL**
Tim **BERRA**
Carl **BLAND**
J. V. **CAIN**
Roger **CARR**
Mark **CARRIER**
Don **CLUNE**
Linzy **COLE**
Aaron **COX**
Paco **CRAIG**
Jerry **DAANEN**
Carroll **DALE**
Wendell **DAVIS**

Bill **DRAKE**
Mark **DUPER**
Hart Lee **DYKES**
Quinn **EARLY**
Henry **ELLARD**
Phillip **EPPS**
Bernard **FORD**
John **GARRETT**
Everett **GAY**
Jack **GEHRKE**
Frank **GRANT**
Mel **GRAY**
Roy **GREEN**
Bob **HAYES**
Freddie **HYATT**
Michael **IRVIN**

Tommy **KANE**
Jeff **KEMP**
Curtis **LEAK**
Gary **LEE**
Jerry **LEVIAS**
Leo **LEWIS**
Louis **LIPPS**
Pete **MANDLEY**
Willie **McGEE**
Ron **MORRIS**
Bobby **MOTEN**
Jimmy **ORR**
Stephone **PAIGE**
Danny **PEBBLES**
Johnny **PERKINS**
Frank **PITTS**
Bucky **POPE**
David **RAY**
Andre **REED**

Jerry **RICE**
Preston **RILEY**
Ricky **SANDERS**
Rod **SHERMAN**
Mike **SIANI**
J. T. **SMITH**
Jack **SNOW**
Paul **STAROBA**
Dwight **STONE**
Otto **STOWE**
Lynn **SWANN**
Steve **SWEENEY**
Al **SYKES**
Jim **THAXTON**
Odessa **TURNER**
Howard **TWILLEY**
Wesley **WALKER**
Bob **WEST**
Eric **YARBER**

```
S R E D N A S E L B E E P P S
E K G R A N T W I L L E Y A H
K A E A I V T O A A E L G A E
Y E H K B D I T D N A B Y C R
D L R E P O P S T D N E T O M
V E K M C G R A Y A S A H T A
P V E P O P O A H K Y C A I N
E I Q G A R R E T T E H X R D
R A N I I B R W I S U S T E L
E S I A E A A I M E I R O N E
I P V R E L P K S W E E N E Y
R E R C K F X T E P O P I E L
R A I E A C O L E R P N L R R
A R R K N N C R I N A I S G A
C L U N E N A A D D R A L L E
```

THE RED ZONE

Bend-don't-break defenses allow opponents to roam freely from 20 to 20. But once an offense crosses that line and enters "the red zone," the defense stiffens. Gaps are plugged. Runners who had seen daylight, see open holes, eclipsed by inside linebackers, turn black. Zones are flooded. Receivers who had found seams, find themselves hemmed in by nickel coverage. The offense sputters. The drive ends. The defense rests.

You have reached the red zone. Until now, the questions have been relatively easy. This chapter is the true test of your football knowledge. Answer the following 50 questions correctly and you will be trivia's reigning champion.

1. Who recorded the longest punt in the NFL in 1989? (Hint: He runs, he passes, but he doesn't normally punt.)

2. In which year was the proposal to hold an annual draft of collegiate players *accepted* by the NFL?

3. Who was the first player selected in the first NFL draft?

4. Who was the first player to be signed by the team that drafted him?

5. In which year did the NFL allow underclassmen to declare themselves eligible for the league's annual collegiate draft?

6. Which three players, as of February 1, 1992, rank as the career leaders in quarterback traps? (Note: The NFL did not begin compiling statistical information concerning sacks until 1982.)

7. Super Bowl fever must be contagious. Rapt by the attention surrounding their second consecutive appearance, Buffalo misguidedly allowed running back Thurman Thomas to skip one of the many mandatory media sessions prior to Super Bowl XXVI. The NFL fined the team for this transgression. How big was the Bills' bill?

8. Name the five men who have been inducted in the Dallas Cowboys' Ring of Honor in Texas Stadium.

9. Prior to the 1992 draft, 27 of today's 28 NFL franchises had, at one point or another, used a first-round pick to select a quarterback. Which

team made it unanimous in '92, and which quarterback did they choose?

1991 proved to be a fairy-tale season for the Lions—a Grimm's fairy tale. For although Detroit did appear blessed in reaching the NFC Championship game with the Washington Redskins, they also were cursed. During the team's playoff drive, both Mike Utley and Jerry Ball were lost to devastating injuries.

10. On November 17, 1991, Mike Utley fell freakishly during a routine pass-play blocking assignment. As a result, he will be paralyzed—permanently—from the chest down. That same day, in a contest between Houston and Cleveland, another player had to be carried off the field on a stretcher. Fortunately, he was paralyzed for only 90 minutes and not a lifetime. Name the Browns' wide-out who will walk, but never onto a football field, again.

11. Three weeks later, Jerry Ball was lost for the season during the Lions' December 8 encounter with the Jets. The All-Pro nose tackle was a victim of a chop-block which, prior to his injury, was deemed legal on running plays, though not on passing plays. Name the two New York players who, some speculate, conspired to "deflate the Ball."

12. By virtue of their 1–15 record in '91, and a clever trade with the Buccaneers, the Indianap-

olis Colts earned the first two picks of the 1992 NFL draft. Which team, in which year, was the last to corral the top two pro prospects?

13. According to NFL regulations, what is the distance between the two goal posts?

14. To whom did New York Head Coach Bill Parcells award a game ball following the Giants 39–20 thrashing of the Denver Broncos in Super Bowl XXI?

15. After polling the managerial staffs of many NFL franchises, *The Sporting News* selects its Executive of the Year. Who was awarded this honor in 1991?

16. Which NFL franchise has gone the longest without winning a league championship?

17. From 1934 through 1991, 236 players have rushed for 1,000 yards or more in a single season. Of these dashers and slashers, who holds the record for the best yards-per-carry average?

18. Which is the oldest stadium currently in use in the NFL?

19. In his four Super Bowl appearances, the 49ers' Joe Montana threw 11 touchdown passes. How many times was he intercepted?

20. On December 16, 1991, New York Jets receiver Dale Dawkins drove home after a 3–6 loss, earlier that day, to the New England Patriots. Dawkins lost control of his Nissan 300ZX after the car careened across an ice patch and rammed into a tree. Fortunately, a teammate who was following 100 yards behind witnessed the crash and rescued Dawkins from the wreck. Who is the Good Samaritan who saved Dawkins' life and, possibly, salvaged his career?

21. Former Pittsburgh Head Coach Chuck Noll has vehemently and repeatedly denied knowledge of and/or responsibility for the accusations made in *False Glory*. The book's author alleges that Noll silently condoned his and his teammates' usage of steroids during the 1980s. Name the retired Steeler lineman who put these charges in print.

22. When did the American Football League conduct its first draft of college players?

23. Which NFL legend, interviewed during the first evening of riots in Los Angeles following the announcement of the verdict in the Rodney King case, lamented: "The modern black athlete is probably the most embarrassing human being from the standpoint of reinvestment in black people that we've ever had."

24. How much did a minute of advertising time cost during Super XXVI?

25. On December 12, 1965, two teams vied for the title in the final AFL Championship game. Which teams were involved and what was the outcome?

26. A touchdown is worth 6 points; the point after adds another. A successful field goal scores 3 points and a safety increases the tally by 2. Is it then possible for an NFL team to record a victory with a 1–0 decision?

27. Each year, a parade is organized in Pasadena to celebrate the dubious achievement of the player who is the last to be selected in the NFL draft. Who was the 336th pick overall in the 1992 draft, and thus, so honored?

28. The American Football League was formed in 1959 and began play in 1960. A year later, this Chicago Bear became the first player to intentionally allow his contract to expire so that he might sign with an AFL squad. Name the offensive end who snubbed his NFL allegiance and the team for which he switched leagues.

29. In 1977, the NFL adopted its restricted free agency policy, which allows an unsigned player to receive "offer sheets" from other clubs. Should the player opt to sign an offer sheet,

his original team may retain his rights by re-warding him with an equal or better contract. If the original team forgoes this right of first refusal, the player may then switch teams, but his former squad must be compensated with draft picks. In return for "losing" a player who has more than three years of league experience and earns more than $290,000, the previous team receives two first-round draft choices. This is a steep price to pay, even for a super-star. Thus, in the 15 years the system has been in place, only five players have received offer sheets. Of those five, only two actually changed teams in exchange for draft choices. Name these two far-from-free agents.

30. The promising career of Los Angeles Raider cornerback Stacey Toran ended in a tragic auto accident. Toran was drunk when the ac-cident occurred. California state law recog-nizes a blood alcohol level of .10 percent as the limit at which one will be considered to be driving under the influence. What was To-ran's blood alcohol level at the time of the crash?

Although Commissioner Paul Tagliabue has de-layed the expansion process, the NFL should still be adding two teams, one to each conference in the next few years. This growth will be the first for the league since Seattle and Tampa Bay were awarded franchises in 1974 (and began play in '76). Five cities remain in the hunt for an NFL berth. The following four questions pertain to those candidates.

31. James Busch Orthwein curried favor with the NFL when he bailed out Victor Kiam, the debt-plagued owner of the New England Patriots. Orthwein purchased the Patriots in 1992 and agreed to "stabilize" the organization until another suitable owner could be located. In doing so, Orthwein greatly enhanced the possibility of which former NFL city being awarded a franchise?

32. Among Orthwien's co-investors is a former NFL star who would become the league's first minority representative. Who is he?

33. Which best-selling author heads one of three parties bidding to return pro football to Baltimore?

34. Which city can take the "sting" out of NFL owners' small-town doubts by boasting that it has recently launched and supported a franchise in the National Basketball Association?

35. Who conceived the NFL's "tradition" of Thanksgiving Day games?

36. In 1992, the Raiders' maverick owner Al Davis, finally and deservedly, was elected to Pro Football's Hall of Fame. This year, he was inducted

into another Hall of Fame as well. Which was it?

37. What was the Bert Bell Benefit Bowl?

38. In 1988, 49er tackle Charlie Krueger sued the San Francisco organization and won a $2.3 million settlement. What was the nature of the charges Krueger brought against his former team?

39. Since 1960, the Raiders have played their regular season home games in six different stadiums. Name them.

40. In what year did the NFL adopt the policy that allowed teams unlimited free substitution of players?

41. Football can be a dangerous and painful sport. Bobby Hebert can testify to that. The Saints' quarterback, who suffered cartilage damage to his knee in '87 and a shoulder separation in '91, has admitted that he consulted with a physician outside the New Orleans organization to procure proper medication for these ailments. Which painkiller did his doctor prescribe?

42. In 1989, the Lions and Steelers selected running backs Barry Sanders and Tim Worley, respectively, in the first round of the NFL draft. On October 1 of that year, the two

teams clashed in an inter-conference match that pitted their freshmen in a battle for rushing supremacy. Which runner outgained the other by only a yard and what were his totals for the day?

43. During the 1920s, Rock Island fielded a professional football franchise. What was the name of that team?

44. Much ado was made of Al Davis' promotion of Art Shell to the Raiders' head coaching position in 1989. Many believe that the former all-star lineman is the first black head coach. They are wrong. Shell is merely the first black head coach of pro football's modern era. Who truly owns the distinction?

45. In their inaugural season, the AFL's New York Titans won seven games and lost seven under head coach Sammy Baugh. Despite their competitiveness, the year was marred by a loss in their encounter with the Houston Oilers on October 9, 1960. Explain.

46. What is defensive end "Natu" Tuatagaloa's full name?

47. Six Degrees of Separation, Part II? In 1992, a con man, posing as a football star, befriended singer Diane Schuur and record exec. Carl Griffin and appeared on *The Maury Povich Show*. The talk-show's topic: athletes and their

obsessive fans. Only after taping the episode did Povich and his staff realize they had been hoodwinked by one such groupie. Name the player who's caught bombs and the imposter who bombed after being caught.

48. Who is the NFL's Director of Player Programs?

49. Jim Thorpe was in demand as much in death as he was in life. After he died on March 28, 1953, two towns united to bid for and win the rights to bury the former Olympian and football legend. Citizens and politicians believed his interment would increase their revenues by attracting tourists to their previously unremarkable locale. They enshrined Thorpe in a $15,000 mausoleum of pink marble and voted to rename their towns in honor of the Native American and ex-Oorang Indian. Name the two towns and the state where Thorpe now resides.

With only seconds remaining in the game and trailing by 5 points, your team faces a fourth and goal from 1 yard out. You have no choice, Coach. You must go for it. Can you punch it into the end zone, or will a heroic goal-line stand deny you the World Championship?

50. With the imminent addition of two more franchises within the next few years, the NFL is considering the possibility of realigning teams in both conferences on the basis of geography

or rivalry or both. If so, it will not be the first time the league has juggled its formation. In 1967, the NFL concocted an unusual three-year arrangement, in which it would be divided into two conferences of two divisions each. In 1968, two teams were instructed to flip-flop their divisional placements, only to revert to their original groupings the following year. Detail the structure of the NFL in 1968, naming the conferences, the divisions, and the teams that played in each.

PAYDIRT!
(ANSWERS)

THE ONE AND ONLY'S

1. The **Miami Dolphins'** 1972 record of 17–0 remains the "perfect season."

2. In 1992, Seattle "promoted" their general manager, **Tom Flores,** to coach the Seahawks squad. Flores was formerly the head coach of the Raiders.

3. Trips to Disneyland were in order for the 49ers' **Joe Montana** who was named MVP for his performances in Super Bowls XVI, XIX, and XXIV. He had to settle for just the NFL title after Super Bowl XXIII, for which teammate Jerry Rice won the honor.

4. **1990**

5. The **Tampa Bay Buccaneers** own a 0–2–0 mark against the Silver & Black.

6. **Chuck Howley** was named the MVP of Super Bowl V. The Cowboy linebacker intercepted two passes and led a defense that held the Colts to a meager 69 yards in 31 rushing attempts. Despite his efforts, Baltimore defeated Dallas, 16–13. (Howley was also the first non-quarterback to receive the MVP trophy.)

7. Running back **Mike Oliphant** has performed with the Washington Redskins and the Cleveland Browns.

8. In 1991, **Dallas Cowboy** running back Emmit Smith led the NFL with 1,563 yards rushing. Concurrently, wide receiver Michael Irvin's 1,523 receiving yards set the league standard.

9. **#33 Sammy Baugh** anchored the Redskins' offensive and defensive backfields from 1937 to 1952. In 1960 and '61, he was the head coach of the New York Titans and in 1964, he coached the Houston Oilers.

10. Detroit advanced to the NFC Championship game in 1991, a feat no one believed possible after their regular-season opener. Without Sanders, the pride of their pride, the Lions were easily housebroken by the Washington Redskins, **45–0.**

11. Over the course of his career, **George Blanda** tallied 2,002, a football odyssey.

12. Washington's commander-in-chief, **Joe Gibbs,** prepares incredible, connect-the-dot game plans for his quarterbacks, which make them appear almost interchangeable at times. The Redskins have captured the Lombardi Trophy with **Joe Theismann** (Super Bowl XVII), **Doug Williams** (Super Bowl XXII), and **Mark Rypien** (Super Bowl XXVI), respectively, at the helm.

13. In 1989, Kansas City's **Christian Okoye** gained 1,480 yards on 370 carries. He averaged 4 yards per carry.

14. 1979 was the last year the **Balimore/Indianapolis Colts** reached the playoffs.

15. **Chuck Knox** coached the following teams to division titles (in these years): the **Los Angeles Rams** (1973–1977), the **Buffalo Bills** (1980), and the **Seattle Seahawks** (1988).

16. Defensive tackle **Randy White** and defensive end **Harvey Martin** shared the award for their contributions to the Dallas Cowboys' 27–10 victory over the Denver Broncos in **Super Bowl XII.**

17. "Let's *Not* Make a Deal" was the motto of the **Cincinnati Bengals** in 1987.

18. The **Washington Redskins** traded up to pick fourth overall in the 1992 NFL draft. They did so in order to select Michigan's **Desmond Howard.**

19. **Jack Pardee** earned his accolades with the WFL's Florida Blazers (1974), the NFL's Washington Redskins (1979), the USFL's Houston Gamblers (1984), and the NCAA's Houston Cougars (1989). He is currently employed by the NFL's Houston Oilers, who expect he will win again.

20. The Rams relocated as defending champions, but would not reclaim the NFL title for their Los Angeles fans until **1951.** Ironically, the 24–17 victory came at the expense of their successors in Cleveland, the **Browns.**

21. Clem Daniels gained no yardage. In fact, he was dropped for a **2-yard loss.** The Texans then dropped Daniels and, wisely, the Raiders recovered him. He would lead Oakland in rushing for six consecutive seasons.

22. On December 5, 1989, Viking **Mike Merriweather** blocked a punt by the Rams' Dale Hatcher. The ball rolled back through **Los Angeles'** end zone and **Minnesota** won, 23–21.

23. 6'3", 235-pound guard **Bob Kalsu** played for the Buffalo Bills in 1968 and joined the military

forces in 1969. He was killed in combat the following year.

24. Fearing the abolishment of the draft in 1993, only the **Vikings** were willing to pull the trigger on a trade. Minnesota sent defensive tackle **Keith Millard** to Seattle for the **Seahawks'** second-round pick in '92 and a conditional pick in '93.

25. On November 5, 1989, the Cowboys (and Coach Johnson) celebrated their only victory of the season, a 13–3 conquest of their division rivals, the **Washington Redskins** in R.F.K. Stadium.

NICKNAMES

1. c	8. c
2. b	9. a
3. a	10. d
4. d	11. b
5. d	12. c
6. a	13. a
7. b	14. d

15. a	21. b
16. b	22. d
17. c	23. a
18. b	24. c
19. c	25. d
20. a	

MUDDLE IN THE HUDDLE #1
(SAFETIES)

A	B	C	D	E	F	G	H	I	J	K	L	M
B	H	N	F	M	A	J	S	Q	U	Z	R	C
N	**O**	**P**	**Q**	**R**	**S**	**T**	**U**	**V**	**W**	**X**	**Y**	**Z**
E	T	W	I	K	Y	D	O	X	V	L	P	G

1. Steve Atwater

2. Bennie Blades

3. Mark Carrier

4. Deron Cherry

5. David Fulcher

6. Brett Maxie

7. Tim McDonald

8. Erik McMillan

9. Louis Oliver

10. Andre Waters

FIRST AND TEN

1. "Sweetness" himself, **Walter Payton.**

2. By now, even Bo knows **Steve Bono.** Bono's stats for 1991 (237 attempts, 141 completions, 1,617 yards, and 11 touchdowns) ranked him third in the NFC. The NFL's leading passer in '91 was teammate Steve Young.

3. If Indianapolis reaches the playoffs again someday, they will do so on the arm of Illinois graduate **Jeff George** rather than on the legs of Eric Dickerson. In 1991, the Colts' first-round pick of 1990 attempted 485 passes and completed 292 for 2,910 yards and 10 touchdowns.

4. In 1991, Buffalo's all-purpose back **Thurman Thomas** rushed 288 times for 1,407 yards and caught 62 passes for an additional 631 yards. Grand total: 2,038 yards.

5. William "The Refrigerator" Perry is only one of **Michael Dean "Gator" Perry**'s 11 siblings.

6. 6'1", 277-pound defensive tackle **Russell Maryland** didn't earn his first starting assignment with Dallas until November 17, 1991, when the Cowboys clashed with the Oilers.

7. Never "dull," **Sterling Sharpe** was the first Packer to lead the NFL in receptions since Don Hutson pulled down 47 in '45.

8. Following his junior season at Penn State, **Blair Thomas** received reconstructive surgery on his right knee. Doctors and coaches have hypothesized that, subsequently, Thomas overcompensated physically. The overdevelopment of the left side of his body consequently limited his playing time and productivity.

9. Saint linebacker **Pat Swilling** is "blessed" with talent.

10. In both 1988 and 1989, Detroit's **Eddie Murray** connected on 20 of his 21 field goal attempts, tying the NFL season record for accuracy with a 95.2 percent mark.

11. Seahawks' wide-out **Brian Blades** was born on July 24, 1965. Brother **Bennie Blades** was born on September 3, 1966.

12. Cincinnati fans hope that **David Klingler** may someday soon "restore the roar" to the Bengals' offense.

13. In 1991, Houston's **Haywood Jeffires** caught 100 passes for 1,181 yards and 7 touchdowns.

14. **Vinny Testaverde** was the last Heisman Trophy winner to be the very first pick in the NFL draft. He has never fulfilled the potential this status would suggest.

15. When St. Louis drafted him in 1979, many anticipated that **Ottis "O. J." Anderson** would be

the next O. J. Simpson. Despite several 1,000-yard seasons, no one confused him with the original O. J. and the Cardinals traded him to the Giants in '86. He may not be "The Juice," but neither has he lost "the juice." Ottis, who turned 35 on January 19, 1992, keeps on running.

16. Overall, the 14th pick of the '91 draft, **Leonard Russell** carried the ball 266 times for 959 yards, a 3.6 average, and 4 touchdowns.

17. The Pats will stand pat with Pat—**Pat Harlow,** that is. The 6′ 6″, 280-pound tackle should anchor New England's offensive line for years to come.

18. Redskins' kicker **Chip Lohmiller** kicked field goals and P.A.T.'s for a total of 149 points. The entire Colts' team tallied six fewer points, 143. Washington finished the season with a 14–2 record; Indianapolis went 1–15.

19. In 1984, Steeler corner **Rod Woodson** qualified for the U.S. Olympic trials in the hurdles.

20. Few would argue with **Bruce Smith**'s self-evaluation. (Except, perhaps, Reggie White.)

21. Al Davis loves projects and **Aundray Bruce**'s potential.

22. In 1991, longtime Seahawk starter **Dave Krieg** attempted 285 passes and completed 187 for a

league-high 65.6 mark, 2,080 yards and 11 touchdowns. On the downside, he threw 12 interceptions.

23. Charger defensive end **Burt Grossman** (6'6", 270 lb.) is a graduate of the University of Pittsburgh.

24. **Joey Browner** and his brothers are a little "defensive." Joey, the perennial Pro-Bowler, played safety for the Vikings 1983–1991. His brother Jim was a defensive back with the Bengals; Keith was a linebacker with the Buc's, 49ers, Raiders, and Chargers; and Ross was a defensive end with the Bengals, Gamblers, and Packers.

25. Though he may not be the flashiest, **Marcus Allen** has proven to be the most reliable Raider running back since he joined the team in 1982.

SCRIMMAGED LINES #1
(DEFENSIVE LINEMEN)

NAME FIND #1
(QUARTERBACKS)

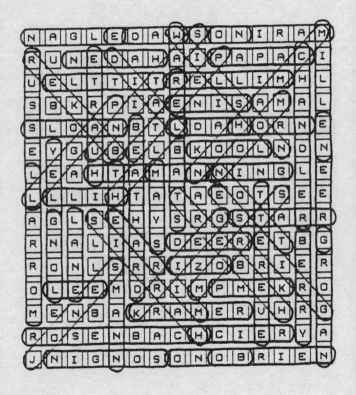

SCORECARD

00. Jim Otto	15. Neil Lomax
1. Warren Moon	16. Joe Montana
2. Mike Horan	17. Dave Krieg
3. Jan Stenerud	18. Mike Tomczak
4. Jim Harbaugh	19. Bernie Kosar
5. Sean Landeta	20. Barry Sanders
6. Kevin Butler	21. Deion Sanders
7. Morten Andersen	22. Erik McMillan
8. Troy Aikman	23. Barry Word
9. Rodney Peete	24. Mel Farr
10. Pete Stoyanovich	25. Bubba McDowell
11. Jim Everett	26. Rod Woodson
12. Chris Miller	27. Steve Atwater
13. Dan Marino	28. Darrell Green
14. Dan Fouts	29. Patrick Allen

30. Dave Meggett

31. Jim Taylor

32. Jim Brown

33. David Fulcher

34. Thurman Thomas

35. Neal Anderson

36. Bennie Blades

37. Nate Odomes

38. Tim Worley

39. Robert Delpino

40. Bill Bates

41. Keith Byars

42. Eric Ball

43. Larry Brown

44. John Stephens

45. Wayne Haddix

46. Marv Cook

47. Joey Browner

48. Lionel Washington

49. Dennis Smith

50. Mike Singletary

51. Mike Croel

52. Pepper Johnson

53. Ray Donaldson

54. Chris Spielman

55. Cornelius Bennett

56. Chris Doleman

57. Mike Merriweather

58. Jack Lambert

59. Kyle Clifton

60. Eric Moore

61. Roy Foster

62. Tunch Ilkin

63. Jay Hilgenberg

64. Randall McDaniel

65. Eric Andolsek

66. Ray Nitschke

67. Doug Widell

68. Russ Grimm

69. Tim Krumrie

70. Rayfield Wright

71. Charles Mann

72. Rod Saddler

73. John Hannah

74. Jim Covert

75. Chris Hinton

76. Steve Wisniewski

77. Tony Mandarich

78. Richmond Webb

79. Bob St. Clair

80. Andre Rison

81. Tim Brown

82. John Taylor

83. Willie Anderson

84. Sterling Sharpe

85. Nick Buoniconti

86. Ernie Jones

87. Charley Hennigan

88. Al Toon

89. Steve Tasker

90. Neil Smith

91. Kevin Greene

92. Reggie White

93. Jerry Ball

94. Charles Haley

95. Michael Carter

96. Cortez Kennedy   98. Eric Swann

97. Renaldo Turnbull   99. Jerome Brown

RUNNING MATES

1. p	11. d
2. m	12. s
3. h	13. e
4. k	14. b
5. q	15. r
6. t	16. f
7. a	17. g
8. n	18. j
9. o	19. c
10. l	20. i

MUDDLE IN THE HUDDLE #2
(TIGHT ENDS)

A	B	C	D	E	F	G	H	I	J	K	L	M
E	C	D	K	L	S	D	Q	V	Z	G	W	F
N	O	P	Q	R	S	T	U	V	W	X	Y	Z
Y	A	N	T	I	U	X	B	M	P	J	R	H

1. Hoby Brenner   3. Austin Denney

2. Bruce Coslet   4. Ferrell Edmunds

5. Eric Green

6. Keith Jackson

7. Brent Jones

8. Ozzie Newsome

9. Jay Novacek

10. Don Warren

SECOND AND EIGHT

1. Fans were particularly kind to kicker **Scott Norwood** whose last-minute attempt in Super Bowl XXV sailed wide to the right.

2. In 1984, the Bears' **Richard Dent** sacked opposing quarterbacks 17½ times. The Tennessee State grad was the MVP of Super Bowl XX.

3. Speedster **Mel Gray** returned 36 kickoffs for 929 yards in 1991. That year, he also led the league in punt returns: 25 for 385 yards and a 15.4 average.

4. Tampa Bay tried to swing a trade with the Cardinals, sending **Chris Chandler** to Phoenix in exchange for a first-round draft choice. The Cards played it cool and, reluctantly, the Buc's released Chandler whom the Cards then claimed off the waiver wire for $100.

5. 1991 MVP and Pro-Bowler **Greg Lloyd** spends two and a half hours every day pumping iron.

6. As good a runner as **Eric Dickerson** once was, it seems ill-advised for him to have made such a statement about the men who protected the ex-Colt each week from those carnivorous Lions, Bears, and Bengals.

7. Penn State's **Mike Munchak** was the eighth pick overall in the '82 draft.

8. **Renaldo "Skeets" Nehemiah** is now a member of a consortium of track and field athletes promoting the use of blood testing, in addition to urine sampling, to guarantee that the sport and its participants are not tainted by performance-enhancing drugs.

9. The Dolphins' **Reggie Roby** had a gross average of 45.7 yards. (Net average: 36.4.)

10. The Cardinals' **Rich Camarillo** averaged 45.3 yards gross per punt, and a league-leading mean of 38.9 yards net.

11. **Dan Saleaumua** was drafted by the Lions in 1987 and released following the '88 season.

(Perhaps Detroit coaches were more comfortable with the name Ball . . . Jerry Ball.)

12. Cowboy cornerback **Larry Brown** was the 320th pick overall in the 1991 draft.

13. Cleveland Brown quarterback **Bernie Kosar** threw 308 consecutive passes without once being intercepted. The old mark had been set by Bart Starr who had thrown unerringly 294 times.

14. Philadelphia's **Ben Smith** intercepted Kosar's 309th pass on November 10, 1991. Smith's pick enabled the Eagles to edge the Browns, 32–30.

15. The Green Bay Packers used the 230th pick overall in the '91 draft to select **Ty Detmer.**

16. On November 3, **Shawn McCarthy** buried the Bills in the coffin corner with his 93-yarder. In '91, the Pat punted 66 times for 2,650 yards and a 40.2 gross average.

17. **Gayle "The Kansas City Comet" Sayers.**

18. The Pro Football Hall of Fame committee elected the Redskins' versatile lineman **Russ Grimm** to the 1980's All-NFL squad.

19. Self-admittedly, **Lyle Alzado** spent an average of $30,000 a year on steroids.

20. Indiana grad **Vaughn Dunbar** will be in that number, when the Saints go marching in . . .

21. In exchange for quarterback **Jim Everett,** the Oilers received the Rams' first- and fifth-round picks in 1987 and their first-round choice in 1988. Additionally, guard Kent Hill and defensive end William Fuller were sent to Houston. In 1991, Everett ranked 27th in the league in passing with a 68.9 rating.

22. New England's **Marv Cook** caught 82 passes for 808 yards, a 9.9 average. He was the Patriots' third-round pick of the 1989 NFL draft.

23. In April 1992, **Joe Namath** had both his knees surgically replaced with artificial ones to increase his stability and decrease his pain.

24. With a name like **Tony Bennett,** the 6'1", 234-pound linebacker may do a better job of singing his own praises.

25. **Bobby Layne** quarterbacked the Bears in 1948, the New York Bulldogs in '49, the Detroit Lions from 1950–1958, and the Pittsburgh Steelers from 1958–1962.

THE HOLLYWOOD BOWL

1. f
2. i
3. b
4. j
5. h
6. a

7. d
8. e
9. k
10. g
11. c

NAME FIND #2
(CENTERS)

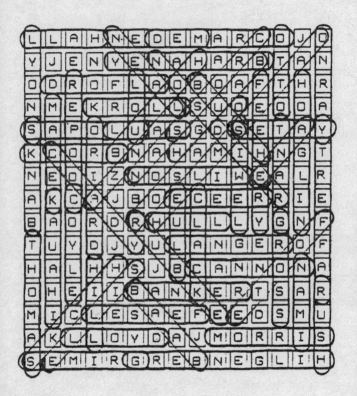

OUT OF BOUNDS

1. a. (True. Aspiring quarterbacks may apply at home-team headquarters.)

2. b. (He's not bragging. It is . . . 70 inches.)

3. d. (Zylocaine is used to deaden pain in non-weight-bearing joints.)

4. b. (Mike Ditka was the cover boy for the sales and marketing publication.)

5. c. (Only $15!)

6. b. (False. Well, they can't all be true!)

7. d. (Appearing before the title, Y. A. Tittle)

8. c. (The "pebbles" of the skin's surface are inverted so as not to protrude from the ball. Apparently, the resulting indentations enhance one's ability to catch the ball.)

9. a. (True. Montana was chosen for his animated personality.)

10. b. (Though there are plans for her someday to succeed her father, Mike Brown, as General Manager.)

11. c. (Adman George "I Want My Maypo" Lois also adopted "In Your Face" as the slogan for ESPN's '92 baseball coverage.)

12. a. (True, White is the co-author with Larry Reid. One can only assume Reggie prefers *two-hand* touch.)

13. d. (Pagliei played fullback for the Philadelphia Eagles in 1959 and the New York Titans in 1960. And yes, Tschappatt and Musgrove are real names of real players.)

14. b. (Even the Eagles, Cardinals, Seahawks, and Falcons leave the flying to American Airlines.)

15. c. (Lombardi went from Titletown, USA, to Middletown, N.J., after he died on September 3, 1970.)

16. a. (Yes. The Bear and the Buc are third cousins . . . on John Mark's mother's side of the family.)

17. b. (The winner and still champ . . . William Perry at 325 pounds! Runners-up: Tootie Robbins—322 lb., Kevin Gogan—311, and Bubba Paris—306.)

18. c. (Tunch Ilkin. Hi, Mom!)

19. a. (True, which just goes to prove today's players are unwilling to use their heads when it counts.)

20. b. (Indianapolis fans hope Steve Emtman will help the Colts capture the Lombardi Trophy, which is accorded Super Bowl champions.)

BY THE BOOK

1. k	7. l
2. i	8. c
3. d	9. e
4. f (available from Penguin USA)	10. b
	11. h
5. a	
	12. g
6. j	

MUDDLE IN THE HUDDLE #3 (LINEBACKERS)

A	B	C	D	E	F	G	H	I	J	K	L	M
F	L	P	K	N	V	B	A	U	S	C	H	R
N	O	P	Q	R	S	T	U	V	W	X	Y	Z
Y	W	G	I	Z	X	D	T	J	O	M	Q	E

1. Michael Cofer	6. Seth Joyner
2. Kevin Greene	7. Karl Mecklenburg
3. Tim Harris	8. John Offerdahl
4. Sam Huff	9. Darryl Talley
5. Vaughan Johnson	10. Derrick Thomas

A WORLD OF THEIR OWN

1. Spoiling the chances of **Raleigh-Durham** being selected for an NFL franchise in '94, the **Sky-hawks** played unprofessionally and were received ambivalently by Carolina fans. The team folded after a single season and was succeeded by the **Ohio Glory,** which knew no glory in '92.

2. Linebacker **George Bethune,** who played for the NFL's Los Angeles Rams in 1989 and 1990, was the first player selected in the WLAF's second annual draft.

3. Fans of Barcelona's **Eric Naposki** may show their support for the linebacker by joining "La Penya Naposki."

4. On April 26, 1992, **Cornell Burbage** of the New York/New Jersey Knights returned a kick 101 yards for a touchdown. The score helped lift

the Knights to a 34–11 victory over division foe, the Montreal Machine.

5. Nose tackle **Chris Williams** of the Frankfurt Galaxy recovered a fumble and returned it for a touchdown on the WLAF's opening weekend of play in 1991.

6. Ohio quarterback **Pat O'Hara** connected with **Melvin Patterson** for a 99-yard touchdown (and an unbeatable league record) in the Glory's 33–39 loss to the New York/New Jersey Knights on May 10, 1992.

7. Tom Landry is a member of the consortium that owns the **San Antonio Riders.** In 1992, the Riders hosted their games in San Marcos, Texas.

8. **Reggie Slack,** the quarterback of the New York/New Jersey Knights completed 16 consecutive passes. On April 12, 1992, he went 7 for 7 against the Orlando Thunder and, two weeks later, he went 9 for 9 versus the Montreal Machine. (Due to a shoulder injury, Slack did not compete in the Knights' April 18 encounter with the Frankfurt Galaxy.)

9. Only **63** of the 110 NFL "loans" were approved by the WLAF, which may indicate that the quality of play in the spring league has improved.

10. A **highway accident** involving a truck delayed Barcelona's team bus in traffic for nearly three hours. Arriving late—very late—the home team dressed and took the field without the benefit of warm-ups. The Dragons, subsequently, were extinguished 0–17.

THIRD AND THIRTEEN

1. Over the course of just 16 months, the All-Pro tackle **Luis Sharpe** competed in 44 professional league games.

2. In the States, **Doug Flutie** forever may be remembered for his heroic feats as a quarterback at Boston College. In Canada, however, his recent accomplishments have been far more dramatic and memorable. In 1991, he led the CFL in attempts, completions, and yardage. Following that season, the free agent left the Lions and signed a four-year deal with the Calgary Stampeders worth a reported $1 million a year.

3. The Seattle Seahawks drafted **Dan McGwire** in 1991 as the heir apparent to Dave Krieg. Dan is the brother of Oakland A's slugger, Mark McGwire.

4. **Mark Herron** totaled 2,444 all-purpose yards in '74, which not only led the Pats, but the league as well.

5. **Carnell Lake,** selected by the Steelers in the second round of the 1989 draft, was named the team's rookie of the year, having started in 15 of 16 games and recovered five fumbles during his first season.

6. The Washington Redskins selected 6'2", 276-pound defensive tackle **Bobby Wilson** from Michigan State with the 17th pick overall of the 1991 draft.

7. When he signed with the Raiders in 1989, wide receiver **Sam Graddy** returned to the site of his Olympic triumph, Los Angeles Memorial Coliseum, where the Raiders play their home games.

8. Since the '84 games, San Francisco's **Michael Carter** has been putting opposing centers in their place rather than putting the shot.

9. Linebacker/center **Chuck Bednarik** played for the Eagles from 1949–1962. During his 14-year career, he appeared in eight Pro Bowl games (1951–55, '57, '58, and '61) and was named the all-star contest's MVP in 1954.

10. Ferocious "lion"-backer **Michael Cofer** regularly devours opposing quarterbacks. The Tennessee graduate was Detroit's third-round selection in the 1983 draft.

11. Green Bay quarterback **Don "Magic Man" Majkowski** was paying his respect to Packer legend, Paul Hornung (who was inducted into the Pro Football Hall of Fame in 1986).

12. **James Brooks** was the Chargers first-round draft choice in 1981 and remained in San Diego until he was traded to Cincinnati in 1984. Brooks had three 1,000-yard seasons with the Bengals and joined the Browns in '92 as a Plan B free agent.

13. Defensive end **Shane Curry** was murdered in what some law-enforcement officials now speculate was a case of mistaken identity.

14. **Hershel Walker** was a member of the U.S. two-man bobsled team in the '92 Winter Games, but his plans for summer gold hit a snag when he learned America would not field a karate squad for the Barcelona games.

15. Voted the World League's Most Valuable Player in 1991, **Stan Gelbaugh** signed with Seattle prior to the '92 season to compete with Kelly Stouffer and Dan McGwire for the starter's assignment.

16. **Les Kelley** had less impact than Saint officials had hoped. The linebacker lasted only three seasons in the NFL, 1967–1969.

17. In his senior season, Cornhusker **Mike Rozier** rushed for 2,148 yards and NCAA records of 29 touchdowns and a 7.86 yards-per-carry average. He was waived by the Falcons following the '91 campaign.

18. Chiefs' safety **Deron Cherry** was honored for his "service to team, community, and country."

19. Dallas Cowboy linebacker **Ken Norton, Jr.,** is the son of . . . drumroll, please . . . Ken Norton, Sr.

20. The days and Knights of **Reggie Williams** have been very productive. The New York/New Jersey franchise, which the former linebacker fielded in 1991, advanced to the World League's championship game in its inaugural season.

21. Since his retirement, **Rocky Thompson,** born Symonds, has run a grain-exporting business in Bermuda and coached high school football in Kentucky.

22. **David Woodley** was only 24 years old in '83 when the Dolphins were scalped by the Redskins, 27–17, in Super Bowl XVII. Today, he deserves all of our prayers for a speedy recovery and a hard-earned "victory" in his battle with liver cancer.

23. In 1967, **Mike Garrett** led the Kansas City Chiefs in rushing with 1,087 yards. Five years

later (1972), he charged to 1,031 yards with San Diego.

24. By contrast, double-teams and knee injuries must seem a pleasure to **Doug Smith.**

25. 6'6", 284-pound tackle **Gary Zimmerman** played for the USFL's Los Angeles Express in 1984 and 1985, before signing with the Vikings in '86. He received his private pilot's license in 1987 and his instrument rating and own aircraft in 1990.

FOOTBALL CONNECTIONS

1. Brown, Csonka, Little, and Nance all graduated from Syracuse University.

2. Montana, Bradshaw, and Starr are the only players to have received the Super Bowl MVP award more than once.

3. Collins, Manley, and Wilson have all received lifetime suspensions from the NFL for having violated the league's drug policies in excess of three times each.

4. Montana, Esiason, and Long have all appeared as television spokespersons for Hanes sportswear.

5. Sanders, Jordan, and Dozier have all played the field—the outfield, that is—in the majors.

Sanders has roamed the field with the New York Yankees and the Atlanta Braves, his Falcon teammate Jordan with the St. Louis Cardinals, and Dozier with the New York Mets.

6. The bittersweet lives of Bell, Piccolo, and Cappeletti were each depicted in movies made for television. The films, respectively: *The Ricky Bell Story, Brian's Song,* and *Something for Joey.*

.7. 1960 marked the inaugural seasons of the Jets, the Oilers, and the Broncos, as well as the New England Patriots and the Buffalo Bills.

8. Prior to the 1992 season, Bates, Ilkin, Brenner, and Reasons (along with Steve Jordan, Luis Sharpe, and Dave Duerson) were named vice-presidents on the executive board of the National Football League Players Association.

9. McMahon, Landry, and Jurgenson are all featured in Kodak's instructional videotape, "How to Play Winning Football."

10. Byars, Jackson, and Dickerson—as well as Calvin Williams and Fred Barnett—were all invited to attend a special mini-camp at the campus of Nevada-Las Vegas prior to the 1992 season, hosted and paid for by Eagles' quarterback Randall Cunningham. Cunningham invested more than $30,000 in this unorthodox preseason program, which he hoped would speed his

recovery from the knee injury he had suffered the year before.

GAME FILMS

1. Shaw thwarted the unsportsmanlike efforts of terrorists Marthe Keller and Dern, but he could not alter the outcome of **Super Bowl X**—Steelers 21, Cowboys 17. Frankenheimer intercut actual footage of the game with the film's dynamite conclusion. (Note: *Black Sunday* was based on the novel by Thomas Harris, author of *Silence of the Lambs*.)

2. Director Francis D. Lyon cast the unforgettable **Elroy "Crazylegs" Hirsch** in the title role of this very forgettable film.

3. *When Harry Met Sally.* Billy Crystal's Harry was crushed, as were the Lions, 0–20.

4. Even Charlton Heston failed to lead the **New Orleans Saints** to the promised land, the Super Bowl.

5. Alan Alda played writer/quarterback **George Plimpton,** who was much in need of a M*A*S*H unit after a few nutcracker drills with the likes of Joe Schmidt and Mike Lucci.

6. The soul of starting quarterback Joe Pendleton, in the body of backup Conrad Jarrett, took the

field and the title for the **Los Angeles Rams** with a fourth-quarter touchdown run against the Pittsburgh Steelers. Beatty portrayed both, in addition to millionaire Leo Farnsworth, in his 1978 remake of *Here Comes Mr. Jordan.*

7. **Jack Lemmon** (Hinkle) and **Walter Matthau** starred in the classic comedy directed by Billy Wilder.

8. Hawkeye Pierce and Trapper John summon "The Hammer" for a scrimmage 3 miles from the front in Robert Altman's **M*A*S*H.**

9. Though set in the future, Caan loved the team of the '70's (and '90's?), the **Dallas Cowboys.**

10. Robert Muldoon became **Roberta Muldoon,** but remained a football fan.

SCRIMMAGED LINES #2
(DEFENSIVE BACKS)

ILLEGAL PROCEDURES

1. New York Jets' running back **Freeman McNeil** claims his attempts to overturn the NFL's current system of restrictive free agency by no means expresses a personal dissatisfaction with the league or team management. He simply believes that a more equitable system for player movement must be established for the benefit of all players, not just the superstars.

2. The reputations of Detroit defensive tackle **Alex Karras** and Green Bay's "Golden Boy" **Paul Hornung** were tarnished by their yearlong suspensions. Five other members of the Lions' squad were fined $2,000 apiece for similar infractions of league policy. Neither Karras nor Hornung were found to have bet against their own teams.

3. Retired Giant linebacker **Brian Kelley** owns a one-third interest in the Lodi, New Jersey, concern.

4. **Chuck Muncie**

5. Denver wide receiver **Vance Johnson** was filmed in the buff during postgame playoff coverage in a segment on HBO's *Inside the NFL.*

6. Cornerback **Terry Taylor** was the seventh player to receive such a lifetime suspension

from the NFL. He was the 22nd player chosen overall in the '84 draft and played for the Seahawks through the 1988 season. In '89, Seattle traded Taylor to the Detroit Lions in exchange for running back James Jones.

7. **Barry Word** played for the Saints in 1987 and 1988 and then announced he was retiring due to his disillusionment with the pro game. He changed his mind and signed with Kansas City in 1990 and is now considered one of the NFL's finer backs. In 1991, he carried the ball 160 times for 684 yards (a 4.3 average) and 4 touchdowns.

8. **True.** Not only did the NFL fine Elway $1,000 (the league's standard fee for such an infraction), the game's referee also assessed the Broncos a 5-yard penalty for the quarterback's charitable deed.

9. Mexican-bred kicker **Rafael Septien** was a hometown hero until his run-in with the law in 1986. Despite having been cleared of the most serious charges levied against him, his career in football was over. When Septien attempted a comeback with the Broncos, a group of Denver women petitioned the team not to employ him. In his nine-year tenure (1978–1986) with the Cowboys, he totaled 874 points.

10. Punter **Ralph Giacomarro,** is the named plaintiff in the class-action suit. He, among others,

claims never to have received severance pay.
(Ain't that a kick in the pants!) A U.S. District
Court in Atlanta, Georgia, ruled in the players'
favor.

FOURTH AND TWO

1. **Rick Casares** compiled 5,675 rushing yards with
the Chicago Bears.

2. On November 13, 1983, Seattle's **Zachary
Dixon** ran one back for six against the St. Louis
Cardinals.

3. Charger cornerback **Gill Byrd** makes his teammates believe they can fly.

4. As a member of the Purple People Eaters' front
four he laid down the law. Today, **Alan Page**
practices law in Minnesota.

5. 6'4", 280-pound guard **Jeff Bregel** was the San
Francisco 49ers second-round draft choice in
1987. The USC grad was the 37th player selected overall.

6. Huskie **Don Heinrich** was inducted into the
College Football Hall of Fame in 1987. After
his coaching stints, he went into broadcasting
serving as an analyst for University of Washington, then 49er telecasts. He died on March 1,
1992.

7. Guard **Joe DeLamielleure** played with the Bills from 1973–1983 and was voted onto the AFC's Pro Bowl squad six times.

8. (Alec Baldwin, look out!) Navy grad **Phil McConkey** caught two passes for 50 yards in Super Bowl XXI, including a 6-yard touchdown reception.

9. Guard/tackle **Ron Mix** (#74) had been the only Charger other than Dan Fouts (#14) to have his number retired.

10. Although he no longer holds the record, don't feel sorry for **Terry Bradshaw;** he does own four Super Bowl rings.

11. Tackle **Ron Heller** reportedly said "let's don't quit," which rankled Coach Perkins despite the context. Perkins fractured two fingers in the off-field fracas.

12. **Scott Appleton** was the first Texas Longhorn to claim the prestigious Outland Trophy. After his retirement from football, he became a minister. He died of heart failure on March 4, 1992.

13. Kevin Murphy is the president and **Chuck Doyle,** the vice-president of N.E. Wear, a San Francisco-based clothing company that special-

izes in casual menswear. Doyle was a running back for the Bills in 1986 and 1987.

14. A jury has ruled that the restaurant outside of which **Joe Phillips** was attacked is liable for 10 percent of the damages the Charger nose tackle will receive. The jury believed that the restaurant should have provided more security in what is known to be a high-crime area.

15. Despite his fantastic '49 season, **Tony "Silver Fox" Canadeo** totaled only 4,197 yards in his 11 seasons with the Packers.

16. **Abdul Salaam** doesn't give a "faulk" what you call him.

17. Perhaps, Eagle defensive tackle **Mike Golic** will consider auditioning for the role of baseball's "Phillies Phanatic" upon retirement from the stressful world of pro football.

18. Defensive end **Marcus Koch** was ready to settle for a life down home rather than the regular home-and-away. (Apparently, he prefers planing boards to boarding planes.) But Redskin officials convinced him to return to camp, and since, has remained, and played, in Washington.

19. Regardless of his heritage, the play of defensive lineman/linebacker **Eric Kumerow** is far from criminal.

20. The Bears' title hopes were crushed when running back **Willie Galimore** (1957–1963) and end **Bo Farrington** (1960–1963) were lost in the training-camp crash.

21. It seems appropriate the event that the first-place finisher in a cutting horse competition should be a cowboy, a Dallas Cowboy, that is. **Jay Novacek** teamed with pro Bill Riddle to score 436.5 points.

22. Like mother, like son: Barbara and **Marvcus Patton.**

23. Running back **Dave Kopay** played for the San Francisco 49ers (1964–1967), the Detroit Lions (1968), the Washington Redskins (1969–1970), the New Orleans Saints (1971), and the Green Bay Packers (1972). The late, great Jerry Smith was the first player whose death has been linked to the AIDS virus.

24. **Ray Isom**

25. Forget Bo! Forget Neon Deion! What? Could it be? You've forgotten . . . **Matt Kinzer.**

NAME FIND #3
(WIDE RECEIVERS)

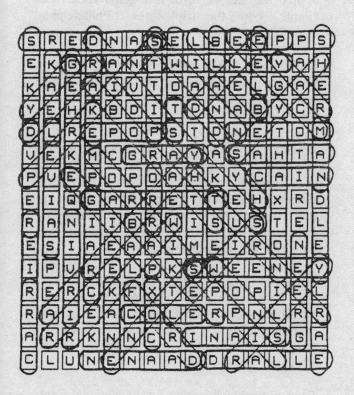

THE RED ZONE

1. **Randall Cunningham** could have cleaned up in one of those Punt, Pass, and Kick competitions! On December 3, 1989, the Eagles' quarterback booted the ball 91 yards in a game versus the Giants. With the triple-threat, Philadelphia won, 24–17.

2. On May 19, **1935,** the NFL *accepted* the proposal for teams to draft in inverse order of the teams' standings from the preceding season. The first draft was *held* on February 8, 1936.

3. Heisman Trophy-winner **Jay Berwanger** was chosen by Philadelphia, but the halfback from the University of Chicago did not sign with the Eagles. He would not sign with the Bears either, to whom the Eagles had traded his rights. Berwanger retired from football without ever playing a down, professionally.

4. After Berwanger's sudden retirement, the Boston Redskins signed blocking back/quarterback/linebacker/kicker **Riley Smith.** The second pick overall of the 1936 draft kicked 14 of 17 P.A.T.s and 4 field goals in his rookie season with the 'Skins.

5. Fearing further litigation by the National Football League Players' Association, the NFL relaxed the eligibility standards for the draft in **1990.**

6. In ascending order:
   #3. **Richard Dent**—Chicago Bears: 103½ sacks
   #2. **Reggie White**—Philadelphia Eagles: 110 sacks
   #1. **Lawrence "L. T." Taylor**—New York Giants: 121½ sacks

7. The Bills were fined **$5,000.** I'm sure there's no doubting Thomas will face the press next time.

8. The magnificent seven ride again: LB **Chuck Howley** (1961–1972), MLB **Lee Roy Jordan** (1963–1976), DT **Bob "Mr. Cowboy" Lilly** (1961–1974), QB **"Dandy" Don Meredith** (1960–1968), RB **Don Perkins** (1961–1968), CB **Mel Renfro** (1964–1977), and QB **Roger "The Dodger" Staubach** (1969–1979). Jerry Jones has extended an offer to Tom Landry to be inducted into the Ring of Honor, but Landry has refused, explaining that he has been much too busy.

9. The **Denver Broncos** employed the 25th pick overall in the 1992 draft to select UCLA's **Tommy Maddox.**

10. Oilers' safety Bubba McDowell collided with Browns wide receiver **Danny Peebles,** ending that particular play and a particularly promising career. The 25-year-old Peebles announced his retirement from football shortly thereafter.

11. **Jim Sweeney** and **Brad Baxter** and Jets head coach, Bruce Coslet have denied accusations that the chop-block and its consequences were premeditated. More important, following the '91 season, the NFL reviewed and altered its chop-block policy, making such blocks below the waist illegal regardless of whether it is a passing or running play.

12. The **Chicago Cardinals** selected first and second in the **1958** draft.

13. The measure between the uprights is **24 feet.**

14. **No one** received a game ball. Coach Parcells believed that the victory was the result of a giant team effort and that everyone was equally deserving of the honor.

15. Buffalo's **Bill Polian** was the recipient . . . again. The Bills' General Manager was named TSN's Executive of the Year in 1988 also.

16. The **Cardinals,** then of Chicago, defeated the Philadelphia Eagles 28–21 for the **1947** NFL Championship. The Cardinals failed to reach a title game after moving to St. Louis, but hope to rise from the ashes during their incarnation in Phoenix.

17. In 1934, the Chicago Bears' **Beattie Feathers** became the first player to top the 1,000-yard mark, rushing 101 times for 1,004 yards. His

9.94 yards per carry that year set a standard unapproached by any superstar since. Feathers' closest challenge came from the legendary Jim Brown, who could muster only 6.4 yards per carry in '63.

18. Erected in 1924, **Los Angeles Memorial Coliseum** has been called home by both the Rams and the Raiders. The Coliseum was also the site of the 1964 and 1984 Olympic Games.

19. **None.** Joe Montana amassed 1,142 yard passing in Super Bowls XVI, XIX, XXIII, and XXIV without throwing to the other team.

20. Though his Nissan was totaled, Dawkins may still have a future in football, thanks to the heroic efforts of fellow wide-out and friend, **Rob Moore.** Dawkins escaped the crash with a shattered femur, which required the insertion of a steel rod in his right leg.

21. **Steve Courson**

22. The AFL held its first draft—of 33 rounds!—on **November 22, 1959.** It held an additional draft 10 days later on December 2 of 20 rounds.

23. **Jim Brown** made his remarks in a taped interview, which appeared on ESPN's *SportsCenter*.

24. For 60 seconds of air time, sponsors paid **$1.7 million.** In 1974, a minute cost advertisers only $217,000.

25. **The Buffalo Bills trampled the San Diego Chargers 23–0.**

26. If an NFL squad is forced to **forfeit** a contest, the game will be logged as a 1-point triumph for the unchallenged opponents.

27. Michigan center **Matt Elliot,** the 336th pick overall, may be just the man Joe Gibbs needs to keep the Redskins on top in the NFL.

28. End **Willard Dewveall** played for the NFL's Chicago Bears in 1959 and 1960. In '61, he struck "black gold" and signed with the AFL's **Houston Oilers.** He "drilled" with the team through the 1964 season.

29. Defensive back **Norm Thompson** left the Baltimore Colts to sign with the St. Louis Cardinals in 1977, the first year of the restricted free agency reform. Eleven years later, Chicago Bear linebacker **Wilber Marshall** earned the nickname "Steve Austin" when he signed a contract with the Washington Redskins, which reportedly made him a "Six Million Dollar Man."

30. Stacy Toran's blood alcohol level was a shocking **.32 percent.** (A blood alcohol level of .40

percent is considered lethal. At that percentage, the average human being fatally succumbs to alcohol poisoning.)

31. James (Anheuser) Busch Orthwein is the majority owner of a group hoping to return pro football to **St. Louis, Missouri.**

32. If Orthwein can woo the NFL to St. Loo, **Walter Payton**'s dreams will come true. Orthwein has already selected "Sweetness" to be the team's representative to the league.

33. **Tom Clancy,** the author of *The Hunt for Red October* and *A Clear and Present Danger,* hopes that the only *Patriot Games* he'll be concerned with in the near future are those between New England and his Baltimore squad.

34. **Charlotte, North Carolina,** has enthusiastically backed the NBA's fledgling franchise, the Hornets.

35. We should all give thanks to **G. A. Richards,** the first owner of the Detroit Lions, for giving us an excuse to not speak to family.

36. Al Davis is also a member of the prestigious **Adelphi University Athletic Hall of Fame** in Garden City, New York.

37. The Bert Bell Benefit Bowl, established in 1961, pitted the second-place finishers from

each conference of the National Football League in a consolation contest. Also known as **The Playoff Bowl,** the first (January 7, 1961) featured the Detroit Lions and the Cleveland Browns. The Lions triumphed 17–16.

38. Charlie Krueger, who played for the 'Niners from 1959 through 1973, claimed that he was both physically and psychologically scarred by the team's mistreatment. Apparently, the training staff did not alert Krueger as to the severity of injuries suffered and placated any concern and masked any pain by feeding him a mix of steroids and painkillers. As a result, he is now **permanently disabled.** He has also been diagnosed as having **"depressive neurosis,"** the latter condition due to a sense of betrayal.

39. These are the sites the Raiders have called home: **Kezar Stadium** (1960), **Candlestick Park** (1961), **Youell Field** (1962–1965), the **Oakland Coliseum** (1966–1981), **California Memorial Stadium** (one game in 1973), and **Los Angeles Memorial Coliseum** (1982–?).

40. The NFL began permitting unlimited substitution in **1950.** This signaled the twilight of the two-way player and the dawn of the situation-specialist.

41. **Darvocet**

42. **Barry Sanders** won the duel, carrying the ball five times for only a single yard. Yes, one yard

more than Worley, who gained zero yards on five attempts also. Despite Sanders' workhorse performance, the Lions were defeated, 3–23.

43. **The Rock Island Independents**

44. Tailback/blocking back **Fritz Pollard** was a player-coach for the Akron Pros (three stints: 1920–1921, 1925, 1926), the Milwaukee Badgers (1922), and the Hammond Pros (1923–1925).

45. The Oilers defeated the Titans that day, 27–21. But far more devastating for the Titans was the loss they suffered as a consequence of the contest. New York guard **Howard Glenn died as a result of a broken neck** incurred during the game.

46. Natu's birth name is more than a mouthful: **Gerardus Mauritius Natuitasina Tuatagaloa.**

47. It's a bird, it's a plane, it's New York Giants' wide receiver **Mark Ingram**—NOT! Con man **Aaron Williams** was exposed after members of the Povich staff contacted Giant officials for background information and learned that the real Mark Ingram had been in Detroit the day of the show's taping. Whoops! The show never aired in its original form.

48. On May 11, 1992, NFL Commissioner Paul Tagliabue appointed **Dr. Len Burnham** as the league's Director of Player Programs.

49. Jim Thorpe has done his part; his body remains in the Jim Thorpe Monument in Jim Thorpe, **Pennsylvania.** Regardless of his presence, few consider what were once the townships of **Mauch Chunk and East Mauch Chunk** in their summer travel plans.

50. It is important to remember that in 1968 the NFL had yet to merge with the AFL, and thus:

THE NATIONAL FOOTBALL LEAGUE

EASTERN CONFERENCE

CAPITOL DIVISION	CENTURY DIVISION
Dallas Cowboys	Cleveland Browns
New York Giants*	New Orleans Saints*
Philadelphia Eagles	Pittsburgh Steelers
Washington Redskins	St. Louis Cardinals

WESTERN CONFERENCE

CENTRAL DIVISION	COASTAL DIVISION
Chicago Bears	Atlanta Falcons
Detroit Lions	Baltimore Colts
Green Bay Packers	Los Angeles Rams
Minnesota Vikings	San Francisco 49ers

*The Giants and the Saints were the teams that swapped divisions in '69

LAST MAN OUT
by Donald Honig

It is February, 1946, in New York. The sensational base-ball rookie Harvey Tippen has just signed on with the Dodgers. Everything is going great until fate throws a sharp curve. A gorgeous, young society heiress is found brutally murdered, and Tippen, who was her last lover, is now tops on the suspect list. Agonizing over a secret he is afraid to confess, Tippen is caught between cops look-ing for a quick conviction and a Dodger ownership seek-ing to sweep the scandal under the carpet. It looks like Tippen's diamond future is over before it's begun when baseball reporter Joe Tinker sends the game into extra innings. But nothing can prepare Tinker for what awaits him at the end of this twisted trail of desire as he hunts for the truth and tries to persuade the police that a vital piece in the puzzle has been overlooked. Ringing with authenticity, this mystery-thriller is as rich in nostalgic magic as it is in spellbinding suspense.

Coming from Dutton Books

27 million Americans can't read a bedtime story to a child.

It's because 27 million adults in this country simply can't read.

Functional illiteracy has reached one out of five Americans. It robs them of even the simplest of human pleasures, like reading a fairy tale to a child.

You can change all this by joining the fight against illiteracy.

Call the Coalition for Literacy at toll-free **1-800-228-8813** and volunteer.

Volunteer Against Illiteracy. The only degree you need is a degree of caring.

FROM CAP ANSON TO HITTING MACHINE DON MATTINGLY ... FROM THE BROOKLYN *EXCELSIORS* TO THE NEW YORK *METS* ... THE ULTIMATE BOOK FOR BASEBALL FANS!

- Do you know whose season and career home run records Babe Ruth broke?

- Do you know what current major league team was originally called the *Invaders*?

- Do you know who was the first player to get hits for two different teams in two different cities on the same day?

Test your memory and knowledge of America's favorite pastime with the most comprehensive sourcebook of every unusual, intriguing and amazing baseball achievement—plus special sections featuring the evolution of season and career hitting, fielding and pitching records— that everyone, from fan to fanatic, will devour.

DAVID NEMEC is a novelist and baseball historian. He has written the historical sections of *The Ultimate Baseball Book*, numerous baseball and memorabilia books, and the franchise histories for major-league team yearbooks.

GREAT BASEBALL FEATS, FACTS & FIRSTS

DAVID NEMEC

A SIGNET BOOK

SIGNET
Published by the Penguin Group
Penguin Books USA Inc., 375 Hudson Street,
New York, New York 10014, U.S.A.
Penguin Books Ltd, 27 Wrights Lane,
London W8 5TZ, England
Penguin Books Australia Ltd, Ringwood,
Victoria, Australia
Penguin Books Canada Ltd, 10 Alcorn Avenue,
Toronto, Ontario, Canada M4V 3B2
Penguin Books (N.Z.) Ltd, 182–190 Wairau Road,
Auckland 10, New Zealand

Penguin Books Ltd, Registered Offices:
Harmondsworth, Middlesex, England

Published by Signet, an imprint of Dutton Signet,
a division of Penguin Books USA Inc.

This book previously appeared in a Plume edition
published by New American Library.

First Signet Printing, April, 1989
16   15   14   13

REGISTERED TRADEMARK—MARCA REGISTRADA

Printed in the United States of America

To my father, Joseph Sylvester Nemec,
who was ahead of his time
but balanced matters by having a son
who is an anachronism in his.

Contents

SECTION 5

SECTION 6

Acknowledgments

A book like this one is often the product of a single, highly skewed imagination, but usually there have been many minds along the way that have triggered, fostered and helped refine it.

Among those I especially wish to cite are: Philip Von Borries, baseball historian, whose favorite province is the old American Association and in particular Pete Browning; Bill Weiss, Pacific Coast League statistician, for providing me with copious material on the minor leagues; Dino Restelli for introducing me to many old players and fans in the San Francisco Bay area; Jill Grossman and Larry Zuckerman for their supportive and helpful editing; and Fran Collin for her representation of my interests in the publishing industry.

Finally, I want to thank the many readers who have written to apprise me of errors they've found in earlier editions. With their help this book is now as accurate as I know how to make it, although I suspect there still may be some glitches. Baseball research, in many areas, is still in its infancy and much new information has been unearthed since I began this project. In any case, I hope readers will continue to let me know where I'm still short of the mark, which is always absolute perfection.

Foreword

It probably won't come as a surprise to those of you familiar with my other baseball history and memorabilia books to learn that I'm in a shrinking minority. I don't believe there is any way at the moment to compare George Brett's accomplishments to those, say, of Home Run Baker. Nor do I think anyone ever will devise a satisfactory method to do it. We are doomed to debate forever whether Babe Ruth would have out-homered Roger Maris if he too had been in his prime in 1961, or whether Cy Young would have won 500 games or just 400, or not even 300, if he had pitched under the same conditions and against the same batters that Dwight Gooden faces. Give me an argument if you like—I'm still open to being convinced that one or the other of our sabermetricians now on the case will discover a system to measure Reggie Jackson against Chuck Klein—but, meanwhile, it doesn't make me overly despondent not to know who was the greatest hitter or pitcher or shortstop of all time. Life—and baseball—are full of uncertainties. Differences of opinion are a large part of what makes them fun.

In the next breath, I'm going to haul off and say that I do have some suggestions that I think will help you make order out of the chaos that exists whenever baseball analysts gather to thrash out and attempt to settle once and for all the metaphysical issues of their profession. First off, many of them like to dismiss all records set before 1893 because the geometry of the playing field hadn't yet been properly established. This is a convenient way to dispose of a lot of unwieldly 50-win and 400-strikeout seasons, but ultimately it's an evasion of the problem. A record achieved in 1886 isn't any less meaningful because it happened when the pitcher's mound was only 50 feet from home plate. That it was accomplished by a pitcher who played left field between starting assignments or had a 6.90 ERA after the mound was moved to its present location is also beside the point. A record is a record regardless of when or under what circumstances it occurred. If five pitchers win 200 games in the course of a decade, but only one wins 250, then we all agree that one pitcher has the best mark for that particular 10-year-period. But if no pitchers win 200 games in the following decade, and only two win as many as 150, we'll all agree again that it doesn't necessarily mean those two pitchers aren't at least the equal of the five who won 200 a decade earlier and perhaps even as good as the 250-game winner. What it comes down to is that for us to grapple successfully with the many enormous disparities that exist between batting averages in the twenties and batting averages in the sixties, pitching strikeouts in 1906 and pitching strikeouts in 1986, shortstops' fielding averages in 1882 and shortstops' fielding averages in 1982, we can't simply call some of the figures unrepresentative and drop them from consideration. Instead, we have to set up a few ground rules. One that I've found helpful in winding my path through the record books is to divide the game into seven periods:

1. 1876, the year the National League began, through 1892
2. 1893, the first year the pitcher's mound was 60 feet six inches from the plate, through 1900
3. 1901, the American League's inaugural year as a major circuit, through 1919
4. 1920, the unofficial beginning of the lively ball era, through 1941
5. 1942, the first year World War II altered the game appreciably, through 1960
6. 1961, the first wave of expansion, through 1976
7. 1977, the third wave of expansion, through the present

To some extent these points of demarkation are arbitrary. Many, for example, feel that the seventh phase really began when the strike zone was redefined after the 1968 season and a second wave of expansion took place, or else when the American League adopted the designated hitter rule in 1973. If you want to side with either of those contentions, I have no quarrel. Neither will I be unhappy if you happen to think the National Association was a major league and the first phase should therefore begin with the 1871 season.

Almost every generalization that is made about baseball invites speculation, if not outright argument. Everybody is in accord that the game entered a new phase when the pitcher's mound was moved 10 feet farther away from the plate, because it altered the balance between batters and pitchers radically in favor of the former and immediately led to more hitting and scoring. But I have yet to unearth a good explanation for why batting averages and run production jumped in 1893, really took off for the stratosphere in 1894 and then returned for the next few years to about the level reached in 1893. What happened during the 1894 season? Why was it that hitters really feasted the second year—rather than the first year—after the mound was moved? I don't know the answer. I can't even make a reasonable guess why somebody like Hugh Duffy hit .440 in 1894, 77 points higher than he did in any other season. The record books are full of feats, facts and firsts that defy logic and leave us hungering for explanations. And the books themselves aren't always logical or consistent. Some claim Christy Mathewson won 374 games, others say 373, and there are a great many today that credit him with only 372 victories. Which figure is the true one? For my purposes, I usually go with the Macmillan *Baseball Encyclopedia* when there is a conflict—but I haven't found the Macmillan so trustworthy that I'd be willing to stake my reputation on its data. What I've done when a serious dispute exists is attach an alert signal, letting you know that before you hold forth on Paul Hines, for one, at your favorite watering hole or the next SABR convention, you ought to be prepared for somebody to jump in and say, "Now wait a minute, ace. According to the *Sporting News*, the first triple Crown winner was . . ."

In any event, I think you'll have a good time looking through this book and seeing who holds a certain record and who held it before him. You'll also note how and why several dozen pitchers who were active before 1920 had career ERAs under 2.50 while only two pitchers who were active between 1920 and 1960 had career ERAs under 3.00. Maybe you already know who those two pitchers are. If so, you can still expect to find a fair amount you don't know, or haven't quite thought of in the same way I have, and will appreciate having it in a compact form. Enjoy yourself.

—*David Nemec*
San Francisco, California

The System for
Evaluating Feats

In college, I had a coach who used to start out each season by telling us that baseball was essentially a simple game. Three strikes, three outs; nine players, nine innings. There was an inherent order to it, and when it was played right it worked like a mathematical equation. Listening to our coach, I always got a bad feeling in my stomach. He wasn't explaining baseball to us but reducing it. Seeing the game merely in terms of numbers and logic was deeply disturbing to me. It was so much more.

Yet, once I began to write about baseball, I realized that he had a point. It really is a game with a magic number, and that number beyond all doubt is three. Along with three strikes and three outs and a structure that is built on multiples of three, in the scheme of things 300 wins and 3000 hits have become the twin pinnacles that, when attained by a pitcher or a batter, assure him of eventual selection to the Hall of Fame. On a seasonal basis, a .300 or higher batting average for a hitter is almost exactly as likely to occur as a 3.00 or lower ERA for a pitcher, and in the utopian year there would be about 10 or 12 of each. To my knowledge that utopia has never been achieved in a season. Probably it never will be. One faction or the other will inevitably hold an edge, and in the ebb and flow of rule changes and developments in equipment and playing surfaces that edge will constantly swing back and forth like a pendulum. Arguably, the balance between hitters and pitchers is more even now than it's ever been. In the past 10 seasons we've had about the same number of .350 hitters and pitchers who have allowed fewer than two earned runs a game, and that, historically, has not always been the case. Indeed there have been times when virtually no pitchers could hold the opposition below three runs a game—forget two—and a .350

batting average just barely got its owner into the top 10 hitters. The 1930 season was like that. The 1968 season, however, in the American League especially, was the exact opposite. Was it because most of the great hitters were born around 1905 and somewhere in the early thirties something in the genes changed around and resulted in a lot of super pitching arms being hatched? Maybe, but there are several much more likely explanations. Wherever the truth lies, though, those two seasons and others like them created scads of records for batting zeniths and pitching nadirs or vice versa—records that in some instances are so skewed as to be all but unbreakable. Nobody in the past 40 years has come anywhere near to collecting 190 RBIs in a season or posting a 7.71 ERA in over 150 innings or rapping 67 doubles. What that means, to me, is that a straight fact and record book, while interesting, leaves something to be desired, namely a perspective that allows for other notable feats to receive their due. I've tried to provide that perspective, first by noting the all-time record and, where it's possible to do it without disrupting the continuity of the book, featuring it in the period in which it occurred, and then by tracing the evolution of the record and noting some of the significant high points and low points since it was set. In other words, touching on not only the major record but the records for each period as well.

It's not an altogether new approach, but what is unique, I think, is the manner in which it's been organized and served up to you. The main course is full of the staples that you rightfully want in a book of feats, facts and firsts, but it's spiced with flavors that ought to do some exciting things to your taste buds.

Introduction

The first section of this book, covering the years from 1846 through 1900, differs somewhat in design from the other sections. Though I'm not writing a history of baseball, I do feel both the obligation and the desire to offer up a backdrop—a setting of the stage, if you will.

In Section 1, along with the great feats and firsts that occurred in the last century, I'll introduce all of the various elements that are present in a typical day or night at a baseball game with the exception of the managers and the stadiums, which we'll meet in Section 2 when both subjects really began to come into their own. Tucked in amid the introductions are chapters on first basemen's records, some of the most interesting teams of the era and a few of the more intriguing bit players who flitted across the stage for only a moment or two but sometimes stole the show before disappearing into the wings. Some comments with regard to chapters on team and individual record holders: Although each for the most part is located in the section focusing on the era when the all-time record was set—i.e., Home Run Feats is found in Section 5, the period when Roger Maris and Hank Aaron set the single-season and career home run marks—all include the bulk of significant records established since 1901. Secondly, the seasons of 1918 and 1919, which were abbreviated due to World War I, and the strike-shortened 1981 season have been omitted from consideration except in cases when the number of games played had no bearing on the record figure. And finally, the names in capital letters designate the all-time record holders for the specified era or position, as distinguished from the names in regular case, which designate either league record holders or runners up to an all-time record.

SECTION 1

Famous Firsts:
1846–1900

The precise origins of many things about baseball that we
take for granted are heavily shrouded by the almost impene-
trable veils of the past. It would be wonderful to know who
first thought of putting webbing in his glove or what pitcher
was the first to pick a runner off base, but it is impossible
even to pinpoint with any degree of certainty the moment of
transition between ancient games like rounders and stoolball
and to say this is how and where baseball began. There are
still many people, some current major-league players among
them, who believe that Abner Doubleday invented the game
as we know it. The more tenable opinion for the past
half-century has been that Alexander Cartwright was the
inventor and that the first game under the Cartwright rules
was played on June 19, 1846, at Elysian Fields in Hoboken,
New Jersey, between the New York Nine and Cartwright's
club, the Knickerbockers. There is no longer any serious
dispute that this game took place; a complete record of it
exists. We know that the final score was 23–1, and the game
ended when the New York Nine scored their 21st run, then
called an ace, in the fourth inning, added two more for safe
measure, and then held the Knickerbockers scoreless in their
last turn at bat. We even know that Cartwright, umpiring
the game, levied a six-cent fine for swearing against a New
York Nine player named Davis.

But was it really the first game? If so, how did the
Knickerbockers, purportedly the first club ever to organize
mainly for the purpose of playing baseball, manage to lose
so egregiously? Who were the New York Nine? When and
where did they assemble and start mastering the intricacies
of the new sport? How sure are we that they didn't secretly
play a slew of games to prepare for Cartwright's bunch and
that those games weren't the first ones? Well, the unhappy

truth is that we're not at all sure; nor, probably, will we ever be. Therefore be warned that some of the firsts you will encounter at the beginning of each section of this book may in fact have been seconds or thirds or, in some instances, no more than myths fashioned by the ageless pairing of a writer with space to fill and a player with an eye to posterity. But in any event, they are well worth sharing.

1849—The Knickerbockers adopt the first official club uniform, which consists of blue woolen pantaloons, a white flannel shirt and a straw hat; in 1855, a broad patent leather belt is added and the straw hat gives way to a mohair cap.

1857—The first league is formed and calls itself the National Association of Baseball Clubs. All games are played at the Fashion Race Course in Jamaica, New York, and spectators are assessed a 50¢ admission fee. The season runs from July to October because some clubs contend the weather is too hot before July.

1857—After the formation of the National Association, a nine-inning format replaces the first-team-to-score-21-runs-wins rule, with five innings constituting a legal contest.

1859—The Brooklyn Excelsiors become the first team to go on tour.

1859—The National Association of Baseball Players is formed, taking control of the game away from the Knickerbockers Club and giving it a national flavor to induce western clubs to participate. The Association also swiftly has the corollary effect of demolishing baseball's image as strictly a gentleman's game.

1862—Jim Creighton of the Brooklyn Excelsiors, highly paid pitcher and the first famous pro player, suffers a ruptured spleen while batting in a game and dies at his home. A large granite monument is erected over his grave in Brooklyn's Greenwood Cemetery. Carved on the granite and encircled by a wreath is a design featuring a pair of crossed bats, a scorebook, a base and a baseball cap. Above the granite design is the single scrolled word *Excelsior*, and balanced on the summit of the granite column rests a stone baseball.

1864—Second baseman Al Reach, later a sporting goods manufacturer and founder of the *Reach Baseball Guide*, becomes the first "revolver" when he jumps the Eckfords club to sign with the Philadelphia Athletics.

186?—Pitcher Candy Cummings discovers how to make a baseball curve . . . maybe. Cummings himself claims not to be the discoverer, but he nevertheless makes the Hall of Fame for it. In the years to come other pitchers will be credited with discovering various new types of deliveries, but it's open to speculation which of them did and which of them didn't. Elmer Stricklett is credited with discovering the spitball; or maybe it was Billy Hart, who claimed he first used it in 1896 after being taught how to throw it by Baltimore catcher Frank Bowerman; or maybe it was Frank Corridon. Nat Hudson is credited with the sinker; Dave Danforth, the shineball; Russ Ford, the emeryball, and maybe the knuckler too, or at least one of the first good ones; Christy Mathewson, the screwball, the first great one anyway, called a fadeaway; and Eddie Plank, the first great palmball.

187?—Nat Hicks of the Mutuals becomes the first catcher to play directly behind the bat; others claim it is Deacon White, who is almost definitely seen doing it in 1875, at any rate with runners on base.

1871—The National Association forms into an organized professional league and plays its first game on May 4, with Cleveland (Forest City) pitted against Fort Wayne (Kekionga). Bobby Mathews of Kekionga pitches a 2–0 shutout over Forest City's Uncle Al Pratt. Deacon White, catcher for Cleveland and the most famous player in the game, goes 3-for-4.

1871—Rynie Wolters, the first Dutch player, debuts with the New York Mutuals.

1871—Boston and Cleveland keep batting averages for all players, and the other National Association clubs soon do likewise. Previously only runs have been recorded.

1872—Oscar Bielaski, the first Polish player, debuts with the Washington Nationals.

1874—The Boston Red Caps and Philadelphia Athletics embark on the first overseas tour to promote baseball, traveling to England in July. While there, the two clubs play a series of exhibition baseball games as well as several cricket matches. The tour is neither a financial nor an artistic success as the British seem singularly uninterested in the new game.

1875—Fred Thayer of Harvard invents the first catcher's mask and shows it to classmate Jim Tyng, who tests it in a college game. Later Thayer is also credited by some with developing the first inflated chest protector.

1875—Joe Borden of the Philadelphias, aka Joe Josephs,

pitches the first recorded no-hitter on July 28 against the Chicago White Stockings.

1875—The Boston Red Caps turn a profit for the season of $2261.07, which is not lost on other National Association club owners and spurs them to begin thinking of forming a more tightly run league and getting rid of weak clubs, corrupt players and lackadaisical team officials.

1876—William Hulbert, taking the bit in his teeth, forms a new circuit and calls it the National League after getting Boston's four star players, Deacon White, Ross Barnes, Al Spalding and Cal McVey, to desert the Red Caps and sign with his Chicago club. Cynics contend Hulbert's motive in forming the National League isn't to provide a better-run operation but because he fears the National Association will expel the four players and his Chicago team in the bargain.

1876—The first National League game is played on April 22 at Philadelphia, with Joe Borden, now with Boston, beating Lon Knight of the Athletics 6–5. Boston's Jim O'Rourke gets the first National League hit, a single in the top of the first inning. Third baseman Ezra Sutton of the A's has the distinction of having also played in the first National Association game, five years earlier, with Cleveland.

1876—Al Spalding appears on the field wearing a black kid glove with layers of padding to reduce the sting of a thrown or hit ball. (If you prefer another player of the time, feel free to substitute his name for Spalding's. Literally dozens are credited with having been the first to use a glove.)

1876—Philadelphia and New York are booted out of the new circuit for failing to complete their last western road trips. Not until 1883 will the two largest cities in the country again be permitted to have franchises in the National League.

1877—The first uniform playing schedule is adopted so that fans in all cities will know in advance which dates their club will be playing at home and can plan accordingly.

1877—The National League starts its second season with a new rule, which states that for a batted ball to be fair it must stay within the foul lines until it passes a base or else is fielded. The rule is put in to curb Ross Barnes, Davy Force and other batsmen who are adept at slicing hits that land in fair territory and then carom foul, forcing infielders to play outside the boundaries when they come to bat. Other players who will force rules to be changed in the years ahead are George Wright and Dickey Pearce, specialists at trapping pop flies before the infield fly rule is created; Will White and Jack Schappert, deft at hitting and intimidating batters without penalty until it occurs to somebody that maybe these wounded batsmen should be awarded first base; King Kelly, who is credited, perhaps falsely, with instigating a rule that prevents him from hopping off the bench when a foul fly heads his way and announcing himself into the game as a substitute in order to catch it; Roy Thomas, so skilled at fouling off pitches that the National League finally, in 1901, decides to start counting foul balls as strikes; and Germany Schaefer, whose crowd-catching device of setting out from second base to steal first causes a rule to be written that the bases can no longer be run backward.

1878—For the first time a commercial league, the National, plays all its scheduled games. Always before at least one team has failed to finish the season.

1879—Boston owner Arthur Soden devises the reserve clause. At first it protects only five players on each team, but with time it's expanded to include the whole roster.

1879—The Providence Grays build the first wire screen behind home plate and across the grandstand in their park to protect spectators from foul tips in a seating area that has become known as the "Slaughter Pens." That same year or maybe a year earlier the Grays are also, some say, the first team to install a turnstile in their park.

1880—Rules are put in to declare a runner out if hit by a batted ball and to award a base on balls on eight balls instead of nine.

1880—The *Chicago Tribune* begins reporting RBIs, but RBI records are not consistently kept until 1907 and then are not officially recognized until 1920.

1881—The pitcher's box is moved to 50 feet from home plate instead of 45 feet.

1882—Denny McKnight of Pittsburgh and Justus Thorner of Cincinnati create the American Association as a competitor to the National League. The AA puts teams in cities dropped by the NL, charges 25¢ admission instead of 50¢, says it's okay to play games on Sunday where the blue laws allow and to sell liquor at them, and outfits its players in gorgeous silk uniforms. Best of all, as far as the players are concerned, it chooses not to honor the NL's blacklist and to go after all players not bound to the NL by the reserve clause. The NL reacts to the threat by trying to ignore it.

1882—The number of balls needed to get a walk is knocked down to seven.

1882—Providence centerfielder Paul Hines trots out to his position wearing sunglasses. Fred Clarke is later credited with being the first player to wear pull-down sunglasses attached to his cap.

1882—Pete Browning of the Louisville Eclipse club wins the American Association batting title with a .378 average, 36 points higher than the runner-up, as only four players in the new league break the .300 mark. Two years later Browning will have the first modern baseball bat made for him by J. A. "Bud" Hillerich, an accidental occurrence that leads to the formation of Hillerich and Bradsby, the world's most famous batmaker. (A century later players credited with inventing curveballs and shin guards will be immortalized on bronze plaques in the Baseball Hall of Fame. Browning, the owner of a .341 career batting average, the first player to have his bats custom made and one of the most colorful and controversial characters in a league replete with them, will not.)

1883—The term *fan* is coined by St. Louis Browns manager Ted Sullivan when team owner Christ Von der Ahe calls the club's followers fanatics. Heretofore the popular word for a baseball fan has been *krank*, and kranks have already been analyzed in depth by Thomas Lawson in his book *The Krank: His Language and What It Means*, which contains a lexicon that includes many phrases that will still be in vogue 100 years later—to wit, the umpire as a 10th man or a robber, a bat as a willow or an ash, outstanding fielding plays as circus catches. The first great krank emerges around the time Sullivan thinks up a shorter word for him. His name is Arthur Dixwell, and he lives in Boston. Independently wealthy, he lavishes rewards on Beaneater players who do something unexpectedly fine and boosts the minor leagues in the New England area with his award of the coveted Dixwell trophy. When excited, Dixwell is heard to scream, "Hi! Hi!" and hence becomes known as Hi! Hi! Dixwell.

1884—Pitchers are allowed to employ shoulder-high deliveries instead of being restricted to those in which their hands must pass below their hips. As a sop to hitters, who now must face overhand fastballs from only 50 feet away, the number of balls needed for a walk is cut to six. In 1886, when observers feel that games are cluttered with too many walks, the figure is again hiked to seven.

1884—Henry Lucas, a young real estate scion who had been operating a minor league called the Union Association, grows convinced that baseball players are little more than chattels and vows to build his minor league into a powerful new major league that will not have the reserve clause. Lucas pilfers many good players from the American Association and National League, but his circuit fails when he stacks his own team, the St. Louis Maroons, with most of the good players and places competing UA teams in such thriving metropolises as Wilmington and Altoona.

188?—Harry Stevens, the "Scorecard Man," aka "Hustling Harry," comes out of the woodwork. By 1900 Harry has nailed down the scorecard and food concessions at most major-league parks, a distinction that his heirs still carry on in 1994. His sales prompt fans to beg owners to put numbers on players' uniforms so that better use can be made of the scorecards; some owners actually oblige their fans for a week or two, but the players resist, not liking the idea of wearing a number. Meanwhile, Stevens is so flush from his commissions that by 1910 he has sent his son to Yale Law School.

1886—The New York Giants set a record when 20,709 attend a Memorial Day game at the Polo Grounds. Later in the season the Giants get nearly 30,000 to a game.

1886—Cincinnati owner Aaron Stern observes that women swarm to the Reds ball park on days that handsome Tony Mullane is scheduled to pitch. Shrewdly, Stern begins designating games that Mullane will work against weak teams that normally draw poorly as special "Ladies Day" events. Mullane becomes known as "The Apollo of the Box" and receives credit from many historians for starting Ladies Days, but further research turns up Ladies Day games as far back as 1876. Whatever the truth of the matter is, Ladies Day games mushroom in the 1880s, and clubs like Brooklyn begin making every day except holidays Ladies Day in the belief that women add a certain tone to the crowd and curtail rowdyism and drunkenness. Brooklyn owner Charles Byrne also points out to his fellow moguls that it's a lot cheaper than hiring special police.

1887—Batters are no longer permitted to call for high or low pitches, and the strike zone is now defined as the area between the tops of the shoulders and the bottoms of the knees rather than above or below the waist. Also in 1887, the NL belatedly goes along with the Association and gives a batter first base if hit by a pitch. To further complicate things for umpires, a base on balls is reduced to five balls, and a strikeout requires four strikes instead of three. major-league rulers, still not content, next decide to count walks as base hits. After all this, Tip O'Neill and Pete Browning post astronomical batting averages in the Association, which are discounted because they were compiled by men who got four strikes and received many walks. (Years later, after statisticians have removed the walks from their hit totals, their averages remain well over .400 and are still viewed as flukes.)

1887—Before the season, Chicago peddles King Kelly to Boston for $10,000, a record transaction. Two years earlier the Detroit Wolverines had shelled out only $7000 to obtain four players nearly as good as Kelly from Buffalo.

1887—Cap Anson takes his champion Chicago White Stockings to Hot Springs, Arkansas, to prepare for a preseason series with the defending AA champion St. Louis Browns and is credited with originating the concept of spring training.

1887—Several St. Louis Browns tout Merrell's Penetrating Oil as a cure for bruises and muscle pulls, the first player endorsement of a product, some say, although players have already begun appearing on cigarette and chewing tobacco cards.

1887—Henry Chadwick decides it's time to revise won-lost records for pitchers. Previously a pitcher who worked the most innings in a game was credited with the decision regardless of the score when he departed. Chadwick, called "the father of the game," was born in England in 1824 and became a sportswriter in 1848. By 1887 he has long since invented the box score, begun editing *Spalding's Official Baseball Guide,* authored the first rule book and originated the scoring system still in use today.

188?—Third baseman Arlie Latham of the St. Louis Browns takes it upon himself to start coaching his teammates when they're on base. A torrential heckler and ace sign stealer, Latham soon becomes so popular with fans that it's feared efforts to control his antics may cut attendance. In 1907, John McGraw pays Latham to do nothing more than act as a base coach for the Giants, making him the first contracted coach.

1888—Detroit begins issuing rainchecks, which state, "In case rain interrupts the game before three innings are played this check will admit the bearer to grounds for the next league game only." Other clubs also adopt the practice, and the next-league-game rule will remain the custom for a long while.

1888—Pitcher Tim Keefe of the New York Giants designs and sells to his team their tight-fitting all-black uniforms with white raised letters that spell NEW YORK across the chest. Called "Funeral" uniforms at first, their color will soon catch on. The 1889 Baltimore Orioles, for one, play in black pants with white side stripes, white shirts and maroon stockings, and black-and-white-striped caps.

1888—Officials finally have it all figured out: Batters should get only three strikes, and that's it. The following year four balls, for the first time, constitute a walk.

188?—Philadelphia manager Harry Wright introduces pregame batting practice and also starts fungoing fly balls to his outfielders before games.

1889—For the first time in major-league history a pennant race is decided on the last day of the season. On October 5, New York beats Cleveland while lowly Pittsburgh is downing Boston's ace pitcher John Clarkson. Had the Beaneaters won, they, and not the Giants, would have claimed the NL flag.

1889—Indianapolis owner John T. "Tooth" Brush waits until Monte Ward, organizer of the first major league players union, goes on a world tour and then sneaks through a classification rule wherein players are graded from A to E, with A players limited to salaries of $2500 and E players able to earn no more than $1500—Ward explodes when he comes home and learns that salaries have been capped.

1890—Ward, Ned Hanlon and several other angry players get Cleveland street railway magnate Albert Johnson to influence other capitalists to loan money to players so that they can build parks in eight cities and start a new league. By the spring of 1890, the Players League has corraled most of the top players in the AA and NL and is a reality. Six months later the Players League concludes its first and only season of play, and Ward and its other leaders are unaware that the AA and NL are near collapse. In their ignorance, the players agree to return to the fold, after getting a few concessions from the owners that are quickly reneged on when the AA ceases operation in the fall of 1891 and the NL absorbs its four strongest franchises, leaving the players with only one major league to which to sell their talents and no recourse but retirement or the minors if they don't like what they're offered.

1890—Harry Decker perfects the "Decker Safety Catching Mitt"—a forerunner of modern mitts. Previously, catchers used heavily padded mittens. Buck Ewing, the first to use Decker's mitt, enthusiastically endorses it.

1891—The substitution rule is liberalized, allowing a player to enter a game at any time and at any position, the only restriction being that the player for which he is substituted cannot reenter the game.

1891—Pittsburgh fines outfielder Pete Browning for not wearing spikes on his shoes. Spikes have been in general use for several years and by now are mandatory equipment.

1892—The new 12-team National League for the first time plays a 154-game schedule, clubs meeting each of their rivals 14 times. (The longer schedule is tried again later in the decade, then reduced to 140 games, where it remains until 1904.)

1892—On June 2, Benjamin Harrison becomes the first president to attend a game while in office, when he watches the Reds beat Washington 7–4 in 11 innings.

1893—The pitcher's mound is moved from 50 feet to 60 feet 6 inches from home plate, and a rule is added that bats must be completely round, eliminating all the bats that are flat on one side or sawed off at the end. It puzzles officials at first why those extra six inches were tacked onto the new mound distance, until they learn that a surveyor misread the blueprint, which correctly read 60 feet 0 inches.

1893—Clifford Spencer proposes that, in conjunction with increasing the mound distance, the field should be made pentagonal with four bases for better balance, fewer foul balls, more stealing and higher status for second basemen. Many are intrigued by the idea, but it's shelved for the moment because the lengthened mound distance immediately leads to more scoring and revitalizes fan interest.

1894—To curb pesky hitters like Willie Keeler who stick out their bats and deliberately poke pitches foul until they get one to their liking, a batter for the first time is charged with a strike for hitting a foul bunt.

1894—Players on the Baltimore Orioles conspire with groundskeeper Tom Murphy to landscape the baselines in their home park in order to prevent their bunts from rolling foul while at the same time leaving the outfield grass high to hide illegal balls that can be put into play at propitious moments. Murphy also loosens the dirt in front of the pitcher's mound to stymie rival hurlers like Cy Young and Amos Rusie and reduce them to a par with Baltimore's moundsmen, who are among the worst in the league.

1895—The infield fly rule is adopted, and a strike is now assessed a batter on a foul tip—but not as yet on a foul ball. Umpires are left to judge between a tipped ball and a fouled one.

1896—A Princeton professor named Hinton invents the first mechanical pitching machine, a smoothbored breech-loading cannon mounted on two wheels and fitted with curved prongs attached to the sides of the muzzle in order to curve a ball.

1897—Eddie Abbaticchio, the first Italian player of note, debuts with Philadelphia.

1897—Oliver Perry Caylor dies. Although never himself a major league player, Caylor helped to found the American Association, managed the Cincinnati Reds and the New York Metropolitans for two seasons and part of a third, subsequently edited *Reach's Official Baseball Guide* and then became baseball editor of the *New York Herald* and official scorer for the Giants. His witty, cutting style and iconoclastic viewpoint are sorely missed in the next decade.

1898—The first modern balk rule is put in the book; also the modern rule for recognizing stolen bases, making it forever impossible to compare Ty Cobb, Lou Brock and Rickey Henderson to Harry Stovey, Billy Hamilton and other early base thieves.

1899—The Cleveland Spiders are the first major league team to become a traveling road show when they play all but a handful of their games in rival cities after the 4th of July owing to poor home attendance; an entirely predictable result after the team's best players are shifted en masse to St. Louis prior to the season, leaving a crew of dregs in the Forest City that lose an ML record 134 games and win a mere 20.

1900—A pentagon-shaped home plate is unveiled, replacing the old diamond-shaped one.

1900—At the conclusion of the season, the infield fly rule is modified so that it's in effect with none out as well as with one out. The National League also decides to start calling foul balls strikes in 1901, unable to care less that the upstart

Western League, which has changed its name to the American League and began billing itself as a major circuit, doesn't want to go along with the foul-strike rule and will not conform until 1903.

Season Record Holders Prior to 1901

It would take an entire book to chronicle the rules that were used to determine batting and pitching records in the 19th century, the exceptions that were made to them, the numerous seasons in which incomplete statistics were kept and the many disputes that are still raging over whether a certain batter hit .492 one year or only .435 and whether a certain pitcher struck out 513 batters another year or only 505. Suffice to say these are the consensus records of an era that was not as yet consumed by the mystique of records and the devotion to minutiae needed to keep them accurately.

The record holders prior to 1893 played when the pitcher's mound was either 45 feet or 50 feet from home plate. The record holders between 1893 and 1900 played under present rules for the most part but in a period when there was only one 12-team league, no meaningful postseason play, and a batter was still allowed to hit an unlimited number of foul balls without a strike being charged against him.

1876 THROUGH 1892

Batting

Department	National League	American Association
Batting Average	.429, Ross Barnes, Chicago, 1876	.435, TIP O'NEILL, St. Louis, 1887
Slugging Average	.581, Dan Brouthers, Detroit, 1886	.691, TIP O'NEILL, St. Louis, 1887
Home Runs	20, SAM THOMPSON, Philadelphia, 1889	19, Harry Stovey, Philadelphia, 1889
		19, Bug Holliday, Cincinnati, 1889

Department	National League	American Association
RBIs	166, SAM THOMPSON, Detroit, 1887	119, Harry Stovey, Philadelphia, 1889
Runs	153, Dan Brouthers, Detroit, 1887	177, TOM BROWN, Boston, 1891
Hits	205, Jack Glasscock, Indianapolis, 1889	225, TIP O'NEILL, St. Louis, 1887
Doubles	49, Ned Williamson, Chicago, 1883	52, TIP O'NEILL, St. Louis, 1887
Triples	26, John Reilly, Cincinnati, 1890	31, DAVE ORR, New York, 1886
Total Bases	311, Sam Thompson, Detroit, 1887	357, TIP O'NEILL, St. Louis, 1887
Bases on Balls	136, JOHN CROOKS, St. Louis, 1892	119, Dummy Hoy, St. Louis, 1891
Stolen Bases	111, Billy Hamilton, Philadelphia, 1891 111, Monte Ward, New York, 1887	138, HUGH NICOL, Cincinnati, 1887

Note: Ned Williamson of the Chicago White Stockings hit 27 home runs in 1884, most of them over a fence so close to the plate that in every other season but 1884 his hits would have been ground-rule doubles—as were the majority of his two-baggers in 1883.

Pitching

Department	National League	American Association
Wins	60, HOSS RADBOURN, Providence, 1884	52, Guy Hecker, Louisville, 1884
Losses	48, JOHN COLEMAN, Philadelphia, 1883	41, Larry McKeon, Indianapolis, 1884
Innings Pitched	680, WILL WHITE, Cincinnati, 1879	671, Guy Hecker, Louisville, 1884
Strikeouts	441, Hoss Radbourn, Providence, 1884	513, MATTY KILROY, Baltimore 1886
Complete Games	75, WILL WHITE, Cincinnati, 1879	72, Guy Hecker, Louisville, 1884
Shutouts	16, GEORGE BRADLEY, St. Louis, 1876	12, Ed Morris, Pittsburgh, 1886
ERA	1.23, George Bradley, St. Louis, 1876	1.21, DENNY DRISCOLL, Pittsburgh, 1882

Batting

Department	Record Holder	Runner-up
Batting Average	.440, HUGH DUFFY, Boston, 1894	424, Willie Keeler, Baltimore, 1897
Slugging Average	.690, HUGH DUFFY, Boston, 1894	686, Sam Thompson, Philadelphia, 1894
Home Runs	25, BUCK FREEMAN, Washington, 1899	19, Ed Delahanty, Philadelphia, 1893
RBIs	165, SAM THOMPSON, Philadelphia, 1895	146, Ed Delahanty, Philadelphia, 1893
Runs	192, BILLY HAMILTON, Philadelphia, 1894	166, Billy Hamilton, Philadelphia, 1895
Hits	243, WILLIE KEELER, Baltimore, 1894	240, Jesse Burkett, Cleveland, 1896
Doubles	55, ED DELAHANTY, Philadelphia, 1899	51, Hugh Duffy, Boston, 1894
Triples	31, HEINIE REITZ, Baltimore, 1894	29, Perry Werden, St. Louis, 1893
Total Bases	372, HUGH DUFFY, Boston, 1894	352, Sam Thompson, Philadelphia, 1895
Bases on Balls	126, BILLY HAMILTON, Philadelphia, 1894	124, John McGraw, Baltimore, 1899
Stolen Bases	98, BILLY HAMILTON, Philadelphia, 1894	87, Billy Hamilton, Philadelphia, 1895

Note: Some sources still credit Werden with 33 triples in 1893.

Pitching

Department	Record Holder	Runner-up
Wins	36, AMOS RUSIE, New York, 1894	35, Cy Young, Cleveland, 1895
Losses	33, RED DONAHUE, St. Louis, 1897	30, Jim Hughey, Cleveland, 1899
Innings Pitched	482, AMOS RUSIE New York, 1893	447, Ted Breitenstein, St. Louis, 1894
Strikeouts	239, CY SEYMOUR, New York, 1898	208, Amos Rusie, New York, 1893

Department	Record Holder	Runner-up
Complete Games	50, AMOS RUSIE, New York, 1893	46, Ted Breitenstein, St. Louis, 1894, 1895
Shutouts	6, WILEY PIATT, Philadelphia, 1898 6, JACK POWELL, Cleveland, 1898	5, done by six different pitchers
ERA	1.88, CLARK GRIFFITH, Chicago, 1898	2.10, Al Maul, Baltimore, 1898

TEAM SEASON RECORD HOLDERS

1876 through 1892

Highest	National League	American Association
Batting Average	.337, CHICAGO, 1876	.307, St. Louis, 1887
Slugging Average	.446, CHICAGO, 1884	.413, St. Louis, 1887
Winning Pct.	.788, CHICAGO, 1880 (67–17)	.705, St. Louis, 1885 (79–33)
Lowest		
Batting Average	.208, Washington, 1888	.204, BALTIMORE, 1886
Slugging Average	.261, New York, 1876	.258, BALTIMORE, 1882
Winning Pct.	.138, CINCINNATI, 1876 (9–56)	.196, Louisville, 1889 (27–111)

1893 through 1900

	Highest	Lowest
Batting Average	.349, Philadelphia, 1894	.247, St. Louis, 1898
Slugging Average	.484, Boston, 1894	.305, St. Louis, 1898 .305, Cleveland, 1899
Winning Pct.	.705, Boston, 1897 (93–39)	.130, Cleveland, 1899 (20–134)

The Four Most
Interesting Teams Before 1901

1884 PROVIDENCE GRAYS
W-84 L-28
Manager: Frank Bancroft

Regular Lineup—1B, Joe Start; 2B, Jack Farrell; SS, Arthur Irwin; 3B, Jerry Denny; RF, Paul Radford; CF, Paul Hines; LF, Cliff Carroll; C, Barney Gilligan: P, Hoss Radbourn; P, Charlie Sweeney.

Fourth in the National League in batting and fifth in runs scored, the Grays nonetheless won the pennant by 10½ games. Their lineup had just one .300 hitter, Hines, and Radford hit only .197, one of the poorest averages ever for a regular outfielder. The Grays had finished third in 1883 and seemed destined to drop out of contention altogether when Sweeney jumped the club midway in the 1884 season and signed with St. Louis in the Union Association. Sweeney reportedly had the best fastball in the game at the time and was, moreover, an excellent hitter—good enough to play the outfield on the days Radbourn pitched. After Sweeney's defection, manager Bancroft tried to find a replacement for him, but there were three major leagues in 1884, and experienced pitchers were scarce. Finally Bancroft in desperation struck a bargain with Radbourn, who had been under suspension for drunkenness when Sweeney left. Radbourn offered to pitch every game for the rest of the season if in return Providence released him from his contract. Then he proceeded to fulfill his part of the deal by posting an all-time record 60 wins. Radbourn didn't literally pitch every game down the stretch—other Providence players, Radford among them, took a turn on the mound now and then to spell him—but he did work far more often than necessary considering the Grays' runaway win, and it took its toll on his arm. After 1884 he was only an average pitcher and was out of baseball entirely eight years later.

Upon leaving the game, Radbourn opened a billiard parlor and spent his days there, drinking and schmoozing with patrons until he suffered an injury that left his face partially paralyzed. Self-conscious, he retired to a back room, where he sat most of the time in dim light, which concealed his disfigurement. He died of paresis in 1897.

His team fared no better. The smallest city in the National League, Providence, despite winning the pennant, could not draw enough fans to meet its payroll and withdrew from the majors after the 1885 season, never to return.

1882 CINCINNATI REDS
W-55 L-25
Manager: Pop Snyder

Regular Lineup—1B, Dan Stearns; 2B, Bid McPhee; SS, Chick Fulmer; 3B, Hick Carpenter; RF, Harry Wheeler; CF, Jimmy Macullar; LF, Joe Sommer; C, Pop Snyder; P, Will White.

Expelled from the National League after the 1880 season for playing games on Sunday and selling beer in its park, the Cincinnati franchise was quick to regroup when the American Association formed in time to begin the 1882 season. The Reds signed White, Sommer, Carpenter and Wheeler, all members of the 1880 team who were either released or left unprotected by National League clubs, and then snatched catcher Snyder away from the Boston Red Stockings to serve as player-manager. These five players became the nucleus of the only Cincinnati club to win a pennant before 1919. Joining with them were 22-year-old second baseman McPhee, getting his first opportunity to play in the majors, and shortstop Fulmer, who had been blacklisted by the National League early in the 1880 season. In the Association's inaugural year, the Reds were easily the class of the league, romping home 11½ games ahead of Philadelphia. Whether they were as good as Chicago, the NL champ in 1882, was never settled—a postseason series between the two teams ended in controversy after each had won a game—but they were undoubtedly the best Cincinnati nine since the legendary Red Stockings. The club remained strong for several more years but was never again able to mount a serious pennant bid as the St. Louis Browns emerged as the league's powerhouse team.

1894 PHILADELPHIA PHILLIES
W-71 L-57
Manager: Arthur Irwin

Regular Lineup—1B, Jack Boyle; 2B, Bill Hallman; SS, Joe Sullivan; 3B, Lave Cross; RF, Sam Thompson; CF, Billy Hamilton: LF, Ed Delahanty; C, Jack Clements; P, Jack Taylor; P, Kid Carsey; P, Gus Weyhing; util., Tuck Turner.

The Phillies had an all-time record team batting average of .349, averaged over nine runs a game and featured three .400 hitters. But the club could do no better than finish a distant fourth, 10 games behind third-place Boston. At a glance, the reason would seem to be inadequate pitching—the Phillies mound staff had an aggregate 5.63 ERA in 1894—but every team except the New York Giants had the same problem that year. With the mound now 60 feet 6 inches from the plate, hitters in 1894 were so far ahead of pitchers that the league batting average was .309, and five teams scored over 1000 runs.

The better explanation for the Phillies' failure to challenge for the pennant probably lay in manager Irwin. Boston, New York and Baltimore, the three clubs that finished ahead of Philadelphia, were piloted by Frank Selee, Monte Ward and Ned Hanlon, three of the best minds in the game, and I have a hunch that Irwin found himself on the wrong end of a lot of 10–9 and 10–8 scores when he came up against them.

1899 CLEVELAND SPIDERS
W-20 L-134
Managers: Lave Cross and Joe Quinn

Regular Lineup—1B, Tommy Tucker; 2B, Joe Quinn; SS, Harry Lockhead; 3B, Suter Sullivan; RF, Sport McAllister; CF, Tommy Dowd; LF, Dick Harley; C, Joe Sugden;

P, Jim Hughey; P, Charlie Kneppei; P, Frank Bates; P, Crazy Schmidt.

One of the National League's best clubs earlier in the decade, the Spiders were disemboweled by their owners, the Robison brothers, after they bought the St. Louis franchise and gauged that its fans would be more supportive of a good team. Syndicate ownership was outlawed shortly thereafter—but too late to save the Spiders. The Robisons shipped every single regular from the 1898 club to St. Louis, leaving manager Cross with only three quality players—himself, Quinn and Dowd—plus aging Tommy Tucker, talked out of retirement to play one more season. After the club lost 30 of its first 38 games, Cross was mercifully transferred to St. Louis, which needed a third baseman, and the reins were handed to Quinn. Under Quinn, the Spiders had a 12–104 record and were so inept that they no longer dared to show their wares in front of a Cleveland crowd. After June, the club played out the season on the road, where it lost 102 of 113 games and became known as the Wanderers. The leading pitcher, Knepper, had a .154 win percentage, and no hurler won more than four games. Amid all this, Tommy Dowd hit a respectable .278 in 147 games. Dowd, in his 10-year career, had the unpleasant distinction of playing on just about every rotten team in the period. Ironically, he began with the pennant-winning 1891 Boston AA team but played only four games with them before being swapped to Washington, which finished in the cellar. There is a theory that Lave Cross, whose career stats are better than many contemporary players who made the Hall of Fame, never got in because he played for and managed—albeit for only a few weeks—the 1899 Spiders, the worst team in history.

Wild Men
On the Mound

Bases-on-balls statistics prior to 1893 require that anyone interested in interpreting them read a rule book for each season. As an illustration, in 1883 Pud Galvin of Buffalo walked only 50 batters in 656 innings; seven years later he walked 62 in 247 innings. What happened to Galvin's control? Nothing—the fact is it probably got better. But in 1883 a batter had to receive seven balls before he drew a walk. By 1889 the number of balls needed for a walk had dropped to four, and the following year Amos Rusie of the Giants set an all-time record when he granted 289 free passes. In 1893 the mound was moved 10 feet 6 inches farther from the plate, but by that time most pitchers, Rusie included, had adapted, at least partially, to the less liberal margin for errant tosses, and pitchers on the whole issued fewer walks at the longer distance.

MOST BASES ON BALLS, SEASON

		Team	League	Year	
1893–1900	Amos Rusie (R)	New York	National	1893	218[1]
	Cy Seymour (L)	New York	National	1898	213
1901–19	Bob Harmon (R)	St. Louis	National	1911	181
	Nap Rucker (L)	Brooklyn	National	1908	125
1920–41	Bob Feller (R)	Cleveland	American	1938	208[2]
	Ken Chase (L)	Washington	American	1941	143
1942–60	Sam Jones (R)	Chicago	National	1955	185[3]

[1] Probably the wildest pitcher in history, Rusie got better as his career went along. By 1897 his control had improved so much that he gave up only 87 walks in 322 innings.

[2] Both the 20th-century record and the American League record.

[3] The 20th-century National League record.

		Team	League	Year	
	Tommy Byrne (L)	New York	American	1949	179[4]
162-Game	Nolan Ryan (R)	California	American	1977	204[5]
Schedule	Sam McDowell (L)	Cleveland	American	1971	153

[4]The 20th-century record for a left-hander.
[5]Walked 202 in 1974 and is the only pitcher in the 20th century to issue 200 or more walks in a season twice.

Most Seasons League Leader in Bases on Balls

AL—6—Nolan Ryan, last in 1978; Ryan also led the NL in 1980 and 1982.
NL—5—Amos Rusie, 1890–94 consecutive
NL since 1901—4—Jimmy Ring, 1922–25 consecutive; Bob Veale, last in 1968

Most Intentional Walks, Season

23—Mike Garman, 1975, St. Louis, NL
Dale Murray, 1978, Cincinnati, NL
Ken Tekulve, 1982, Pittsburgh, NL

Most Hit Batsmen, Season, Since 1893

NL—41—Joe McGinnity, 1900, Brooklyn
AL—31—Chick Fraser, 1901, Philadelphia

Fewest Bases on Balls, Season, by League Leader in Bases on Balls

NL—82—David Cone, New York, 1992
AL—97—Jimmy Dygert, Philadelphia, 1908

Most Bases on Balls, Game, Nine Innings

NL—16—Bill George, New York Giants, May 30, 1887, versus the Chicago White Stockings. George, a 22-year-old rookie left-hander, set the record in a season when five balls were still needed for a walk. Some sources contend that in 1887 White Stockings rookie George Van Haltren also gave up 16 walks in a game.

NL since 1893—14—Henry Mathewson, New York, October 5, 1906, versus Boston. Christy's younger brother, Mathewson set the modern NL record while making his only major-league start.

AL—16—Bruno Haas, Philadelphia, June 23, 1915, versus New York. In 1915 A's pitchers issued an all-time record

827 walks—only 28 of them by Haas, who was released soon after his record-shattering performance. Six years later, however, he resurfaced as a halfback in the newly formed National Football League.

Most Consecutive Bases on Balls, Game

7—Dolly Gray, Washington, AL, August 28, 1909. Gray walked eight batters altogether in the course of the inning, also a record. But it must have been only a momentary lapse, for he walked just 77 batters in 218 innings that season.

Co-Winners of the "Why Let a Few Walks Bother You" Award

Yankees Hall of Famer Lefty Gomez pitched a shutout on August 1, 1941, despite giving up 11 walks. On May 21, 1970, Mel Stottlemyre of the Yankees was relieved with one out in the ninth inning after surrendering 11 walks in a game that also ended as a shutout.

MOST BASES ON BALLS, CAREER, TOP 10

		Years Active	BB
1.	Nolan Ryan	1966–93	2795
2.	Steve Carlton	1965–88	1833[1]
3.	Phil Niekro	1964–87	1809
4.	Early Wynn	1939–63	1775
5.	Bob Feller	1936–56	1764
6.	Bobo Newsom	1929–53	1732
7.	Amos Rusie	1889–1900	1704
8.	Charlie Hough	1970–	1613[2]
9.	Gus Weyhing	1887–1901	1566[3]
10.	Red Ruffing	1924–47	1541

[1]The lefty career record.
[2]When Hough garnered his 200th career win in 1992, it meant, for what it's worth, that all ten hurlers on the most walks list have notched at least 200 victories, led by Carlton with 329.
[3]Like Rusie, his control began to improve dramatically after the mound distance was increased.

Most Hit Batsmen, Career

206—Walter Johnson, 1907–27. He also once held the AL record for wild pitches with 21, but the mark now belongs to Juan Guzman with 26 in 1993.

pitches in a season—21. The NL record since 1901 is held by Red Ames of the Giants, who let 30 pitches get away from him in 1905.

The Amos Rusie Award for the Most Consistent Lack of Control

Left-hander—Tommy Byrne, 1943–57. Byrne spent most of his career with the Yankees, but in 1951, while pitching for the St. Louis Browns, he walked 16 Washington Senators in a 13-inning game. Over his career, he gave up 1037 bases on balls in only 1362 innings.

Right-hander—Dick Weik, active between 1948 and 1954 with the Senators, Indians and Tigers. Weik made only 26 starts but four times walked 10 or more batters in a game. In 1949 he issued 103 walks in only 95 innings, and if his control improved after that his stats didn't show it. Lifetime, he had a 6–22 won-lost record and 237 walks in 214 innings. Despite it all the Indians liked him enough to trade Mickey Vernon for him in 1950. Three years later Vernon won his second AL batting crown while Weik had a 13.97 ERA in 12 games.

Weik's control problems were equally manifest in the minors. In his very first pro game, with Charlotte in the Tri-State League in 1946, he walked 15 men. Two years later he led the Southern Association in bases on balls, issuing 173 in just 132 innings.

Owners

George Steinbrenner, Marge Schott, Ted Turner and Tom Werner are poles apart in their philosophies on operating a major-league baseball franchise, and each may seem like one of a kind. But the truth is that each of them has had numerous prototypes throughout the game's history. Here are fourteen of my favorite owners; by no means the most famous fourteen, nor the most influential, nor the wackiest—just a representative selection from the legion of fascinating men and women who have had a hand in shaping events.

The First Steinbrenner

Aaron Champion became president of the Cincinnati Red Stockings baseball club in 1867 and immediately embarked on a no-holds-barred commercial expansion program. He pushed through an $11,000 stock issue so that the Red Stockings could refurbish their home grounds, Union Field, and then set out with manager Harry Wright to obtain the best players available regardless of the price. The Red Stockings were not, as some historians have written, the first professional team. Rather, they were the first nationally successful one by dint of being the first all-salaried team, a device to hold players to full-season contracts and prevent them from "revolving," or jumping to rival teams. For more about the Red Stockings see "Team Records," but let's look for a moment at the salaries of the 1869 Red Stockings as a point of comparison to, say, what Red Sox regulars got in 1993.

Harry Wright, CF	$1800
George Wright, SS	$1800
Asa Brainard, P	$800
Charlie Gould, 1B	$800

Fred Waterman, 3B	$800
Charlie Sweazy, 2B	$700
Doug Allison, C	$700
Andy Leonard, LF	$700
Cal McVey, RF	$700
Dick Hurley, Sub	$600
Total salaries:	$9400

The First Tom Werner

Arthur Soden was principal owner and team president of the Boston Beaneaters from 1877 through 1906. To stop revolving, Soden instituted the reserve clause and later was a leader in the movement to limit players' salaries. Tight-fisted, intransigent, Soden was nevertheless highly successful —Boston was the National League's strongest team as late as 1898—until the American League arrived on the scene. Refusing to match the huge sums of money dangled in front of his stars by AL clubs, Soden had lost virtually every player of merit by the time the two leagues reached a peace settlement in 1903. Boston deservedly finished deep in the cellar in 1906—his last season as its owner.

The First August Busch/Charlie Finley/Ted Turner

Chris Von der Ahe was owner and sometimes manager of the St. Louis Browns in the American Association. Von der Ahe was just one of several brewery magnates who helped start the Association in 1882, but by the middle of the decade he stood alone. Outfitting his players in elegant multicolored silk uniforms, bickering with umpires and rival owners, getting more press than all the other club officials combined, Von der Ahe at the same time gave Browns fans high-quality baseball. Sadly, the game swiftly passed him by when the Association folded after the 1891 season, and he died nearly broke.

The Biggest Reason the American Association Failed

The Metropolitan Exhibition Company owned both the American Association New York Metropolitans and the National League New York Giants in the mid-1880s. Convinced that the NL would survive the civil war between the two circuits, company officials stocked the Giants with many of the Mets' best players after the club won the 1884 Association pennant and even included in the package the Mets manager, Jim Mutrie. When the Pittsburgh Alleghenies switched to the National League after the 1886 season, the Association was left without any strong owners except Von der Ahe. The Metropolitan Exhibition Company's machinations were a forerunner of the syndicate ownership practices of the Robison brothers and the von der Horsts, which nearly ruined the National League too in the late 1890s.

Big City Versus Little City I

When Fredrick Stearns bought the Detroit National League franchise in the mid-1880s, the automobile was still only a fantasy, and Detroit was one of the smallest cities to have a major-league team. The Buffalo franchise, likewise serving a small city, was on the verge of collapsing, and Stearns, thinking he saw a quick way to enliven his franchise, purchased Buffalo's four best players—Deacon White, Dan Brouthers, Jack Rowe and Hardy Richardson—at the close of the 1885 season. With the addition of the "Buffalo Four," Detroit became an instant contender in 1886 and won the NL pennant the following year, but Stearns was thwarted from reaping the benefits he had anticipated. His plan, since Detroit had too small a population to draw many fans regardless of the quality of the team, was to make the Wolverines the top road attraction in the game and earn the bulk of his money on visits to Chicago, Boston, Philadelphia and New York. But team owners in these cities abruptly changed the rules governing the sharing of gate receipts when they fathomed Stearn's strategy, and by 1889 Detroit had folded and would be without major-league baseball again until 1901.

Big City Versus Little City II

Andrew Freedman, the New York Giants owner in the late 1890s, believed that having possession of the team in the largest population center in the country entitled him to run it any way he pleased, and for eight years he did. Even more penurious than Arthur Soden and far and away the most loathed baseball mogul in his day, Freedman aborted the career of his star pitcher Amos Rusie by forcing Rusie to hold out one entire season. By the end of the decade the Giants had sunk to last place and seemed destined to stay there unless Freedman was removed. After a bitter struggle, he sold out to a group headed by John Brush, and within a few months Brush had induced John McGraw to desert the American league for the Giants managerial post, and the franchise was on its way to becoming once again the most financially successful in the game.

Big City Versus Little City III
Horace Fogel was part of the new regime that Brush brought with him when he took over the Giants—Fogel even managed the club for a while in 1902—but by 1912 he had switched allegiance to Philadelphia and bought a chunk of the moribund Phillies. He was forced to divest himself of his stock and barred from the game when he allegedly charged that St. Louis manager Roger Bresnahan had allowed the Giants to beat the Cardinals in a crucial series near the end of the 1912 season so that Bresnahan's crony John McGraw would be assured of winning the pennant. The accusation had really emanated not from Fogel and the Phillies camp but from Cubs owner Charles Murphy, who headed the one NL franchise that was on a par at the time with New York's and was thus too powerful to oust. Interestingly, the only other owner ever banned was another Phillies mogul, Billy Cox, who was given the gate by Commissioner Judge Landis early in World War II for betting on his own team. Cox departed meekly and sold the club to the Carpenters, who installed their youngest son, Bob, as team president.

The First Marge Schott
Helen Britton assumed control of the St. Louis Cardinals in 1911 after her uncle, Stanley Robison, died, and she ran them through 1916 when her marriage came apart and she sold the team. After Britton and her husband separated, she took over his post as club president for the 1916 season, making her the first woman ever to act in that capacity on a major league level.

The Federal League Legacy I
In 1915 Harry Sinclair bought a controlling interest in the Newark Federal League franchise and quickly found a way to recoup his losses—and then some—after the Feds closed up shop. As part of the peace settlement with organized baseball, Sinclair was allowed to take over the contracts of many Federal League players and sell them to major-league clubs, earning himself a sizable piece of change and in the process becoming a broker of players and the greatest trader in human merchandise since the abolition of slavery. If the

name seems to ring a bell, you're right—it's the same Harry Sinclair who was later implicated in the Teapot Dome Scandal.

The Federal League Legacy II

Another stipulation of the peace settlement with the Federal League granted Fed moguls Phil Ball and Charles Weeghman the privilege of purchasing the St. Louis Browns and the Chicago Cubs respectively. Ball did little to improve the Browns plight, but Weeghman provided a sharp contrast to former Cubs owner Charles Murphy and indeed to most major-league magnates of his time. In 1916 Weeghman began the groundwork that would soon make Wrigley Field a national treasure. Among his many innovations was to build concession booths in back of the stands so that fans weren't continually being disturbed by hawkers peddling scorecards and refreshments.

The Braves Have That History

Atlanta owner Ted Turner decided in 1977 that he could manage his team better than anyone else and handled the Braves for one game before Commissioner Bowie Kuhn, probably fearing that George Steinbrenner, Ray Kroc and Charlie Finley would soon get the same brainstorm, ordered Turner to cut out the nonsense. Back in 1929, however, Commissioner Landis sat quietly by while Braves owner Judge Fuchs ran the club. Manager Fuchs, the last mogul foolish enough to station himself in his team's dugout for a full season, finished a dreary last, thanks largely to the assistance he'd received from owner Fuchs, who sent Rogers Hornsby to the Cubs prior to the season for a packet of cash, a pocketful of minor leaguers and second baseman Freddie Maguire, whom Hornsby outhit in 1929 by a mere 128 points.

The Greatest Innovator Prior to World War II

Many would vote for Branch Rickey, who brought Jackie Robinson to the majors and was the first major-league mogul to operate a minor-league "farm" system to develop young players, but equally high marks should go to Larry MacPhail. As owner of the Cincinnati Reds in 1935, MacPhail introduced night baseball to the majors and later brought it to Brooklyn and the Yankees when he took over those clubs. Furthermore, he orchestrated the first televised World Series in 1947 and the first official old-timers' game, also in

1947, to commemorate Babe Ruth, ill with throat cancer, Ruth's Foundation for Boys receiving the entire proceeds. But perhaps his most significant act of all was to bring Red Barber with him when he moved from Cincinnati to Brooklyn. Try, if you can, to summon back a vision of Ebbets Field in the forties and fifties without hearing Barber's voice as a counterpoint to it.

The Greatest Innovator Since World War II

Bill Veeck—and there's no one else even close. Over and above the countless zany and delightful spectacles he gave his fans, Veeck owned the last Cleveland team to win a World Championship, the last Chicago team to win a pennant and the last team, in 1953, to play under a name that will always be among the most tradition-laden in history—the St. Louis Browns.

The Greatest Innovator Since Veeck

Charlie Finley has been with us too recently to get into perspective. We laughed when he adorned his Kansas City A's in green, white and gold uniforms in the fifties, and we groaned when he scheduled weekday World Series games exclusively at night, but history, I think we're going to find, will be very generous to him.

Famous Brother Acts

After the Cincinnati Red Stockings broke up, Harry Wright and his brother George signed with the Boston Red Caps in the newly formed National Association. In 1876 they were joined on the Boston club, now in the National League, by a third brother, Sam, for a short time. Hence the Wrights were not only the first brothers to play in the major leagues, they were also the first trio of brothers. In 1877 a second set of brothers arrived on the scene in Boston when Deacon White was joined on the Red Caps by his younger brother Will. The following season both White brothers jumped to the Cincinnati club and formed the first sibling battery in the National League, with Deacon catching and Will pitching. They stayed together through the 1880 season; when the Cincinnati franchise folded, Deacon caught on with Buffalo while Will was cast adrift until the American Association was organized two years later.

First Brother Battery in the American League
Homer and Tommy Thompson with the 1912 Yankees. You might have missed seeing them since Tommy pitched only 33 innings and Homer didn't even catch one entire game.

Second Brother Battery in the American League
Milt and Alex Gaston with the 1929 Red Sox. Both played several seasons in the AL but were together only in 1929.

First Brother Battery in the National League after 1900
Jack and Mike O'Neill with the 1902–3 Cardinals. Mike, the pitching half, also served as the Cardinals' main pinch hitter—on June 30, 1902, he hit the first pinch grand slam in history, off Togie Pittinger of the Braves. A few years

later, two younger brothers, Steve and Jim, arrived in the majors. Steve, who managed the 1945 Tigers to a World Championship, is the lone O'Neill remembered today, but all four brothers made a dent.

Most Successful Brother Battery

AL—Rick and Wes Ferrell played together from 1934 through 1938 with the Red Sox and Senators. Rick is in the Hall of Fame, and Wes not only won nearly 200 games but was perhaps the best hitting pitcher ever. In 1948, seven years after leaving the majors, he led the Western Carolina League with a .425 average while serving as a player-manager for Marion.

NL—Mort and Walker Cooper helped power the Cardinals to three pennants in the early forties. Mort won 20 games three years in a row, and Walker was voted to several All-Star squads.

Oldest Player to Act as His Brother's Batterymate

Johnny Riddle, nearly 43 years old, caught his brother Elmer for the 1948 Pirates.

First Brothers to Oppose Each Other as Starting Pitchers

Jesse and Virgil Barnes on May 3, 1927; pitching for the Dodgers, Jesse beat Virgil and the Giants 7–6. Earlier in the decade the two had both been with the Giants and formed the first brother starter-reliever combo, Virgil acting the part of savior.

Second Brothers to Oppose Each Other as Starting Pitchers

Joe Niekro, then with the Cubs, faced his brother Phil on July 5, 1967, the first of what would be many duels between them, Phil and the Braves winning 8–3.

Only Pitcher to Start Against His Brother in His First Major-League Game

By special arrangement, Pat Underwood of the Tigers faced his brother Tom of the Blue Jays in his major-league debut on May 31, 1979.

First Brothers Each to Win 20 Games in a Season

Harry and Stan Coveleski. Harry first collected 20 wins with the 1914 Tigers, Stan with the 1918 Indians. The Coveleskis played for rival teams in the AL for several years but made a pact not to pitch against each other and never did.

Only Brothers to Win a Combined 40 Games in a Season as Teammates
Dizzy Dean won 30 games and brother Paul won 19 for the 1934 Cardinals.

Only Brothers to Pitch a Combined Shutout
Rick and Paul Reuschel of the Cubs on August 21, 1975, 7–0 over the Dodgers.

Brothers with the Best Combined Career Winning Percentage, Each Winning at Least One Game
The famous Hovlik brothers. Ed was 2–1 with the 1918–19 Senators, and Joe was 3–0 with the 1911 White Sox, giving them a family winning percentage of .833.

Among brothers with more than 250 career decisions combined, the Deans rank first with a .631 winning percentage. The three Clarksons, thanks chiefly to John, posted a combined winning percentage of .622 to top all brothers who figured in more than 500 career decisions.

First Twins to Play in the Major Leagues
John and Phil Reccius with the 1882–83 Louisville Eclipse club in the American Association. For a time the Louisville manager was their older brother Bill.

Only Twins in the 20th Century to Play Beside Each Other
Johnny and Eddie O'Brien formed a keystone combination for the 1953 Pirates; later they both also pitched for the Pirates.

First Brothers to Play Beside Each Other in the Outfield
Jim and John O'Rourke of the 1880 Boston Red Stockings.

First Brothers to Play Beside Each Other in the Infield
Bill and Jack Gleason of the 1882 St. Louis Browns, Bill at shortstop and Jack at third base.

First Brothers to Oppose Each Other in a World Series
Doc and Jimmy Johnston in 1920, Doc with Cleveland and Jimmy with Brooklyn. The second pair of brothers to face each other in the Series were the Meusels in 1921, Bob

with the Yankees and Emil with the Giants. In 1908 the
Clarke brothers, Fred and Josh, narrowly missed becoming
the first brothers to play against each other in a Series when
Fred's Pirates lost the NL pennant on the last day of the
season and Josh's Naps finished ½ game behind the victorious Tigers.

First Black Siblings to Play in the Major Leagues
Fleet and Welday Walker, in 1884, with Toledo in the
American Association.

First Black Siblings to Play in the Major Leagues in the 20th Century
Sammy and Solly Drake, Solly with the 1956 Cubs and
Sammy four years later, also with the Cubs.

Only Brothers to Have 100 or More RBIs, Season, in the Same League
Bob and Roy Johnson, Bob with the Philadelphia A's and
Roy with the Red Sox. Two other sets of brothers—the
Meusels and Joe and Vince DiMaggio—also had 100 RBI
seasons but in different leagues.

Most Home Runs, Season, by Brothers Who Were Teammates
54—Tony Conigliaro (36) and Billy Conigliaro (18), 1970
Red Sox.

Brothers With the Highest Combined Career Batting Average
The Sherlocks. Monk hit .324 for the 1930 Phillies, and
Vince hit .462 for the 1935 Dodgers; their combined career
average is .335.

Brothers With the Highest Combined Season Batting Average
The Waners. Playing side by side in the outfield for the
1927 Pirates, they hit a combined .367, Paul leading the NL
with a .380 average and Lloyd hitting .355—between them
they also had a brother-record 460 hits.

Only Brothers Who Celebrated Their Major-League Debuts More Than 25 Years Apart
Jesse and Art Fowler. Born in 1898, Jesse broke in with
the 1924 Cardinals. Art, 24 years younger, first appeared
with the 1954 Reds.

First Brothers to Share the Same Position for the Same Team

Patsy and George Tebeau. When Patsy, the Cleveland Spiders' manager-first baseman, was injured in 1895, brother George, previously a spare outfielder, replaced him at the initial sack. A third Tebeau, Pussy, also played two games for the 1895 Spiders.

Player With the Most Brothers Who Preceded Him in the Major Leagues

Joe Delahanty. By the time he broke in with the 1907 Cardinals, four of his brothers—Ed, Tom, Jim and Frank—had paved the way for him. Hall of Famer Ed, who drowned in 1903 after falling from a railroad trestle over Niagara Falls, was the best of the Delahantys, and Tom was the only one never a big-league regular.

Last Trio of Brothers to Play in the Same League

AL—Bob, Ted and Ed Sadowski; all were active in the AL in 1962.

NL—Technically, the Cruzes—Jose, Hector and Cirilio—but Cirilio played only a few innings. Felipe, Matty and Jesus Alou were the last trio of brothers in the NL who were all quality players.

TOP 10 BROTHERS, CAREER HITS*

1.	Paul and Lloyd Waner	5611
2.	Felipe, Matty and Jesus Alou	5094
3.	Joe, Dom and Vince DiMaggio	4853
4.	Ed, Jim, Frank, Joe and Tom Delahanty	4217
5.	Hank and Tommy Aaron	3987
6.	Joe and Luke Sewell	3619
7.	Ken, Clete and Cloyd Boyer	3559
8.	Honus and Butts Wagner	3474
9.	Bob and Roy Johnson	3343
10.	George and Ken Brett	3245

*Including only brothers who contributed to the family's total figure. For example, Cloyd Boyer had 20 hits but no home runs; Tommy Sewell was hitless in one at bat; and the Mathewsons, Whites and Galvins were omitted from the pitchers' list because in each case one brother failed to win a game.

BROTHERS WITH 1,750 OR MORE CAREER RBIS

1. Joe, Dom and Vince DiMaggio	2739
2. Hank and Tommy Aaron	2391
3. Ed, Jim, Frank, Joe and Tom Delahanty	2153
4. Paul and Lloyd Waner	1907
5. Bob and Emil Meusel	1886
6. Bob and Roy Johnson	1839
7. Ken, Clete and Cloyd Boyer	1803
8. Lee and Carlos May	1780
9. Honus and Butts Wagner	1766

BROTHERS WITH 300 OR MORE CAREER HOME RUNS

1. Hank and Tommy Aaron	768
2. Joe, Vince and Dom DiMaggio	573
3. Eddie and Rich Murray	445
4. Lee and Carlos May	444
Ken and Clete Boyer	444
6. Graig and Jim Nettles	406
7. Dick, Hank and Ron Allen	358
8. Bob and Roy Johnson	346

BROTHERS WITH 1,800 OR MORE CAREER RUNS

1. Joe, Dom and Vince DiMaggio	2927
2. Paul and Lloyd Waner	2828
3. Ed, Jim, Frank, Joe and Tom Delahanty	2309
4. Hank and Tommy Aaron	2276
5. Felipe, Matty and Jesus Alou	2213
6. Bob and Roy Johnson	1956

BROTHERS WITH 200 OR MORE CAREER WINS

1. Phil and Joe Niekro	539
2. Gaylord and Jim Perry	529
3. John, Dad and Walter Clarkson	385
4. Hoss and George Radbourn	311
5. Stan and Harry Coveleski	297
6. Bob and Ken Forsch	282
7. Gus and John Weyhing	267
8. Jesse and Virgil Barnes	214
9. Dizzy and Paul Dean	200

Invisible Men:
Umpires

Don Denkinger achieved a unique distinction in 1985—he became the first umpire ever to be the most memorable performer in a World Series. Years from now, long after it has grown misty whose pinch single finally won Game Six, his controversial safe call on Jorge Orta's seeming ground-out will still seem vivid. But whether Denkinger himself will become a major figure in the umpires' pantheon remains to be determined. If he does, he'll have a lot of company.

The First Famous Umpire

In the early days umpires were required to be consummate gentlemen, and the man appointed to umpire a game was generally deemed to be both the most honorable and the most knowledgeable club member. But when baseball became a business and players were no longer necessarily of the gentleman class, a new breed of umpire appeared. The first such man was probably Bill McLean, an ex-prizefighter. Officiating in the National Association in the early 1870s, McLean earned the nickname "King of Umpires" because of the vigorous manner in which he took charge of games. McLean later umpired in the National League through the 1884 season. Living in Providence, he customarily walked from his home to work an afternoon game in Boston, rising at 4:00 A.M.

First to Make Umpiring a Full-Time Profession

Nobody knows for sure, but a good guess would be "Honest" John Gaffney, who joined the National League in 1884 and introduced the style of working behind the catcher with no runners on base. By 1888 Gaffney was paid $2500 plus expenses for a season's work, more than most players received. Only a few years earlier umpires had earned just $5 a game, paid by the visiting team while the home team absorbed all other expenses.

First League to Put Its Umpires on a Regular Salary

In 1883 the American Association paid its umpires $140 a month and $3 per diem for travel expenses. Accordingly, the AA had a better overall caliber of umpiring than the National League in the early eighties. The AA's most highly esteemed umpire was probably Ben Young, who pioneered in forming a code of ethics for umpires before he was killed in a railway accident en route to an assigned game. Before his death, Young was also instrumental in getting the AA to provide training for its umpires, issue them blue coats and caps, and experiment with a double umpire system. The NL regarded two umpires as a needless extravagance and preferred to put each game in charge of just one man like Gaffney or Bob Ferguson, a former NL player and manager, whose philosophy after becoming an umpire was "Never change a decision, never stop to talk to a player—make 'em play ball and keep their mouths shut and never fear but the people will be on your side and you'll be called the king of umpires." As late as 1908, in fact, both the National and the American League had a staff of only six umpires, one of whom served as an alternate, meaning that three umpires each day worked a game entirely alone.

Most Difficult Call for an Umpire Prior to 1884

Whether or not a pitch was legally delivered. Until 1884 pitchers were restricted to below-the-waist deliveries, much like fast-pitch softball pitchers. Umpires in the early days often consulted with players and sometimes even with fans before rendering a decision on a play or a pitch.

Only Umpire Banned for Rigging Games

Dick Higham, a former National League player and a good one. Higham was suspected of throwing games while playing, which makes you wonder what the NL expected when he was hired in 1882 to umpire. His downfall came midway in the season while he was umpiring a string of games that involved Detroit and kept making questionable calls against the Wolverines. Detroit officials were finally led to inspect his mail, much of which was in code and not a particulary sophisticated one. From it, they were easily able to deduce that Higham was in collusion with gamblers who were making a nifty sum, thanks to his help, by betting against Detroit.

First Former Player to Have a Lengthy Career as an Umpire

Bob Emslie joined the National League umpiring staff in 1891 after pitching for three seasons with Baltimore in the American Association and remained an umpire until 1924. Emslie was working the bases in the famous "Merkle Game" between the Giants and the Cubs in 1908, and it was actually his responsibility to decide whether Giants rookie Fred Merkle touched second base after Al Bridwell singled home the apparent winning run. But when Emslie claimed not to have seen the play, the onus fell on home plate umpire Hank O'Day, himself a former National League pitcher. O'Day ruled that Merkle was out, and pandemonium reigned at the Polo Grounds, making it impossible for O'Day and Emslie to clear the field and resume the game. Instead it had to be replayed at the end of the season when the Giants and Cubs wound up in a dead heat. The Cubs won the makeup game and the pennant and then went on to win their second and—to date—last World Championship in the Series that fall against the Tigers. Hence Emslie and O'Day are well remembered by both Giants and Cubs fans for their role in the Merkle game, and the game itself was pivotal for major league baseball as a whole in that it, along with several other controversial games in that same period, eventually forced officials to realize that more umpires were needed.

First World Series Game to Have More Than Two Umpires

The fourth game of the 1909 Series between the Pirates and the Tigers found Bill Klem behind the plate, Billy Evans working the bases and Silk O'Loughlin and Jimmy Johnstone on the foul lines after a bitter dispute in Game Three over whether a batted ball had been fair or foul.

Umpire with Most Seasons of Service

NL—Bill Klem. In 1909 Klem was in the fifth season of what would be a record 37-year career. He also officiated in a record 18 World Series, the last in 1940.

AL—Tommy Connolly served 31 years, from 1901 through 1931, and umpired in eight World Series. He, Klem, Hank O'Day, Cy Rigler, Billy Evans and Jocko Conlon are the only umpires to work more than five Series.

Active Umpire with Most Seasons of Service
   AL—Larry Barnett and Don Denkinger, 25 seasons
   NL—Bruce Froemming, 23 seasons

Umpire Who Started the Custom of Raising His Right Arm to Signal a Strike
   Cy Rigler. He reputedly initiated it so that Dummy Hoy, a deaf-mute, could keep track of the count while on base or playing in the outfield. The problem with this story is that Rigler first raised his arm to call a strike around 1905, by which time Hoy had already been out of the game for several years.

First Hall of Fame Player Later to Umpire
   Tim Keefe. But many outstanding players became umpires after their playing careers ended. Among them were the aforementioned O'Day and Emslie, plus George Moriarty, Babe Pinelli, Lon Warneke, George Pipgras, Al Orth, Sherry Magee, Charlie Berry, Bob Caruthers, Firpo Marberry, Ed Rommel, Mal Eason, Butch Henline, Bill Dinneen, Lip Pike, Chief Zimmer and Ed Swartwood.

Men Who Both Played and Umpired in a World Series
   Dinneen, Warneke, Rommel, Pipgras and Frank Secory, a substitute with the 1945 Cubs. Former umpires Ken Burkhart and Bill Kunkel were also members of World Series teams, but neither got into a game.

The "Right Man for the Job" Award
   The home plate umpire for the famous double no-hit game on May 2, 1917, between Fred Toney of the Reds and Hippo Vaughn of the Cubs was former pitcher Al Orth. In 1908 Orth and Vaughn had been teammates on the Yankees for a brief while.

The "Lou Gehrig in Blue" Award
   Bill McGowan, who worked in the American League from 1925 through 1954, umpired a record 2541 consecutive games over a 16½ year period without missing a single inning. Born in 1896, McGowan began his umpiring career in the Tri-State League in 1913 at age 17.

The "Going Out with a Bang" Award
   Babe Pinelli served as a home plate umpire for the final

time in his long career on October 8, 1956. His last official action that day was to signal a called third strike on Dodgers pinch hitter Dale Mitchell and thus ring down the curtain on Don Larsen's perfect World Series game.

The "Umpires' Best Friend" Award

Tom Lynch, former National League umpire, became the NL president after Harry Pulliam committed suicide in 1909. Lynch was the first official to back umpires to the hilt in their war to reduce player rowdyism. He was so successful that he became despised by owners and players alike and was soon fired.

First Umpire to Wear Glasses on the Field

Ed Rommel on April 18, 1956, at Washington in a game between the Senators and Yankees. Larry Goetz was the first National League umpire to do it.

The "Longest Day" Award

On October 2, 1920, the Pirates and Reds played the last major-league tripleheader. Peter Harrison worked behind the plate in all three games—until darkness began to descend over Forbes Field in the sixth inning of the finale, with the Pirates ahead 6–0, and he was at last able to call a halt to the marathon without argument.

First Basemen's Records

Prior to 1900 most of the dominant hitters in the major leagues were first basemen. Then as now size and batting prowess were the key qualities sought by managers when testing players at the position. Four first sackers of the game's first phase—Dan Brouthers, Roger Connor, Cap Anson and Dave Orr—hold most of the pre-1900 career batting records. Others, like Harry Stovey, Long John Reilly, Tommy Tucker, and Jake Beckley, also ranked consistently among the leading hitters and sluggers. Connor, Anson, Beckley, and Brouthers are in the Hall of Fame, and several more of their contemporary gateway guardians probably should be. Achieved during a time when the season schedule called for far fewer games than are played today, the bulk of their season and career marks have long since been eclipsed. So too have the fielding standards that were set by men, like Joe Start and Charlie Comiskey, who used rudimentary gloves and in some cases none at all. In fact, only one first baseman's season record that was established before 1900 is still on the books—for most triples.

SEASON BATTING RECORDS

Department	National League	American League
Batting Average	.401, Bill Terry, New York, 1930	.420, GEORGE SISLER, St. Louis, 1922
Slugging Average	.656, Willie McCovey, San Francisco, 1969	.765, LOU GEHRIG, New York, 1927
Home Runs	51, Johnny Mize, New York, 1947	58, HANK GREENBERG, Detroit, 1938
RBIs	143, Don Hurst, Philadelphia, 1932	184, LOU GEHRIG, New York, 1931

Department	National League	American League
Runs	139, Bill Terry, New York, 1930	167, LOU GEHRIG, New York, 1936
Hits	254, Bill Terry, New York, 1930	257, GEORGE SISLER, St. Louis, 1920
Doubles	48, Keith Hernandez, St. Louis, 1979	64, GEORGE BURNS, Cleveland, 1926
Triples	29, PERRY WERDEN, St. Louis, 1893 22, Jake Daubert, Cincinnati, 1922*	20, Lou Gehrig, New York, 1926
Total Bases	392, Bill Terry, New York, 1930	447, LOU GEHRIG, New York, 1927
Stolen Bases	67, FRANK CHANCE, Chicago, 1903	52, Frank Isbell, Chicago, 1901
Bases on Balls	137, WILLIE MCCOVEY, San Francisco, 1969	137, ROY CULLENBINE, Detroit, 1947
Strikeouts	169, Andres Galarraga, Montreal, 1990	182, CECIL FIELDER, Detroit, 1990
Fewest Strikeouts (Minimum 500 ABs)	6, Stuffy McInnis, Boston, 1924	5, STUFFY MCINNIS, Cleveland, 1922

*Record since 1901. Records are otherwise since 1893 for NL players and 1901 for AL players with the all-time holder's name in caps.

Note: Some sources still credit Werden with 33 triples in 1893, but most reference works have now uniformly credited him with 29. In 1932 Jimmie Foxx hit 58 homers for the Philadelphia A's but played 13 games at third base; similarly, Stan Musial of the Cardinals had 50 doubles in 1946 but played 42 games in the outfield. Hence both Foxx and Musial are not recognized as record holders here because a significant portion of their accomplishments occurred while they were playing other positions.

Most Games, Career, at First Base
2377—Jake Beckley, 1888–1907

Most Consecutive Games at First Base
885—Lou Gehrig, New York Yankees, June 6, 1925, through September 27, 1930

EVOLUTION OF SEASON RECORD FOR BEST FIELDING AVERAGE

	Team	League	Year	Average
Joe Start	New York	National	1876	.964[1]
Joe Start	Hartford	National	1877	.964
Chubb Sullivan	Cincinnati	National	1878	.975
Cap Anson	Chicago	National	1879	.975
Cap Anson	Chicago	National	1880	.977
Joe Start	Providence	National	1884	.980
Dave Orr	New York	Amer. Assoc.	1886	.981
Roger Connor	New York	National	1887	.993
Patsy Tebeau	Cleveland	National	1897	.994
Dan McGann	New York	National	1906	.995
Ed Konetchy	St. Louis	National	1913	.995[2]
Ed Konetchy	Pittsburgh	National	1914	.995
Stuffy McInnis	Philadelphia	American	1914	.995
Fritz Mollwitz	Cincinnati	National	1915	.996
Chick Gandil	Chicago	American	1919	.997[3]
Stuffy McInnis	Boston	American	1921	.999[4]
Frank McCormick	Philadelphia	National	1946	.999
Wes Parker	Los Angeles	National	1968	.999
Jim Spencer	Texas	American	1973	.999
Steve Garvey	Los Angeles	National	1981	.999
Eddie Murray	Baltimore	American	1981	.999
Steve Garvey	San Diego	National	1984	1.000

[1]Several sources credit him with being the first first sacker to play off the bag with the bases empty.

[2]Among the better first basemen in his time, but hidden away on bad teams until late in his career.

[3]He and Hal Chase were two of the *enfants terribles* in the teens. Chase got all the raves for his glove, but Gandil got the stats—he led the AL in fielding four consecutive years, 1916–19, whereas Chase, ironically, was never a fielding leader.

[4]For a player who was never considered among the greats, even in his time, McInnis holds an awful lot of records. His .999 average was better than any of the .999 FAs that followed in that he handled more chances.

Best Career Fielding Average, Minimum 1,000 Games
.996—Steve Garvey, 1969–87

Most Seasons League Leader in Fielding Average
NL—9—Charlie Grimm, last in 1933
AL—6—Joe Judge, last in 1930

Most Consecutive Errorless Games
    193—Steve Garvey, San Diego Padres, June 26, 1983, through April 14, 1985

Most Consecutive Errorless Chance
    1700—Stuffy McInnis, Boston Red Sox and Cleveland Indians, May 31, 1921, through June 2, 1922

Most Chances Accepted, Career
    25,505—Jake Beckley, 1888–1907

Most Chances Accepted, Season
    1986—Jiggs Donahue, Chicago White Sox, 1907

Most Chances Accepted, Game, Nine Innings
    NL—22—Ernie Banks, Chicago, May 9, 1963 (22 putouts)
    AL—22—Done several times; last by Alvin Davis, Seattle, May 28, 1988 (22 putouts)

Most Assists, Season
    184—Bill Buckner, Boston Red Sox, 1985: breaking his old record of 161, set in 1983 with the Cubs, which in turn had broken his 1982 mark of 159. The current NL mark is 180, set in 1990 by Sid Bream of Pittsburgh.

Most Seasons League Leader in Assists
    NL—8—Fred Tenney, last in 1907
    AL—6—George Sisler, last in 1927
            Vic Power, last in 1962

Most Double Plays, Season
    194—Ferris Fain, Philadelphia A's, 1949. That year the A's turned 217 double plays, an all-time team record, and then topped 200 again in 1950 and 1951.

Best Glove Man Ever at First Base
    Hal Chase had the rep, Vic Power was compared to him, and Keith Hernandez has the most Gold Gloves—ten—but don't overlook Paul Campbell. In 1941, playing with Montreal in the International League, Campbell set an all-time record for first basemen by starting 26 double plays; the major league record is 18. Furthermore, Campbell tied a major-league single-game mark on May 14, 1949, when he performed two unassisted double plays for the Tigers.

Under the Lights

If you thought night baseball was a comparatively recent innovation, you might be surprised to learn that the first night game was played on September 2, 1880, between Jordan Marsh & Company and R. H. White & Company, two Boston department stores. The two company nines battled to a 16–16 tie at Nantasket Bay near Hull, Massachusetts, as part of a series of lighting displays put on by the Northern Electric Company of Boston to prove the far-reaching value of the incandescent lamp, invented by Thomas Edison only the year before.

There were other night games during the latter part of the 19th century, but few had the foresight to envision that night baseball would ever be anything more than a novelty. One who did was sportswriter O. P. Caylor. In 1893 Caylor wrote:

> Should the time ever come when by some system of illumination base ball could be played as well at night as in the daytime the possibilities of the game's earnings could hardly be estimated. . . . But the chances are that the time will never come when base ball at night will be possible. . . . However, it is a subject which will be worth consideration. If any one ever does discover a system of out-of-door lighting sufficiently good for base ball playing in the open air at night he will at once take ranks with the millionaires of the land.

Caylor's remarks are quite prescient in all, but his last statement makes me wince each time I read it. George Cahill, the man who first discovered a way of economically staging night games, never made anything close to a million from his invention and indeed is largely forgotten today.

By 1910 Cahill had devised a portable lighting system good enough to get the grudging permission of Charlie Comiskey to stage a game under artificial glare at the new White Sox park. Some 20,000 fans watched two local amateur teams play a full nine innings under the gleam of twenty 137,000-candlepower arc lights and from all accounts thoroughly enjoyed the proceedings. But Comiskey and other major-league owners saw no future in night baseball, and it would be another 25 years before Cahill realized his dream.

The first major-league night game did not take place until 1935. On May 24, at Crosley Field, Paul Derringer of the Reds beat the Phillies 2–1 after President Franklin Roosevelt turned on the lights by pushing a button in the White House. The first to bat under artificial light in a major-league game was Phillies outfielder Lou Chiozza. Among the 20,422 in attendance, though no great ceremony was made of it, was the man who had the largest hand in making it all possible, George Cahill.

Although the first major-league team to install lights, the Reds were far from being the first team in organized baseball to do so. On April 28, 1930, Independence, Kansas, of the Class C Western Association staged the first offical pro night game, losing 13–3 to Muskogee, and by 1935 many other minor-league clubs had already begun playing under the lights.

Second Major-League Team to Install Lights

The Dodgers, and they could not have had a better sense of timing. Their guests on June 15, 1938, for the inaugural night game at Ebbets Field, were the Reds. Four days earlier the Reds scheduled starting pitcher, left-hander Johnny Vander Meer, had pitched a no-hitter against the Braves, and in case you don't know what he did to the Dodgers in front of the first crowd in the New York area to witness a major-league game under the lights, see "No-hitters and Perfect Games."

First American League Team to Install Lights

The Indians, but the Athletics were the first team actually to play at home under the lights. A complete list follows of the opening night games for the 16 franchises that were around when it all started.

Stadium	Date	Result
At Crosley Field	May 24, 1935	Reds 2, Phillies 1
At Ebbets Field	June 15, 1938	Reds 6, Dodgers 0
At Shibe Park	May 16, 1939	Indians 8, A's 3, 10 innings
At Shibe Park (Phillies)	June 1, 1939	Pirates 5, Phillies 2
At Cleveland Stadium	June 27, 1939	Indians 5, Tigers 0
At Comiskey Park	August 14, 1939	White Sox 5, Browns 2
At Polo Grounds	May 24, 1940	Giants 8, Braves 1
At Sportsman's Park	May 24, 1940	Indians 3, Browns 2
At Sportsman's Park (Cards)	June 4, 1940	Dodgers 10, Cardinals 1
At Forbes Field	June 4, 1940	Pirates 14, Braves 2
At Griffith Stadium	May 28, 1941	Yankees 6, Senators 5
At Braves Field	May 11, 1946	Giants 5, Braves 1
At Yankee Stadium	May 28, 1946	Senators 2, Yankees 1
At Fenway Park	June 13, 1947	Red Sox 5 White Sox 3
At Briggs Stadium	June 15, 1948	Tigers 4, A's 1
At Wrigley Field	August 6, 1988	Cubs 6, Mets 4

First Night All-Star Game
June 13, 1943, at Shibe Park, won by the American League 5–4. However, the last part of the 1942 game, at the Polo Grounds, was played under the lights when darkness began to set in after a lengthy rain delay.

First Night World Series Game
October 13, 1971, at Three Rivers Stadium, when the Pirates beat the Orioles 4–3 to even the Series at two games apiece.

Players We Wish We'd Seen More of: 19th Century

Now that there are 26 teams and baseball is no longer the only professional sport to attract the nation's top athletes, there is enough room in the major leagues to accommodate just about every player who has the talent and the desire to make the game a career. But prior to expansion, free agency and changes in the minor league draft rules, every era had its share of shooting stars, players who crossed our line of vision for only a few short moments, just long enough to light up the sky brightly—in some instances brilliantly—before they were inexplicably sent back to the minors or otherwise allowed to fade off, often disappearing so completely that nothing at all is known about them today. Here are my top seven choices from the 19th century.

1. Jocko Flynn. As a 22-year-old rookie with the 1886 Chicago White Stockings, he won 24 games and led the National League in winning percentage. Used also on occasion in the outfield, he played part of one game there in 1887 and then was gone.

2. George Nicol. A pitcher-outfielder, Nicol threw a seven-inning no-hitter for the St. Louis Browns as a rookie in 1890, beating Philadelphia 21–2. It was by far his best mound effort, but before departing at age 23 in 1894, he hit .362 with 25 RBIs and 51 hits in 141 at bats, the second-highest career average in history among players with over 100 at bats.

3. Harry Moore. Playing left field for the Washington Union Association team in 1884, he hit .336 in 111 games, the third-best average in the league, but then departed so precipitously that not a single morsel of biographical information is known about him.

4. Levi Meyerle. One of the game's first great stars, he led all National Association batters in 1871 with a .492 average, the highest in major-league history if you're among those who consider the NA a major league. Meyerle hit .346 with Philadelphia in 1876, the National League's inaugural season, and then was mysteriously blacklisted by Cincinnati the following season, at age 28, despite carrying a .327 average after 27 games.

5. Walter Thornton. A pitcher-outfielder, Thornton broke in with Chicago in 1895 at age 20 and exited in 1898 with a 23–18 career pitching record and a .312 career batting average in 154 games.

6. Jack Rothfuss and Jesse Hoffmeister. For years Pittsburgh was plagued with first base problems, and they may have begun in 1897 when the Pirates cut Rothfuss after he hit .313 in 35 games and showed good power, knocking home 18 runs in 115 at bats. In 1897 the Pirates also had a gaping hole at third base where Jim Donnelly, the incumbent, hit only .193. They tried Hoffmeister for 48 games, and he hit .309 and had 36 RBIs but fielded only .792 with 31 errors. His glove convinced the Pirates to drop him in 1898 and go with Bill Grey, who hit a robust .229 and made 59 errors.

7. Herb Goodall and Charlie Hamburg. After finishing deep in the American Association cellar in 1889, Louisville won the pennant the following year, mostly because manager Jack Chapman lost fewer players than the other AA clubs to the Players League. But among the key regulars who did jump to the PL were leftfielder Pete Browning, two-time AA batting champ, and pitcher John Ewing, brother of Hall of Fame catcher Buck Ewing. They were replaced by two rookies, Hamburg and Goodall. In 133 games Hamburg hit .272 and scored 93 runs while Goodall won eight games, led the AA with four saves and batted a phenomenal .422 with 19 hits in 45 at bats. Despite their large contributions to the team's revival, both were dropped from the roster in the 1891 season, and without them Louisville fell all the way to seventh place.

World Series Play:
1876–1900

FRANCHISE SUMMARY

Team	League	WS Record	Years in Series
New York Giants	National	2–0–0	1888, 1889
Providence Grays	National	1–0–0	1884
Detroit Wolverines	National	1–0–0	1887
Louisville Eclipse	Association	0–0–1	1890
Cincinnati Red Stockings	Association	0–0–1	1882
St. Louis Browns	Association	1–2–1	1885, 1886, 1887 1888
Chicago White Stockings	National	0–1–2	1882, 1885, 1886
Brooklyn Bridegrooms	Both	0–1–1	1889, 1890
New York Metropolitans	Association	0–1–0	1884

Yearly Highlights
1882—Cincinnati (AA) and Chicago (NL) tied 1 game to 1

At the conclusion of the American Association's first season as a major league, the pennant winners in the AA and the National League played a "World Series" to settle which circuit was superior. But the Series ended abortively after two games when AA president Denny McKnight wired the Red Stockings that they would be expelled if they continued play. Cincinnati was prepared to defy McKnight, but Chicago manager Cap Anson withdrew his White Stockings from the Series in what he believed was the best interest of both teams.

1884—Providence (NL) defeated New York (AA) 3 games to 0

Responding to a challenge from New York manager Jim Mutrie, Providence manager Frank Bancroft brought his Grays to the Mets' home park, the original Polo Grounds, for a three-game World Series. The first contest was played on October 23, 1884, before a crowd of 2500 in blustery conditions and under Association rules, which called for hit batsmen to be given first base. As a result, both Providence leadoff batter Paul Hines and second batter Cliff Carroll reached base after being hit by the Mets' Tim Keefe. Hines scored the first run on a wild pitch and a passed ball, and the Grays won 6–0 behind their 60-game winner Hoss Radbourn. The following day Radbourn won 3–1 on a three-run homer by Jerry Denny and then closed out the Series with 11–2 win in even rawer conditions, which caused the third game to be terminated after six innings. The Grays played all three games without using a single substitute.

1885—St. Louis (AA) and Chicago (NL) tied 3 games to 3

The Browns and White Stockings played seven games and wound up deadlocked at three-all, with one contest a tie, in what was now called "The World Championship Series," so named by Alfred Spink, the creator of the *Sporting News*. Players did not take the games seriously because the owners, in their greed, were more concerned with attracting spectators than making for good baseball, and the crowds at times overran the field. Neither team's players received a penny for participating in this Series, which was sloppily played and ineptly umpired.

1886—St. Louis (AA) defeated Chicago (NL) 4 games to 1

The first best-four-of-seven Series played to a conclusion. After splitting the first two games in Chicago, the teams moved to St. Louis, where the Browns won three straight, the finale in the 10th inning when Curt Welch scored from third base on a wild pitch that sailed over the head of Chicago catcher King Kelly. Welch was the first Series hero to be immortalized for a feat that was largely fiction. His "$15,000 Slide," which was made to seem the tail end of a brazen dash for the plate, wasn't even necessary—he could have jogged home and scored standing up.

1887—Detroit (NL) defeated St. Louis (AA) 8 games to 3

Frederick Stearns, eager to take full advantage of his slugging Wolverines, challenged Browns owner Chris Von der Ahe to a 15-game Series, with the two teams traveling in a special train of parlor cars and playing in all major cities as well as St. Louis and Detroit. Von der Ahe further agreed to hiking admission prices to one dollar and to Stearns's suggestion that two umpires be used, "Honest John" Kelly and "Honest John" Gaffney. In search of a way to plug her acting career, Helen Dauvray, wife of New York Giants shortstop Monte Ward, hit upon the notion of awarding a cup in her name to the winning team. Detroit won the first Dauvray Cup, which has disappeared over the years, by taking 8 of the first 11 games, but the teams played the last four anyway.

1888—New York (NL) defeated St. Louis (AA) 6 games to 2

Jim Mutrie, having switched his loyalty to the NL in 1885, became the first man to manage Series teams in two leagues. His war cry to herald his Giants was "We are the people!" Nobody quite knew what it meant, least of all Mutrie, but it sounded good and a song went with it. A 10-game Series was arranged and played out even though the Giants won six of the first eight games. Von der Ahe, supported by his players and in particular Arlie Latham, a notorious rabble-rouser, blamed the umpires for his club's defeat, even accusing umpires Kelly and Gaffney of betting on the Giants. This Series also had the first goat, Browns shortstop Bill White, who had replaced the popular Bill Gleason after Gleason was traded to Philadelphia. White was unfairly chastised—his fielding cost St. Louis one game at most—and never again played in the majors. The Dauvray Cup came to Helen's husband and his Giants, to be kept by them pending the results of the following year's Series.

1889—New York (NL) defeated Brooklyn (AA) 6 games to 3

The Giants played the Bridegrooms in what would have been the first subway Series if there had been subways in 1889—at the time New York and Brooklyn were still separate cities. The Giants won in nine games, making the 10th game unnecessary, and now had two legs up on the three Series wins required to take permanent possession of the Dauvray Cup.

1890—Louisville (AA) tied Brooklyn (NL) 3 games to 3

It was the last Dauvray Cup World Series, as the war between the two leagues in 1891 made postseason play between their pennant winners out of the question. The Bridegrooms, after switching to the NL intact with no key players lost to Players League raids, beat Louisville three of the first four games. But Louisville won the next two, in Brooklyn no less, evening the Series. The weather was so dreadful for the deciding seventh game that only 300 fans showed up and the contest was called off, the Series ending, as it had begun eight years earlier, in a tie.

Postscript

In 1892 the National League, now inflated to 12 teams after absorbing 4 clubs from the defunct Association, played a split schedule for the first and only time in major-league history, the Cleveland Spiders winning the first half season and the Boston Beaneaters the second. After the first game of the postseason series ended in a tie, Boston swept five in a row and terminated proceedings. No championship was played in 1893, but William Temple, president of the Pittsburgh Pirates, which unexpectedly finished second to Boston that year, felt cheated of a crack at the Beaneaters and proposed a plan whereby the second-place team at the end of each season would challenge the first-place team to a best four-of-seven series and win by default if the first place team refused the challenge. He then ordered a cup in his name for $800 from New York jeweler A. E. Thrall and stipulated that, like the Dauvray Cup, permanent possession of the Temple Cup would go to the first team to win it three times. To Temple's chagrin, the Baltimore Orioles won easily in 1894, and the Giants finished second while his Pirates plummeted to seventh place. To the chagrin of all club owners in the league, the Orioles merely went through the motions in their series with the Giants and dropped four straight games. When the same lack of player enthusiasm persisted the next three years, the Temple Cup series was scrapped, owners citing low motivation and secret agreements between teams to split the take fifty-fifty regardless of the result. The irony was that the Orioles, after dismal performances in the 1894 and 1895 series, had revved up their act and taken the next two series in a row, putting them on the brink of seizing permanent ownership of the Temple Cup, which now resides, instead, in the Hall of Fame.

SECTION 2

Famous Firsts:
1901–19

1901—The American League opens its first season as a major league on April 24 but runs into bad luck—three of the four scheduled lid-lifters are rained out. Hence the honor of playing the first AL game falls exclusively to Chicago and Cleveland, which meet at the Chicago Cricket Club in front of 14,000 or so. Chicago, behind rookie right-hander Roy Patterson, wins 8–2. Bill Hoffer, himself a record-shattering rookie 31-game winner in the National League only six years earlier, goes all the way for Cleveland in defeat but is released a few weeks later with a 3–8 record. Cleveland outfielder Ollie Pickering earns the distinction of being the first player to bat in an AL game while his teammate, second baseman Erv Beck, goes 2-for-2 and gets the game's only extra-base hit, a double. The following day Beck hits the first AL home run.

1902—Tom Rice of the *Brooklyn Eagle* begins campaigning for scoreboards and other fan conveniences like having teams announce lineup changes; his efforts lead, among other things, to announcers with megaphones strolling about the grounds and calling out starting lineups and substitutions.

1903—The first moving picture of a baseball game is made, featuring Nap Lajoie and Harry Bay of Cleveland during a post-season series with Cincinnati. In 1910 the National Commission receives $500 for World Series movie rights; the figure climbs to the gigantic sum of $3500 in 1911. Four years later Harry Aitken of the Mutual Film Corporation talks John McGraw of the Giants into becoming the first manager to film his players during spring training for instructional purposes.

1905—Roger Bresnahan experiments with a batting helmet—called a "pneumatic head protector"—after being beaned. In 1907 Bresnahan catches the opening game of the season for the Giants wearing shin guards. The game winds up being forfeited to the Phillies when the Polo Grounds crowd gets unruly, but Bresnahan nonetheless makes the Hall of Fame, in part for his experimentation with headgear and shin guards. Nig Clarke, a rookie catcher for Cleveland who regularly wore soccer guards under his socks in 1905, becomes a footnote in the shin guard story.

1907—Albert Spalding creates a commission to unearth the origins of baseball and names A. G. Mills to head it. Mills, a former National League president, after some months of digging attributes the game's invention to his old friend Gen. Abner Doubleday, who purportedly concocted it one afternoon in 1839 in Cooperstown, New York, while still a West Point cadet. Mills's report is nine-tenths fiction and one-tenth the vague testimony of Abner Graves, a boyhood friend of Doubleday's who claimed to have seen the first game. On the basis of Mills's findings, the Hall of Fame and National Baseball Museum are placed in Cooperstown, and a centennial celebration of the game's birth is planned for 1939. Long before 1939 all the historical material accumulated by Mills is reportedly destroyed in a fire, making verification of it impossible. But the hoopla attending the centennial celebration is so vast that it reaches all the way to Hawaii, where Bruce Cartwright, grandson of a man named Alexander Cartwright, writes a letter in 1938 and encloses supporting evidence that touches off an investigation that seems to prove beyond all doubt that the Mills Commission's findings were phony and Alexander Cartwright was the true inventor of baseball. Hall of Fame committee members, upon deliberation, buy grandson Bruce's evidence, and Doubleday, the man responsible for the shrine's placement in Cooperstown, is himself never enshrined.

1908—George Baird of Chicago invents an electric scoreboard that instantly records balls, strikes, runs, etc.

1908—In July the Giants stun the baseball world by paying $11,000 for Rube Marquard, an unproven minor-league pitcher.

1908—On August 4 the Cardinals and Dodgers play a full game at Brooklyn's Washingtion Park using only one ball. There is nothing to attest that this was the last time it was done, only that it was still something that happened as late as 1908.

1909—On July 18 Cleveland shortstop Neal Ball, in a game against the Red Sox, performs the first unassisted triple play. The previous year, while playing for the Yankees, Ball led the majors with 80 errors and fielded .898.

1910—President Taft throws out the first ball at the Senators' opener on April 14, then watches Walter Johnson pitch a one-hit 3–0 shutout over the Athletics. Taft likes the experience so much that he decides to make it an annual event.

1911—It becomes mandatory for home teams to wear white uniforms and visiting teams dark uniforms. The Giants and the Phillies are the first to start doing this as a way for both fans and players to distinguish one team from the other.

1911—A cork-and-rubber-center ball replaces the dead-as-duck-feathers rubber-core ball; Ty Cobb hits .420, Wildfire Schulte of the Cubs cracks 21 homers, and batting averages as a whole in the American League skyrocket 30 points.

1912—Ty Cobb is suspended by AL president Ban Johnson for going into the Hilltop Park stands on May 15 and fighting with Yankees fan Claude Lueker. The Tigers react to Cobb's suspension by going on strike before their game on May 18 against the Athletics, forcing Detroit manager Hugh Jennings to use Philadelphia seminary student Aloysius Travers, later a priest, on the mound, local amateurs at other positions, and 48-year-old coach Deacon McGuire behind the bat. Travers pitches a complete-game 26-hitter, losing 24–2, while McGuire singles and scores a run, and 30-year-old third baseman Ed Irvin, playing his only major-league game, raps two triples in three at bats, giving him a record 2.000 career slugging average. Late in the game, Jennings inserts himself as a pinch hitter and avoids getting hit by a pitch, thereupon failing in his last big-league at bat to increase his all-time career record for being hit 260 times by pitches.

1914—The Federal League opens its first of two seasons as a major circuit after luring many major-league players into its camp. The first to jump ship is St. Louis Browns first baseman George Stovall. Joe Tinker is the first star to join the Feds. Walter Johnson signs a Fed contract, then recants when Washington owner Clark Griffith gives him a raise, plus a healthy bonus, which is subsidized by other American League owners to keep him out of the Feds' clutches.

1915—The Tigers, the last team to wear collars on their uniforms, finally abandon them. The Yankees, meanwhile, wear pinstriped uniforms for the first time.

1915—The National League makes it a rule that all clubs must have canvases to cover their fields in the event of rain so that play can resume when it stops without resorting to the ancient method of burning wood and spreading oil and sawdust.

1915—The American League starts the policy of giving each player two passes, good for any park in the league.

1915—Cardinals officials, convinced that St. Louis can't support two major-league teams and the Browns are the stronger franchise, attempt to move the team to Baltimore when Federal League owners of the Baltimore club express an interest in buying the Cardinals and transfering them, but other National League owners block the move. Thirty-nine years later the Browns move to Baltimore.

1916—Cubs owner Charles Weegham comes up with the revolutionary idea of allowing fans to keep balls hit into the stands, seemingly bringing to an end the warfare between park policemen and fans trying to obtain souvenir balls. But as late as 1923 a Philadelphia boy is arrested and housed overnight in the slammer for keeping a ball hit into the Baker Bowl bleachers, and in 1937 a Yankees fan is vigorously pummeled by ushers when he attempts to retrieve a ball lodged in the home plate screen. His suit against the Yankees, in which he wins $7,500, results in a sort of truce between club officials and fans on the issue.

1917—The Cardinals establish the first "Knothole Gang" for kids. The brainchild of St. Louis insurance man W. E. Bilheimer to combat juvenile delinquency, it is so successful that in 1920 the Cardinals admit an estimated 64,000 boys to their games for free.

1917—On June 27 Braves catcher Hank Gowdy becomes the first major leaguer to enter the military service in World War I. In October of the following year, former Phillies third baseman Eddie Grant becomes the first major-leaguer player ever to be killed in combat.

1919—The Cardinals pay $10,000 to Kansas City for pitcher Jesse Haines. Haines is the last minor leaguer to be purchased by the Cardinals until World War II, as their farm system, for the next quarter of a century, supplies them with all the talent they need.

A Short History of Team Names

Unlike the Kansas City Royals and several other expansion teams whose names were chosen logically and systematically by their fans, most of the 16 teams that constituted the major leagues from 1901 through 1960 had a number of names before settling on the one now in vogue. To eliminate confusion, all references to teams for the remainder of the book will use their current names.

American League

California Angels (1961)—Originally the Los Angeles Angels, the name of the Pacific Coast League team in the "City of Angels," they became the California Angels when the franchise moved to its new stadium in Anaheim.

Baltimore Orioles (1901)—During the 1901 season the franchise was located in Milwaukee. Moving to St. Louis in 1902, the team became known as the Browns because of the brown trim on its uniforms, a carryover from the old St. Louis Browns in the American Association. When the franchise shifted to Baltimore in 1954, team officials and fans were eager to rid the club of all association with the losing Browns and revive the old Orioles tradition. All Baltimore major league teams since 1885, with the exception of the Federal League Terrapins, had been called the Orioles, as had the International League franchise, the city's lone link to organized baseball from 1916 through 1953.

Boston Red Sox (1901)—Called the Pilgrims or the Puritans in the early years of the American League, and also for a time the Somersets—after owner Charles Somers—they became the Red Sox when new owner John Taylor decided the club needed a zippier name. For a time the club was labeled the Red Stockings, the name of the original Boston

National League team, but sportswriters soon shortened it to Red Sox, and in later years, to BoSox.

Chicago White Sox (1901)—Called the Invaders at first when the American League "invaded" Chicago before the opening of the 1900 season, the club then assumed the name White Stockings, which had been discarded by its National League counterpart in the late 1890s, but the sobriquet was immediately abbreviated to fit into sports page headlines. Within a few years it began being shortened, still more, to ChiSox. Also called the Pale Hose, as opposed to the Red Sox, who are known as the Crimson Hose.

Cleveland Indians (1901)—Known as the Broncos in 1901, then the Blues because of their uniforms, and then the Naps when Nap Lajoie became the team's player-manager, the Indians didn't settle finally on a name until 1915. From 1912 through 1914 they were called the Mollie McGuires since many of their players were Irish, but when they finished last in 1914, it seemed time for a completely fresh start. Some believe the name Indians was chosen to commemorate Louis Sockalexis, the ill-fated Penobscot Indian who played with the Cleveland Spiders in the 1890s. Also called the Tribe.

Detroit Tigers (1901)—The team began as the Wolverines, after the Detroit National League entry which had adopted the name of the state animal, but sportswriter Phil Reid of the *Detroit Free Press* noticed that the blue-and-orange-striped stockings worn by the 1901 club resembled Princeton's colors and started calling them the Tigers. Also known as the Bengals.

Kansas City Royals (1969)—The name was chosen by the team's fans.

Milwaukee Brewers (1970)—The name of the first National League team representing Milwaukee in 1878; also the name of the first American League team in 1901 and the minor-league American Association team.

Minnesota Twins (1901)—Named for the twin cities of Minneapolis and St. Paul. From 1901 through 1960, the team was known as both the Senators and the Nationals, sometimes abbreviated to Nats, because its home was the nation's capital.

New York Yankees (1901)—Began in 1901 as the Baltimore Orioles. Shifted to New York in 1903, the team was called the Highlanders because its home ground, Hilltop Park, was so high and also because its first president was Joseph Gordon, whose name suggested the Gordon Highlanders, at the time a crack regiment in the British army. Around 1914 Jim Price of the *New York Press* coined the current name. Also called the Bronx Bombers.

Oakland Athletics (1901)—Began in 1901 as the Philadelphia Athletics; moved to Kansas City in 1955 and then to Oakland in 1968. The name has a long and rich history that both Kansas City and Oakland officials fortunately chose to preserve. In 1871 the Philadelphia Athletics won the first National Association pennant. Also called the A's.

Seattle Mariners (1977)—The name was adopted to honor the nautical tradition of the Pacific Northwest. The first major-league team in Seattle survived only one season—1969—before moving to Milwaukee, and was called the Pilots. There was some sentiment to name the team the Rainiers, after the Seattle club in the Pacific Coast League, but Mariners was a more popular choice.

Texas Rangers (1961)—Upon leaving Washington after the 1971 season, the franchise assumed the name of the state's traditional lawmen and took the example of the Minnesota team by coupling it with Texas so as not to slight either Dallas or Forth Worth.

Toronto Blue Jays (1977)—Name chosen in a fan contest.

National League

Atlanta Braves (1876)—The team moved from Boston to Milwaukee in 1953—the first franchise since 1903—then abandoned Milwaukee for Atlanta after the 1965 season. While in the National Association the team was dubbed the Red Caps. The red hosiery they sported led to their being called the Red Stockings after they joined the National League, but by the 1890s they were more commonly known as the Beaneaters. The name Braves came into existence in 1912 because owner Jim Gaffney was a Tammany Hall chieftain. Prior to that they had also been known as the Doves, while the team president was George Dovey, and the Pilgrims after the Red Sox dropped that name. A horrible season in 1935 spurred team officials and fans to call the club the Bees from 1936 to 1940, but the name never really caught on.

Chicago Cubs (1876)—Originally the White Stockings, the team became known as the Colts after player-manager Cap Anson appeared on stage in a play called *Runaway Colt* in the mid-1890s. When Anson left the club after being denied the share of the franchise he'd been promised, people began calling them the Orphans. For several years they were also known as the Cowboys and the Broncos, but in 1901 Chicago sportswriters George Rice and Fred Hayner began referring to them as the Cubs because their roster was stocked with so many young players after American League raids had depleted it. Also known as the Bruins.

Cincinnati Reds (1890)—Short for Red Stockings, the name of the great Cincinnati team in the late 1860s. Briefly called the Red Legs in the 1940s when *reds* was an evil word in America.

Colorado Rockies (1993)—Team based in Denver, where several teams have carried the nickname.

Florida Marlins (1993)—Named after the Miami Marlins, former Triple A team.

Houston Astros (1962)—First called the Colt 45s. Became the Astros when the Astrodome was opened in 1965.

Los Angeles Dodgers (1890)—Based in Brooklyn until 1958, the club shrewdly kept the Dodgers name after moving to the West Coast, thereby retaining the loyalty of its East Coast fans and also appealing to the many transplanted New Yorkers in the L.A. area. In 1889, while the franchise was still in the American Association, the team acquired the name Bridegrooms after three players got married in the off-season. When Ned Hanlon became manager in 1899, the team was called the Superbas because there was a popular vaudeville troupe at the time known as "Hanlon's Superbas." The club was also called the Atlantics—after the old Brooklyn National Association team—and later the Robins when Wilbert Robinson became manager, but by World War I the Dodgers name had taken hold. It had its roots in "Trolley Dodgers," the pejorative sobriquet given turn-of-the-century Brooklynites by New Yorkers.

Montreal Expos (1969)—Named after Expo '67, the World's Fair exposition.

New York Mets (1962)—Short for Metropolitans, a revival of the name borne by the New York American Association franchise in the 1880s.

Philadelphia Phillies (1883)—The original name of the Philadelphia team in the National League, it was spelled Fillies at first, as in female horses. Also briefly called the Quakers and later the Bluejays when the Carpenters bought the team during World War II and tried to create a new image, but neither name stuck.

Pittsburgh Pirates (1887)—The team was called the Alleghenies while it was in the American Association and then, facetiously, the Innocents after the franchise traitorously deserted the AA and switched to the National League. Became the Pirates in 1891 when the club "pirated" Lou Bierbauer and Harry Stovey, two star players the Philadelphia American Association team neglected to protect after they jumped to the Players League. Also called the Bucs or the Corsairs.

St. Louis Cardinals (1892)—Originally the St. Louis Browns American Association franchise, accepted into the National League when the AA folded after the 1891 season. Also known in the 1890s as the Maroons and the Perfectos. In 1899 the Robison brothers, who owned both the Cleveland and the St. Louis franchises, not only stocked St. Louis with all of Cleveland's best players but also brought along the Spiders' uniforms. St. Louis sportswriter Willie McHale, observing the red trim, coined the name Cardinals.

San Diego Padres (1969)—Assumed the nickname of the old Pacific Coast League team whose place they took in town.

San Francisco Giants (1883)—Like the Dodgers, the Giants retained their name when they moved from New York to the West Coast in 1958. But though the Dodgers also successfully kept their identity, the Giants failed. It is doubtful that very many San Francisco fans know much about the franchise's history, let alone that the team name was originated in 1885 by manager Jim Mutrie, who called his charges "My boys, my Giants!" Before Mutrie came along the club was known as the Green Stockings or the Gothams.

Team Records since 1901

On September 7, 1916, the New York Giants embarked on a 26-game winning streak, the longest victory skein since the National League was formed in 1876, by beating the Dodgers 4–1 at the Polo Grounds. All 26 victories came in their home park, giving them a second record for the most consecutive wins at home. In the course of the streak the Giants beat every National League rival at least once. The only blemish on their record was a 1–1 tie with the Pirates on September 18 in the second of three straight doubleheaders that postponements forced the two clubs to play.

Earlier in the 1916 season the Giants had rattled off 17 straight victories away from the Polo Grounds, the last coming on May 29 when Christy Mathewson beat the Braves 3–0 and registered the final shutout of his career. On the strength of Mathewson's arm, the Giants broke the previous record for most consecutive road wins—16, set by the Washington Senators between May 30 and June 15, 1912. The two long streaks gave the Giants 43 wins without a loss; their record when they weren't on a tear also included 43 wins—but against 66 losses. Overall, the club finished with an 86–66 mark, good only for fourth place.

Most Consecutive Wins without a Tie
NL—21—Chicago, 1935. The 1881 Chicago White Stockings also won 21 in a row, but tied a game with Providence.
AL—19—New York, 1947. In 1906 the White Sox also won 19 straight but had one tie.

Most Consecutive Wins Prior to 1876
The National Association Boston Red Caps won 26 straight in 1875. If you recognize the NA as a major league—and many do—then the 1875 Red Caps share the all-time major-

league record with the 1916 Giants. The record for the most consecutive wins by a professional team was set by the 1869–70 Cincinnati Red Stockings, who won 130 straight games with one tie before losing 8–7 to the Brooklyn Atlantics on June 14, 1870, in 11 innings. After scoring two runs in the top of the 11th to go ahead 7–5, the Red Stockings let the game slip away when second baseman Charlie Sweazy muffed a throw from shortstop George Wright, who was trying for a double play on a ground ball with runners on first and second. Bob Ferguson, the lead runner, scored the winning run on the error. Ironically, at the end of the nine innings the Red Stockings had refused the Atlantics' offer of a tie and insisted on playing to a decision.

Most Consecutive Doubleheaders Won
5—New York Yankees, 1906; the last one on September 4 when they beat the Red Sox 7–0 and 1–0

Most Consecutive Wins, Start of Season
NL—13—Atlanta, April 6 to April 21, 1982
AL—13—Milwaukee, April 6 to April 20, 1987

Most Consecutive Wins, Start of Season, before 1901
20—St. Louis Maroons, Union Association, April 20 to May 22, 1884. The runaway UA pennant winners didn't suffer their first loss until May 24, when they were beaten 8–1 by Boston's Tommy Bond.

Most Consecutive Losses
NL—23—Philadelphia, 1961; the streak ended on August 20 when the Phils beat the Braves in the second game of a doubleheader
AL—21—Baltimore, 1988

Most Consecutive Losses Prior to 1901
26—Louisville Eclipse, American Association, May 22 to June 22, 1889. Louisville finished in the cellar with a 27–111 record. In 1890 the club won 61 more games, the largest improvement in major-league history, and became the first major-league team to vault from last place to a pennant the following season.

Most Consecutive Losses, Expansion Team
NL—20—Montreal, 1969
AL—15—Texas, 1972

Most Consecutive Losses on the Road

NL—22—New York Mets, June 16 through July 28, 1963. The Mets played some home games, which they won, in the midst of their road losing streak, but the Pittsburgh Innocents, co-holders of the all-time record, in 1890 dropped 22 straight, all on the road.

AL—19—Philadelphia, July 25 through August 8, 1916; in the process the A's also set an all-time record for the most losses—19—in a two-week span.

Most Consecutive Losses at Home

AL—20—St. Louis, June 3 through July 7, 1953
NL—14—Boston, May 8 through May 24, 1911

Most Consecutive Doubleheaders Lost

In 1929 weather postponements forced the Boston Braves to play a record nine doubleheaders in a row from September 4 through September 15; at one point in their travails they lost five consecutive twin bills, one at Philadelphia and four straight to the Giants in Boston.

Most Consecutive Losses, Start of the Season

AL—21—Baltimore, 1988
NL—9—Brooklyn, 1918; Boston, 1919; New York Mets, 1962

Special Mention

In 1899 the Cleveland Spiders, playing their final season in the National League, had losing streaks of 24 games, 16 games and 14 games.

Highest Batting Average, Season

NL—.319—New York Giants, 1930
AL—.316—Detroit, 1921

Lowest Batting Average, Season

AL—.212—Chicago, 1910
NL—.213—Brooklyn, 1908

Highest Slugging Average, Season

AL—.489—New York, 1927
NL—.481—Chicago, 1930

Lowest Slugging Average, Season
AL—.261—Chicago, 1910. Patsy Dougherty led the club with a .300 slugging average, 85 points below Ty Cobb's *batting* average that season.
NL—.274—Boston, 1909

Most Runs, Season
AL—1067—New York, 1931
NL—1004—St. Louis, 1930

Fewest Runs, Season
NL—372—St. Louis, 1908; only three fewer than Brooklyn scored that year
AL—380—Washington, 1909

Most Home Runs, Season
AL—240—New York, 1961, including a record 128 on the road
NL—221—New York Giants, 1947; Cincinnati, 1956

Fewest Home Runs, Season
AL—3—Chicago, 1908; pitcher Ed Walsh tied for the club lead with one homer.
NL—7—Pittsburgh, 1917

Most Pennants
AL—33—New York, last in 1981
NL—18—Brooklyn-Los Angeles, last in 1988

Fewest Pennants
AL—0—Seattle; Washington-Texas; Los Angeles-California
NL—0—Houston; Montreal

Most Consecutive Pennants
AL—5—New York, 1949–53; 1960–64
NL—4—New York Giants, 1921–24

Most Consecutive Seasons without Winning a Pennant
NL—48—Chicago, 1946–93
AL—42—St. Louis, 1902–43

Most Seasons Finishing in Last Place
NL—24—Philadelphia, last in 1971
AL—25—Philadelphia-Kansas City-Oakland, last in 1993

Most Consecutive Seasons Finishing in Last Place
    AL—7—Philadelphia, 1915–21
    NL—5—Philadelphia, 1938–42

Most Consecutive Seasons Avoiding a Last-Place Finish
    NL—86—Brooklyn-Los Angeles, 1906–91
    AL—61—Boston, 1933–93; no, the Sox, unlike L.A., didn't finish last in 1992, just last in the AL East

Highest Winning Percentage, Season
    NL—.763, Chicago, 1906 (116–36)
    AL—.721, Cleveland, 1954 (111–43)

Highest Winning Percentage, Season, 162 Games
    AL—.673—New York, 1961; Baltimore, 1969 (109–53)
    NL—.667—Cincinnati, 1975 (108–54)
      New York Mets, 1986 (108–54)

Lowest Winning Percentage, Season
    AL—.235—Philadelphia, 1916 (36–117)
    NL—.248—Boston, 1935 (38–115)

Lowest Winning Percentage, Season, 162 Games
    NL—.250—New York Mets, 1962 (40–120)
    AL—.327—Toronto, 1979 (53–109)

Lowest Winning Percentage, Pennant Winner
    NL—.509—New York Mets, 1973 (82–79)
    AL—.525—Minnesota, 1987 (85–77)

Highest Winning Percentage, Non-Pennant Winner
    NL—.680—Chicago, 1909 (104–49)
    AL—.669—New York, 1954 (103–51)

Fewest Games Needed to Clinch Pennant, 154-Game Schedule
    AL—136—New York, 1941
    NL—137—New York, 1904

Fewest Games Needed to Clinch Pennant or Division, 162-Game Schedule
    NL—142—Cincinnati, 1975
    AL—146—Baltimore, 1969

Largest Margin of Victory by Pennant Winner
    NL—27½ games—Pittsburgh, 1902
    AL—19½ games—New York, 1936. (In 1983 Chicago won the Western Division by 20 games but lost the League Championship Series for the pennant.)

Most Games Finishing behind Pennant Winner
    NL—66½—Boston, 1906
    AL—64½—St. Louis, 1939

Fewest Games Finishing behind Pennant Winner, Last Place Team, Prior to 1969
    NL—21—New York Giants, 1915
    AL—25—Washington, 1944

Largest Improvement by Pennant Winner over Previous Season's Record
    AL—33 games—Boston, 1946
    NL—29 games—Atlanta Braves, 1991

Most Consecutive Years Finishing in First Division
    39—New York Yankees, 1926–64

Most Consecutive Years Finishing in Second Division
    20—Chicago Cubs, 1947–66

Best Home Record, Season
    AL—.805—New York, 1932 (62–15)
    NL—.789—Pittsburgh, 1902 (56–15)

Worst Home Record, Season
    AL—.234—St. Louis, 1939 (18–59)
    NL—.260—Boston, 1911 (19–54)

Best Road Record, Season
    NL—.800—Chicago, 1906 (60–15)
    AL—.730—New York, 1939 (54–20)

Worst Road Record, Season
    NL—.167—Boston, 1935 (13–65)
    AL—.169—Philadelphia, 1916 (13–64)

Most Consecutive Games Won from One Club
    AL—23—Baltimore from Kansas City Royals, May 10, 1969, through August 12, 1970

NL—20—Pittsburgh from Cincinnati, last 17 in 1937, first 3 in 1938

Most Games Won from One Club, Season

AL—21—New York from St. Louis, 1927

NL—21—Chicago from Cincinnati, 1945; Chicago from Boston, 1909. In 1909 the Braves also lost 20 of 21 games to Pittsburgh, giving them a 2–41 record against the NL's top two teams that year.

Where the Games Are Played

During the period between 1909 and 1915 more than half the teams then in the major leagues either built new stadiums or made massive renovations in the parks they were using. There were several reasons for the feverish construction, not the least of which were the ever-present threat of fire in the old wood parks and the many lawsuits the Phillies faced when a section of the rickety Baker Bowl grandstand collapsed in 1903, killing several spectators.

The first ballpark on record was built in 1862 when William Cammeyer, the owner of the Union Club's grounds in Brooklyn, conceived the notion of enclosing his field and charging admission to games. Cammeyer's park did not survive long, nor did the majority of other parks that were built in the last century—the lifespan for most was only a few years—but Sulphur Dell, built in 1866, was the home of the Southern Association Nashville Volunteers until 1963 and set an all-time park longevity record of 97 years. Prior to 1991 the oldest major-league park was Comiskey, home of the White Sox, which opened in 1910. To keep you abreast of who is playing where at the moment, and how long they have been there, here is a list—which excludes for the moment the parks to be unveiled in 1994 by Cleveland and Texas.

AMERICAN LEAGUE
Oriole Park at Camden Yards, Baltimore Orioles
First game—April 6, 1992; Baltimore 2, Cleveland 0.
Seating capacity—48,000. Natural surface.

The Yard is a new stadium deliberately built to look like an old one. In 1992, their first year of occupancy, the Orioles drew 3,567,819 fans. The Yard marks the third new AL park to open in the past four seasons; Cleveland and Texas bid to make it five by 1994.

Fenway Park, Boston Red Sox
First game—April 20, 1912; Boston 7, New York 6, 11 innings.
Seating capacity—33,583. Natural surface.
Considered the ultimate in parks when it was built, but within a year the Red Sox already had a sneaking suspicion it was too small and that its left-field wall would always be both a boon and a burden.

Anaheim Stadium, California Angels
First game—April 19, 1966; Chicago 3, California 1.
Seating capacity—64,573. Natural surface.
Clean, efficient, yet spacious and without a single major flaw. The Angels first played in tiny Wrigley Field, which they inherited from the Los Angeles franchise in the Pacific Coast League, and then, for several years, shared Chavez Ravine with the Dodgers while waiting for their own new park to be completed.

Comiskey Park II, Chicago White Sox
First game—April 18, 1991; Detroit 16, Chicago 0.
Seating capacity—42,250. Natural surface.
With the closing of Comiskey Park I at the finish of the 1990 season, Tiger Stadium and Fenway Park became the oldest facilities in the majors. Ironically, the White Sox also lost their lid-lifter in Comiskey I, 2–0 to the St. Louis Browns on July 1, 1910.

Cleveland Stadium, Cleveland Indians
First game—July 31, 1932; Philadelphia 1, Cleveland 0.
Seating capacity—74,208. Natural surface.
The inaugural game drew 80,284, the largest crowd ever for a major-league stadium opening. Formerly called Municipal Stadium, it was the last of the cavernous stadiums to be built. So mammoth that until the late forties the Indians continued to use smaller, cozier League Park, their former home, except on weekends and holidays.

Tiger Stadium, Detroit Tigers
First game—April 20, 1912; Detroit 6, Cleveland 5, 11 innings.
Seating capacity—52,806. Natural surface.
Probably the most esthetically pleasing of the still-extant old stadiums and definitely the favorite park for power hitters. Formerly called Briggs Stadium and prior to that Navin Field. Before it was built, the Tigers played in Bennett Park, named after Charlie Bennett, a catcher with the Detroit Wolverines who lost both legs in a railway accident.

Bennett Park seated only 8500 and was the smallest park in the majors when it closed.

Royals Stadium, Kansas City Royals
First game—April 10, 1973; Kansas City 12, Texas 1.
Seating capacity—40,625. Artificial surface.

Features a 322-foot-wide water spectacular with a fountain and a 10-foot waterfall from the upper cascade plus two lower pools that empty into five more 10-foot falls. The Royals played in Municipal Stadium, with a seating capacity of 30,611, until their new park was finished.

County Stadium, Milwaukee Brewers
First game—April 14, 1953; Milwaukee 3, St. Louis 2, 10 innings.
First AL game—April 7, 1970; California 12, Milwaukee 0.
Seating capacity—53,192. Natural surface.

Used by the Milwaukee Braves in the National League through 1965, then sat idle until the Seattle Pilots franchise shifted to Milwaukee in 1970 except for some "home" games played there by the White Sox. At one time had a seating capacity of only 46,625.

The Metrodome, Minnesota Twins
First game—April 6, 1982; Seattle 11, Minnesota 7.
Seating capacity—55,244. Artificial surface and sky.

The Twins' home from 1961 until 1982 was Metropolitan Stadium.

Yankee Stadium
First game—April 18, 1923; New York 4, Boston 1.
Seating capacity—57,545. Natural surface.

Closed for two years in the middle seventies, the Yankees sharing Shea Stadium with the Mets during the hiatus. Before it was built the Yankees shared Polo Grounds with the Giants from 1912 through 1922 after forsaking Hilltop Park, their original home field. Yankee Stadium took 284 days to build—the renovation took more than twice that long and reduced the capacity by some 13,000 seats.

Oakland Coliseum, Oakland Athletics
First game—April 17, 1968; Baltimore 4, Oakland 1.
Seating capacity—50,219. Natural surface.

The park was there waiting for the A's when they moved from Kansas City, where they used Municipal Stadium. While the franchise was based in Philadelphia, the A's played in Columbia Park, located at Twenty-ninth and Columbia Avenue, until 1909 when Shibe Park was completed. Shibe was the first all concrete-and-steel stadium in the majors.

The Kingdome, Seattle Mariners
First game—April 6, 1977; California 7, Seattle 0.
Seating capacity—59,438. Artificial surface and sky.

The only home the Mariners have known. Their predecessors in Seattle, the Pilots, in 1969 were forced to use Sicks Stadium, former home of the Seattle Pacific Coast League team, which seated only 25,000, and moved to Milwaukee partly because their home facility was so inadequate.

Arlington Stadium, Texas Rangers
First game—April 21, 1972; Texas 7, California 6.
Seating capacity—43,508. Natural surface.

A former minor-league stadium, upgraded to major-league capacity. During the franchise's last years in Washington, RFK Stadium was its home, but Griffith Stadium was where the original Senators played before moving to Minnesota. Decrepit, archaic, it was the second-oldest park in the majors when it closed and seated only 29,731.

Skydome, Toronto Blue Jays
First game—June 5, 1989; Milwaukee 5, Toronto 3.
Seating capacity—48,378. Artificial surface.

A triumph of modern architecture and technology, the Blue Jays' space-age facility helped them to set a new American League attendance record in its first year of operation.

NATIONAL LEAGUE

Fulton County Stadium, Atlanta Braves
First game—April 12, 1966; Pittsburgh 4, Atlanta 3, 13 innings.
Seating capacity—52,006. Natural surface.

Also used by the Atlanta Falcons in the NFL, finished in 1965 in preparation for the Braves' move from Milwaukee. Before transferring to Milwaukee from Boston, the team played in Braves Field, which opened in 1915, replacing South End Grounds, the oldest park in the majors, home to the Boston Red Caps in the National Association as far back as 1873.

Wrigley Field, Chicago Cubs
First game—April 23, 1914; Chicago Whales 9, Kansas City Packers 1.
First NL game—April 20, 1916; Chicago 7, Cincinnati 6, 11 innings.
Seating capacity—38,040. Natural surface, natural everything.

Called North Side Park originally, it was taken over by the Cubs from the Whales when the Federal League folded.

The Cubs had previously played in West Side Park at Polk and Lincoln. Plans to install lights in time for the opening of the 1942 season had to be put on hold after Pearl Harbor because electrical equipment was needed for defense purposes—and stayed on hold until 1988.

Riverfront Stadium, Cincinnati Reds
First game—June 30, 1970; Atlanta 8, Cincinnati 2.
Seating capacity—52,392. Artificial surface.

Until 1970 the Reds played in Crosley Field which held fewer than 30,000, making it the smallest park in the majors. Called Redland Field when it opened in 1912, it also had the distinction of having the first "artificial" surface—in 1937, when the Reds dyed the sun-burned outfield grass green.

Mile High Stadium, Colorado Rockies
First game—April 9, 1993; Montreal 11, Colorado 4.
Seating capacity—76,100. Natural surface.

Began in 1947 as Bears Stadium, expanded 1959; holds minor league single-game attendance record as well as major league season attendance record, set in 1993 (4,483,270).

Joe Robbie Stadium, Florida Marlins
First game—April 5, 1993; Florida 6, Los Angeles 3.
Seating capacity—46,500. Natural surface.

The summer heat in Florida makes night baseball a must at Joe Robbie. In 1993, their inaugural season, the Marlins played just 35 day games, the fewest in the majors.

The Astrodome, Houston Astros
First game—April 12, 1965; Philadelphia 2, Houston 0.
Seating capacity—45,011. Artificial surface and sky.

The Astrodome cost $31,600,000 to construct and was first used on April 9, 1965, for an exhibition game between the Astros and Yankees. Prior to 1965 the Astros played in Colts Stadium, built in 1962 for the new Houston National League team.

Dodger Stadium, Los Angeles Dodgers
First game—April 10, 1962; Cincinnati 6, Los Angeles 3.
Seating capacity—56,000. Natural surface.

Their first four seasons in L.A., the Dodgers played in Memorial Coliseum where they set an all-time attendance record on May 7, 1959, when they drew 93,103 for an exhibition game honoring Roy Campanella. They also set an Opening Day attendance record of 78,672 in their first game in the Coliseum on April 18, 1958, against the Giants. In Dodger Stadium, also known as Chavez Ravine, they set a single-season attendance record in 1982. Before transferring to L.A. from Brooklyn, the team played at Ebbets Field, which held only 32,111; nevertheless the Dodgers attracted 1,807,526 fans in 1947, at the time an NL record.

Olympic Stadium, Montreal Expos
First game—April 15, 1977; Philadelphia 7, Montreal 2.
Seating capacity—59,149. Artificial surface.

The Expos originally played in Jarry Park, home of the minor-league Montreal Royals. The last games in Jarry Park were on September 26, 1976, when the Phillies won a divison-clinching doubleheader from the Expos, their first title of any sort in 26 years.

Shea Stadium, New York Mets
First game—April 17, 1964; Pittsburgh 4, New York 3.
Seating capacity—55,601. Natural surface.

Windy, too close to the airport, a tough place to spend an evening in the fall or early spring—unless you're a pitcher. While waiting for Shea to be built, the Mets played their first two seasons in the Polo Grounds.

Veterans Stadium, Philadelphia Phillies
First game—April 10, 1971; Philadelphia 4, Montreal 1.
Seating capacity—66,271. Artificial surface.

Features a monstrous TV screen and probably the fastest turf in the majors. The Phillies played in Shibe Park from July 4, 1938, through 1970. Prior to switching to Shibe and sharing it with the A's, the club had called Baker Bowl home for over half a century. Refurbished a number of times, especially after the 1903 disaster, the Baker Bowl seated just 18,000 and hosted its first game on April 30, 1887, the Phils beating the Giants 15–9.

Three Rivers Stadium, Pittsburgh Pirates
First game—July 16, 1970; Cincinnati 3, Pittsburgh 2.
Seating capacity—58,438. Artificial surface.

When Three Rivers took longer to complete than expected, the Pirates had to open the 1970 season in Forbes Field, giving baseball fans a last opportunity to attend a game in the oldest concrete-and-steel stadium still extant. The first fully modern park in the majors when it opened in 1909, Forbes had triple-decker stands, elevators, electric lights, telephones, inclined ramps instead of stairs and maids in the ladies' restrooms. Moreover, it shared with Shibe Park the distinction of having the first visitors' dressing room, ending the custom of visiting teams dressing at their hotels and then riding to the park in open horse-drawn buses.

Busch Stadium, St. Louis Cardinals
First game—May 16, 1966; St. Louis 4, Atlanta 3, 12 innings. Seating capacity—50,222. Artificial surface.

Before 1966 the Cardinals played in Sportsman's Park, a relic that dated back to 1876 when it was used by the first St. Louis team in the National League. The park was later taken over by Chris Von der Ahe's American Association Browns and then renovated by the St. Louis Browns American League team and used by them until they moved to Baltimore. Until 1920 the Cardinals played in Robison Field, built by the St. Louis Maroons for their 1884 season in the Union Association. The final game played at Robison Field, the last wood park in the majors, was on July 6, 1920.

Jack Murphy Stadium, San Diego Padres
First game—April 8, 1969; San Diego 2, Houston 1. Seating capacity—58,433. Natural surface.

Underrated, in some ways the best all-around facility in the majors. The last major-league park to be built without a carpet prior to the new White Sox stadium.

Candlestick Park, San Francisco Giants
First game—April 12, 1960; San Francisco 3, St. Louis 1. Seating capacity—58,000. Natural surface.

The Giants had a carpet for a while but wisely removed it. While waiting for Candlestick to be finished, the team played in Seals Stadium, which was built in 1931 exclusively for baseball and was still one of the finest parks in the country when it went the way of all abandoned inner-city sports facilities. Before moving to the Bay Area, the Giants called the Polo Grounds home. Polo Grounds was famed for 250-foot home runs and 450-foot outs. Candlestick is famed for being the only major-league park where a pitcher—Stu Miller, in the 1961 All-Star Game—committed a balk when he was blown off the mound.

Managers' Records

Connie Mack took over the Pittsburgh manager's job late in the 1894 season, lasted through 1896 and then was replaced by Patsy Donovan. He had to wait until 1901 to get a second opportunity to manage in the majors. John McGraw had a similar experience, guiding the Baltimore Orioles to an unexpectedly high fourth-place finish in 1899 and then having to endure a one-year hiatus in St. Louis as a player only before Baltimore was granted an American League franchise and he was given the reins in 1901. By the time Mack and McGraw were done managing, they held almost every dugout longevity record.

Most Years as Manager, League
AL—50—Connie Mack, Philadelphia, 1901 through 1950
NL—32—John McGraw, Baltimore, 1899; New York Giants, 1902 through 1932

Most Games Won as Manager, League
AL—3582—Connie Mack, Philadelphia. Mack also holds the AL record for most losses, 3814.
NL—2690—John McGraw, Baltimore and New York Giants. McGraw also suffered the most losses in the NL, 1863.

Most Pennants Won as Manager, League
AL—10—Casey Stengel, New York, last in 1960
NL—10—John McGraw, New York, last in 1924

Most World Series Won as Manager, League
AL—7—Joe McCarthy, New York, last in 1943; Casey Stengel, New York, last in 1958
NL—4—Walter Alston, Brooklyn-Los Angeles, last in 1965

Most Consecutive Pennants Won as Manager, League
   AL—5—Casey Stengel, New York, 1949–53
   NL—4—John McGraw, New York, 1921–24
   AA—4—Charlie Comiskey, St. Louis, 1885–88

Most Clubs Managed
   7—Frank Bancroft, Worcester, NL; Detroit, NL; Cleveland, NL; Providence, NL; Philadelphia, AA; Indianapolis, NL; Cincinnati, NL. Bancroft managed less than nine full seasons and had just one pennant winner, the 1884 Providence Grays, but he spread his work over a 22-year period and was the only man to manage in the NL before the American Association came into existence and after the American League replaced the Association as the NL's rival. One of the game's first great promoters and missionaries, Bancroft took a team to Cuba in 1879, the first such expedition in history, and later staged a wedding at home plate. He spent the last 30 years of his life as the Cincinnati Reds business manager and traveling secretary.

Most Clubs Managed, since 1901
   6—Jimmy Dykes, Chicago AL; Philadelphia, AL; Baltimore, AL; Cincinnati, NL; Detroit, AL; Cleveland, AL. Dykes also used to hold the record for most years as a manager without winning a pennant.
   John McNamara, Oakland, AL; San Diego, NL; Cincinnati, NL; California, AL; Boston, AL; Cleveland, AL. Thus far, in 18 seasons McNamara has won just one pennant.

Most Clubs Managed to Pennants
   3—Bill McKechnie, Pittsburgh, NL; St. Louis, NL; Cincinnati, NL
   Dick Williams, Boston, AL; Oakland, AL; San Diego, NL

Most Clubs Managed to Division Titles
   4—Billy Martin, Minnesota, AL; Detroit, AL; New York, AL; Oakland, AL

Only Manager to Lead Same Club to Consecutive Pennants in Two Different Leagues
   Bill McGunnigle steered Brooklyn to the American Association flag in 1889, then repeated in 1890 after the Bridegrooms transferred to the National League.

First Manager to Pilot Two Clubs to Pennants, Same League, since 1901
NL—Pat Moran, Philadelphia, 1915; Cincinnati, 1919
AL—Joe Cronin, Washington, 1933; Boston, 1946

First Manager to Pilot Pennant Winners in Two Leagues, since 1901
Joe McCarthy, Chicago, NL, 1929; New York, AL, 1932

Most Years Managed Without Winning a Pennant
26—Gene Mauch, Philadelphia, NL, 1960 into 1968; Montreal, NL, 1969 through 1975; Minnesota, AL, 1976 into 1980; California, AL, 1981 through 1982, 1985 through 1987

Only Man to Win a Pennant in His Lone Season as a Manager
George Wright, Providence, NL, 1879

First Man to Win a World Championship in His First Full Season as Manager
AL—Tris Speaker, Cleveland, 1920
NL—Rogers Hornsby, St. Louis, 1926

First Manager to Pilot Club in World Series without Managing It for Full Season
NL—Charlie Grimm, Chicago, 1932
AL—Bob Lemon, New York, 1978. Lemon piloted the Yankees in two Series—1978 and 1981—without ever managing the club a full season.

Only Manager to Win Four Pennants since 1901 and Not Make the Hall of Fame
Billy Southworth, St. Louis, NL, 1942, 1943, 1944; Boston, NL, 1948

Only Manager to Win Back-to-Back World Championships and Not Make the Hall of Fame
Bill Carrigan, Boston, AL, 1915 and 1916. Carrigan retired after the 1916 triumph but in the late twenties was coaxed into returning to manage a string of awful Red Sox teams, tarnishing his reputation as a great manager.

Last Manager to Win Three Consecutive Pennants
    Tony LaRussa, Oakland, AL, 1988–90. The last NL manager to win three flags in a row was Billy Southworth with the 1942–44 Cardinals.

Highest Career Winning Percentage as Manager
    .615—Joe McCarthy, 24 seasons, 2125 wins and 1333 losses

Lowest Career Winning Percentage as Manager, Minimum 1000 Games
    .401—Jimmy Wilson, nine seasons, 493 wins and 735 losses. Wilson's best team was the 1943 Cubs, who finished fifth.

Lowest Career Winning Percentage as Manager, Minimum 500 Games
    .313—John McCloskey, five seasons, 190 wins and 417 losses. McCloskey, who helped found the Texas League, skippered the 1908 Cardinals, probably the National League's most dismal team in the deadball era.

First Great Manager Who Was Never a Major-League Player
    Frank Selee. After managing the Boston Beaneaters to five pennants in the 1890s, Selee moved to the lackluster Chicago Cubs in 1902. Within a year he had the Cubs in contention and was just putting the finishing touches on a club that would win three consecutive pennants (1906–8) when failing health forced him to step down in 1905 and turn the reins over to Frank Chance, his personal choice as his replacement.

First Manager to Win 1000 Games
    Cap Anson of the Chicago White Stockings and Harry Wright, then in his last season as the Philadelphia Phils skipper, both went over the 1000 mark in 1893.

Youngest Manager to Win 1000 Games
    Fred Clarke, who became player-manager of the Louisville Colonels in 1897 when he was only 24 years old, collected his 1000th win at age 35 in 1908 while at the helm of the Pittsburgh Pirates. Only 42 when he stepped down at the end of the 1915 season, Clarke departed with 1602 wins, the most by any manager in history to that point.

Oldest Rookie Manager

Tom Sheehan was 66 years old when he took over the San Francisco Giants in June 1960 and steered them to a 46–50 record for the remainder of the season before giving way to Al Dark.

Youngest Rookie Manager, since 1901

Roger Peckinpaugh was only 23 years old when he served as the Yankees player-manager for the last 17 games of the 1914 season.

Youngest Player-Manager to Lead Club for Full Season, since 1901

Lou Boudreau bid for and was given the Cleveland manager's post at age 24 in 1942. Six years later he became the last player-manager to steer his club to a pennant.

Last Player-Manager to Win a National League Pennant

Technically, Leo Durocher, who played a few games for his Brooklyn Dodgers in 1941. The last to do it while still a full-time player was Gabby Hartnett with the 1938 Chicago Cubs.

Last Year Both Teams in World Series Were Led by Player-Managers

1934—Frankie Frisch, St. Louis Cardinals, and Mickey Cochrane, Detroit Tigers. The Tigers repeated in 1935 under Cochrane and played the Cubs, led by Charlie Grimm, who'd played two games during the regular season but didn't appear at all in the Series.

First Year Both Teams in World Series Were Led by Player-Managers

1903—Jimmy Collins, Boston Red Sox, and Fred Clarke, Pittsburgh Pirates. Player-managers were so common then that the 1905 World Series, when McGraw's Giants played Mack's A's, was the only one until 1911 in which neither team was led by a manager who was also a full-time player.

Only Pitchers to Win a Pennant as Player-Managers

NL—Al Spalding, Chicago, 1876
AL—Clark Griffith, Chicago, 1901

Only American League Manager to Win Two Pennants between 1936 and 1968 for Teams Other Than the Yankees
  Al Lopez, Cleveland, 1954; Chicago, 1959

Winners of the "Might Have Been Another Casey Stengel" Award

Burt Shotton. Fired by the Phillies in 1933 after managing a string of rotten teams, he lucked into the Dodgers' managerial post in 1947 when Leo Durocher was suspended for the season, won a pennant and then won again in 1949 as Durocher's replacement after Durocher was axed. In 1950 Shotton lost the NL pennant to the Phillies in the last game of the season when he failed to replace slow-footed Cal Abrams with a pinch runner and saw Abrams thrown out at the plate trying to bring home the run that would have tied the Dodgers with the Phillies and forced a pennant playoff. That lapse as much as anything else caused the Dodgers to can him. Over the next six seasons Brooklyn won four pennants under Chuck Dressen and Walter Alston with basically the same team that Shotton had in 1950. If Shotton had stayed with the club, we can only wonder now what might have happened—but it's a fairly strong possibility that fans in the 1950s would have had the treat of watching two eccentric senior citizens trying to outmaneuver one another each fall.

The Three Most Interesting Teams Between 1901 and 1919

1908 PITTSBURGH PIRATES
W-98 L-56
Manager: Fred Clarke

Regular Lineup—1B, None; 2B, Eddie Abbatichio; 3B, Tommy Leach; SS, Honus Wagner. RF, Owen Wilson; CF, Roy Thomas; LF, Fred Clarke; C, George Gibson; P, Vic Willis; P, Nick Maddox; P, Howie Camnitz; P, Lefty Leifield; P, Sam Leever.

Led by Wagner and player-manager Clarke, this team finished only one game shy of the pennant and in so doing immortalized Fred Merkle and the Cubs infield of Tinker, Evers and Chance. Merkle's "boner" probably would have been overlooked amid the welter of strange occurrences in 1908 if the Pirates had won their final game of the season, against the Cubs, clinching the pennant and making it unnecessary for the Cubs and Giants to replay the game in which Merkle neglected to touch second base. As it is, the Pirates' own boner that year has been largely overlooked. The club played all season without a decent first baseman after cutting Jim Nealon, who had an off year in 1907 after leading the National League in RBIs as a rookie in 1906. In preference to Nealon, the Pirates alternated Harry Swacina, Jim Kane and Al Storke, none of whom could do the job. The following year the Pirates picked up Bill Abstein, won the pennant and then released him after he had a poor World Series. Without Abstein, the club once again had a gaping hole at first base that would go unplugged until 1920, when Charlie Grimm emerged.

1913 WASHINGTON SENATORS
W-90 L-64
Manager: Clark Griffith

Regular Lineup—1B, Chick Gandil; 2B, Ray Morgan; 3B, Eddie Foster; SS, George McBride; RF, Danny Moeller; CF, Clyde Milan; LF, Howard Shanks; C, John Henry and Eddie Ainsmith; P, Walter Johnson; P, Joe Boehling; P, Bob Groom.

After finishing second to the Red Sox in 1912, the Senators seemed ready to provide Washington fans with their first major-league pennant, especially when rookie left-hander Boehling looked sharp in spring training. Boehling continued to shine when the season started—he finished with a 17–7 record, combining with Johnson to post 54 wins and only 14 losses. But the rest of the mound staff had a dismal 37–50 record, and the Senators again could do no better than second place. Griffith, in his search for supporting moundsmen, tried 23 pitchers all told in 1913, ranging from his own 43-year-old arm to that of 18-year-old Jack Bentley. It was a shame none of them worked out because Johnson had an incredible season. In 1913 he won 36 games, lost only 7 and had a 1.14 ERA and an .837 win percentage. All of his stats towered over those of the second-best pitcher in the league, Cleveland's Cy Falkenberg, who had a 23–10 record. The following year Boehling slumped to only 12 wins, and the Senators slipped to third place and did not seriously contend again until a decade later.

1916 PHILADELPHIA ATHLETICS
W-36 L-117
Manager: Connie Mack

Regular Lineup—1B, Stuffy McInnis; 2B, Nap Lajoie; 3B, Charlie Pick; SS, Whitey Witt; RF, Jimmy Walsh; CF, Amos Strunk; LF, Rube Oldring; C, Wally Schang; P, Elmer Myers; P, Joe Bush; P, Jack Nabors; P, Tom Sheehan.

The A's had the worst team in this century only two years after they won their fourth pennant in five seasons. Mack blamed Federal League defections and his having to sell stars like Home Run Baker, who wanted more money than he could pay, but his explanation didn't quite wash then, and history has made it look even lamer. After the Federal League folded, there were a number of good players floating loose whom Mack could have gotten cheaply, but they weren't his kind of people, and he played out the season instead with the few members of the 1914 crew who'd remained loyal to him, plus 41-year-old Lajoie and a pack of rejects from other clubs. Myers and Bush, two quality pitchers, had a combined 29–45 record, but the rest of the staff lost 72 games and won only 7. A truly embarrassing operation, from 1915 through 1921 the A's finished in the cellar a record seven straight years.

ERA Records

The National League didn't officially begin keeping earned run averages until 1912, and the American League didn't follow suit until the following year. As a result, many of the ERA records that were set before 1912 have been unearthed only after today's standards were applied to what, in some cases, were previously uncalculated statistics.

Lowest ERA, Season, 1901 through 1919
AL—0.96—Dutch Leonard, Boston, 1914; the all-time season record
NL—1.04—Three Finger Brown, Chicago, 1906; the all-time National League record

Lowest ERA, Season, 1920 through 1941
NL—1.66—Carl Hubbell, New York Giants, 1933
AL—2.06—Lefty Grove, Philadelphia, 1931

Lowest ERA, Season, 1942 through 1960
AL—1.64—Spud Chandler, New York, 1943
NL—1.75—Howie Pollet, St. Louis, 1943

Lowest ERA, Season, 1961 through 1976
NL—1.12—Bob Gibson, St. Louis, 1968
AL—1.65—Dean Chance, Los Angeles, 1964

Lowest ERA, Season, since 1977
NL—1.53—Dwight Gooden, New York, 1985
AL—1.74—Ron Guidry, New York, 1978

Only Pitcher to Lead League in ERA Both before and after 1893
Billy Rhines, Cincinnati, led the NL in 1890 and again in 1896.

Most Seasons League Leader in ERA
    AL—9—Lefty Grove, last in 1939
    NL—5—Pete Alexander, last in 1920; Sandy Koufax, 1962–66 consecutive

Lowest ERA, Season, Team, since 1901
    NL—1.73—Chicago, 1907
    AL—1.78—Philadelphia, 1910

Last Team with an ERA below 2.25, Season
    NL—Chicago, 1919 (2.21); Cincinnati, 1919 (2.23)
    AL—Washington, 1918 (2.14)

Last Team with an ERA below 2.50, Season
    NL—St. Louis, 1968 (2.49)
    AL—Chicago, 1967 (2.45); the best ERA by any team since 1919

Lowest Team ERA, Season, since 1968
    AL—Baltimore, 1972 (2.54)
    NL—Houston, 1981 (2.66)

TOP 10 IN ERA, CAREER, SINCE 1893

(Minimum 1500 innings)

		Years Active	*ERA*
1.	Ed Walsh	1904–17	1.82
2.	Addie Joss	1902–10	1.89
3.	Joe Wood	1908–20	2.03
4.	Three Finger Brown	1903–16	2.06
5.	Christy Mathewson	1900–16	2.13
6.	Rube Waddell	1897–1910	2.16[1]
7.	Walter Johnson	1907–27	2.17[2]
8.	Orval Overall	1905–13	2.24
9.	Ed Reulbach	1905–17	2.28
10.	Jim Scott	1907–17	2.30

[1]Lefty record holder.
[2]Only member of the career top 10 who pitched in the lively ball era.

Lowest Career ERA, Pitcher Active Exclusively after 1910
    2.43—Jeff Tesreau, 1912–18

Lowest Career ERA, Pitcher Active Exclusively between 1920 and 1945
2.98—Carl Hubbell, 1928-43. Hubbell is the only pitcher in that period who had an ERA under 3.00 in over 1500 innings.

Lowest Career ERA, Pitcher Active Exclusively between 1940 and 1960 at Least Ten Full Seasons
2.92—Harry Brecheen, 1940–53. Brecheen and Hubbell are the only two pitchers active between 1920 and 1960 who had career ERAs under 3.00.

TOP 10 IN ERA, CAREER, SINCE 1920
(Minimum 1500 innings)

		Years Active	ERA
1.	Hoyt Wilhelm	1952–72	2.52
2.	Whitey Ford	1950–67	2.75
3.	Sandy Koufax	1955–66	2.76
4.	Jim Palmer	1965–84	2.86
5.	Andy Messersmith	1968–79	2.86
6.	Tom Seaver	1967–86	2.86
7.	Juan Marichal	1960–75	2.89
8.	Rollie Fingers	1968–85	2.90
9.	Bob Gibson	1959–75	2.91
10.	Roger Clemens	1984–	2.94

Only Pitchers since 1901 with Career 0.00 ERA, Minimum Nine Innings
Tim Jones, Pittsburgh, 1977, in 10 innings had a 1–0 record and 0.00 ERA.
John Dagenhard, Boston Braves, 1943, hurled a complete-game win in his only big league start and also threw two relief innings without giving up an earned run to compile a career 0.00 ERA in 11 innings.

On the Black

Which pitcher had the best control? It all depends on what standard you use to measure control and whether you accept that different eras require different standards. Cy Young gave up 103 bases on balls in 423 innings in 1893 and walked just 37 batters in 342 innings 10 years later. Had Young's control really improved that much by 1903, or were other factors operating? On the evidence Young definitely got sharper as his career progressed—he may even have had the best control of any pitcher in history—but it's also true that he was playing in a time that was extremely forgiving of pitchers who disdained nibbling at the corners of the plate and elected simply to come in with the ball. A very dead ball it was, scuffed up, dirt-stained and often laden with other foreign substances as well—a ball that was usually kept in play for several innings and sometimes even for an entire game. In any event, virtually all the career and season records for control were set in the early part of the 20th century.

Best Control, Career, since 1893, Minimum 2500 Innings
Deacon Phillippe issued 363 walks in 2608 innings, an average of 1.25 walks per nine innings. Phillippe pitched in the National League, mostly with the Pirates, from 1899 to 1911. In 1910 he walked only nine batters in 122 innings, a National League record low among pitchers in over 100 innings. Phillie won 188 games, plus three more in the 1903 World Series when he started five games, completed them all, and relieved in two others. Almost as remarkable as his iron-man Series effort was the fact that he gave up only four walks in 50 innings.

Best Control, Career, since 1920, Minimum 2500 Innings
Red Lucas, 455 walks in 2542 innings. Active in the

National League between 1923 and 1938, Lucas only once gave up more than 50 walks in a season. See "Pinch-Hitting Feats," page 254, for more about Lucas.

Best Control, Career, since 1893, Left-hander
Noodles Hahn, 380 walks in 2021 innings, an average of 1.70 walks per nine innings. Hahn, a 22-game winner for the Reds in 1901, is also the only lefty in this century besides Steve Carlton to win 20 games for a last-place team.

Best Control, Career, since 1920, Left-hander
Fritz Peterson, 426 walks in 2218 innings, and never more than 49 in a season

Best Control, Career, 300-Game Winner
Cy Young, hands down. With 1217 walks in 7357 innings —an average of only 1.49 walked per nine innings—Young begs that anyone seriously interested in determining who was the best pitcher ever examine his overall record carefully.

Best Control, Career, 1920 through 1941, Minimum 3000 Innings
First Prize—Carl Hubbell, 724 walks in 3589 innings
Second Prize—Paul Derringer, 761 walks in 3645 innings

Best Control, Career, 1942 through 1960, Minimum 3000 Innings
First Prize—Robin Roberts, 902 walks in 4689 innings
Second Prize—Lew Burdette, 628 walks in 3068 innings

Best Control, Career, since 1961, Minimum 3000 Innings
First Prize—Juan Marichal, 709 walks in 3509 innings
Second Prize—Fergie Jenkins, 967 walks in 4499 innings. Jenkins is also the only pitcher to record more than 3000 K's and fewer than 1000 walks.

Best Control, Season, Minimum 250 Innings
AL—Cy Young, Boston, 1904, 29 walks in 380 innings
NL—Babe Adams, Pittsburgh, 1920, 18 walks in 263 innings. Adams also set an NL record in 1913 when he worked 314 innings without hitting a batter. The major-league record for kindness to hitters is held by Al Crowder, who pitched 327 innings for Washington in 1932 without incurring a single hit batsman. That same season, Crowder set a

second all-time record when he went the entire year without uncorking a wild pitch. Crowder's remarkable control exhibition helped him to end the season with 15 straight wins.

Most Consecutive Innings without Giving up a Base on Balls

AL—84⅓—Bill Fischer, Kansas City A's, 1962. Largely because of his long skein, Fischer also set an AL season record in 1962 for pitchers in over 100 innings, walking only eight batters in 128 innings.

NL—68—Christy Mathewson, New York Giants, 1913; Randy Jones, San Diego, 1976

Second Basemen's Records

Three names head almost everyone's list of the greatest second basemen, and all three were active between 1901 and 1919. In the new century's first decade the dominant player in the American League was Nap Lajoie. By the end of the century's second decade Rogers Hornsby was emerging as the best player in the N. L. Between their periods of dominance was Eddie Collins, viewed by many as the finest second basemen ever.

SEASON BATTING RECORDS

Department	National League	American League
Batting Average	.424, Rogers Hornsby, St. Louis, 1924	.426, NAP LAJOIE, Philadelphia, 1901
Slugging Average	.756, ROGERS HORNSBY, St. Louis, 1925	.643, Nap Lajoie, Philadelphia, 1901
Home Runs	42, ROGERS HORNSBY, St. Louis, 1922 42, DAVE JOHNSON, Atlanta, 1973	32, Joe Gordon, Cleveland, 1948
RBIs	152, ROGERS HORNSBY, St. Louis, 1922	125, Nap Lajoie, Philadelphia, 1901
Runs	156, ROGERS HORNSBY, Chicago, 1929	145, Nap Lajoie, Philadelphia, 1901
Hits	250, ROGERS HORNSBY, St. Louis, 1922	232, Nap Lajoie, Philadelphia, 1901
Doubles	57, Billy Herman, Chicago, 1935, 1936	60, CHARLIE GEHRINGER, Detroit, 1936
Triples	31, HEINIE REITZ, Balt., 1894 25, Larry Doyle, N.Y. Giants, 1911*	22, Snuffy Stirnweiss, New York, 1945

Department	National League	American League
Total Bases	450, ROGERS HORNSBY, St. Louis, 1922	356, Charlie Gehringer, Detroit, 1936
Bases on Balls	148, EDDIE STANKY, Brooklyn, 1945	128, Max Bishop, Philadelphia, 1929, 1930
Stolen Bases	77, Davey Lopes, L.A., 1975	81, EDDIE COLLINS, Philadelphia, 1910
Strikeouts	168, JUAN SAMUEL, Philadelphia, 1984	144, Bobby Knoop, California, 1966
Fewest Strikeouts (Minimum) 500 ABS)	8, EMIL VERBAN, Philadelphia, 1947	8, Eddie Collins, Chicago, 1923

*Record since 1901.

Note: Dave Johnson also had one home run as a pinch hitter, giving him a total of 43 in 1973.

Most Games, Career, at Second Base
2650—Eddie Collins, 1906–30

Most Consecutive Games at Second Base
798—Nellie Fox, Chicago White Sox, August 7, 1955, through September 3, 1960.

EVOLUTION OF SEASON RECORD FOR BEST FIELDING AVERAGE

	Team	League	Year	Average
Ross Barnes	Chicago	National	1876	.910
Jack Burdock	Boston	National	1878	.918
Joe Quest	Chicago	National	1879	.925
Davy Force	Buffalo	National	1880	.939[1]
Charlie Bastian	Philadelphia	National	1886	.945[2]
Fred Dunlap	Pittsburgh	National	1889	.950
Charlie Bassett	New York	National	1890	.952
John Crooks	Columbus	Amer. Assoc.	1891	.957[3]
Lou Bierbauer	Pittsburgh	National	1893	.959
Heinie Reitz	Baltimore	National	1894	.968
Bid McPhee	Cincinnati	National	1896	.978[4]
Gus Dundon	Chicago	American	1905	.978
George Cutshaw	Pittsburgh	National	1919	.980
Aaron Ward	New York	American	1923	.980
Sparky Adams	Chicago	National	1925	.983

	Team	League	Year	Average
Max Bishop	Philadelphia	American	1926	.987[5]
Max Bishop	Philadelphia	American	1932	.988
Ski Melillo	St. Louis	American	1933	.991
Snuffy Stirnweiss	New York	American	1948	.993[6]
Al Schoendienst	St. Louis-New York	National	1956	.993
Jerry Adair	Baltimore	American	1964	.994
Bobby Grich	Baltimore	American	1973	.995
Rob Wilfong	Minnesota	American	1980	.995[7]
Bobby Grich	California	American	1985	.997

[1]Force also played a slew of games at shortstop, a more error-prone position, in 1880, and his average combines his work at both spots. A weak hitter, if not the weakest ever, he relied heavily on his fielding to keep him in the league.

[2]Another extraordinarily inept hitter who got by on his fielding.

[3]The American Association consistently had poorer fielding averages than the National League during its decade as a major circuit, leading to the surmise that either the NL had better fielders—unlikely since the two leagues were about equal in every other respect—or else scorers were tougher in the AA. If the latter was the case, and I tend to think it probably was, Crooks must have been quite a good fielder.

[4]The record crept up a point or two every couple of years until Reitz and McPhee came along. McPhee had actually been around a good while by 1896 but didn't start using a glove until late in his career. Considering that his record stood for 23 years, you have to wonder if he wouldn't have been close to perfect with one of today's models.

[5]A good ballplayer whose skills weren't the sort that were highly regarded in his time. Comparable to Johnny Evers, who's in the Hall of Fame, and Nellie Fox, who one day will be.

[6]Bobby Doerr also fielded .993 in 1948, but Stirnweiss won the fielding crown that year and also became the record holder, because his average was a shade higher.

[7]Wilfong's 1980 average was .99481 in 120 games; Grich's 1973 average was .99471 in 162 games. In 1970 Ken Boswell of the Mets fielded .9956 but wasn't in enough games to qualify as the fielding leader.

Best Career Fielding Average
.990—Ryne Sandberg, 1981–

Most Seasons League Leader in Fielding Average
AL—9—Eddie Collins, last in 1924
NL—7—Red Schoendienst, last in 1958

Most Consecutive Errorless Games
123—Ryne Sandberg, Chicago Cubs, 1989–90. Sandberg's streak ended on May 18, 1990, when he made a wild throw in a game against Houston.

Most Consecutive Errorless Chances Accepted
582—Ryne Sandberg, Chicago Cubs, 1989–90. During his skein Sandberg broke Manny Trillo's record for consecutive errorless chances (479) and Joe Morgan's for consecutive errorless games (91).

Most Chances Accepted, Career
14,156—Eddie Collins, 1906–30

Most Chances Accepted, Season
1059—Frankie Frisch, St. Louis Cardinals, 1927; Frisch also set an all-time record that season when he had 641 assists.

Most Chances Accepted, Game, Nine Innings
NL—18—Terry Harmon, Philadelphia, June 12, 1971
AL—18—Julio Cruz, Seattle, June 7, 1981, first nine innings of an 11-inning game; he handled 19 chances altogether before the game was over.

Most Gold Glove Awards
9—Ryne Sandberg, 1983–91 consecutive

Triples Records

After a little more juice was added to the ball prior to the 1911 season, the scale on the hitters' side once again began to rise—but not so markedly that it can account for Owen Wilson's staggering all-time record achievement. In 1912 Wilson clubbed 36 triples, easily the most by any player in this century and 22 more than Wilson himself collected in his second-best season. There has never been a satisfactory explanation for how he did it. True, Joe Jackson of Cleveland hit 26 triples that same season, the American League record, and Detroit's Sam Crawford tied Jackson's mark just two years later, a lusty sign that the period was probably the most sanguine one in history for triples. True also that Wilson played in Forbes Field, which for many years was sculpted in such a way that balls hit between outfielders frequently grew into triples, helping the Pirates to total 110 or more three-baggers in a season seven times between 1902 and 1930, something that all the other 15 teams combined were able to do only five times. But that still doesn't begin to tell us why it was Wilson who set the record and not Honus Wagner or Fred Clarke or Tommy Leach or Max Carey, four teammates of his who were all much more prolific triples hitters over their careers than he was. To understand why, you had to be in Forbes Field that year, evidently, and even then it might not have come clear. In all likelihood, Wilson's record is just one of the many inexplicable feats that we call a fluke for the lack of a more adequate word.

Most Career Triples by Player Active Exclusively since 1941
   177—Stan Musial, 1941–63

Most Career Triples by Player Active since Musial Retired
   166—Roberto Clemente, 1955–72

TOP 10 IN CAREER TRIPLES

		Years Active	Triples
1.	Sam Crawford	1899–1917	309
2.	Ty Cobb	1905–28	294
3.	Honus Wagner	1897–1917	252
4.	Jake Beckley	1888–1907	243[1]
5.	Roger Connor	1880–97	233[2]
6.	Tris Speaker	1907–28	223
7.	Fred Clarke	1894–1915	220[3]
8.	Dan Brouthers	1879–1904	205
9.	Joe Kelley	1891–1908	194
10.	Paul Waner	1926–45	190[4]

[1]Held the career record before Crawford broke it in 1912.

[2]Held the career record before Beckley broke it in 1904. Prior to Connor, the record belonged to Harry Stovey with 185 career triples.

[3]Clarke's career total is disputed, as are the totals of everyone on the list who played before 1900.

[4]The most career triples by a player active exclusively since 1920.

Most Career Triples by Player Active since 1977
135—Pete Rose, 1963–86

Most Seasons League Leader in Triples
AL—5—Sam Crawford, last in 1915; Willie Wilson, last in 1988
NL—5—Stan Musial, last in 1951

Most Consecutive Seasons League Leader in Triples
AL—3—Sam Crawford, 1913–15; Elmer Flick, 1905–07
NL—3—Garry Templeton, 1977–79

Most Triples, Season, 1920 through 1941
NL—26—Kiki Cuyler, Pittsburgh, 1925
AL—23—Earle Combs, New York, 1927

Most Triples, Season, 1942 through 1960
AL—23—Dale Mitchell, Cleveland, 1949
NL—20—Stan Musial, St. Louis, 1946; Willie Mays, New York Giants, 1957

Most Triples, Season, 1961 through 1977
NL—17—Ralph Garr, Atlanta, 1974
AL—15—Gino Cimoli, Kansas City A's, 1962

Most Triples, Season, since 1977
AL—21—Willie Wilson, Kansas City Royals, 1985
NL—19—Garry Templeton, St. Louis, 1979; Juan Samuel, Philadelphia, 1984; Ryne Sandberg, Chicago, 1984

Fewest Triples, Season, League Leader in Triples
AL—8—Del Unser, Washington, 1969
NL—10—Johnny Callison, Philadelphia, 1962; Willie Davis, Los Angeles, 1962; Maury Wills, Los Angeles, 1962; Dickie Thon, Houston, 1982

Fewest Triples, Season, 600 or More at Bats
AL—0—Cal Ripken, Jr., Baltimore, 1989, 646 at bats
NL—0—Mickey Witek, New York, 1943, 622 at bats

Only Catchers Ever to Lead League in Triples
NL—Tim McCarver, St. Louis, 1966, led with 13 triples.
AL—Carlton Fisk, Boston, 1972, tied Joe Rudi, Oakland, for the lead with nine triples.

Last First Baseman to Lead League in Triples
NL—Stan Musial, St. Louis, 1946, led with 20 triples.
AL—Vic Power, Kansas City A's and Cleveland, 1958, led with 10 triples.

Last Team to Hit 100 Triples in a Season
NL—Pittsburgh, 1930, 119 triples
AL—Washington, 1932, 100 triples

Last Team to Hit More Triples Than Home Runs
AL—Chicago, 1949, 66 triples and 43 home runs
NL—Houston, 1979, 52 triples and 49 home runs

Only Player to Lead League in RBIs Two Years in a Row Without Hitting a Triple
Jackie Jensen, Boston Red Sox, 1958–59. Ironically, just two years earlier, in 1956, Jensen had led the American League in triples with 11.

Pitching Records for
Most Wins

Among the many records Jack Chesbro established in 1904, probably the most significant occurred when he achieved his 41st victory. Only one other pitcher in major-league history, Ed Walsh in 1908, has had a 40-win season since the mound was moved to its present 60-foot-6-inch distance from the plate. Ironically, both Chesbro and Walsh fell just short of bringing pennants to their teams by losing games on the last day of the season.

TOP 10 IN SEASON WINS SINCE 1901

	Team	League	Year	Wins
1. Jack Chesbro	New York	American	1904	41
2. Ed Walsh	Chicago	American	1908	40[1]
3. Christy Mathewson	New York	National	1908	37[2]
4. Walter Johnson	Washington	American	1913	36
5. Joe McGinnity	New York	National	1904	35
6. Joe Wood	Boston	American	1912	34
7. Cy Young	Boston	American	1901	33
Christy Mathewson	New York	National	1904	33
Pete Alexander	Philadelphia	National	1916	33
10. Cy Young	Boston	American	1902	32
Walter Johnson	Washington	American	1912	32

[1]Disputed. Some sources say he had only 39 wins.
[2]20th-century National League record.

TOP 10 IN SEASON WINS SINCE 1920

		Team	League	Year	Wins
1.	Jim Bagby	Cleveland	American	1920	31
	Lefty Grove	Philadelphia	American	1930	31[1]
	Denny McLain	Detroit	American	1968	31
4.	Dizzy Dean	St. Louis	National	1934	30[2]
5.	Hal Newhouser	Detroit	American	1944	29
6.	Dazzy Vance	Brooklyn	National	1924	28
	Dizzy Dean	St. Louis	National	1935	28
	Lefty Grove	Philadelphia	American	1930	28
	Robin Roberts	Philadelphia	National	1952	28
10.	12 with 27 wins, last done by Bob Welch, Oakland A's, 1990.				

[1]20th-century lefty record.
[2]One of Dean's wins in 1934 is disputed. On June 27 he was credited with a victory in relief over the Giants that even by the scoring rules of that time should have gone to Jim Mooney.

TEAM MILESTONE PITCHERS (SINCE 1893)

National League

Team	Last 30-Game Winner	Last 25-Game Winner	Last 20-Game Winner
Astros	None	None	Mike Scott, 20 (1989)
Braves	Kid Nichols, 30 (1897)	Dick Rudolph, 27 (1914)	Tom Glavine, 22 (1993)
		Bill James, 26 (1914)	Greg Maddux, 20 (1993)
Cardinals	Dizzy Dean, 30 (1934)	Dizzy Dean, 28 (1935)	John Tudor, 21 (1985)
			Joaquin Andujar, 21 (1985)
Cubs	None	Charlie Root, 26 (1927)	Greg Maddux, 20 (1992)
Dodgers	None	Sandy Koufax, 27 (1966)	Ramon Martinez, 20 (1990)
Expos	None	None	Ross Grimsley, 20 (1978)
Giants	Christy Mathewson, 37 (1908)	Juan Marichal, 26 (1968)	John Burkett, 22 (1993)
			Bill Swift, 21 (1993)

Team	Last 30-Game Winner	Last 25-Game Winner	Last 20-Game Winner
Mets	None	Tom Seaver, 25 (1969)	Frank Viola, 20 (1990)
Padres	None	None	Gaylord Perry, 21 (1978)
Phillies	Pete Alexander, 30 (1917)	Steve Carlton, 27 (1972)	Steve Carlton, 23 (1982)
Pirates	Frank Killen, 30 (1896)	Burleigh Grimes, 25 (1928)	John Smiley, 20 (1991)
Reds	None	Bucky Walters, 27 (1939)	Danny Jackson, 23 (1989)

American League

Team	Last 30-Game Winner	Last 25-Game Winner	Last 20-Game Winner
A's	Lefty Grove, 31 (1931)	Bob Welch, 27 (1990)	Dave Stewart, 22 (1990)
Angels	None	None	Nolan Ryan, 22 (1974)
Blue Jays	None	None	Jack Morris, 21 (1992)
Brewers	None	None	Ted Higuera, 20 (1986)
Indians	Jim Bagby, 31 (1920)	Bob Feller, 26 (1946)	Gaylord Perry, 21 (1974)
Mariners	None	None	None
Orioles	None	Steve Stone, 25 (1980)	Mike Boddicker, 20 (1984)
Rangers	None	Fergie Jenkins, 25 (1974)	Kevin Brown, 21 (1992)
Red Sox	Joe Wood, 34 (1912)	Mel Parnell, 25 (1949)	Roger Clemens, 21 (1990)
Royals	None	None	Bret Saberhagen, 23 (1989)
Tigers	Denny McLain, 31 (1968)	Mickey Lolich, 25 (1971)	Bill Gullickson, 20 (1991)
Twins	Walter Johnson, 36 (1913)	Jim Kaat, 25 (1966)	Roger Erickson, 20 (1991)
White Sox	Ed Walsh, 40 (1908)	Red Faber, 25 (1921)	Jack McDowell, 22, (1993)
Yankees	Jack Chesbro, 41 (1904)	Ron Guidry, 25 (1978)	Ron Guidry, 22 (1985)

Last Pitcher to Win 30 Games Three Years in a Row
    Pete Alexander, 1915–17. Christy Mathewson, 1903–5, is the only other pitcher to do it since 1901.

Last Pitcher to Win 25 or More Games Three Years in a Row
 Hal Newhouser, 1944–46

Most Seasons League Leader in Wins
 NL—9—Warren Spahn, last in 1961
 AL—6—Walter Johnson, last in 1924; Bob Feller, last in 1951

Most Seasons 30 or More Wins
 Right-hander—7—Kid Nichols, 1891–97 consecutive
 Left-hander—2—Frank Killen, 1893 and 1896

Most Seasons 20 or More Wins
 Right-hander—16—Cy Young, last in 1908
 Left-hander—13—Warren Spahn, last in 1963

Most Wins, Season, Against One Team
 9—Ed Walsh, Chicago White Sox, 1908, was a perfect 9–0 versus the Red Sox and 9–1 versus the Yankees. His record when he opposed the other five AL clubs was "only" 22–14. Also in 1908, Ed Reulbach of the Cubs beat Brooklyn nine times.

Best Pitching Duo, Season, since 1901
 NL—Joe McGinnity (35) and Christy Mathewson (33) won 68 games between them for the 1904 Giants.
 AL—Jack Chesbro (41) and Jack Powell (23) won 64 games between them for the 1904 Yankees.

Best Pitching Duo, Season, since 1920
 AL—Hal Newhouser (29) and Dizzy Trout (27) won 56 games between them for the 1944 Tigers.
 NL—Bucky Walters (27) and Paul Derringer (25), 52 wins between them for the 1939 Reds

Best Pitching Duo, Season, since 1961
 NL—Sandy Koufax (26) and Don Drysdale (23), 49 wins between them for the 1965 Dodgers
 AL—Bob Welch (27) and Dave Stewart (22), 49 wins between them for the 1990 Oakland A's, topping by one the 48 games Mike Cuellar and Dave McNally won between them for the 1970 Orioles.

Best Pitching Trio, Season, since 1901
   Joe McGinnity (35), Christy Mathewson (33) and Dummy
Taylor (21), 89 wins among them for the 1904 New York
Giants

Best Pitching Trio, Season, since 1920
   Jim Bagby (31), Stan Coveleski (24) and Ray Caldwell
(20), 75 wins among them for the 1920 Cleveland Indians

Best Pitching Trio, Season, since 1961
   Mike Cuellar (24), Dave McNally (24) and Jim Palmer
(20), 68 wins among them for the 1970 Baltimore Orioles

Best Pitching Quartet, Season, since 1901
   Joe McGinnity (35), Christy Mathewson (33), Dummy
Taylor (21) and Hooks Wiltse (13), 102 wins among them
for the 1904 New York Giants

Best Pitching Quartet, Season, since 1920
   Red Faber (23), Lefty Williams (22), Eddie Cicotte (21)
and Dickie Kerr (21), 87 wins among them for the 1920
Chicago White Sox

Best Pitching Quartet, Season, since 1961
   Dave McNally (21), Mike Cuellar (20), Pat Dobson (20)
and Jim Palmer (20), 81 wins among them for the 1971
Baltimore Orioles

**Fewest Wins, Club Leader in Wins, World Championship
Team**
   NL—14—John Candelaria, Pittsburgh, 1979
   AL—15—Lefty Gomez and Red Ruffing, New York, 1941

First League Champion without a 20-Game Winner
   AL—Philadelphia, 1914, led by Chief Bender and Joe
Bush with 17 wins each
   NL—New York, 1922, led by Art Nehf with 19 wins. The
Giants also won in 1923 and again in 1924 without a 20-game
winner.

**First Season Neither World Series Team Had a 20-Game
Winner**
   1975—Rick Wise led the Red Sox with 19 wins, and Gary
Nolan, Jack Billingham and Don Gullett led the Reds with
only 15 wins.

First Pitcher to Win 20 Games in a Season Divided Between Two Leagues, since 1901
    Joe McGinnity, 1902, 13 wins for Baltimore in the AL and then 8 more in the NL, for a total of 21, after jumping to the Giants. Pat Flaherty with the White Sox and Pirates in 1904, Hank Borowy with the Yankees and Cubs in 1945, and Rick Sutcliffe with the Indians and Cubs in 1984 have also done it.

Most Wins by Pitcher on a Last-Place Team
    NL—27—Steve Carlton, Philadelphia, 1972; NL record .459 percent of team's wins
    AL—22—Nolan Ryan, California, 1974

Most Career Wins, Relief Pitcher
    124—Hoyt Wilhelm, 1952–72

Most Games Won, Career, From One Team
    NL—70—Pete Alexander, 1911–30, from Cincinnati
    AL—66—Walter Johnson, 1907–27, from Detroit

300-GAME WINNERS

		Years Active	*Wins*
1.	Cy Young	1890–1911	511
2.	Walter Johnson	1907–27	417
3.	Pete Alexander	1911–30	373
4.	Christy Mathewson	1900–1916	372
5.	Warren Spahn	1942–65	363
6.	Kid Nichols	1890–1906	362
7.	Pud Galvin	1879–92	361
8.	Tim Keefe	1880–93	342
9.	Steve Carlton	1965–88	329
10.	John Clarkson	1882–94	327
11.	Eddie Plank	1901–17	326
12.	Don Sutton	1966–88	324
	Nolan Ryan	1966–93	324
14.	Phil Niekro	1964–87	318
15.	Gaylord Perry	1962–83	314
16.	Tom Seaver	1967–86	311
17.	Hoss Radbourn	1881–91	310
18.	Mickey Welch	1880–92	307
19.	Early Wynn	1939–63	300
	Lefty Grove	1925–41	300

Pitchers Who Won 100 or More Games in Each League (In Order Accomplished)
1. Cy Young
2. Al Orth
3. Jim Bunning
4. Gaylord Perry
5. Fergie Jenkins
6. Nolan Ryan
7. Dennis Martinez

Fewest Full Seasons Needed to Win 200 Games, since 1901
Pete Alexander had 190 wins after his first seven seasons, won two more in 1918 before he was inducted into the army, then had 16 wins in 1919 after he was discharged, giving him 208 wins in his first eight full seasons. Christy Mathewson had a 0–3 record in 1900, won 174 games in his first seven full seasons and had 211 wins after his eighth. Hence Mathewson achieved more wins in his first eight full seasons, but Alexander had more after his first seven seasons and probably would have had more after his eighth season, too, if his career hadn't been interrupted by military service.

Fewest Full Seasons Needed to Win 300 Games, since 1901
12—Christy Mathewson; he had 312 wins at the end of his 12th full season

Fewest Wins at Age 30, 300-Game Winner
31—Phil Niekro. The record was formerly held by Gaylord Perry, who had only 76 wins on his 30th birthday. Early Wynn, with 83 wins when he turned 30, was the record-holder before Perry. Niekro also holds the record for the fewest wins at age 40—he had only 197—by a future 300-game winner.

Pitching Records for Most Starts and Complete Games

In 1904 Jack Chesbro of the Yankees set a post-1893 record when he started 51 games. The modern National League record holder is the Giants' Joe McGinnity, who made 48 starts in 1903. McGinnity's record is in some ways the more remarkable because it came in the last major-league season that the schedule called for only 140 games.

Most Games Started, Career
815—Cy Young, 1890 through 1911. Young made 30 or more starts in 19 consecutive seasons (1891–1909), another all-time record.

Most Games Started, League, Career
NL—677—Steve Carlton, 1965 through 1986
AL—665—Walter Johnson, 1907 through 1927

Most Seasons League Leader in Starts
NL—6—Robin Roberts, 1950–55. consecutive
AL—5—Bob Feller, last in 1948; Early Wynn, last in 1959

Most Games Started, Season, 1920 through 1941
AL—44—George Uhle, Cleveland, 1923
NL—40—Pete Alexander, Chicago, 1920

Most Games Started, Season, 1942 through 1960
AL—42—Bob Feller, Cleveland, 1946
NL—42—Bob Friend, Pittsburgh, 1956

Most Games Started, Season, 1961 through 1976
AL—49—Wilbur Wood, Chicago, 1972. Wood also made 48 starts in 1973, as did Mickey Lolich of the Tigers in 1971.

Wood's 49 starts in 1972 were the most by any pitcher since Ed Walsh made 49 for the 1908 White Sox.

NL—42—Fergie Jenkins, Chicago, 1969; Don Drysdale, Los Angeles, 1963 and 1965; Jack Sanford, San Francisco, 1963

Most Games Started, Season, Since 1977
NL—44—Phil Niekro, Atlanta, 1979; the most by an NL pitcher since Alexander made 44 starts in 1917

AL—40—Mike Flanagan, Baltimore, 1978; Dennis Leonard, Kansas City, 1978; Jim Clancy, Toronto, 1982

Most Consecutive Starting Assignments, No Relief Appearances
NL—534—Steve Carlton, May 15, 1971, through August 5, 1986

AL—492—Jack Morris, September 30, 1978, through 1993

ML—594—Nolan Ryan, July 30, 1974, through 1993

Most Opening Day Starting Assignments
AL—14—Walter Johnson, all of them with Washington

NL—14—Steve Carlton, 13 with Philadelphia and one with St. Louis

Most Consecutive Opening Day Starting Assignments
16—Tom Seaver, 13 in the National League and three in the American League

Chesbro also set a modern record when he completed 48 games in 1904. Two years earlier Vic Willis of the Boston Braves set the National League record when he went the route 45 times in his 46 starts.

Most Complete Games, Season, 1920 through 1941
NL—33—Pete Alexander, Chicago, 1920; Burleigh Grimes, Brooklyn, 1923

AL—32—Red Faber, Chicago, 1922; George Uhle, Cleveland, 1926

Most Complete Games, Season, 1942 through 1960
AL—36—Bob Feller, Cleveland, 1946

NL—33—Robin Roberts, Philadelphia, 1953

Most Complete Games, Season, 1961 through 1976
AL—30—Catfish Hunter, New York, 1975

NL—30—Steve Carlton, Philadelphia, 1972; Fergie Jenkins, Chicago, 1971; Juan Marichal, San Francisco, 1968

Most Complete Games, Season, since 1977
    AL—28—Rick Langford, Oakland, 1980
    NL—23—Phil Niekro, Atlanta, 1979

Most Complete Games, Season, since 1901, Left-hander
    NL—41—Noodles Hahn, Cincinnati, 1901
    AL—39—Rube Waddell, Philadelphia, 1904

Last Team with Three Pitchers Who Completed 20 or More games
    The 1980 Oakland A's registered 94 complete games, led by Rick Langford with 28, Mike Norris with 24 and Matt Keough with 20.

Most Consecutive Complete Games
    188—Jack Taylor, St. Louis Cardinals and Chicago Cubs, June 20, 1901, through August 9, 1906. On August 13, 1906, Taylor was knocked out in the third inning by the Dodgers, ending a record string of 1,727 consecutive innings without being relieved; altogether, he threw the last pitch for his team in 203 straight games in which he appeared.

Most Seasons League Leader in Complete Games
    NL—9—Warren Spahn, last in 1963
    AL—6—Walter Johnson, last in 1916

First Season League Leader Had Fewer Than 30 Complete Games
    NL—1910—Three Finger Brown of the Cubs, Nap Rucker of the Dodgers and Christy Mathewson of the Giants all tied for the lead with 27 complete games.
    AL—1923—George Uhle of Cleveland led with 29 complete games.

First Season League Leader Had Fewer Than 20 Complete Games
    AL—1955—Whitey Ford of the Yankees led with only 18.
    NL—1957—Warren Spahn of the Milwaukee Braves led with 18; 1957 was also the first season that neither league had a pitcher who completed 20 games.

Fewest Complete Games, League Leader in Complete Games
   NL—8—Greg Maddux, Atlanta, 1993
   AL—11—Jack Morris, Detroit; Dave Stewart, Oakland, 1990

Most Starts, Season, without Completing a Game
   NL—37—Steve Bedrosian, Atlanta, 1985. Shipped to the Phillies in 1986, Bedrosian was sent to the bullpen and proceeded to notch 29 saves, a club record.
   AL—34—Kirk McCaskill, Chicago, 1992

Most Starts, Career, without Completing a Game
   63—Scott Scudder, 1989 through 1992; Wally Whitehurst, with 51 through 1993, ranks second at the moment.

Most Complete Games, League, Career
   AL—531—Walter Johnson, 1907 through 1927
   NL—437—Pete Alexander, 1911 through 1930

Most Complete Games, League, Career, Since 1920
   NL—382—Warren Spahn, 1942 through 1965
   AL—356—Ted Lyons, 1923 through 1946

TOP TEN IN COMPLETE GAMES, CAREER, SINCE 1893

		Years active	CG
1.	Cy Young	1890–1911	643[1]
2.	Walter Johnson	1907–27	531
3.	Pete Alexander	1911–30	438
4.	Christy Mathewson	1900–1916	434
5.	Jack Powell	1897–1912	422
6.	Eddie Plank	1901–17	410[2]
7.	Kid Nichols	1890–1906	391[3]
8.	Vic Willis	1898–1910	388
9.	Warren Spahn	1942–65	382
10.	Ted Lyons	1923–46	356

[1]Had 106 CGs prior to 1893.
[2]The most by a left-hander.
[3]Had 142 CGs prior to 1893.

Players We Wish We'd Seen More of: 1901–19

The deadball era was loaded with ephemeral performers. Some, like Judge McCreedie and Ham Iburg, simply preferred life on the Pacific Coast to life in the eastern major-league cities. Others, like Bill Keister, never found a team that could tolerate their abundant talents. Keister hit with power, scored a goodly number of runs, stole plenty of bases and compiled a .312 career batting average in seven seasons. Yet no team kept him for longer than a year, and he was permanently jettisoned from the majors after the 1903 season in which he led the Phillies in slugging average, homers and RBIs despite playing in only 100 games. Here are some of the many other fine players in the early part of the century who appeared on the major-league stage all too briefly.

1. Erv Beck. Cleveland's regular second baseman as a rookie in 1901, he not only hit the American League's first home run, but at the end of the season he had a .289 batting average and 79 RBIs. Beck lost his job when Cleveland obtained Nap Lajoie from Philadelphia and was sent to Cincinnati. In 1902, split between the Reds and Detroit, he hit .301 and finished the season as the Tigers' starting first baseman. Notwithstanding his two fine years, he never again played in the majors.

2. Irv Waldron. In 1901, his one and only major-league season, he started out with Milwaukee, then was shipped to Washington, where he hit .322. Overall, Waldron had a .311 batting average in 141 games, scored 102 runs and led the American League in at bats.

3. Pop Foster. Another who dropped from view after the 1901 American League season, split between Washington and Chicago. In his finale he cracked seven homers and had a .422 slugging average. Despite his nickname, Foster was only 23 when he left the majors.

4. Dave Rowan. Aside from Terry Foster, he has the record for the highest career batting average among players with 50 or more at bats. Rowan hit .385 for the 1911 St. Louis Browns in an 18-game trial and collected 11 RBIs in only 65 at bats, but wasn't invited back in 1912.

5. Tacks Neuer. Threw a shutout in his first start for the 1907 Yankees and was 4–2 with a 2.17 ERA and three shutouts in six career starts. Neuer died at 86 in 1966 leaving no record with which arm he threw, let alone why that arm got such short shrift in the majors.

6. Horace Milan. Most younger brothers of star players get lengthy trials if they show any promise at all. Clyde Milan's brother was the rare exception; despite hitting .320 and swiping six bases, he got into only 42 games with the Senators in the mid-teens.

7. Henry Schmidt. If you're into baseball history and you haven't discovered him yet, you've missed one. Schmidt left the majors after posting 22 wins as a Brooklyn rookie in 1903.

8. Elmer Stricklett. The distinction of being the first spitballer may or may not have been his, but what indisputably belongs to him are three solid major-league seasons, all of them unfortunately with Brooklyn. In the last one, 1907, he completed 25 of 26 starts and racked up four shutouts and a 2.27 ERA—yet had only a 12–14 record. With a contender he might have became a star; like so many pitchers of that era who labored for Brooklyn, he just became disenchanted.

9. Erwin Harvey. Called "Zaza" and used as a pitcher by the White Sox for most of the 1901 season, he had a mediocre mound record, but his bat was so good that the Sox tried him in the outfield. He hit .333 in 1901 and then .348 with Cleveland the following year, but after a few weeks the Indians mysteriously cut him. For his career, Harvey hit .332 and stole 17 bases in only 76 games.

10. Bud Ryan. Came to the majors with Cleveland in 1912 after he hit .339 for Portland in the Pacific Coast League, but was sent back to the minors after stroking .296 in 1913. The following year, without him, Cleveland plummeted to the American League cellar and had only one player, Joe Jackson, whose batting average was higher than Ryan's career .282.

11. The Federal League Four. Supposedly all the players

who jumped to the Federal League were welcomed back to the majors when the Feds folded after the 1915 season, but don't you believe it. If there wasn't an unwritten blacklist in operation, how else can what happened to Steve Evans, Vin Campbell, Rebel Oakes and Ted Easterly be explained? The Cardinals' best outfielder in the early teens, Evans in 1915 led the Federal League in doubles and hit .308 after topping the Feds in slugging average and triples on a .348 average in 1914. Campbell led the National League in batting much of the 1910 season, yet was reduced by the Pirates to a part-time outfielder in 1911. Sent to the Braves the following year, he hit .296 and led the NL in at bats—then was cut. Two .300-plus seasons in the Federal League gave him, at age 27, a .310 career batting average. Oakes, a teammate of Evans's on the Cardinals, became the player-manager of the Pittsburgh Rebels after joining the Feds in 1914 and nearly spearheaded the Rebels to the 1915 FL pennant. One of the best-hitting catchers in the deadball era and an outstanding pinch hitter, Easterly was just 29 after the 1915 season and boasted a .300 career batting average, second at the time among catchers only to Chief Meyers. Evans, Campbell, Oakes and Easterly were all top-notch players, all seemingly with several years of good play left in them, and yet all four were left without a home in the majors after the 1915 season ended.

The Great Scandals

In 1920 eight members of the Chicago White Sox were barred for life from organized baseball for their part in throwing the 1919 World Series. The eight players were Chick Gandil, Eddie Cicotte, Swede Risberg, Lefty Williams, Happy Felsch, Fred McMullin, Joe Jackson and Buck Weaver, and the order in which they are listed may also reflect their degree of guilt. Gandil, the ringleader, quit after the 1919 season and never attempted to deny or mitigate his actions. The next five players acknowledged their complicity but offered extenuating circumstances to explain their lapse from grace. Jackson admitted he took money but claimed he played his best in the Series. Weaver admitted only that he knew the fix was on and that he chose not to betray his teammates by informing on them. Although brought to trial, none of the eight players was ever convicted in court of the slightest wrongdoing. Because of testimony he gave at their trial, St. Louis Browns second baseman Joe Gedeon was also barred from the game, as were a host of former players and hangers-on. Gedeon and the Chicago Eight were neither the first nor the last players banished from the game, however. Nor were they necessarily the worst offenders. Here is a partial list of baseball's top malefactors.

The First Great Scandal

In 1865 three players with the New York Mutuals, Thomas Devyr, Edward Duffy and William Wamsley, were accused of conspiring with gamblers to lose a game to the Brooklyn Eckfords. All three players admitted their guilt and were expelled by the Mutuals, only to be reinstated a few months later without further penalty.

The Louisville Four

Major-league baseball in its infancy was rife with gamblers and players suspected of dumping games. One reason the National Association collapsed was its inability to police itself, and there is ample evidence that the National League, which replaced it, improved matters only slightly. At the close of the 1877 season, NL President William Hulbert was faced with a situation he could not ignore when evidence was given to him that four Louisville players, Jim Devlin, George Hall, Al Nichols and Bill Craver, had thrown games on the team's final eastern road trip. Devlin had reputedly been approached by a gambler named McLeod and Hall simultaneously approached by his own brother-in-law. Both were urged to see to it that Louisville found a way to blow its 3½-game lead with 12 contests to play and swing the pennant to Boston. Nichols was made part of the plot and led to its unraveling when Louisville team officials, noting the deluge of telegrams he suddenly began receiving, examined their contents and discovered they were from gamblers informing him which games to lose. A case has been made that Craver wasn't one of the conspirators and was banned solely because he stood on his constitutional right not to have his mail opened without his permission.

In any event, the Louisville Four were probably not the only dishonest players in 1877—they were merely the most flagrant. In subsequent years, players under suspicion were blacklisted rather than barred, a practice that soon included not only the game's shady characters but also those who exhibited rebellious tendencies. In 1881 a formal blacklist was drawn up; on it were nine players: Mike Dorgan, Buttercup Dickerson, Emil Gross, Lipman Pike, Sadie Houck, Edward "The Only" Nolan, Bill Crowley, John Fox and Blower Brown. All except Nolan and Pike were later reinstated without undue disruption to their careers. Pike, who had first been blacklisted back in 1878 for an unrecorded offense, was 36 years old in 1881 and near the end anyway, while Nolan, who had also been blacklisted in 1878 for lying to the owner of his Indianapolis team, in disgust dropped down to the minor leagues, where he starred for years.

The Scots Verdict

In 1904, St. Louis Cardinals pitcher Jack Taylor fell under suspicion of throwing games. Testimony was heard for and against him, and he received what sources in the period called a "Scots Verdict," meaning there was good reason to believe him to be guilty but insufficient evidence to convict him.

The Corkscrew Brain

It belonged, Fred Lieb wrote, to Hal Chase, quite possibly the greatest fielding first baseman ever and a fine all-around player—when he wanted to be. Much has been written about Chase in recent years, all of it condemnatory and perhaps justly so, but too many sources would have you believe that Chase all by himself undermined the fabric of baseball and created the climate for the Black Sox scandal. This is ludicrous. Chase was first and foremost an opportunist. As a rookie with the Yankees in 1905, he found himself on a team that had lost the pennant the previous year on a ninth-inning wild pitch on the last day of the season, an occurrence that did not seem to overly depress team owners Frank Farrell and Big Bill Devery. Both men were gamblers by occupation and surrounded themselves with others of their breed, a combination that Chase no doubt viewed as license to do his thing. In support of this are the numerous instances when Yankees managers begged Farrell to get rid of Chase and found themselves axed instead, plus the fact that Chase was himself named manager of the club while supposedly under clouds of suspicion.

How far up into the front office and how wide on the field Chase's chicanery extended can only be guesswork now, but it is intriguing that despite his reputation for wrecking the morale of every team he played for, John McGraw hired him in 1919 and gave him the Giants first-base job. True, McGraw released him at the end of the season, along with Heinie Zimmerman and Jean Dubuc, two other questionable figures of the era, and none of the three ever played in the majors again—but where had McGraw's head been back in the spring? Did he discredit all the rumors about Chase? Had he seen Chase as still capable of being reformed? Or does the full story, for some reason, remain buried?

The Douglas Incident

Subsequent to the Black Sox scandal, a number of players found themselves outside the barred gates of organized baseball. Among them were Gene Paulette of the Phillies, who was banned for betting on games and being foolish enough to admit it, pitchers Paul Carter and Claude Hendrix of the

Cubs, who were never formally banished but were rather declared personae non grata, and Benny Kauff, expelled in 1920 by Commissioner Landis after he was accused of being part of a stolen car ring. Three ex-big leaguers, Bill Rumler, Gene Dale and Harl Maggert, were also dismissed by Landis in 1920 for dumping Pacific Coast League games, and pitcher Ray Fisher incurred Landis's wrath when he refused to sign the contract the Reds tendered him and instead took a coaching job at the University of Michigan. When Fisher applied for reinstatement at the close of the college season, Landis refused to grant it, and Fisher, unfairly, found himself on the same list with all the crooked players who had been booted from the game in the massive effort to clean it up and restore its image. The effort seemed at an end in 1922, until pitcher Phil Douglas jumped the league-leading Giants and then sent a letter to Cardinals outfielder Les Bell, offering to make himself scarce for the rest of the season if the Cardinals would send him a little travel money. Bell, one of the most strait-laced players in the twenties, instead turned the letter over to team officials, it soon wound up on Landis's desk, and Douglas found himself out of the game.

A Double Standard?

Rube Benton, another ex-Giants pitcher, was let go by McGraw in 1921 after admitting he bet on games. When Benton had an outstanding season with St. Paul in the American Association in 1922, the Reds tried to bring him back to the majors, but McGraw blocked the move, claiming Benton had been blacklisted. Forced by the Reds to decide the issue, Landis ruled that since Benton had never been officially expelled he was eligible to pitch for any team that would have him. So Benton, a self-confessed friend to gamblers, returned to the majors with the Reds in 1923 while Ray Fisher, whose only crime had been to reject a contract he considered to be inadequate, was left permanently outside the walls.

The Last Major-League Player to Be Barred

In the final days of the 1924 season, with the Giants rolling to their fourth straight pennant, Giants outfielder Jimmy O'Connell sidled up to Phillies shortstop Heinie Sand before a game and offered him $500 to go easy on the Giants that day. Sand reported the bribe attempt to his manager, and the machinery was quickly set into motion that would expel both O'Connell and Giants coach Cozy Dolan, who had allegedly put O'Connell up to approaching Sand. But few at the time believed that O'Connell, a Santa Clara graduate, had been either the instigator of the bribe offer or Dolan's unwitting dupe. There was testimony from O'Connell that several other Giants players had a hand in it and statements from them that it had all been meant as a joke. In any event, O'Connell went down alone, and Dolan, after bitterly shouting that the real story had yet to be told, then decided he wasn't going to be the one to tell it and remained mum until his death. What really happened that September afternoon in 1924? Probably no one will ever know, but, for whatever it means, it was the last scandal involving a New York Giants player, and 1924 was the last season that a club managed by John McGraw won a pennant.

Cobb and Speaker Dodge a Bullet

In 1926 an event that threatened for a time to eclipse even the Black Sox scandal erupted when former Tigers pitcher Dutch Leonard let it be known that he had certain incriminating letters from Smokey Joe Wood regarding bets that Leonard, Wood, Tris Speaker and Ty Cobb had made on a 1919 game between the Tigers and Indians. According to Leonard, the bet was an added thought after Speaker agreed to let the Tigers win the game so that they could beat the Yankees out of second-place money. Speaker and Cobb were at first persuaded to retire in exchange for having the matter left unexplored; then they reconsidered and decided to fight the charge. When Leonard refused to appear publicly to confront them, Landis let the issue die—although neither Speaker nor Cobb, both player-managers at the time, was ever offered a manager's job again—and the popular theory was that Leonard was merely trying to retaliate against Cobb for releasing him during the 1926 season and against Speaker for not giving him a chance to catch on with the Indians. Yet the possibility is strong that if Leonard's letters had come to light a few years earlier, when Landis was mercilessly striving to rid baseball of even the smallest hint of corruption, the game might have been shorn of its two greatest stars as it was about to enter its golden era.

Player Takes on Commissioner and Wins

In 1946 Jorge Pasquel, a wealthy customs broker in Mexico who had a financial interest in the Mexican professional league, after a chance meeting with Giants outfielder Danny Gardella at Al Roon's gymnasium in Manhattan seized upon the notion of spiriting major-league players south of the border. Soon thereafter, Gardella and several dozen other players had been induced to play in Mexico, and alarmed major-league owners looked to newly appointed commissioner Happy Chandler for help. Chandler ruled that all players who did not leave Mexico by his deadline were automatically barred from organized baseball for five years. The ban stuck until 1949 when a flurry of legal suits, most of them initiated by Gardella, made Chandler recant and take wayward players back into the fold. Gardella, a mediocre player, benefited little himself from his besting Chandler and was released after a few games. But Sal Maglie, another Mexican League renegade, became one of the National League's top pitchers.

Most Recent Player Suspended for Gambling

Pitcher Denny McLain of the Tigers was made to sit out much of the 1970 season by Commissioner Bowie Kuhn after being implicated in a bookmaking operation. In recent years several players have been suspended for parts of a season upon being convicted of using and/or trafficking in drugs, but no one has been suspected of allowing his drug involvement to affect the honesty with which he approached the game. To date, not even Cincinnati Manager Pete Rose, who was banished in 1989 for betting on baseball games, is thought to have allowed his gambling activities to influence in any way a game upon which he wagered.

World Series Play: 1901–19

FRANCHISE SUMMARY

Team	League	WS Record	Years in Series
Boston	American	5–0	1903, 1912, 1915, 1916, 1918
Cincinnati	National	1–0	1919
Boston	National	1–0	1914
Chicago	American	2–1	1906, 1917, 1919
Philadelphia	American	3–2	1905, 1910, 1911, 1912, 1914
Pittsburgh	National	1–1	1903, 1909
Chicago	National	2–3	1906, 1907, 1908, 1910, 1918
New York	National	1–4	1905, 1911, 1912, 1913, 1917
Philadelphia	National	0–1	1915
Brooklyn	National	0–1	1916
Detroit	American	0–3	1907, 1908, 1909

Yearly Highlights

1903—Boston (AL) defeated Pittsburgh (NL) 5 games to 3

The first "World Series" since 1890 and the first between the NL and the AL was a five-of-nine affair, Boston winning despite yeoman's work by the Pirates' Deacon Phillippe, who pitched five complete games and had three wins. Boston was led by Bill Dinneen, who won three of his four starts. Phillippe was called on so often because Sam Leever had injured his shoulder in a trapshooting tournament prior to the Series, and another Pirates pitcher, Ed Doheny, was committed to a mental hospital. Jimmy Sebring of the Pirates was the batting star, starting a Series tradition wherein lightly regarded players were often the ones to shine most brilliantly. The teams hit a record 25 triples between them due to a ground rule that any ball going into the overflow crowds that ringed the outfield rated three bases. Members of the Pirates received a larger Series share than the winning

Red Sox because Pittsburgh owner Barney Dreyfuss gave all of the club's take to his players while Boston owner Henry Killilea pocketed his portion and then sold the team to John Taylor, son of the owner of the *Boston Globe*.

1905—New York (NL) defeated Philadelphia (AL) 4 games to 1

There was no World Series in 1904, largely because Giants manager John McGraw and team owner John Brush feared the Yankees would win the AL pennant and were loath to risk their supremacy against a rival New York team. The Giants made this decision in July while the Yankees were leading the AL and then were stuck with it when Yankees ace Jack Chesbro, on the last day of the season, wild-pitched home the run that handed Boston the game and the pennant. In October of 1904, Brush issued an announcement that if the Giants won again in 1905 they would play the AL champ, regardless of who it was. When the Giants repeated, Christy Mathewson, their star pitcher and a Bucknell graduate, found himself pitted against the A's Eddie Plank of Gettysburg College. It was the first time two college grads faced each other in a Series, and the Giants prevailed easily, with all five contests ending in shutouts, three of them pitched by Mathewson.

1906—Chicago (AL) defeated Chicago (NL) 4 games to 2

The Cubs were 26–3 in August and 24–5 down the stretch to finish with a 50–8 surge that gave them a record 116 victories. Against their vaunted pitching staff, the White Sox, known at "The Hitless Wonders," seemed hopelessly overmatched. But after holding the Sox to 6 runs in the first four games, Cubs pitchers gave up 16 runs in the last two contests. Ed Walsh of the triumphant Sox struck out 12 batters in Game Three, a Series nine-inning record that stood until 1929.

1907—Chicago (NL) defeated Detroit (AL) 4 games to 0

The first game ended in a 12-inning deadlock after the Cubs scored the tying run in the ninth on a passed ball. The Cubs then swept the next four games.

1908—Chicago (NL) defeated Detroit (AL) 4 games to 1

In the first Series that matched repeat pennant winners, the Cubs again won easily as Orval Overall and Three

Finger Brown each won two games and allowed only two earned runs between them.

1909—Pittsburgh (NL) defeated Detroit (AL) 4 games to 3

It was the first Series to go the distance. In his third and final try to win a World Championship, Ty Cobb of the Tigers once again came up on the short end. Pirates rookie Babe Adams became the second pitcher to win three games in a seven-game Series, and Pittsburgh stole 18 bases, tying the Series record set in 1906 by the Cubs.

1910—Philadelphia (AL) defeated Chicago (NL) 4 games to 1

Jack Coombs of the A's won three games and hit .385. The Cubs won Game Four after a last-ditch ninth inning rally to avert a Series sweep.

1911—Philadelphia (AL) defeated New York (NL) 4 games to 2

Home Run Baker earned his nickname by hitting two key four-baggers in the Series. Giants second baseman Larry Doyle, carrying the winning run in Game Five, missed home plate on his slide, but none of the A's noticed, and home plate umpire Bill Klem rightfully held silent. The A's lapse became unimportant when they won Game Six 13–2.

1912—Boston (AL) defeated New York (NL) 4 games to 3

The first Series played in Fenway Park and the first truly great one. Art Irwin, who played with Providence in the 1884 World Series, attended the opener and lamented that he'd been born too soon when he saw the size of the crowd. The Series was decided in the bottom of the 10th inning of the seventh game when the Red Sox, trailing 2–1, scored two runs after Giants outfielder Red Snodgrass muffed a fly ball, Christy Mathewson issued an uncharacteristic walk to weak-hitting Steve Yerkes, Tris Speaker singled home the tying run after Fred Merkle and Chief Meyers of the Giants let his pop foul drop between them, Duffy Lewis was intentionally walked, and Larry Gardner then brought Yerkes home with the Series-ending run on a sacrifice fly. The overall hitting star was Buck Herzog of the Giants with 12 hits, while Joe Wood, who won three games for the Red Sox, topped all pitchers.

1913—Philadelphia (AL) defeated New York (NL) 4 games to 1

Home Run Baker was again the hitting star, rapping his third Series four-bagger. Chief Bender of the A's won two complete games despite being hit hard while Christy Mathewson, in his final Series, lost the last game 3–1 to Eddie Plank.

1914—Boston (NL) defeated Philadelphia (AL) 4 games to 0

The only team to win a pennant after being in last place on July 4, the Braves were accorded little chance in the Series. But they swept the A's behind pitchers Bill James and Dick Rudolph, who won two games apiece and allowed only one earned run between them. The Braves, who played in decrepit South End Grounds, borrowed Fenway Park for the Series. A year later the Red Sox borrowed brand-new Braves Field, which was larger than Fenway.

1915—Boston (AL) defeated Philadelphia (NL) 4 games to 1

Babe Ruth made his first Series appearance, as a pinch hitter, in Baker Bowl, where 400 extra seats were put in right field, reducing the park's dimensions and enabling Red Sox outfielder Harry Hooper to bounce two balls into the temporary seats in Game Five—hits that now would be ground-rule doubles that then counted as home runs. The Phils, in a sense, were the victims of their own greed, losing their fourth Series game in a row by one run when Hooper's second park-created homer came in the ninth inning.

1916—Boston (AL) defeated Brooklyn (NL) 4 games to 1

In the longest Series game in history—Game Two on October 2—it took Babe Ruth 14 innings to beat Sherry Smith of the Dodgers 2–1. The following day Jack Coombs edged Carl Mays, 4–3, to give Brooklyn its only win.

1917—Chicago (AL) defeated New York (NL) 4 games to 2

In Game Four, Benny Kauff became the first National Leaguer to hit two homers in a Series game; Patsy Dougherty of Boston had been the first American Leaguer, in 1903. Heinie Zimmerman of the Giants was tagged the Series goat when Eddie Collins was trapped off third base in the fourth inning of the sixth game but darted past Giants catcher Bill Rariden, leaving Zimmerman to chase Collins helplessly across the plate when neither pitcher Rube Benton nor first baseman Walter Holke covered home. Red Faber of the White Sox won three games and lost one, making him the only pitcher ever to post four decisions in a seven-game Series.

1918—Boston (AL) defeated Chicago (NL) 4 games to 2

In anticipation of big crowds that never materialized, the Cubs borrowed Comiskey Park from the White Sox. George Whiteman of the Red Sox hit .250 and knocked in only one run but is still remembered as one of the Series heroes, whereas Cubs second baseman Charlie Pick, who, like Whiteman, came up from the minors in midseason and played only because his team was short-handed, isn't remembered at all despite batting .389 and leading both clubs with seven hits. The Red Sox scored only nine runs in the Series and hit just .186 but won because Carl Mays and Babe Ruth held the Cubs to only four runs and won two games each.

1919—Cincinnati (NL) defeated Chicago (AL) 5 games to 3

Aiming for increased gate receipts to make up for the short—140-game—regular-season schedule, the National Commission, comprising the two league presidents, Ban Johnson and John Heydler, plus Gary Herrmann, president of the Reds, expanded the Series to a best-five-of-nine format but could have halted proceedings after the first game because the verdict was already self-evident to many in attendance. The signal that the Series was fixed came in the bottom of the first inning when Eddie Cicotte of the White Sox deliberately plunked Reds leadoff hitter Morrie Rath in the back. Joe Jackson, one of the fixers, led all batters with 12 hits and a .375 average, giving credence to his lifelong contention that he promised his worst to gamblers but played his best.

SECTION 3

Famous Firsts:
1920–41

1920—The pall that hangs over baseball after the 1919 World Series leads officials to abolish the spitball and all other pitches that involve applying foreign substances to the ball in an effort to sanitize the game and increase hitting. A select few pitchers are exempted from the abolition and allowed to continue throwing spitters until their careers are over.

1920—The Bill Doak fielder's glove is introduced by the Rawlings Sporting Goods Company of St. Louis. In contrast to the old pancake glove, it has a natural pocket whose size can be adjusted by leather laces.

1920—Cleveland shortstop Ray Chapman becomes the first player to die as a result of an injury incurred in a major-league game when he succumbs after Carl Mays of the Yankees beans him with a submarine pitch on August 16 in a game at the Polo Grounds.

1921—On August 25, Harold Arlen, the voice of radio station KDKA in Pittsburgh, broadcasts the first baseball game over the air, from Philadelphia, the Pirates winning 8–5 over the Phillies. In the fall of that year KDKA installs a wire between Pittsburgh and New York, which Grantland Rice uses to issue sporadic reports from the Polo Grounds, where the World Series is being played between the Yankees and Giants. Another radio station, WJZ in Newark, New Jersey, is even more ambitious and manages to broadcast the Series in its entirety by relay as Sandy Hunt of the *Newark Sunday Call* reports play-by-play action from his seat in the Polo Grounds to the WJZ radio shack, where Tommy Cowan then repeats Hunt's account to station listeners.

1921—American League pitcher Al Sothoron sets a post-deadball era record when he works the entire season—178 innings—without surrendering a home run.

1921—Eppa Rixey of the Reds gives up only one homer in 301 innings—an NL post-deadball record.

1922—The Williams shift is introduced—not to frustrate Ted Williams, who's only about four years old at the moment, but rather to combat lefty pull-hitters Ken Williams of the Browns and Cy Williams of the Phillies.

1922—George Uhle of the Indians wins 22 games with a 4.07 ERA, the first pitcher since 1901 to achieve 20 victories despite allowing over four runs a game.

1922—White Sox owner Charlie Comiskey, anxious to shed his miserly image, forks over $125,000 to the San Francisco Seals for the contract of third baseman Willie Kamm, the first $100,000 purchase of a minor leaguer.

1923—The Giants buy pitcher/first baseman Jack Bentley from the Baltimore club in the International League for $65,000, but Bentley refuses to report unless he's given a piece of his sale price. The first minor leaguer to demand a cut of the action, Bentley finally relents—but the suspicion will always linger that the Giants secretly gave him signing money after extracting a pledge from him to deny it.

1923—Graham McNamee, the first famous baseball announcer, begins his career. Although not terribly knowledgeable about baseball McNamee has personality—or what in later years is called "charisma." By profession a singer, McNamee obtains his first radio job on a lunch break while serving on jury duty and shortly thereafter is heard for the first time over the air on WEAF in New York, a forerunner of WNBC. From the start it is obvious that McNamee's enthusiastic cultivated delivery gives his audience the feeling that it is part of whatever he is describing, and he is the natural choice to handle the microphone when WEAF decides to broadcast the 1923 World Series.

1924—WMAQ of Chicago broadcasts the home games of both the Cubs and the White Sox, with Hal Totten the voice. Totten is later joined by Pat Flaherty.

1925—The American League permits resin bags to counteract somewhat the ruinous effect that banning foreign substances has had on pitchers.

1929—The Indians and the Yankees become the first teams to put numbers on the backs of their uniforms and leave them there. On May 13, at League Park in Cleveland, fans for the first time are treated to the sight of two teams wearing numbered uniforms and get an additional charge when Willis Hudlin beats the Yankees 4–3. Two years later the American League makes numbered uniforms mandatory for all teams.

1929—On July 5, the Giants use the first public address system in a major-league park for a game against Pittsburgh.

1929—Cincinnati's Harry Hartman becomes the first radio announcer to say "Going, going, gone," whenever a fair-hit ball is headed over the wall.

1932—Jack Graney, former Cleveland outfielder and the first major-league player to hit a home run off Babe Ruth, in 1914, starts as the voice of the Indians, a job he will hold until his retirement after the 1954 World Series. Since announcers in the early days of radio don't travel with teams, Graney becomes a master at re-creating road games, play-by-play reports of which he receives by wire. (In the late 1950s, long after most other teams have begun putting their announcers on the scene, Waite Hoyt and Les Keiter, the twin voices of the Cincinnati Reds, will still be re-creating away games.) To Graney falls the honor of being the first ex–major-leaguer to become a play-by-play announcer, with Hoyt not far behind him—but the first future Hall of Famer to hold down the job is Harry Heilmann, the longtime voice of the Detroit Tigers.

1932—The Kessler brothers provide a harbinger of what fans in Philadelphia will be like in another few decades when they heap so much abuse on A's third baseman Jimmy Dykes that manager-owner Connie Mack finally gives Dykes a break and sells him to the White Sox.

1933—Washington deals first baseman Joe Judge to Brooklyn, ending the record 18 consecutive years that Judge and Senators outfielder Sam Rice have been road roommates.

1934—On Sunday, April 29, the Pirates entertain the Reds in Forbes Field and beat them 9–5 as Pittsburgh becomes the last major-league city to lift its blue laws and host a Sunday game.

1934—Burleigh Grimes wins his 270th and final victory on May 30 when he beats Washington 5–4 while pitching in a relief role for the Yankees. Grimes's win is the last in major-league history by a pitcher legally permitted to throw a spitball.

1934—A few members of the Cincinnati Reds fly to a game in Chicago, the first major-league team to travel together by air.

1935—William Wrigley of the Cubs becomes the first owner to allow all his team's games to be broadcast.

1935—Augie Galan of the Cubs sets a major-league record when he becomes the first player to play an entire 154-game season without grounding into a double play.

1938—The Giants, Dodgers and Yankees for the first time allow their home games to be broadcast on a regular basis. The Yankees hire Mel Allen and team him with Arch McDonald.

1938—Ernie Lombardi of the Reds grounds into 30 double plays, a National League record.

1939—The *Reach Baseball Guide* merges with the *Spalding Baseball Guide*. The two publish under the *Spalding-Reach Baseball Guide* name through 1941, then both bow out after over half a century in the business as the *Sporting News* takes over the publication of the annual guide.

1939—The 25-player limit, reduced to 23 in the depression, is restored and, with the exception of the 1946 season when teams are allowed to carry more players to accommodate returning service vets, remains unchanged until 1986 when the owners, locked in a power struggle with the players' union, cut back to 24-man rosters.

1939—On May 17, W2XBS of New York televises a college contest between Princeton and Columbia, the first baseball game ever to appear on the new video device. On August 26 of that same year, also over W2XBS, the first major-league game is telecast when a TV camera is lugged into Ebbets Field, where the Dodgers are hosting the Reds.

1939—Lou Gehrig becomes the first player to have his uniform number retired. By 1994 the Yankees will have permanently removed 13 numbers from circulation.

1940—Ernest Thayer dies without revealing what player was his real-life model for the 52-line poem he published in 1888. Former Philadelphia Phillies pitcher Dan Casey and his three children contend that he was the inspiration for Thayer's "Casey at the Bat," while others believe that it was his brother Dennis, an outfielder with the Baltimore Orioles in the mid-1880s. But there is no evidence that Thayer ever saw either of the Casey brothers play, and, moreover, neither Philadelphia nor Baltimore particularly wants the honor of being Mudville, the city in the poem.

1941—The Dodgers become the first team to wear plastic batting helmets after Pee Wee Reese and Peter Reiser are idled by beanings.

1941—The Tigers give $52,000 to University of Michigan student Dick Wakefield, making him the first big "bonus baby."

1941—On March 8, Phillies pitcher Hugh Mulcahy becomes the first major-leaguer to be drafted in the prelude to World War II; Tigers outfielder Hank Greenberg becomes the second after playing 19 games. Within two years over 100 major leaguers are involved in the war effort, but only two, Elmer Gedeon and Harry O'Neill, are killed in action.

RBI Records

The official tabulation of RBIs was not adopted by both major leagues until 1920 when all slugging statistics suddenly took on an increased importance with Babe Ruth's emergence as the game's greatest home run hitter and the accompanying surge in attendance. Prior to 1920 RBI statistics were kept unofficially, and there were many seasons, especially in the 1880s, when some team scorers noted how runs were brought home and others didn't. As a result it is now impossible to reconstruct who led the American Association in RBIs in 1885, for example, or how many career RBIs Pete Browning, Dave Orr, Deacon White and many other early-day stars had.

EVOLUTION OF THE SEASON RBI RECORD

		Year	Team	League	RBIs
1.	Sam Thompson	1887	Detroit	National	166[1]
2.	Babe Ruth	1921	New York	American	171
3.	Lou Gehrig	1927	New York	American	175[2]
4.	Hack Wilson	1930	Chicago	National	190[3]

[1]Some purists prefer to start with the 1888 season when both the National League and the American Association began keeping reasonably accurate RBI data. Even if you align yourself with their thinking, Thompson remains the pre-Ruth record holder, with 165 RBIs for the 1895 Philadelphia Phillies. In addition, Thompson was the most prolific player ever at knocking in runs—.921 per game. Lou Gehrig ranks second with .919 per game; Hank Greenberg is third with .915 per game.

[2]In 1931 Gehrig set an American League record, which still stands, when he had 184 RBIs; six years later Hank Greenberg of Detroit had 183.

[3]In 1930 Gehrig led the AL with 174 RBIs, and Chuck Klein of the Phillies had 170 RBIs; the season was so skewed that Bill Terry's RBI total of 129, good for only fifth place in 1930, would have led the NL the following year.

Most RBIs, Season, 1901 through 1919
AL—130—Home Run Baker, Philadelphia, 1912, although some sources still credit Ty Cobb with 144 RBIs in 1911
NL—128—Gavvy Cravath, Philadelphia, 1913

Most RBIs, Season, 1941 through 1960
AL—159—Vern Stephens and Ted Williams, Boston, 1949
NL—143—Ernie Banks, Chicago, 1959

Most RBIs, Season, 1961 through 1977
NL—153—Tommy Davis, Los Angeles, 1962
AL—142—Roger Maris, New York, 1961

Most RBIs, Season, since 1977
NL—149—George Foster, Cincinnati, 1977
AL—145—Don Mattingly, New York, 1985

Most Seasons League Leader in RBIs
AL—6—Babe Ruth, last in 1928 when he tied with Gehrig
NL—5—Honus Wagner, last in 1912

Fewest RBIs, Season, League Leader in RBIs, since 1920
AL—105—Al Rosen, Cleveland, 1952
NL—105—Gary Carter, Montreal, and Mike Schmidt, Philadelphia, 1984

Fewest RBIs, Season, League Leader in RBIs, Prior to 1920
NL—80—Bill Dahlen, New York Giants, 1904
AL—83—Harry Davis, Philadelphia, 1905

Most RBIs, Game
NL—12—Jim Bottomley, St. Louis, September 16, 1924
—12—Mark Whiten, St. Louis, September 7, 1993
AL—11—Tony Lazzeri, New York, May 24, 1936

Most RBIs, Game, Pitcher, since 1900
9—Tony Cloninger, Atlanta, July 3, 1966, including two grandslams

Most RBIs, Doubleheader
NL—13—Nate Colbert, San Diego, August 1, 1972
—13—Mark Whiten, St. Louis, September 7, 1993
AL—No American League player has ever collected more than 11, the number Lazzeri amassed in a single game.

Fewest RBIs, Season, Outfielder, Minimum 400 at Bats
  11—Charlie Jamieson, Philadelphia A's, 1918, 416 at bats

Fewest RBIs, Season, First Baseman, Minimum 400 at Bats
  20—Ivy Griffin, Philadelphia A's, 1920, 467 at bats, and Joe Agler, Buffalo Buffeds (FL), 1914, 463 at bats

Fewest RBIs, Season, Third Baseman, Minimum 400 at Bats
  14—Bobby Byrne, St. Louis Cardinals, 1908, 439 at bats, and Eddie Yost, Washington, 1947, 428 at bats

Fewest RBIs, Season, Minimum 500 at Bats
  12—Enzo Hernandez, San Diego Padres, 1971, 549 at bats

Fewest RBIs, Season, Minimum 150 Games
  19—Morrie Rath, Chicago White Sox, 1912, 157 games

Fewest RBIs, Season, Minimum 100 Games and 300 at Bats
  6—Dick Howser, Cleveland Indians, 1965, 307 at bats

Greatest Margin, Season, Between Runs and RBIs, since 1901
  106—Lloyd Waner, Pittsburgh Pirates, 1927, scored 133 runs and had only 27 RBIs. The all-time record for the greatest margin between runs and RBIs is held by John McGraw, with 140 runs and 33 RBIs for the 1899 Baltimore Orioles, a difference of 107.

PLAYERS WHO HAD 40 HOMERS AND FEWER THAN 100 RBIS IN A SEASON

	Year	Team	League	Homers	RBIs
Duke Snider	1957	Brooklyn	National	40	92
Mickey Mantle	1958	New York	American	42	97
Mickey Mantle	1960	New York	American	40	94
Harmon Killebrew	1963	Minnesota	American	45	96
Hank Aaron	1969	Atlanta	National	44	97
Rico Petrocelli	1969	Boston	American	40	97
Hank Aaron	1973	Atlanta	National	40	96
Davy Johnson	1973	Atlanta	National	43	99
Darrell Evans	1985	Detroit	American	40	94

Most RBIs, Season, with Fewer Than 10 Home Runs
   NL—128—Pie Traynor, Pittsburgh, 1928, 3 home runs
   AL—127—Ty Cobb, Detroit, 1911, 8 home runs

Most Seasons with 100 or More RBIs and Fewer Than 10 Home Runs
   7—Honus Wagner, last in 1912

Last Player to Collect 100 or More RBIs and Fewer Than 10 Home Runs
   Tommy Herr, St. Louis Cardinals, 1985; 8 home runs and 110 RBIs. Herr was the first player to do it since George Kell of the Tigers in 1950.

Most RBIs, Season, With No Home Runs
   121—Hugh Jennings, Baltimore Orioles, 1896

Last Player to Lead League in RBIs with Fewer Than 10 Home Runs
   Dixie Walker, Brooklyn, led the National League in 1945 with 124 RBIs despite hitting only eight homers.

Special Mention
   In 1979 Jim Rice of the Boston Red Sox became the first player ever to string together three successive seasons in which he had, at minimum, 110 RBIs, 35 home runs and 200 hits.

Most Seasons 150 or More RBIs
   7—Lou Gehrig, last in 1937

Most Consecutive Seasons 100 or More RBIs
   13—Lou Gehrig, 1926–38; Jimmie Foxx, 1929–41

Most RBIs Per Each Home Run, Career
   1.77—Lou Gehrig, 873 RBIs on 493 home runs

First Player to Lead Majors in RBIs Three Years in a Row
   Cecil Fielder, 1990–92

TOP TEN IN CAREER RBIS

		Years Active	RBIs
1.	Hank Aaron	1954–76	2297[4]
2.	Babe Ruth	1914–35	2209[3]
3.	Lou Gehrig	1923–39	1990
4.	Stan Musial	1941–63	1951
5.	Ty Cobb	1905–28	1933[2]
6.	Jimmie Foxx	1925–45	1922
7.	Willie Mays	1951–73	1903[5]
8.	Cap Anson	1876–97	1879[1]
9.	Mel Ott	1926–47	1860
10.	Carl Yastrzemski	1961–83	1844

[1] The first player to accumulate 1,000 RBIs.
[2] Broke Anson's career RBI record in 1927.
[3] Broke Cobb's career mark in 1931.
[4] Broke Ruth's career mark in 1975 while serving as a DH for the Milwaukee Brewers.
[5] Although seventh on the all-time list, Mays never led the National League in RBIs.

TOP 10 IN CAREER RBIS,
PLAYERS ACTIVE THROUGH 1993 SEASON

		First Year	RBIs
1.	Dave Winfield	1973	1786
2.	Eddie Murray	1977	1662
3.	George Brett	1972	1595
4.	Andre Dawson	1976	1492
5.	Robin Yount	1974	1406
6.	Harold Baines	1980	1144
7.	Cal Ripken, Jr.	1981	1104
8.	Kent Hrbek	1981	1033
9.	George Bell	1981	1002
10.	Don Mattingly	1982	999

Total Bases Records

In 1921 Babe Ruth set an all-time major-league record when he collected 457 total bases. The following year Rogers Hornsby amassed 450 total bases, setting the National League mark. Since 1930 no player has seriously threatened either record.

TOP 10 IN TOTAL BASES, SEASON

		Year	Team	League	Total Bases
1.	Babe Ruth	1921	New York	American	457
2.	Rogers Hornsby	1922	St. Louis	National	450
3.	Lou Gehrig	1927	New York	American	447
4.	Chuck Klein	1930	Philadelphia	National	445
5.	Jimmie Foxx	1938	Boston	American	438
6.	Stan Musial	1948	St. Louis	National	429[1]
7.	Hack Wilson	1930	Chicago	National	423
8.	Chuck Klein	1932	Philadelphia	National	420[2]
9.	Lou Gehrig	1930	New York	American	419
10.	Joe DiMaggio	1937	New York	American	418

[1] The only player on the list who didn't do it in a season between 1920 and 1941.
[2] The only player to have two seasons with 420 or more total bases.

Most Total Bases, Season, 1901 through 1919
    AL—367—Ty Cobb, Detroit, 1911
    NL—325—Cy Seymour, Cincinnati, 1905

Most Total Bases, Season, 1942 through 1960
    NL—429—Stan Musial, St. Louis, 1948
    AL—376—Mickey Mantle, New York, 1956

Most Total Bases, Season, 1961 through 1976
NL—382—Willie Mays, San Francisco, 1962
AL—374—Tony Oliva, Minnesota, 1964

Most Total Bases, Season, since 1977
AL—406—Jim Rice, Boston, 1978
NL—388—George Foster, Cincinnati, 1977

Fewest Total Bases, Season, League Leader in Total Bases
NL—237—Honus Wagner, Pittsburgh, 1906
AL—260—George Stone, St. Louis, 1905

Most Seasons 400 or More Total Bases
AL—5—Lou Gehrig, last in 1936
NL—3—Chuck Klein, last in 1932

Most Seasons 300 or More Total Bases
NL—15—Hank Aaron, last in 1971
AL—13—Lou Gehrig, 1926 through 1938 consecutive

TOP 10 IN TOTAL BASES, CAREER

		Years Active	Total Bases
1.	Hank Aaron	1954–76	6856[3]
2.	Stan Musial	1941–63	6134[2]
3.	Willie Mays	1951–73	6066
4.	Ty Cobb	1905–28	5856[1]
5.	Babe Ruth	1914–35	5793
6.	Pete Rose	1963–86	5752[4]
7.	Carl Yastrzemski	1961–83	5539
8.	Frank Robinson	1956–76	5373
9.	Tris Speaker	1907–28	5104
10.	Lou Gehrig	1923–39	5060

[1]The first player to collect 5000 total bases.
[2]Broke Cobb's career total bases record in 1962.
[3]Broke Musial's career total bases record in 1972.
[4]The only player on the top 10 list who never had a season in which he was a league leader in total bases.

Fewest Total Bases, Season, Minimum 500 Plate Appearances
   NL—117—Leo Durocher, St. Louis, 1937
   AL—115—Hunter Hill, St. Louis-Washington, 1904. A member of one of the worst teams in history, the 1904 Senators, Hill retained his third base job despite posting a .197 BA and a .224 SA.

Most Total Bases, Game
   NL—18—Joe Adcock, Milwaukee Braves, July 31, 1954, against Brooklyn in Ebbets Field; four home runs and a double
   AL—16—Held by several players. The first to do it was Ty Cobb, who hit three home runs, two singles and a double in six at bats against the St. Louis Browns in Sportsman's Park on May 5, 1925. The next day Cobb hit two more homers, making him the first player since Cap Anson in 1884 to hit five home runs in two games.

Record Slugging Averages

Once again we find the same two names at the head of the class. In 1920 Babe Ruth compiled an all-time record .847 slugging average when he clubbed 54 home runs in only 458 at bats. Five years later Rogers Hornsby slugged at a .756 clip to set the National League record.

Highest Slugging Average, Season, 1901 through 1919
AL—.657—Babe Ruth, Boston, 1919
NL—.571—Heinie Zimmerman, Chicago, 1912

Highest Slugging Average, Season, 1941 through 1960
AL—.731—Ted Williams, Boston, 1957; the last player to slug .700
NL—.702—Stan Musial, St. Louis, 1948

Highest Slugging Average, Season, 1961 through 1976
AL—.687—Mickey Mantle, New York, 1961
NL—.669—Hank Aaron, Atlanta, 1971

Highest Slugging Average, Season, since 1977
NL—.677—Barry Bonds, San Francisco, 1993
AL—.664—George Brett, Kansas City, 1980

Most Seasons League Leader in Slugging Average
AL—13—Babe Ruth, last in 1931
NL—9—Rogers Hornsby, last in 1929

Highest Slugging Average, Season, by Runner-up to League Leader
AL—.765—Lou Gehrig, New York, 1927; second to Babe Ruth who slugged .777
NL—.687—Chuck Klein, Philadelphia, 1930; second to Hack Wilson, Chicago, who slugged .723

All-time Highest Slugging Average, Season, by Player Who Hit No Home Runs
.488—Hugh Jennings, Baltimore, 1896

Lowest Slugging Average, Season, League Leader in Slugging Average
NL—.436—Hy Myers, Brooklyn, 1919
AL—.466—Elmer Flick, Cleveland, 1905

Lowest Slugging Average, Season, since 1920, League Leader in Slugging Average
AL—.476—Snuffy Stirnweiss, New York, 1945
NL—.521—Johnny Mize, New York Giants, 1942

Lowest Slugging Average, Season, since 1961, League Leader in Slugging Average
AL—.502—Reggie Jackson, Baltimore, 1976
NL—.536—Will Clark, San Francisco, 1991

Lowest Slugging Average, Season, Minimum 400 at Bats
19th Century—.197—Jim Lillie, Kansas City, National League, 1886, 416 at bats and 82 total bases
20th Century—.206—Pete Childs, Philadelphia, National League, 1902, 403 at bats and 83 total bases

Lowest Slugging Average, Season, since 1901, Minimum 500 at Bats
AL—.240—Jim Levey, St. Louis, 1933; 529 at bats and 127 total bases
NL—.242—Al Bridwell, Boston, 1907; 509 at bats and 123 total bases

Smallest Differential between Slugging Average and Batting Average, Season, since 1901, Mininum 500 at Bats
NL—19 points—Spike Shannon, St. Louis and New York Giants, 1906; .256 batting average and .275 slugging average
AL—36 points— Ed Hahn, New York and Chicago, 1906; .221 batting average and .257 slugging average

Special Mention
Only one player in major-league history, Roger Metzger, was a league leader more than once in an extra-base hit department and yet retired with a career slugging average

that was under .300. Metzger tied for the National League lead in triples in 1972, then led alone in 1974 before an amputated finger forced him to quit in 1980 with a .231 career batting average and a .293 career slugging average.

THE 10 HIGHEST CAREER SLUGGING AVERAGES

	Years Active	SA
1. Babe Ruth	1914–35	.690
2. Ted Williams	1939–60	.634
3. Lou Gehrig	1923–39	.632
4. Jimmie Foxx	1925–45	.609
5. Hank Greenberg	1930–47	.605
6. Joe DiMaggio	1938–51	.579
7. Rogers Hornsby	1915–37	.577
8. Johnny Mize	1936–53	.562
9. Stan Musial	1941–63	.559
10. Willie Mays	1951–73	.557

Highest Career Slugging Average, Player Active Primarily between 1901 and 1919
.517—Joe Jackson, 1908–20

Highest Career Slugging Average, Player Active Primarily between 1942 and 1960
.559—Stan Musial, 1941–63

Highest Career Slugging Average, Player Active Primarily after 1961
.557—Willie Mays, 1951–73

Highest Career Slugging Average, Player with under .300 Career Batting Average
First Place—.557—Mickey Mantle, 1951–68; .298 batting average. Mantle ranks 11th on the career list, a fraction below Mays.
Second Place—.548—Ralph Kiner, 1946–55; .279 batting average

Lowest Career Slugging Average, Player with .300 Career Batting Average
.355—Patsy Donovan, 1890–1907; .301 batting average.

Among players with 2,000 hits, Donovan also has the second-fewest extra-base hits. Of his 2,253 hits, .868 percent of them were singles. Maury Wills, with a single percentage of .874, ranks first in fewest extra-base hits.

ACTIVE PLAYERS WITH CAREER SLUGGING AVERAGES OVER .500
(Minimum 2000 at bats)

		First Year	SA
1.	Fred McGriff	1986	.531
2.	Barry Bonds	1986	.526
3.	Ken Griffey, Jr.	1989	.520
4.	Kevin Mitchell	1984	.515
5.	Mark McGwire	1986	.509
6.	Darryl Strawberry	1983	.508
7.	Jose Canseco	1986	.507
8.	Cecil Fielder	1985	.500

Long Day's Journey

The 1920 season was less than a month old when a reminder was served that even though the deadball era was over a whiff of it still lingered. On May 1, in Boston, the Brooklyn Dodgers hooked up in a 26-inning 1–1 tie with the Braves that will probably always stand as both the longest game in major-league history and the longest game not played to a decision. What made the game most seem like a throwback to an earlier time, however, was not its extraordinary length but the fact that both starting pitchers, Leon Cadore of the Dodgers and Joe Oeschger of the Braves, went all the way. The following day the Dodgers played 13 innings against the Phillies and then went into overtime again on May 3 against the Braves, losing to them 2–1 in 19 innings. Brooklyn's three-game total of 58 innings played—the equivalent of six and a half games—is a record that has never been even remotely challenged.

Longest Game Played to a Decision, Same Day

NL—25 innings—St. Louis 4, New York Mets 3, September 11, 1974; also the longest night game in major-league history

AL—24 innings—Philadelphia 4, Boston 1, September 1, 1906. Both Jack Coombs of the A's and Joe Harris of the Red Sox went all the way. Harris, rarely the recipient of any support from his teammates, had a dreadful 3–21 record and .087 winning percentage in 1906, the second-worst performance since 1901 by a 20-game loser, behind only Jack Nabors who was 1–20 in 1916.

Longest 1–0 Game, since 1901

24 innings—Houston 1, New York Mets 0, April 15, 1968

Most Innings without Scoring, One Day

27—St. Louis Cardinals, July 2, 1933, lost the first game of a double-header 1–0 to Carl Hubbell and the New York Giants in 18 innings, then were blanked 1–0 again in the nightcap by Roy Parmalee.

Longest Day's Work to No Avail

On May 31, 1964, the New York Mets lost a double-header to San Francisco that consumed an all-time record 10½ hours; the nightcap, in addition, lasted 23 innings.

Longest Game in Organized Baseball History

33 innings—Pawtucket 3, Rochester 2, International League, April 19, 1981. The game was suspended at 4:07 A.M. after 32 innings with the score 2–2, then completed that night, with Pawtucket pushing across the winning run almost as soon as the game was resumed. The longest game that was not interrupted by suspension was played on June 14, 1966, between Miami and St. Petersburg of the Class A Florida State League, Miami, managed by Billy DeMars, winning 4–3 in 29 innings over Sparky Anderson's St. Pete Club.

Last Team to Play Two Opponents in One Day

Rainouts in 1951 forced the Cardinals into a situation whereby they had to entertain the pennant-bound New York Giants on the afternoon of September 13 in a makeup game at Sportsman's Park, then shower, change uniforms and return to the field that night for a regularly scheduled game against the Boston Braves.

Most Days in a Row, since 1901, Playing No Opponents

10—Philadelphia Phillies, 1909. On August 19 a prolonged spell of poor weather in the East resulted in the Phillies being rained out for the 10th straight day.

Only Tripleheader in Which All Three Games Went the Full Nine Innings

September 1, 1890—Brooklyn Bridegrooms (NL) versus Pittsburgh Innocents (NL). The Bridegrooms swept the triple bill—10–9, 3–2, and 8–4—and went on to win the National League pennant that season. Not surprisingly, Pittsburgh finished in the cellar, 66 ½ games behind Brooklyn.

Shortest Day's Work by Pitcher Hurling Complete Game

Red Barrett of the Boston Braves pitched a 2–0 shutout against Cincinnati on August 10, 1944, in which he threw only 58 pitches—an average of 6.4 pitches per inning.

Iron-Man Pitchers

On June 19, 1927, Jack Scott of the Phillies pitched both ends of a double-header against the Reds, winning the first game 3–1 and then losing the nightcap 3–0. Thirty-five at the time, Scott became the oldest major-league player ever to pitch two complete games in one day. No one realized then that he would also be the last major-league player to do it.

First Pitcher to Win Two Complete Games in One Day
    Candy Cummings, Hartford, beat Cincinnati 14–4 and 8–4 on September 9, 1876.

First Pitcher to Win Two Complete Games in One day, Mound at Its Present Distance
    Cy Seymour of the New York Giants, while beating Louisville 11–1 and 4–3 on May 30, 1898, became the first pitcher to win a doubleheader after the mound was moved to 60 feet 6 inches from the plate. The second game was called after seven innings.

First Pitcher to Pitch Two Complete Games in One Day, since 1901
    Joe McGinnity of the Baltimore Orioles worked both ends of a doubleheader twice in 1901, splitting on each occasion. On August 1, 1903, McGinnity became the first pitcher in this century to win both ends of a doubleheader. With the Giants by then, he won two more complete-game doubleheaders before the month was out, the last on August 31.

Only Pitcher since 1901, Besides McGinnity, to Win Two Complete Games in One Day More Than Once
    Pete Alexander of the Phillies in 1916 and again in 1917

Only Pitcher since 1901, Besides McGinnity, to Pitch More Than Two Complete-Game Doubleheaders

Mule Watson did it twice with the Philadelphia A's in 1918 and a third time in 1921 with the Boston Braves. His record for the six games was three wins, two losses and one tie.

Only Pitcher to Hurl Two Complete-Game Shutouts in One Day

Ed Reulbach of the Cubs, in the thick of the 1908 pennant race, beat Brooklyn 5–0 and 3–0 on September 26.

Only Pitcher to Be Involved in Two Complete-Game 1–0 Decisions in One Day

On July 31, 1915, Dave Davenport, pitching for the St. Louis Terriers in the Federal League, beat Buffalo 1–0 and then lost the second game of the twin bill 1–0. Davenport gave up only five hits that day—and just one in the game he lost.

Last Pitcher to Win Two Complete Games in One Day

Emil Levsen, Cleveland, beat the Boston Red Sox 6–1 and 5–1 on August 28, 1926. Levsen did it without striking out a batter in either game. Johnny "Stud" Stuart of the St. Louis Cardinals also pitched a double-header win against the Boston Braves in 1923 without registering a single strikeout that day. Stuart's performance enabled rookie Harry McCurdy, who caught both games, to set a major-league mark when he completed the twin bill without handling a single chance.

First Pitcher to Lose Two Complete Games in One Day

Dave Anderson of Pittsburgh lost two of the three games the Innocents dropped in their tripleheader loss to the Brooklyn Bridegrooms on September 1, 1890.

Only Pitcher in This Century to Lose Two Complete Games in One Day

Wiley Piatt, Boston Braves, lost 1–0 and 5–3 to Pittsburgh on June 25, 1903.

Closest Any Pitcher Has Come since 1927 to Hurling Two Complete Games in One Day

On September 6, 1950, Don Newcombe of the Brooklyn

Dodgers started both ends of a doubleheader against the league-leading Phillies. Newcombe shut out the Phils 2–0 in the opener but left in the sixth inning of the nightcap, trailing 2–0.

Last Pitcher to Start Both Ends of a Doubleheader

Wilbur Wood, Chicago White Sox, on July 20, 1973, against the Yankees. He was knocked out in both games and wound up with two losses that day.

No-Hitters and Perfect Games

On April 30, 1922, Charlie Robertson of the White Sox became the first pitcher in major-league history to hurl a perfect game on the road when he beat Detroit 2–0 at Navin Field. It was the fourth perfect game in the American League since 1904, but after Robertson's masterpiece there was a 34-year drought before Don Larsen of the Yankees pitched a perfect game in the 1956 World Series.

CHRONOLOGY OF FULL-LENGTH PERFECT GAMES

June 12, 1880	Lee Richmond; Worcester defeated Cleveland (NL) 1–0.[1]
May 5, 1904	Cy Young; Boston defeated Philadelphia (AL) 1–0.
October 2, 1908	Addie Joss; Cleveland defeated Chicago (AL) 1–0.[2]
June 23, 1917	Ernie Shore; Boston defeated Washington (AL) 4–0.[3]
April 30, 1922	Charlie Robertson; Chicago defeated Detroit (AL) 2–0.
October 8, 1956	Don Larsen; New York (AL) defeated Brooklyn (NL) 2–0.[4]
May 29, 1959	Harvey Haddix; Pittsburgh lost to Milwaukee (NL) 1–0 in 13 innings.[5]
June 21, 1964	Jim Bunning; Philadelphia defeated New York Mets (NL) 6–0.
September 9, 1965	Sandy Koufax; Los Angeles defeated Chicago (NL) 1–0.[6]
May 8, 1968	Catfish Hunter; Oakland defeated Minnesota (AL) 4–0.

May 15, 1981	Len Barker; Cleveland defeated Toronto (AL) 3–0.
September 30, 1984	Mike Witt; California defeated Texas (AL) 1–0.
September 16, 1988	Tom Browning, Cincinnati, defeated Los Angeles (NL) 1-0.
July 28, 1991	Dennis Martinez, Montreal, defeated Los Angeles (NL) 2–0.

[1]Richmond's and perfect game, even though it was the first of its kind, attracted little attention at the time. Some newspaper accounts didn't even note that Richmond had allowed no opposition base runners, let alone that his was the first such pitching feat in history. Richmond was a left-hander, the only one besides Koufax and Haddix to pitch a perfect game.

[2]Probably the greatest clutch pitching job ever. Cleveland and Chicago were locked, along with Detroit, in the closest pennant race in American League history when Joss took the mound that day; his opponent was 40-game winner Ed Walsh.

[3]See "Relievers' Records" for details of Shore's game.

[4]Larsen beat Sal Maglie in his perfect game; the last batter he faced, pinch hitter Dale Mitchell, took a called third strike on a 3–2 count. Three days earlier, in Game Two of the Series, Larsen had been knocked out by the Dodgers in the second inning.

[5]The final score should have been 3–0, but Joe Adcock of the Braves, who homered with two on, was declared out for passing Hank Aaron on the bases.

[6]Koufax's opponent, Bob Hendley, pitched a one-hitter.

Close But No Cigar Award

On April 20, 1990, Brian Holman of the Mariners lost his bid to become the first hurler to toss a perfect game against a reigning world champion when Ken Phelps of the A's hit a pinch homer with two out in the bottom of the ninth inning, but many other pitchers on the brink of immortality have also suffered crushing disappointments.

First Prize—Hooks Wiltse. Hurling for the Giants on July 4, 1908, Wiltse had a perfect game with two out in the ninth inning of a scoreless contest and two strikes on his mound opponent, George McQuillan of the Phils. Wiltse then nicked McQuillan with a pitch to spoil his perfecto, although he did win 1–0 in ten innings.

Second Prize—Milt Pappas. On September 2, 1972, Pappas, working for the Cubs, was one pitch away from a perfect game when he walked San Diego pinch hitter Larry Stahl on a 3–2 count.

Third Prize—In 1958 Billy Pierce of the White Sox had a 1–0 lead over Washington and was one out away from a perfect game, the first by an American League left-hander, when pinch hitter Ed Fitzgerald stroked an opposite-field double.

Fourth Prize—Tommy Bridges of the Tigers shut out Washington 13–0 on August 15, 1932, but lost a perfect game with two out in the ninth inning when pinch hitter Dave Harris hit a bloop single.

Fifth Prize—In 1983 another Tigers pitcher, Milt Wilcox, saw his try for a perfect game slip away when Jerry Hairston of the White Sox singled with two out in the ninth inning.

On June 15, 1938, in the initial night game played at Ebbets Field, Johnny Vander Meer of the Reds no-hit the Dodgers 6–0 four days after he'd held the Braves hitless. Vander Meer's back-to-back gems were the first no-hitters in the National League since 1934 and made him the first player to pitch consecutive no-hitters as well as the first to throw two in the same season. Fifteen years earlier an American League pitcher, Howard Ehmke with the last-place Red Sox, narrowly missed earning the dual distinction that fell to Vander Meer. Ehmke no-hit the Athletics on September 7, 1923, and then lost his chance at a second straight no-hitter four days later when the official scorer called a ground ball that was misplayed by the Red Sox third baseman a single. The muffed grounder turned out to be the only hit off Ehmke, but the scorer might have only been trying to even up the breaks. While Ehmke had a valid argument that he'd been cheated out of a second no-hitter, he could not deny that his first one was a gift from Athletics pitcher Slim Harriss, who doubled off the right-field wall early in the game but was called out for missing first base.

Pitcher Who Came the Closest After 1938 to Equaling Vander Meer's Feat

Ewell Blackwell of the Reds no-hit the Braves 6–0 on June 18, 1947. Following the same pattern as Vander Meer, he started against the Dodgers four days later and was working on a second consecutive no-hitter when Eddie Stanky singled with one out in the ninth inning.

Second Pitcher to Throw Two No-Hitters in a Season

Allie Reynolds, New York Yankees, 1951. Three other pitchers have also done it—Virgil Trucks, Detroit Tigers, 1952; Jim Maloney, Cincinnati Reds, 1965; and Nolan Ryan, California Angels, 1973. Trucks, who had only a 5–19 record for the season, won both his no-hitters by a 1–0 score and also hurled a 1–0 one-hit victory over Washington that year that was marred only by leadoff batter Eddie Yost's single on the first pitch of the game.

First Pitcher to Hurl Three Career No-Hitters
Larry Corcoran, Chicago White Stockings, 1880, 1882 and 1884

First Pitcher to Hurl Four Career No-Hitters
Sandy Koufax, Los Angeles Dodgers, threw no-hitters in four consecutive seasons (1962–65), the last one a perfect game.

First Pitcher to Hurl Seven Career No-Hitters
Nolan Ryan (7), California Angels, 1973 (2), 1974, 1975; Houston Astros, 1981; and Texas Rangers, 1990, 1991

First Pitcher to Hurl Two No-Hitters after 1901
Christy Mathewson, New York Giants, 1901 and 1905

First Pitcher to Hurl Three No-Hitters after 1901
Bob Feller, Cleveland Indians, 1940, 1946 and 1951. Feller won all three of his no-hitters by one run and also pitched a record 12 complete-game one-hitters.

First Major-League No-Hitter
It depends on what you believe was the first major league. On July 28, 1875, a couple of months before the National Association concluded its final season, Philadelphia's Joe Borden, aka Joe Josephs, no-hit Chicago 4–0. The following year, in the National League's first season, George Bradley of St. Louis no-hit Hartford 2–0 on July 28.

Only Pitcher since 1893 to Hurl a No-Hitter in His First Start
Bobo Holloman, St. Louis Browns, held the Philadelphia A's hitless on May 6, 1953; it was his only complete game in the majors. Before the mound was moved to its present distance from the plate, Ted Breitenstein of the American Association St. Louis Browns, in 1891, and Bumpus Jones of the Cincinnati Reds, in 1892, also threw no-hitters in their first starts. On April 14, 1967, Red Sox rookie Bill Rohr, pitching in his first major-league game, saw his no-hit

bid in Yankee Stadium disappear when Elston Howard of the Yankees singled with two out in the ninth inning. Similarly, Padres yearling Jimmy Jones lost a no-hitter in his first major-league game on September 22, 1986, when Bob Knepper of the Astros, Jones's mound opponent, tripled for the lone hit the rookie surrendered in his 5–0 win.

Most Famous No-Hit Game

A close call among several possible choices, but most pitching afficionados vote for the double no-hit duel on May 2, 1917, between the Reds' Fred Toney and Hippo Vaughn of the Cubs, won 1–0 by Toney in the 10th inning when Jim Thorpe drove in the winning run. The only other two double no-hit games in organized baseball history occurred in the minor leagues. The first came in 1952 in a Pony League game between Bradford and Batavia, and the second happened in 1992 when Andy Carter of the Clearwater Phillies in the Florida State League topped Scott Bakkum of the Winter Haven Red Sox, 1–0.

First American League No-Hitter

On May 9, 1901, Cleveland's Earl Moore no-hit the White Sox for nine innings but lost 4–2 in the 10th, making him also the first pitcher in this century to lose a no-hit game.

First Pitcher to Hurl a No-Hitter In Each League after 1900

Tom Hughes, Boston Braves, pitched a no-hitter against Pittsburgh in 1916 six years after he'd pitched a nine-inning no-hitter for the Yankees before losing 5–0 to Cleveland in the 11th. Jim Bunning was the second pitcher to throw a no-hitter in each league; Nolan Ryan was the third and last to do it.

Only Teammates to Pitch No-Hitters on Consecutive Days

In 1917 two St. Louis Browns pitchers, Ernie Koob and Bob Groom, no-hit that year's World Champion, the White Sox, on consecutive days—May 5 and May 6—but not in consecutive games; Groom's no-hitter came in the second half of a double-header. Less than a month earlier, on April 14, 1917, Eddie Cicotte of the White Sox had no-hit the Browns 11–0. After May, the White Sox went the rest of the year without being involved in any more hitless games, but they still remain the only World Champion to be victimized twice in a season by no-hitters.

Only No-Hitters Lost in Nine Innings

NL—On April 23, 1964, Ken Johnson of Houston became the only pitcher ever to lose a complete-game no-hitter in nine innings when he was beaten 1–0 by the Reds.

AL—On April 30, 1967, Steve Barber of the Orioles carried a no-hitter into the ninth inning against the Tigers, then was relieved by Stu Miller, who lost the game 2–1 on an error by shortstop Mark Belanger.

Only Fans to See Their Team No-Hit Twice in Three Years and Yet Win Both Games

On May 26, 1956, Milwaukee fans watched Johnny Klippstein, Hersh Freeman and Joe Black of the Reds combine to no-hit the Braves through nine innings before losing in the tenth. Exactly three years later, on May 26, 1959, County Stadium hosted another no-hitter—indeed, the first perfect game in the National League since 1880—when the Pirates' Harvey Haddix held the Braves without a base runner for 12 innings before losing 1–0 in the 13th.

Only Opening Day No-Hitters

NL—Red Ames, New York Giants, lost 3–0 to the Dodgers in 13 innings on April 15, 1909, after holding them hitless until the 10th inning.

AL—Bob Feller, Cleveland, defeated Chicago 1–0 on April 16, 1940.

First Independence Day No-Hitters

NL—Hooks Wiltse, New York Giants, defeated Philadelphia 1–0 in 10 innings on July 4, 1908.

AL—George Mullin, Detroit, defeated St. Louis 7–0 on July 4, 1912, which also happened to be his 32nd birthday.

Only No-Hitters to Clinch Titles

AL—Allie Reynolds, New York, 8–0 over Boston on September 28, 1951.

NL—Mike Scott, Houston, 2–0 over San Francisco on September 25, 1986.

Pitcher Receiving the most Support While Throwing a No-Hitter

Frank Smith, Chicago White Sox, defeated Detroit 15–0 on September 6, 1905. Twenty years later, on September 19, 1925, Ted Lyons of the White Sox, about to put the final touch on a 17–0 no-hitter against Washington, instead became the first of many pitchers to fall prey to a Senators pinch hitter when Bobby Veach singled with two out in the ninth inning.

First No-Hitter by Pitcher With Expansion Team

AL—Bo Belinsky, Los Angeles, defeated Baltimore 2–0 on May 5, 1962.

AL—Don Nottebart, Houston, defeated Philadelphia 4–1 on May 17, 1963.

FIRST NO-HITTER FOR EACH TEAM AFTER 1900

(Present Franchise Location Only)

National League

Team	Pitcher	Date	Opponent	Score
Atlanta	Phil Niekro	August 7, 1973	San Diego	9–0[1]
Chicago	Bob Wicker	June 11, 1904	New York	1–0, 12 innings
Cincinnati	Fred Toney	May 2, 1917	Chicago	1–0, 10 innings
Houston	Don Nottebart	May 17, 1963	Philadelphia	4–1
Los Angeles	Sandy Koufax	June 30, 1962	New York	5–0[2]
Montreal	Bill Stoneman	April 17, 1969	Philadelphia	7–0
New York	None			
Philadelphia	Chick Fraser	September 18, 1903	Chicago	10–0
Pittsburgh	Nick Maddox	September 20, 1907	Brooklyn	2–1[3]
St. Louis	Jesse Haines	July 17, 1924	Boston	5–0[4]
San Diego	None			
San Francisco	Juan Marichal	June 15, 1963	Houston	1–0[5]

[1]Frank Pfeffer pitched the first Boston Braves no-hitter, beating Cincinnati 6–0 on May 8, 1907; Jim Wilson pitched the first Milwaukee Braves no-hitter, beating Philadelphia 2–0 on June 12, 1954.

[2]Mal Eason pitched the first Brooklyn Dodgers no-hitter, beating St. Louis 2–0 on July 20, 1906.

[3]Maddox's no-hitter was the last by a Pittsburgh pitcher at home until John Candaleria no-hit Los Angeles 2–0 on August 9, 1976, at Three Rivers Stadium. No Pirate ever pitched a no-hitter at Forbes Field (1909–70)—nor, for that matter, did any pitcher for a visiting team.

[4]The last team to register a no-hitter in this century. Moreover, Haines's no-hitter was the first by a pitcher on a St. Louis National League team since 1876.

[5]Christy Mathewson pitched the first New York Giants no-hitter, beating St. Louis 5–0 on July 15, 1901.

Most One-Hitters, Season
4—Pete Alexander, Philadelphia, 1915. Alexander never pitched a no-hitter.

Special Mention
Jim Barr also never pitched a no-hitter, but he once did something far more extraordinary. With the Giants in 1972, he retired a record 41 batters in a row over the course of two games before surrendering a double to Bernie Carbo of the Cardinals.

American League

Team	Pitcher	Date	Opponent	Score
Baltimore	Hoyt Wilhelm	September 2, 1958	New York	1–0[1]
Boston	Cy Young	May 5, 1904	Philadelphia	3–0[2]
California	Bo Belinsky	May 5, 1962	Baltimore	2–0
Chicago	Nixey Callahan	September 20, 1902	Detroit	3–0
Cleveland	Earl Moore	May 9, 1901	Chicago	2–4, 10 innings
Detroit	George Mullin	July 4, 1912	St. Louis	7–0
Kansas City	Steve Busby	April 27, 1973	Detroit	3–0
Milwaukee	Juan Nieves	April 15, 1987	Baltimore	7–0
Minnesota	Jack Kralick	August 26, 1963	Kansas City	1–0[3]
New York	Tom Hughes	August 30, 1910	Cleveland	0–5, 11 innings
Oakland	Catfish Hunter	May 8, 1968	Minnesota	4–0[4]
Seattle	Randy Johnson	June 2, 1990	Detroit	2–0
Texas	Jim Bibby	July 7, 1973	Oakland	6–0[5]
Toronto	Dave Stieb	September 2, 1990	Cleveland	3–0

[1] Earl Hamilton pitched the first St. Louis Browns no-hitter, beating Detroit 5–1 on August 30, 1912.

[2] Perfect game. Young's mound opponent that day was Rube Waddell.

[3] Walter Johnson pitched the first Washington Senators no-hitter, beating Boston 1–0 on July 1, 1920.

[4] Perfect game. Weldon Henley pitched the first Philadelphia A's no-hitter, beating St. Louis 6–0 on July 22, 1905. No A's pitcher threw a no-hitter while the franchise was in Kansas City.

[5] The franchise's first no-hitter. No member of the expansion Washington Senators ever threw one.

Record-breaking Scorers

In 1939 third baseman Red Rolfe of the New York Yankees set a 20th-century record when he scored at least one run in 18 consecutive games; the all-time record is held by Billy Hamilton of the Philadelphia Phillies, who scored in 24 straight games in 1894. Rolfe was typical of a kind of player who flourished in the 1930s when runs were scored at a record rate, especially by the Yankees, but would have been only a footnote in any other era. Between 1934 and 1941 Rolfe scored 846 runs—an average of 105.8 per year—without ever having more than 14 home runs, 90 walks or 80 RBIs in a season. Moreover, his batting average during that span was under .300.

Most Runs, Season, since 1901
    AL—177—Babe Ruth, New York, 1921
    NL—158—Chuck Klein, Philadelphia, 1930

Most Runs, Season, 1901 through 1919
    AL—147—Ty Cobb, Detroit, 1911
    NL—139—Jesse Burkett, St. Louis, 1901

Most Runs, Season, 1942 through 1960
    AL—150—Ted Williams, Boston, 1949
    NL—137—Johnny Mize, New York Giants, 1947

Most Runs, Season, 1961 through 1976
    NL—137—Billy Williams, Chicago, 1970
    AL—132—Mickey Mantle and Roger Maris, New York, 1961

Most Runs, Season, since 1977
    AL—146—Rickey Henderson, New York, 1985
    NL—143—Lenny Dykstra, Philadelphia, 1993

Most Years League Leader in Runs
    AL—8—Babe Ruth, last in 1928
    NL—5—George Burns, last in 1920; Rogers Hornsby, last in 1929; Stan Musial, last in 1954

Most Years 150 or More Runs, since 1901
    AL—6—Babe Ruth, last in 1930
    NL—2—Chuck Klein, last in 1932

Only Player to Score Six Runs in a Game Twice
    Mel Ott, New York Giants, August 4, 1934, and again on April 30, 1944. The all-time record for the most runs scored in a game is seven, on August 15, 1886, by Guy Hecker of the Louisville Eclipse team in the American Association.

Highest Percentage of Team's Runs Scored, Season
    AL—.199—Burt Shotton, St. Louis, 1913, scored 105 of the Browns' 528 runs.
    NL—.196—Tim Raines, Montreal, 1983, scored 133 of the Expos' 677 runs.

Fewest Runs, Season, League Leader in Runs
    NL—89—Gavvy Cravath, Philadelphia, 1915
    AL—92—Harry Davis, Philadelphia, 1905

CAREER TOP 10 IN RUNS

		Years Active	Runs
1.	Ty Cobb	1905–28	2245
2.	Babe Ruth	1914–35	2174
	Hank Aaron	1954–76	2174
4.	Pete Rose	1963–86	2165
5.	Willie Mays	1951–73	2062
6.	Stan Musial	1941–63	1949
7.	Lou Gehrig	1923–39	1888[1]
8.	Tris Speaker	1907–28	1881[2]
9.	Mel Ott	1926–47	1859
10.	Frank Robinson	1956–76	1829

[1]In the 14 full seasons he played—1925–38—Gehrig *averaged* 134 runs per year.
[2]Eighth on the career list, although he was never a league leader in runs.

The Three Most Interesting Teams between 1920 and 1941

1921 NEW YORK YANKEES
W-98 L-55
Manager: Miller Huggins

Regular Lineup—1B, Wally Pipp; 2B, Aaron Ward; 3B, Home Run Baker; SS, Roger Peckinpaugh; RF, Bob Meusel; CF, Elmer Miller; LF, Babe Ruth; C, Wally Schang; P, Carl Mays; P, Waite Hoyt; P, Bob Shawkey.

The first Yankees team to win a pennant and the first club in the 20th century to post a slugging average above .450, they also had the league's best pitching staff and could even run when necessary. Ruth, Meusel and Pipp, the three top RBI men, all tied for the club lead in stolen bases with 17, not a bad figure in 1921—only three players in the AL had as many as 25. Yankees pitchers led the AL with a 3.79 ERA and 481 strikeouts, the first number reflecting the sudden surge in run production, the latter number indicating that even with the increase in scoring batters weren't as yet swinging from the heels. Mays topped the AL with 27 wins a year after the Chapman tragedy. On the club also was Shotgun Rogers, who had killed John Dodge, a former major-league infielder, with a pitch in a 1916 Southern Association game.

1930 PHILADELPHIA PHILLIES
W-52 L-102
Manager: Burt Shotton

Regular Lineup—1B, Don Hurst; 2B, Fresco Thompson; 3B, Pinky Whitney; SS, Tommy Thevenow; RF, Chuck Klein; CF, Denny Sothern; LF, Lefty O'Doul; C, Spud Davis; P, Phil Collins; P, Ray Benge; P, Les Sweetland; P, Claude Willoughby; P, Hap Collard; P, Hal Elliott.

Spearheaded by Klein and O'Doul, the Phils scored 944 runs and had a .315 batting average. Yet they finished last, attributable mostly to their grisly pitching staff, which was the worst in this century. Collins posted a fine 16–11 record and Benge finished at 11–15, but the rest of the Phillies hurlers had a combined 25–76 mark and surrendered over 7.5 runs a game. Sweetland, Willoughby and Elliott were the leading culprits (see "Astronomical ERAs" for more about them), but Collard was only a notch better. Dead last in every pitching department except strikeouts, the 1930 Phillies allowed 1199 enemy base runners to cross the plate, a record that will almost surely never be broken. A year later the Phils still had the poorest pitching in the league but improved to sixth place when some of the rabbit was siphoned from the ball, reducing the number of runs they surrendered to 828. Twenty years later Shotton repaid Phillies fans for their patience with his efforts in 1930 by mismanaging a Brooklyn Dodgers team that lost the pennant to the Phils on the last day of the season.

1936 CLEVELAND INDIANS
W-80 L-74
Manager: Steve O'Neill

Regular Lineup—1B, Hal Trosky; 2B, Roy Hughes; 3B, Bad News Hale; SS, Bill Knickerbocker; RF, Roy Weatherly; CF, Earl Averill, LF, Joe Vosmik; C, Billy Sullivan; P, Johnny Allen; P, Mel Harder; P, Oral Hildebrand; P, Denny Galehouse; P, Lloyd Brown.

The Indians led the AL with a .304 batting average, had the league's RBI leader in Trosky, got a .351 season from catcher Sullivan, a .378 season from Averill, and 20 wins from Allen—yet finished in fifth place, albeit one game short of the best ever AL record for a second division team. The reasons they faltered were obvious; Harder, who posted 223 career wins, had an off year with a 15–15 record and a 5.16 ERA, and Joe Vosmik, after losing the 1935 batting crown on his last at bat of the season, sagged to a .287 mark. Apart from Harder and Vosmik, the team got good numbers from all its regulars and seemed only to be waiting on the development of a 17-year-old rookie phenom Bob Feller to make its move. By 1938 Feller was ready, but the Indians, it turned out, had peaked two years too early. They would not contend until 1940 and then only for that one season before once again falling back into the pack.

Doubles Records

Owen Wilson's 36 triples in 1912, the most improbable feat in the deadball era, had its counterpart in the lively ball era when Earl Webb of the Boston Red Sox socked an all-time major-league record 67 doubles in 1931. In 1931 Webb also led American League outfielders in errors, a stat that was probably more indicative of his talent. The 1931 season was the only one in which Webb collected more than 30 doubles. In contrast, Joe Medwick, who set the National League record when he rapped 64 doubles in 1936, had 40 or more doubles seven years in a row.

Most Doubles, Season, 1901 through 1919
    AL—53—Tris Speaker, Boston, 1912
    NL—44—Honus Wagner, Pittsburgh, 1904

Most Doubles, Season, 1942 through 1960
    AL—56—George Kell, Detroit, 1950
    NL—53—Stan Musial, St. Louis, 1953

Most Doubles, Season, 1961 through 1976
    NL—51—Frank Robinson, Cincinnati, 1962
    AL—47—Fred Lynn, Boston, 1975

Most Doubles, Season, since 1977
    AL—54—Hal McRae, Kansas City Royals, 1978
      —54—John Olerud, Toronto, 1993
    NL—51—Pete Rose, Cincinnati, 1978

Most Seasons League Leader in Doubles, since 1901
    AL—8—Tris Speaker, last in 1923
    NL—8—Stan Musial, last in 1954

Most Seasons 50 or More Doubles
AL—5—Tris Speaker, last in 1926
NL—3—Paul Waner, last in 1936; Stan Musial, last in 1953

Most Doubles, Season, All-time Organized Baseball Record
100—Lyman Lamb, Tulsa (Western League), 1924. The St. Louis Browns gave Lamb short trials in 1920 and again in 1921, mostly at third base, and he did well enough to make one wonder whether the Browns, lacking a third baseman in 1922 when they missed the pennant by one game, would have won if he'd been given a full shot at the job.

Most Doubles, Season, Team
373—St. Louis Cardinals, 1930; eight players had 32 or more doubles.

Most Doubles, Season, Team, since 1942
310—Boston Red Sox, 1979

Fewest Doubles, Season, League Leader in Doubles
AL—32—Sal Bando, Oakland, and Pedro Garcia, Milwaukee, 1972
NL—32—Sam Mertes, New York Giants, Harry Steinfeldt, Cincinnati, and Fred Clarke, Pittsburgh, 1902

Fewest Doubles, Season, since 1901, Minimum 500 at Bats
NL—4—Roy Thomas, Philadelphia, 1902; 531 at bats
AL—5—Donie Bush, Detroit, 1915, 542 at bats

TOP 10 IN CAREER DOUBLES

		Years Active	*Doubles*
1.	Tris Speaker	1907–28	793
2.	Pete Rose	1963–	746
3.	Stan Musial	1941–63	725
4.	Ty Cobb	1905–28	724
5.	Nap Lajoie	1896–1916	657
6.	Carl Yastrzemski	1961–83	646
7.	Honus Wagner	1897–1917	640
8.	Hank Aaron	1954–76	624
9.	Paul Waner	1926–45	603
10.	Charlie Gehringer	1924–42	574

Fewest Doubles, Career, Minimum 5000 at Bats

100—Roy Thomas, 1899–1911. Thomas also has the fewest extra-base hits—160—among players with over 1500 career hits.

MVP Award Winners

Between 1911 and 1914 the Chalmers Award, in the form of a new car, was given each season to the most valuable players in both leagues but was stopped largely because the rules stipulated that no player could win it twice. From 1922 through 1928 the American League gave a most valuable player award, with the voting limited to eight players, one from each team, and the National League followed suit, beginning in 1924 and continuing through 1929. But the league awards never quite managed to capture public fancy, and the concept of choosing a most valuable player was shelved until 1931 when the Baseball Writers Association of America revived it. They have selected two Most Valuable Players, one in each league, ever since.

First BWAA Most Valuable Player Award Winners
  AL—Lefty Grove, Philadelphia
  NL—Frankie Frisch, St. Louis

First Player to Win Two MVP Awards
  AL—Jimmie Foxx, Philadelphia, 1932 and 1933; also the first to win consecutive MVP Awards
  NL—Carl Hubbell, New York Giants, 1933 and 1936

First Player to Win Three MVP Awards
  AL—Jimmie Foxx, Philadelphia, Boston, 1932, 1933 and 1938
  NL—Stan Musial, St. Louis, 1943, 1946 and 1948

Other Three-time MVP Award Winners
  AL—Joe DiMaggio, New York, 1939, 1941 and 1947; Yogi Berra, New York, 1951, 1954 and 1955; Mickey Mantle, New York, 1956, 1957 and 1962

NL—Roy Campanella, Brooklyn, 1951, 1953 and 1955; Mike Schmidt, Philadelphia, 1980, 1981, and 1986. Barry Bonds, Pittsburgh–San Francisco, 1990, 1992 and 1993

First Player on a Second-Division Team to Win an MVP Award
NL—Hank Sauer, Chicago, 1952; the Cubs finished fifth.
AL—None

First Player to Win MVP Award and Cy Young Award in Same Season
NL—Don Newcombe, Brooklyn, 1956
AL—Denny McLain, Detroit, 1968

Youngest Player to Win MVP Award
AL—Vida Blue, Oakland, 1971; 22 years old
NL—Johnny Bench, Cincinnati, 1970; 22 years old but nearly eight months older than Blue.

Oldest Player to Win MVP Award
NL—Willie Stargell, Pittsburgh; 39 years old
AL—Spud Chandler, New York, 1943; 36 years old

First Catcher to Win MVP Award
AL—Mickey Cochrane, Detroit, 1934
NL—Gabby Hartnett, Chicago, 1935

First Shortstop to Win MVP Award
NL—Marty Marion, St. Louis, 1944
AL—Lou Boudreau, Cleveland, 1948

First Third Baseman to Win MVP Award
NL—Bob Elliott, Boston, 1947
AL—Al Rosen, Cleveland, 1953

First Relief Pitcher to Win MVP Award
NL—Jim Konstanty, Philadelphia, 1950
AL—Rollie Fingers, Milwaukee, 1981

Only Second Baseman to Win Two MVP Awards
Joe Morgan, Cincinnati, 1975 and 1976

Only Third Baseman to Win Two or More MVP Awards
Mike Schmidt, Philadelphia Phillies, (3) 1980, 1981 and 1986.

Only Shortstop to Win Two MVP Awards
Ernie Banks, Chicago Cubs, 1958 and 1959

Only Player to Win MVP Awards in Both Leagues
Frank Robinson, Cincinnati (NL), 1961; Baltimore (AL), 1966.

Only Pitcher to Win Consecutive MVP Awards
Hal Newhouser, Detroit, 1944 and 1945.

Only Rookie to Win MVP Award
Fred Lynn, Boston Red Sox, 1975

First Unanimous Selection for MVP Award
AL—Hank Greenberg, Detroit, 1938
NL—Orlando Cepeda, St. Louis, 1967

Teams That Have Never Had an MVP Award Winner
NL—New York Mets, Houston, Montreal, Florida, Colorado and San Diego
AL—Toronto and Seattle. No St. Louis Browns player ever won an MVP Award before the franchise moved to Baltimore, nor did any player on either the original or the expansion Washington Senators.

Teams with the Most MVP Winners
AL—19—New York; but only two—Thurman Munson in 1976 and Don Mattingly in 1985—since 1963
NL—14—St. Louis

Players We Wish We'd Seen More of: 1920-41

The list of players in the 1920s and 1930s who were blocked either because they were on the wrong team or played the wrong position is a long one, and only some perverse streak in me, I suppose, caused me to limit it to a luckless 13.

1. Red Dorman. Like Ty Cobb, Dorman had a .360+ career batting average in the major leagues (.364), and also like Cobb, his last season came in 1928. But there the similarity ends. An outfielder, he was dropped by Cleveland after shining in a 24-game late-season trial.

2. Suds Sutherland. Won six games and lost only two as a rookie with the 1921 Tigers. But it wasn't good enough to earn him an encore—not even when coupled with a .407 batting average.

3. Herm Merritt. A 20-year-old shortstop, he hit .370 in 20 games for the 1921 Tigers but suffered the same fate as Sutherland.

4. Tripp Sigman. Had a .326 batting average and a .519 slugging average for the 1929-30 Phillies, but room couldn't be found for him in an outfield that featured Chuck Klein and Lefty O'Doul, and he got into only 62 games before being given a pink slip.

5. Pete Scott. Another outfielder in the late 1920s whose path was blocked by players like the Waner brothers and Hack Wilson. After three half-time seasons with the Cubs and Pirates, he departed in 1928 with a .303 career batting average and 88 RBIs in 522 at bats.

6. Jack Cummings. Had a .341 career batting average, showed good power and was an excellent pinch hitter, yet played in only 89 games between 1926 and 1929 with the Giants and Braves. A catcher, he hit .363 in 1927 and had 14 RBIs in 80 at bats, but was only rarely used by McGraw to spell Zack Taylor, who hit .233.

7. Babe Twombley. A singles hitter who was sent packing by the Cubs after he batted .377 in 1921, including a remarkable 15-for-38 as a pinch hitter.

8. Chicken Hawkes. Unlike Twombley, Hawkes had some power, but not enough to impress the Phillies, who dumped him after he hit .322 in 105 games in 1925. The following season they gave his first base job to Jack Bentley, who hit .258.

9. Tom Hughes. An outfielder with the 1930 Tigers, he hit .373 in 17 games but never got another crack at a major-league job.

10. Johnnie "Ty Ty" Tyler. Hit .340 and slugged .553 in 47 at bats with the 1935 Boston Braves, one of the most dismal teams ever, but was nevertheless let go.

11. Ben Paschal. Hit .357 for the 1920 Red Sox in a brief look but then bounced around the minors until the Yankees purchased him to serve as a backup outfielder to Babe Ruth, Earle Combs and Bob Meusel. Played six years with the Yankees without ever getting a shot at a full-time job even though he hit .360 in 1925 while filling in for an ailing Ruth. Apart from Buzz Arlett and Ike Boone, Paschal was probably the best player in this era who never got a full opportunity to showcase his talent in the majors.

12. Roy Carlyle. Another outfielder who wound up, to his detriment, with the Yankees. Released after hitting .377 for the 1926 team. Career batting average of .318 in 174 games and a fine 18-for-47 as a pinch hitter.

13. Merv Connors. Unable to wrest the White Sox first-base job away from Zeke Bonura and Joe Kuhel, Connors spent most of his career in the minors even though he hit .355 in his second and last big-league trial in 1938 and became the first White Sox player to hit three homers in a game at Comiskey Park. For more about Connors, Buzz Arlett, Ike Boone and other stars of the period who were denied major-league exposure, see "Minor League Feats and Firsts," page 229.

All-Star Game Feats

In 1933 Arch Ward of the *Chicago Tribune* hit upon the notion of holding a major-league all-star game as an adjunct to the World's Fair in Chicago that year, and it has been an annual event ever since with the exception of 1945, the final year of World War II.

First All-Star Game Home Run
AL—Babe Ruth, New York, in the very first game, July 6, 1933, at Comiskey Park
NL—Frankie Frisch, St. Louis, also in the inaugural game

First All-Star Game Won, League
AL—1933 at Comiskey Park, by a 4–2 score
NL—1936 at Braves Field, by a 4–3 score. A record-low crowd of 25,556 attended after a story was circulated around Boston that the game was sold out when in fact there were still plenty of seats available.

First Pitcher to Win Two All-Star Games
AL—Lefty Gomez, New York, 1933 and 1935. Gomez won a record third game in 1937 and then was the losing pitcher the following year, giving him an additional record of four decisions in All-Star play.
NL—Bob Friend, Pittsburgh, 1956 and 1960 (first game)

First Player to Hit Two Home Runs in All-Star Competition
NL—Frankie Frisch, St. Louis, 1933 and 1934
AL—Lou Gehrig, New York, 1936 and 1937

First Player to Hit Two Home Runs in One Game
Arky Vaughan, Pittsburgh, 1941 at Briggs Stadium, Detroit

First Player to Get Four Hits in One Game

Joe Medwick, St. Louis Cardinals, 1937 at Griffith Stadium, Washington

Longest Pitching Stint in an All-Star Game

Lefty Gomez of the Yankees went six innings as the starting pitcher for the American League in 1935, at Cleveland, as the AL won 4–1. The rules then did not limit pitchers to three innings.

Most Memorable Single Feat in All-Star Play

Probably Carl Hubbell's five consecutive strikeouts at the Polo Grounds in 1934. Hubbell opened the game by giving up a single to Charlie Gehringer and a walk to Heinie Manush. Then he fanned Babe Ruth, Lou Gehrig and Jimmie Foxx to end the first inning and began the second inning by whiffing Al Simmons and Joe Cronin. Hubbell's record for consecutive strikeouts in an All-Star Game was tied in 1986 by Fernando Valenzuela, who fanned Don Mattingly, Cal Ripken, Jesse Barfield, Lou Whitaker and Ted Higuera in order.

Most Serious Injury in All-Star Play

NL—Dizzy Dean's broken toe, suffered when Earl Averill of Cleveland hit a line drive off Dean's foot in the first inning of the 1937 game. Dean pitched three innings before giving in to the injury, then tried to come back from it too soon, hurt his arm and was never the same pitcher.

AL—Ted Williams's broken elbow, sustained when he crashed into the left-field wall in the first inning of the 1950 game at Comiskey Park. The injury kayoed Williams until late in the season, and without him the Red Sox lost the pennant by four games.

Most Exciting All-Star Game

The 1950 game gets my vote for several reasons. Not only was it the first extra-inning game and the first one televised, but when Red Schoendienst homered in the top of the 14th inning to win 4–3 for the NL, it seemed to have an odd impact on the American League that has lasted ever since. Prior to 1950, the AL held a 12–4 lead in games; by 1964 the NL had caught up. A year later the NL took the lead for the first time in games won and is now ahead 36 to 23 with 1 tie.

Second Most Exciting Game

The 1957 game at Sportsman's Park, won by the AL 6–5. After scoring three runs in the top of the ninth inning, the AL led 6–2, but the NL came back with three runs in the bottom half and had the tying run on base when Minnie Minoso speared Gil Hodges's line drive to end the game.

Highest-Scoring Game

The 1954 game at Cleveland Stadium won by the AL 11–9. You won't get much of an argument from my corner if you vote this also the most exciting game.

Most Lop-sided Game

The 1946 game at Fenway Park, won by the AL 12–0 as Ted Williams hit two home runs, compiled a record 10 total bases and five RBIs, also a record, later tied by Al Rosen in the 1954 game.

Last Time Prior to 1989 AL Won Two Games in a Row

In 1958 at Baltimore. The following year two games were played, an experiment that lasted until 1962; in that four-year span the NL won seven of the eight games with one a tie, in 1961 at Fenway Park, when rain began falling after the ninth inning with the score knotted 1–1.

First Indoor Game

In 1968 at the Astrodome. It was also the first 1–0 game and the only game in which no player had an RBI. The NL's winning run scored in the bottom of the first inning as Willie McCovey of the Giants hit into a double play.

First Game Played Outside the United States

In 1982 at Montreal, won by the NL 4–1.

Last of the 16 Teams that Existed in 1933 to Host a Game

The Philadelphia Phillies. The 1943 game was played in Shibe Park, their home ground, but the Athletics were the hosts. By the time the Phillies finally got the honor in 1952 both the White Sox and Tigers had hosted two games. To add to the grief of Phillies fans, who'd waited nearly 20 years to see their club in the host's role, rain forced the game to be called after five innings.

Best Pitcher in All-Star Play
AL—Mel Harder, Cleveland, appeared in four games, a total of 13 innings, without allowing an earned run.

NL—Juan Marichal, San Francisco, in 18 innings of All-Star play gave up only one earned run.

Most Career Strikeouts by Pitcher in All-Star Play
19—Don Drysdale, Los Angeles. But his record probably won't last much longer now that Gooden and Clemens are on the scene.

Most All-Star Appearances
24—Stan Musial, Willie Mays and Hank Aaron

Most Career Hits in All-Star Play
23—Willie Mays

Most Career Home Runs in All-Stay Play
6—Stan Musial

Most Career Total Bases in All-Star Play
40—Stan Musial and Willie Mays

Most Career RBIs in All-Star Play
12—Ted Williams

First Player to Win Two All-Star Game MVP Awards
Willie Mays, 1963 and 1968

Most Recent Player to Win Two All-Star Game MVP Awards
Gary Carter, 1981 and 1984

Most Recent Player to Win All-Star Game MVP Award Playing for Losing Team
Carl Yastrzemski, 1970, when the AL lost 5–4 in 12 innings. Altogether there have been seven extra-inning All-Star Games, and the NL has won all seven.

Shortstops' Records

I'm probably going to make myself even more unpopular with sabermetricians when I say that there is no way we are ever going to be able to gauge which shortstop had the greatest range, the best arm or the surest glove. Statistics alone can't give us any of these answers, and no one has had the fortune to see all of the contenders for the title of best-ever play, let alone play under conditions similar enough to allow meaningful comparisons to be made. But statistics do tell us that two of the top-hitting shortstops of all time were Luke Appling and Arky Vaughan, and that both were active in the 1930s. Appling and Vaughan were not just offensive standouts, however. Both were also among the best glovemen of the era, and Vaughan regularly led the NL in double plays and assists. By the time World War II began they had been joined by five outstanding young shortstops— Lou Boudreau, Marty Marion, Pee Wee Reese, Eddie Miller and Phil Rizzuto—perhaps the most massive gathering of fielding talent at the position in history. These five men would sweep the vast majority of fielding honors in both leagues during the 1940s, and three of them would win Most Valuable Player Awards.

SEASON BATTING RECORDS

Department	National League	American League
Batting Average	.401, HUGHIE JENNINGS, Baltimore, 1896	.388, Luke Appling, Chicago, 1936
	.385, Arky Vaughan, Pittsburgh, 1935*	
Slugging Average	.614, ERNIE BANKS, Chicago, 1958	.578, Robin Yount, Milwaukee, 1982

Department	National League	American League
Home Runs	47, ERNIE BANKS, Chicago, 1958	40, Rico Petrocelli, Boston, 1969
RBIs	143, Ernie Banks, Chicago, 1959	159, VERN STEPHENS, Boston, 1949
Runs	159, HUGHIE JENNINGS, Baltimore, 1895 132, Pee Wee Reese, Brooklyn, 1949*	137, Frank Crosetti, New York, 1936
Hits	211, Garry Templeton, St. Louis, 1978	213, TONY FERNANDEZ, Toronto, 1986
Doubles	48, Dick Bartell, Philadelphia, 1932	51, JOE CRONIN, Boston, 1938
Triples	24, ED McKEAN, Cleveland, 1893 20, Honus Wagner, Pittsburgh, 1912*	21, Bill Keister, Baltimore, 1901
Total Bases	379, ERNIE BANKS, Chicago, 1958	368, Cal Ripken, Jr., Baltimore, 1991
Stolen Bases	104, MAURY WILLS, Los Angeles, 1962	62, Bert Campaneris, Oakland, 1968
Bases on Balls	118, Arky Vaughan, Pittsburgh, 1936	149, EDDIE JOOST, Philadelphia, 1949
Strikeouts	114, Roy Smalley, Chicago, 1950 114, Bill Almon, San Diego, 1977 114, Shawon Dunston, Chicago, 1986	144, TRAVIS FRYMAN, Detroit, 1992
Fewest Strikeouts	5, Charlie Hollocher, Chicago, 1922	4, JOE SEWELL, Cleveland, 1925

*Record since 1901
Note: Cecil Travis of Washington had 218 hits in 1941, but a number of them came while he was playing third base.

Most Games, Career, at Shortstop
2581—Luis Aparicio, 1956–73

Most Consecutive Games at Shortstop
Cal Ripken, Jr., has now played in 1897 consecutive games, including 1770 straight games at shortstop to break Everett Scott's old mark of 1307.

Best Career Fielding Average
.980—Larry Bowa, 1970–85

EVOLUTION OF SEASON RECORD FOR BEST FIELDING AVERAGE

	Team	League	Year	Average
Johnny Peters	Chicago	National	1876	.932
George Wright	Boston	National	1878	.947[1]
George Davis	Chicago	American	1902	.951[2]
Tommy Corcoran	Cincinnati	National	1905	.952
Terry Turner	Cleveland	American	1906	.960
Terry Turner	Cleveland	American	1910	.973[3]
Everett Scott	Boston	American	1919	.976[4]
Eddie Miller	Boston	National	1942	.981
Buddy Kerr	New York	National	1946	.982
Lou Boudreau	Cleveland	American	1947	.982[5]
Phil Rizzuto	New York	American	1950	.982
Ernie Banks	Chicago	National	1959	.985
Larry Bowa	Philadelphia	National	1971	.987
Ed Brinkman	Detroit	American	1972	.990
Larry Bowa	Philadelphia	National	1979	.991
Tony Fernandez	Toronto	American	1989	.992
Cal Ripken	Baltimore	American	1990	.996

[1]Though documented, many of the relatively high fielding averages in the National League's early years are suspect, Wright's among them. Official scorers of that period were notoriously uneven. Testimony to this is that despite continuous improvements in gloves and overall playing conditions Wright's mark stood unchallenged, even by Wright himself, until 1895 when Hughie Jennings of Baltimore became only the second shortstop to field .940 or better.

[2]Seldom mentioned anymore by historians, Davis was not only a fine fielder but also at one time held the record for most career hits by a switch hitter.

[3]Turner's 1910 mark includes games he played at other infield positions. Even so, he was undoubtedly one of the top fielders of his era, good enough to be the only player ever to hold simultaneously a season record for the best fielding average at two different positions—shortstop and third base.

[4]Scott's record, long forgotten, can now be seen to have been a quantum leap; he also fielded just a hair lower in 1918.

[5]Boudreau fielded .983 in 1944, but injuries kept him from playing in enough games to qualify as a record breaker. His 1947 mark is actually a shade higher than Rizzuto's .982 average four years later; though both made the same number of errors, Boudreau handled 27 more chances.

Most Seasons League Leader in Fielding Average

AL—8—Everett Scott, 1916 through 1923 consecutive; Lou Boudreau, last in 1948; Luis Aparicio, 1959 through 1966 consecutive.

NL—6—Larry Bowa, last in 1983

Most Consecutive Errorless Games
95—Cal Ripken, Jr., Baltimore Orioles; April 14, 1990, through July 27, 1990

Most Consecutive Errorless Chances
During his record errorless games streak Ripken also broke the mark for errorless chances (431) before committing a bobble on July 28, 1990.

Most Chances Accepted, Career
12,564—Luis Aparicio, 1956–73

Most Chances Accepted, Season
984—Dave Bancroft, New York Giants, 1922

Most Chances Accepted, Game, Nine Innings, since 1902
19—Eddie Joost, Cincinnati Reds, May 7, 1941

Most Consecutive Games, No Chances Accepted
3—Tommy Tresh, New York Yankees, August 30, August 31 and September 1, 1968

Most Assists, Season
621—Ozzie Smith, San Diego Padres, 1980

Most Assists, Game, Nine Innings, since 1901
14—Tommy Corcoran, Cincinnati Reds, August 7, 1903

Most Seasons League Leader in Assists
AL—7—Luke Appling, last in 1946
    Luis Aparicio, last in 1968
NL—8—Ozzie Smith, last in 1989

Most Double Plays, Season
AL—147—Rick Burleson, Boston, 1980
NL—137—Bobby Wine, Montreal, 1970

Most Years League Leader in Double Plays
AL—6—George McBride, last in 1914; Cal Ripken, Jr., last in 1992
NL—5—Mickey Doolan, last in 1913; Dick Groat, last in 1964; Ozzie Smith, last in 1991

Most Gold Glove Awards
14—Ozzie Smith, last in 1992

Astronomical ERAs

The law that for every action there is an equal and opposite reaction applies not only in physics but also in baseball. While slugging statistics and scoring totals were soaring in the 1920s and 1930s so were pitchers' ERAs. In 1930 Remy Kremer of the Pirates became the first pitcher in major-league history to win 20 games despite allowing over five earned runs (5.02) per each nine innings he worked. Before the decade was out Bobo Newsom had won 20 games with an even higher ERA, and Roxie Lawson of the Tigers had somehow managed to achieve an 18–7 record and a dazzling .720 winning percentage in 1937 on a 5.27 ERA. But Kremer, Newsom and Lawson were stingy with enemy batters compared to three other pitchers in the 1930s who posted the three worst season ERAs in history among hurlers in 150 or more innings.

The Terrible Trio
   First Prize—Les Sweetland, Philadelphia Phillies, 1930; 7.71 ERA in 167 innings
   Second Prize—Claude Willoughby, Philadelphia Phillies, 1930; 7.59 ERA in 153 innings
   Third Prize—Jim Walkup, St. Louis Browns, 1937; 7.36 ERA in 150 innings

Highest ERA, Season, since 1942, Minimum 150 Innings
   First Prize—Ken Schrom, Cleveland Indians, 1987, 6.50 ERA in 153.2 innings
   Second Prize—Jack Morris, Toronto Blue Jays, 1993, 6.19 ERA in 152.2 innings

Highest ERA, Season, 1901 through 1919, 150 Innings
   5.30—Orlie Weaver, Chicago Cubs and Boston Braves, 1911; 165 innings

Highest ERA, Season, Prior to 1901, Minimum 10 Starts
    10.32—Charlie Stecher, Philadelphia, American Association, 1890

Highest ERA, Season, since 1901, Minimum 10 Starts
    9.85—Steve Blass, Pittsburgh Pirates, 1973. After a 19–8 season in 1972, Blass suffered a mysterious loss of control the following season and gave up 84 walks and 109 hits in 89 innings. A career .172 hitter, he ironically discovered the secret of hitting while forgetting everything he knew about pitching and rapped .417 (10-for-24) in 1973.

Highest ERA, Season, League Leader in ERA
    AL—3.20—Early Wynn, Cleveland, 1950
    NL—3.08—Bill Walker, New York Giants, 1929

Highest ERA, Season, 20-Game Winner
    1893–1900—4.92—Kid Carsey (24–16), Philadelphia, 1895
                    Brickyard Kennedy (22–19), Brooklyn,
                    1894, Clark Griffith (21–11), Chicago,
                    1894
    1901–19—3.83—Henry Schmidt (22–13), Brooklyn, 1903
    1920–41—5.08—Bobo Newsom (20–16), St. Louis Browns,
                    1938
    1942–60—4.07—Lew Burdette (21–15), Milwaukee Braves,
                    1959
    1961–76—4.08—Jim Merritt (20–12), Cincinnati Reds,
                    1970
    1977–92—4.04—Jack Morris (21–6), Toronto Blue Jays,
                    1992

Highest Career ERA, 300-Game Winner
    3.54—Early Wynn, 1939–63

HALL OF FAME PITCHERS WITH THE HIGHEST CAREER ERAS

		Years Active	Wins	ERA
1.	Red Ruffing	1924–47	273	3.80
2.	Ted Lyons	1923–46	260	3.67
3.	Jesse Haines	1918–37	210	3.64
4.	Herb Pennock	1912–34	241	3.61
5.	Waite Hoyt	1918–38	237	3.59

Highest Career ERA, 200-Game Winner

4.36—Earl Whitehill, 1923–39. Lew Burdette has never revealed whom he chose as his model when he was learning to pitch, but Whitehill would be a good guess. In 3566 innings he gave up 3917 hits and 1431 walks while striking out only 1350 batters. Yet he won 218 games and lost only 185.

Winner of the "Where Did He Go Wrong?" Award

Russ Van Atta. As a rookie with the 1933 Yankees, Van Atta pitched a shutout in his first major-league start and finished with a 12–4 record. Traded to the Browns in 1935, he twice led the American League in mound appearances and lasted until 1939 solely, it would seem, in the hope that he'd recover his early form. But Van Atta only got worse and worse. By the time he retired he'd absorbed so many fearful shellings that he had a 5.60 career ERA, the third highest in history among pitchers in over 700 innings. Whatever the Browns' strategy was in those years, it apparently didn't include molding a decent pitching staff. While they were clinging to Van Atta and Jim Walkup, they cut people like Fay Thomas, who won seven games in 1935 on a respectable (for the Browns) 4.78 ERA and all during the 1930s was regarded as one of the top pitchers in the minors.

Winner of the "Team That Never Learned How to Pick Them" Award

The Browns. In their 52-year history they never had a single ERA leader, and in 1951 they contrived to put together a mound staff that for a time had on it possibly the two worst pitchers ever—Sid Schacht and Irv Medlinger. Schacht, mainly a relief pitcher, worked in 19 games in 1950–51, gave up 44 hits and 21 walks in 22 innings and left with a 14.34 ERA, the all-time highest among pitchers in more than 20 innings. Medlinger, who had a 13.83 ERA in 14 innings, is fifth on the all-time list among pitchers who worked more than 10 innings.

The All-Time Worst Career ERAs

100 Innings—8.30—John McDougal, 125 innings (1895–96)
7.60—Bill Rhodes, 152 innings, (1893)
7.20—Jake Boyd, 136 innings (1894–96)
100 Innings—since 1901—7.19—Chet Nichols, 123 innings (1926–32)

7.17—Luther Roy, 171 innings (1924–29)

7.06—Lauren Pepper, 110 innings (1954–57)

6.95—Carl Doyle, 223 innings (1935–40)

250 Innings—6.99—Bill Kissinger, 319 innings (1895–97)

6.95—Hal Elliott, 322 innings (1929–32)

400 Innings—6.74—Jim Walkup, 462 innings (1934–39)

6.06—Lefty Mills, 435 innings (1934–40)

700 Innings—6.10—Les Sweetland, 741 innings (1927–31)

5.84—Claude Willoughby, 841 innings (1925–31)

1000 Innings—5.11—Mike Sullivan, 1123 innings (1889–99)

5.02—Chief Hogsett, 1222 innings (1929–44)

5.01—Roy Mahaffey, 1056 innings (1926–36)

4.97—Jack Knott, 1557 innings (1933–46)

4.95—Kid Carsey, 2222 innings (1891–1901)

4.94—Buck Ross, 1365 innings (1936–45)

4.91—Alex Ferguson, 1236 innings (1918–29)

The Hall of Fame

In the mid-1930s Ford Frick, then the National League president, was the prime mover behind the sentiment that a Hall of Fame to commemorate the game's greatest players should be opened in 1939, marking the centennial season for those who believed the Mills Commission's report that Abner Doubleday invented baseball. Acting on Frick's lead, Henry Edwards, secretary of the American League Service Bureau, polled the 226 members of the Baseball Writers Association of America for their choices from a list of 33 players. Two-thirds of the ballots cast were needed for selection. Ty Cobb led with 222 votes, Babe Ruth and Honus Wagner both had 215, Christy Mathewson had 205, and Walter Johnson received 189 votes. Before 1939 two more pollings were done, resulting in the selection of Nap Lajoie, Tris Speaker, Eddie Collins, George Sisler, Cy Young, Willie Keeler, Peter Alexander and Lou Gehrig (by special election) as well as 13 pre-1900 figures chosen by the Centennial Commission and the Committee on Old-Timers. These 26 immortals had their plaques installed in the Hall of Fame in a special induction ceremony in 1939 and have been joined in the years since by a long list. Although exceptions have been made in special cases, the three original criteria for selection have remained constant. A player must be active at least 10 seasons, must be retired at least 5 and must receive at least 75 percent of the vote.

In 1971 a Special Negro League Committee was formed to select players from the defunct Negro Leagues. Names followed by (NL) designate Negro League players who never played in the majors. Starred names belong to figures who were selected to the Hall of Fame as nonplayers.

Members of the Hall of Fame

1936 Ty Cobb, Honus Wagner, Babe Ruth, Christy Mathewson, Walter Johnson

1937 Nap Lajoie, Tris Speaker, Cy Young, Morgan Buckley,* Ban Johnson,* Connie Mack, John McGraw, George Wright.

1938 Pete Alexander, Alexander Cartwright,* Henry Chadwick*

1939 George Sisler, Eddie Collins, Willie Keeler, Lou Gehrig, Cap Anson, Charlie Comiskey, Candy Cummings, Buck Ewing, Hoss Radbourn, Al Spalding

1942 Rogers Hornsby

1944 Judge K. M. Landis*

1945 Roger Bresnahan, Dan Brouthers, Fred Clarke, Jimmy Collins, Ed Delahanty, Hugh Duffy, Hughie Jennings, Mike Kelly, Jim O'Rourke, Wilbert Robinson

1946 Jesse Burkett, Frank Chance, Jack Chesbro, Johnny Evers, Clark Griffith, Tom McCarthy, Joe McGinnity, Eddie Plank, Joe Tinker, Rube Waddell, Ed Walsh

1947 Carl Hubbell, Frank Frisch, Mickey Cochrane, Lefty Grove

1948 Herb Pennock, Pie Traynor

1949 Charlie Gehringer, Three Finger Brown, Kid Nichols

1951 Mel Ott, Jimmie Foxx

1952 Harry Heilmann, Paul Waner

1953 Dizzy Dean, Al Simmons, Ed Barrow,* Chief Bender, Tom Connolly,* Bill Klem,* Bobby Wallace, Harry Wright*

1954 Rabbit Maranville, Bill Dickey, Bill Terry

1955 Joe DiMaggio, Ted Lyons, Dazzy Vance, Gabby Hartnett, Frank Baker, Ray Schalk

1956 Hank Greenberg, Joe Cronin

1957 Sam Crawford, Joe McCarthy*

1959 Zack Wheat

1961 Max Carey, Billy Hamilton

1962 Bob Feller, Jackie Robinson, Bill McKechnie,* Edd Roush

1963 John Clarkson, Elmer Flick, Sam Rice, Eppa Rixey

1964 Luke Appling, Red Faber, Burleigh Grimes, Miller Huggins, Tim Keefe, Heinie Manush, John Ward

1965 Pud Galvin

1966 Ted Williams, Casey Stengel

1967 Red Ruffing, Branch Rickey,* Lloyd Waner

1968 Joe Medwick, Kiki Cuyler, Goose Goslin

1969 Stan Musial, Roy Campanella, Stan Coveleski, Waite Hoyt

1970 Lou Boudreau, Earle Combs, Ford Frick,* Jesse Haines

1971 Jake Beckley, Dave Bancroft, Chick Hafey, Harry Hooper, Joe Kelley, Rube Marquard, George Weiss,* Satchel Paige

1972 Sandy Koufax, Yogi Berra, Early Wynn, Lefty Gomez, Will Harridge,* Ross Youngs, Josh Gibson (NL), Buck Leonard (NL)

1973 Warren Spahn, Billy Evans,* George Kelly, Mickey Welch, Monte Irvin, Roberto Clemente

1974 Mickey Mantle, Whitey Ford, Jim Bottomley, Jocko Conlan,* Sam Thompson, Cool Papa Bell (NL)

1975 Ralph Kiner, Earl Averill, Bucky Harris,* Billy Herman, Judy Johnson (NL)

1976 Robin Roberts, Bob Lemon, Roger Connor, Fred Lindstrom, Cal Hubbard,* Oscar Charleston (NL)

1977 Ernie Banks, Amos Rusie, Joe Sewell, Al Lopez,* Martin Dihugo (NL), John Henry Lloyd (NL)

1978 Eddie Mathews, Addie Joss, Larry MacPhail*

1979 Willie Mays, Warren Giles,* Hack Wilson

1980 Al Kaline, Duke Snider, Chuck Klein, Tom Yawkey*

1981 Bob Gibson, Johnny Mize, Rube Foster (NL)

1982 Hank Aaron, Frank Robinson, Travis Jackson, Happy Chandler*

1983 Brooks Robinson, Juan Marichal, George Kell, Walter Alston*

1984 Luis Aparicio, Harmon Killebrew, Don Drysdale, Rick Ferrell, Pee Wee Reese

1985 Hoyt Wilhelm, Lou Brock, Enos Slaughter, Arky Vaughan

1986 Willie McCovey, Bobby Doerr, Ernie Lombardi

1987 Billy Williams, Catfish Hunter, Ray Dandridge (NL)

1988 Willie Stargell

1989 Johnny Bench, Carl Yastremski, Red Schoendienst, Al Barlick*

1990 Joe Morgan, Jim Palmer

1991 Rod Carew, Gaylord Perry, Fergie Jenkins, Tony Lazzeri, Bill Veeck*

1992 Rollie Fingers, Tom Seaver, Hal Newhouser, Bill McGowan

1993 Reggie Jackson

Individual Batting and Pitching Streaks

A significant majority of the great batting and pitching streaks occurred between 1920 and 1941. Foremost among them is probably Joe DiMaggio's hitting streak in 1941, which began inauspiciously on May 15 when DiMaggio collected a meager single off Eddie Smith of the White Sox. Two months later the streak reached 56 games after DiMaggio rapped a double and two singles against Al Milnar and Joe Krakauskas of the Indians. The following night, on July 17, at Cleveland Stadium, DiMaggio was stopped by Al Smith and Jim Bagby but more by third baseman Ken Keltner and shortstop Lou Boudreau. Keltner converted two hard shots down the third-base line into outs, and in DiMaggio's last at bat, in the eighth inning, Boudreau fashioned a double play out of a smash that DiMaggio later said was among the hardest balls he ever hit. During his 56-game streak DiMaggio hit .408 with 91 hits in 223 at bats. That same year Ted Williams of the Boston Red Sox lost the MVP Award to DiMaggio although he hit .406 for the entire season.

Longest National League Hitting Streak

44 games—Pete Rose, Cincinnati, 1978; stopped on August 1 by Larry McWilliams and Gene Garber of the Atlanta Braves.

Willie Keeler, Baltimore, 1897. Prior to Keeler's 44-game streak, the record was held by Bill Dahlen of the Chicago White Stockings, who hit safely in 42 straight games in 1894, breaking George Davis's year-old mark of 33 games. Dahlen's streak ended on August 7 against Cincinnati in a game in which the White Stockings made 20 hits, five each by Bill Lange and Cap Anson, who preceded and followed Dahlen in the Chicago batting order. According to some record books, Dahlen began a 28-game streak the next day, meaning that he narrowly missed putting together a 71-game skein, but the second streak is still the subject of dispute.

Most Consecutive Base Hits, No Bases on Balls Intervening
AL—12—Walt Dropo, Detroit, July 14 and 15, 1952
NL—10—Jake Gettman, Washington, September 10 and 11, 1897; Ed Konetchy, Brooklyn, June 28, June 29 and July 1, 1919

Most Consecutive Games Hitting at Least One Home Run
NL—8—Dale Long, Pittsburgh, May 19 through May 28, 1956
AL—8—Don Mattingly, New York, July 8 through July 18, 1987
—8—Ken Griffey, Jr., Seattle, July 20 through July 28, 1993

Most Consecutive Games Collecting at Least One RBI
NL—17—Ray Grimes, Chicago, 1922. For many years Grimes's mark went unrecognized because a back injury sidelined him for a nine-day stretch during the streak.
AL—13—Taft Wright, Chicago, 1941.

Most Consecutive Games Played
2130—Lou Gehrig, New York Yankees, 1925–39. Unquestionably the most remarkable streak of this or any other era, Gehrig's skein began on June 1, 1925, when he pinch-hit for shortstop Pee Wee Wanninger; continued because regular first baseman Wally Pipp was beaned in batting practice by Charlie Caldwell (who later earned fame for a streak of his own when he coached Princeton to two straight undefeated football seasons); seemed destined for an early end on July 5, 1925, until Fred Merkle fainted from the heat in the ninth inning after playing the whole game at first base for the Yankees; took a small detour on September 28, 1930, when Gehrig played left field while Babe Ruth pitched and Harry Rice played first base; aroused only mild attention until 1933 when Gehrig surpassed the previous record of 1,307 games set by former Yankees shortstop Everett Scott (whose own streak ended when he was replaced by Pee Wee Wanninger, the man Gehrig pinch-hit for to start his skein); came within a hair of being terminated in 1934 when Gehrig was beaned in a midseason exhibition game; and seemed definitely over a month later when he had to be carried off the field after suffering a back injury, only to see

him penciled in the lineup the following day at shortstop and then replaced by a pinch runner after leading off the game with a single. The streak finally ended on May 2, 1939, when Gehrig, already showing the debilitating effects of the neuromuscular disease that just two years later would claim his life, removed himself from the lineup, allowing Babe Dahlgren to play the entire game at first base. Prior to Scott, the consecutive game record was held by third baseman George Pinkney, who played 577 straight games for the old Brooklyn Bridegrooms. Steve Garvey holds the National League record, playing in 1207 consecutive games before a thumb injury ended his string on July 30, 1983.

Most Consecutive Wins by a Pitcher, League
NL—24—Carl Hubbell, New York Giants, 1936–37
AL—17—Johnny Allen, Cleveland, 1936–37
          Dave McNally, Baltimore, 1968–69

Most Consecutive Wins by a Pitcher, Season, League
NL—19—Tim Keefe, New York Giants, 1888
Rube Marquard, New York Giants, 1912. On July 3, 1912, after beating Brooklyn 2–1, Marquard had an incredible 19–0 record, which should actually have been 20–0. Earlier in the season Jeff Tesreau had been credited with a victory that ought to have gone to Marquard, who relieved Tesreau in the top of the ninth inning of a game in which the Giants were trailing and then saw them come back and win in their final turn at bat.
   AL—16—Walter Johnson, Washington, 1912
Joe Wood, Boston, 1912; beating Johnson on September 1 to tie Johnson's brand-new record
Lefty Grove, Philadelphia, 1931; missing his chance for an AL season-record 17th straight win when he lost 1–0 to the Browns on August 23, after left-fielder Jimmy Moore, spelling Al Simmons, who took the day off, misplayed a fly ball, leading to the game's only run.
Schoolboy Rowe, Detroit, 1934

Most Consecutive Wins by a Pitcher in His Home Park
20—Lefty Grove, Boston Red Sox, May 3, 1938, through May 12, 1941. In the process Grove forever buried the notion that a southpaw could not win in Fenway Park.

Most Consecutive Wins by a Relief Pitcher

22—Roy Face, Pittsburgh Pirates, 1958–59. Face was only two short of Hubbell's alltime-record 24 straight wins when he lost his next-to-last decision in 1959 after getting off to a 17–0 start.

Most Consecutive Wins by a Pitcher with a Last-Place Team

15—Steve Carlton, Philadelphia Phillies, 1972. Carlton's record streak helped make him a 27-game winner with a team that won only 59 games.

World Series Play: 1920–41

FRANCHISE SUMMARY

Team	League	WS Record through 1941	Last year in WS
Boston	American	5–0	1918
Cleveland	American	1–0	1920
Boston	National	1–0	1914
New York	American	9–3	1941
Cincinnati	National	2–1	1940
Chicago	American	2–1	1919
Philadelphia	American	5–3	1931
St. Louis	National	3–2	1934
Pittsburgh	Natonal	2–2	1927
New York	National	4–8	1937
Washington	American	1–2	1933
Chicago	National	2–7	1938
Detroit	American	1–5	1940
Philadelphia	National	0–1	1915
Brooklyn	National	0–3	1941

Yearly Highlights
1920—Cleveland (AL) defeated Brooklyn (NL) 5 games to 2

Indians player-manager Tris Speaker platooned at three positions—first base, left field and right field—and got a trio of wins from Stan Coveleski, the last pitcher until 1946 to win three in a Series. The Indians also received the first Series grand-slam homer from Elmer Smith, the first Series homer by a pitcher from Jim Bagby, and Bill Wamby's unassisted triple play, the only one in Series history. Cleveland won the pennant despite losing the AL's premier shortstop, Ray Chapman, who was killed by a Carl Mays pitch in August.

1921—New York (NL) defeated New York (AL) 5 games to 3

The first Subway Series and also the last Series played on a best-five-of-nine format. Waite Hoyt of the Yankees pitched three complete games without allowing an earned run but lost one of them, the Series finale, on an error by shortstop Roger Peckinpaugh. In Game Three, the Giants pounded a Series-record 20 hits while winning 13–5.

1922—New York (NL) defeated New York (AL) 4 games to 0

When the best the Yankees could do was a tie in Game Two, manager Miller Huggins was nearly fired, and John McGraw and his Giants seemed to have permanently cemented the Yankees into place as the city's second-best team. Of Babe Ruth, who hit only .118 in the Series, sportswriter Joe Vila wrote: "The exploded phenomenon didn't surprise the smart fans who long ago realized that he couldn't hit brainy pitching. Ruth, therefore, is no longer a wonder. The baseball public is onto his real worth as a batsman and in the future, let us hope, he will attract just ordinary attention."

1923—New York (AL) defeated New York (NL) 4 games to 2

Casey Stengel hit two game-winning homers for the Giants, the first one inside the park, but Ruth, just a year after Vila's put-down, broke out of his Series slump with a vengeance, hitting .368 and hammering three homers.

1924—Washington (AL) defeated New York (NL) 4 games to 3

The most exciting Series to date. Washington won the deciding game in 12 innings, Walter Johnson getting the victory in relief. The winning run came home when Earl McNeely's ground ball hit a pebble and bounced over Giants third baseman Fred Lindstrom's head. In McGraw's last Series game he was outfoxed by Senators manager Bucky Harris, who started right-hander Curly Ogden, allowed him to pitch to just two batters and then brought in lefty George Mogridge, saddling the Giants with a lineup of left-handed hitters.

1925—Pittsburgh (NL) defeated Washington (AL) 4 games to 3

In the eighth inning of Game Three, with the Senators leading 4–3 and two out, Earl Smith of the Pirates hit a drive headed into the temporary right-centerfield seats in Griffith Stadium, but Sam Rice dove over the wall and came out of the crowd clutching the ball. Second base umpire Rigler signaled the catch, but many observers felt that Rice had wrestled the ball out of a fan's hand. On his way to becoming the Series hero when he also led both teams with 12 hits, Rice saw his dream fade when the Pirates, down three games to one, pulled out the next two contests and then rallied to win the seventh game, getting 15 hits and nine runs off Walter Johnson, who was making his last Series appearance. Roger Peckinpaugh, the AL's MVP in 1925, once again became the Series goat when he made eight errors.

1926—St. Louis (NL) defeated New York (AL) 4 games to 3

For the third year in a row the Series went the full seven games. The deciding clash was played in a steady drizzle at Yankee Stadium. Pitching in relief, Pete Alexander struck out the Yankees' Tony Lazzeri with the bases loaded and two out in the seventh inning, preserving a 3-2 Cardinals lead. The Series ended when Babe Ruth was caught trying to steal second base with two out in the ninth inning.

1927—New York (AL) defeated Pittsburgh (NL) 4 games to 0

Herb Pennock of the Yankees had a perfect game going in Game Three until Pie Traynor ended it with one out in the eighth. Ruth and Lou Gehrig between them knocked in 12 runs while the Pirates scored only 10.

1928—New York (AL) defeated St. Louis (NL) 4 games to 0

Ruth set several Series records as he hit three homers and batted .625 while Gehrig knocked home nine runs against a Cardinals pitching staff that had a 6.09 Series ERA.

1929—Philadelphia (AL) defeated Chicago (NL) 4 games to 1

Howard Ehmke broke Ed Walsh's Series record when he fanned 13 Cubs in the opener. The Cubs led 8–0 in the seventh inning of Game Four but lost 10–8 as the A's put on the most amazing one-inning rally in Series history.

1930—Philadelphia (AL) defeated St. Louis (NL) 4 games to 2

Al Simmons and Jimmie Foxx both had a good Series, but it was the pitching of Lefty Grove and George Earnshaw, each of whom won two games, that beat the Cards.

1931—St. Louis (NL) defeated Philadelphia (AL) 4 games to 3

The Cards were led by Pepper Martin, who hit .500 and stole five bases, and Bill Hallahan, who recorded two wins and saved the seventh game.

1932—New York (AL) defeated Chicago (NL) 4 games to 0

Ruth may or may not have "called" his shot in Game Three, but in any event it was his second homer of the game and last in Series play. It came in the fifth inning of a 4–4 game, against Charlie Root, on an 0–2 pitch, a high inside change-up. The homer overrode Gehrig's overall Series effort of three homers and eight RBIs.

1933—New York (NL) defeated Washington (AL) 4 games to 1

In their first Series, Carl Hubbell and Mel Ott of the Giants were the pitching and hitting stars. Hubbell won two games without giving up an earned run, and Ott slugged two homers, the second bringing home the deciding run in the 10th inning of the final game.

1934—St. Louis (NL) defeated Detroit (AL) 4 games to 3

In the sixth inning of the final game, Joe Medwick of the Cardinals slid hard into Tigers third baseman Marv Owen, nearly triggering a riot in Briggs Stadium. When Detroit fans pelted Medwick with fruit and vegetables as he tried to take his left-field post in the bottom of the inning, Commissioner Landis ordered him removed from the game for his own protection. The Cardinals were ahead at the time 9–0 and didn't protest Landis's decision, but if the score had been closer, one wonders whether Landis would not have been forced to declare the first forfeit in Series history.

1935—Detroit (AL) defeated Chicago (NL) 4 games to 2

Lon Warneke's two fine pitching efforts were all the Cubs could point to, as the Tigers made do without Hank Greenberg, who was injured early in the Series.

1936—New York (AL) defeated New York (NL) 4 games to 2

After losing the opener 6–1 to Carl Hubbell, the Yankees scored 42 runs in the next five games, including a record 18 in Game Two.

1937—New York (AL) defeated New York (NL) 4 games to 1

Hubbell's win in Game Four was all that prevented the Yankees from sweeping.

1938—New York (AL) defeated Chicago (NL) 4 games to 0

Stan Hack of the Cubs hit .471 to lead all Series batters. The rest of the accolades once again belonged to the Yankees.

1939—New York (AL) defeated Cincinnati (NL) 4 games to 0

The Reds hung tough before losing the opener 2–1 in the ninth inning and took the Yankees to 10 innings before dropping Game Four but managed only 12 singles in the other two contests.

1940—Cincinnati (NL) defeated Detroit (AL) 4 games to 3

Two complete-game victories by both Bucky Walters and Paul Derringer sparked the Reds to their first untainted World Championship.

1941—New York (AL) defeated Brooklyn (NL) 4 games to 1

In Game Three, Fred Fitzsimmons of the Dodgers blanked the Yankees for seven innings before a line drive off the bat of Yankees pitcher Marius Russo broke his kneecap and forced him to leave the game. The Dodgers ultimately lost 2–1 and then dropped Game Four in the ninth inning when Tommy Henrich fanned for what should have been the final out of a 4–3 Dodgers victory, only to have the third strike elude catcher Mickey Owen and Henrich reach first base. Before the Yankees were retired they scored four runs and broke open the most competitive Series they had been in since 1926.

SECTION 4

Famous Firsts:
1942–60

1942—Ted Lyons sets a post deadball era record when he makes 20 starts and completes all 20 games.

1943—To save on rubber, which is in short supply during the war, a new balata baseball is manufactured and used. It results in no home runs being hit in the first 11 games of the season and shutouts in 11 of the first 29 games. Finally, the balls left over from 1942 are brought out of the closet while balls with a better quality of rubber cement are rushed into production.

1944—On July 20, in a game against the Yankees, Nels Potter of the Browns becomes the first pitcher ever to be ejected expressly for violating the spitball rule.

1945—The Washington Senators miss becoming the only team in modern history to vault from last place to a pennant the following year when they lose on the final day of the season to the A's in extra innings on a fly ball that outfielder Bingo Binks, who's neglected to don sunglasses after the sun breaks through late in the day, loses in the brightness.

1945—The National League's leader in pitching wins, leader in pitching losses, runner-up in stolen bases and the Red Sox leader in saves all have the same last name—Barrett—and no two of them are related.

1947—Pitcher Bill Voiselle of the Braves, who resides in Ninety-Six, North Carolina, becomes the first player to wear the name of his hometown on the back of his uniform when he appears on the field bearing number 96.

1947—Bonus baby Joe Tepsic stings the Dodgers and quits rather than be sent to the minors after spending the 1946 season with the club.

1947—"Howling Hilda" Chester, now at her peak, lets other Dodgers fans know how she feels about Tepsic's betrayal. With her ringing cow bells and shouts to Dodgers players until they wave to her in their seat in the Ebbets Field bleachers, Chester prefers the sobriquet "Queen of the Bleachers" to "Howling Hilda." Before each game she can be seen carrying a banner with her name on it and earning the price of admission by selling songsheets at the corner of Dekalb Avenue and Flatbush Extension. When the Dodgers are out of town, she bides her time by selling newspapers in downtown Brooklyn. Chester has her counterparts in Mary Ott, the "Horse Lady of St. Louis," who for 25 years has been the scourge of umpires and visiting players to Sportsman's Park, and "Megaphone Lolly" Hopkins in Boston. Hopkins, however, is considerably more genteel than Ott and much less partisan than Chester; she bestows her cheers not only on Braves and Red Sox players but also on players from visiting teams should they happen to do something that pleases her.

1948—There are no Hildas or Lollys or Marys in Cleveland, but there is Joe Early, a night watchman, who writes to Indians owner Bill Veeck, asking how come players are always honored—why not a fan every now and then? Why not indeed, responds Veeck, and he has a special night for Early at which Early receives an outhouse, a backfiring Model T and some weird animals, plus a Ford convertible, luggage, a refrigerator, a washing machine, a watch, a stereo, clothes and lots more. Between Veeck's promotions and the first Cleveland pennant-winner in 28 years, the Indians draw 2,620,627 and shatter every all-time attendance record.

1949—Mel Allen is first heard to utter the line that made him famous, "How about that?" when Joe DiMaggio returns to the New York lineup after being disabled by a bone spur and cracks a hit his first time up. Another colorful bit of work from that same era, though never heard nationally, comes from Pittsburgh's Rosie Rosewell, who says, each time Ralph Kiner cranks one out of Forbes Field, "Open the window, Aunt Minnie, here it comes!" pauses a moment, and then shatters a light bulb over the air.

1951—Bill Veeck, now the owner of the Browns, hires Eddie Gaedel, a three-foot-seven-inch midget, and uses him as a pinch hitter for leadoff man Frank Saucier in the bottom of the first inning of a game on August 19 against Detroit. Pitcher Bob Cain of the Tigers, after he realizes it isn't a gag and stops laughing, walks Gaedel on four pitches. American League president Will Harridge is appalled when he learns of Veeck's latest innovation and orders Gaedel's at-bat stricken from the record book until it's pointed out to him by Veek that the game's stats will thereupon make it seem that Cain pitched to no one.

1951—Russ Hodges utters the most famous single line ever mouthed by a play-by-play announcer when he ecstatically shouts, shrieks and sobs, "The Giants win the pennant!" over and over again after Bobby Thomson's three-run homer abruptly ends the National League pennant playoff series between the Giants and the Dodgers.

1953—Paul Pettit, the Pirates' $100,000 bonus baby, posts a 7.11 ERA but manages to win a game, for which the Pirates are grateful. Cleveland's $100,000 bonus baby, Billy Joe Davidson, in contrast, never even throws a single pitch in a major-league game.

1954—The sacrifice fly rule, tinkered with for years, sometimes in effect and other times not, is once again adopted and this time remains on the books; a batter who hits a run-scoring fly ball is henceforth not charged with time at bat.

1954—Players for the first time are no longer allowed to leave their gloves on the playing field while their team is at bat.

1950s—Warning tracks are at last required in the outfields of all major-league parks. Padded fences, however, will not be mandatory until the 1970s.

1956—Robin Roberts of the Phillies is tagged for a National League record 46 home runs on his way to surrendering an all-time career record 502 homers.

1957—The American League makes batting helmets mandatory. Prior to this many players have already begun wearing them.

1957—Pedro Ramos of the Senators surrenders 43 home runs, a new American League season record.

1960—Jerry Holtzman of the *Chicago Sun Times* helps initiate the crediting of "saves" to relief pitchers.

1960—White Sox owner Bill Veeck is the first to put names on the backs of his team's uniforms. Veeck also unveils an exploding scoreboard in Comiskey Park. On the other hand, Veeck's crosstown rival, the Chicago Cubs, calmly ally themselves with the Red Sox and remain the last clubs to have a manually operated scoreboard until 1986, when the Oakland A's turn back the clock and convert their scoreboard to a human-run operation.

Batting Title
Record Holders

Ted Williams and Stan Musial were unquestionably the elite hitters in their respective leagues during the period between 1942 and 1960. The last two players to retire with career averages above .330, they each set numerous offensive records, not the least of which are their league marks for the longest span of time between their first and last batting titles. Williams took his initial American League crown in 1941 and his final crown an all-time record 17 years later; Musial holds the National League record with a 14-year spread between his first triumph in 1943 and his last in 1957.

Most Batting Titles Won
    AL—12—Ty Cobb, last in 1919
    NL—8—Honus Wagner, last in 1911

Other Players Who Won Four or More Batting Titles
    7—Rod Carew (AL), last in 1978
       Stan Musial (NL), last in 1957
       Rogers Hornsby (NL), last in 1928
    6—Ted Williams (AL), last in 1958
    5—Wade Boggs (AL), last in 1988
    4—Bill Madlock (NL), last in 1983
       Roberto Clemente (NL), last in 1967
       Harry Heilmann (AL), last in 1927
       Tony Gwynn (NL), last in 1989

Most Batting Titles Won Prior to 1901
    5—Dan Brouthers led the National League in 1882, 1883, 1889 and 1892 and the American Association in 1891. The only other players ever to lead two different major leagues batting were Pete Browning, who won the American Association batting crown in 1882 and 1885 and the Players

League batting crown in 1890, and Ed Delahanty, National League in 1899 and American League in 1902.

Most Consecutive Batting Titles Won
AL—9—Ty Cobb, 1907–15
NL—6—Rogers Hornsby, 1920–25

Youngest Batting Title Winner
AL—Al Kaline, Detroit, 1955; 20 years old
NL—Pete Reiser, Brooklyn, 1941; 22 years old

Oldest Batting Title Winner
AL—Ted Williams, Boston, 1958; 40 years old
NL—Honus Wagner, Pittsburgh, 1911; 37 years old

Oldest Player to Win His First Batting Title
NL—Al Oliver, Montreal, 1982; 35 years old
AL—Charlie Gehringer, Detroit, 1937; 34 years old

Most Batting Title Winners, Team
NL—22—Pittsburgh; won by 10 different players; last winner was Bill Madlock in 1983.
AL—20—Boston, six won by Ted Williams, five by Wade Boggs, three by Carl Yastrzemski, two by Pete Runnels and one each by four other players

Fewest Batting Title Winners, Team
NL—0—New York Mets; Houston Astros; Giants while in San Francisco; Florida Marlins
AL—0—Milwaukee Brewers; A's while in Oakland

Most Seasons Since Last Batting Title Winner, Team
AL—50—Chicago; last winner was Luke Appling in 1943. Appling, who also won in 1938, is the only White Sox player ever to lead the AL in batting.
NL—39—New York–San Francisco Giants; last winner was Willie Mays in 1954

Only Third Basemen to Win More Than One Batting Title
NL—4—Bill Madlock, 1975, 1976, 1981 and 1983
AL—5—Wade Boggs, 1983, 1985, 1986, 1987, 1988
—3—George Brett, 1976, 1980 and 1990

Last Shortstop to Win a Batting Title
AL—Lou Boudreau, Cleveland, 1944

NL—Dick Groat, Pittsburgh, 1960. Only three shortstops have won NL batting titles since 1901—Honus Wagner, Arky Vaughan and Groat—and all three played for the Pirates.

Only Catchers to Win a Batting Title
NL—Bubbles Hargrave, Cincinnati, 1926
      Ernie Lombardi, Cincinnati, 1938, and Boston, 1942
AL—None

Only Pitcher Ever to Win a Batting Title
Guy Hecker, Louisville (AA), 1886. Hecker was one of a kind. Nicknamed "The Big Blond," he didn't begin his professional career until he was in his mid-twenties and played only nine seasons in the majors after his belated start. But he packed so many extraordinary feats into his brief career that he could occupy a full page in the all-time record book by himself. As a rookie with Louisville in 1882, Hecker authored a no-hitter, only the second in American Association history, which was further distinguished by the fact that his teammates made six errors behind him. Two years later he won 52 games for Louisville, an Association record. In 1886 Hecker slipped to only 27 wins but hit .342, edging out teammate Pete Browning for the AA batting crown by two points. That same season, in a game against Baltimore on August 15, Hecker hit three home runs, the only AA player ever to do so, and in addition crossed the plate seven times, an all-time one-game record. Now the possessor of batting, slugging and pitching marks that can never be surpassed, Hecker was still not done. Versatile enough to play elsewhere when he wasn't pitching, he set an unsurpassable *fielding* record on October 9, 1887, when he became the first player in major-league history to play an entire game at first base without handling a single chance.

Most Recent Batting Title Winner to Repeat the Following Season
NL—Tony Gwynn, San Diego, 1987–89
AL—Wade Boggs, Boston, 1985–88

Most Recent Player to Win a Batting Title without Hitting a Home Run
AL—Rod Carew, Minnesota, 1972
NL—Zack Wheat, Brooklyn, 1918

Fewest Base Hits by a Batting Title Winner
    NL—102—Ernie Lombardi, Boston, 1942
    AL—127—Ty Cobb, Detroit, 1914

Biggest Leap in Average from Previous Season by Batting Title Winner (qualifiers only)
    NL—97 points—Carl Furillo, Brooklyn, 1953; hit .247 in 1952, .344 in 1953
    AL—85 points—Mickey Vernon, Washington, 1946; hit .268 in 1943, .353 in 1946 after losing two years to military service

Biggest Drop in Average Season after Winning Batting Title
    AL—118 points—Norm Cash, Detroit, 1962; hit .361 in 1961, .243 in 1962
    NL—99 points—Willie McGee, St. Louis, 1986; hit .353 in 1985, .254 in 1986

Most Discouraging Season after Winning Batting Title
    NL—Rico Carty, Atlanta, 1971. Carty hit .366 to win the NL batting title in 1970, then missed all of 1971 after suffering a severe knee injury.
    AL—George Sisler, St. Louis, 1923. After Sisler won the AL batting crown in 1922, surgery for sinus blockages that affected his eyesight idled him for the entire 1923 season; he was never again the same player.

Only Players to Win Two Batting Titles with Averages Below Their Career Averages
    Ty Cobb, Detroit, 1906 (.350), 1907 (.324); .367 career average
    Ted Williams, Boston Red Sox, 1947 (.343), 1958 (.328); .344 career average

Multiple Batting Title Winners Who Retired with Career Averages Below .300
    AL—Carl Yastrzemski, Boston, 1963, 1967 and 1968; .285 career average
        Pete Runnels, Boston, 1960 and 1962; .291 career average
        Ferris Fain, Philadelphia, 1950 and 1951; .290 career average
        Mickey Vernon, Washington, 1946 and 1953; .286 career average
    NL—Tommy Davis, Los Angeles, 1962 and 1963; .294 career average

Highest Batting Average to Win Batting Title, since 1901
AL—.426—Nap Lajoie, Philadelphia, 1901
NL—.424—Rogers Hornsby, St. Louis, 1924

Highest Batting Average Failing to Win Batting Title, since 1901
   AL—.408—Joe Jackson, Cleveland, 1911; runner-up to Ty Cobb's .420. Cobb's .401 average in 1922, second to George Sisler's .420, is the only other .400 season in this century that failed to win a batting crown.
   NL—.393—Babe Herman, Brooklyn, 1930; runner-up to Bill Terry's .401

Lowest Average to Win Batting Title
AL—.301—Carl Yastrzemski, Boston, 1968
NL—.313—Tony Gwynn, San Diego, 1988

Closest Batting Title Races
   First place—Snuffy Stirnweiss of the Yankees won the AL batting crown in 1945 by less than a thousandth of a point, hitting .30854 to Tony Cuccinello's .30845. After missing the batting title by the narrowest margin in history, Cuccinello was released by the White Sox and never again played in the majors.
   Second Place—George Kell, Detroit, won the AL batting crown in 1949 by .00016 of a point over Ted Williams, Boston Red Sox.
   Third Place—Chick Hafey, St. Louis Cardinals, won the NL batting crown in 1931 by .00028 of a point over Bill Terry, New York Giants. Both hit .349 when their averages were rounded off. In third place with a .348 average was Jim Bottomley of the Cardinals.
   Fourth Place—Alex Johnson, California Angels, won the AL batting crown in 1970 by .00037 of a point over Carl Yastrzemski, Boston Red Sox.

Most Disputed Batting Title
   First Place—For 70 years Ty Cobb was credited with winning the 1910 AL batting title by a single point—.385 to .384—over Nap Lajoie of Cleveland despite efforts on Lajoie's behalf by St. Louis Browns manager Jack O'Connor and coach Harry Howell, who instructed rookie third baseman Red Corriden to play deep each time Lajoie batted in a doubleheader on the last day of the season. Corriden's

positioning allowed Lajoie to beat out eight bunts and resulted in both O'Connor and Howell being barred from future major-league jobs. In 1981 the *Sporting News* discovered that Lajoie had won after all—.384 to .383—because Cobb received double credit for a 2-for-3 game, and two hitless at bats were omitted from his statistics. The *Sporting News* is right, yet it's also true that Lajoie's season-ending flurry of hits was tainted. Your choice who the real winner was.

Second Place—In 1976 George Brett of the Kansas City Royals won the AL batting title over teammate Hal McRae when outfielder Steve Brye of the Minnesota Twins allowed a fly ball Brett hit on his last at bat of the season to fall safely. Brye made only a token attempt to deny he'd deliberately engineered Brett's batting title win and justified his machinations by claiming that Brett, a third baseman, was more deserving of the crown than McRae, a designated hitter. Again, your choice who really won.

Handicapped Players

In 1945 the St. Louis Browns purchased Pete Gray, the MVP the previous year in the Southern Association. Gray, who had only one arm, played 77 games for the 1945 Browns, a remarkable achievement for a man missing a limb, but it was surpassed in 1989 when rookie Jim Abbott, lacking the use of his right arm owing to a birth defect, leaped from the Michigan University campus to win 12 games for the Angels.

Most Successful One-Armed Player

Hugh "One Arm" Daily. Daily pitched in the National League, Union Association and American Association from 1882 to 1887. In 1883, pitching for Cleveland, he led the National League in bases on balls and threw a no-hitter against Philadelphia; the following year he led all Union Association hurlers in strikeouts. No known photographs of Daily in action have survived, but we know it was his left arm that was lacking and that, since he was a pitcher, he couldn't have worn a glove while in the field. Reportedly, Daily fielded hard-hit balls by first blocking them with a pad attached to his truncated left forearm.

Major-League Pitcher Overcoming the Greatest Handicap

Bert Shepard, a former minor-league pitcher, lost a leg after being shot down over Germany in World War II while serving as an Army Air Corps pilot. Outfitted with an artificial leg, he was signed as a coach by the Washington Senators in 1945. After pitching in several exhibition games, he made a relief appearance on August 14 in the regular-season game against the Red Sox and gave up only one run in five innings. Shepard, who came to bat three times during his relief stint, also classifies as the hitter overcoming the greatest handicap. In 1948, while managing the Class B Waterbury, Connecticut, club, he played several games at first base.

Most Successful Handicapped Pitcher, since 1901

Luther "Dummy" Taylor, a deaf-mute, won 21 games for the New York Giants in 1904 and 112 games over a nine-year career. One of only two deaf-mutes to play in the majors, after leaving baseball Taylor worked as a housefather at the Illinois School for the Deaf in Jacksonville, where he helped Dick Sipek, who was partly deaf, to become a good enough outfielder to play with the Cincinnati Reds in the middle 1940s.

Most Successful Handicapped AL Pitcher, prior to Abbott

Many players have had lengthy major-league careers despite missing toes and fingers, two Hall of Famers, Three Finger Brown and Red Ruffing, among them; Gray, Shepard and Daily were the only three who managed to play without a limb. But another Daley—Buddy Daley—pitched in the American League for 10 years with nearly as great a handicap. Daley had a withered right arm, the result of an injury incurred at birth, but was still able to win 60 games, plus one in the 1961 World Series.

Smallest Player

Eddie Gaedel, the midget Bill Veeck hired in 1951, stood three feet seven inches and weighed 67 pounds. Prior to Gaedel, there were a goodly number of fringe players who barely topped the five-foot mark, but the smallest player to play a full season in the majors was probably Dicky Pearce, listed as having been only five feet, three-and-a-half inches. The smallest player to become a star was Dummy Hoy, who was five foot four inches and weighed 148 pounds. Hoy was easily the most successful handicapped player of all time; not only was he diminutive but he was a deaf-mute. His dual handicap kept him from making the major leagues until he was given a chance in 1888 by Washington at age 26. He went on to play 14 seasons and compile over 2000 hits. Among the many other successful small players were Harry Chappas, five feet, three inches; Hugh Nicol, five feet, four inches; Davy Force, five feet, four inches; Willie Keeler, five feet, four-and-a-half inches; Sparky Adams, five feet, four-and-a-half inches; Freddy Patek, five feet, five inches; Albie Pearson, five feet, five inches; and Bobby Shantz, five feet, six inches but only 139 pounds. Special mention: Ernie Oravetz, an outfielder with the Washington Senators for two years in the 1950s, was not only five feet, four inches but also wore glasses.

Tallest Player Prior to Randy Johnson
Johnny Gee, who won seven games in the National League between 1939 and 1946, was six feet, nine inches—an inch taller than Gene Conley, the most successful tall player. Conley won 91 games for the Braves, Phillies and Red Sox in the 1950s and early 1960s. At one point in his career Conley also played with the NBA Boston Celtics during the winter months.

First Player to Wear Glasses
Will White, pitcher, 1877–86, and a 229-game winner

First Player in the 20th Century to Wear Glasses
Lee Meadows, St. Louis Cardinals, 1915

First Player Other Than a Pitcher to Wear Glasses
George Toporcer, St. Louis Cardinals, 1921

First Catcher to Wear Glasses
Clint Courtney, New York Yankees, 1951

First Winner of Most Valuable Player Award to Wear Glasses
NL—Jim Konstanty, Philadelphia, 1950
AL—Dick Allen, Chicago, 1972

First League Leader in a Major Hitting Department to Wear Glasses
NL—Chick Hafey, St. Louis, 1931, won the batting title.
AL—Bob Dillinger, St. Louis, 1948, had the most base hits.

First 20-Game Winner to Wear Glasses, since 1901
NL—Lee Meadows, Pittsburgh, 1926 (20–9)
AL—Mel Harder, Cleveland, 1934 (20–12)

First Player With One Eye

AA—Billl Irwin, Cincinnati pitcher, 1886

AL—Hi Jasper, pitcher for Chicago, Cleveland and St. Louis from 1914 to 1919.

NL—Tom Sunkel, pitcher for St. Louis, New York and Brooklyn from 1937 to 1944

Firsts by Black Players

The first black professional baseball player, according to most sources, was John Jackson, who played under the name of Bud Fowler with the Newcastle, Pennsylvania, club in 1872. During the next two decades a number of other black players made their marks in the minor leagues. The two best probably were second baseman Frank Grant, who broke in with Buffalo in the International League in 1886 and was called the "Black Fred Dunlap," and George Stovey, the leading pitcher in the International League in the mid-1880's. Grant and Stovey would have both undoubtedly played in either the American Association or the National League, along with many other black players who were their contemporaries, had they not encountered a latent prejudice that emerged and soon permeated all of organized baseball when the Toledo American Association club hired the Walker brothers in 1884.

First Black Major-League Player

Probably catcher Fleet Walker with Toledo in 1884, followed shortly thereafter by his younger brother Welday, an outfielder. Fleet actually made his professional debut with Toledo a year earlier when the team was in the Northwest League. In 50 games he batted .251, and the following season, facing stronger AA pitching, raised his average to .263, a highly respectable showing for a catcher in an era when many backstoppers hit below .200. The Walkers first attracted the attention of Toledo manager Charlie Morton while they were playing for Oberlin College. Welday did little in the few major-league games he played, but Fleet was good enough to keep another rookie catcher, Deacon McGuire, on the bench for much of the 1884 season. McGuire would go on to become the first player to catch in over 1500 major-league games, while Walker's big-league experience would last only a few months. Not all historians agree, however, that the Walkers were the first black major leaguers. In 1882 the Providence Grays signed catcher Sandy Nava and used him for the next three seasons to spell their regular backstopper Barney Gilligan. Nava, the first native San Franciscan to play in the majors, explained his dark complexion by saying he was Cuban. Whether or not Nava was actually black is impossible to determine now, but it may be significant that when prejudice began mushrooming later in the decade he was phased out of the major leagues.

First Professional Black Player in the 20th Century

Technically, it was Jimmy Claxton, who pitched briefly in 1916 for the Oakland Oaks in the Pacific Coast League, but once again there is lots of room for debate. In 1901 John McGraw tried to sign Charlie Grant, a black second baseman, to a contract with the Baltimore Orioles, who were about to begin their fledgling season in the American League. To circumvent the issue of Grant's color, McGraw presented him as Tokohama, a full-blooded Cherokee Indian, after he saw a creek with that name on a wall map in the Hot Springs, Arkansas, hotel where the Orioles were staying during spring training. But White Sox owner Charlie Comiskey, among others, saw through the hoax and blocked Grant's signing. A few years later, as manager of the New York Giants, McGraw attempted to hire a Cuban pitcher named Jose Mendez, but Mendez's nickname alone—"the Black Matty"—unified rival National League clubs against McGraw's integration effort. In 1911, however, the Cincinnati Reds successfully managed to sign two light-skinned Cubans named Rafael Almeida and Armando Marsans. Almeida failed to stick, but Marsans proved to be a pretty good outfielder and paved the way for other clubs, the Washington Senators in particular, to import more Cuban players. All of course were light-skinned, but there have been numerous light-skinned Latin players who, since the color line was finally broken, have acknowledged their ancestry was at least partially black. So it's safe to say, I think, that one or two black players besides the Walkers—and one hopes a lot more than that—found ways before 1946 to get past the color barrier.

First Black American Player Officially Accepted by Organized Baseball in the 20th Century
Jackie Robinson in 1946 with the Montreal Royals, Brooklyn's International League farm club. In his first game in organized baseball, on April 18, 1946, at Roosevelt Stadium in Jersey City, Robinson collected three singles and a home run off Jersey City's Phil Oates.

First Black American to Play in the National League
Jackie Robinson. He made his major-league debut with Brooklyn on April 15, 1947, against the Boston Braves, went hitless, and was 0-for-20 after his first five games. Robinson ended the 1947 season with a .297 batting average, led the National League in stolen bases, and was named Rookie of the Year.

First Black American to Play in the American League
Larry Doby, Cleveland, 1947. Used mainly at second base and as a pinchhitter, Doby hit only .156 in 29 games. Moved to center field the following spring, he hit .301 and sparked the Indians to their first pennant since 1920.

First Black American to Pitch in the National League
Dan Bankhead, Brooklyn, 1947. Used as a reliever in four games, he had an 0–0 record but homered in his first major-league at bat. In the fall he became the first black pitcher to play in a World Series—though not the first to pitch in one—when he got into a game as a pinch runner.

First Black American to Pitch in the American League
Satchel Paige, Cleveland, 1948. Paige was also the first black to win a game and the first to pitch a shutout, both occurring in his first major-league start. On October 10, 1948, he became, in addition, the first black to pitch in a World Series game when he worked two-thirds of an inning in relief.

First Black Pitcher to Win a World Series Game
Joe Black, Brooklyn, started and won the first game of the 1952 Series.

First Black Pitcher to Throw a No-Hitter
Sam Jones, Chicago Cubs, May 12, 1955, against Pittsburgh

First Black Pitcher to Win 20 Games in a Season
NL—Don Newcombe, Brooklyn, 1955 (20–5)
AL—Mudcat Grant, Minnesota, 1965 (21–7)

First Black Manager
AL—Frank Robinson, Cleveland, 1975
NL—Frank Robinson, San Francisco, 1981

First Black to Be a League Leader in Fielding Average
NL—Jackie Robinson, Brooklyn, 1948, led all second basemen with a .980 FA.
AL—Vic Power, Kansas City A's, 1957, led first basemen with a .998 FA.

First Black Umpire
Emmett Ashford, American League, 1965. Ashford retired in 1970 and died of a heart attack in 1980.

YOUR FAVORITE TEAM'S FIRST BLACK PLAYERS

(Teams in Existence Prior to 1961)

Team	First Black Player	Second Black Player	First Black Regular
Brooklyn Dodgers	Jackie Robinson, 1947	Dan Bankhead, 1947	Jackie Robinson, 1947
Cleveland Indians	Larry Doby, 1947	Satchel Paige, 1948	Larry Doby, 1948
St. Louis Browns	Hank Thompson, 1947	Willard Brown, 1947	Satchel Paige, 1952
New York Giants	Hank Thompson, 1949	Monte Irvin, 1949	Hank Thompson, 1950
Boston Braves	Sam Jethroe, 1950	Luis Marquez, 1951	Sam Jethroe, 1950
Chicago White Sox	Minnie Minoso, 1951	Sam Hairston, 1951	Minnie Minoso, 1951
Philadelphia A's	Bob Trice, 1953	Vic Power, 1954	Vic Power, 1954
Chicago Cubs	Ernie Banks, 1953	Gene Baker, 1953	Banks and Baker, 1954
Pittsburgh Pirates	Curt Roberts, 1954	Sam Jethroe, 1954	Curt Roberts, 1954
St. Louis Cards	Tom Alston, 1954	Brooks Lawrence, 1954	Curt Flood, 1958
Cincinnati Reds	Nino Escalera, 1954	Chuck Harmon, 1954	Frank Robinson, 1956
Washington Senators	Carlos Paula, 1954	Joe Black, 1957	Carlos Paula, 1954

Team	First Black Player	Second Black Player	First Black Regular
New York Yankees	Elston Howard, 1955	Harry Simpson, 1957	Elston Howard, 1959
Philadelphia Phillies	John Kennedy, 1957	Chuck Harmon, 1957	Pancho Herrera and Tony Taylor, 1960
Detroit Tigers	Ozzie Virgil, 1958	Larry Doby, 1958	Jake Wood, 1961
Boston Red Sox	Pumpsie Green, 1959	Earl Wilson, 1959	Willie Tasby, 1960

Note: The St. Louis Browns, the third team to integrate, never had a black regular until after the franchise moved to Baltimore (Bob Boyd, 1956). Paige, who had a 12–10 record in 138 innings in 1952, was the first black to see more than token action with the team.

Thompson and Irvin debuted in the same game with the Giants in 1949; ditto Banks and Barker with the Cubs in 1953 and Escalera and Harmon with the Reds in 1954.

Some sources credit Hairston with being the White Sox first black player in July 1951; by then, however, Minoso had already been with the team for several weeks.

FIRST BLACK LEAGUE LEADERS

Batting

Department	National League	American League
Batting Average	Jackie Robinson, Brooklyn, 1949	Tony Oliva, Minnesota, 1964
Slugging Average	Willie Mays, N.Y. Giants, 1954	Larry Doby, Cleveland, 1952
Home Runs	Willie Mays, N.Y. Giants, 1955	Larry Doby, Cleveland, 1952
RBIs	Monte Irvin, N.Y. Giants, 1951	Larry Doby, Cleveland, 1954
Stolen Bases	Jackie Robinson, Brooklyn, 1947	Minnie Minoso, Chicago, 1951
Hits	Willie Mays, S.F. Giants, 1960	Minnie Minoso, Cleveland, 1960
Runs	Frank Robinson, Cincinnati, 1956	Larry Doby, Cleveland, 1952
Doubles	Hank Aaron, Milwaukee, 1955	Minnie Minoso, Chicago, 1957
Triples	Hank Thompson, N.Y. Giants, 1952	Minnie Minoso, Chicago, 1951

Department	National League	American League
Bases on Balls	Jim Gilliam, Los Angeles, 1959	Dick Allen, Chicago, 1972 Roy White, New York, 1972
Strikeouts	Pancho Herrera, Philadelphia, 1960	Larry Doby, Cleveland, 1952
Total Bases	Willie Mays, N.Y. Giants, 1955	Tony Oliva, Minnesota, 1964

Pitching

Wins	Don Newcombe, Brooklyn, 1957	Mudcat Grant, Minnesota, 1965
Losses	Sam Jones, Chicago, 1955	Orlando Pena, Kansas City A's, 1963
Winning Pct.	Don Newcombe, Brooklyn, 1955	Mudcat Grant, Minnesota, 1965
Shutouts	Bob Gibson, St. Louis, 1962	Mudcat Grant, Minnesota, 1965
Strikeouts	Don Newcombe, Brooklyn, 1951	Al Downing, New York, 1964
ERA	Sam Jones, San Francisco, 1959	Luis Tiant, Cleveland, 1968
Bases on Balls	Sam Jones, Chicago, 1955	Earl Wilson, Boston, 1963
Complete Games	Juan Marichal, San Francisco, 1964	Fergie Jenkins, Texas, 1974

Awards

Rookie of the Year	Jackie Robinson, Brooklyn, 1947	Tony Oliva, Minnesota, 1964
Most Valuable Player	Jackie Robinson, Brooklyn, 1949	Elston Howard, New York, 1963
Cy Young	Don Newcombe, Brooklyn, 1956	Vida Blue, Oakland, 1971

Eagle-eyed Hitters

Ted Williams owned many records when he retired in 1960. Most have since been broken, but one that still stands is his career mark for the highest bases on balls average. Williams walked .208 percent of the times he stepped to the plate: Max Bishop, with a career bases on balls average of .204, is the only other player above .200. Williams also still holds the record for the most consecutive seasons as a league leader in bases on balls—six, from 1941 through 1949, excepting the 1943, 1944 and 1945 seasons when he was in the military service.

Most Seasons League Leader in Bases on Balls
    AL—11—Babe Ruth, last in 1933
    NL—6—Mel Ott, last in 1942

Most Seasons 100 or More Bases on Balls
    AL—13—Babe Ruth, last in 1934
    NL—10—Mel Ott, last in 1942. Ott also set an all-time major-league record in 1942 when he received 100 or more walks for he seventh consecutive season.

Most Bases on Balls, Season
    AL—170—Babe Ruth, New York, 1923
    NL—148—Eddie Stanky, Brooklyn, 1945
            Jimmy Wynn, Houston, 1969

Fewest Bases on Balls, Season, Minimum 500 at Bats
    AL—6—George Stovall, Cleveland, 1909; 565 at bats
    NL—9—Virgil Stallcup, Cincinnati, 1949; 575 at bats

Fewest Bases on Balls, 154-Game Season, League Leader in Bases on Balls
    NL—69—Hack Wilson, Chicago, 1926
    AL—90—Willie Kamm and Johnny Mostil, Chicago, 1925

Most Intentional Bases on Balls, Season
   45—Willie McCovey, San Francisco, 1969

Most Bases on Balls, Season, Pinch Hitter
   AL—18—Elmer Valo, Washington, 1960
   NL—16—Harry McCurdy, Philadelphia, 1933
            Merv Rettenmund, San Diego, 1977

Most Consecutive Games Receiving at Least One Base on Balls
   AL—22—Roy Cullenbine, Detroit, July 2 through July 24, 1947
   NL—15—Darrell Evans, Atlanta, April 9 through April 27, 1976

Most Bases on Balls, Game, Since 1893
   AL—6—Jimmie Foxx, Boston, June 16, 1938
   NL—5—held by many players, but Mel Ott of the New York Giants, who walked five times in a game on four separate occasions, is the only player ever to do it more than twice.

MOST BASES ON BALLS, CAREER, TOP 10

	Years Active	Bases on Balls
1. Babe Ruth	1914–35	2056[1]
2. Ted Williams	1939–60	2019
3. Joe Morgan	1963–84	1865
4. Carl Yastrzemski	1961–83	1845
5. Mickey Mantle	1951–68	1734
6. Mel Ott	1926–47	1708
7. Eddie Yost	1944–62	1614[2]
8. Darrell Evans	1969–89	1605
9. Stan Musial	1941–63	1599
10. Pete Rose	1963–86	1566[3]

[1]The only player on the top 10 list who was active before 1920.

[2]The only leadoff hitter on the list and also the only player with fewer than 2000 career hits.

[3]With so many modern players on the list, you should rightfully wonder where the eagle-eyed hitters of the game's early days rank. Ty Cobb, for one, is only 17th in career bases on balls. Willie Keeler, five feet, four-and-a-half inches and reputedly the most deft bat handler ever, is nowhere to be found—he had just 524 walks in 8594 at bats.

Most Intentional Bases on Balls, Game

5—Mel Ott, New York Giants, on October 5, 1929, in the second game of a doubleheader against the Phillies and the last game of the season. Ott began the game one home run behind the Phillies Chuck Klein in the NL home run derby; to ensure Klein of the crown, Phillies pitchers purposely passed Ott every time he came to bat.

First Player to be Given an Intentional Pass with the Bases Loaded

Nap Lajoie, Philadelphia Athletics, May 23, 1901.

Most Bases on Balls, Season, Team

AL—835—Boston, 1949
NL—732—Brooklyn, 1947

Fewest Bases on Balls, Career, Minimum 5000 at Bats

172—George Stovall, 1904–15; 5222 at bats

Fewest Bases on Balls, Career, Minimum 4000 at Bats

138—Jesus Alou, 1963–79; 4345 at bats. Alou also seldom struck out, so fielders, knowing that contact was imminent, were unusually alert when he came to bat.

Fewest Bases on Balls, Career, Minimum 1500 at Bats

25—Rob Picciolo, 1977–85; 1628 at bats. In 1979 Picciolo, probably the most impatient hitter in history, walked only three times in 348 at bats.

HIGHEST ON-BASE PERCENTAGE, CAREER, TOP TEN RETIRED PLAYERS

(Minimum 1000 games)

		Years Active	On Base Pct.
1.	Ted Williams	1939–1960	.483
2.	Babe Ruth	1914–35	.474
3.	John McGraw	1891–1906	.460[1]
4.	Billy Hamilton	1888–1901	.455
5.	Lou Gehrig	1923–39	.447
6.	Rogers Hornsby	1915–37	.434
7.	Ty Cobb	1905–28	.432

	Years Active	On Base Pct.
8. Jimmie Foxx	1925–45	.428
9. Tris Speaker	1907–28	.427
10. Ferris Fain	1947–55	.425[2]

[1]McGraw and Hamilton were two of the best players in the 1890s at coaxing walks. Even so, the generally inflated batting averages of the period resulted in their being higher on the list than they probably deserve to be.

[2]The one real surprise on the list. Eddie Yost, Ted Williams, Eddie Joost and Eddie Stanky were the recognized masters at drawing walks in the late 1940s and early 1950s, but Fain was just as good. One illustration of how difficult it is to achieve a career on-base percentage of .400 or better: Mike Hargrove is the only player to retire in the past 20 years with a .400 career on-base percentage. However, Wade Boggs is certain to retire with a career OBA well above .400, and Frank Thomas is also a virtual lock to top that figure.

The Four Most Interesting
Teams between 1942 and 1960

1946 BROOKLYN DODGERS
W-96 L-60
Manager: Leo Durocher

Regular Lineup—1B, Ed Stevens; 2B, Eddie Stanky; 3B, Cookie Lavagetto; SS, Pee Wee Reese; RF, Dixie Walker; CF, Carl Furillo; LF, Pete Reiser; C, Bruce Edwards; P, Joe Hatten; P, Kirby Higbe; P, Vic Lombardi; P, Hank Behrman; P, Hugh Casey.

With only one regular, Walker, hitting .300 and Higbe's 17 wins leading the pitching staff, the Dodgers nevertheless succeeded in ending the regular season tied with the heavily favored Cardinals. They were swept in the two-of-three pennant playoff series yet seemed on the verge of replacing the Cards as the NL's next great dynasty, especially when they won the flag in 1947. And while it's true that the Dodgers did win five more pennants in the next decade, many observers felt they perennially seemed to fall short of expectations—one game short each season, to be exact. The 1946 club set a painful pattern; it was the first of three Dodgers teams in a six-year period to lose the pennant by dint of dropping its last game of the season. Moreover, of the six World Series the Dodgers participated in between 1947 and 1956, they lost five of them, all to the Yankees. Had the Dodgers defeated the Cards in 1946 and thereupon started off their reign as the NL's top team by proving to themselves that they could win the big game, it is conceivable that they would have won 9 pennants in the next 11 years rather than 6, and that they, and not the Yankees, would have been the era's dominant club.

1950 BOSTON RED SOX
W-94 L-60
Manager: Joe McCarthy/Steve O'Neill

Regular Lineup—1B, Walt Dropo; 2B; Bobby Doerr; 3B Johnny Pesky; SS, Vern Stephens; RF, Al Zarilla; CF, Dom DiMaggio; LF, Ted Williams; C, Birdie Tebbetts; P. Mel Parnell; P, Ellis Kinder; P, Joe Dobson; P, Chuck Stobbs.

This team ought to have won its third consecutive pennant but instead ended up with three hairline misses, losing in 1948 to the Indians in a pennant playoff game, to the Yankees in 1949 by dropping the last two games after leading by one game with two to go, and to the Yankees again in 1950 despite hitting .302 as a unit and scoring 1027 runs, both figures records for the era. Analysts pointed to the season-ending broken elbow Ted Williams sustained in the All-Star Game as the reason the Sox came up short in 1950, yet it's hard to see how they could have needed more hitting. What did them in was a dreadful 4.88 staff ERA—a full run worse than in 1949—and an AL-high 748 bat on balls. Mel Parnell, with an 18–10 record, was the only pitcher whose ERA was under 4.00, but even Parnell failed to match his 1949 performance, when he won 25 games. The most exciting post-World War II offensive show, the Sox featured a utilityman, Billy Goodman, who wasn't good enough to crack the regular lineup even though he won the AL batting crown with a .354 average. It was sad to see them fade. The 1950 season was both their last gasp and McCarthy's; he quit in mid-campaign, the team slipped to a distant third in 1951 and then started tumbling swiftly toward mediocrity. Those who loved hitting in those years still talk wistfully about the classic Series matchup they never got to see—the Rex Sox versus the Dodgers.

1956 CINCINNATI REDS
W-91 L-63
Manager: Birdie Tebbetts

Regular Lineup—1B, Ted Kluszewski; 2B, Johnny Temple; 3B, Ray Jablonski; SS, Roy McMillan; RF, Wally Post; CF, Gus Bell; LF, Frank Robinson; C, Ed Bailey; P, Brooks

Lawrence; P, Johnny Klippstein; P, Joe Nuxhall; P, Art Fowler; P, Hal Jeffcoat; P, Hersh Freeman.

McMillan hit three home runs and Temple hit just two, but the rest of the team clubbed 216, spurring Reds fans to vote the entire starting lineup to the All-Star team the following year, and who can argue that their chauvinism was all that wrongheaded? Had Bell hit one more four-bagger, the Reds would have been the first team in history to have four 30-homer men; as it was, they tied the 1947 Giants' record for the most home runs in a 154-game season. Weak pitching did them in—what else?—but the Big Red Machine in the 1970s was pallid in comparison to this team. The only comparable club in recent history was the 1963 Twins.

1959 MILWAUKEE BRAVES
W-86 L-70
Manager: Fred Haney

Regular Lineup—1B, Joe Adcock; 2B, Felix Mantilla; 3B, Eddie Mathews; SS, Johnny Logan; RF, Hank Aaron; CF, Billy Bruton; LF, Wes Covington; C, Del Crandall; P. Warren Spahn; P, Lew Burdette; P, Bob Buhl; P, Joey Jay; P, Don McMahon.

Not a great team in any sense but good enough to have easily won its third consecutive pennant if Red Schoendienst hadn't been idled for the entire season by tuberculosis. Minus Schoendienst, the Braves tried seven players at second base before going with 35-year-old Bobby Avila in the stretch drive. Avila had been on the downside of the hill for about five years by then and played his last innings in the two-game pennant playoff loss to the Dodgers. Equally responsible for the Braves' also-ran status, though not as well publicized, was Haney's stubborn insistence on platooning lefty Frank Torre at first base with righty Joe Adcock. Torre hit .228 and had one homer; Adcock batted .292 and clubbed 25 homers. No one could fault Haney for the loss of Schoendienst, but his Adcock-Torre experiment played a large hand in his being replaced at the close of the season by Chuck Dressen.

First Relief Pitcher to Win 3 Cy Young
NL—Mike Marshall, Los Angeles, 1974
AL—Sparky Lyle, New York 1977 (7/18

Minor League Feats and Firsts

The first minor league was the International Association, formed in 1877. A second minor-league circuit, the League Alliance, also tried to get off the ground that same year but failed to complete its schedule. In 1879 the Western League, the first minor league to endure for a substantial length of time, was founded by Ted Sullivan. Five years later the International League, the oldest minor league still in existence, began as the Eastern League. By 1903 there were 13 minor-league teams, and ten years later the total had climbed to 40. In 1949, the peak of what is now seen to have been the golden age of organized baseball, there were 59 minor leagues in operation. Many were forced to close their doors, however, when major-league teams began televising games into their areas. Even the relatively stable Triple A leagues underwent severe upheavals once the two major leagues began transferring franchises in the 1950s and placed teams in Milwaukee, Kansas City, Baltimore, San Francisco and Los Angeles, all former AAA bastions. Major-league expansion in the 1960s and 1970s removed several more Triple A strongholds from minor-league circuits. In 1993 there were 17 minor leagues, about the same number there have been for the past decade, with four of them organized exclusively for first-year professional players.

First Minor-League Pennant Winner
The Tecumseh club of London, Ontario, which won the 1877 International Association flag with a team batting average of .191; St. Paul was leading the League Alliance that same year when it disbanded.

Biggest Crowd to See a Minor-League Game
In 1982, 65,666 fans turned out for an American Associa-

tion game between Denver and Omaha. The previous record had been held by the Miami Marlins, who drew 57,000 to the Orange Bowl on August 7, 1956, to watch Satchel Paige beat Columbus in an International League game. In 1941 the Jersey City Giants of the IL set a record when they sold 65,391 tickets for their home opener at Roosevelt Stadium, but since the park held only 40,000 all ticket buyers could not, and obviously did not, attend the game.

First Minor-League Team to Draw 1 Million Fans in a Season

The Louisville Redbirds in 1983 had a total attendance of 1,052,438.

Best Minor-League Team Ever

By almost unanimous consensus the 1919–25 Baltimore Orioles, who won an organized-baseball record seven pennants in a row after losing their star southpaw Ralph Worrell, who won 25 games in 1918 at age 19 and then perished in the flu epidemic. In 1919 the Orioles featured Max Bishop at second base; 23-year-old coal miner Joe Boley at shortstop; Fritz Maisel, down from the majors, at third base; Merwin Jacobson in center field; and Otis Lawry, the International League's top hitter with a .364 average. A year later Jacobson led the IL with a .404 mark, the league's highest average since 1897, and 20-year-old Lefty Grove was purchased from Martinsburg in the Blue Ridge League to augment an already solid mound staff that was led by Harry Frank, Jack Ogden and Jack Bentley. The 1920 Orioles won the IL flag by a record 26½ games and demolished St. Paul in the Little World Series.

In 1921 the Orioles won 119 games in a 168-game season and a record 27 games in a row. The team easily triumphed again in 1922 as owner-manager Jack Dunn continued to resist offers from major-league teams for his stars like Grove and Bishop, although he did auction off Jack Bentley to the Giants for $65,000 at the end of the season.

Good as Grove was, however, the club's best pitcher in 1923 was Rube Parnham with a 33–7 record and a season-ending string of 20 wins in a row. Parnham had earlier pitched briefly with the Philadelphia A's, but several other Orioles stars like outfielder Clarence Pitt, the IL's top hitter in 1923, and first baseman Clayton Sheedy, never got a major-league opportunity at all, in part because of Dunn's refusal to let go of his players until his price was met. At the conclusion of the 1923 season, with rival IL clubs tiring of the Orioles' dominance and pressing league officials to end the circuit's holdout against the major-league draft system that embraced the rest of organized baseball, Dunn finally agreed to sell Max Bishop to the A's for $25,000 but held on to Joe Boley until 1927 when the A's forked over $65,000. By then Boley was 31 years old and on the downside of his career.

Lefty Grove was more fortunate; he went to the A's for $100,600 after a 26–6 season in 1924. In his five years with the Orioles, Grove won 108 games and lost only 36, giving him a combined major- and minor-league record of 411 wins and 190 losses, easily the highest winning percentage in organized baseball history. Preparing for Grove's departure, the Orioles signed 24-year-old amateur pitching star George Earnshaw late in the 1924 season and kept him until the spring of 1928 when he too was sold to the A's—for $70,000. In 1925 Earnshaw, Jack Ogden and Tommy Thomas still gave the Orioles the most formidable pitching staff in the minors and spurred the club to its seventh straight pennant with help from outfielders Maurice Archdeacon and Twitchy Dick Porter, the IL's batting champ in 1924 and again in 1927. Earnshaw, Ogden and Thomas were all in the majors by the 1928 season, but Dunn clung to Porter until a few weeks before his death in October of 1928 when Porter was finally sold to Cleveland for $40,000. By the time Porter left the Orioles he was 28 years old.

A few last comments. Great as the Orioles were, they had one glaring weakness. At no time during their seven-year rein could Dunn manage to land a top-flight catcher. On that count, and that count alone, the team was below major-league caliber. Many observers believed that in all other respects the Orioles were better than most of the teams in the majors. The best evidence of that was that the A's, who wound up with the majority of Dunn's stars, emerged as the game's strongest team by the end of the decade.

Now, to answer your two questions. How did Connie Mack corral so many of those great Orioles? Well, it didn't hurt that he and Dunn were both Irish. The more interesting question is how did the A's come up with all that dough in the mid-1920s after suffering a long series of last-place clubs that drew hardly any fans at all and then, despite winning three pennants in a row, fall on such hard times by the early 1930s that Mack had to sell almost all of his purchased Orioles? There was a depression on, sure, but was that the whole story? It would take space that I don't have to spare in this book and a grasp of Mack's rather strange psychological makeup that no one may ever have to tell you why I don't think it was.

Second-Best Minor-League Team Ever

Ironically, while the Orioles were dashing to seven straight International League pennants, the Fort Worth Panthers of the Texas League won seven consecutive percentage championships between 1919 and 1925, losing the pennant only in 1919 in a split-season playoff to the Shreveport Gassers, the first-half winner, and then sweeping both halves of the league race for the next six years. Managed by Jake Atz, the "Cats" featured first baseman Clarence "Big Boy" Kraft, who collected 55 homers in 1924 (at the time a minor-league record) and 196 RBIs, still a Texas League record, then retired and was replaced in 1925 by Ed Konetchy, a former longtime major-league star. Atz's top moundsmen were Paul Wachtel, who won a Texas League-record 232 games, and Joe Pate. Many of the Cats stars saw big-league duty at some point in their careers, but apart from Konetchy only pitcher Wilcy Moore and infielders Jackie Tavener and Topper Rigney were significant performers in the majors.

Worst Minor League Team Ever

In 1926 Reading of the International League posted a 31–129 record and .194 winning percentage while finishing an organized baseball-record 75 games behind pennant-winning Toronto.

Most Recent Minor-League Team that Staked a Legitimate Claim to Being Major League

In 1945 Paul Fagan bought a one-third interest in the San Francisco Seals from owner Charlie Graham and immediately vowed to bring major-league baseball to San Francisco and soon—as soon, the fact was, as he succeeded in having the Pacific Coast League certified as a third major league. Fagan, the scion of a San Francisco banking family, was at first viewed as a crackpot by members of the major-league establishment, but his vision suddenly took on a frightening tinge of reality when he began implementing it. Fagan believed that the path to big-league recognition lay in getting all PCL teams to stop selling their star players to major-league clubs and start paying them big-league salaries. Accordingly, he saw to it that the 1946 Seals were better paid than many of their major-league counterparts and arranged for them to travel first class and stay in the best hotels. His reward in 1946 was a new minor-league attendance record, and San Francisco's reward was a Seals pennant behind pitcher Larry Jansen's 30–6 season and the stellar work of second baseman Hugh Luby, the PCL's Most Valuable Player that year, and first baseman Ferris Fain. Fagan's plan collapsed when other PCL club owners refused to match his largesse and undermined him by arranging working agreements with major-league teams that cemented the PCL's minor-league status, but for that one year the Seals looked, traveled, played and were paid like major leaguers. Ferris Fain, for one, balked when he was sold to the Philadelphia A's because he would have to take a cut in salary.

Number of Home Runs Babe Ruth Hit in the Minor Leagues

Just one. It came in 1914 while Ruth was with Providence, on loan from the Red Sox to whom he'd been sold earlier in the year by Baltimore. Ruth was the first great star that Jack Dunn auctioned to a major-league club. Dunn had hoped to hang onto Ruth awhile longer but encountered money problems when the Federal League put a team in Baltimore to compete with the Orioles. Why did Ruth go to the Boston Red Sox instead of Philadelphia like so many of Dunn's latter-day stars? Actually Ruth came very close to winding up with the A's. Connie Mack was given first crack at him but declined, and Dunn then contacted Boston owner Joe Lannin, who also happened to be Irish, as was the Red Sox player-manager, Bill Carrigan. John McGraw, of the same persuasion, felt betrayed when Dunn sold Ruth without first offering the Babe to the Giants.

All-time Organized-Baseball Record for Most Home Runs in an Inning

3—Gene Rye, Waco, Texas League, May 6, 1930, against Beaumont; Waco scored 18 runs in the inning and won 22–4. Rye, whose real name was Mercantelli, appeared briefly with the Boston Red Sox the following year and went 7-for-39, all singles.

Organized Baseball Record for Best Season by a Pitcher
Bob Riesener had a perfect 20–0 record in 1957 for Alexandria in the Evangeline League; in 1949, 40-year-old right-hander Orie Arntzen of Albany in the Eastern League posted a 25–2 record and was voted the Minor League Player of the Year by the *Sporting News*; but many consider Bill Kennedy's 1946 season with Rocky Mount in the Coastal Plains League to be the most awesome year ever by a minor-league hurler. Kennedy, who later had an eight-year major-league career, mainly as a reliever, had a 28–3 record, with 456 strikeouts and a 1.03 ERA in 280 innings.

Longest Hitting Streak in Organized Baseball History
Joe DiMaggio went on a 61-game tear for the San Francisco Seals in 1933 as a prelude to his major-league 56-game record, but the all-time record belongs to outfielder Joe Wilhoit of Wichita in the Western League, who in 1919 hit in 69 straight games. Wilhoit had earlier played four seasons in the majors and hoped his skein would earn him a return ticket, but it didn't happen.

Organized Baseball Record for Highest Season Batting Average (USA leagues only)
.441—Bob Schmidt, Duluth, Northern League, 1939

Organized Baseball Record for Most Home Runs in a Season
72—Joe Bauman, Roswell Rockets, Longhorn League, 1954. Bauman, a 32-year-old first baseman, also had 224 RBIs, hit an even .400 and had a .916 slugging average.

Organized Baseball Record for Most RBIs in a Season
254—Bob Crues, Amarillo, West Texas–New Mexico League, 1948. In addition, Crues hit .404 and had 69 home runs.

Organized Baseball Record for Most Home Runs in a Game
8—Nig Clarke, Corsicana, Texas League, June 15, 1902. That day Corsicana and Texarkana moved their game to Ennis and played in the morning to circumvent the Sunday blue laws then in force. In the tiny Ennis park, Corsicana eked out a 51–3 win as Clarke went 8-for-8, all four-baggers. The class of the Texas League at the time, Corsicana posted a record 27 straight wins in 1902, led by Clarke, who later made the major leagues as a catcher with Cleveland.

Organized Baseball Record for Best Single-Game Performance by a Pitcher

On May 13, 1952, Ron Necciai, pitching for Bristol, a Pittsburgh farm club in the Class D Appalachian League, threw a no-hitter and struck out 27 batters in a nine-inning game. That same summer a teammate of his, Bill Bell, threw three no-hitters, two of them back-to-back. By the end of the 1952 season Pittsburgh owner Branch Rickey, groping for ways to bolster the last-place Pirates, had rushed both Necciai and Bell up to the majors, where they were hit hard, lost confidence and never recovered it.

Best Minor-League Player Prior to World War II

Plenty of grist for argument here, but I recommend Ike Boone, who won five minor league batting titles in four different circuits—the Southern Association in 1921, the Texas League in 1923, the Pacific Coast League in 1929 and the International League in 1931 and 1934. With the San Francisco Mission Reds in 1929, Boone hit .407 and had 55 homers and 323 hits, leading the Pacific Coast League in all these departments; in addition, he collected 553 total bases, an all-time organized-baseball season record. A year later Boone was hitting .448 for the Mission Reds after 83 games when he was acquired by Brooklyn. Boone was among the rare minor-league *wunderkinds* who hit nearly as well in the majors—.319 in 356 games and .330-plus in his only two seasons as a regular. The rap against him was that he was slow afoot and a lackadaisical outfielder, the same rap borne by Smead Jolley and, to a lesser extent, Buzz Arlett, two PCL contemporaries of Boone's who many contend were his superiors. Another PCL star of the same vintage, Ox Eckhardt, was lightly regarded by major-league scouts because he fashioned his astronomical minor-league batting averages by hitting to the opposite field rather than with power.

Best Minor League Player since World War II

Rocky Nelson gets my vote. Unlike Boone, Arlett and Jolley, who hit well when given opportunities in the majors, and Eckhardt, who never got a real opportunity, Nelson was given chance after chance in the late 1940s and early 1950s but flopped so many times that it seemed inevitable he would finish out his career in the International League, where he won two Triple Crowns. But then Pittsburgh gave him one last shot in 1959 at age 34, and he responded with two good seasons while sharing first base with Dick Stuart, another minor-league sensation no one really believed would ever produce in the majors.

Career Home Run Leader, American Association
Bunny Brief, 256. Brief also led the PCL in 1916 with 33 homers. In 569 major-league at bats, he hit .223 and had only five homers.

Career Home Run Leader, International League
Ollie Carnegie, 258. Frozen for years in the high minors, Carnegie never played a single game in the majors.

Career Home Run Leader, Pacific Coast League
Buzz Arlett, 251. Arlett began as a pitcher with the Oakland Oaks and still holds the PCL record for the most putouts in a season by a pitcher, one of the many paradoxes in a career that was restricted to the minors for all but one year supposedly because of weak glovework. Like Brief, Arlett cut a swath in more than one Triple A league. In 1932 he twice hit four home runs in a game for Baltimore and led the International League with 54 homers and 144 RBIs. For how he did in his lone year in the majors, see both "Rookie Records" and "Final Season Records."

MINOR LEAGUE CAREER PITCHING LEADERS

Wins

		Minor-League Wins	Major-League Wins
1.	Bill Thomas	384	—[1]
2.	Joe Martina	349	6[2]
3.	George Payne	348	1
4.	Tony Freitas	342	25
5.	Alex McColl	332	4[3]

[1]Thomas collected 384 wins despite losing three full seasons, from 1947 through 1949, when he was declared ineligible after being implicated in an Evangeline League betting scandal.

[2]All six wins came as a 35-year-old rookie with the 1924 Washington Senators. His last major-league appearance was a perfect relief inning in the World Series that fall.

[3]Another longtime minor leaguer who got his sole major-league chance with a pennant-bound Washington team. McColl came to the Senators when he was 39—in time to pitch two perfect relief innings in the 1933 World Series.

Most Wins in One League
  295—Frank Shellenback, Pacific Coast League. Won 10 games as a 19-year-old rookie with the 1918 White Sox, then was cut when he started poorly in 1919 and never again made it out of the high minors.

Most Losses in One League
  235—Herman Pillette and Spider Baum, Pacific Coast League

Most Games Pitched
  1015—Bill Thomas

MINOR LEAGUE CAREER BATTING LEADERS
Highest Average

		Minor League	Major League
1.	Ike Boone	.370	.319
2.	Ox Eckhardt	.367	.192[1]
3.	Smead Jolley	.366	.305
4.	Don Stokes	.365	—

Most Home Runs

1.	Hector Espino	484	—
2.	Buzz Arlett	432	18
3.	Nick Cullop	420	11[2]
4.	Andres Mora	404	27
5.	Merv Connors	400	8
6.	Joe Hauser	399	79[3]

Most RBIs

1.	Nick Cullop	1857	67
2.	Buzz Arlett	1786	72
3.	Jim Poole	1785	140[4]
4.	Spencer Harris	1769	46
5.	Larry Barton	1751	—

Most Hits

1.	Spencer Harris	3617	94
2.	Harry Strohm	3486	—
3.	Eddie Hock	3474	1
4.	George Whiteman	3388	70
5.	Snake Henry	3384	14[5]
6.	Jigger Statz	3356	737[6]

Most Stolen Bases

	Minor League	Major League
1. George Hogriever	947	48[7]
2. Kid Mohler	776	0
3. Count Campau	682	63
4. Duke Reilley	676	5

[1]Holds the all-time organized-baseball record for highest career batting average, even ahead of Ty Cobb's, which is lowered by his minor-league stats.

[2]One of the last American Indian players, he also showed good power in the majors but struck out too much to stick.

[3]Both preceded and followed Jim Poole as the Philadelphia A's regular first baseman. A knee injury gave the job to Poole, but Hauser later reclaimed it for a time while Jimmie Foxx was still learning the position. Small for a first sacker, only five-feet, ten-and-a-half inches—but a bomber in the high minors. In 1930 Hauser hit 63 home runs for Baltimore and had 443 total bases, an International League record. With Minneapolis in the American Association three years later, he set an all-time Triple A record when he clubbed 69 homers.

[4]Became expendable when the A's acquired Jimmie Foxx and Hauser recovered from his knee injury. His 29 seasons in organized baseball are the most by any player who wasn't a pitcher. Among pitchers, George Brunet leads with 33 seasons, followed by Herman Pillette who, like Poole, put 29 years into the game. Brunet is an original. Apart from being the only minor-league pitching great to have a significant major-league career—324 games and 15 seasons—he's one of the small number of post-1950 players to forge a second life for himself in the minors after his major-league days ended. Still active in 1985 at age 50, Brunet had a 244–242 minor-league record in 668 games.

[5]Did poorly when the Braves gave him a crack at their first-base job in the early 1920s—but at least he got a chance in the majors, however brief. Larry Barton, who came along a few years later when the game was overstocked with good-hitting first basemen, never did.

[6]His 3356 hits all came with the Los Angeles Angels in the PCL. When his major-league total is added to them, he stands fourth on the all-time organized-baseball career hit list, behind only Pete Rose, Ty Cobb and Hank Aaron.

[7]Many of his minor-league seasons were in the 1890s before the modern rule for determining a stolen base was evolved. As a result, his true stolen base total is probably quite a bit less.

Switch Hitters' Records

In 1950 Jim Russell of the Brooklyn Dodgers became the first switch hitter in major-league history to homer from both sides of the plate for the second time in the same game. Russell's record lasted less than six years. On May 18, 1956, Mickey Mantle of the New York Yankees had his third switch-hit homer game. By the time he was done Mantle would have 10 of them and hold most of the other all-time switch-hit slugging records as well.

First Switch Hitter to Homer from Both Sides of the Plate in the Same Game
  AL—Wally Schang, Philadelphia, September 8, 1916, at Shibe Park off Allan Russell and Slim Love of the Yankees
  NL—Augie Galan, Chicago, June 15, 1937

First Switch Hitter of Note
  Bob "Death to Flying Things" Ferguson, New York Mutuals, 1871. Active in the major leagues until 1884, Ferguson was the first switch hitter to collect 1000 career hits.

First Switch Hitter to Collect 2000 Career Hits
  George Davis, Chicago White Sox, 1902. Davis collected 2688 hits altogether, the switch-hit career record until Pete Rose broke it in 1976.

First Switch Hitter to Collect 3000 Career Hits
  Pete Rose, Cincinnati Reds, 1978. In 1984 Rose also of course became the first switch hitter to make 4000 hits.

First Switch Hitter to Collect 100 Hits from Each Side of the Plate in a Season
  NL—Garry Templeton, St. Louis, 1979
  AL—Willie Wilson, Kansas City Royals, 1980

First Switch Hitter to Win a Batting Title
  AA—Tommy Tucker, Baltimore Orioles, 1889
  AL—Mickey Mantle, New York, 1956
  NL—Pete Rose, Cincinnati, 1968

SEASON BATTING RECORDS

Department	National League	American League
Batting Average	.362, George Davis, New York, 1893 .353, Willie McGee, St. Louis, 1985*	.365, MICKEY MANTLE, New York, 1956**
Slugging Average	.615, Ripper Collins, St. Louis, 1934	.705, MICKEY MANTLE, New York, 1956
Home Runs	38, Howard Johnson, New York, 1991	54, MICKEY MANTLE, New York, 1961
RBIs	134, GEORGE DAVIS, New York, 1897 128, Ripper Collins, St. Louis, 1934*	130, Mickey Mantle, New York, 1956*
Hits	230, PETE ROSE, Cincinnati, 1973	230, WILLIE WILSON, K.C. Royals, 1980
Doubles	51, PETE ROSE, Cincinnati, 1978	46, John Anderson, Milwaukee, 1901
Triples	27, GEORGE DAVIS, New York, 1893 19, Max Carey, Pittsburgh, 1923* 19, Garry Templeton, St. Louis, 1979*	21, Willie Wilson, K.C. Royals, 1985
Total Bases	369, Ripper Collins, St. Louis, 1934	376, MICKEY MANTLE, New York, 1956
Bases on Balls	116, Miller Huggins, St. Louis, 1910	146, MICKEY MANTLE, New York, 1957
Runs	140, MAX CAREY, Pittsburgh, 1922	133, Willie Wilson, K.C. Royals, 1980
Pinch Hits	22, Red Schoendienst, St. Louis, 1962	24, DAVE PHILLEY, Baltimore, 1961
Stolen Bases	110, VINCE COLEMAN, St. Louis, 1985	83, Willie Wilson, K.C. Royals, 1979

Department	National League	American League
At Bats	695, Maury Wills, Los Angeles, 1962	705, WILLIE WILSON, K.C. Royals, 1980
Strikeouts	126, Vince Coleman, St. Louis, 1987	160, MICKEY TETTLETON, Detroit, 1991
	126, Howard Johnson, New York, 1989	
Fewest Strikeouts (Minimum 500 ABs)	10, FRANKIE FRISCH, St. Louis, 1927	21, Buck Weaver, Chicago, 1919

*Record since 1901
**In 1956 Mantle became the only switch hitter ever to win a Triple Crown.
Note: Tommy Tucker of the Baltimore Orioles (AA) hit .372 in 1889, the all-time highest season average by a switch hitter.

First Switch Hitter to Hit for the Cycle
NL—Max Carey, Pittsburgh, June 20, 1925
AL—Mickey Mantle, New York, May 23, 1957

CAREER BATTING RECORDS

Department	Name	Years Active	Record No.
Batting Average	Frankie Frisch	1919–37	.316
Slugging Average	Mickey Mantle	1951–68	.557
Home Runs	Mickey Mantle	1951–68	536
RBIs	Mickey Mantle	1951–68	1509
Hits	Pete Rose	1963–86	4256
Doubles	Pete Rose	1963–86	746
Triples	George Davis	1890–1909	167
Total Bases	Pete Rose	1963–86	5752
Bases on Balls	Mickey Mantle	1951–1968	1734
Runs	Pete Rose	1963–86	2165
Pinch Hits	Dave Philley	1941–62	93
	Jerry Hairston	1973–88	93
Stolen Bases	Max Carey	1910–1929	738
At Bats	Pete Rose	1963–86	14,053
Strikeouts	Mickey Mantle	1951–68	1710

Most Unsung Career Record Held by a Switch Hitter
Don Buford grounded into only 33 double plays in 4553 at bats—a ratio of one to every 138 at bats, the best in history.

Great Batting Debuts

Late in the 1951 season the St. Louis Browns brought outfielder Bob Nieman up from Oklahoma City in the Texas
League. On September 14 Brownie fans watched him face
pitcher Mickey McDermott of the Red Sox and become the
first—and to date only—player to homer in his first two at
bats in the majors. Bert Campaneris of the Kansas City A's
is otherwise the only player in this century to hit two homers
in his initial major-league game—in his first and fourth at
bats on July 23, 1964. The first player to homer twice in his
inaugural game was Princeton Charlie Reilly, who did it
with Columbus in the American Association on October 9,
1889. Reilly, a switch hitter, played in five more games and
batted .478 before the curtain descended on the 1889 season. It was mostly downhill for him after his great debut—he
hit only .250 in an eight-year career—although in 1892 he
became one of the first three players in history to get a
pinch hit.

First National League Player to Homer in His Initial at Bat
    Bill Duggleby, Philadelphia Phillies, April 21, 1898.
Duggleby, a pitcher, did it up big, bringing home four runs
with his circuit clout. Nearly 90 years have passed since that
spring afternoon, but Duggleby remains the only player to
hit a grand slam in his first at bat.

Second Player to Homer in His First at Bat
    Johnny Bates, Boston Braves, April 12, 1906

First American League Player to Homer in His First at Bat
    Earl Averill, Cleveland Indians, April 16, 1929. Averill
was also the first future Hall of Famer to break in with a
homer. The only other Hall of Famer to debut similarly was

pitcher Hoyt Wilhelm of the New York Giants on April 25, 1952. He then played 20 years in the majors without ever hitting another home run and in fact collected just 45 total bases in 408 at bats.

Second Pitcher to Homer in His First at Bat
Clise Dudley, Brooklyn Dodgers, April 29, 1929

First American League Pitcher to Homer in His First at Bat
Bill Lefebvre, Boston Red Sox, June 10, 1938

First Black Player to Homer in His First at Bat
Dan Bankhead, Brooklyn Dodgers, August 20, 1947. It was his only hit that year and the only homer in his career.

First American League Black Player to Homer in His First at Bat
Gates Brown, Detroit Tigers, June 19, 1963

Only Expansion Team Player to Homer in His First at Bat in Team's Inaugural Game
Al Woods, Toronto Blue Jays, April 7, 1977, as a pinch hitter in the fifth inning

Only Players on Opposing Teams to Homer in Their First at Bats in the Same Game
Emmett Mueller, Philadelphia Phillies, and Ernie Koy, Brooklyn Dodgers, April 19, 1938

Winners of the "Three Musketeers" Award
On September 20, 1981, Gary Gaetti, Tim Laudner and Kent Hrbek of the Minnesota Twins all homered in their first-major league games, Gaetti's coming in his first at bat.

Most Unlikely Player to Homer in His First at Bat (Pitchers Excluded)
Shortstop Buddy Kerr of the New York Giants hit one out the first time he stepped to the plate on September 8, 1943. Five years later Kerr became the last Giants regular to play a full season in the Polo Grounds without hitting a single home run.

Most Significant Homer by Player in His First at Bat
Jay Bell, Cleveland Indians, September 29, 1986, off Bert Blyleven of the Twins. Bell's clout—on the first pitch he saw

in the major leagues—was the record-breaking 47th gopher ball Blyleven served up in 1986.

Winner of the "Not Easily Intimidated" Award

Facing Warren Spahn in his initial major-league game, on May 24, 1957, Cubs outfielder Frank Ernaga homered in his first at bat and then tripled his next time up against Spahn.

Greatest Debut by a Hall of Famer

On June 30, 1894, Louisville outfielder Fred Clarke introduced himself by clubbing five hits in his first game. The only other player to debut with a five-hit game was Cecil Travis of the Senators on May 16, 1933, in a 12-inning contest.

Players Who Got Four Hits in Their First Games

Ray Jansen, St. Louis Browns, September 30, 1910
Casey Stengel, Brooklyn Dodgers, July 27, 1912
Art Shires, Chicago White Sox, August 20, 1928
Ed Freed, Philadelphia Phillies, September 11, 1942
Spook Jacobs, Philadelphia A's, April 13, 1954
Willie McCovey, San Francisco Giants, July 30, 1959
Mack Jones, Milwaukee Braves, July 13, 1961
Ted Cox, Boston Red Sox, September 17, 1977
Kirby Puckett, Minnesota Twins, May 8, 1984
Bill Bean, Detroit Tigers, April 25, 1987
Delino DeShields Montreal Expos, April 9, 1990
Special Mention—Pitcher Russ Van Atta debuted with the Yankees on April 25, 1933, by collecting four hits in the process of shutting out the Senators 16–0.

The Five Greatest One-Game Wonders

First Place—The Houston Colt 45s started an all-rookie lineup on September 29, 1963, including outfielder Johnny Paciorek, who was a perfect 3-for-3, walked twice, scored four runs and drove in three. A back injury felled Paciorek in 1964, and he never worked his way back to the majors.

Second Place—Third baseman Ray Jansen of the St. Louis Browns went 4-for-5 on September 30, 1910, in his only look at major-league pitching.

Third Place—In 1933 catcher Aubrey Epps of the Pirates went 3-for-4 in his only big-league game and knocked in three runs.

Fourth Place—White Sox catcher Chuck Lindstrom, son of Hall of Famer Fred Lindstrom, tripled and walked in his lone game in 1958, then quit with a perfect 1.000 career batting average and a record 3.000 slugging average, breaking the old mark of 2.000 set in 1912 by Ed Irvin, another one-game wonder.

Fifth Place—In 1944 Steve Biras of the Indians went 2-for-2 in his only game, singling as a pinch hitter and then staying in the game at second base and singling again, giving him a 1.000 career batting average and two RBIs.

Catchers' Records

The period between 1942 and 1960 was a prime time for receivers. In 1942 Ernie Lombardi won a batting title, the last catcher ever to do so, and four years later Buddy Rosar became the first backstopper to post a perfect 1.000 fielding average. Furthermore, the 1951 season was the first in which catchers were chosen as the Most Valuable players in both leagues, something that has happened only one other time in history—at the close of the 1955 season.

SEASON BATTING RECORDS

Department	National League	American League
Batting Average	.394, JACK CLEMENTS, Philadelphia, 1895 .367, Babe Phelps, Brooklyn, 1936*	.362, Bill Dickey, New York, 1936
Slugging Average	.630, GABBY HARTNETT, Chicago, 1930	.617, Bill Dickey, New York, 1936
Home Runs	41, ROY CAMPANELLA, Brooklyn, 1953	37, Carlton Fisk, Chicago, 1985
RBIs	142, ROY CAMPANELLA, Brooklyn, 1953	133, Bill Dickey, New York, 1937
Runs	103, Roy Campanella, Brooklyn, 1953	118, MICKEY COCHRANE, Philadelphia, 1932
Hits	193, TED SIMMONS, St. Louis, 1975	192, Yogi Berra, New York, 1950
Doubles	42, Terry Kennedy, San Diego, 1982	42, MICKEY COCHRANE, Philadelphia, 1930
Triples	13, TIM McCARVER, St. Louis, 1966 JOHNNY KLING, Chicago, 1903	12, Mickey Cochrane, Philadelphia, 1928

Department	National League	American League
Total Bases	317, Roy Campanella, Brooklyn, 1953	318, YOGI BERRA, New York, 1950
Bases on Balls	125, GENE TENACE, San Diego, 1977	121, Darrell Porter, K.C. Royals, 1979
Stolen Bases	25, John Stearns, New York, 1977	36, JOHN WATHAN, K.C. Royals, 1982
Strikeouts	113, Randy Hundley, Chicago, 1966	126, RON KARKOVICE, Chicago, 1993
Fewest Strikeouts (Minimum 400 ABs)	14, Ernie Lombardi, Cincinnati, 1938	7, MICKEY COCHRANE, Philadelphia, 1927

*Record since 1901

Note: All catchers' seasons that contained 15 or more games at other positions are excluded, and where ties exist—i.e., between Kennedy and Cochrane for most doubles—the all-time record holder is considered to be the catcher who played the fewest games elsewhere. The lone exceptions are Fisk, Tenace and Porter, all of whom played more than 15 games at other positions but collected so many more home runs and bases on balls respectively than the runners-up to their league records that excluding them would result in recognizing a much lesser achievement.

Most Games, Career, at Catcher

2225—Carlton Fisk, 1969–93. Fisk lasted just long enough to break Bob Boone's old record of 2223 games.

Most Consecutive Games at Catcher

312—Frankie Hayes, Philadelphia A's and Cleveland Indians, October 3, 1943, through April 21, 1946

EVOLUTION OF SEASON RECORD FOR BEST FIELDING AVERAGE

	Team	League	Year	Average
Doug Allison	Hartford	National	1876	.881[1]
Pop Snyder	Louisville	National	1877	.910[2]
Pop Snyder	Boston	National	1878	.912
Pop Snyder	Boston	National	1879	.925
Silver Flint	Chicago	National	1880	.932
Charlie Bennett	Detroit	National	1881	.962[3]
Chief Zimmer	Cleveland	National	1896	.972

	Team	League	Year	Average
Malachi Kittredge	Boston	National	1901	.984
Ossee Schrecken- gost	Philadelphia	American	1905	.984
Johnny Kling	Chicago	National	1907	.987
Bill Bergen	Brooklyn	National	1908	.989
George Gibson	Pittsburgh	National	1912	.990[4]
Hank Severeid	St. Louis	American	1923	.993
Mickey Cochrane	Philadelphia	American	1930	.993
Shanty Hogan	New York	National	1931	.996
Bill Dickey	New York	American	1931	.996
Earl Grace	Pittsburgh	National	1932	.998
Buddy Rosar	Philadelphia	American	1946	1.000[5]

[1]The catcher for the 1869–70 Cincinnati Red Stockings, Allison was 30 years old by the time the National League was formed, and 1876 was his last season as a regular.

[2]May have been the best catcher of his era, but he jumped to the American Association in 1882, thereby sacrificing the disproportionate recognition that National League players have received from historians.

[3]Bennett had a .966 fielding average in 1888 but in only 74 games, fewer than the 60 percent of his team's games required to qualify as a fielding leader. Another catcher, Farmer Vaughn, fielded .969 in 1893, but included in his average were some 40 games he played at other positions.

[4]In only 94 games, just barely qualifying as the new record holder.

[5]Yogi Berra fielded 1.000 in 1958 but caught only 85 games. The National League record was set by Wes Westrum of the New York Giants when he fielded .999 in 1950.

Best Career Fielding Average
.993—Bill Freehan, 1961–76

Most Seasons League Leader in Fielding Average
AL—8—Ray Schalk, last in 1922
NL—7—Gabby Hartnett, last in 1937

Most Consecutive Errorless Games
148—Yogi Berra, New York Yankees, July 28, 1957 through May 10, 1959. During his streak Berra also set the record for most consecutive errorless chances—950.

Most Chances Accepted, Career
12,988—Gary Carter, 1974–92

Most Chances Accepted, Season
1221—Johnny Edwards, Houston Astros, 1969. That year the Astros' pitchers set the all-time season record for most strikeouts. All the one-game records for most chances accepted are similarly held by the batterymates of strikeout record-setters.

Most Assists, Season
NL—214—Pat Moran, Boston 1903; he did it while catching only 107 games.
AL—212—Oscar Stanage, Detroit, 1911

Most Seasons League Leader in Assists
AL—6—Jim Sundberg, last in 1981
NL—6—Gabby Hartnett, last in 1935
       Del Crandall, last in 1960

Most No-hitters Caught, Career
4—Ray Schalk; the last one was Charlie Robertson's perfect game on April 30, 1922

Only Catcher since Ernie Lombardi to Hit .300 or More Five Times
Thurman Munson, last in 1977

Most Recent Left-hander to Catch in a Major-League Game
Mike Squires, Chicago White Sox, last in 1980

Most Games Caught by Left-hander, Since 1901
43—Jiggs Donahue, Pittsburgh Pirates, 1901 (1); Milwaukee Brewers, 1901 (19); St. Louis Browns, 1902 (23).

Greatest Left-handed Catcher
Jack Clements, 1884–1900; .286 career batting average in 1157 games

Most Gold Glove Awards
10—Johnny Bench, 1967–83

Men for All Seasons

Heisman Trophy Winners to Play Major-League Baseball

On June 20, 1986, Auburn running back Bo Jackson, the number one pick in the NFL draft, spurned a reported $7 million deal with the Tampa Bay Buccaneers to sign a baseball contract with the Kansas City Royals. When Jackson was added to the Royals' roster in September, he became only the second former Heisman Trophy winner to play in a major-league game. Those of you who are up on your general sports history can not only name the first but also remember him as one of the last great single-wing tailbacks: Vic Janowicz, Ohio State, 1950. Janowicz won as a junior, then floundered through his final college season after the new Buckeye coach, Woody Hayes, installed a T-formation, which diluted his triple-threat talents. But the Pirates still thought enough of Janowicz's overall athletic ability to make him a bonus baby. After two undistinguished seasons with the Pirates in the mid-1950s, Janowicz opted to pursue a pro football career with the Washington Redskins instead, but that too ended when he was in a near-fatal auto accident.

Members of the Pro Football Hall of Fame Who Played Major League Baseball

There are seven: Jim Thorpe, Paddy Driscoll, Red Badgro, Ernie Nevers, George Halas, Greasy Neale and Ace Parker. None of them even remotely threatened to become a Hall of Famer in both sports, but all except Driscoll and Badgro had their moments. Parker homered in his first major-league at bat; Nevers surrendered two of Babe Ruth's 60 home runs in 1927; Thorpe drove in the winning run in the famous double no-hit game in 1917; Neale starred for the Reds in the 1919 World Series; and Halas played a few games for the 1919 Yankees in right field, a position that would be occupied the following year by Babe Ruth.

Only Member of Both the Pro Football and Pro Baseball Hall of Fame
Cal Hubbard, a star tackle in the NFL, was enshrined in Cooperstown as well as in Canton, Ohio, after a long career as a National League umpire. Hank Soar, Charlie Moran and George Magerkurth were other umpires who played in the NFL. Soar also coached the Providence Steamrollers in the Basketball Association of America, a forerunner of the NBA.

Only Major-League Manager Who also Served as Head Coach in the NFL
Hugo Bezdek managed the Pirates from 1917 through 1919 and later coached the Pittsburgh Steelers.

First Athlete to Play in Both a Rose Bowl Game and a World Series
Jackie Jensen, an All-American running back at Cal, played in the 1949 Rose Bowl game against Northwestern and later played for the Yankees in the 1950 World Series. Chuck Essegian, who teamed with Gary Kerkorian and Harry Hugasian to give Stanford the nation's best-ever Armenian backfield, in 1959 became the second athlete to play in both a Rose Bowl game and a World Series.

Other College Football Stars Who Played in the Major Leagues
The list is too long to mention everyone. Among those who had successful major-league careers were Jackie Robinson, Glenn Wright, Lou Gehrig, George Stirnweiss, Spud Chandler, Blondie Ryan, Billy Werber, Del Pratt, Luke Sewell, Ted Kluszewski, Sam Chapman, Eldon Auker, Lloyd Merriman, Frank Grube, Harvey Hendrick, Wes Schulmerich, Eddie Morgan, Rick Leach, Bill Carrigan, Red Wilson, Joe Sparma, Tom Haller, Galen Cisco, Harry Agganis, Carl Reynolds, Riggs Stephenson, Gee Walker, Kirk Gibson, Al Dark, Jake Gibbs, Bernie Allen, Ron Darling, Norm Cash and Frankie Frisch. Bud Metheny, Eric Tipton and Bob Finley were three outstanding running backs who played in the majors during World War II when rosters were thinned by the draft; Finley, the catalyst on the top-ranked SMU

Mustangs in 1935, was never more than a reserve catcher even with draft-depleted Philadelphia Phillies and might have done better to consider a pro football career. Among the others who achieved stardom on college gridirons but were only marginal major leaguers were Jesse Hill, Johnny Herrnstein, Tom Gastall, Dean Look, Bill Renna, Harley Boss, Chink Outen, Larry Bettencourt, Don Lund, Steve Korcheck, Carroll Hardy, Jerry Schoonmaker, Paul Giel, David Morey, Tom Yewcic, Haywood Sullivan, George Spencer and Mike Miley.

Athletes who Played Both Pro Football and Major-League Baseball Prior to World War II

In the 1920s and 1930s it was not at all uncommon for major-league baseball players to give pro football a whirl during the off-season. Among the many not previously mentioned who did were Chuck Dressen, Evar Swanson, Tom Whelan, Mike Wilson, Russ Young, Ab Wright, Ernie Vick, Pid Purdy, Jim Levey, Hoge Workman, Joe Vance, Al Pierotti, Ossie Orwoll, Garland Buckeye, Walt Masters, Bert Kuczynski, Red Smith, Walter French, Bob Fothergill, Charlie Berry and Walt Gilbert.

Athletes Who Played Both Pro Football and Major-League Baseball after World War II

Beginning in the early 1940s it became increasingly difficult to combine both sports. Until Bo Jackson came along and played for both the Royals and the NFL Raiders, the last athlete to play both pro sports on a major-league level was Tom Brown, an outfielder with the 1963 Senators who later played on the first Super Bowl winner, the 1966 Green Bay Packers. Among the other two-sport pro athletes since 1941 are Jim Castiglia, Steve Filipowicz, Pete Layden, Norm Bass, Rex Johnston, Cliff Aberson and Deion Sanders.

Only College Basketball All-American to Win a Major-League MVP Award

Dick Groat, winner of the National League MVP award in 1960, had been an All-American at Duke before he signed a bonus contract with the Pirates. Groat also played for a short time in the National Basketball Association.

Athletes Who Played Both Pro Basketball and Major-League Baseball Prior to World War II

Before World War II a number of major leaguers regularly switched their sliding pads for short pants during the winter months. Pro basketball was a loose operation then at best with a short season and lots of franchise transfers, but the biggest reason it was relatively simple for major leaguers to play both sports was that pro basketball teams hadn't yet become repositories for seven-footers. The game still had plenty of room for a good small man, and there were many of them, including several of the following two-sporters: Harry Riconda, Ralph Miller, Ed Wineapple, Bert Lewis and Rusty Saunders. No famous baseball names here, but Saunders, a four-game outfielder with the 1927 Philadelphia A's, was well-known among court followers. He played some 20 years on the pro circuit and was deep into his forties before he finally put away his sneakers.

Athletes Who Played Both Pro Basketball and Major-League Baseball after World War II

The most recent athlete to play both is Boston Celtics star Danny Ainge, who dropped baseball after being stymied by major-league pitching—he hit .187 in 88 games for Toronto in 1981. Others who have had dual careers since World War II are Frankie Baumholtz, Howie Schultz, Chuck Connors, Del Rice, Bill McCahan, Hank Biasetti, George Crowe, Irv Noren, Steve Hamilton, Cotton Nash, Dave Debusschere, Ron Reed, Johnny Gee, Dick Ricketts and Gene Conley. Conley was the best in both worlds; DeBusschere, the best pro basketball player also to play major-league baseball; and Reed, a teammate of DeBusschere's on the 1966–67 Detroit Pistons, the best baseball player also to play pro basketball.

Other Athletes for All Seasons

The best major-league baseball player who later became a pro golfer was Ken Harrelson, but Sammy Byrd, known in his days with the Yankees as "Babe Ruth's Caddy" because he often served as a late-inning defensive replacement for Ruth, was the best pro golfer who had been a former major-league baseball player. The greatest track-and-field athlete who also played major-league baseball was of course Jim Thorpe. Not far behind Thorpe, who was probably the greatest all-around athlete in major-league history, was Vern Kennedy, a 21-game winner for the White Sox in 1936 and winner of the decathlon at the Penn Relays in 1927.

Pinch-hitting Feats

Pinch hitters really began to come into their own in the 1950s, and no player did more to elevate their status than Peanuts Lowrey when he tagged 22 pinch bingles for the Cardinals in 1953. Close on Lowrey's heels followed Ron Northey, Dave Philley, Elmer Valo, Smokey Burgess and Jerry Lynch, and by the end of the decade most teams had at least one player whose sole job was to sit patiently in the dugout and await pivotal situations, usually late in a game, when his bat was needed.

First Pinch Hitter
Most sources agree that it was pitcher Mickey Welch of the New York Giants, on September 10, 1889, and that he fanned.

First Player to Be Used as a Pinch Hitter Twice in a Season
In 1891 the rules were changed, allowing teams to substitute for any player during a game at any time. Previously substitutes could be used only in the event of an injury or with the opposing team's permission, which was not always granted. The St. Louis Browns of the American Association used pitcher Jack Stivetts as a pinch hitter twice in 1891, but he failed to deliver on both occasions. Yet the choice was a sound one, for Stivetts went on to post a .297 career batting average, the all-time highest among pitchers who worked at least 2000 innings.

First Successful Pinch Hitter
Jack Doyle of the Cleveland Spiders. In a game at Brooklyn on June 7, 1892, he batted for pitcher George Davies and singled. Doyle was also successful in two of his next three tries in the role, but strangely was used as a pinch

hitter only five times in his long career and not at all in the six seasons he played in the 1900s. He retired in 1905 with a .301 career batting average and a .600 (3-for-5) batting average as a pinch hitter.

EVOLUTION OF THE SEASON PINCH-HIT RECORD

Player	Team	League	Year	Pinch Hits
Jack Doyle	Cleveland	National	1892	1[1]
John Sharrott	Philadelphia	National	1893	2[2]
Doggie Miller	Louisville	National	1896	6
Duke Farrell	Washington	National	1897	8[3]
Sammy Strang	New York	National	1905	8
Howard Wakefield	Washington	American	1906	9
Dode Criss	St. Louis	American	1908	12[4]
Ted Easterly	Cleveland-Chicago	American	1912	13
Doc Miller	Boston	National	1913	20[5]
Sam Leslie	New York	National	1932	22[6]
Peanuts Lowrey	St. Louis	National	1953	22[7]
Dave Philley	Baltimore	American	1961	24
Vic Davalillo	St. Louis	National	1970	24
Jose Morales	Montreal	National	1975	25

[1]Two members of the Pittsburgh Pirates, Princeton Charlie Reilly and none other than Connie Mack, also had pinch hits in 1892.

[2]Tied by several players between 1893 and 1896.

[3]The first great pinch hitter. Until he went 1-for-11 in 1904, Farrell was averaging close to .500 in pinch-hit roles.

[4]The only player to be a league leader in pinch hits four consecutive seasons (1908–11), Criss was also the first pitcher in the American League to serve as a pinch-hitting specialist.

[5]Pinch hitters have generally followed great seasons with poor ones. Miller was one of the rare exceptions. After setting a new season pinch-hit record in 1913, he averaged .343 as a pinch hitter the following year—yet was released by the Reds.

[6]Leslie's feat was so unpublicized that when Lowrey collected 22 pinch hits in 1953 many sportswriters thought he'd set a new record and that the old one belonged to Ed Coleman of the Browns, who made 20 pinch hits in 1936.

[7]Lowrey's season is viewed as something of a fluke because he went 9-for-69 as a pinch hitter in 1954-55, but check what he did in 1952—13-for-27—one of the best years ever among pinch hitters with more than 25 at bats.

.400 SEASONS BY PINCH HITTERS
(Minimum 35 at bats)

Player	Team	Year	Hits/AB's	Average
Ed Kranepool	New York Mets	1974	17–35	.486
Frenchy Bordagaray	St. Louis Cards	1938	20–43	.465
Rick Miller	Boston Red Sox	1983	16–35	.457
Jose Pagan	Pittsburgh Pirates	1969	19–42	.452
Gates Brown	Detroit Tigers	1968	18–40	.450
Joe Cronin	Boston Red Sox	1942	18–42	.429
Don Dillard	Cleveland Indians	1961	15–35	.429
Candy Maldonado	San Francisco Giants	1986	17–40	.425
Merritt Ranew	Chicago Cubs	1963	17–41	.415
Carl Taylor	Pittsburgh Pirates	1969	17–41	.415
Dave Philley	Philadelphia Phils	1958	18–44	.409
Frankie Baumholtz	Chicago Cubs	1955	15–37	.405
Jerry Lynch	Cincinnati Reds	1961	19–47	.404
Jerry Turner	San Diego Padres	1978	20–50	.400
Chet Laabs	St. Louis Browns	1940	14–35	.400

Best World Series Performance by a Pinch Hitter
Dusty Rhodes of the New York Giants hit a home run and two singles and netted six RBIs as a pinch hitter in the first three games of the 1954 World Series.

First Player to Hit a Pinch Home Run in a World Series
Yogi Berra, New York Yankees, October 2, 1947, at Ebbets Field. The first player to hit two pinch homers in a World Series was Chuck Essegian of the Los Angeles Dodgers in the second and sixth games of the 1959 Series, both coming at Comiskey Park.

First Player to Hit Pinch Home Runs in Successive Games
Ray Caldwell, New York Yankees, June 10 and June 11, 1915. Caldwell was a pitcher.

First Player to Hit Pinch Home Runs in Both Games of a Doubleheader
AL—Joe Cronin, Boston, June 17, 1943
NL—Hal Breeden, Montreal, July 13, 1973

Most Pinch Home Runs, Season
NL—6—Johnny Frederick, Brooklyn, 1932
AL—5—Joe Cronin, Boston, 1943

First Player to Homer as a Pinch Hitter in Three Consecutive Plate Appearances

Del Unser, Philadelphia Phillies, 1979. A year earlier Lee Lacy of the Dodgers homered in three consecutive official at bats but received a base on balls during his streak.

First Player to Homer As a Pinch Hitter in His First Major League at Bat

NL—Eddie Morgan, St. Louis, April 14, 1936
AL—Ace Parker, Philadelphia, April 30, 1937

Most Plate Appearances, Season, by a Pinch Hitter

NL—86—Merv Rettenmund, San Diego, 1977
AL—81—Elmer Valo, Washington and New York, 1960; including a pinch-hit record 18 bases on balls.

Lowest Season Batting Average by a Pinch Hitter, Minimum One Hit

.030—Chink Outen, Brooklyn, 1933; one hit in 33 at bats. An outstanding hitter in the minors—he rapped .341 for Jersey City in 1932—Outen batted .248 overall for Brooklyn in 1933, his lone test against big-league pitching.

TOP 10 IN CAREER PINCH HITS

		Years Active	Pinch Hits
1.	Manny Mota	1962–80	150
2.	Smokey Burgess	1949–67	145[1]
3.	Greg Gross	1973–89	143
4.	Jose Morales	1973–85	123
5.	Jerry Lynch	1954–66	116
6.	Red Lucas	1923–38	114[2]
7.	Steve Braun	1971–85	113
8.	Terry Crowley	1969–83	108
9.	Dennis Walling	1975–92	108
10.	Gates Brown	1963–75	107

[1]Gets my vote as the best ever. Even as a rookie he was a rugged pinch hitter—he had 12—and if it hadn't been for a terrible final season, he would have had a career pinch-hit average of well over .300.

[2]Lucas, a pitcher, in 1935 became the first player to make 100 pinch hits, and he held the career record for most pinch hits until 1965 when Burgess broke it. Ham Hyatt, in 1917, was the first player to collect 50 career pinch hits. In 1913 Hyatt also became the first player to hit three pinch home runs in a season.

First Player to Hit 10 Pinch Home Runs
Cy Williams. He retired in 1930 with only 41 career pinch hits, but 11 of them were homers.

Most Career Pinch Home Runs
20—Cliff Johnson. Playing for Toronto, he broke Jerry Lynch's old mark of 18 when he hit his 19th on August 5, 1984, against Oakland.

First Player to Hit Three Pinch Grand Slam Home Runs
Ron Northey, Chicago Cubs, September 18, 1950. Willie McCovey and Rich Reese have since tied Northey's record for the most pinch grand slams. In 1956 Northey hit .376 as a pinch hitter for the White Sox (15-for-39), remarkable in itself, but even more extraordinary is that 13 of his 15 hits came with two strikes on him.

THE TOP 10 CAREER PINCH HITTERS
(Minimum 100 Pinch-hit at Bats)

		Years Active	At Bats	Hits	Average
1.	Gordy Coleman	1959–67	120	40	.333
2.	Ward Miller	1909–17	110	36	.327
3.	Doc Miller	1910–14	120	39	.325
4.	Rod Carew	1967–85	124	40	.323
5.	Al Kaline	1953–74	115	37	.322[1]
6.	Tommy Davis	1959–76	197	63	.320
7.	Elmer Smith	1914–25	123	39	.319
8.	Estel Crabtree	1929–44	116	37	.319
9.	Earl Smith	1919–30	129	41	.318
10.	Bibb Falk	1920–31	114	36	.316[2]

[1]Hall of Famers, for the most part, have been undistinguished pinch hitters. Aside from Kaline, only Bill Terry and Red Schoendienst among those with 100 or more pinch-hit at bats have career averages of over 300.

[2]The difference of only 17 points between the 1st and 10th players on the list indicates how difficult it is to be consistently successful as a pinch hitter. Among players with 200 or more pinch-hit at bats, only Bob Fothergill, who hit exactly .300, was able to post a .300 career batting average.

Lowest Career Batting Average as Pinch Hitter, Minimum 300 at Bats
.204—Mike Jorgensen, 1968–85; 72 hits in 353 bats

Lowest Career Batting Average as Pinch Hitter, Minimum 200 at Bats
  .176—Russ Snyder, 1959–70; 49 hits in 278 at bats

THE 10 WORST PINCH HITTERS OF ALL TIME
(Minimum 100 Pinch-hit at Bats)

		Years Active	At Bats	Hits	Average
1.	Ivan Murrell	1963–74	180	21	.117
2.	Ted Kubiak	1967–76	123	15	.122
3.	Al Zarilla	1943–53	120	15	.125
4.	Woody Held	1954–69	147	19	.129
5.	Lou Klimchock	1958–70	161	21	.130
6.	J. C. Martin	1959–72	109	16	.148
7.	Dick Nen	1963–70	102	15	.147
8.	Hector Cruz	1973–82	128	19	.148
9.	Billy Klaus	1952–63	120	18	.150
10.	Roger Repoz	1964–72	133	20	.150

Cy Young Award Winners

The Cy Young Award was originated in 1956. It was initially intended to honor only the top major-league pitcher each season, but by 1967 the feeling that the best pitcher in each league should be honored yearly had gained sway, and a second award was added.

First Cy Young Winner
Don Newcombe, Brooklyn Dodgers, 1956

First Left-hander to Win a Cy Young
Warren Spahn, Milwaukee Braves, 1957

First American League Pitcher to Win a Cy Young
Bob Turley, New York Yankees, 1958

First Cy Young Winner for a Team Other Than a Pennant Winner
NL—Don Drysdale, Los Angeles, 1962
AL—Dean Chance, Los Angeles, 1964

First to Win Two Cy Youngs
Sandy Koufax, Los Angeles Dodgers, 1965. When he won again in 1966, Koufax also became the first three-time winner.

Other Three-Time Winners
NL—Tom Seaver, New York Mets, 1969, 1973 and 1975
AL—Jim Palmer, Baltimore, 1973, 1975 and 1976
AL—Roger Clemens, Boston, 1986, 1987, 1991

Only Four-Time Winner
Steve Carlton, Philadelphia Phillies, 1972, 1977, 1980 and 1982. When he won in 1972, Carlton also became the only pitcher to cop the award while playing for a last-place team.

First Relief Pitcher to Win a Cy Young
NL—Mike Marshall, Los Angeles, 1974
AL—Sparky Lyle, New York, 1977

Only Rookie to Win a Cy Young
Fernando Valenzuela, Los Angeles Dodgers, 1981

Youngest Cy Young Winner
NL—Dwight Gooden, New York Mets, 1985, age 20; 15 days younger than Valenzuela the year he won
AL—Bret Saberhagen, Kansas City Royals, 1985, age 21

Oldest Cy Young Winner
AL—Early Wynn, Chicago, 1959, age 39
NL—Steve Carlton, Philadelphia, 1982, age 37

Most Wins by Starting Pitcher Who Won a Cy Young
AL—31—Denny McLain, Detroit, 1968
NL—27—Steve Carlton, Philadelphia, 1972

Fewest Wins by Starting Pitcher Who Won a Cy Young, 1981 Excepted
AL—18—Pete Vuckovich, Milwaukee, 1982; Roger Clemens, Boston, 1991
NL—18—Mike Scott, Houston, 1986

Lowest ERA by Cy Young Winner
AL—1.04—Rollie Fingers, Milwaukee, 1981
NL—1.12—Bob Gibson, St. Louis, 1968

Highest ERA by Cy Young Winner
AL—3.66—LaMarr Hoyt, Chicago, 1983
NL—3.12—Bob Gibson, St. Louis, 1970

Only Pitcher to Win a Cy Young after Being Traded in Midseason
Rick Sutcliffe, Chicago Cubs, 1984. Sutcliffe, who started the year with Cleveland, is also the only winner to play in both leagues in the same season.

25-Game Winners Who Failed to Win a Cy Young
NL—Juan Marichal, San Francisco, and on three different occasions, no less—1963, 1966 and 1968

AL—Jim Katt, Minnesota, 1966; Mickey Lolich, Detroit, 1971

Only Pitcher to Win a Cy Young in Both Leagues
Gaylord Perry, Cleveland (AL), 1972; San Diego (NL), 1978

AL—Jim Katz, Minnesota, 1306; Mickey Lolich, Detroit,
1971, ...

Once a century ...

In the National League, ... C, D, E, H, W, ... Sam Dugan 418, a ...

Batters' Strikeout Records

In 1956 outfielder Jim Lemon of the Washington Senators fanned 138 times, setting a new all-time record. Four years later Mickey Mantle of the Yankees collected his 1000th strikeout in only his 10th season, and another Senator, Harmon Killebrew, completed his second of a record six straight seasons in which he fanned over 100 times. Twenty years later Lemon, Mantle and Killebrew would no longer hold any major season or career strikeout records, yet they still loom today as probably the three leading harbingers of the home-run-or-bust syndrome that had already begun to permeate the game by the late 1950s.

The National League began keeping accurate batters' strikeout stats in 1910, and the American League followed suit three years later. From 1876 to 1896 the National League had counted batters' strikeouts and then, for no overwhelming reason, ceased doing it for the next 14 years. The American Association kept track of the batters' strikeouts in only 2 of its 10 seasons as a major league—1889 and again in 1891. Records of batters' strikeouts are also available for the lone Players League season in 1890.

Since foul balls were not universally counted as strikes until 1903, and batters received four strikes as late as 1887, the natural assumption is that strikeouts in the game's early years were relatively infrequent. But the stats that are available to us indicate otherwise. In 1886, with the mound still only 50 feet from the plate and pitchers now allowed to throw overhand, Matty Kilroy, a rookie left-hander with the Baltimore Orioles in the American Association, fanned 513 hitters. An individual breakdown of Kilroy's victims is impossible to reconstruct a century later, but Tom Brown, rightfielder for the Pittsburgh Alleghenies, was quite likely his main one. Brown led the Players League in fanning the air in 1890, the American Association in 1891 and the National League in three of the next four seasons. Even without the strikeout totals from 6 of the 16 years he played, Brown finished in 1898 with 708 whiffs. Including his six lost years, he probably struck out around 1,100 times, making him the only player to top 1,000 until Babe Ruth came along.

Chronology of Significant Strikeout Milestones

1884—Sam Wise, shortstop for the Boston Red Stockings, struck out 104 times, a record that stood until 1914.

1887—John Morrill of the Boston Red Stockings became the first player to strike out 500 times in his career.

1892—Tom Brown, playing with Louisville in the National League, became the first player to strike out 90 or more times two years in a row.

1892—Pud Galvin concluded his career with 630 strikeouts in only 2702 at bats; a pitcher, Galvin sometimes played the outfield between mound assignments and had a .202 batting average despite the frequency with which he fanned.

1930—Babe Ruth became the first player to strike out 1000 times in his career

1932—Bruce Campbell of the St. Louis Browns struck out 104 times, the first to top 100 since 1914.

1934—Harlond Clift of the Browns became the first third baseman to strike out 100 or more times in a season.

1935—First baseman Dolf Camilli of the Phillies became the first National Leaguer since 1884 to strike out 100 times in a season.

1937—Frank Crosetti of the Yankees became the first shortstop to strike out 100 or more times in a season.

1940—Chet Ross of the Boston Braves set a new rookie strikeout record when he fanned 127 times.

1949—The last season in which neither league had a player who struck out 100 times.

1958—Harry Anderson of the Phillies topped the National League with 95 strikeouts, the last league leader to fan less than 100 times.

1963—John Bateman of the Houston Colt 45s became the first catcher to fan 100 or more times in a season.

1966—Mickey Mantle of the Yankees became the first player to fan 1500 times.

1966—George Scott of the Boston Red Sox set an American League rookie strikeout record by fanning 152 times.

1978—In his 11th season Bobby Bonds of the Texas Rangers struck out for the 1500th time, the quickest any player has ever reached 1500 K's.

1978—Pirates leadoff hitter Omar Moreno had only two home runs yet struck out 104 times.

1979—Lou Brock retired with 1730 strikeouts and only 149 home runs, further proof that it isn't only sluggers who have fallen prey to the whiff syndrome.

1983—Reggie Jackson of the Angels became the first player to strike out 2000 times.

1984—Juan Samuel of the Phillies fanned 168 times, setting an all-time rookie record.

1986—Pete Incaviglia of the Rangers fanned 185 times to set both a new all-time rookie and American League record, José Canseco of the A's (175) and Danny Tartabull of the Mariners (157) also topped George Scott's old AL rookie mark.

1987—Rob Deer of the Brewers K's 186 times to set a new American League record.

EVOLUTION OF BATTERS' SEASON STRIKEOUT RECORD
(Since 1913)

	Team	League	Year	K's
Danny Moeller	Washington	American	1913	103[1]
Gus Williams	St. Louis	American	1914	120
Vince DiMaggio	Boston	National	1938	134
Jim Lemon	Washington	American	1956	138
Jake Wood	Detroit	American	1961	141[2]
Harmon Killebrew	Minnesota	American	1962	142
Dave Nicholson	Chicago	American	1963	175[3]
Bobby Bonds	San Francisco	National	1969	187
Bobby Bonds	San Francisco	National	1970	189

[1]The 1913 season was the first in which both leagues began keeping complete and official strikeout records. Moeller was the first documented player to fan 100 times in a season since Sam Wise in 1884.

[2]Also broke Chet Ross's rookie record in 1961; the new mark lasted only until 1966.

[3]Nicholson fanned 573 times in 1419 career at bats—a strikeout average of .404. Counting only those times his bat made contact, he hit .356, making him an even more exciting player than Dave Kingman or Reggie Jackson, if they happen to be your brand of excitement. Kingman's strikeout average

at retirement was .272; Jackson's was a mere .263. They rank one and two as the easiest strikeout victims among modern players with over 5000 career at bats, but in comparison to Nicholson they both seem like Joe Sewell. But before we get to Sewell and the other players at the opposite end of the spectrum from Nicholson, Kingman and Jackson, consider this: Through the 1992 season 105 players had topped 1000 career strikeouts, but only two of them—Babe Ruth and Jimmie Foxx—finished their careers prior to 1959.

TOP 10 IN CAREER STRIKEOUTS

		Years Active	K's
1.	Reggie Jackson	1967–87	2597
2.	Willie Stargell	1961–82	1936
3.	Mike Schmidt	1972–89	1883
4.	Tony Perez	1964–86	1867[1]
5.	Dave Kingman	1971–86	1816
6.	Bobby Bonds	1968–81	1757
7.	Dale Murphy	1976–92	1733
8.	Lou Brock	1961–79	1730[1]
9.	Mickey Mantle	1951–68	1710
10.	Harmon Killebrew	1954–75	1699

[1]Never a league leader in K's.

THE 10 HARDEST BATTERS TO STRIKE OUT

(Minimum 10 Seasons since 1901)

		Years Active	AB's	K's	AB/K Ratio
1.	Joe Sewell	1920–33	7132	114	63 to 1
2.	Lloyd Waner	1927–45	7732	173	45 to 1[1]
3.	Nellie Fox	1947–65	9232	216	43 to 1
4.	Tommy Holmes	1942–52	4992	122	41 to 1[2]
5.	Tris Speaker	1907–28	7899	220	36 to 1[3]
6.	Stuffy McInnis	1909–27	6667	189	35 to 1
7.	Andy High	1922–34	4440	130	34 to 1
8.	Sam Rice	1915–34	9269	275	34 to 1
9.	Frankie Frisch	1919–37	9112	272	34 to 1
10.	Dale Mitchell	1946–56	3984	119	34 to 1

[1]As a part-time outfielder and pinch hitter with the Pirates, Braves and Reds in 1941, Waner made over 230 plate appearances without striking out a single time.

[2]In 1945 Holmes led the National League in home runs with 28 and in fewest strikeouts with nine, the only such double winner in history.

[3]Speaker's and McInnis's stats prior to 1913 are excluded because their strikeout totals for their earlier seasons are unavailable.

The Five Most Remarkable Batters' Strikeout Feats in This Century

First Place—Tommy Holmes's all-time record double win in 1945

Second Place—Ted Williams hit 521 career home runs and fanned only 709 times.

Third Place—Joe DiMaggio hit 361 career home runs and fanned only 369 times.

Fourth Place—Joe Sewell's last strikeout in the 1930 season came on May 26 when White Sox lefty Pat Caraway zapped him twice in the same game. The only other pitcher ever to fan Sewell twice in a game was the equally obscure Cy Warmoth, who did it in 1923. Warmoth had a mere 54 strikeouts in his career. In 1931 Caraway totaled only 55 strikeouts in 220 innings.

Fifth Place—Nellie Fox played 98 consecutive games in 1958 without striking out, breaking the old record of 89 games, set in 1932 by third baseman Carey Selph of the White Sox shortly before he was released.

Special Mention—In 1935 catcher Lee Head of Knoxville in the Southern Association fanned only one time in 122 games and 402 at bats.

World Series Play: 1942–60

FRANCHISE SUMMARY

Team	League	WS Record Through 1960	Last Year in WS
Los Angeles	National	1–0	1959
Boston	American	5–1	1946
New York	American	18–7	1960
St. Louis	National	6–3	1946
Cleveland	American	2–1	1954
Cincinnati	National	2–1	1940
Pittsburgh	National	3–2	1960
Chicago	American	2–2	1959
Milwaukee	National	1–1	1958
Washington	American	1–2	1933
Detroit	American	2–5	1945
Chicago	National	2–8	1945
Philadelphia	National	0–2	1950

Became Defunct between 1942 and 1960

Team	League	WS Record	Last Year
Philadelphia	American	5–3	1931
Boston	National	1–1	1948
New York	National	5–9	1954
Brooklyn	National	1–8	1956
St. Louis	American	0–1	1944

Yearly Highlights
1942—St Louis (NL) defeated New York (AL) 4 games to 1

After dropping the Series opener, the Cards got two complete-game wins from rookie Johnny Beazley, plus a shutout from Ernie White, and took the next four games to hand the Yankees their first Series loss since 1926.

1943—New York (AL) defeated St. Louis (NL) 4 games to 1

The Yankees' retaliation for the 1942 wipeout featured two superbly pitched games by Spud Chandler, the AL's MVP in 1943.

1944—St. Louis (NL) defeated St. Louis (AL) 4 games to 2

The last series to be played entirely in one stadium—antiquated Sportsman's Park—was also the Browns' one and only fall appearance. Their pitchers allowed only 16 runs in the six games, but Cardinals pitchers gave up just 12.

1945—Detroit (AL) defeated Chicago (NL) 4 games to 3

Hal Newhouser of the Tigers had a Series ERA of 6.10 but won two games, including the clincher. Hank Borowy of the Cubs became the first pitcher since Jack Coombs in 1916 to win a Series game in both leagues.

1946—St. Louis (NL) defeated Boston (AL) 4 games to 3

Considered one of the great Series, but only the first and last games were tight. Moreover, the two stars, Ted Williams and Stan Musial, hit .200 and .222 respectively. But Harry Brecheen of the Cardinals won three games, and Enos Slaughter tallied the run that won the Series in the eighth inning of Game Seven by scoring all the way from first base on Harry Walker's single when Red Sox shortstop Johnny Pesky hesitated a fraction of a second before relaying Leon Culberson's throw to the plate.

1947—New York (AL) defeated Brooklyn (NL) 4 games to 3

The first Series to be televised. The opener drew a record 73,365 to Yankee Stadium as Guy Lombardo and his orchestra entertained and Met Opera soprano Helen Jepson sang the national anthem. Although sloppily played for the most part, this Series ranks among the most exciting because of two events: Bill Bevens's near no-hitter in Game Five and Al Gionfriddo's catch of Joe DiMaggio's 415-foot drive the following day with two Yankees aboard.

1948—Cleveland (AL) defeated Boston (NL) 4 games to 2

The last Series until 1967 that did not include either a New York team or a former New York team. The Braves won the opener 1–0 on a single by Tommy Holmes, which drove home Phil Masi from second base after Masi had seemingly been picked off in a carefully timed play between Indians pitcher Bob Feller and shortstop Lou Boudreau. It was the closest Feller would ever come to a Series victory. The fifth game, in Cleveland, drew an all-time Series record crowd of 86,288.

1949—New York (AL) defeated Brooklyn (NL) 4 games to 1

The 1949 Series also began with a 1–0 game, won by the Yankees on Tommy Henrich's homer leading off the bottom of the ninth inning. It was the closest Don Newcombe of the Dodgers would ever come to a Series victory. Brooklyn's lone bright spot came in Game Two when Preacher Roe turned the tables on the Yankees and blanked them 1–0.

1950—New York (AL) defeated Philadelphia (NL) 4 games to 0

Phillies manager Eddie Sawyer pulled the biggest Series surprise since Connie Mack started Howard Ehmke in the 1929 opener when he named reliever Jim Konstanty to start the lid-lifter. But for the third straight year the Series began with a 1–0 game, won once again by the Yankees behind Vic Raschi. Although swept, the Phils were in every game except the last one until the final out.

1951—New York (AL) defeated New York (NL) 4 games to 2

The Giants, sparked by Eddie Stanky, won two of the first three games but then fell prey to Joe DiMaggio, playing in his last Series, and a 13-run assault in Game Five.

1952—New York (AL) defeated Brooklyn (NL) 4 games to 3

The Dodgers went up three games to two, but superlative relief pitching by Allie Reynolds helped the Yankees snatch the last two contests. Reynolds also pitched a 2–0 shutout in Game Four.

1953—New York (AL) defeated Brooklyn (NL) 4 games to 2

Billy Martin became the only player to make 12 hits in a 6-game Series and drove in the winning run in the ninth inning of the last game. The Dodgers became the first team to hit .300 in a Series and lose.

1954—New York (NL) defeated Cleveland (AL) 4 games to 0

Dusty Rhodes of the Giants delivered three game-winning hits, two of them as a pinch hitter, and Willie Mays broke hearts all over Cleveland when he robbed Vic Wertz of a probable game-winning two-run triple with a back-to-the-plate catch in the eighth inning of the opener.

1955—Brooklyn (NL) defeated New York (AL) 4 games to 3

In their eighth try the Dodgers finally managed to win their first and only Series while in Brooklyn. The hero was Johnny Podres with two complete-game victories, including a 2–0 shutout in the finale.

1956—New York (AL) defeated Brooklyn (NL) 4 games to 3

Don Larsen's perfect game gave the Yankees a 3–2 lead in the Series, but Clem Labine pitched a brilliant 10-inning 1–0 win for the Dodgers the following day, setting up what promised to be a highly dramatic final game. It disappointed—the Yankees won 9–0 behind Johnny Kucks—which is why this Series, aside from Larsen's perfect game, is seldom mentioned among the great ones even though it was Brooklyn's last fall appearance.

1957—Milwaukee (NL) defeated New York (AL) 4 games to 3

Lew Burdette of the Braves pitched three complete-game victories, the last two of them shutouts, and Hank Aaron had 11 hits and seven RBIs.

1958—New York (AL) defeated Milwaukee (NL) 4 games to 3

Down three games to one, the Yankees beat Burdette twice and Warren Spahn once to become the first team since the Pirates in 1925 to come back from so large a Series deficit. Bob Turley pitched a 7–0 shutout in Game Five, saved Game Six and then won the final game with a six-and-two-thirds-inning relief stint.

1959—Los Angeles (NL) defeated Chicago (AL) 4 games to 2

The first Series involving a West Coast team and the last one involving a Chicago team. Ted Kluszewski provided most of the White Sox offense with three homers and 10 RBIs but could do little with Dodgers relief ace Larry Sherry, who won two games and saved the other two L.A. victories. Charlie Neal of the Dodgers knocked in six runs and led all batters with 10 hits.

1960—Pittsburgh (NL) defeated New York (AL) 4 games to 3

For the first time a seven-game Series ended with a home run when Bill Mazeroski of the Pirates led off the bottom of the ninth inning by depositing a Ralph Terry pitch over the Forbes Field left-field wall. In his last World Series as a manager, Casey Stengel saw his Yankees hit .338, set a Series record for runs and total bases, and still contrive to lose. Pittsburgh pitchers had a collective 7.11 ERA, the poorest ever by a Series participant, let alone a winner.

SECTION 5

Famous Firsts:
1961–76

1961—For the first time in 60 years two cities are given new major-league franchises. One of them, the Washington Senators, replacing the old Washington Senators, who have moved to Minnesota, plays the first game involving an expansion team on April 10 at Griffith Stadium, a 4–3 loss to the Chicago White Sox, the team that, perhaps fittingly, played the very first American League game back in 1901.

1962—The National League reluctantly follows the American League's lead and swells to 10 teams by granting franchises to groups representing Houston and New York. Houston plays the first game involving an NL expansion team on April 10 and, perhaps fittingly, triumphs over the Chicago Cubs, the lone participant in the very first major-league season back in 1876 that has survived until 1962 without any interruptions or franchise transfers.

1962—Borrowing a page from the old Baltimore Orioles' scrapbook, the San Francisco Giants win the NL pennant after groundskeeper Matty Schwab drenches the infield at Candlestick Park, supposedly to keep the dust from billowing in the stiff winds there—but the Dodgers scream that it was done to slow down their leading base thief, Maury Wills, the first player in modern history to swipe more than 100 sacks in a season. Significantly, perhaps, Schwab is voted a full World Series share by Giants players.

1965—An amateur rookie draft is at long last instituted, major-league teams selecting free-agent players in the reverse order of their finish. The Yankees, the leading opponents of the draft, immediately topple to sixth place, their first second-division finish in 40 years.

1965—As a signal that the complete game is soon to become an endangered species, the Dodgers use three pitchers to shut out the Astros on September 3 and then need four pitchers to shut them out again the following day.

1966—Red Barber, possibly the finest baseball broadcaster ever, is fired after 34 years in the booth when he appalls the Yankees brass by asking his TV cameraman to pan the stands in Yankee Stadium on an afternoon when only 413 fans turn out to watch the Yankees first cellar finisher since 1912.

1968—Dick McAuliffe of the Tigers sets a record when he becomes the first American League player to play more than 150 games in a season without grounding into a double play.

1969—Both major leagues expand to twelve teams and divide into two divisions, the champs in each division meeting in a best-three-of-five League Championship Series at the end of the regular season to determine the pennant winner and World Series representative.

1969—The "Bleacher Bums" make their official debut at Wrigley field and root the Cubs to their highest finish since 1945. They are too far from the action, however, to follow the movements of the Cubs catcher Randy Hundley's flip-over mitt, the first of its kind, or to see the hands of Expos outfielder Rusty Staub, the first to popularize batting gloves.

1969—John Hollison dies in Chicago. His obituary neglects to mention that he was the last surviving major-league pitcher to hurl from a rectangular box only 50 feet from home plate.

1970—The average player's salary reaches a new high of $25,000 per year.

1970—Tommy Agee of the Mets becomes the first outfielder to win a Gold Glove in each league.

1970—Traded by the Cardinals to the Phillies, outfielder Curt Flood refuses to report to his new team and elects to test the reserve clause instead. Flood sets off a chain of events that within six years will merit him a few moments of silent thanks each evening around the dinner table of every major-league player.

1970—Major-league umpires refuse to work the League Championship Series games and force a settlement that increases their salaries and benefits. During the coming decade the umpires will repeatedly display their willingness to strike until their demands are met.

1971—The Pirates begin wearing form-fitting double-knit uniforms. Later in the decade the White Sox will experiment with short pants. In 1990 the White Sox will turn back the sartorial clock when they wear 1917-style uniforms for a home game to commemorate their last world championship.

1971—Ron Hunt of the Expos sets a modern record when he's hit by 50 pitches. In 1974 Hunt will retire with a 20th-century record of 243 HBP's.

1972—The players stage a 13-day strike, the first general strike in major-league history, and delay the opening of the season for 10 days. Commissioner Bowie Kuhn rules that games lost due to the strike will not be made up. As a result, the Tigers win the AL Eastern Division by dint of playing and winning one more game than the Red Sox. The Tigers half-game margin of victory is the smallest in either major league since 1908 when a similar ruling against playing makeup games gave the Tigers the flag by half a game over Cleveland.

1972—Milt Pappas of the Cubs becomes the first pitcher in history to post 200 career wins without ever winning 20 games in a season.

1973—The American League, after voting unanimously in favor of the designated hitter rule, uses designated hitters for pitchers for the first time in major-league history. The National League disdains the notion of a designated hitter and refuses to go along with the rule. Research into the history of the designated hitter idea reveals that it was first suggested in 1928 by National League president John Heydler, and that NL owners were all for it but couldn't get the support of the AL, which roundly vetoed it.

1974—Fergie Jenkins of the Texas Rangers becomes the last AL starting pitcher to appear in the batting order. In the game against the Twins, he singles in the sixth inning to break up a no-hitter and then goes on to triumph 2–1 for his 25th win.

1975—Catfish Hunter, the first star player to get himself declared a free agent, starts his first season with the Yankees, the team that won the bidding war for his services.

1975—Pitchers Andy Messersmith and Dave McNally, having played all season without signing contracts, demand free agency and are granted it by arbitrator Peter Seitz, the same man who declared Hunter a free agent. Seitz's decision results in a modification of the reserve clause and a shift in the balance of power from the owners to the players.

1976—Dan Driessen of the Reds becomes the first player to serve as a dh in a World Series game.

First Second-Wave Expansion Team to Win a Division Title
AL—Kansas City Royals, 1976
NL—Montreal ...
First Second-Wave Expansion Team to Win a Pennant

Expansion Team Firsts

On April 11, 1961, the Los Angeles Angels became the first major-league expansion team to register a victory when they bested Baltimore 7–2 in their very first game. The following year the Houston Colt 45s became the first National League expansion team to win a game when they blasted the Cubs 11–2 in their inaugural contest. In contrast, the New York Mets debuted by losing their first nine games and went on to set a new 20th-century record for the most losses in a season. But in 1969 the Mets rewarded their followers and flabbergasted their critics by becoming the first expansion team to win a division title, a pennant and a World Championship.

First American League Expansion Team to Win a Division Title
Kansas City Royals, 1976

First American League Expansion Team to Win a Pennant
Kansas City Royals, 1980

First American League Expansion Team to Win a World Championship
Kansas City Royals, 1985

First Expansion Team to Occupy Sole Possession of First Place
AL—The Los Angeles Angels swept a twin bill from the Senators on July 4, 1962, and moved briefly into first place. They ultimately finished third, making them the first expansion club to achieve a first-division finish.

NL—The Mets surged past the Cubs into the NL Eastern Division lead for the first time on September 10, 1969, after taking a doubleheader from the Expos.

First Second-Wave Expansion Team to Win a Division Title
AL—Kansas City Royals, 1976
NL—Montreal, 1981

First Second-Wave Expansion Team to Win a Pennant
AL—Kansas City Royals, 1980
NL—San Diego, 1984

First Second-Wave Team to Win a World Championship
AL—Kansas City Royals, 1985
NL—None

First Third-Wave Expansion Team to Win a Division Title
AL—Toronto, 1985

First Season Two Expansion Teams Opposed Each Other in a League Championship Series
AL—1982—California versus Milwaukee
NL—1986—New York Mets versus Houston

FIRST EXPANSION TEAM PLAYERS TO BE LEAGUE LEADERS

Batting

Department	National League	American League
Batting Average	Al Oliver, Montreal, 1982	ALEX JOHNSON, California, 1970
Slugging Average	Darryl Strawberry, New York, 1988	FRANK HOWARD, Washington, 1968
Home Runs	Dave Kingman, New York, 1982	FRANK HOWARD, Washington, 1968
RBIs	Dave Winfield, San Diego, 1979	FRANK HOWARD, Washington, 1970
Hits	Al Oliver, Montreal, 1982	GEORGE BRETT, Kansas City, 1975
Runs	Tim Raines, Montreal, 1983	ALBIE PEARSON, Los Angeles, 1962*
Doubles	RUSTY STAUB, Houston, 1967	Amos Otis, Kansas City, 1970
Triples	Roger Metzger, Houston, 1971 Joe Morgan, Houston, 1971	BOBBY KNOOP, California, 1966

Department	National League	American League
Total Bases	Dave Winfield, San Diego, 1979	FRANK HOWARD, Washington, 1968
Stolen Bases	Ron Le Flore, Montreal, 1980	TOMMY HARPER, Seattle Pilots, 1969
Bases on Balls	JOE MORGAN, Houston, 1965**	FRANK HOWARD, Washington, 1970
Strikeouts	JIM WYNN, Houston, 1967	FRANK HOWARD, Washington, 1967

*First AL major offensive department leader from an expansion team.
**First NL major offensive department leader from an expansion team.

Pitching

Wins	Tom Seaver, New York, 1969	DEAN CHANCE, Los Angeles, 1964
Losses	ROGER CRAIG, New York, 1962	George Brunet, California, 1967
Winning Pct.	TOM SEAVER, New York, 1969	Paul Splittorff, Kansas City, 1979
Starts	JERRY REUSS, Houston, 1973	Dennis Leonard, Kansas City, 1978
Complete Games	Tom Seaver, New York, 1973	DEAN CHANCE, Los Angeles, 1964
Innings	Randy Jones, San Diego, 1976	DEAN CHANCE, Los Angeles, 1964
Shutouts	John Matlack, New York, 1974	DEAN CHANCE, Los Angeles, 1964
ERA	Tom Seaver, New York, 1970	DICK DONOVAN, Washington, 1961*
Strikeouts	TOM SEAVER, New York, 1970	Nolan Ryan, California, 1972
Bases on Balls	Bill Stoneman, Montreal, 1969	BO BELINSKY, Los Angeles, 1962
Games Pitched	RON HERBEL, N.Y.-S.D., 1970	Ken Sanders, Milwaukee, 1971
Saves	HAL WOODESHICK, Houston, 1964**	Minnie Rojas, California, 1967

Awards

Cy Young	Tom Seaver, New York, 1969	DEAN CHANCE, Los Angeles, 1964

Department	National League	American League
MVP	None	JEFF BURROUGHS, Texas, 1974
Rookie of the Year	TOM SEAVER, New York, 1967	Lou Piniella, Kansas City, 1969

*First AL leader from an expansion team.
**First NL leader from an expansion team in a department other than losses.

Home Run Feats

In 1961, to the dismay of many who regarded Babe Ruth's slugging records as inviolate, Roger Maris of the Yankees clubbed 61 home runs, breaking Ruth's season record of 60, set in 1927. Thirteen years later Hank Aaron of the Braves shattered Ruth's career record of 714 circuit clouts. Many of Ruth's home run marks still stand, however, and among them are two that will surely never be broken. In 1927 Ruth hit more home runs all by himself than every team in the American League except his own Yankees. Eight years later, upon joining the Boston Braves for what would be his final major-league season, he became the first player to hit three home runs in a game in both leagues when he thrice found the seats on May 25, 1935, at Forbes Field. Another of Ruth's records that seems likely to endure is his season mark for most homers on the road—32—also set in 1927, although George Foster of the Reds came remarkably close to equaling it in 1977 before finishing with 31.

Most Home Runs at Home, Season
    AL—39—Hank Greenberg, Detroit, 1938; he had 58 altogether
    NL—34—Ted Kluszewski, Cincinnati, 1954; but only 15 on the road

Most Seasons League Leader in Home Runs
    AL—12—Babe Ruth, last in 1931
    NL—7—Ralph Kiner, 1946 through 1952 consecutive

Most Home Runs, Season, 1901 through 1919
    NL—24—Gavvy Cravath, Philadelphia, 1915
    AL—29—Babe Ruth, Boston, 1919; breaking Socks Seybold's league record of 16, set in 1902 with Philadelphia

Most Home Runs, Season, 1920 through 1941
    AL—60—Babe Ruth, New York, 1927
    NL—56—Hack Wilson, Chicago, 1930, the all-time NL record

Most Home Runs, Season, 1942 through 1960
    NL—54—Ralph Kiner, Pittsburgh, 1949
    AL—52—Mickey Mantle, New York, 1956

Most Home Runs, Season, 1961 through 1976
    AL—61—Roger Maris, New York, 1961
    NL—52—Willie Mays, San Francisco, 1965

Most Home Runs, Season, Since 1977
    NL—52—George Foster, Cincinnati, 1977
    AL—51—Cecil Fielder, Detroit, 1990

First Player to Homer in Every Park in Use During His Career
    Harry Heilmann. He homered in Braves Field, Forbes Field, Ebbets Field, Wrigley Field, Crosley Field and the Baker Bowl for the first time in 1930, the season he came to Cincinnati from the Tigers. Previously he had homered in all nine American League stadiums in which he'd played— Shibe Park, Comiskey Park, Sportsman's Park (used also by the Cardinals), Cleveland's League Park, Navin Field, Fenway Park, Yankee Stadium, the Polo Grounds (used by both the Yankees and the Giants until 1923) and Griffith Stadium.

First Player to Hit 30 or More Home Runs in a Season in Both Leagues
    Dick Stuart, Pittsburgh (NL) 1961, Boston (AL) 1963

First Player to Hit 40 or More Home Runs in a Season in Both Leagues
    Darrell Evans, Atlanta (NL) 1973, Detroit (AL) 1985

Most Times Hitting Three or More Home Runs in a Game
    6—Johnny Mize. First done while with the Cardinals on July 13, 1938; last done on September 15, 1950, while with the Yankees

Most Times Hitting Two or More Home Runs in a Game
    72—Babe Ruth. He hit three homers in a game twice, once in each league, and never hit four in a game.

Players Who Hit Four Home Runs in a Game

AL—Lou Gehrig, New York, June 3, 1932. The first player to hit four in a game in the 20th century, he picked the day John McGraw quit as manager of the Giants to do it and so got second billing in the sports pages.

Pat Seerey, Chicago, July 18, 1948, in an 11-inning game. He hit only .231 that season with 19 homers and was cut early the following year.

Rocky Colavito, Cleveland, June 10, 1959. He did it in Baltimore's Memorial Stadium, at the time a very tough park to homer in.

NL—Bobby Lowe, Boston, May 30, 1894. In Boston's 20–11 win over Cincinnati, Lowe also singled, giving him 17 total bases.

Ed Delahanty, Philadelphia, July 13, 1896. At Chicago, in a 9–8 loss to the Colts.

Chuck Klein, Philadelphia, July 10, 1936. In a 10-inning game at Forbes Field, a rugged place for sluggers prior to 1947.

Gil Hodges, Brooklyn, August 31, 1950. He did it at Ebbets Field, making him the lone player in this century prior to Bob Horner—Lowe is the only other one—to hit four homers in a game in his home park.

Joe Adcock, Milwaukee, July 31, 1954. Also at Ebbets Field. Adcock had a double in addition, giving him 18 total bases, the one-game record.

Willie Mays, San Francisco, April 30, 1961.

Mike Schmidt, Philadelphia, April 17, 1976. At Wrigley Field in a 10-inning game won 18–16 by the Phillies.

Bob Horner, Atlanta, July 6, 1986. At Atlanta, in an 11–8 loss to Montreal, making him the first player since Delahanty to hit four homers in a losing cause.

Mark Whiten, St. Louis, September 7, 1993. At Cincinnati, in a 15–2 Cardinals win in which he also had 12 RBIs.

The "Lucky Spectator" Award

Pitcher Billy Loes was either a teammate or an opponent of four players who hit four homers in a nine-inning game—Hodges, Adcock, Colavito and Mays—and so was on hand when each of them did it.

Only Pitchers to Hit Three Home Runs in a Game

Guy Hecker, Louisville (AA), August 16, 1886

Jim Tobin, Boston (NL), May 13, 1942. A good hitter,

Tobin hammered six homers in 1942, more than anyone else on the club except Max West and Ernie Lombardi.

Last Player to Hit Two Grand Slam Homers in a Game
Frank Robinson, Baltimore Orioles, June 26, 1970; in a 12–2 win over Washington.

First Player to Hit Three Grand Slam Homers in a One-Week Span
Lou Gehrig, New York Yankees, August 29, August 31 and September 1, 1931. Jim Northrup of the Tigers and Larry Parrish of the Rangers have also hit three four-run homers in a week's time.

First Team to Hit Two Grand Slam Homers in the Same Inning
Minnesota, July 18, 1962, Harmon Killebrew and Bob Allison doing the damage

Most Grand Slam Home Runs in a Season
6—Don Mattingly, New York Yankees, 1987, breaking Ernie Banks' record of five, set in 1955

Only Pitcher to Hit Two Grand Slam Home Runs in a Game
Tony Cloninger, Atlanta Braves, July 3, 1966. Moreover, Cloninger is the only National League player ever to do it.

Most Consecutive Games Hitting at Least One Home Run, Pitcher
4—Ken Brett, Philadelphia Phillies, June 9, 13, 18 and 23, 1973. His only home runs that season.

Last American League Pitcher to Homer in a Regular-Season Game, Batting as Pitcher
Roric Harrison, Baltimore, October 3, 1972

Most Home Runs, Season, as Team's Leadoff Batter in Game
11—Bobby Bonds, San Francisco Giants, 1973. Rickey Henderson holds the career record with 61 leadoff homers.

Most Home Runs, Season, Against One Team
14—Lou Gehrig, New York Yankees, 1936; against Cleveland

Most Home Runs, Season, by Runner-up to League Leader
    AL—54—Mickey Mantle, New York, 1961
    NL—47—Ted Kluszewski, Cincinnati, 1955

Most Home Runs, Season, through April 30
    11—Willie Stargell, Pittsburgh Pirates, 1971
        Graig Nettles, New York Yankees, 1974
        Mike Schmidt, Philadelphia Phillies, 1976

Most Home Runs, Season, through May 31
    20—Mickey Mantle, New York Yankees, 1956

Most Home Runs, Season, through June 30
    30—Babe Ruth, New York Yankees, 1928

Most Home Runs, Season, through July 31
    41—Babe Ruth, New York Yankees, 1928
        Jimmie Foxx, Philadelphia A's, 1932

Most Home Runs, Season, through August 31
    51—Roger Maris, New York Yankees, 1961

Most Home Runs, Season, through September 30
    60—Babe Ruth, New York Yankees, 1927
        Roger Maris, New York Yankees, 1961

Only Team with Two Players Who Hit 50 or More Home Runs
    The 1961 New York Yankees. Roger Maris, 61, and Mickey Mantle, 54.

Only Team with Three Players Who Hit 40 or More Home Runs
    The 1973 Atlanta Braves. Dave Johnson, 43, Darrell Evans, 41, and Hank Aaron, 40.

Only Team with Four Players Who Hit 30 or More Home Runs
    The 1977 Los Angeles Dodgers. Steve Garvey, 33, Reggie Smith, 32, Ron Cey, 30, and Dusty Baker, 30.

PLAYERS WITH 50 OR MORE HOMERS
IN A SEASON

	Team	League	Year	Home Runs
Roger Maris	New York	American	1961	61[1]
Babe Ruth	New York	American	1927	60
Babe Ruth	New York	American	1921	59
Hank Greenberg	Detroit	American	1938	58
Jimmie Foxx	Philadelphia	American	1932	58
Hack Wilson	Chicago	National	1930	56
Babe Ruth	New York	American	1920	54
Babe Ruth	New York	American	1928	54
Ralph Kiner	Pittsburgh	National	1949	54
Mickey Mantle	New York	American	1961	54
Mickey Mantle	New York	American	1956	52
Willie Mays	San Francisco	National	1965	52
George Foster	Cincinnati	National	1977	52
Ralph Kiner	Pittsburgh	National	1947	51
Johnny Mize	New York	National	1947	51
Willie Mays	New York	National	1955	51
Cecil Fielder	Detroit	American	1990	51
Jimmie Foxx	Boston	American	1938	50[2]

[1]Had only one homer before May 3, 1961, the Yankees' 17th game, but then hit 11 in the rest of May.

[2]The only player to hit 50 in a season with two different franchises and also the only player besides Mantle to hit 50 in a season and fail to win his league's home run crown.

Most Controversial Home Run Ever

AL—George Brett's two-run "pine tar" blast for the Royals on July 24, 1983, which beat the Yankees 5–4 and had the odd effect, after all the disputes were settled, of causing *both* clubs to go into a tailspin and fall out of contention.

NL—The famous homer that should have been but wasn't. Dave Augustine's seeming game-winning blast for the Pirates in the 13th inning on September 20, 1973, against the Mets was ruled to have bounced off the top of the wall, allowing Cleon Jones to retrieve the ball and the Mets to throw the potential winning run out at the plate. The Mets ultimately won the game and the NL Eastern Division title. The Pirates will always feel they were robbed, and Augustine never hit another home run in the majors.

Last Team to Go a Full Season without Finding the Seats in Its Home Park
The 1945 Washington Senators. Their only homer at Griffith Stadium was an inside-the-park four-bagger by first baseman Joe Kuhel. Griffith Stadium was so cavernous that Sam Rice played a record 19 seasons with the Senators without ever hitting a fair ball into the seats in his home park.

Last Player to Hit Two Inside-the-Park Home Runs in a Game
Greg Gagne, Minnesota, October 4, 1986; against the White Sox. Gagne was the first player to accomplish this feat since Dick Allen of the White Sox on July 31, 1972, who did it, oddly enough, against Minnesota.

First Player to Hit One over the Green Monster
Hugh Bradley of the Red Sox tagged the first homer over the left-field wall in Fenway shortly after the park first opened its doors in 1912. It was his only homer all season. In 1914, playing for the Pittsburgh Rebels in the Federal League, Bradley had no homers in 427 at bats.

First Player to Clear the Left-Field Wall in Braves Field
Frank Snyder, New York Giants, 1926, more than 11 years after Braves Field hosted its first game. The place was so mammoth that between 1915 and 1928, when the fences were moved in, only seven balls were hit out of the park.

Fewest Home Runs, Season, Since 1901, by League Leader in Home Runs
NL—6—Tommy Leach, Pittsburgh, 1902. Leach hiked his total to seven in 1903, but all of them were inside-the-park—as were most of his four-baggers in 1902.
    AL—7—Sam Crawford, Detroit, 1908
            Braggo Ruth, Cleveland, 1915

Home Run Leaders Who Never Hit Another Four-Bagger in the Majors
Fred Odwell, Cincinnati Reds, 1905; Dave Brain, Boston Braves, 1907

Most At Bats, Season, without Hitting a Home Run
    NL—672—Rabbit Maranville, Pittsburgh, 1922
    AL—658—Doc Cramer, Boston, 1938

PLAYERS WITH 500 OR MORE
CAREER HOME RUNS

	Years Active	Home Runs
Hank Aaron	1954–76	755
Babe Ruth	1914–35	714[1]
Willie Mays	1951–73	660
Frank Robinson	1956–76	586
Harmon Killebrew	1954–75	573
Reggie Jackson	1967–87	563
Mike Schmidt	1972–89	548
Mickey Mantle	1951–68	536
Jimmie Foxx	1925–45	534
Ted Williams	1939–60	521
Willie McCovey	1959–80	521
Eddie Mathews	1952–68	512
Ernie Banks	1953–71	512
Mel Ott	1926–47	511[2]

[1] Total would be 715 if Ruth were credited with a game-winning homer he hit in 1918 that rules of that time rated only a triple because the winning run scored from first base.

[2] Was third on the all-time career list as recently as the spring of 1960.

Most Home Runs, Career, by a Pitcher
38—Wes Ferrell, 1927–41. Right behind Ferrell are Bob Lemon with 37, Red Ruffing with 36 and Warren Spahn and Earl Wilson with 35.

Most Grand Slam Home Runs, Career
23—Lou Gehrig, 1923–39

Most Inside-the-Park Home Runs, Career
51—Sam Crawford, 1899–1917

Most Home Runs, Career, All of Them Inside-the-Park
9—Miller Huggins, 1904–16

Most Home Runs, Career, without Ever Being a League Leader in Home Runs
475—Stan Musial, 1941–63

Most Seasons Homering in All Parks Played In

11—Babe Ruth, last in 1931. Even granting that in Ruth's day there were only 8 parks, as opposed to 14 now in the American League, it's still an extraordinary record. Hank Aaron, the NL record holder, did it nine times, last in 1966 when there were 10 different parks to conquer.

Not with a Whimper

In 1966 an arthritic condition in his left elbow forced Sandy Koufax to retire after he'd enjoyed one of the finest seasons ever by a pitcher. Koufax easily broke Henry Schmidt's 63-year-old record for most wins by a pitcher in his final major-league season and went out with the biggest bang of any pitcher in history.

RECORD HIGHS BY PLAYERS IN THEIR FINAL SEASON*
Pitching

Department	Name	Team	League	Year	Record No.
Wins	Sandy Koufax	Los Angeles	National	1966	27
ERA	Ned Garvin	Brooklyn-N.Y.	Nat.-Am.	1904	1.72
Winning Pct.	Larry French	Brooklyn	National	1942	.789
Losses	Pete Dowling	Mil.-Cleve.	American	1901	26
Innings	Sandy Koufax	Los Angeles	National	1966	323
Starts	Sandy Koufax	Los Angeles	National	1966	41
Complete Games	Jack Cronin	Brooklyn	National	1904	33[1]
Shutouts	Henry Schmidt	Brooklyn	National	1903	5[2]
	Buttons Briggs	Chicago	National	1905	5
	Joe McGinnity	New York	National	1908	5
	George Kaiserling	Newark	Federal	1915	5
	Sandy Koufax	Los Angeles	National	1966	5
Strikeouts	Sandy Koufax	Los Angeles	National	1966	317
Bases on Balls	Henry Schmidt	Brooklyn	National	1903	120
Games	Bill Wakefield	N. Y. Mets	National	1964	62

Depart-ment	Name	Team	League	Year	Record No.
Saves	Russ Christopher	Cleveland	American	1948	17
	Rollie Fingers	Milwaukee	American	1985	17

*Excluding players who retired before 1901 or were declared ineligible.
[1]Quit at age 30 rather than suffer through another season with Brooklyn like 1904 when he had a 2.70 ERA but lost 23 games.
[2]Even though Schmidt won 22 games in 1903, Brooklyn didn't retain him. Another of the many outstanding pitchers the club let slip through its fingers in the early part of the century, he played only that one season in the majors.

Batting

Depart-ment	Name	Team	League	Year	Record No.
Batting Ave.	Sam Dungan	Washington	American	1901	.320[1]
	Bill Keister	Philadelphia	National	1903	.320[2]
Slugging Ave.	Buzz Arlett	Philadelphia	National	1931	.538[3]
Home Runs	Dave Kingman	Oakland	American	1986	35
RBIs	Dave Kingman	Oakland	American	1986	94
Hits	Irv Waldron	Mil.-Wash.	American	1901	186[4]
Runs	Ike Davis	Chicago	American	1925	105
Doubles	Jack Burns	St. L.-Detroit	American	1936	37
Triples	Ernie Gilmore	Kansas City	Federal	1915	15[5]
Total Bases	Dave Kingman	Oakland	American	1986	242
Games	Chick Stahl	Boston	American	1906	155
	Al Scheer	Newark	Federal	1915	155
Stolen Bases	Dave Fultz	New York	American	1905	44
Bases on Balls	Roy Cullenbine	Detroit	American	1947	137[6]
Strikeouts	Howie Goss	Houston	National	1963	128
Fewest Strikeouts	Joe Sewell	New York	American	1933	4
At Bats	Tony Lupien	Chicago	American	1948	617[7]

[1]Played in the National League in the early 1890s and did fairly well, then slipped down to the minors. In 1900, the American League's last year as a minor league, Dungan was its leading hitter.
[2]Probably the most enigmatic figure of all time, Keister hit at least .300 in every one of his five seasons as a regular and showed good power, yet never

found a team or a position he could call home. The Phillies dropped him after 1903 even though he led the club in RBIs and was second in batting.

[3]In 1960, Ted Williams had a .645 slugging average in his final season but batted only 310 times. Similarly, Chicken Hawkes of the Phillies hit .322 in 1925 but had only 320 at bats. The all-time record for the highest batting average by a player in his final season belongs to Dave Orr, who hit .373 for the Brooklyn Players League entry in 1890 before he suffered a stroke and had to quit. Orr also holds the all-time record for most triples, RBIs and total bases.

[4]Almost as mysterious as Keister, Waldron hit .311 in 141 games and led the American League in at bats in its inaugural season. Like Arlett, he got only that one taste of major-league life; and also like Arlett, he played most of his career in the Pacific Coast League.

[5]For those of you who are unwilling to acknowledge the Federal League was a major circuit, the alternate record holder is: Tommy Long, 14 triples with the 1917 Cardinals.

[6]Granted, Cullenbine hit only .224 in 1947. But he led the American League in walks, ranked fourth in home runs and was second on the Tigers in RBIs. Like Lupien, he was cut; and like Lupien's replacement, George Vico, his replacement in 1948, was gone by the end of the following year.

[7]Another first baseman who got short-changed in the late 1940s. An excellent fielder and a deft base thief, Lupien wasn't considered a strong enough hitter for a first sacker—he had just six homers in 1948—and lost his job to Charlie Kress, who had all of one homer in 1949.

Outfielders' Records

Outstanding outfielders were probably more plentiful during the 1960s and 1970s than at any other time in history. Six of the top 10 in career games played in the outfield—Willie Mays, Hank Aaron, Lou Brock, Al Kaline, Roberto Clemente and Vada Pinson—were active throughout most of the period; Curt Flood set the all-time record for the best season fielding average and several other glove marks; Aaron broke Babe Ruth's career record for home runs; Roger Maris broke Ruth's season home run record; and Brock established many new season and career stolen base standards.

SEASON BATTING RECORDS

Batting Average	National League	American League
Batting Average	.440, HUGH DUFFY, 1894 .398, Lefty O'Doul, Philadelphia, 1929*	.420, Ty Cobb, Detroit, 1911
Slugging Average	.723, Hack Wilson, Chicago, 1930	.847, BABE RUTH, New York, 1920
Home Runs	56, Hack Wilson, Chicago, 1930	61, ROGER MARIS, New York, 1961
RBIs	190, HACK WILSON, Chicago, 1930	171, Babe Ruth, New York, 1921
Hits	254, LEFTY O'DOUL, Philadelphia, 1929	253, Al Simmons, Philadelphia, 1925
Runs	196, BILLY HAMILTON, Philadelphia, 1894 158, Chuck Klein, Philadelphia, 1930*	177, Babe Ruth, New York, 1921

Batting Average	National League	American League
Doubles	64, Joe Medwick, St. Louis, 1936	67, EARL WEBB, Boston, 1931
Triples	36, OWEN WILSON, Pittsburgh, 1912	26, Joe Jackson, Cleveland, 1912 26, Sam Crawford, Detroit, 1914
Total Bases	445, Chuck Klein, Philadelphia, 1930	457, BABE RUTH, New York, 1921
Bases on Balls	148, Jim Wynn, Houston, 1969	170, BABE RUTH, New York, 1923
Stolen Bases	118, Lou Brock, St. Louis, 1974	130, RICKEY HENDERSON, Oakland, 1982
Strikeouts	189, BOBBY BONDS, San Francisco, 1970	186, Rob Deer, Milwaukee, 1987
Fewest Strikeouts (Minimum 500 ABs)	5, LLOYD WANER, Pittsburgh, 1936	8, Tris Speaker, Washington, 1927

*Record since 1901

Most Games, Career, in the Outfield
2935—Ty Cobb, 1905–1928

Most Consecutive Games in the Outfield
897—Billy Williams, Chicago Cubs, September 11, 1963, through June 13, 1969

Best Career Fielding Average
.993—Terry Puhl, 1977–90

Most Seasons League Leader in Fielding Average
AL—6—Amos Strunk, last in 1920
NL—5—Mike Griffin, last in 1898

Most Consecutive Errorless Games
316—Darren Lewis, Oakland A's and San Francisco Giants, August 21, 1990, through the 1993 season. As the 1994 season begins, Lewis has yet to make his first error in the majors.

Most Consecutive Errorless Chances
770—Darren Lewis, Oakland A's and San Francisco Giants, August 21, 1990, through the 1993 season

EVOLUTION OF SEASON RECORD FOR BEST FIELDING AVERAGE

	Team	League	Year	Average
Paul Hines	Chicago	National	1876	.923
John Glenn	Chicago	National	1877	.948
Joe Hornung	Boston	National	1881	.948
Tom Dolan	St. Louis	Association	1883	.957[1]
Jim O'Rourke	New York	National	1888	.960
Jim Fogarty	Philadelphia	National	1889	.961[2]
Jim Fogarty	Philadelphia	Players	1890	.963
Mike Griffin	Brooklyn	National	1892	.986[3]
Harry Bay	Cleveland	American	1904	.987
Sam Crawford	Detroit	American	1905	.988
Fielder Jones	Chicago	American	1906	.988
Ed Hahn	Chicago	American	1907	.990
Wildfire Schulte	Chicago	National	1908	.994
Sammy West	Washington	American	1928	.996[4]
Dick Porter	Cleveland	American	1933	.996
Harry Craft	Cincinnati	National	1940	.997
Danny Litwhiler	Philadelphia	National	1942	1.000
Rocky Colavito	Cleveland	American	1965	1.000
Curt Flood	St. Louis	National	1966	1.000[5]

[1]May have been one of the greatest outfielders ever but was so poor a hitter that no team could afford to carry him for his fielding alone. Set an all-time record in 1883 when he threw out 62 base runners trying to advance.

[2]Among the very best outfielders in his day but took ill late in the 1890 season and died early in 1891 at 27.

[3]Not a fluke season by any means. Griffin owned the surest outfield glove in the game for nearly a decade.

[4]The best fielder in his time. His arm went dead in 1930 but came back as strong as ever—he led the AL in double plays in 1932.

[5]Several outfielders have had perfect fielding averages since 1966, but none had as many chances as Flood with 396.

Most Chances Accepted, Career
7461—Tris Speaker, 1907-28

Most Chances Accepted, Season
566—Taylor Douthit, St. Louis Cardinals, 1928. It was the only year Douthit handled anywhere near that number of chances. Second to Douthit is Richie Ashburn, who had 560 chances in 1951. Ashburn is the only outfielder to han-

dle over 520 chances in a season more than once—he did it four times, last in 1957.

Most Chances Accepted, Game, Nine Innings

13—Earl Clark, Boston Braves, May 10, 1929. Clark was only 21 at the time and seemed ready to take over the Braves' regular centerfield slot, but he never made it.

Most Assists, Season, Since 1901

44—Chuck Klein, Philadelphia Phillies, 1930. Klein played shallow in his home park, the Baker Bowl, which had a short right field, and threw out several batters at first base on what ought to have been singles.

Most Runners Thrown Out at Plate, Game

3—Jack McCarthy, Chicago Cubs, April 26, 1905. The Pirates provided the opposition that day and repeatedly challenged McCarthy's 36-year-old arm on short fly balls. Notwithstanding his having risen to the test, McCarthy lost his job to Wildfire Schulte.

Most Gold Glove Awards

12—Roberto Clemente, 1955–72
  Willie Mays, 1951–73.

Triple Crown Winners

In 1967 Carl Yastrzemski won the Triple Crown when he led the American League in batting and RBIs and tied Harmon Killebrew of the Twins for the top spot in home runs. Only a year earlier Frank Robinson had won the Triple Crown after the Orioles acquired him from the Reds. After a ten-year hiatus since Mickey Mantle's Triple Crown season in 1956, Robinson's and Yastrzemski's triumphs seemed to signal that hitters like Chuck Klein, Jimmie Foxx, Lou Gehrig and Ted Williams, who were capable of winning a Triple Crown and who had been relatively abundant in the 1930s and 40s, were once again going to emerge. Instead however, 19 seasons have passed since 1967, and Yastrzemski still remains the last Triple Crown winner.

Closest Since 1967 to Winning a Triple Crown

AL—Dick Allen, Chicago, led in homers and RBIs and was third in batting in 1972. Jim Rice, Boston, also led in homers and RBIs and was third in batting in 1978.

NL—Mike Schmidt, Philadelphia, led in homers and RBIs and was fourth in batting in 1981

TRIPLE CROWN WINNERS

	Team	League	Year	HRs	RBIs	BA
Paul Hines	Providence	National	1878	4	58	.358[1]
Tip O'Neill	St. Louis	Association	1887	14	123	.435[2]
Hugh Duffy	Boston	National	1894	18	145	.440
Nap Lajoie	Philadelphia	American	1901	14	125	.422
Ty Cobb	Detroit	American	1909	9	115	.377[3]
Heinie Zimmerman	Chicago	National	1912	14	103	.372
Rogers Hornsby	St. Louis	National	1922	42	152	.401[4]

	Team	League	Year	HRs	RBIs	BA
Rogers Hornsby	St. Louis	National	1925	39	143	.403
Chuck Klein	Philadelphia	National	1933	28	120	.368[5]
Jimmie Foxx	Philadelphia	American	1933	48	163	.356
Lou Gehrig	New York	American	1934	49	165	.363
Joe Medwick	St. Louis	National	1937	31	154	.374[6]
Ted Williams	Boston	American	1942	36	137	.356[7]
Ted Williams	Boston	American	1947	32	114	.343
Mickey Mantle	New York	American	1956	52	130	.353[8]
Frank Robinson	Baltimore	American	1966	49	122	.316
Carl Yastrzemski	Boston	American	1967	44	121	.326

[1]Disputed. Some sources give the batting title in 1878 to Abner Dalrymple.

[2]Led the American Association in every major hitting department in 1887—runs, hits, total bases, slugging average, doubles and triples as well as the three TC departments.

[3]The only TC winner also to lead his league in stolen bases.

[4]The case against Hornsby being the all-time greatest second baseman always starts with the fact that everybody hit a ton during his peak years. Really? Who else between 1920 and 1940 won two Triple Crowns, let alone hit .400 three times?

[5]Despite winning the Triple Crown, he wasn't selected the MVP.

[6]Last National League player to win a Triple Crown.

[7]Lost out in the MVP voting to Joe Gordon of the Yankees.

[8]The only TC winner who also hit 50 homers in the same season.

NUMBER OF TIMES LED THE THREE TC DEPARTMENTS*

	BA	HRs	RBIs	Total Wins
Babe Ruth	1	12	6	19
Ty Cobb	12	1	4	17
Ted Williams	6	6	4	16
Rogers Hornsby	7	2	4	13
Honus Wagner	8	0	4	12
Hank Aaron	2	4	4	10
Stan Musial	7	0	2	9
Lou Gehrig	1	3	5	9
Jimmie Foxx	2	4	3	9
Johnny Mize	1	4	3	8
Dan Brouthers	5	2	1	8[1]
Cap Anson	3	0	4	7
Nap Lajoie	3	1	3	7
Chuck Klein	1	4	2	7
Ed Delahanty	2	1	3	6

	BA	HRs	RBIs	Total Wins
Mickey Mantle	1	4	1	6
Joe DiMaggio	2	2	2	6
Sam Thompson	1	2	2	5
Carl Yastrzemski	3	1	1	5
Willie Mays	1	4	0	5
Joe Medwick	1	1	3	5

Active Players

	BA	HRs	RBIs	Total Wins
Dave Parker	2	0	1	3^2
Don Mattingly	1	0	1	2

*Includes only players who won at least one batting title and one of the other two TC departments.

[1]RBI totals for Brouthers and Anson are incomplete. It is possible, even likely, that each won at least one more RBI crown.

[2]Mattingly is the only active player who has won a batting title and a second TC department. Gary Sheffield now looks to be the only active player who has more than an outside shot to win a Triple Crown.

Close, But No Cigar, Awards

First Prize—Cy Seymour of the Reds led the National League in every major hitting department except home runs in 1905. He lost the TC by the margin of one home run; the NL leader in homers that year was a teammate of Seymour's, Fred Odwell, who never hit another home run in the majors.

Second Prize—Ted Williams led the AL in homers and RBIs in 1949 but missed taking his third Triple Crown when he lost the batting title to George Kell by .00016 of a point.

Third Prize—Stan Musial missed a Triple Crown in 1948 by a single home run; that season he led the National League in every other major hitting department.

Fourth Prize—Al Rosen of the Indians led the American League in homers and RBIs in 1953 but lost the batting title to Mickey Vernon by a single point when he failed by an eyelash to beat out an infield hit in his last at bat of the season.

Fifth Prize—By today's rules Jimmie Foxx would have won a Triple Crown in 1932 as well as in 1933. He led in homers and RBIs but lost the AL batting title by three points to Dale Alexander, who had only 392 at bats. Foxx came close again in 1938 when he led in batting and RBIs and clubbed 50 homers but lost the home run crown to Hank Greenberg, who had 58.

Sixth Prize—Ty Cobb led the AL in batting and RBIs in 1911 but fell one home run short of winning his second TC. In 1907 Cobb also missed a TC when he finished tied for second in homers.

Seventh prize—Rogers Hornsby came nearly as close as Ted Williams to winning three TCs. In 1921 he led the NL in batting and RBIs but trailed home run leader George Kelly by two circuit clouts.

Eighth Prize—Gavvy Cravath of the Phillies led the NL in homers and RBIs in 1913 but lost the batting crown to Jake Daubert of the Dodgers by nine points.

Closest Babe Ruth Came to Winning a Triple Crown

In 1924 Ruth led the AL in homers and batting average but finished second in RBIs, eight behind Goose Goslin of the Senators. Two years later Ruth won the homer and RBI crowns but trailed batting leader Heinie Manush of the Tigers by six points.

Closest Hank Aaron Came to Winning a Triple Crown

In 1963 Aaron led the NL in homers and RBIs but finished third in batting seven points behind the winner, Tommy Davis.

Great Shutout Feats

More shutouts were pitched in 1968 than in any other season since the end of the deadball era as pitchers savored their last months before mound heights were shaved and the strike zone was reduced to edge the balance of power once again toward the batters' side of the scale. That year Don Drysdale established a new all-time record for consecutive shutout innings, Bob Gibson fashioned the most shutouts by any pitcher since the end of the deadball era, and the Mets' Jim McAndrew also set a shutout record, albeit one he would rather not own.

Most Shutout Games, Season, since 1901
NL—16—Pete Alexander, Philadelphia, 1916
AL—13—Jack Coombs, Philadelphia, 1910

Most Shutout Games, Season, since 1920
NL—13—Bob Gibson, St. Louis, 1968
AL—11—Dean Chance, Los Angeles, 1964

Most Shutout Games, Season, 1920 through 1941
NL—10—Carl Hubbell, New York Giants, 1933
AL—6—Done by nine pitchers, last by Bob Feller, Cleveland, 1941

Most Shutout Games, Season, 1942 through 1960
NL—10—Mort Cooper, St. Louis, 1942
AL—9—Bob Feller, Cleveland, 1946
Bob Lemon, Cleveland, 1948

Most Shutout Games by Left-hander, Season, since 1901
NL—11—Sandy Koufax, Los Angeles, 1963. Second only to Ed Morris of the Pittsburgh Alleghenies in the American Association, who had 12 in 1886.

AL—9—Ron Guidry, New York, 1978
　　　Babe Ruth, Boston, 1916

Most Seasons League Leader in Shutouts
NL—7—Pete Alexander, last in 1921
AL—7—Walter Johnson, last in 1924

Most Consecutive Shutouts Pitched
NL—6—Don Drysdale, Los Angeles, 1968
AL—5—Don White, Chicago, 1904

Most Consecutive Shutout Innings Pitched
NL—59—Orel Hershiser, Los Angeles, 1988. Hershiser's streak was maintained at one point by a questionable interference call, but Don Drysdale of the Dodgers, the previous record-holder with 58 consecutive innings, was the beneficiary of an even more controversial ruling. In 1968, after pitching four shutouts in succession, he led the Giants 3–0 in the ninth inning on May 31 at Dodger Stadium and then filled the bases with none out. With a 2–2 count, Drysdale's next pitch hit Giants catcher Dick Dietz, apparently forcing home a run and ending the shutout skein. But plate umpire Harry Wendelstadt ruled that Dietz hadn't tried to dodge the pitch. With the count now 3–2, Dietz popped out to short left field, and Drysdale then got the next two batters, preserving his streak. The Dodgers claimed that Wendelstadt's call was both correct and courageous; Giants vice president Chub Feeney said it would have been courageous if he'd made it in San Francisco.
AL—55⅔—Walter Johnson, Washington, 1913; including two relief appearances

Most Consecutive Shutout Innings Pitched by Left-hander
45⅓—Carl Hubbell, New York Giants, 1933

Most Consecutive Shutout Innings Pitched, Beginning of Career
NL—25—George McQuillan, Philadelphia, 1908
AL—22—Boo Ferriss, Boston, 1945. Ferriss is one of nine pitchers who threw shutouts in their first two major-league games. McQuillan, whose shutout string included relief appearances, is not among them.

Most Spectacular Pitching Job, First Two Major-League Games

Jim Hughes of the Baltimore Orioles threw a two-hit shutout in his major-league debut on April 18, 1898, then no-hit the Boston Beaneaters four days later in his second start. Hughes won 23 games as a rookie and 28 in his sophomore year, then got married and spent the 1900 season pitching in a California outlaw league after his new bride refused to go East.

Most Innings Needed to Win Shutout in First Start

11—Jesse Stovall, Cleveland September 3, 1903. Stovall, brother of Cleveland first baseman George Stovall, beat Detroit 1–0. The Tigers were so impressed by his overtime masterpiece that they acquired him after the season, then cut him loose when he had a 3–13 record in 1904.

Most Unusual League Leader in Shutouts

In 1935, Freddie Fitzsimmons of the New York Giants hurled just 94 innings and had an uninspiring 4–8 record. He nevertheless tied for the NL lead in shutouts when all four of his wins were whitewashes.

Most Hits Surrendered While Pitching a Shutout

NL—14—Larry Cheney, Chicago, versus the New York Giants on September 14, 1913

AL—14—Milt Gaston, Washington, versus Cleveland on July 10, 1928

The Team That Never Learned How to Pick Them II

The only time a St. Louis Browns pitcher led the American League in whitewashes was in 1929 when three Brownies —Sam Gray, George Blaeholder and Al Crowder—all tied for the top spot with four shutouts.

Most Shutout Games Lost, Season

NL—11—Bugs Raymond, St.Louis, 1908

AL—10—Walter Johnson, Washington, 1909; five of them to the White Sox

Most Consecutive Shutout Games Lost, Season

4—Jim McAndrew, New York Mets, 1968; he gave up only six runs in his four losses. No other pitcher has ever lost more than two shutouts in a row.

Pitcher with Whom McAndrew Could Most Sympathize
Erv Kantlehner, Pittsburgh, had a 2.26 ERA in 1915 but only a 6–12 record as the Pirates were blanked 8 times in his 18 starts.

Most Consecutive Shutout Wins, Team
NL—6—Pittsburgh, June 2 through June 6, 1903, amid an all-time record 56 straight shutout innings from June 1 to June 9
AL—5—Baltimore, September 2 through September 6, 1974

Most Shutout Games Won in a Season, Team
NL—32—Chicago, 1907 and 1909
AL—30—Chicago, 1906

Most Shutout Games Lost in a Season, Team
NL—33—St. Louis, 1908; 11 of them behind Bugs Raymond
AL—29—Washington, 1909; 10 of them behind Walter Johnson

Most Consecutive Games Without Being Shut Out, Team
AL—308—New York, August 3, 1931, through August 2, 1933. The streak was ended by Lefty Grove of the A's, who blanked the Yankees 7–0.
NL—182—Philadelphia, August 17, 1893, through May 10, 1895

TOP 10 IN CAREER SHUTOUTS

		Years Active	Shutouts
1.	Walter Johnson	1907–27	110
2.	Pete Alexander	1911–30	90
3.	Christy Mathewson	1900–1916	78
4.	Cy Young	1890–1911	76
5.	Eddie Plank	1901–17	69[1]
6.	Warren Spahn	1942–65	63
7.	Tom Seaver	1967–86	61
	Nolan Ryan	1966–93	61
9.	Bert Blyleven	1970–92	60
10.	Don Sutton	1966–88	58

[1]Southpaw record.

Most Consecutive Innings Without Scoring, Team
    AL—48—Philadelphia, September 22 to September 26, 1906
    NL—48—Chicago, June 15 to June 21, 1968. During their scoreless skeins both the A's and the Cubs lost four consecutive shutout games, tying a record held by several teams but most notably the Astros, who had it happen to them in 1963 and again only three years later.

Most 1–0 Games Won, Career
    38—Walter Johnson, Johnson also lost an all-time record 26 1–0 games and 65 shutout games altogether, also an all-time record.

Only Pitcher to Complete 100 or More Games without Ever Pitching a Shutout
    Jim Hughey, 1891–1900, registered exactly 100 complete games but no shutouts. His career record was 29–80, giving him a .266 winning percentage, the all-time poorest among pitchers in over 100 decisions. In Hughey's defense he pitched for the 1898 St. Louis Browns and the 1899 Cleveland Spiders, two of the worst teams in the last century.

Most Complete Games since 1901 without Pitching a Shutout
    45—Roy Mahaffey, 1927–36

Only Pitcher since 1901 to Throw a No-hitter But Never a Shutout
    Ed Lafitte of the Brooklyn Tip Tops in the Federal League held the Kansas City Packers hitless on September 19, 1914, while beating them 6–2. Lafitte, whose family tree included the pirate Jean Lafitte, won 35 games in the majors between 1909 and 1915, but none was a shutout. Bumpus Jones, who no-hit Pittsburgh 7–1 on October 15, 1892, in his first major-league game, also never pitched a shutout. The following year the mound was moved 10½ feet farther from the plate, and Jones, unable to adjust to the added distance, was cut by Cincinnati after being battered to the tune of a 10.32 ERA in his first seven games.

The Three Most
Interesting Teams Between
1961 and 1976

1967 CHICAGO WHITE SOX
W-89 L-73
Manager: Eddie Stanky

Regular Lineup—1B, Tom McCraw; 2B, Wayne Causey; 3B, Don Buford; SS, Ron Hansen; RF, Ken Berry; CF, Tommy Agee; LF, Pete Ward; C, J. C. Martin; P, Gary Peters; P, Joel Horlen; P, Tommy John; P, Bob Locker; P, Hoyt Wilhelm; P, Wilbur Wood.

Nobody ever thought much of Stanky as a manager, but he kept this club in the tight 1967 American League race until the last week of the season when a doubleheader loss to Kansas City left the battle to the Red Sox, Twins and Tigers. The White Sox best hitters in 1967, Buford and Berry, batted .241; Ward led in RBIs with 62; Agee in runs with 73 and total bases with 196; and the club scored almost 200 runs less than pennant-winning Boston. But Stanky's pitching tandem of Peters and Horlen, coupled with a superlative bullpen crew of Wilhelm, Locker and Wood, made for a lot of close low-scoring games. The Sox team batting average of .225 and slugging average of .320 are both record lows for a first-division team since the end of deadball era. Peters, Horlen and John ranked first, second and fourth in the AL in ERA, but John's 2.47 figure was a shade too high for a team that averaged just over three runs a game, and he finished with a 10–13 record.

1972 CINCINNATI REDS
W-95 L-59
Manager: Sparky Anderson

Regular Lineup—1B, Tony Perez; 2B, Joe Morgan; 3B, Dennis Menke; SS, Dave Concepcion; RF, Cesar Geronimo; CF, Bobby Tolan; LF, Pete Rose; C, Johnny Bench; P, Jack Billingham; P, Ross Grimsley; P, Gary Nolan; P, Clay Carroll, P, Tom Hall; P, Pedro Borbon; P, Don Gullett; P, Wayne Simpson; P, Jim McGlothlin.

The Reds easily won the NL Western Division by 10½ games over the Astros, beat the favored Pirates in the LCS when Bob Moose wild-pitched home the pennant-winning run in the bottom of the ninth inning of Game Five, then took the A's to seven games in the World Series before losing the finale 3–2. Unlike Cincy teams later in the decade, this club had only one .300 hitter, Rose at .307, and only Bench with 100 RBIs. The Reds trailed the Astros uncharacteristically in batting, runs and even home runs and got a league-low 25 complete games from their starters. But what Anderson lacked in mound quality he made up for in depth. Much like the 1939 Yankees, who lacked a real staff leader but had nine heavy contributors, the Reds had eight pitchers who worked in more than 120 innings and a ninth, Carroll, who saved 37 games. The staff workhorse was Billingham with only 218 innings, and fragile Nolan, the top winner, had just 15 victories. The team won the division with timely hitting and a strong bullpen, but in the postseason the hitters did little, and it was the starting pitchers who, unexpectedly, came through. In the Series the Reds got only one poor starting effort—from McGlothlin in Game Five. Likewise, only Gullett in the first game of the LCS put on a bad show. The 1972 season was Joe Morgan's first as a Red—and the first time the public really became aware of his tremendous versatility, as he led the NL in runs, bases on balls, steals and fielding while hitting .292.

1974 OAKLAND ATHLETICS
W-90 L-72
Manager: Al Dark

Regular Lineup—1B, Gene Tenace; 2B, Dick Green; 3B, Sal Bando; SS, Bert Campaneris; RF, Reggie Jackson; CF, Bill North; LF, Joe Rudi; C, Ray Fosse; P, Catfish Hunter; P, Vida Blue; P, Ken Holtzman; P, Rollie Fingers.

The A's won their division with the second-lowest team batting average in the AL, no reliable dh's, no .300 hitters and only Catfish Hunter of the starters having a good season—Holtzman was 19–17, Blue was 17–15—but the staff had the league's top ERA, and Fingers posted 17 saves. In the LCS the A's beat Baltimore in four games, losing only the first one, and then almost swept the Dodgers in the Series before dropping the fifth game. Dark got solid years from Rudi and Jackson and 103 RBIs from Bando on a .243 average, but the A's hit only .183 as a team in the LCS and .211 in the Series, creating the impression, in retrospect, that they won their third straight world title on habit as much as anything else.

Relievers' Records

In 1970 Hoyt Wilhelm became the first pitcher to appear in 1000 games, Mike Marshall gave up trying to be a starter and moved permanently to the bullpen, and Rollie Fingers, after registering only one complete game in 19 starts, began thinking that he might be wise to do the same. Fifteen years later the three of them held almost every major season and career relief record and were all strong candidates for the title of best relief pitcher ever.

Asked to name the first great reliever, most historians cite Firpo Marberry, but I'd split the honor between Three Finger Brown and Ed Walsh, with Christy Mathewson and Chief Bender only a notch beyond. When those four pitched, a "save" was still some 50 years away from being added to the game's vocabulary, but managers were already well aware that certain pitchers were especially adept at protecting a late-inning lead and were not at all hesitant to yank their starters when the game was on the line and to bring on the staff ace. Brown, for example, averaged over 10 relief appearances a season, and after it was decided what constituted a save and today's standards were applied to yesterday's box scores, he was credited with leading the National League in saves four consecutive years and being the first pitcher to chalk up more than 10 saves in a season. Walsh was only slightly less prized for his relief work. Four of his 40 wins in 1908 came as a reliever, and in addition he collected seven saves.

Just as effective as Brown and Walsh, a generation later, was Lefty Grove. During his peak years he was probably the best southpaw bullpen stopper in the game. After he was traded to the Red Sox, Grove was used almost exclusively as a starter, but between 1925 and 1933 he won 28 games in relief and saved 51 others.

Greatest Season by a Relief Pitcher Prior to 1893
First Prize—Jack Manning, Boston Red Caps, 1876. Manning, a rightfielder, doubled as a change pitcher and won four games and saved five others in relief of starters.
Second Prize—Bill Hutchinson, Chicago White Stockings, 1891. The last pitcher to win 40 games two years in a row, Hutchinson numbered 7 relief victories and a save among his 43 wins in 1891.

Greatest Season by a Relief Pitcher Between 1893 and 1920
First Prize—Tom Hughes, Boston Braves, 1915. He had a 16–14 record overall but was a perfect 6–0 as a reliever and led the NL in saves with nine.
Second Prize—Nig Cuppy, Cleveland Spiders, 1894. He was 8–0 in relief, the first great season by a bullpenner after the mound was moved to its present location.

First Relief Pitcher to Collect 100 Saves
Firpo Marberry, in 1934, pitching for the Tigers. He retired with 101 saves and also won 94 games as a starter.

First Relief Pitcher to Collect 200 Saves
Hoyt Wilhelm, in 1969, pitching for the Angels. He finished with 227 saves.

First Relief Pitcher to Collect 300 Saves
Rollie Fingers, in 1982, pitching for the Brewers. He retired at the end of the 1985 season with 347 saves, the all-time career record.

First Relief Pitcher Selected for an All-Star Game
Jack Russell, Washington Senators, 1934. The first reliever to pitch in an All-Star Game was Mace Brown of the Pirates, in 1938.

First Relief Pitcher to Appear in 60 or More Games Two Consecutive Seasons
Ace Adams, New York Giants, 1942–43. He went on to appear in 60-plus games four straight seasons during World War II.

First Relief Pitcher to Appear in Half His Team's Games
John Wyatt, Kansas City A's, 1964. He had a 9–8 record in 81 games.

First Relief Pitcher to Appear in 90 Games in a Season
Wayne Granger, Cincinnati Reds, 1969. Posted 27 saves in 90 games.

First Relief Pitcher to Appear in 100 Games in a Season
Mike Marshall, Los Angeles Dodgers, 1974. He made 106 appearances, the all-time record, and also set the current American League record in 1979 when he appeared in 90 games for the Twins.

Most Relief Appearances, Season, by a Left-hander
NL—87—Rob Murphy, Cincinnati, 1987
AL—86—Wilbur Wood, Chicago, 1968

Most Relief Innings, Season
NL—208—Mike Marshall, Los Angeles, 1974, shattering the old all-time record of 167 innings, set in 1945 by Andy Karl of the Phillies
AL—168⅓—Bob Stanley, Boston, 1982

Season Tandem Record for Relief Appearances
NL—178—Kent Tekulve (94) and Enrique Romo (84), Pittsburgh, 1979
AL—160—Wilbur Wood (88) and Hoyt Wilhelm (72), Chicago, 1968

Relief Pitcher with the Most Underappreciated Career
Lindy McDaniel. He pitched in 987 games and 2140 innings between 1955 and 1975. Never on a pennant winner, let alone a division winner, he had 172 saves and also won 22 games as a starter.

Best Career by a Reliever Who Began as a Starter
Phil Regan. Dropped in 1965 by the Tigers after successive seasons in which he went 4–10 and 1–5 as a starter, Regan was used exclusively in relief by the Dodgers in 1966 and responded with a 14–1 record and 21 saves, the best all-around season ever by a National League reliever. He finished in 1972 with 92 career saves and 58 relief wins.

Best Career by a Starter Who Began as a Reliever
Phil Niekro, hands down. The runner-up is just as clearcut. Wilbur Wood, after eight years in the bullpen, was made a starter by the White Sox in 1971 and won 20 games the next four years in a row.

Best Final Season by a Reliever

Jim Willoughby departed in 1978 after registering 13 saves in 59 games for the White Sox, and Rollie Fingers collected 17 saves in 1985, his final season, but neither had a particularly overwhelming ERA. Hence the award must go to Russ Christopher, who had 17 saves and a 2.90 ERA as the Indians bullpen ace in 1948 before a weak heart forced him to retire prematurely.

Greatest One-Game Relief Performance

Ernie Shore. On June 23, 1917, in the first game of a doubleheader at Fenway Park, Shore relieved Babe Ruth after Ruth was booted by homeplate umpire Brick Owens for arguing a ball-four call to Washington leadoff hitter Ray Morgan. Red Sox catcher Pinch Thomas was also ejected for joining Ruth's protest. The new catcher, Sam Agnew, cut down Morgan trying to steal second base, and Shore then retired the next 26 batters in a row and is credited with having pitched a perfect game despite not pitching a complete game.

Relief Pitcher Who Did the Most to Aid His Own Cause

NL—Emil Yde, Pittsburgh, June 15, 1924. Trailing the Cubs in the ninth inning, Yde doubled home the tying run and then tripled home the winning run in the 14th inning.

AL—Babe Birrer, Detroit, July 19, 1955. After entering the game in relief, he hit two three-run homers.

Relief Pitcher Who Did the Least to Aid His Own Cause

Ed Rommel, Philadelphia A's, July 10, 1932. In the process of working an American League-record 17 innings in relief, he gave up 29 hits and 14 runs to Cleveland batters, yet emerged the winning pitcher when the A's pushed across their 18th run in the top of the 18th inning. It was Rommel's 171st and last major-league victory, and he had the additional distinction of helping Johnny Burnett of the Indians make nine hits, an all-time one-game record. The A's stuck with Rommel because they brought only two able-bodied pitchers to Cleveland that day and had no one left after Connie Mack lifted starter Lew Krausse.

Least Productive Season by a Reliever

In 1986 Ed Vande Berg of the Dodgers pitched in 60 games without recording a single save and collected just one win. Only one other reliever, Arnie Earley of the Red Sox in 1965, has had a less productive season. In 57 games Earley posted an 0–1 record and no saves.

Most Career Mound Appearances by a Reliever Who Never Started a Game
1050—Kent Tekulve, 1974–89

Winners of the "You-Had-to-Be-Paying-Attention-to-See-Them-in-Action" Award
First Prize—Joe Hoerner (1963–77) appeared in 493 games but logged only 563 innings of work.

Second Prize—Fred Gladding (1961–73), 450 games and 601 innings

Third Prize—Ron Willis (1966–70), 188 games and 238 innings

Fourth Prize—Randy Moffitt (1972–83), 534 games and 782 innings

Fifth Prize—Steve Hamilton (1961–72), 421 games and 664 innings. Included in his career stats are 17 starts and three complete games.

Special Award—Bill Henry (1952–69) appeared in 527 games and made 44 starts in his 16-year career but only once, in 1965, worked 100 innings.

Proof That It Doesn't Pay for a Reliever to Start Off Too Meteorically
Butch Metzger began his career in the mid-1970s with 12 straight wins in relief, breaking the rookie record of 10 straight relief wins set in 1952 by Eddie Yuhas of the Cardinals. Before Yuhas, the record belonged to Joe Pate, who was 9–0, all in relief, for the 1926 Athletics. Now you probably know that Metzger won only 18 games before his arm went, but Yuhas and Pate fared even worse. Neither ever won another game after his rookie season.

Best Season Ever by a Reliever
True, Roy Face was 18–1 in 1959, Phil Regan went 14–1 in 1966, Jim Konstanty and Willie Hernandez both were selected MVPs, and Hernandez, Rollie Fingers and Sparky Lyle all won Cy Young Awards, but John Hiller still gets my vote. In 1973 he had a 10–5 record in relief, a 1.44 ERA, 124 strikeouts in 125 innings—but the clincher was his 38

saves, a southpaw record until 1986 when Dave Righetti of the Yankees netted 46 saves.

EVOLUTION OF THE SEASON SAVE RECORD SINCE 1901

	Team	League	Year	Saves
Joe McGinnity	New York	National	1904	5[1]
Claude Elliott	New York	National	1905	6[2]
George Ferguson	New York	National	1906	7
Ed Walsh	Chicago	American	1908	7
Frank Arellanes	Boston	American	1909	8[3]
Three Finger Brown	Chicago	National	1911	13
Firpo Marberry	Washington	American	1924	15
Firpo Marberry	Washington	American	1925	15
Firpo Marberry	Washington	American	1926	26[4]
Joe Page	New York	American	1949	27
Ellis Kinder	Boston	American	1953	27
Luis Arroyo	New York	American	1961	29
Ted Abernathy	Chicago	National	1965	31[5]
Jack Aker	Kansas City	American	1966	32
Wayne Granger	Cincinnati	National	1970	35
Clay Carroll	Cincinnati	National	1972	37
John Hiller	Detroit	American	1973	38
Dan Quisenberry	Kansas City	American	1983	45
Bruce Sutter	St. Louis	National	1984	45
Dave Righetti	New York	American	1986	46
Bobby Thigpen	Chicago	American	1990	57[6]

[1]Before 1904 the 20th-century record was three, held by many. McGinnity tied Jack Manning's all-time record, set in 1876.

[2]Never pitched again in the majors after 1905.

[3]The only saves of his career.

[4]By 1926 Marberry, you'd think, would have spawned an onslaught of bullpen records, but over the next 30 years Johnny Murphy was the only other relief pitcher to collect 100 saves, and as late as 1946 Ken Raffensberger, mainly a starter, led the National League in saves with just six.

[5]Had 148 career saves, all of them after he passed his 30th birthday.

[6]The current NL record for saves is held by Randy Myers of the Cubs, with 53 in 1993.

EVOLUTION OF SEASON RECORD FOR RELIEF WINS, SINCE 1893

	Team	League	Year	Relief Wins
Frank Killen	Pittsburgh	National	1893	5
Nig Cuppy	Cleveland	National	1894	8
Tom Hughes	Boston	National	1915	10
Elam Vangilder	St. Louis	American	1925	11
George Dauss	Detroit	American	1926	11[1]
Wilcy Moore	New York	American	1927	13[2]
Mace Brown	Pittsburgh	National	1938	15[3]
Jim Konstanty	Philadelphia	National	1950	16[4]
Roy Face	Pittsburgh	National	1958	18[5]

[1]The final 11 wins of a career in which he won 221, all for the Tigers.
[2]Won 19 games altogether in this, his rookie season, and also had 13 saves.
[3]Lost the most important game played that season when he surrendered the famous "homer in the gloamin' " to Gabby Harnett of the Cubs.
[4]Probably the finest season by a reliever prior to Hiller's 1973 season—he also had 22 saves and appeared in 74 games, the most ever by a pitcher in a 154-game season.
[5]The American League record belongs to John Hiller, who won 17 for the Tigers in 1974; Hiller also lost 14 games that year and holds the all-time season record for most relief decisions—31.

TOP 10 IN CAREER SAVES

	Years Active	Saves
1. Lee Smith	1980–	401
2. Jeff Reardon	1979–	365
3. Rollie Fingers	1968–85	341
4. Goose Gossage	1972–	309
5. Bruce Sutter	1976–89	300
6. Dennis Eckersley	1975–	275
7. Tom Henke	1982–	260
8. Dave Righetti	1979–	252
9. Dan Quisenberry	1979–89	244
10. Sparky Lyle	1967–82	238

TOP 10 IN CAREER RELIEF WINS

		Years Active	Relief Wins
1.	Hoyt Wilhelm	1952–72	123
2.	Lindy McDaniel	1955–75	119
3.	Goose Gossage	1972–	109
4.	Rollie Fingers	1968–85	107
5.	Sparky Lyle	1967–85	99
6.	Roy Face	1953–69	96
7.	Kent Tekulve	1974–89	94
	Gene Garber	1969–88	94
9.	Mike Marshall	1965–81	92
10.	Don McMahon	1957–74	90

The 20 Most Lopsided Trades since 1901

At the conclusion of the 1965 season the Reds felt they needed more quality pitchers to become a contender and sent Frank Robinson to Baltimore for starting pitcher Milt Pappas, reliever Jack Baldschun and a promising young outfielder named Dick Simpson. Simpson never panned out, Baldschun proved to be almost through, and the trade began to seem just about the worst one ever made when Robinson won the American League Triple Crown in 1966 and led Baltimore to its first World Championship while the Reds faded from fourth place to seventh. No question the swap worked out badly for the Reds, but it was far from being the all-time worst deal. While Robinson went on to hit 586 career home runs and make the Hall of Fame, Pappas didn't do all that shabbily either. He won 99 games in the National League before retiring and 207 altogether, not exactly the figures of a washout. Here are 20 swaps that, I think, make the Robinson-Pappas transaction look rather good. Excluded are all deals in which a sizable chunk of cash—more than $25,000—sweetened the package and made it too tempting for impoverished club owners to resist. Also excluded is the infamous trade in which the Giants got Christy Mathewson from the Reds for a washed-up Amos Rusie. Not only did it occur near the end of 1900, but the prime mover in the deal, John Brush, knew that he'd soon be leaving the Reds to join the Giants and hence was acting clandestinely in his own best interest.

1905—The Red Sox send rookie George Stone to the Browns for aging Jesse Burkett. Stone leads the American League in total bases in 1905; Burkett hits .257. The following year Stone wins the AL batting title, Burkett is playing out the string in the minors, and the Red Sox plummet to the cellar two years after winning the pennant.

1907—Cleveland deals rebellious holdout pitcher Earl Moore to the Yankees for Walter Clarkson, brother of 328-game winner John Clarkson. Moore doesn't get along in New York either and drops to the minors but resurfaces with the Phillies late in the 1908 season and becomes the ace of their staff. Walter Clarkson wins four games for Cleveland and is cut in 1908 as the Indians, short of pitching, lose the pennant by half a game.

1910—The Cardinals swindle the Reds out of Miller Huggins, Rebel Oakes and Frank Corridon for the price of Fred Beebe and Al Storke. Storke dies before spring training begins, and Beebe plays only one year for the Reds.

1919—Cleveland gets Larry Gardner, Charlie Jamieson and Elmer Myers from the A's for Braggo Roth. Gardner and Jamieson became vital cogs in the Indians' 1920 World Championship team; the A's ship Roth to the Red Sox in midseason. For the Indians, the deal makes up, partially, for the 1915 transaction with the White Sox in which they got Roth for Shoeless Joe Jackson.

1934—Convinced that Wes Ferrell's lame arm won't recover, the Indians send him to the Red Sox along with Twitchy Dick Porter in return for Bob Weiland and Bob Seeds. Ferrell wins 59 games for the Red Sox over the next three seasons, Weiland wins one game for Cleveland, and Seeds is cut after being unable to crack the Indians lineup.

1938—The Phillies send Dolf Camilli to Brooklyn for Eddie Morgan. Morgan never plays a single game for the Phils; Camilli has four 100-plus RBI seasons for the Dodgers and in 1941 leads the NL in both homers and RBIs. (In the Phillies' defense, some sources claim that owner Gerry Nugent got a fair-sized wad of cash too.)

1947—The Phils get Al Lakeman from the Reds for Ken Raffensberger and Hugh Poland. Lakeman hits .159 as the Phils' backup catcher; for the next six years Raffensberger is one of the NL's top pitchers. With Raffensberger, the Phils conceivably could have won two more pennants in that period; without him they are lucky to win one.

1950—The A's send Nellie Fox to the White Sox for catcher Joe Tipton. Tipton never becomes more than a sub; Fox should one day become a Hall of Famer.

1954—The Orioles give up on Roy Sievers and send him to Washington for Gil Coan. Coan turns out to be about finished; in 1957 Sievers becomes the Senators' first home run king.

1959—The Pirates package Frank Thomas, Jim Pendleton, Whammy Douglas and Johnny Powers and ship them to the Reds for Harvey Haddix, Smokey Burgess and Don Hoak. Thomas is a bust in 1959 for the Reds; the others are even bigger disappointments. In 1960 Haddix, Burgess and Hoak lead the Pirates to their first flag since 1927.

1960—The Indians get Norm Cash in a deal with the White Sox and swiftly present him to the Tigers in return for Steve Demeter, whom they expect will fill their third base hole. Which Demeter does—for all of three games. Cash leads the AL in batting in 1961 and goes on to a long and productive career.

1969—The Seattle Pilots snare Lou Piniella from Cleveland in the expansion draft, grow disenchanted with him in spring training and swap him to their sister expansion club, the Kansas City Royals, for John Gelnar and Steve Whitaker. Piniella wins the Rookie of the Year award in 1969; Seattle wins a move to Milwaukee.

1969—Not content with aging third baseman Ed Charles, the Mets deal Amos Otis and Bob Johnson to the Royals for Joe Foy. Foy hits .236 in 1970 and is out of the majors the following year; Otis plays until 1985 and posts higher career totals in every major batting department than any of the Mets' career leaders by the time he retires.

1971—The greatest year ever for trades if you're not a fan of the Mets, Giants or Astros. The Giants start off the season by passing future home-run king George Foster along to the Reds for Frank Duffy and Vern Geishert.

1971—Still in quest of a third baseman, the Mets grab Jim Fregosi from the Angels for Leroy Stanton, Don Rose and Francisco Estrada . . . and throw in pitcher Nolan Ryan.

1971—At the end of the season the Astros deliver John Mayberry to the Royals for Jim York and Lance Clemons. In a three-year period the Royals have now acquired Mayberry, Lou Piniella and Amos Otis just about for free.

1971—Duffy's not what they're looking for, so when the season's over the Giants send him to Cleveland for sore-armed Sam McDowell and manage in the same deal to unload aging Gaylord Perry, who has only 179 wins left in his right arm.

1972—To get Danny Carter the Red Sox divest themselves of Sparky Lyle. Lyle posts 35 saves for the Yankees in 1972 and later wins the Cy Young award; Carter never again plays regularly.

1975—In December, the Yankees obtain Willie Randolph, Dock Ellis and Ken Brett from the Pirates for Doc Medich. Medich wins eight games for Pittsburgh in 1976; Ellis wins 17 for the Yankees, and Randolph becomes one of the top second baseman in the American League for the next decade.

1978—The Indians test switch-hitting shortstop Alfredo Griffin in a few games, find him wanting and ship him to Toronto for reliever Victor Cruz. Cruz wins three games for Cleveland in 1979; Griffin wins the Rookie of the Year award and becomes one of the AL's best glove men at shortstop for the next decade.

Workhorse Records

In 1971 Mickey Lolich of the Tigers pitched 376 innings, the most by any hurler since 1917. The following year Wilbur Wood topped Lolich's post-deadball record when he logged 377 innings for the White Sox. Wood's total was the most by a left-hander since Irv Young pitched 378 innings for the Boston Braves in 1905.

Before 1893, when the mound distance was increased by 10½ feet, pitchers routinely worked 500 or more innings in a season, led by Will White of Cincinnati, who pitched 683 innings in 1879 while the mound was still only 45 feet from the plate. Until the early 1920s pitchers were still expected to finish almost every game they started and paced themselves accordingly. After that, inning totals dipped so sharply that in 1925, for the first time in major-league history, a league leader in innings pitched worked fewer than 300 innings.

Most Innings Pitched, Season, since 1901
AL—464—Ed Walsh, Chicago, 1908
NL—434—Joe McGinnity, New York Giants, 1903

Most Innings Pitched, Season, 1920 through 1941
NL—363—Pete Alexander, Chicago, 1920
AL—358—George Uhle, Cleveland, 1923

Most Innings Pitched, Season, 1942 through 1960
AL—371—Bob Feller, Cleveland, 1946; the post-deadball record for a 154-game season
NL—347—Robin Roberts, Philadelphia, 1953

Most Innings Pitched, Season, 1961 through 1976
AL—377—Wilbur Wood, Chicago, 1972
NL—346—Steve Carlton, Philadelphia, 1972

Most Innings Pitched, Season, since 1977
    NL—342—Phil Niekro, Atlanta, 1979
    AL—319—Jim Palmer, Baltimore, 1977

Most Seasons League Leader in Innings Pitched
    NL—7—Pete Alexander, last in 1920
    AL—5—Bob Feller, last in 1947
            Walter Johnson, last in 1916

Fewest Innings Pitched by League Leader in Innings Pitched, 1981 Excluded
    NL—250—Frank Viola, New York, 1990
    AL—256—Early Wynn, Chicago, 1959

First Season League Leader in Innings Pitched Had Fewer than 300 Innings
    AL—1925—Herb Pennock, New York, led with 277 IPs
    NL—1926—Pete Donohue, Cincinnati, led with 286 IPs

Most Seasons 400 or More Innings Pitched, since 1901
    2—Ed Walsh, Chicago White Sox, 1907 and 1908; Joe McGinnity, New York Giants, 1903 and 1904

Most Seasons 300 or More Innings Pitched, since 1901
    11—Christy Mathewson, last in 1914

Most Consecutive Seasons 300 or More Innings Pitched, since 1901
    9—Walter Johnson, 1910–18

Most Consecutive Seasons 300 or More Innings Pitched, since 1920
    NL—6—Robin Roberts, Philadelphia, 1950–55
    AL—4—Wilbur Wood, Chicago, 1971–74

Most Innings Pitched, Game
    NL—26—Leon Cadore, Brooklyn, and Joe Oeschger, Boston, May 1, 1920
    AL—24—Jack Coombs, Philadelphia, and Joe Harris, Boston, September 1, 1906

Second-Most Innings Pitched, Game
NL—22—Bob Smith, Boston, May 17, 1927. Smith lost 4–3 to the Cubs in 22 innings, the longest complete-game decision in National League history.
AL—21—Ted Lyons, Chicago, May 24, 1929, lost 6–5 to Detroit in 21 innings.

Most Relief Innings Pitched, Game
NL—18⅓—Zip Zabel, Chicago, June 17, 1915, winning 4–3 in 19 innings over Jeff Pfeffer of the Dodgers, who went all the way
AL—17—Ed Rommel, Philadelphia, July 10, 1932, winning 18–17 in 18 innings over Cleveland.

Most Relief Innings Pitched, Career
1870—Hoyt Wilhelm, 1952–72

TOP 10 IN CAREER INNINGS PITCHED

		Years Active	*Innings*
1.	Cy Young	1890–1911	7357
2.	Pud Galvin	1879–92	5941
3.	Walter Johnson	1907–27	5925
4.	Phil Niekro	1964–87	5404
5.	Nolan Ryan	1966–93	5386
6.	Gaylord Perry	1962–83	5352
7.	Don Sutton	1966–88	5282
8.	Warren Spahn	1942–65	5246
9.	Steve Carlton	1965–88	5217
10.	Pete Alexander	1911–30	5189

Great Feats of Precocity

Robin Yount became the youngest regular in American League history when he won the Brewers shortstop job in 1974 shortly after celebrating his 18th birthday. The youngest National League regular, also only 18 at the time, was Johnny Lush, who alternated between first base and the outfield for the 1904 Phillies. Unlike Yount who went on to become a long-time star, Lush was gone from the majors by the age of 24 after leading a hapless Cardinals team in wins and ERA. Trapped on weak clubs, embroiled in frequent holdouts and disputes with managers, he took his talented arm to the Pacific Coast League where he pitched with equal distinction—and bad luck—for several more seasons. With Portland in 1914 for example, he tossed a no-hitter against Venice that he lost 1–0 on a teammate's two-base error followed by a passed ball. Lush was the first player in this century to leave his mark on the game before the age of twenty, but he and Yount were far from being the only players who carved their first niches in the record book while they were still teenagers.

Youngest Player to Hit a Home Run since 1901
   Tommy Brown, who in 1944 played 46 games at shortstop for the Dodgers as a 16-year-old high school student, banged a circuit clout off Preacher Roe of the Pirates on August 20, 1945, when he was just 17 years, 4 months and 14 days old.

Youngest Player to Get a Pinch Hit since 1901
   AL—Mel Acosta, Washington, 1913, at age 17
   NL—Mel Ott, New York Giants, 1926, at age 17; he was 9-for-24 that season as a pinch hitter.

Youngest to Pitch in a Game since 1901

NL—Joe Nuxhall, still a month and a half shy of his 16th birthday, pitched two-thirds of an inning for Cincinnati on June 10, 1944, in the Reds' 18–0 loss to the Cardinals.

AL—Carl Scheib, Philadelphia, September 6, 1943, when he was 16 years, 8 months and 5 days old

Youngest Pitcher to Start a Game since 1901

Bonus baby Jim Derrington was still a couple of months shy of his 17th birthday when the White Sox gave him a starting assignment in 1956. He lost it, was 0–1 in 20 games in 1957 and was gone from the majors before he turned eighteen.

Youngest 20-Game winner

No pitcher has been a 20-game winner before his 20th birthday since the mound was moved to its present distance from the plate. But before that happened there were several teenage 20-game winners. The youngest was Willie McGill, who won 20 in the American Association in 1891 at age 17; as a 16-year-old McGill had become the youngest ever to pitch a complete-game victory when he beat Buffalo on May 20, 1890, while toiling for Cleveland in the Players League. By 1896 McGill, one of the more prodigious imbibers of his day, was finished.

Youngest 25-Game Winner

Jumbo McGinnis, St. Louis Browns (AA), 1882, at age 18 won 25 games; the following year he won 28, giving him 53 wins before his 20th birthday.

First Teenage 20-Game Winner

Among those who consider the National Association a major league, Tommy Bond is regarded as the first teenage 20-game winner—he had a 22–32 record at age 18 with the 1874 Brooklyn Atlantics. In any case, Bond became the youngest 30-game winner in 1876 when he racked up 31 victories for Hartford while still just 20 years old, as well as being the youngest 40-game winner the following season with Boston.

Most Luckless Teenage Pitcher

Larry McKeon set an American Association record for most losses in a season when he was beaten 41 times in 1884 as an 18-year-old rookie with Indianapolis.

Best Debut by a Teenager Pitcher

Von McDaniel of the Cardinals threw a two-hit 2–0 shutout against the Dodgers at age 18 on June 15, 1958.

All-Time Youngest Player

Fred Chapman, Philadelphia, American Association, pitched a game in 1887 when he was just 14.

BEST SEASONS BY TEENAGERS*

Batting

Department	National League	American League
Batting Average	.322, MEL OTT, New York, 1928	.290, Tony Conigliaro, Boston, 1964
Slugging Average	.524, Mel Ott, New York, 1928	.530, TONY CONIGLIARO, Boston, 1964
Home Runs	18, MEL OTT, New York, 1928	24, TONY CONIGLIARO, Boston, 1964
RBIs	82, PHIL CAVARRETTA, Chicago, 1935	52, Tony Conigliaro, Boston, 1964
Hits	162, PHIL CAVARRETTA, Chicago, 1935	139, Al Kaline, Detroit, 1954
Runs	85, PHIL CAVARRETTA, Chicago, 1935	45, Ty Cobb, Detroit, 1906
Doubles	28, PHIL CAVARRETTA, Chicago, 1935	21, Tony Conigliaro, Boston, 1964
Triples	12, PHIL CAVARRETTA, Chicago, 1935 12, FRED LINDSTROM, New York, 1925	7, Ty Cobb, Detroit, 1906
Total Bases	238, PHIL CAVARRETTA, Chicago, 1935	214, Tony Conigliaro, Boston, 1964
Stolen Bases	17, Cesar Cedeno, Houston, 1970	23, TY COBB, Detroit, 1906
Bases on Balls	59, RUSTY STAUB, Houston, 1963	35, Tony Conigliaro, Boston, 1964
Strikeouts	61, Phil Cavarretta, Chicago, 1935	78, TONY CONIGLIARO, Boston, 1964

Pitching

Wins	17, Dwight Gooden, New York, 1984	19, WALLY BUNKER, Baltimore, 1964
Losses	10, Cal McLish, Brooklyn, 1944	12, FRANK SHELLENBACK, Chicago, 1918

Department	National League	American League
Starts	32, Gary Nolan, Cincinnati, 1967	36, BOB FELLER, Cleveland, 1938
Complete Games	8, Gary Nolan, Cincinnati, 1967	20, BOB FELLER, Cleveland, 1938
Innings	227, Gary Nolan, Cincinnati, 1967	278, BOB FELLER, Cleveland, 1938
Games	40, BILLY McCOOL, Cincinnati, 1964	39, Bob Feller, Cleveland, 1938
Shutouts	5, GARY NOLAN, Cincinnati, 1967	4, Joe Wood, Boston, 1909
Bases on Balls	73, Dwight Gooden, New York, 1984	208, BOB FELLER, Cleveland, 1938
Strikeouts	276, DWIGHT GOODEN, New York, 1984	240, Bob Feller, 1938
ERA	2.58, Gary Nolan, Cincinnati, 1967	2.21, JOE WOOD, Boston, 1909

*Includes players since 1901 who ended the season still short of their 20th birthday—batters in at least 100 games, pitchers in at least 154 innings.

Great Milestone Achievements

On April 8, 1974, Hank Aaron of the Braves surpassed what had once seemed an unattainable milestone when he hit his 715th home run off Al Downing of the Dodgers. The only comparable achievement occurred on September 11, 1985, at Riverfront Stadium when Pete Rose singled off Eric Show of San Diego to collect his 4192d career hit 57 years to the day after Ty Cobb played his last game and retired with a record that for the next half-century was believed to be even more unassailable than Ruth's. Here is a partial chronology of other great milestone achievements.

1897—On July 18 Cap Anson became the first player in history to make 3000 hits.

1910—Pitching for Cleveland, Cy Young won his 500th game on July 19, beating Washington 5–4 in 11 innings.

1914—On June 9 Honus Wagner of the Pirates became the first player in this century and only the second in history to make 3000 career hits.

1915—Eddie Plank of the Federal League St. Louis Terriers became the first southpaw to win 300 games.

1916—Sam Crawford of Detroit collected his 309th and final triple.

1921—Still in the early stages of his career, Babe Ruth of the Yankees hit his 137th home run, breaking Roger Conner's career record of 136.

1923—On May 25 Ty Cobb scored his 1741st run, moving him ahead of Wagner. Cobb retired with 2244 runs, an all-time record that has since been challenged only by Pete Rose and Hank Aaron.

1923—Cobb went 4-for-4 on September 20 against the Red Sox at Fenway Park, breaking Wagner's record for career hits.

1927—On July 19, now with the Athletics, Cobb wreaked revenge on Detroit for letting him go by garnering his 4000th career hit, a double, off Sam Gibson of the Tigers. Remarkably, Cobb himself didn't realize what he'd achieved in that less record-concerned time until he read about it in the paper that evening.

1927—On September 30 Babe Ruth shattered his own record of 59 when he hammered his 60th homer of the season off Tom Zachary of Washington.

1928—Tris Speaker of the A's collected his 793d and last career double.

1929—Pete Alexander of the Cardinals netted his 373d career victory, staggering to a 19–16 decision over the Phillies. Released shortly thereafter by the Cards, Alexander left convinced that his last victory had put him one ahead of Christy Mathewson and given him the National League record for career wins, but 15 years later a review of Mathewson's stats revealed he'd been deprived of a win in 1902 that ought to have been credited to him, bringing his total also up to 373. Not long ago it was again reduced to 372.

1935—Babe Ruth, wearing a Boston Braves uniform, collected his 2056th and last walk.

1936—Outfielder Woody Jensen of the Pirates totaled 696 at bats, the all-time record for a 154-game season. The quintessential contact hitter, Jensen struck out only 19 times that year and picked up just 16 walks.

1937—Rogers Hornsby hit .321 in 20 games for the St. Louis Browns and then retired at 41 with a .358 career average, the all-time highest by a right-handed hitter.

1939—On May 2 the Yankees beat Detroit 22–2 at Briggs Stadium without Lou Gehrig's name appearing in the box score for the first time in 2131 games played by the Yankees.

1941—Lefty Grove of the Red Sox, after a long struggle, became the second left-hander to win 300 games.

1942—Paul Waner of the Braves made his 3000th career hit, the last player to do so until 1957.

1960—On July 19 Juan Marichal of the Giants experienced the best mound debut ever by a future Hall of Famer when he pitched a 2–0 one-hitter against the Phillies.

1961—Roger Maris of the Yankees broke Ruth's season home run record when he hit his 61st round-tripper on October 1 off Tracy Stallard of the Red Sox.

1963—Warren Spahn's first win of the season gave him 328 career victories, breaking Eddie Plank's southpaw record.

1963—Early Wynn became the First American League hurler since 1941 to win 300 games when he beat Kansas City.

1970—Willie Mays became the first black player to make 3000 hits.

1972—Roberto Clemente made his 3000th and final career hit, a double off John Matlack of the Mets in the Pirates' last night home game of the season.

1974—Al Kaline of the Tigers became the first American Leaguer since Tris Speaker in 1925 to collect 3000 hits when he doubled on September 24 against Dave McNally of Baltimore.

1975—Bob Watson of Houston scored the 1,000,000th major-league run on May 4 in a game against the Giants.

1979—On September 23, against the Mets, Lou Brock of the Cardinals stole his 938th and final base.

1981—On June 10, just before the players went out on strike, Pete Rose of the Phillies made his 3630th hit to tie Stan Musial's National League record.

1981—Steve Carlton of the Phillies broke Bob Gibson's National League record when he recorded his 3118th career strikeout on September 21 in a 17-inning 1–0 loss to Montreal.

1983—Cal Ripken of the Orioles set a new all-time record when he played every inning of every regular-season, League Championship Series and World Series game played by his team.

1984—Pete Rose played in his 3309th game, breaking Carl Yastrzemski's all-time record for the most games played.

1984—Pete Rose collected his 4000th hit, a double off Jerry Koosman of the Phils, exactly 21 years after making his first hit.

1985—On July 11 Nolan Ryan of the Astros became the first pitcher in history to notch 4000 strikeouts when he fanned Danny Heep of the Mets.

1985—Rod Carew of the Angels collected his 3000th hit on August 4 off Frank Viola of the Twins, making him the first infielder since Eddie Collins to attain the 3000-hit circle. That same day Tom Seaver of the White Sox beat the Yankees 4–1 at Yankee Stadium for his 300th win. It was the first time in history that two players had achieved such important milestone figures on the same date.

1985—Cal Ripken of the Orioles played his 5342d consecutive inning, breaking the all-time record of 5341 consecutive innings, set by Brick Freeman of the Red Sox on June 5, 1905.

1985—Phil Niekro of the Yankees nailed his 300th win on October 6, the last day of the season, by beating Toronto 8–0. It was the first time since 1890 that two pitchers picked up their 300th wins in the same year.

1986—Steve Carlton of the Giants on August 5 became the first southpaw to collect 4000 strikeouts.

1987—Lou Whitaker and Alan Trammell of the Tigers become the first keystone combo to play regularly for the same team for ten years.

1988—Jose Canseco of the A's became the first player in history to hit 40 home runs and steal 40 bases in the same season.

1989—Nolan Ryan of the Rangers notched his 5000th strikeout en route to becoming the first pitcher ever to collect 300 K's in a season after age 40.

1990—George Brett of the Royals became the first player to win a batting title in three different decades (1976, 1980 and 1990).

1991—Cal Ripken Jr. of the Orioles became the first shortstop in AL history to collect 30 or more home runs, 100 or more RBIs and hit .300.

1993—Sparky Anderson of Detroit became the first pilot since Connie Mack retired in 1950 to manage 24 consecutive seasons in the majors.

1993—Carlos Baerga of Cleveland became the first second baseman in major league history to collect 20 or more home runs, 200 or more hits, 100 or more RBIs and hit .300 two years in a row.

World Series Play: 1961–76

FRANCHISE SUMMARY

Team	League	WS Record Thru 1976	Last WS	LCS Record Thru 1976	Last LCS
Oakland	American	3–0	1974	3–2	1975
New York	American	20–10	1976	1–0	1976
St. Louis	National	8–4	1968	—	—
Pittsburgh	National	4–2	1971	1–4	1975
Cleveland	American	2–1	1954	—	—
Boston	American	5–3	1975	1–0	1975
Los Angeles	National	3–2	1974	1–0	1974
Cincinnati	National	4–4	1976	4–1	1976
Chicago	American	2–2	1959	—	—
Baltimore	American	2–2	1971	3–2	1974
New York	National	1–1	1973	2–0	1973
Detroit	American	3–5	1968	0–1	1972
Chicago	National	2–8	1945	—	—
Minnesota	American	0–1	1965	0–2	1970
San Francisco	National	0–1	1962	0–1	1971
Philadelphia	National	0–2	1950	0–1	1976
Atlanta	National			0–1	1969

Became Defunct between 1961 and 1976

Milwaukee	National	1–1	1958	

Yearly Highlights

1961—New York (AL) defeated Cincinnati (NL) 4 games to 1

Whitey Ford broke Babe Ruth's World Series record for consecutive scoreless innings as the Yankees won easily under their new manager, Ralph Houk.

1962—New York (AL) defeated San Francisco (NL) 4 games to 3

Ralph Terry nearly became the first pitcher to lose the seventh game in two World Series on the final pitch of the game. Instead he became the first pitcher to win a seventh game 1–0 as Yankees second baseman Bobby Richardson speared Willie McCovey's line drive in the bottom of the ninth inning with two out and runners on second and third.

1963—Los Angeles (NL) defeated New York (AL) 4 games to 0

The first renewal of the Yankees-Dodgers rivalry since the Brooklyn franchise had fled to the West coast, and the first time the Yankees had been swept in a Series since the Giants did it to them in 1922.

1964—St. Louis (NL) defeated New York (AL) 4 games to 3

Also for the first time since 1922, the Yankees lost back-to-back Series—despite Bobby Richardson's all-time record 13 hits—when a weary Bob Gibson of the Cardinals staggered to a 7–5 win in the deciding game.

1965—Los Angeles (NL) defeated Minnesota (AL) 4 games to 3

The Dodgers dropped the first two games in Minnesota but then got three shutouts, two of them by Sandy Koufax, to win a Series that had only one close game, the finale.

1966—Baltimore (AL) defeated Los Angeles (NL) 4 games to 0

The Dodgers were held scoreless the last 33⅔ innings of the Series by Orioles reliever Moe Drabowsky, who fanned a record-tying six in a row in the opener, followed by three Orioles starting pitchers—Jim Palmer, Wally Bunker and Dave McNally—who had notched only one shutout among them during the regular season.

1967—St. Louis (NL) defeated Boston (AL) 4 games to 3

The seventh game found both Bob Gibson of the Cardinals and Jim Lonborg of the Red Sox shooting for their third wins, the first time that so dramatic a matchup had ever occurred in a Series. Gibson emerged with the victory but shared laurels with teammate Lou Brock, who hit .414 and stole a record seven bases.

1968—Detroit (AL) defeated St. Louis (NL) 4 games to 3

Once again Brock hit over .400 and swiped seven bases, and Gibson and his mound rival both started the seventh game in search of their third Series victories. But this time Gibson's opponent, Mickey Lolich, prevailed as Curt Flood of the Cardinals misplayed a long fly ball into a two-run triple. An inning earlier Lolich had extinguished a St. Louis rally by picking both Flood and Brock off first base. The Series MVP, Lolich brought the Tigers back after they trailed three games to one and aided his own cause in his first Series win by hitting the only home run of his long major-league career. Gibson achieved a measure of solace when he set an all-time Series record by fanning 17 Tigers in the opener.

1969—New York (NL) defeated Baltimore (AL) 4 games to 1

The most improbable world champs ever, the Mets fulfilled their fans' wildest fantasy by capturing four straight after dropping the opener. Prior to the 1969 season each league had expanded to 12 teams and split into two divisions, necessitating a best-three-of-five league Championships Series to determine the pennant winner. The Mets won the first National League LCS, besting the Atlanta Braves three games to none. The Orioles likewise won the first American League LCS three games to none over Minnesota.

1970—Baltimore (AL) defeated Cincinnati (NL) 4 games to 1

The Reds won the fourth game to avert a sweep. Both LCS runners-up, Minnesota and Pittsburgh, once again fell in three straight.

1971—Pittsburgh (NL) defeated Baltimore (AL) 4 games to 3

Led by Roberto Clemente's bat, Nelson Briles's shutout in Game Four and Steve Blass's two complete-game wins, including the series finale, the Pirates rallied after being down two games to none. Game Three, in Pittsburgh, was the first Series contest to be played at night. In LCS play, the Orioles swept Oakland and Pittsburgh bested San Francisco three games to one.

1972—Oakland (AL) defeated Cincinnati (NL) 4 games to 3

The A's Series hero, Gene Tenace, hit .348 and collected four homers and nine RBIs after hitting .225 in the regular season. For the first time in Series history no pitcher on either team registered a complete game. Also for the first time, both LCSes were competitive, the A's needing five games to dispose of Detroit and Pittsburgh taking the Reds to the full five games before losing on a ninth-inning wild pitch.

1973—Oakland (AL) defeated New York (NL) 4 games to 3

Well-pitched games from starters Jerry Koosman and John Matlack, abetted by Tug McGraw's superb relief work, nearly brought the Mets their second World Championship in five years, but the A's got even better relief pitching from Rollie Fingers, who had two saves, and Darold Knowles, who also had two saves and became the first pitcher to appear in every game of a seven-game Series. Again, both LCSes went down to the wire, the Mets beating the Reds in five behind Tom Seaver while Catfish Hunter shut down the Orioles in the fifth game without a single Baltimore runner getting as far as third base.

1974—Oakland (AL) defeated Los Angeles (NL) 4 games to 1

The A's got complete games from Vida Blue and Ken Holtzman to beat the Orioles 3–1 in the LCS, and Don Sutton blanked the Pirates in the opener of the National League LCS, which the Dodgers also won three games to one. But in the World Series, for the third year in a row, no pitcher tossed a complete game. Reliever Rollie Fingers, with a win and two saves, was the Series MVP. The A's, in becoming the first team other than the Yankees to win three straight World Championships, also may have become, in the opinion of many observers, the last team ever to do it.

1975—Cincinnati (NL) defeated Boston (AL) 4 games to 3

In LCS play, the Reds took out the Pirates in three straight, and the Red Sox did the same to Oakland, setting up what promised to be one of the better Series of the decade. It turned out to be possibly the best Series ever. Boston's Luis Tiant broke what was becoming a disturbing pattern by pitching two complete-game victories, and the

Red Sox came from three runs back in the eighth inning of Game Six to tie the Reds in regulation length and then even the Series on a 12th-inning homer by Carlton Fisk. But in Game Seven, the Red rallied from a 3–0 deficit to win their first World Championship in 35 years on Joe Morgan's two-out single in the ninth inning. The Reds scored 29 runs in the Series, the Red Sox scored 30, and both pitching staffs had an identical 3.88 ERA. The most even matchup in history, both statistically and on the field, was probably resolved by the Reds having a deeper bullpen. At the wire, Red Sox manager Darrell Johnson found himself with no one to bring in but rookie lefty Jim Burton. Burton's loss in the seventh game was the last decision he recorded in the majors.

1976—Cincinnati (NL) defeated New York (AL) 4 games to 0

The most one-sided Series since 1963—the Yankees were competitive only in the second game—followed the Reds' three-zip blowout of the Phillies in the National League LCS. The Yankees, on the other hand, needed five games in the LCS to shake the Kansas City Royals, the first American League expansion team to qualify for postseason play. The fifth game seemed headed for extra innings until Chris Chambliss of the Yankees snapped a 6–6 deadlock by leading off the bottom of the ninth inning with a homer off Royals reliever Mark Littell. Mobbed by Yankees fans, Chambliss was unable to complete his home run trot around the bases. Hours later he crept out of the clubhouse, accompanied by two policemen, and touched home plate to make his pennant-winning run official.

SECTION 6

Famous Firsts:
1977–93

1977—The American League bloats to 14 teams after granting new franchises to Toronto and Seattle. There are now 26 clubs in the major leagues, the most since the frantically unstable 1884 season when the uninvited Union Association joined the American Association in its war with the National League.

1977—Paddy Livingston dies in Cleveland. His obituary notes that he played for the Indians but neglects to mention that he was the last surviving member of the American League's class of 1901, its first year as a major circuit.

1978—The Yankees beat the Red Sox 5–4 at Fenway Park to cop the first division playoff game in history.

1979—Willie Stargell of the Pirates and Keith Hernandez of the Cardinals become the first players to be selected co-MVPs.

1981—On June 12 the players go on strike for the second time in history and shut down the season for 50 days.

1982—Joel Youngblood becomes the first player to get hits for two different teams in two different cities on the same day when he's traded by the Mets to the Expos following an afternoon game on August 4 and scurries to Philadelphia in time to play in the game that night for Montreal.

1982—Relief pitcher Greg Minton of the Giants sets a new major-league record when he twirls 269⅓ innings over four seasons without surrendering a home run.

1982—In the wake of dire forecasts that the 1981 strike will disenchant fans with the game, the Dodgers demolish the season attendance record by drawing 3,608,881 fans.

1983—First baseman Pete Rose of the Phillies becomes the first player since the end of the deadball era to play a full season at the position for a pennant winner without hitting a home run.

1984—Jim Rice of the Red Sox sets a new major-league record when he grounds into 36 double plays.

1985—Don Sutton, never a strikeout leader, becomes the first pitcher ever to fan 100 or more hitters in 20 consecutive seasons. By September he is on the same team with Reggie Jackson, the first hitter to fan 100 or more times in 17 consecutive seasons (1981 excepted).

1985—The two League Championship Series are expanded to a best 4-of-7 format, and the Kansas City Royals promptly establish the record for being the first team to rally from a 3–1 deficit to win an LCS.

1986—Don Sutton of the Angels beats the Texas Rangers 5–1 on June 18 for his 300th career victory, making him the first 300-game winner in history who needed more than 20 full seasons to do it and only once was a 20-game winner.

1986—Don Baylor of the Red Sox breaks the American League record that he previously shared with Kid Elberfeld when he is hit by 35 pitches. His career total of 227 leaves him only 16 short of Ron Hunt's modern record.

1986—Bert Blyleven of the Twins surrenders 50 home runs, shattering Robin Roberts's former all-time record of 46 by a comfortable margin.

1986—On September 29, for the first time in history, two brothers face each other as rookie starting pitchers when Greg Maddux of the Cubs beats older brother Mike of the Phillies 8–3.

1987—Benito Santiago of the Padres sets a new rookie record when he hits safely in 34 straight games.

1988—Jerry Reuss of the White Sox becomes the first southpaw to collect 200 career victories without ever winning 20 games in a season.

1989—The Orioles post an 87–75 record, an improvement of 32½ games over their 1988 mark, the largest gain in history by an American League cellar dweller.

1990—Willie McGee becomes the first absentee batting titlist in history when he is traded from the National League to the American League shortly after he collected enough plate appearances to qualify for the NL crown.

1991—The Braves become the first NL or AL team to leap from worst to first when they win the NL pennant after posting the poorest record in the majors in 1990.

1992—Tim Wakefield of Pittsburgh becomes the first rookie to hurl two complete game wins in an LCS.

1993—The Oakland A's become the first defending division champions to finish in the league cellar the following season.

pitcher-a liner sometimes is either a standing catch or a base hit, but pitchers seldom fan 100 or more batters by 30 consecutive by......... Roberts could be is almost the same man with Waddel

The Most Difficult Pitchers to Beat

His 24–4 record and .857 winning percentage in 1986 not only brought Boston's Roger Clemens the Cy Young and MVP awards but narrowly missed equalizing Ron Guidry's incredible performance eight years earlier for the Yankees. In 1978 Guidry had the greatest season ever by a left-hander, a 25-game winner and, for that matter, a 20-game winner when he posted a 25–3 record and an .893 winning percentage. Guidry's mark shattered the old record for the highest winning percentage by a 20-game winner—.880—set by Preacher Roe of the Brooklyn Dodgers in 1951 when he won 22 games and lost only 3. But Roe still holds the National League record.

Highest Winning Percentage, Season, Minimum 15 Wins
   NL—.947—Roy Face, Pittsburgh, 1959 (18–1). At one point in the season Face had a 17–0 record.
   AL—.938—Johnny Allen, Cleveland, 1937 (15–1). Allen was 15–0 until he lost his last start of the season.

Most Wins in a Season without a Loss
   Al—12—Tom Zachary, New York, 1928. The runner-up is Dennis Lamp, who had a perfect 11–0 record for Toronto in 1985.
   NL—10—Howie Krist, St. Louis, 1942. The runner-up, Ken Holtzman of the Cubs, began the 1967 season by winning his first nine games, then was called away to do military service.

Highest Winning Percentage by a Rookie 20-Game Winner
   NL—.838—Bill Hoffer, Baltimore, 1895 (31–6)
   AL—.813—Russ Ford, New York, 1910 (26–6)

Highest Winning Percentage by a Rookie since 1893, Minimum 10 Decisions
 NL—.900—Al Orth, Philadelphia, 1895 (9–1)
 AL—.923—Jim Nash, Kansas City A's, 1966 (12-1). In 1926 Joe Pate of the Philadelphia A's was a perfect 9–0 as a reliever.

Most Wins without a Loss, Only Season in Majors
 3—Luke Nelson, New York Yankees, 1919.
     Danny Osborn, Chicago White Sox, 1975

Most Seasons League Leader in Winning Percentage
 AL—5—Lefty Grove, last in 1939
 NL—3—Ed Reulbach, 1906–08 consecutive

Only Pitcher to Lead Both the NL and the AL in Winning Percentage
 Jack Chesbro, Pittsburgh (NL), 1901 and 1902; New York (AL), 1904

Most Seasons League Leader in Winning Percentage before 1901
 3—Bob Caruthers, St. Louis (AA), 1885 and 1887; Brooklyn (AA), 1889

Only Two-Time League Leader in Winning Percentage with a Career WP below .500
 Larry Benton of the New York Giants led the National League in winning percentage in 1927 and again in 1928 but finished with a 127–128 record.

Highest Career Winning Percentage, Minimum 150 Decisions
 .717—Spud Chandler, 1937–47 (109–43). Chandler didn't win his first game until he was nearly 30. He lost almost two full seasons to military service during World War II and parts of several other seasons to arm ailments. Against that he played for the Yankees, who won seven pennants while he was with them. Prior to joining the Yankees, Chandler posted a mediocre 47–41 record in six minor-league seasons.

Highest Career Winning Percentage, Pitcher Never on a Pennant Winner, Minimum 150 Wins
 .626—Addie Joss, Cleveland, 1902–10 (159–95)

TOP 10 IN CAREER WINNING PERCENTAGE*

(Minimum 200 Decisions)

		Years Active	Wins	Losses	Pct.
1.	Whitey Ford	1950–67	236	106	.690[1]
2.	Dave Foutz	1884–94	147	66	.690
3.	Bob Caruthers	1884–92	218	99	.688[2]
4.	Lefty Grove	1925–41	300	141	.680[3]
5.	Christy Mathewson	1900–16	372	187	.665
6.	Larry Corcoran	1880–87	177	89	.665
7.	Sam Leever	1898–1910	195	100	.661[4]
8.	Sandy Koufax	1955–66	165	87	.655
9.	Dwight Gooden	1984–	154	81	.655
10.	Johnny Allen	1932–44	142	75	.654

[1]Had a .720 winning percentage through 1964, then lost 22 games and won only 20 in his last three seasons.

[2]Had a .708 winning percentage before posting a 2–10 record for the 1892 St. Louis Browns in his final season as a pitcher.

[3]The top winning percentage among 300-game winners.

[4]Had a 36–38 career record after his first three seasons but then fashioned an incredible .718 winning percentage from 1901 through 1910.

Highest Career Winning Percentage since 1961 (Retired Pitchers Only)
.686—Don Gullett, 1970–78 (109–50). In his last four seasons he won 44 games, lost only 13 and had a .772 winning percentage.

Highest Career Winning Percentage, Minimum 40 Decisions
.771—Howie Krist, 1937–46 (37–11). After his first four seasons he had an unbelievable 26–4 career record.

Highest Career Winning Percentage, Minimum 20 Decisions
.871—Luis Aloma, 1950–53 (18–3). In between bouts of arm trouble he also netted 15 saves and pitched a shutout in his only starting assignment.

Most Career Wins without a Loss
4—Ben Shields, 1924–31. Although pounded in almost every game he pitched—he had an 8.27 career ERA—he was somehow never beaten.

Highest Career Winning Percentage as a Relief Pitcher, Minimum 50 Decisions

.718—Hugh Casey, 1935–49 (51–20).

Only Pitcher with a .600 Career Slugging Average and Winning Percentage

Babe Ruth, 1914–35; had a .671 winning percentage (94–46) and a .690 slugging average.

The All-time Worst Fielders

When third baseman Butch Hobson of the Red Sox fielded .899 in 133 games in 1978, he became the first regular player in 62 years to post a fielding average that was below .900.

Last Regular Prior to Hobson to Field below .900
Charlie Pick, Philadelphia A's, 1916. Primarily a third baseman, Pick fielded .899 in 116 games.

Last National Leaguer to Field Below .900 in More Than 100 Games
Heinie Zimmerman, Chicago Cubs, 1914, had an .897 fielding average in 146 games, most of them at third base. Playing shortstop right beside Zimmerman was Red Corriden, who fielded .894 in 107 games. Somehow the Cubs still managed to finish in the first division.

Lowest Fielding Average by a National League Regular since 1914
Dick Allen, Philadelphia, 1967, fielded .908 at third base. The following season he was put in the outfield.

Last Regular Outfielder to Field Below .900
Guy Zinn, New York Yankees, 1912; fielded .893 in 106 games.

Lowest Fielding Average by a Regular Player since 1901
If we drop back a year to 1900, we find Piano Legs Hickman at third base for the New York Giants fielding a grand .842 and making 86 errors. But the record since 1901, when the majors became a two-league operation, belongs to Bill Keister, who fielded .851 and made 97 errors while playing shortstop for the 1901 Baltimore Orioles.

Most Errors, Season, by a Player since 1901

Johnny Gochnauer, Cleveland shortstop, 1903; made 98 errors and fielded .869.

Most Errors, Season, by First Baseman since 1901

Once again, by dropping back a year to 1900, we find Jack Doyle, who made 43 errors with the Giants, most of them, we might imagine, while trying to handle Piano Legs Hickman's throws. The record since 1901 is held by Jerry Freeman, who racked up 41 miscues with Washington in 1908.

Most Errors, Season, by a Catcher since 1901

41—Oscar Stanage, Detroit Tigers, 1911. Rather bizarrely, Stanage also holds the American League record for most assists in a season.

First Player to Make 100 Errors in a Season

Frank Fennelly, shortstop for Cincinnati in the American Association in 1886, collected 117 boots, a figure that was tied by shortstop Herman Long of the Kansas City AA team in 1889. In addition, Long made five errors while playing five games at second base, tying him with Billy Shindle of the 1890 Philadelphia Players League club for the all-time season record of 122 miscues.

Last Player to Make 100 Errors in a Season

Rookie shortstop Joe Sullivan was charged with 102 errors and had an .860 fielding average for Washington in 1893.

Last Player to Make 90 or More Errors in a Season

Johnny Gochnauer, Cleveland, 1903; along with his 98 errors he batted .185.

Last Player to Make 80 or More Errors in a Season

Neal Ball, shortstop New York Yankees, 1908; a year before he became the first player to perform an unassisted triple play.

Last Player to Make 70 or More Errors in a Season

Buck Weaver, shortstop Chicago White Sox, made exactly 70 errors in 1913. The year before he had 71 boots. Despite his high number of miscues, Weaver had relatively decent fielding averages for that time, and one suspects that he accumulated so many errors mostly because he got to more balls than the average shortstop. Switched to third base in 1916, he became one of the outstanding hot corner glove men of his era.

Last Player to Make 60 or More Errors in a Season
Al Brancato, shortstop Philadelphia A's, 1941; 61 errors and a .915 fielding average.

Last Player to Make 50 or More Errors in a Season
Roy Smalley, shortstop Chicago Cubs, 1951; 51 errors and a .945 fielding average. No apologies here. Cubs fans in the early fifties, harkening back to Tinker to Evers to Chance, cynically coined the chant "Miksis to Smalley to Addison Street." When Cubs managers Frankie Frisch and Phil Cavarretta wanted to rest Smalley's scatter-arm, they were stuck with Tommy "Buckshot" Brown at shortstop. In 1951 Brown fielded .911 and was second on the team in errors to Smalley, although he played in just 61 games.

during 57 years when Newark rallies by 11 not something of the season
AL—Willie Wilson, Kansas City, Royals, 1980. The record covers the season he struck out

Base-stealing Feats

What player was the most proficient base thief ever? The most prolific? We're watching both of them perform right now. Indeed the majority of season and career base-stealing records have been set in the past 15 years.

Most Stolen Bases, Season
AL—130—Rickey Henderson, Oakland, 1982; also swiped 108 bases in 1983 and 100 in 1980.
NL—118—Lou Brock, St. Louis, 1974. The only other players who stole 100 or more bases in a season were Maury Wills, who grabbed 104 with the 1962 Dodgers, and Vince Coleman, 110, as a rookie with the 1985 Cardinals and 107 in 1986, his sophomore season.

Most Stolen Bases, Season, 1901 through 1919
AL—96—Ty Cobb, Detroit, 1915
NL—81—Bob Bescher, Cincinnati, 1911

Most Stolen Bases, Season, 1920 through 1941
AL—63—Sam Rice, Washington, 1920
NL—52—Max Carey, Pittsburgh, 1920

Most Stolen Bases, Season, 1942 through 1960
AL—61—George Case, Washington, 1943
NL—50—Maury Wills, Los Angeles, 1960

Most Stolen Bases without Being Caught, Season
NL—21—Kevin McReynolds, New York, 1988
AL—16—Jimmy Sexton, Oakland, 1982

Most Consecutive Stolen Bases without Being Caught
NL—50—Vince Coleman, St. Louis, 1988–89; streak ended

on July 28, 1989, when he was nailed by Nelson Santovenia of the Expos.

AL—32—Willie Wilson, Kansas City Royals, 1980; Tod Cruz, Chicago, 1980–81. Prior to Wilson and Cruz, the AL record was 26, set in 1977 by Mitchell Page of Oakland.

Most Successful Thefts of Home, Season
AL—7—Rod Carew, Minnesota, 1969
NL—7—Pete Reiser, Brooklyn, 1946

First Player to Steal Home Twice in a Game
Joe Tinker, Chicago Cubs, June 28, 1910

Last Pitcher to Steal Home
NL—Rick Sutcliffe, Chicago, July 29, 1988
AL—Harry Dorish, St. Louis Browns, June 2, 1951

Most Stolen Bases, Game
6—Eddie Collins, Philadelphia A's, September 11 and September 22, 1912. Collins's dual feats, occurring only 11 days apart, were the only times in modern history that a player stole more than five bases in a game.

Most Seasons League Leader in Stolen Bases
NL—10—Max Carey, last in 1925
AL—9—Luis Aparicio, 1956–64 consecutive
        Rickey Henderson, last in 1989

Most Seasons 50 or More Stolen Bases
AL—13—Rickey Henderson, last in 1993
NL—12—Lou Brock, last in 1976

Most Players with 50 or More Stolen Bases in a Season, Team
AL—3—Oakland, 1976: Bill North (75), Bert Campaneris (54), Don Baylor (52)
NL—3—San Diego, 1980: Gene Richards (61), Ozzie Smith (57), Jerry Mumphrey (52).

Most Stolen Bases, Season, Team
NL—347—New York Giants, 1911
AL—341—Oakland, 1976

Best Stolen Base Percentage, Season, Minimum 35 Attempts
NL—.962—Max Carey, Pittsburgh, 1922; 51 steals in 53 tries
AL—.943—Amos Otis, Kansas City Royals, 1970; 33 steals in 35 tries

Lowest Stolen Base Percentage, Season, Minimum 20 Attempts
.133—Larry Gardner, Cleveland Indians, 1920; three steals in 23 tries

Most Times Caught Stealing, Season
AL—42—Rickey Henderson, Oakland, 1982; 130 steals in 172 tries.
NL—36—Miller Huggins, St. Louis, 1914; 32 steals in 68 tries. Huggins's stolen base percentage that season—well below .500— was not atypical of the deadball era.

Most times Caught Stealing, Season, Team
NL—149—Chicago, 1924; 137 steals in 286 tries
AL—123—Oakland, 1976; 341 steals in 464 tries

Fewest Stolen Bases, Season, by League Leader in Stolen Bases
AL—15—Dom DiMaggio, Boston, 1950
NL—18—Stan Hack, Chicago, 1938

Fewest Stolen Bases, Season, by Team
AL—13—Washington, 1957; club leader was Julio Becquer with 3
NL—17—St. Louis, 1949; club leader was Red Schoendienst with 8

Highest Batting Average, Season, since 1901, by League Leader in Steals
AL—.420—Ty Cobb, Detroit, 1911
NL—.354—Honus Wagner, Pittsburgh, 1908

Lowest Batting Average, Season, since 1901, by League Leader in Steals
NL—.219—Danny Murtaugh, Philadelphia, 1941
AL—.225—George Case, Cleveland, 1946

Winner of the "Making Them Count" Award
In 1958 Vic Power stole only three bases all year, but two of them were thefts of home—and in the same game, no less.

Winner of the "Right Man for the Job" Award
Inserted as a pinch runner on September 1, 1909, rookie Bill O'Hara of the New York Giants promptly stole both second and third base; called on again to pinch run the following day, he did the same thing. Not only is O'Hara the only pinch runner to swipe two bases on consecutive days, he's the lone pinch runner to swipe two sacks on more than one occasion.

Winner of the "Stemming the Tide" Award
On May 11, 1897, catcher Duke Farrell of Washington threw out a record eight would-be base thieves.

Most Combined Home Runs and Stolen Bases, Season, Minimum 30 Home Runs
87—Eric Davis, Cincinnati Reds, 1987.

MEMBERS OF THE 30/30 CLUB

	Team	Year	Thefts	Homers	Total
Ken Williams	St. Louis Browns	1922	47	39	86
Willie Mays	New York Giants	1956	40	36	76
Willie Mays	New York Giants	1957	38	35	73
Hank Aaron	Milwaukee Braves	1963	31	44	75
Bobby Bonds	San Francisco Giants	1969	45	32	77
Tommy Harper	Milwaukee Brewers	1970	38	31	69
Bobby Bonds	San Francisco Giants	1973	43	39	82
Bobby Bonds	New York Yankees	1975	30	32	62
Bobby Bonds	California Angels	1977	41	37	78
Bobby Bonds	Chicago-Texas	1978	43	31	74
Dale Murphy	Atlanta Braves	1983	30	36	66
Eric Davis	Cincinnati Reds	1987	50	37	87
Darryl Strawberry	New York Mets	1987	36	39	75
Howard Johnson	New York Mets	1987	32	36	68
Joe Carter	Cleveland Indians	1987	31	32	63
Jose Canseco	Oakland A's	1988	40	42	82
Howard Johnson	New York Mets	1989	41	36	77
Barry Bonds	Pittsburgh Pirates	1990	53	33	86
Ron Gant	Atlanta Braves	1990	33	32	65
Howard Johnson	New York Mets	1991	30	38	68
Ron Gant	Atlanta Braves	1991	34	32	66
Barry Bonds	Pittsburgh Pirates	1992	39	34	73
Sammy Sosa	Chicago Cubs	1993	36	33	69

Most Consecutive Games without Being Caught Stealing
  1,206—Gus Triandos, 1953–65. Triandos played his entire career without ever being caught stealing. He tried only once to swipe a base, and that was while playing for Baltimore in 1958 in a game the Orioles were losing so badly to the Yankees that the Yankees didn't bother to make a play on him.

Fewest Stolen Bases, Career, 2,400 or More Games Played
  19—Harmon Killebrew, 1954–75 (2,435 games). Nearly half of Killebrew's thefts—8—came in 1969. Killebrew also has the fewest triples (24) of any player in over 2000 games.

TOP 10 IN CAREER STOLEN BASES

		Years Active	Stolen Bases
1.	Rickey Henderson	1979–	1095[1]
2.	Lou Brock	1961–79	938
3.	Ty Cobb	1905–28	892
4.	Tim Raines	1979–	751
5.	Eddie Collins	1906–30	743
6.	Max Carey	1910–29	738
7.	Honus Wagner	1897–1917	703[2]
8.	Joe Morgan	1963–84	689
9.	Willie Wilson	1976–	667
10.	Bert Campaneris	1964–83	649[3]

[1]The most prolific base thief in history, he has averaged 74.5 stolen bases a season.

[2]In 1897, Wagner's rookie year, a stolen base was still customarily awarded whenever a runner advanced an extra base on a hit or an out. As a result, all stolen base records set before 1898, when the modern scoring rule was established, are impossible to compare to records set afterward and have been omitted from this section.

[3]In 1969 he stole 62 bases in 70 tries, the highest success rate of any American League player with more than 60 attempts in a season. Tim Raines of the Expos, who swiped 70 sacks in 79 attempts for an .886 percentage in 1985, holds the all-time record; in 1986 Raines posted identical stolen base stats to tie his own mark.

Most Career Thefts of Home
  35—Ty Cobb, 1905–28. George Burns, 1911–25, is second with 27.

Most Times Caught Stealing, Career
  307—Lou Brock, 1961–79. No other player is even close.

Highest Stolen Base Percentage, Career, Minimum 400 Attempts
  .849—Tim Raines. At the conclusion of the 1993 season Raines had 751 thefts in 885 attempts, still the best average ever among players with a minimum of 400 career steal attempts although his success rate has been steadily declining the past few years.

Loyalty Records

In 1982 Carl Yastrzemski completed his 23d season in a Boston Red Sox uniform, tying Brooks Robinson's all-time record for playing the most seasons with the same team. Yastrzemski's retirement left Bill Russell heir to the loyalty record among active players. In 1986 Russell played his 18th consecutive season with the Dodgers. Since free agency was made part of the game in 1975, only nine other players who began their careers before then—Mike Schmidt, Robin Yount, Dave Concepcion, Dennis Leonard, Dwight Evans, Bob Forsch, Jim Rice, Charlie Moore and George Brett—were still playing with their original teams during the 1986 season.

Record for Most Seasons with One Team Before Brooks Robinson Broke It
  22—Al Kaline, Detroit Tigers, 1953–74
      Mel Ott, New York Giants, 1926–47
      Stan Musial, St. Louis Cardinals, 1941–63
      Cap Anson, Chicago White Stockings, 1876–97. Anson's share of the record is open to dispute since he played with the Rockford Forest Citys and Philadelphia Athletics in the National Association for five seasons prior to 1876.

Team That for Some Perverse Reason Inspired the Most Loyalty
  The Chicago White Sox from 1914 through 1950. Beginning in 1914, Red Faber pitched 20 years for them without ever playing with another team. Ted Lyons pitched 21 years for the Pale Hose from 1923 through 1946. And shortstop Luke Appling gave the Sox his entire 20-year career from 1930 through 1950. Faber came to the club in time to play on two pennant winners, but Lyons and Appling were not so fortunate. Lyons holds the record for playing the most

pennantless seasons with the same team, and Appling is second to him.

ENTIRE CAREER WITH ONE TEAM
RECORD HOLDERS

Batting

Department	Name	Years Active	Team	Record
Games	Carl Yastrzemski	1961–83	Boston Red Sox	3308
At Bats	Carl Yastrzemski	1961–83	Boston Red Sox	11,988
Hits	Stan Musial	1941–63	St. Louis Cardinals	3630
Home Runs	Mickey Mantle	1951–68	New York Yankees	536
RBIs	Lou Gehrig	1923–39	New York Yankees	1991
Runs	Stan Musial	1941–63	St. Louis Cardinals	1949
Doubles	Stan Musial	1941–63	St. Louis Cardinals	725
Triples	Bid McPhee	1882–99	Cincinnati Reds	189
Total Bases	Stan Musial	1941–63	St. Louis Cardinals	6134
Stolen Bases	Clyde Milan	1907–22	Washington Senators	495
Bases on Balls	Ted Williams	1939–60	Boston Red Sox	2019
Strikeouts	Mickey Mantle	1951–68	New York Yankees	1710
Batting Average	Ted Williams	1939–60	Boston Red Sox	.344
Slugging Average	Ted Williams	1939–60	Boston Red Sox	.634

Pitching

Wins	Walter Johnson	1907–27	Washington Senators	416
Losses	Walter Johnson	1907–27	Washington Senators	279
Winning Pct.	Whitey Ford	1950–67	New York Yankees	.690
Games	Walter Johnson	1907–27	Washington Senators	802

Department	Name	Years Active	Team	Record
Innings Pitched	Walter Johnson	1907–27	Washington Senators	5924
Starts	Walter Johnson	1907–27	Washington Senators	666
Complete Games	Walter Johnson	1907–27	Washington Senators	532
ERA	Addie Joss	1902–10	Cleveland Indians	1.88
Strikeouts	Walter Johnson	1907–27	Washington Senators	3508
Bases on Balls	Bob Feller	1936–56	Cleveland Indians	1764

The All-time Loyalty All-Star Team*

Position	Name	Team	Years Played	Total
First Base	Cap Anson	Chicago White Stockings	1879–97	19
Second Base	Bid McPhee	Cincinnati Reds	1882–99	18
Third Base	Brooks Robinson	Baltimore Orioles	1958–75	18
Shortstop	Dave Concepcion	Cincinnati Reds	1970–86	17
Outfield	Al Kaline	Detroit Tigers	1954–72	19
Outfield	Roberto Clemente	Pittsburgh Pirates	1955–72	18
Outfield	Clyde Milan	Washington Senators	1908–21	14
Catcher	Bill Dickey	New York Yankees	1929–43	15
Pitcher	Walter Johnson	Washington Senators	1907–27	21
Pitcher	Ted Lyons	Chicago White Sox	1923–46	21
Pitcher	Red Faber	Chicago White Sox	1914–33	20
Pitcher	Mel Harder	Cleveland Indians	1928–47	20

*Limited to players who became institutions both because they spent their entire careers with the same team and because they were regulars at the same positions without any interruptions during the years cited. The lone exceptions are Lyons, who lost years to the military service, Kaline, who was a utility outfielder during the regular season in 1968 but played every game in the World Series, and Concepcion, the Reds regular shortstop in 1986 until injured in mid-season.

Mobility Records

Carl Yastrzemski and Alex Johnson dovetailed in 1970 when they fought it out all season for the American League batting crown, which Johnson won by a fraction of a point, but from then on their careers diverged probably as much as those of any two players in modern history. By the time Johnson left in 1976 he had played at least one full season with eight different teams, a 20th-century record.

Most Teams Played for between 1901 and 1960

Since 1961, when expansion increased the number of teams in the major leagues, Ken Brett, Bob Miller and Tommy Davis have all worn a record 10 different uniforms, but prior to expansion the record was held by Dick Littlefield, who pitched for nine different teams between 1950 and 1958. He appeared with the Red Sox, the White Sox, the Tigers, the Browns, the Pirates, the Cardinals, the Giants, the Cubs and the Milwaukee Braves—and, in addition, pitched three games in a Baltimore uniform after the Browns franchise was transferred there in 1954.

One of a Kind

Mike Torrez. Between 1974 and 1978 he pitched for the Expos, the Orioles, the A's, the Yankees and the Red Sox, winning at least 14 games with each club. No other player in history has done so much for so many teams in such a short space of time.

Proof That the More Things Change the More They Stay the Same

Due to the expansion and free agency, player mobility seems to be at an all-time apex in the 1990s, but that isn't really the case. Exactly a century ago things were equally in a state of flux, as can be seen by the career of Jersey Bakely. In 1884 Bakely embarked on an odyssey that took him not only to four different teams in his next four seasons in the majors but also to four different leagues. Bakely actually pitched for six different clubs during that span. He spent the 1884 season with Philadelphia, Wilmington and Kansas City in the Union Association, then was out of the majors until 1888, when he pitched for Cleveland in the American Association. The following year he found himself still with Cleveland but in the National League, and in 1890 he jumped to the Cleveland entry in the Players League. In each of the four seasons he pitched at least 300 innings, giving him an additional record for being the only pitcher ever to figure in a minimum of 30 decisions in four different major leagues.

Proof That the More Things Change the More They Stay the Same, II

Don Mincher broke in with the Washington Senators in 1960, then went to Minnesota when the franchise transferred there the following year. In 1971 he found himself with the expansion Washington Senators and must have felt that he'd come full circle upon learning that the franchise would be transferring to Texas in 1972 and he'd be going with it.

Players in 1000 or More Games at Two Different Positions

Ernie Banks (1953–71); 1259 games at first base, 1125 games at shortstop

Stan Musial (1941–1963); 1896 games in the outfield, 1016 games at first base

Ron Fairly (1958–1978); 1218 games at first base; 1037 games in the outfield.

Rod Carew (1967–75); 1128 games at second base, 1065 games at first base

Robin Young (1974–   ); 1479 games at shortstop, 1230 games in the outfield.

Only Player in 500 or More games at Four Different Positions

Pete Rose (1963–); 1327 games in the outfield, 948 games at first base, 634 games at third base, 628 games at second base. Rose is the only player ever to have played regularly at four different positions.

Players Who Were Regulars at Three Different Positions
(since 1893)

Wid Conroy, 1901–11; shortstop, third base, outfield

Frankie Gustine, 1939–50; second base, third base, shortstop

Nixey Callahan, 1894–1913; pitcher, outfield, third base

Eric McNair, 1929–42; shortstop, second base, third base

Billy Goodman, 1947–62; second base, first base, third base

Ray Boone, 1948–60; shortstop, third base, first base

Gill McDougald, 1951–60; third base, shortstop, second base

Harmon Killebrew, 1954–75; third base, first base, outfield
Joe Torre, 1960–77; catcher, third base, first base
Pete Runnels, 1951–64; shortstop, second base, first base
Dick Allen, 1963–77; third base, outfield, first base
Jimmy Brown, 1937–46; second base, shortstop, third base
Don Buford, 1963–72; second base, third base, outfield
Buddy Myer, 1925–41; second base, shortstop, third base
Dan Meyer, 1974–85; outfield, first base, third base
Don Money, 1968–83; third base, second base, shortstop
Deron Johnson, 1960–76; first base, third base, outfield
Bill Keister, 1896–1903; second base, shortstop, outfield
Barry McCormick, 1895–1904; second base, shortstop, third base

Players since 1893 Who Pitched in 100 games and Had 1000 hits

Babe Ruth (1914–1935); 163 games pitched, 2873 hits.
Cy Seymour (1896–1913); 140 games pitched, 1723 hits.

Players since 1893 to qualify for the Batting Title and ERA Crown in Same Season

Nixey Callahan, Chicago Colts, 1897; 190 innings pitched, 94 games played
Harry Howell, Baltimore Orioles, 1902; 199 innings pitched, 96 games played

Only Player since 1901 to Play 15 or More Games at Every Position

Art Hoelskoetter, 1905–08. The all-time jack-of-all-trades, in his four seasons with the St. Louis Cardinals, he was tried at every job, including that of pinch hitter, in at least 15 games.

The Hitless Wonders

Duane Kuiper and Johnnie LeMaster both finished their careers in 1985 with performances that cemented their rankings among the leading Hitless Wonders of all time. Kuiper, by failing to hit a home run, kept intact his record for the fewest home runs of any player in history with 3000 or more career at bats, and LeMaster's .119 season vaulted his career batting average into 11th place on the list of the all-time weakest hitters.

THE 20 WORST HITTERS*

		Years Active	At Bats	Batting Ave.	Slugging Ave.
1.	Davy Force	1876–88	2950	.211	.249
2.	Jerry Kindall	1956–65	2057	.213	.327
3.	Bobby Wine	1960–72	3172	.215	.286
4.	Dal Maxvill	1962–75	3443	.217	.259[1]
5.	Joe Quest	1878–88	2282	.217	.267
6.	Darrell Chaney	1969–79	2113	.217	.288
7.	George McBride	1901–20	5526	.218	.264[2]
8.	Skeeter Webb	1932–48	2274	.219	.268
9.	Lee Tannehill	1903–12	3778	.220	.273
10.	Rob Deer	1984–	3831	.220	.445
11.	Johnnie LeMaster	1978–87	3191	.222	.289
12.	Art Whitney	1880–91	3681	.223	.285
13.	Jimmy Canavan	1891–97	2064	.223	.344
14.	Ed Brinkman	1961–75	6045	.224	.300
15.	Pop Smith	1880–91	4176	.224	.317
16.	George Strickland	1950–60	2824	.224	.311
17.	Enzo Hernandez	1971–78	2327	.224	.266[3]
18.	Roger Repoz	1964–72	2145	.224	.390[4]

	Years Active	At Bats	Batting Ave.	Slugging Ave.
19. John Kennedy	1962–74	2110	.225	.323[5]
20. Gorman Thomas	1973–86	4677	.225	.448[6]

*Minimum 2000 career at bats. Pitchers and catchers excluded.

[1]Has the lowest slugging average of any player in this century who batted over 3000 times.

[2]A model of consistency. As Washington's regular shortstop from 1908 through 1916, he never hit more than .235 or less than .203.

[3]No fewer than six of the top 15 on this list were shortstops active in the last 15 years. Hernandez was the prototype—low average, low on base percentage, little run production.

[4]If you remember Repoz at all, you remember him as one of a host of slugging outfielders in the 1960s who connected now and then but mostly just struck out a lot. More than that, he had the lowest career average ever among outfielders with 2000 or more at bats until Rob Deer recently surpassed him. In 1992, however, Deer hiked his career BA four points, putting Repoz once again in jeopardy of being the negative record-holder.

[5]The list, as you've already spotted, is constituted almost entirely of players active before 1920 and after 1960. The weakest hitter between 1920 and World War II, and also the only member of the top 25, was Rabbit Warstler, a shortstop and second baseman, who hit .229 between 1930 and 1940.

[6]Despite his low average, Thomas was a steady, and sometimes spectacular, run producer. In contrast, Rick Miller, also an outfielder from the same period, had a .269 career average on 3887 at bats but only 369 RBIs and 552 runs.

LOWEST SEASON BATTING AVERAGE BY POSITION

(Minimum 300 at Bats)

Position	Name	Team	Year	At Bats	BA	SA
First Base	George Scott	Boston Red Sox	1968	350	.171	.237
Second Base	Mickey Doolan	Brooklyn Dodgers	1918	308	.179	.218
Third Base	Dave Roberts	San Diego Padres	1974	318	.167	.252
Shortstop	George McBride	St. Louis Cards	1906	313	.169	.208
Outfield	George Wright	Texas Rangers	1985	363	.190	.242
Catcher	Bill Bergen	Brooklyn Dodgers	1909	346	.139	.156

Position	Name	Team	Year	At Bats	BA	SA
First Base	Mark McGwire	Oakland A's	1991	483	.201	.383
Second Base	Billy Hallman	Cleveland-Phillies	1902	464	.185	.235[1]
Third Base	Eddie Zimmerman	Brooklyn Dodgers	1911	417	.185	.264
Shortstop	Ed Brinkman	Washington Senators	1965	444	.185	.257[2]
Outfield	Rob Deer	Detroit Tigers	1991	448	.178	.386
Catcher	Billy Sullivan	Chicago White Sox	1908	430	.191	.228

(Minimum 500 at Bats)

Position	Name	Team	Year	At Bats	BA	SA
First Base	Dave Kingman	New York Mets	1982	535	.204	.432
Second Base	Bobby Lowe	Detroit Tigers	1904	507	.207	.258
Third Base	Charles Moran	Wash.-St. Lou.	1904	515	.196	.225
Shortstop	Monte Cross	Philadelphia A's	1904	503	.189	.256
Outfield	Charlie Jones	Washington Senators	1905	544	.208	.267
Catcher	Randy Hundley	Chicago Cubs	1968	553	.226	.311[3]

(Prior to 1901*)

Position	Name	Team	Year	At Bats	BA	SA
First Base	Milt Scott	Baltimore (AA)	1886	482	.190	.242
Second Base	Joe Gerhardt	New York (NL)	1885	399	.155	.195[4]
Third Base	Art Whitney	Kansas City (AA)	1891	358	.193	.240
Shortstop	Charlie Bastian	Philadelphia (NL)	1885	389	.167	.252[5]
Outfield	Jim Lillie	Kansas City (NL)	1886	416	.175	.197
Catcher	Henry Sage	Toledo (AA)	1890	275	.149	.229[6]

*Minimum 350 at bats; for catchers, participation in at least half of team's games.

[1] In 1902 the Phillies replaced Hallman with Pete Childs, who hit .194 and had a .206 slugging average, the lowest in this century among players with over 400 at bats.

[2] Cleveland shortstop Johnny Gochnauer hit .185 both in 1902 and 1903, but each year his average was a few thousandths of a point higher than Brinkman's.

[3] Hundley's not-all-that-terrible batting average in 1968 ranks as the worst mostly because catchers who aren't hitting much seldom got 500 at bats in a season.

[4] Called "Move Up Joe," Gerhardt did anything but that with men on base.

A decent hitter early in his career, he tailed off dramatically after pitchers began throwing overhand.

[5]Bastian, Tom McLaughlin and Henry Easterday were the three most inept of the many weak-hitting shortstops in the 1880s, suggesting that the philosophy then with regard to shortstops may have been very like that in our own time.

[6]Because there were three major leagues in 1890, the supply of good catchers was short. Another AA receiver, Herman Pitz of Brooklyn and Syracuse, hit .165 in 90 games and collected just 47 hits in 284 at bats, all of them singles, making him the only player in history without an extra base hit in over 200 at bats.

Most Consecutive at Bats without Hitting a Home Run

3278—Eddie Foster, 1910–23. Foster collected six career home runs in 5652 at bats, but all came early in his career. He connected for the last time near the beginning of the 1916 season.

Most Career at Bats without Hitting a Home Run, since 1901

1931—Tom Oliver, 1930–33. Second to Oliver is Irv Hall, an infielder with the Philadelphia A's during World War II who went homerless in 1904 at bats.

THE 12 LOWEST CAREER HOME RUN PERCENTAGES*

		Years Active	At Bats	Home runs	HR Pct.
1.	Bill Holbert	1876–88	2335	0	.00000[1]
2.	Duane Kuiper	1975–85	3379	1	.00029
3.	Davy Force	1876–86	2950	1	.00034
4.	Emil Verban	1944–50	2911	1	.00034[2]
5.	Jimmy Slagle	1899–1908	4994	2	.00040
6.	Johnny Bassler	1913–27	2319	1	.00043[3]
7.	Bob Ferguson	1876–84	2306	1	.00043
8.	Floyd Baker	1938–49	2280	1	.00044
9.	Woody Woodward	1963–71	2187	1	.00047
10.	Freddie Maguire	1922–31	2120	1	.00047
11.	Al Bridwell	1905–15	4169	2	.00048
12.	Tommy Thevenow	1924–38	4164	2	.00048[4]

*Players who had home run percentages below .00050 in 2000 or more career at bats.

[1]Holds the all-time record for the most career at bats without hitting a home run.

[2]Got his chance during the war when he was 29. Did little his rookie year, but then hit .412 in the 1944 World Series and went on to a productive career. In 1949 he struck out only twice in 343 at bats.

[3]Shared the Detroit catching job during the 1920s with Larry Woodall, who hit only one home run in 1317 career at bats. The only .300 career hitter on the "Powerless" list, Bassler was still catching in the Pacific Coast League when he was in his middle forties.

[4]Hit his only two home runs in 1926 and also homered in the 1926 World Series. All three were inside-the-park circuit clouts. Thevenow's bizarrely condensed power display is second only to Johnny Cooney's. In 3372 at bats between 1921 and 1944, Cooney hit just two home runs—and they came on successive days in 1939.

Lowest Career Batting Average, Minimum 1,000 at Bats

.175—Ray Oyler, 1965–70. Detroit won the pennnat in 1968 with Oyler playing shortstop and hitting .135 in 111 games. The only other player in this century who posted a sub-.200 career batting average in 1000 or more at bats— catchers again excepted—was Rich Morales, 1967–74, who finished at .195.

Lowest Career Batting Average, Minimum 500 at Bats

.161—John Vukovich, 1970–81. In 1971, while sharing the Phillies' third-base job with Don Money, Vukovich hit .166 in 74 games and had a .189 slugging average.

Most Career at Bats without Ever Getting a Hit, Pitchers Included

41—Randy Tate, New York Mets, 1975; went 0-for-41 in his only season. Excluding pitchers, the lowest career average among players who got at least one hit belongs to Skeeter Shelton, an outfielder who was give a 10-game trial by the Yankees in 1915 and went 1-for-40, giving him an .025 career mark.

Most Career at Bats without Ever Getting a Hit, Pitchers Excluded

23—Mike Potter, St. Louis Cardinals, 1976–77
    Larry Littleton, Cleveland Indians, 1981

Most Career at Bats Exclusively as a Pinch Hitter, .000 Career Batting Average

13—Paul Dicken, Cleveland Indians, 1964, 1966

LOWEST CAREER BATTING AVERAGE
BY POSITION
(Minimum 3,000 at Bats)

Position	Name	Years Active	At Bats	BA
First Base	Steve Balboni	1981–	3120	.229[1]
Second Base	Bobby Knoop	1964–72	3622	.236
Shortstop	Bobby Wine	1960–72	3172	.215
Third Base	Lee Tannehill	1903–12	3778	.220[2]
Outfield	Rob Deer	1984–	3831	.220[1]
Catcher	Bill Bergen	1901–11	3028	.170[3]
Pitcher	Ron Herbel	1963–71	206	.029[4]
(Minimum 200 ABs)				

[1] Also played as a designated hitter.

[2] Also played some at shortstop and second base; the only Hitless Wonder who was actually a member of the original Hitless Wonders—the 1906 Chicago White Sox.

[3] Had only a .201 career slugging average. Reportedly a great defensive catcher, but I'm more inclined to believe he stuck around so long because he spent his last eight seasons with Brooklyn. The Dodgers in those years seemed to have entered into some sort of Faustian compact to make their pitchers survive on as little hitting support as possible.

[4] Went 0-for-47 in 1964, his worst season, but the record belongs to Bob Buhl, who went 0-for-70 in 1962 for the Braves and Cubs. The AL Season record for futility is held by Bill Wight of the White Sox, who went 0-for-61 in 1950.

The Three Most Interesting Teams since 1977

1977 KANSAS CITY ROYALS
W-102 L-60
Manager: Whitey Herzog

Regular Lineup—1B, John Mayberry; 2B, Frank White; 3B, George Brett; SS, Freddie Patek; RF, Al Cowens; CF, Amos Otis; LF, Tom Poquette; C, Darrell Porter; P, Dennis Leonard; P, Jim Colborn; P, Paul Splittorff; P, Andy Hassler; P, Marty Pattin; P, Doug Bird; P, Larry Gura.

After posting the best regular-season record ever by an AL expansion club, the Royals were only three outs away from winning the American League pennant. Before they got them the Yankees scored three runs and beat them in the ninth inning of the fifth and final LCS game for the second year in a row. Probably the finest Royals team ever, much stronger than either the 1980 or 1985 clubs, they not only had a solid lineup but a good bench and the deepest pitching staff in the league. With just a very slight reordering of events, Herzog could have taken them to four pennants in five years—and they didn't miss by all that much in 1979, either. The Yankees, Reds and A's are remembered as the dominant teams of the 1970s, but the Royals were on a par with them and may even have been the best of them all.

1980 HOUSTON ASTROS
W-93 L-70
Manager: Bill Virdon

Regular Lineup—1B, Art Howe; 2B, Joe Morgan; 3B, Enos Cabell; SS, Craig Reynolds; RF, Terry Puhl; CF, Cesar Cedeno; LF, Jose Cruz; C, Alan Ashby; P, Joe Niekro; P, Nolan Ryan; P, Ken Forsch; P, Vern Ruhle; P, J. R. Richard; P, Joe Sambito; P, Dave Smith; P, Frank LaCorte.

The Astros came to Dodger Stadium on the last weekend of the season needing to win only one game of a three-game set to clinch their first division title. They lost all three but won the one-game playoff for the right to meet the Phillies in the LCS. After splitting the first two games in Philadelphia, Virdon got a super 11-inning 1–0 shutout from Niekro in Game Three. Playing at home and only one step away from taking the pennant, the Astros then dropped two straight 10-inning games. In Game Five, they led 5–2 in the top of the eighth with Ryan pitching, but Ryan couldn't hold off the Phillies, nor could relief ace Sambito. For the first time in their history the Astros, in 1980, had two .300 hitters, Cedeno and Cruz, plus a pitching staff that could have been unstoppable if Richard hadn't suffered a midseason stroke. An ill-fated club, tenacious to the end, but one break short of winning it all. The same could be said for the 1981 team, which lost the division playoff by a hair to the Dodgers, who went on to win the World Series, and, of course, the 1986 team.

1983 PHILADELPHIA PHILLIES
W-90 L-72
Manager: Pat Corrales and Paul Owens

Regular Lineup—1B, Pete Rose; 2B, Joe Morgan; 3B, Mike Schmidt; SS, Ivan DeJesus; RF, Von Hayes; CF, Gary Maddox; LF, Gary Matthews; C, Bo Diaz; P, Steve Carlton; P, John Denny; P, Ron Reed; P, Charlie Hudson; P, Al Holland, P, Marty Bystrom.

Maddox, their top-hitting regular, hit only .275; they had only one regular younger than 30, no 20-game winners, got only a 15–16 season from staff ace Carlton, eight wins from their number three starter Hudson, and a 6–9 record from Bystrom, their fourth starter. Yet they won their division by six games, romped over the Dodgers in the LCS and won the World Series opener before the Orioles burst their bubble and took four straight. The three big reasons for their unexpected win were Denny's 19 victories, Holland's 25 saves and Schmidt's 40 homers and 109 RBIs. But other contenders got equally good seasons from their top players, and none had a first baseman who hit .245 and had just 45 RBIs. The real catalyst on this club was 39-year-old Morgan, who hit only .230 but scored 72 runs and collected 89 walks in just 404 at bats. Many believe this team, and not the 1973 Mets, was the weakest pennant winner since the 1944 St. Louis Browns—but it may also have been the most savvy team ever. Whether they would have come together if Corrales had remained at the helm may be the only real grist for argument here.

Third Baseman's Records

The proliferation of great third basemen in the past 20 years has yet to be studied and understood. As a point of comparison, only one third baseman active before 1908—Jimmy Collins—is in the Hall of Fame. No one can predict for sure how many third basemen active at the moment will make it, but three seems an extremely conservative guess, and it may be as many as six or seven. From whence did they suddenly all appear?

SEASON BATTING RECORDS

Department	National League	American League
Batting Averages	.391, JOHN MCGRAW, Baltimore, 1899 .379, Fred Lindstrom, New York, 1930*	.390, George Brett, K.C. Royals, 1980
Slugging Average	.644, Mike Schmidt, Philadelphia, 1981	.664, GEORGE BRETT, K.C. Royals, 1980
Home Runs	48, MIKE SCHMIDT, Philadelphia, 1980	43, Al Rosen, Cleveland, 1953
RBIs	135, Eddie Mathews, Boston, 1953	145, AL ROSEN, Cleveland, 1953
Runs	143, John McGraw, Baltimore, 1898 130, Pete Rose, Cincinnati, 1976*	145, HARLOND CLIFT, St. Louis, 1936
Hits	231, Fred Lindstrom, New York, 1928, 1930	240, WADE BOGGS, Boston, 1985
Doubles	51, Pete Rose, Cincinnati, 1978	56, GEORGE KELL, Detroit, 1950

Department	National League	American League
Triples	27, GEORGE DAVIS, New York, 1893 27, JIMMY WILLIAMS, Pittsburgh, 1899 22, Tommy Leach, Pittsburgh, 1902*	22, Bill Bradley, Cleveland, 1903
Total Bases	363, Eddie Mathews, Boston, 1953	367, AL ROSEN, Cleveland, 1953
Bases on Balls	131, Bob Elliott, Boston, 1948	151, EDDIE YOST, Washington, 1956
Stolen Bases	59, Art Devlin, New York, 1905	74, FRITZ MAISEL, New York, 1914
Strikeouts	180, MIKE SCHMIDT, Philadelphia, 1975	172, Jim Presley, Seattle, 1986
Fewest Strikeouts (Minimum 500 ABs)	7, Pie Traynor, Pittsburgh, 1929	3, JOE SEWELL, New York, 1932

*Record since 1901.

Note: Harmon Killebrew of the Twins hit 49 homers in 1969 but played almost half the season at first base. Woody English of the Cubs scored 152 runs in 1930 while playing 83 games at third base and 78 games at shortstop; since his total is higher than the record at both positions, he can conceivably be regarded as the all-time record holder at either.

Most Games, Career, at Third Base
  2,870—Brooks Robinson, 1955–77

Most Consecutive Games at Third Base
  576—Eddie Yost, Washington, July 3, 1951, through May 11, 1955

Best Career Fielding Average
  .971—Brooks Robinson, 1955–77

Most Seasons League Leader in Fielding Average
  AL—11—Brooks Robinson, last in 1975
  NL—6—Heinie Groh, last in 1924
    Ken Reitz, last in 1981

EVOLUTION OF SEASON RECORD FOR BEST FIELDING AVERAGE

	Team	League	Year	Average
Joe Battin	St. Louis	National	1876	.867[1]
Bill Hague	Providence	National	1879	.925[2]
Chappy McGarr	Boston	National	1890	.933
Billy Nash	Boston	National	1894	.933[3]
Lave Cross	Philadelphia	National	1895	.940
Bill Clingman	Louisville	National	1897	.947
Lave Cross	Cleveland-St. Louis	National	1899	.959[4]
Harry Steinfeldt	Chicago	National	1907	.967
Terry Turner	Cleveland	American	1911	.970[5]
Hans Lobert	Philadelphia	National	1913	.974
Larry Gardner	Cleveland	American	1920	.976
Heinie Groh	New York	National	1924	.983[6]
Willie Kamm	Cleveland	American	1933	.984[7]
Hank Majeski	Philadelphia	American	1947	.988
Don Money	Milwaukee	American	1974	.989

[1]A victim of the fair-foul rule change. Slumped to .199 in 1877 after hitting .300 the previous year.

[2]A fluke season—Hague never again came within 80 points of his record. Art Whitney's .924 FA with Pittsburgh in 1887 is probably a truer peak figure for the period.

[3]Rated by many the best fielding third baseman prior to 1900.

[4]Never received anywhere near the press that Hall of Famer Jimmy Collins did, but had better career stats in almost every major department.

[5]Also played shortstop and second base in 1910 but was in enough games at third base to be the recognized fielding leader. Led AL third basemen in FA again in 1912.

[6]Still the NL season record; broke his own former record of .975, set in 1923.

[7]Those who saw both Kamm and Brooks Robinson play rank them about equal and, in any case, the two best glovemen ever at third base.

Most Consecutive Errorless Games

97—Jim Davenport, San Francisco, July 29, 1966, through April 28, 1968. Davenport was a utility infielder by the late 1960s and during the skein also played other positions where he did make errors.

Most Consecutive Errorless Chances

261—Don Money, Milwaukee Brewers, September 28, 1973, through July 16, 1974. Money's season FA record was largely the result of his long errorless streak.

Most Chances Accepted, Career
   8,902—Brooks Robinson, 1955–77

Most Chances Accepted, Season
   603—Harlond Clift, St. Louis Browns, 1937

Most Chances Accepted, Game, Nine Innings
   13—Done by several third basemen; last by Roy Hughes, Chicago Cubs, August 29, 1944

Most Assists, Season
   412—Graig Nettles, Cleveland Indians, 1971

Most Seasons League Leader in Assists
   AL—8—Brooks Robinson, last in 1974
   NL—7—Ron Santo, 1962–68 consecutive

Greatest Left-handed Third Baseman
   Hick Carpenter, 1879–92, played 1,059 games at third base and a scattering of games at shortstop and second base. Carpenter was probably not only the best southpaw third baseman but the best southpaw infielder, period. The last lefty infielder of note was Kid Mohler, a second baseman with the San Francisco Seals in the Pacific Coast League as late as the early teens. Mohler played three games in the majors at age 19 in 1894 before commencing his long minor-league career. The last southpaw infielder to play regularly in the majors was Bill Huhlen, a shortstop with the 1896 Phillies. Don Mattingly of the Yankees, who played several games at third base in 1986, is the most recent southpaw infielder.

Most Gold Glove Awards
   16—Brooks Robinson, 1955–77. Only pitcher Jim Kaat has won as many Gold Gloves.

Red-hot Rookies

Fernando Valenzuela and Dwight Gooden, the most exciting rookie pitchers since Herb Score, exploded onto the
scene in the 1980s only four years apart, and in 1986 Todd
Worrell of the Cardinals shattered the yearling record for
saves by a wide margin in the process of copping the NL
Rookie of the Year Award. None of the three managed to
win 20 games, something only one first-year pitcher—Tom
Browning of the Reds—has done in this decade, but
Valenzuela and Gooden also each set an all-time rookie
record. Gooden's is well known, but you may need to check
the list below before you remember Valenzuela's.

ROOKIE RECORD HOLDERS*

Batting

Department	National League	American League
Batting Average	.373, George Watkins, St. Louis, 1930	.408, JOE JACKSON, Cleveland, 1911
Slugging Average	.621, GEORGE WATKINS, St. Louis, 1930	.609, Ted Williams, Boston, 1939
Home Runs	38, Wally Berger, Boston, 1930 38, Frank Robinson, Cincinnati, 1956	49, MARK MCGWIRE, Oakland, 1987
RBIs	119, Wally Berger, Boston, 1930	145, TED WILLIAMS, Boston, 1939
Hits	223, LLOYD WANER, Pittsburgh, 1927	217, Tony Oliva, Minnesota, 1964

*Qualifications for rookie status are the same as those employed by the
Official Major League Scoring Committee as of 1971.

Department	National League	American League
Runs	135, ROY THOMAS, Philadelphia, 1899 133, Lloyd Waner, Pittsburgh, 1927**	132, Joe DiMaggio, New York, 1936
Doubles	52, JOHNNY FREDERICK, Brooklyn, 1929	47, Fred Lynn, Boston, 1975
Triples	27, JIMMY WILLIAMS, Pittsburgh, 1899 25, Tommy Long, St. Louis, 1915**	19, Home Run Baker, Philadelphia, 1909 19, Joe Cassidy, Washington, 1904
Total Bases	352, Dick Allen, Philadelphia, 1964	374, HAL TROSKY, Cleveland, 1934 374, TONY OLIVA, Minnesota, 1964
Stolen Bases	110, VINCE COLEMAN, St. Louis, 1985	66, Kenny Lofton, Cleveland, 1992
Bases on Balls	115, ROY THOMAS, Philadelphia, 1899 100, Jim Gilliam, Brooklyn, 1953**	107, Ted Williams, Boston, 1939
Pinch Hits	20, JOE FRAZIER, St. Louis, 1954	17, Sammy Hale, Detroit, 1920
Strikeouts	168, Juan Samuel, Philadelphia, 1984	185, PETE INCAVIGLIA, Texas, 1986
Fewest Strikeouts (Minimum 500 ABs)	17, BUDDY HASSETT, Brooklyn, 1936	25, Tom Oliver, Boston, 1930

Pitching

Department	National League	American League
Wins	30, BILL HOFFER, Baltimore, 1895 28, Pete Alexander, Philadelphia, 1911**	26, Russ Ford, New York, 1910
Losses	28, STILL BILL HILL, Louisville, 1896 25, Harry McIntyre, Brooklyn, 1905**	26, Bob Groom, Washington, 1901
Games	78, Tim Burke, Montreal, 1985	80, MITCH WILLIAMS, Texas, 1986
Starts	41, IRV YOUNG, Boston, 1905	36, Roscoe Miller, Detroit, 1901

Department	National League	American League
Complete Games	41, IRV YOUNG, Boston, 1905	35, Roscoe Miller, Detroit, 1901
Innings Pitched	378, IRV YOUNG, Boston, 1905	332, Roscoe Miller, Detroit, 1901
Winning Pct.	.838 BILL HOFFER, Baltimore, 1895 .833, King Cole, Chicago, 1910**	.813, Russ Ford, New York, 1910
Strikeouts	276, DWIGHT GOODEN New York, 1984	245, Herb Score, Cleveland, 1955
Bases on Balls	185, SAM JONES, Chicago, 1955	168, Elmer Myers, Philadelphia, 1916
Shutouts	8, FERNANDO VALEN-ZUELA, L.A., 1980	8, RUSS FORD, New York, 1910 8, REB RUSSELL, Chicago, 1913
Saves	36, TODD WORRELL, St. Louis, 1986	27, Greg Olson, Baltimore, 1989
ERA	1.11, BABE ADAMS, Pittsburgh, 1909	1.39, Harry Krause, Philadelphia, 1909

**Record since 1901.

Only Rookie to Win a Batting Title
Tony Oliva, Minnesota Twins, 1964 (.323)

Only Rookies to Be League Leaders in Home Runs
Al Rosen, Cleveland Indians, 1950 (37); Mark McGwire, Oakland A's, 1987 (49), Ralph Kiner, Pittsburgh, 1946 (23).

Oldest Rookie 20-Game Winner
Jim Turner, Boston Braves, 1937, 34 years old (20–11). Lou Fette, a rookie 30-year-old teammate of Turner's, also won 20.

Only Rookie Pitcher to Win 20 Games While Pitching Less Than 200 Innings
Bob Grim, New York Yankees, 1954 (20–6; 199 innings pitched). Grim is not only the only rookie to accomplish this, but the only pitcher in history.

Most Recent Rookie 20-Game Winners
NL—Tom Browning, Cincinnati, 1985 (21-9)
AL—Bob Grim, New York, 1954 (20-6)

Best Season by Rookie Batter Who Failed to Win Rookie of the Year Award

Minnie Minoso, Chicago White Sox, 1951, hit .326, led the AL in triples and stolen bases and was fifth in slugging, but lost out to the Yankees Gil McDougald.

Best Season by Rookie Pitcher Who Failed to Win Rookie of the Year Award

Gene Bearden, Cleveland Indians, 1948, had a 20–7 record and led the AL with a 2.43 ERA, but lost the award to Al Dark of the Boston Braves in the last season only one rookie honor was given.

Only Team in Existence since 1947 That Has Never Had a Rookie of the Year Winner

Pittsburgh. Ironically, in 1946, the last season no official rookie award was given, Ralph Kiner of the Pirates was generally regarded to be the top rookie in the majors, although Del Ennis of the Phillies copped the *Sporting News* yearling award.

Life-Begins-At-40 Records

When 46-year-old Phil Niekro garnered his 300th win by blanking Toronto 8–0 on the last day of the 1985 season, he also became the oldest major-league pitcher ever to toss a shutout, replacing Satchel Paige, who was a few months younger when he whitewashed the Tigers 1–0 in 12 innings on August 6, 1952. Between them Niekro and Paige hold a number of the "Life-Begins-at-40" records.

Oldest Player to Hit a Home Run
AL—46—Jack Quinn, Philadelphia, 1930. Quinn, a pitcher, is also the oldest player to make more than one hit in a season—he collected four in 1932 when he was 48.
NL—46—Cap Anson, Chicago, 1897

Oldest Player to Hit a Grand Slam Home Run since 1901
43—Tony Perez, Cincinnati, in 1985

Oldest Player to Participate in a Major-League Game
Satchel Paige pitched three shutout innings for the Kansas City A's at age 59 (or maybe older) on September 25, 1965, against the Boston Red Sox. The only hit off Satch was a double by Carl Yastrzemski.

Oldest Player to Hit Safely in a Major-League Game
Minnie Minoso went 1-for-8 at age 53 as a dh for the Chicago White Sox in 1976; his lone hit, a single, came on September 12. Nick Altrock was a slightly younger 53-year-old when he played right field for the White Sox on October 6, 1929, and got a hit in his only trip to the plate.

First 40-Year-Old to Play in a Major-League Game

Dickey Pearce, a standout shortstop in the 1850s, hung on long enough to play 25 games with St. Louis in 1876, the National League's inaugural year. But if you're among those who credit the National Association with being a major league, the honor goes to Harry Wright, who played a single game in the outfield for the 1875 Boston Red Caps after he turned 40. Wright also played one game for Boston in 1876.

First Player Who Was Still a Regular at Age 40

Joe Start, Providence Grays, 1883. Start, a first baseman, remained a regular player until he was nearly 44 years old.

Oldest Rookie

NL—43—Diomedes Olivo, Pittsburgh, 1962, had a 5–1 record and seven saves in 62 games.

AL—42—Satchel Paige, Cleveland, 1948, had a 6–1 record in 27 games.

Oldest Rookie to Play in Over Half His Team's Games

Chuck Hostetler hit .298 in 90 games as a 41-year-old rookie outfielder with the 1944 Detroit Tigers.

Oldest Rookie to Play Enough to Qualify for a Batting Title

Earle Brucker played 102 games for the 1937 Philadelphia A's at age 36—the rules then required a player to participate in two-thirds of his team's games to qualify for a batting title. In 1938 Brucker actually did lead all American League batters when he hit .374—but in only 53 games.

Oldest Rookie to Go on to a 20-Year Career

Hoyt Wilhelm, 29 when he came to the New York Giants in 1952, retired in 1972 after playing 21 years in the majors.

Most Games Caught after Age 40 Prior to 1980s

220—Deacon McGuire, 1884–1912. Some historians, myself among them, consider this to be the most impressive of all the "Life-Begins-at-40" accomplishments.

Oldest 20-Game Winner

NL—42—Warren Spahn, Milwaukee, 1963 (23–7)
AL—41—Cy Young, Boston, 1908 (21–11)

Oldest League Leader in a Major Pitching Department
    NL—48—Jack Quinn, Brooklyn, 1932; led in saves with
8. Also the NL save leader in 1931 with 15.
    AL—42—Jim Turner, New York, 1945, led in saves with
10.

Oldest League Leader in a Major Batting Department
    AL—40—Ted Williams, Boston, 1958, hit .328 to win the
batting title.
    NL—40—Cap Anson, Chicago, 1891, led in RBIs with
120.

LIFE-BEGINS-AT-40 SEASON BATTING RECORDS

Department	National League	American League
Batting Average	.335, Cap Anson, Chicago, 1895 .325, Pete Rose, Philadelphia, 1981*	.357, TY COBB, Philadelphia, 1927
Slugging Average	.508, STAN MUSIAL, St. Louis, 1962	.501, Darrell Evans, Detroit, 1987
Home Runs	20, Hank Aaron, Atlanta, 1974	34, DARRELL EVANS, Detroit, 1987
RBIs	120, CAP ANSON, Chicago, 1891 82, Stan Musial, St. Louis, 1962*	108, Dave Winfield, Toronto, 1992
Hits	172, Pete Rose, Philadelphia, 1982	207, SAM RICE, Washington, 1930
Runs	87, Cap Anson, Chicago, 1895 82, Willie Mays, San Francisco, 1971*	121, SAM RICE, Washington, 1930
Doubles	32, Honus Wagner, Pittsburgh, 1915	35, SAM RICE, Washington, 1930
Triples	17, HONUS WAGNER, Pittsburgh, 1915	13, Sam Rice, Washington, 1930
Total Bases	243, Honus Wagner, Pittsburgh, 1915	286, DAVE WINFIELD Toronto, 1992
Stolen Bases	25, DAVEY LOPES, Chicago-Houston, 1986	22, Ty Cobb, Philadelphia, 1927

Department	National League	American League
Bases on Balls	112, Willie Mays, San Francisco, 1971	121, LUKE APPLING, Chicago, 1949
Strikeouts	123, WILLIE MAYS, San Francisco, 1971	115, Reggie Jackson, California, 1986
Fewest Strikeouts (Minimum 500 ABs)	32, Pete Rose, Philadelphia, 1982	14, SAM RICE, Washington, 1930

*Record since 1901.

Note: Record holders are players who were at least 40 years old before the end of the season in which they set the mark. Batting and slugging average record holders must have had enough plate appearances to qualify for the batting title.

The Leading Losers

Hugh Mulcahy is the only major leaguer who has ever been saddled with the unwelcome nickname of "Losing Pitcher," but rather surprisingly he owns none of the major records for pitching losses. Three of them have been set since 1981—by Jose DeLeon, Terry Felton and George Frazier. Do you know what they are?

Lowest Winning Percentage, Season, Minimum 20 Decisions
AL—.048—Jack Nabors, Philadelphia, 1916 (1–20)
NL—.095—Jose DeLeon, Pittsburgh, 1985 (2–19)

Most Losses, Season, without a Win
AL—12—Steve Gerkin, Philadelphia, 1945
NL—12—Russ Miller, Philadelphia, 1929

Most Consecutive Losses, Season
AL—19—Bob Groom, Washington, 1909
       Jack Nabors, Philadelphia, 1916
NL—18—Roger Craig, New York Mets, 1963
       Cliff Curtis, Boston, 1910. Curtis also lost his first five decisions in 1911, giving him 23 consecutive losses, a record that lasted until 1993 when Anthony Young of the New York Mets dropped 27 straight decisions before beating Florida in relief, 5–4, on July 28.

Most Seasons League Leader in Losses
NL—4—Phil Niekro, Atlanta, 1977–80 consecutive
AL—4—Bobo Newsom, last in 1945; done with four different teams
       Pedro Ramos, 1958-61, consecutive

Most Consecutive Losses, Start of Career
16—Terry Felton, Minnesota, April 18, 1980, through September 12, 1982; breaking Guy Morton's record of 13, set with Cleveland in 1914.

Last 25-Game Loser
Ben Cantwell, Boston Braves, 1935. His 4–25 record is the worst since 1901 by a 25-game loser. Just two years earlier, in 1933, Cantwell had rung up a 20–10 record with the Braves to lead all National League pitchers in *winning* percentage.

Most Losses, Season, 162-Game Schedule
24—Roger Craig, New York Mets, 1962
  Jack Fisher, New York Mets, 1964

Most Losses, Season, by Relief Pitcher
NL—16—Gene Garber, Atlanta, 1979 (6–16)
AL—14—Darold Knowles, Washington, 1970 (2–14 but
      had 27 saves)
      John Hiller, Detroit, 1974 (17–14)
      Mike Marshall, Minnesota, 1979 (10–14)

Most Losses, Season
48—John Coleman, Philadelphia Phillies, 1883 (12-48). Despite his monstrous number of losses, Coleman was the Phillies' ace—the rest of their mound staff had an aggregate 5–33 record.

Most Losses, Season, since 1893
33—Red Donahue, St. Louis Browns, 1897. But Donahue was not the last 30-game loser. That distinction belongs to Jim Hughey of Cleveland, who had a 4–30 record in 1899.

Most Losses, Season, since 1901
29—Vic Willis, Boston Braves, 1905. He also dropped 25 decisions in 1904, making him the last pitcher to lose 24 or more games two years in a row.

Most Losses, Season, since 1920
27—Paul Derringer, St. Louis Cardinals–Cincinnati Reds, 1933

Most Losses, Only Major-League Season

37—George Cobb, Baltimore Orioles, 1892 (10–37). In 1876, his one and only season, Dory Dean had a 4–26 record with Cincinnati, which played just 65 games. Cobb's record, in contrast, came in the first season that the National League experimented with a 154-game schedule. Another one-year hurler, Florence Sullivan of the AA Pittsburgh Alleghenies, lost 35 of his team's 108 decisions in 1884.

Most Losses, Only Major-League Season, since 1901

NL—18—Ham Iburg, Philadelphia, 1902
AL—13—Orie Arntzen, Philadelphia, 1945
       Troy Herriage, Kansas City A's, 1956
       Jeff Byrd, Toronto, 1977
FL—20—Hank Keupper, St. Louis, 1914

Only 30-Game Winner Who Later Lost 20 Games in a Season

Denny McLain, Washington, 1971 (10–22); Detroit, 1968 (31–6)

Only Pitcher since 1901 to Lose 20 Games for a Pennant-winning Team

George Mullin, Detroit, 1907 (20–20)

Lowest Winning Percentage by Pitcher on a Pennant-Winner, Minimum 20 Decisions

NL—.345—Larry French, Chicago, 1938 (10–19)
AL—.350—Bill Bevens, New York, 1947 (7–13). In 1986 Tom Seaver of the pennant winning Red Sox also had a 7–13 record, but six of his losses came with the second-division White Sox.

Most Losses, Season, in a World Series (Best 4-of-7)

3—George Frazier, New York Yankees, 1981; all of them in relief

Most Fantastic Turnaround from One Season to the Next

Earl Hamilton was cut by the St. Louis Browns after he had a 0–9 record in 1917. Brought back to the majors by Pittsburgh in 1918, Hamilton posted a perfect 6-0 record and an 0.83 ERA in six starts.

TOP 10 IN CAREER LOSSES

		Years Active	Losses
1.	Cy Young	1890–1911	316
2.	Pud Galvin	1879–92	308
3.	Nolan Ryan	1966–93	292
4.	Walter Johnson	1907–27	279
5.	Phil Niekro	1964–87	274
6.	Gaylord Perry	1962–83	265
7.	Don Sutton	1966–88	256
8.	Jack Powell	1897–1912	254[1]
9.	Eppa Rixey	1912–33	251
10.	Robin Roberts	1948–66	245
	Warren Spahn	1942–65	245

[1]Has a .492 career winning percentage, one of only two 200-game winners who finished below .500. The other is Bobo Newsom with a .487 winning percentage.

MOST LOSSES, CAREER, WITH .000 WINNING PERCENTAGE

	Years Active	Career Record
Terry Felton	1979–82	0–16
Steve Gerkin	1945	0–12
Charlie Stecher	1890	0–10
Ed Albosta	1941, 1946	0–8
Archie Reynolds	1968–72	0–8
Paul Brown	1961–63, 1968	0–8
Walter Craddock	1955–58	0–7
Tommy McCarthy	1884–94	0–7[1]
Roy Bruner	1939–41	0–7
Walter Moser	1906, 1911	0–7
Ed O'Neil	1890	0–7[2]
Charlie Barnabe	1927–28	0–7

[1]Made the Hall of Fame as an outfielder, but his first season, as a 19-year-old pitcher-outfielder with the 1884 Boston Union Association team, is best forgotten. He was 0–7 on the mound and hit only .215.

[2]O'Neil and Charlie Stecher were teammates in 1890 on the AA Philadelphia A's, who ended the season with probably the worst pitching staff in history.

Lowest Career Winning Percentage since 1901, Minimum 200 Decisions

.372—Milt Gaston, 1924–34 (97–164). Gaston, who never pitched in the minor leagues, had a 5–3 record as a 28-year-old rookie with the 1924 Yankees and was 15–14 with the Browns in 1925 after being traded to them but finished below .500 every other season.

Lowest Career Winning Percentage since 1901, Minimum 150 Decisions

.331—Buster Brown, 1905–13 (51–103); died before the 1914 season began.

Lowest Career Winning Percentage since 1901, Minimum 100 Decisions

.299—Happy Townsend, 1901–06 (35–82). Townsend spent the bulk of his career with dismal Washington teams, and it's impossible now to gauge whether he was unlucky or simply a poor pitcher carried by a club that could find no one better.

Lowest Career Winning Percentage since 1901, Minimum 50 Decisions

.206—Ike Pearson, 1939–48 (13–50); including a 7–40 record as a starter. Signed by the pitcher-hungry Phillies after graduating from the University of Mississippi, Pearson was thrown into the breech without a minor-league apprenticeship and suffered for it his whole career.

Lowest Career Winning Percentage, Cy Young Award Winner

.381—Mark Davis (1980–   ) 51–83

Lowest Career Winning Percentage, Pitcher with ERA below 3.00 in over 100 Decisions

.352—George Bell, 1907–11 (43–79). Seventeen of Bell's 43 wins were shutouts, and he had a fine 2.85 ERA. One of the most luckless pitchers ever, his misfortune was twofold: He was bound by the reserve clause to Brooklyn, at the time a rotten team, and he didn't get to the majors until he was 32 years old.

All-time Winner of the Hugh Mulcahy Award

Ike Butler had a 1–10 record with the 1902 Baltimore

Orioles in his only year in the majors. Discouraged, he signed with Portland, where he set a Pacific Coast League record in 1903 when he lost 31 games and then tied his own mark the following year when he dropped 31 more.

Father-and-Son Firsts

In 1989, Ken Griffey of the Reds not only had the ultimate
thrill a baseball-playing parent can receive when his son
Ken, Jr., cracked the Mariners' starting lineup, he became
the elder half of the first father-son duo to be active in the
majors in the same season.

First Son to Play for a Team Managed by His Father
Earl Mack, Philadelphia A's, 1910; son of Connie Mack.
When Dale Berra played with the Yankees for a short while
under his father's tutelage in 1985, it was only the second
time in major-league history a son had been managed by his
father. In 1987 Cal Ripken became the first son to play as
a regular for his father.

First Father and Son to Play in the Majors
Herman and Jack Doscher. A third baseman with Troy,
beginning in 1879, Herman wasn't much of a player, nor
was his son, who pitched briefly for the Cubs and Dodgers
in the early 1900s. The second father-and-son combo to
make the majors, the Meinkes—Frank and son Bob—had
even less impact.

First Father and Son Who Both Had Lengthy Careers
The Sullivans, Billy, Sr., and Billy, Jr. The elder Sullivan
played for the White Sox in the first part of the century and
was a fine catcher but a weak hitter. His son, also a catcher,
was the antithesis. Billy, Jr., hit .351 for Cleveland in 1935,
but his defensive skills were such that he caught more than
half his team's games only once and was moved behind the
plate after failing to cut it as both a third baseman and a
first baseman. The Sullivans were also the first father and

son to play in a World Series—Billy I in 1906 with the White Sox, and Billy II in 1940 with the Tigers.

Other Fathers and Sons Who Both Had Lengthy Careers
Earl Averill, Sr., and Jr. George and Dick Sisler. Ray and Bob Boone. Marty and Matt Keough. Ernie and Don Johnson. Mike and Tommy Tresh. Pinky and Milt May. Joe Schultz, Sr., and Jr. Mel Queen and son Mel. Dick Schofield and son Dick. Yogi and Dale Berra. Bob and Terry Kennedy. Maury and Bump Wills. Joe Coleman and son Joe. Dizzy and Steve Trout. Jim Bagby, Sr., and Jr. Vern and Vance Law. Jim and Mike Hegan. Max and Hal Lanier. Dolf and Doug Camilli. Gus and Buddy Bell. Roy Smalley, II and III. Oscar Ray Grimes, Sr., and Jr. Thornton and Don Lee.

First Father and Son to Play for the Same Team in the Same Decade
Earle Brucker, Sr., and Jr., both caught for the A's in the 1940s. Although he didn't make the majors until he was 36 years old, the elder Brucker, a long-time A's coach under Connie Mack, posted a .290 average over a five-year career. The Griffeys in 1990 of course became the first father and son to play for the same team in the same *season*.

First Father and Son Both to Pitch in the Majors
Willie Mills, New York Giants, 1901; Art Mills, Boston Braves, 1927. Neither ever won a game.

Only Father and Son Each to Win a Game before His 20th Birthday
Lew Krausse, Sr., Philadelphia A's, 1931; Lew Krausse, Jr., Kansas City A's, 1961.

Only Father and Son Each to Be a League Leader in Innings Pitched
Jim Bagby, Sr., Cleveland, 1920, led the AL with 340 innings pitched; Jim Bagby, Jr., Cleveland, 1943, equaled his father's feat by pitching in 273 innings.

Only Father and Son Each to Be a League Leader in Losses
Herman Pillette, Detroit, 1923, led the AL with 19 losses; Duane Pillette, St. Louis, 1951, tied for the AL lead with 14 losses.

Only Father and Son Each to Be a League Leader in Pinch Hits

Joe Schultz, Sr., St. Louis Cardinals, 1919, led the NL with eight pinch hits; Joe Schultz, Jr., St. Louis Browns, led the AL in pinch hits in both 1945 and 1946.

First Black Father and Son to Play in the Majors

Sam Hairston, Chicago White Sox, 1951, saw two of his sons make the majors—John in 1969 with the Cubs, and later Jerry, who broke in with the 1973 White Sox. Maury Wills became the second black father to have a son make it when Bump won the Rangers' second base job in 1977.

Longest Span between First Games Played in Majors by a Father and Son, Since 1901

36 years—Jack Lively, Detroit Tigers, 1911; Bud Lively, Cincinnati Reds, 1947. Both were pitchers; Jack was 62 years old when his son reached the majors.

All-time Longest Span between First Games Played in Majors by a Father and Son

43 years—Charlie Ganzel, St. Paul (UA), 1884; Babe Ganzel, Washington Senators, 1927. The elder Ganzel, among the game's leading catchers in the 1890s, had been dead 13 years by the time Babe made the majors, but his younger brother John, a first baseman with several teams in the early part of the century, was still alive to see it.

Only Father to Have Two Sons Who Won Batting Titles

Ewart Walker, who pitched for Washington between 1909 and 1912, fathered both Dixie and Harry Walker. Dixie won the NL batting title in 1944; Harry won it in 1947. Moreover, Ewart's brother Ernie played in the majors for the Browns in the mid-teens, giving the Walkers a second record for being the only family who had two generations of brothers make it to the top.

First Three-Generation Family in Majors

When Bret Boone joined Seattle in 1992, following on the heels of his grandfather Ray and his father Bob, the Boones became the first father-son-grandson trio in big league history.

LEADERS IN COMBINED CAREER HITS*

1.	Gus and Buddy Bell	4337
2.	George, Dick and Dave Sisler	3557
3.	Eddie Collins, Sr. and Jr.	3377
4.	Ray, Bob and Bret Boone	3191
5.	Bobby and Barry Bonds	3051
6.	Maury and Bump Wills	2941
7.	Ewart, Dixie and Harry Walker	2883
8.	Yogi and Dale Berra	2753

LEADERS IN COMBINED CAREER WINS*

1.	Dizzy and Steve Trout	258
2.	Jim Bagby, Sr. and Jr.	224
3.	Ed Walsh and son Ed	206
4.	Joe Coleman and son Joe	194

*Batters contributing at least one hit and pitchers at least one win to the family total.

When both teams joined Seattle in 1976, following the
birth of his grandchild, Ray and the father hung up receivers.
On the other teams. New York, New Jersey.

The Most Prolific Hitters

In 1985 Pete Rose established a new all-time record for
career base hits and Wade Boggs became the first American
League player since 1928 to make 240 hits in a season.

PLAYERS WHO MADE 240 OR MORE HITS IN A SEASON

	Team	League	Year	Hits
George Sisler	St. Louis.	American	1920	257
Lefty O'Doul	Philadelphia	National	1929	254
Bill Terry	New York	National	1930	254
Al Simmons	Philadelphia	American	1925	253
Rogers Hornsby	St. Louis	National	1922	250
Chuck Klein	Philadelphia	National	1930	250
Ty Cobb	Detroit	American	1911	248
George Sisler	St. Louis	American	1922	246
Babe Herman	Brooklyn	National	1930	241
Heinie Manush	Detroit	American	1928	241
Jesse Burkett	Cleveland	National	1896	240
Wade Boggs	Boston	American	1985	240

Most Seasons League Leader in Hits
    AL—8—Ty Cobb, last in 1919
    NL—7—Pete Rose, last in 1981

Most Seasons 200 or More Hits
    NL—10—Pete Rose, last in 1979
    AL—9—Ty Cobb, last in 1924

Most Consecutive Seasons 200 or More Hits
  NL—8—Willie Keeler, 1894 through 1901
  NL since 1901—5—Chuck Klein, 1929 through 1933
  AL—7—Wade Boggs, 1983 through 1989

Most Consecutive Seasons 200 or More Hits, Start of Career
  3—Johnny Pesky, Boston Red Sox, 1942, 1946 and 1947; he missed the 1943 through 1945 seasons while in military service.

First Players to Make 200 or More Hits in a Season
  NL—Sam Thompson, Detroit, 1887 (203 hits)
  AA—Tip O'Neill, St. Louis, 1887 (225 hits)
      Pete Browning, Louisville, 1887 (220 hits)
      Denny Lyons, Philadelphia, 1887 (209 hits)
  AL—Nap Lajoie, Philadelphia, 1901 (232 hits)

All-Time Organized-Baseball Record for Most Hits in a Season
  325—Paul Strand, Salt Lake City, Pacific Coast League, 1923. Strand, who had earlier flopped as a teenage pitcher with the Boston Braves, returned to the majors at age 30 in 1924, but finished his career in the minors after hitting .228 in 47 games for the Philadelphia A's.

Fewest Hits, Season, Minimum 150 Games
  NL—80—Dal Maxvill, St. Louis, 1970; batted 399 times in 152 games.
  AL—82—Ed Brinkman, Washington, 1965; batted 444 times in 154 games.

Most Hits in a Nine-Inning Game
  NL—7—Wilbert Robinson, Baltimore, June 10, 1892; went 7-for-7. Rennie Stennett, Pittsburgh, September 16, 1975; went 7-for-7 and twice had two hits in an inning as the Pirates blasted the Cubs 22–0, the worst shutout shellacking in this century.
  AL—6—Held by many players. Only one AL player, Cesar Gutierrez of Detroit, has ever gone 7-for-7, and that was in a 12-inning game on June 21, 1970. For the season Gutierrez netted only 101 hits and hit .243; after 1970 he made just seven more hits in the majors.

All-Time Major-League Record for Most Hits in a Game
   9—Johnny Burnett, Cleveland, July 10, 1932; went 9-for-11 in an 18-inning game against Philadelphia.

First Player to Go 6-For-6 in a Nine-Inning Game
   Davy Force, Philadelphia, June 27, 1876.

First Teammates Each to Get Six Hits in the Same Nine-Inning Game
   Hick Carpenter and Long John Reilly of the American Association Cincinnati Red Stockings on September 12, 1883.

PLAYERS WHO MADE 3,000 OR MORE CAREER HITS

	Years Active	*Hits*
Pete Rose	1963–	4256[1]
Ty Cobb	1905–28	4191[2]
Hank Aaron	1954–76	3771
Stan Musial	1941–63	3630
Tris Speaker	1907–28	3515
Carl Yastrzemski	1961–83	3419[3]
Honus Wagner	1897–1917	3415
Eddie Collins	1906–30	3310
Willie Mays	1951–73	3251
Nap Lajoie	1896–1916	3242
George Brett	1973–93	3154
Paul Waner	1926–45	3152
Robin Yount	1974–	3142
Rod Carew	1967–85	3053
Lou Brock	1961–79	3023
Dave Winfield	1973–	3014
Al Kaline	1953–74	3007
Roberto Clemente	1955–72	3000

[1]Holds the record for the most hits in the National League, having played his entire career there. Cobb is of course the American League record holder.
[2]Disputed figure. Many historians believe that Cobb was credited with an extra hit in 1910 and his correct total should be 4190.
[3]The first player to make 3000 hits on less than a .290 career batting average, Yaz was down to .285 by the time he retired. Kaline and Brock are the only other members of the 300-hit club who finished with career batting averages below .300.

The Strikeout Kings

On April 30, 1986, in the course of beating Seattle, Roger Clemens of the Red Sox became the first pitcher in history to fan 20 batters in a nine-inning game. Less than a month later, on May 28, Joe Cowley of the White Sox set a modern record when he started off his game against the Rangers by striking out the first seven hitters who faced him. Cowley's record lasted only until September 23, 1986, when Jim Deshaies of the Astros fanned the first eight Dodgers he faced in the course of pitching his first Major League complete game. Clemens, Cowley and Deshaies are just three of the multitude of pitchers in recent years who have toppled almost all the existing season and career strikeout records.

Most Consecutive Strikeouts, Game

10—Tom Seaver, New York Mets, April 22, 1970. Seaver fanned 19 San Diego Padres in the game, tying the former nine-inning record, and broke Mickey Welch's old mark of nine consecutive strikeouts, set against Philadelphia on August 28, 1884, when Welch, pitching for the New York Gothams (soon to become the Giants), opened the game by fanning the first nine Phillies he faced—the all-time record Deshaies was shooting for until he faltered after striking out Jose Gonzalez.

Most Consecutive Strikeouts by a Rookie in His First Game

7—Sammy Stewart, Baltimore Orioles, September 1, 1978, against Cleveland. A starting pitcher at the time, Stewart failed to finish the game despite his strikeout skein and was also knocked out early in his next start. The following season Earl Weaver made him a reliever.

Most Strikeouts by a Rookie in His First Start
  NL—15—Karl Spooner, Brooklyn, September 22, 1954
          J. R. Richard, Houston, September 5, 1971
  AL—12—Elmer Myers, Philadelphia, October 6, 1915.
Moreover, Myers threw a two-hit shutout. The following
season he led the AL in losses with 23 and set the AL
rookie record for most bases on balls.

First Pitcher to Strike out 19 Batters in a Game
  Charlie Sweeney, Providence Grays, June 7, 1884. Exactly one month later Hugh Daily of Chicago fanned 19
hitters in a Union Association game. Daily, as you no doubt
know, had only one arm, but Sweeney apparently had a less
overt but ultimately more insidious handicap. He jumped to
the Union Association in the midst of the 1884 season,
paving the way for Hoss Radbourn to set all sorts of iron-
man records while bringing Providence the pennant. By
1887 Sweeney, possibly the most gifted pitcher of his time,
had drifted from the majors altogether although just 24 years
old, and shortly thereafter he wound up in San Quentin,
convicted of manslaughter.

**First Pitcher to Strike out 18 Batters in a game, Mound 60
Feet 6 Inches From The Plate**
  AL—Bob Feller, Cleveland, October 2, 1938, against
Detroit
  NL—Sandy Koufax, Los Angeles, August 31, 1959, against
San Francisco. Koufax also fanned 18 Cubs on April 24,
1965, making him the only NL pitcher who twice struck out
18 or more batters in a game.

**First Pitcher to Strike Out 19 Batters in a Game, Mound 60
Feet 6 Inches From The Plate**
  NL—Steve Carlton, St. Louis, September 15, 1969, against
the pennant-winning Mets. The following year Tom Seaver
of the Mets, while breaking Welch's consecutive strikeout
mark, became the second pitcher to do it.
  AL—Nolan Ryan, California, August 12, 1974. In 1976
Ryan also had an 18-K effort and became the first AL
hurler who twice fanned 18 or more batters in a game.

Most Strikeouts, Game, by a Rookie
  18—Bill Gullickson, Montreal, September 10, 1980

Most Strikeouts, Game, Extra Innings Included
21—Tom Cheney, Washington Senators, September 12, 1962, against Baltimore, in 16 innings

Most Strikeouts, Season
AL—383—Nolan Ryan, California, 1973. His record-breaking strikeout was Rich Reese of the Twins—on his last pitch of the season.
NL—382—Sandy Koufax, Los Angeles, 1965

Most Strikeouts, Season, 1901 Through 1919
AL—349—Rube Waddell, Philadelphia, 1904. Waddell's total is now universally accepted, but after Bob Feller notched 348 K's in 1946 it was hotly contested for some while by many authorities, who felt that Waddell had been credited with more strikeouts in 1904 than he'd earned and Feller was now the true modern record holder.
NL—267—Christy Mathewson, New York Giants, 1903

Most strikeouts, Season, 1920 through 1941
NL—262—Dazzy Vance, Brooklyn 1924
AL—261—Bob Feller, Cleveland, 1940

Most Strikeouts, Season, 1942–60
AL—348—Bob Feller, Cleveland, 1946
NL—246—Don Drysdale, Los Angeles, 1960

Most Strikeouts, Season, since 1977
AL—341—Nolan Ryan, California, 1977
NL—313—J. R. Richard, Houston, 1979

Most Seasons League Leader in Strikeouts
AL—12—Walter Johnson, last in 1924
NL—7—Dazzy Vance, 1922–28 consecutive

Most Seasons 300 or More Strikeouts
6—Nolan Ryan, last in 1989. Ryan also holds the record (14) for the most seasons with 200 or more strikeouts.

Most Consecutive Seasons 200 or More Strikeouts
9—Tom Seaver, 1968–76

Most Seasons 100 or More Strikeouts
24—Nolan Ryan, 1968, 1970–92 consecutive

Most Significant Milestone Strikeout
My vote goes to Ryan's whiff of the Expos' Brad Mills on April 27, 1983, giving him his 3509th career strikeout and tying him with Walter Johnson.

Most Strikeouts, Season, Team
NL—1221—Houston, 1969; led by Don Wilson with 235
AL—1189—Cleveland, 1967; led by Sam McDowell with 236

First Team to Top 1000 Strikeouts in a Season
Los Angeles Dodgers, 1959, notched 1077; led by Don Drysdale with 242

Fewest Strikeouts, Season, Since 1901, by League Leader in Strikeouts
AL—113—Bobo Newsom, Washington, and Tex Hughson, Boston, 1942
NL—134—Dazzy Vance, Brooklyn, 1922

Most Recent League Leader to Have Fewer Than 200 Strikeouts (1981 Excluded)
AL—187—Len Barker, Cleveland, 1980
NL—188—Jack Sanford, Philadelphia, 1957

Most Consecutive Years, League, without a Pitcher Who Had 200 or More Strikeouts
NL—16—1942 through 1957, from Johnny Vander Meer, who had 202 K;s in 1941, to Sam Jones with 205 K's in 1958
AL—13—1917 through 1929, from Walter Johnson with 228 K's in 1916 to Lefty Grove, 209 K's in 1930

Most Consecutive Years, Individual, without Registering 100 Strikeouts in a Season
21—Ted Lyons, 1923–46. Lyons, a 260-game winner, never once in his long career came even close to notching 100 strikeouts in a season; his high was 74 in 1933.

TOP 10 IN CAREER STRIKEOUTS

	Years Active	Strikeouts
1. Nolan Ryan	1966–93	5714
2. Steve Carlton	1965–88	4136[1]
3. Bert Blyleven	1970–92	3701[2]
4. Tom Seaver	1967–86	3640
5. Don Sutton	1966–88	3574
6. Gaylord Perry	1962–83	3534[3]
7. Walter Johnson	1907–27	3509[4]
8. Phil Niekro	1964–87	3342[5]
9. Fergie Jenkins	1965–83	3192
10. Bob Gibson	1959–75	3117

[1]Southpaw record. Mickey Lolich, the runner-up, is 12th on the all-time list. Jerry Koosman, if you can believe it, is the fourth-most prolific lefty strikeout king in history and 16th on the all-time list.

[2]Replaced Jim Bunning on the top 10 list in 1985. Bunning's departure from it left Johnson as the lone member who collected a significant portion of his career strikeouts—let alone all of them—prior to expansion.

[3]Never a league leader in strikeouts; nor, for that matter, was Sutton.

[4]The only top 10 member who was active before 1959.

[5]Niekro, Jenkins, Gibson and Blyleven all were league leaders in strikeouts just once.

World Series Play: 1977–93

FRANCHISE SUMMARY

Team	League	WS Record through 1993	Last WS	LCS Record through 1993	Last LCS
Toronto	American	2–0	1993	2–3	1993
Pittsburgh	National	5–2	1979	2–7	1992
New York	American	22–11	1981	4–1	1981
Oakland	American	4–2	1990	6–4	1992
Cleveland	American	2–1	1954	—	—
New York	National	2–1	1986	3–1	1988
Minnesota	American	2–1	1991	2–2	1991
St. Louis	National	9–6	1987	3–0	1987
Cincinnati	National	5–4	1990	5–2	1990
Los Angeles	National	5–4	1988	5–2	1988
Boston	American	5–4	1986	2–2	1990
Baltimore	American	3–3	1983	5–2	1983
Chicago	American	2–2	1959	0–2	1993
Kansas City	American	1–1	1985	2–4	1985
Detroit	American	4–5	1984	1–2	1987
Philadelphia	National	1–4	1993	3–3	1993
Chicago	National	2–8	1945	0–2	1989
San Francisco	National	0–2	1989	1–2	1989
Atlanta	National	0–2	1992	2–3	1993
Milwaukee	American	0–1	1982	1–0	1982
San Diego	National	0–1	1984	1–0	1984
California	American	—	—	0–3	1986
Houston	National	—	—	0–2	1986
Montreal	National	—	—	0–1	1981

Yearly Highlights

1977—New York (AL) defeated Los Angeles (NL) 4 games to 2

The Royals for the second year in a row took the Yankees to five games in the LCS before succumbing in the ninth inning of the finale. The Dodgers beat the Phillies 3–1 in the LCS but fell prey in the Series to Mike Torrez's two complete-game wins and Reggie Jackson's three-homer barrage in Game Six. Jackson had five homers and 10 RBIs in the Series.

1978—New York (AL) defeated Los Angeles (NL) 4 games to 2

For the first time all four divisions had repeat winners. Both the Yankees and the Dodgers won their LCSes three games to one, and the Yankees then completed the reprise of the 1977 season by winning the Series in six after losing the opening two games in Los Angeles. Bucky Dent, whose three-run homer sparked the Yankees in their division playoff win over the Red Sox, had 10 hits in the Series, and his Dodgers counterpart at shortstop, Bill Russell, led all players with 11.

1979—Pittsburgh (NL) defeated Baltimore (AL) 4 games to 3

The Orioles held a 3–1 lead in games and had their three mound aces, Mike Flanagan, Jim Palmer and Scott McGregor, ready to apply the clincher. But all three lost, giving the Pirates their second seven-game Series win over Baltimore in the decade. The Orioles beat California 3–1 in the LCS while the Pirates swept Cincinnati.

1980—Philadelphia (NL) defeated Kansas City (AL) 4 games to 2

To win their first world title in their 98-year history, the Phillies beat not only a hot Kansas City team that had knocked off the Yankees three straight in the LCS, but the Astros with a pair of come-from-behind 10th-inning victories in the final two games of the National League LCS. After a disappointing LCS, Mike Schmidt had two homers and seven RBIs in the Series and was outdone only by Amos Otis of the Royals, who led both clubs with 11 hits and a .438 average.

1981—Los Angeles (NL) defeated New York (AL) 4 games to 2

The Dodgers came back from a 2–1 deficit in the LCS to defeat the Expos, then lost the first two Series games. Returning to Los Angeles, they took three straight from the Yankees and then journeyed back to Yankee Stadium and won the closer 9–2 in a fashion that made Yankees owner George Steinbrenner apoplectic and spoiled for him the taste of the Yankees' LCS sweep of Oakland, managed by Billy Martin.

1982—St. Louis (NL) defeated Milwaukee (AL) 4 games to 3

The Brewers became the first team to win an LCS after trailing two games to zip when they took three straight from the Angels at Milwaukee. But in the Series the Brewers had to play the last two games on the road, and the Cardinals won both, led by Keith Hernandez's eight RBIs and Joaquin Andujar's two wins. Mike Caldwell of the Brewers also had two wins and was only one out away, in Game Five, from being the first pitcher since 1977 to complete two games in a Series. To earn the right to meet the Brewers, the Cardinals pasted Atlanta three straight times in the National League LCS.

1983—Baltimore (AL) defeated Philadelphia (NL) 4 games to 1

The Phillies rode Steve Carlton's two wins to a victory over the Dodgers in the LCS, then took the Series opener before the Orioles got untracked. For the Orioles, Cal Ripken hit only .167 in the Series and Gary Roenicke went 0-for-7 after both had murdered White Sox pitchers in the American League LCS.

1984—Detroit (AL) defeated San Diego (NL) 4 games to 1

The Tigers swept the Royals in the LCS and had little trouble in the Series with the Padres as Jack Morris posted two complete-game wins and Alan Trammell hit .450 and knocked in six runs. All the postseason drama occurred in the National League LCS when the Padres took three straight from Chicago after the Cubs were poised to win their first pennant since 1945.

1985—Kansas City (AL) defeated St. Louis (NL) 4 games to 3

The majors changed to a best-four-of-seven format in the LCSes, giving the Royals an opportunity to snatch the AL pennant from the Blue Jays after trailing three games to one. In the Series they likewise fell behind the Cardinals 3–1 but then won three straight to become the first AL expansion team to win a world title. The Cardinals cited umpire Don Denkinger's questionable safe call in Game Six as the reason for their defeat, but their .185 team batting average was a much larger factor. In the LCS, the Cardinals beat the Dodgers 4 games to 2, homers by Jack Clark and switch hitter Ozzie Smith—his first ever left-handed—hanging consecutive defeats on Dodgers reliever Tom Niedenfuer in the final two contests.

1986—New York (NL) defeated Boston (AL) 4 games to 3

After an uneventful regular season in which all four division races were resolved by Labor Day, the Mets beat the Astros four games to two in a National League LCS that was arguably the best-played and most dramatic fall series ever. It culminated in a see-saw 16-inning game—the longest post-season contest in history—which the Mets won 7–6 behind Jesse Orosco, the first relief pitcher to win three games in a championship series. Orosco saved two more contests in the World Series, including the deciding seventh game, but was only one of many Mets heroes in the most remarkable comeback in Series history. Trailing 5–3 with two out in the bottom of the 10th inning of Game 6 and only one strike away from elimination, the Mets rallied for three runs and thereby became the first team on the brink of extinction to overcome so large a deficit in its last turn at bat and then go on to win the Series. The Mets' triumph deprived Boston pitcher Bruce Hurst of the MVP Award—he had already been voted the trophy on the basis of his two Series wins before New York launched its last-ditch comeback—but the Red Sox, although frustrated once again in a bid to claim their first World Championship since 1918, had the satisfaction of staging an equally incredible come-from-behind win in the AL LCS. Down three games to one, Boston trailed the Angels 5–4 in the top of the ninth inning of Game 5 when Red Sox centerfielder Dave Henderson uncorked a two-out, two-strike, two-run homer. The Angels fought back to tie the game in the bottom of the ninth, but lost 7–6 in 11 innings and then were blown out in the final two contests in Boston. Houston starter Mike Scott and Boston second baseman Marty Barrett were the individual pitching and hitting standouts in post-season play, but in the end the Mets superior bullpen, one of the deepest in recent history, was the deciding factor.

1987—Minnesota (AL) defeated St. Louis (NL) 4 games to 3

The Twins posted the poorest road record of any flag winner in history and then won only one away game in post-season play, that against the Tigers in the AL LCS. But that win was enough to bring Minnesota its first world championship when neither Detroit nor the Cardinals, the NL champs, could manage a win in the Metrodome, the first indoor park to host a World Series game. Minus their top slugger, Jack Clark, who was idled by an ankle injury, the Cards needed seven games to defeat the Giants, the NL West winners. The crucial contest—and probably the 1987 post-season highlight—was the third NL LCS game at Candlestick Park when St. Louis rallied from a 4–0 deficit to triumph 6–5. Frank Viola of the Twins, who sandwiched wins in the Series opener and finale around a shellacking in Game 4, copped the Series MVP Award, and Minnesota outfielder Dan Gladden was the top offensive performer in fall play, knocking home five runs in the LCS and seven more in the Series.

1988—Los Angeles (NL) defeated Oakland (AL) 4 games to 1

In perhaps the most stunning Series upset since the Mets beat the vaunted Orioles in 1969, Dodgers pitchers held Oakland hitters to a .177 batting average and just 11 runs. Led by Orel Hershiser's two complete-game wins and Kurt Gibson's two-strike, two-out, two-run homer in the bottom of the ninth inning in Game 1, Los Angeles lost only the third Series game—on a dramatic solo homer in the last of the ninth by the A's Mark McGwire. That four-bagger was McGwire's lone Series hit. Jose Canseco, the other half of the A's heralded slugging duo, also was held hitless save for a grandslam homer in the opening game. In contrast, Mickey Hatcher of the Dodgers, a sub during the regular season, hit .368 and clubbed two key homers. Hatcher typified the outstanding efforts Los Angeles received from unlikely sources. Gibson's homer, for example, came in his lone

Series appearance after he injured his knee. To add insult, his victim was Dennis Eckersley, who set an LCS record when he saved all four of the A's wins in their AL LCS sweep of the Red Sox. Gibson's long-ball heroics and Hershiser's four-star pitching likewise thwarted the heavily favored Mets in the NL LCS. Hershiser deservedly was an easy winner of both the LCS and the Series MVP Awards.

1989—Oakland (AL) defeated San Francisco (NL) 4 games to 0

The long-awaited first Bay Area World Series—and the Giant's first fall appearance in 27 years—was on course to being the most one-sided championship match since 1976 before a massive earthquake interrupted play for ten days with the A's ahead 2 games to 0. When action resumed Oakland completed its sweep of San Francisco. The A's were so thoroughly dominant that for the first time in Series history the losing team not only never had the lead in any of the four games but never once had the tying run at the plate in its final turn at bat. Dave Stewart was voted the MVP, but the award could as easily have gone to any one of several A's. The Giant's Will Clark, who had destroyed the Cubs in the NL LCS, was held in check by A's pitchers throughout the Series, and none of the other San Francisco hitters was able to take up the slack. Indeed, the Blue Jays, who fell to the A's in five games in the AL LCS, may well have been the second-best team in post-season action—albeit a very distant second best. In any case, the A's ended the 1980s as probably the strongest team since the 1975–76 Reds.

1990—Cincinnati (NL) defeated Oakland (AL) 4 games to 0

In their first year under manager Lou Piniella, the Reds became one of the few teams in history to lead their league from wire to wire and then capped their remarkable season by defeating the Pirates in the National League LCS and sweeping the heavily favored defending-champion A's in the World Series. Billy Hatcher of the Reds set a new Series BA record and Cincinnati third sacker Chris Sabo had nine hits and five RBIs in the four-game fray. The MVP award was copped by Reds hurler Jose Rijo, who bested A's ace Dave Stewart twice after Stewart had beaten the Red Sox a pair of games in the American League LCS. Boston fireballer Roger Clemens exemplified the Sox frustration in their second one-sided loss to the A's in three years when he was heaved out early in the final ALCS game for moaning too graphically about ball and strike calls.

1991—Minnesota (AL) defeated Atlanta (NL) 4 games to 3

The Twins continued to be winless on the road in fall classics since moving to Minnesota, but nevertheless snatched their second World Championship in five years when ex-Tiger ace Jack Morris won a gutty 1–0 ten-inning verdict in Game 7. The best Series since 1975 featured two of the poorest teams in the majors in 1990, both of which had been revitalized by free-agent signings and an influx of young talent. Atlanta took seven games to edge Pittsburgh in the NLCS, while the twins needed only five ALCS contests to polish off Toronto. The 1991 Series was the first seven-game affair since 1962 with a 1–0 finale, and the first fall fray since 1924 to go the ultimate limit—an extra-inning contest won by the home team in its final at bat.

1992—Toronto (AL) defeated Atlanta (NL) 4 games to 2

An electrifying extra-inning triumph in Game 6 rendered the Blue Jays the first team outside the USA to cop a World Championship and put Jack Morris on his third different title team in a nine-year period. Morris failed in his bid to become the first hurler to bag Series wins with three different clubs, but Juan Guzman and the other Jays pitchers more than took up the slack. After becoming the oldest to homer in a Series earlier in the affair, 41-year-old Dave Winfield garnered the Series-winning hit. Toronto catcher Pat Borders meanwhile grabbed the Series MVP prize, mainly on the strength of his timely hitting. The Jays needed only six games to dispose of Oakland in the ALCS, but Pittsburgh took the Braves to the absolute limit before falling 3–2 in Game 7 of the NLCS to a two-out two-run single by seldom used backup catcher Francisco Cabrera.

1993—Toronto (AL) defeated Philadelphia (NL) 4 games to 2

Joe Carter's three-run homer in the bottom of the ninth inning of Game 6 gave the Blue Jays a come-from-behind 8–6 win against Phils reliever, Mitch Williams, and made them the first team since the 1977–78 Yankees to bag consecutive world titles. Williams was also the loser in Game 4, a 15–14 slugfest that broke the record for the most runs in a post-season fray (25), last done by the St. Louis Browns and New York Giants in the finale of the 1888 World Series. Paul Molitor was the Series MVP as he continued to excel in post-season action, but the award could well have gone to Phils centerfielder Len Dykstra in a losing cause. Molitor's bat also sparked the Jays in their six-game triumph over the White Sox in the ALCS. Led by Dykstra and pitcher Curt Schilling, the Phils likewise put away the favored Braves in six rounds in the NLCS by rebounding from a 2–1 deficit to stifle the meat of Atlanta's batting order in the next three games and earn their third Series appearance in the past 14 seasons after making just two stabs at the world title in the previous 97 years.

WORLD SERIES RECORDS

Batting

Department	Single Series	Career (Minimum 20 games)
Batting Average	.750, Billy Hatcher, Cincinnati, NL, 1990	.391, Lou Brock, St. Louis, NL
Slugging Average	1.727, Lou Gehrig, New York, AL, 1928	.744 Babe Ruth, New York, AL
Home Runs	5, Reggie Jackson, New York, AL, 1977	18, Mickey Mantle, New York, AL
RBIs	12, Bobby Richardson, New York, AL, 1960	40, Mickey Mantle, New York, AL
Runs	10, Reggie Jackson, New York, AL, 1977	42, Mickey Mantle, New York, AL
	10, Paul Molitor, Toronto, AL 1993	
Hits	13, Bobby Richardson, New York, AL, 1964	71, Yogi Berra, New York, AL
	13, Lou Brock, St. Louis, NL, 1968	
	13, Marty Barrett, Boston, AL, 1986	
Total Bases	25, Reggie Jackson, New York, AL, 1977	123, Mickey Mantle, New York, AL
Stolen Bases	7, Lou Brock, St. Louis, NL, 1967	14, Lou Brock, St. Louis, NL
	7, Lou Brock, St. Louis, NL, 1968	14, Eddie Collins, Philadelphia and Chicago, AL

Pitching

Department	Single Series	Career (Minimum 20 games)
Wins	3, achieved by many pitchers, last by Mickey Lolich, Detroit, AL, 1968	10, Whitey Ford, New York, AL
Losses	3, George Frazier, New York, AL, 1981 3, Lefty Williams, Chicago AL, 1919	8, Whitey Ford, New York, AL
Complete Games	3, achieved by many pitchers, last in 1968	10, Christy Mathewson, New York, NL
ERA	0.00, Christy Mathewson, New York, NL, 1905 0.00, Waite Hoyt, New York, AL, 1921 (27 innings)	0.83, Harry Brecheen, St. Louis, NL
Saves	3, Roy Face, Pittsburgh, NL, 1960 3, Kent Tekulve, Pittsburgh, NL, 1979	6, Rollie Fingers, Oakland, AL
Shutouts	3, Christy Mathewson, New York, NL, 1905	4, Christy Mathewson, New York, NL
Strikeouts	35, Bob Gibson, St. Louis, NL, 1968	94, Whitey Ford, New York, AL

Lowest Batting Average, Single Series, Minimum 15 at Bats

NL—.000—Dal Maxvill, St. Louis, 1968 (0-for-22)
            Gil Hodges, Brooklyn, 1952 (0-for-21)
            Jimmy Sheckard, Chicago, 1906 (0-for-2)
AL—.000—Mike Epstein, Oakland, 1972 (0-for-16)
            Flea Clifton, Detroit, 1935 (0-for-16)

Lowest Batting Average, Career, Minimum Two World Series and 40 at Bats

AL—.061—Marv Owen, Detroit, 1934, 1935 (3-for-49)
NL—.117—Dal Maxvill, St. Louis, 1964, 1967 and 1968 (7-for-61)

Most World Series Wins By Pitcher without a Loss

6—Lefty Gomez, New York, AL

Most World Series Losses By Pitchers without a Win

4—Don Newcombe, Brooklyn, NL

GAME TIME!

☐ **THE ULTIMATE BASEBALL QUIZ BOOK by Dom Forker.** A mound of tantalizing trivia for the baseball buff. You're up against a full count of questions about the American national pastime. See if you can touch all the bases, but look out! This newly revised edition just might throw you a curve!   (152360—$4.99)

☐ **GREAT BASEBALL FEATS, FACTS & FIRSTS by David Nemec.** Thousands of scores, stats and stories in one amazingly complete volume! Discover the unconventional records, the offbeat feats, the historic scores and the one-of-a-kind characters that keep baseball flying—in this comprehensive up-to-the-minute encyclopedia.   (161246—$4.99)

☐ **GREAT AMERICAN BASEBALL TEAM BOOK by David Nemec.** More than 100 years of scores, stats, and stories in one amazingly complete volume. It's a baseball memoir, a reference, and a terrific read that puts all the facts at your fingertips as it brings the history of the game to life in your imagination.   (175670—$4.99)

Prices slightly higher in Canada.

ARE YOU FAN ENOUGH TO FACE A MOUND OF TRIVIA QUESTIONS?

You're up! But be careful. Even a baseball-trivia pinch-hitter can strike out. . . .

1. Who pitched three doubleheaders in one month and won all six games, none of which lasted more than one hour and fifty minutes?
2. Who hit two game-winning home runs for the Giants against the Yankees in the 1923 series?
3. Who is the manager who is nicknamed the "White Rat"?
4. Who is the present-day pitcher who has won the American League ERA title with the lowest numbers?
5. Who hit the single that scored Enos Slaughter from first base for the winning run in the 1946 series?
   a) He won a batting title.
   b) His brother won one, too.
6. Who is the Met player who got married at home plate?

The Ultimate Baseball Quiz Book

Revised and Updated Edition

Dom Forker

A SIGNET BOOK

SIGNET
Published by the Penguin Group
Penguin Books USA Inc., 375 Hudson Street,
New York, New York 10014, U.S.A.
Penguin Books Ltd, 27 Wrights Lane,
London W8 5TZ, England
Penguin Books Australia Ltd, Ringwood,
Victoria, Australia
Penguin Books Canada Ltd, 10 Alcorn Avenue,
Toronto, Ontario, Canada M4V 3B2
Penguin Books (N.Z.) Ltd, 182–190 Wairau Road,
Auckland 10, New Zealand

Penguin Books Ltd, Registered Offices:
Harmondsworth, Middlesex, England

Published by Signet, an imprint of Dutton Signet,
a division of Penguin Books USA Inc.

First Printing, Revised and Updated Edition, March, 1988
First Printing, March, 1981
14   13   12   11

REGISTERED TRADEMARK—MARCA REGISTRADA

Printed in the United States of America

To my lifetime heroes:
Ellen Gallagher Forker, my mother,
and Columb Forker, my father

Contents

Introduction

Forty-one summers have rolled by since that sudden spring when Jackie Robinson broke the color barrier of "organized" baseball, but I still fondly remember, as though it was yesterday, that unusually warm April afternoon of 1946 when he first crossed the foul line of a "white" diamond.

At the time I was an avid fan of Frank Hague, the larcenous mayor of Jersey City, and a bitter foe of Jackie Robinson, the felonious base thief of the Montreal Royals.

Looking back to that eventful day, however, I find it easy to justify the prejudices of my nine-year-old self.

First Mayor Hague had indirectly provided me with the ticket that gained me access to Roosevelt Stadium, which was filled with 26,000 pennant-waving fans on that historic occasion.

Little did I know, at the time, that Mayor Hague expected every city employee in Jersey City to buy a quota of tickets for the opening-day game every year in order to insure a sellout. He sold so many tickets, it seemed, that he could have turned people away from the Los Angeles Coliseum.

Fortunately for the grade-school baseball fans in the Jersey City–Bayonne area, not all of the people who bought tickets for the opener wished to attend it. Better still, many of them felt that they were getting at least part of their money's worth if they could give them away to appreciative young boys who would put them to their proper use. I was just one of many grateful youths who received free tickets for the 1946 opening-day game. We proudly presented our prized possessions to the good Sisters of St. Joseph's, and we promptly got excused from all afternoon classes on that special day.

Second, I was an ardent fan of the Jersey City Giants, the Triple-A International League farm team of the parent New York Giants.

Manager Mel Ott's players were, of course, the bitter

rivals of the Brooklyn Dodgers, who just happened to be the parent organization of the Montreal Royals. If you rooted for the Big Giants, you rooted for the Little Giants; if you cheered for the Dodgers, you cheered for the Royals. The rivalry was as simple as that.

So, when Jackie Robinson stepped into the batter's box in the first inning, I cheered the Jersey City Giants' pitcher and booed the Montreal Royals' second baseman. But Robinson, leaning forward like a cobra with his bat held straight up and down, seemed eager to give me a reception of his own.

And he did!

He led the Royals to a 14–1 victory with four hits, including a home run, two stolen bases, and four runs scored. By the time the game had ended, there seemed to be a lot of converts and very few Giants' fans left in the sparsely populated park.

That's the way it was back then, and in the 1950s, when we were growing up on the streets of Bayonne. From morning to night, we would form baseball comparisons that would inevitably lead to disputed deadlocks. Who's the best center fielder in New York: Joe DiMaggio, Willie Mays, or Duke Snider? Wow! Who's the best team in New York: the Yankees, the Dodgers, or the Giants? Dynamite! Who's the best manager in New York: Casey Stengel, Leo Durocher, or Charlie Dressen? Division!

I've never grown tired of talking about baseball: arguing the indefensible, conjuring up the possible, and predicting the might-have-beens. Facts, patterns, and ironic twists have always been especially appealing to me. Somehow none of it seems trivial. Anything that is connected with baseball is just too important to me.

Maybe you feel the same way! If you do, maybe you can help me. Who was that Jersey City Giants' pitcher whom I wanted to strike out Jackie Robinson, when I was young?

(Answer appears on page 321.)

Dom Forker
June 1, 1987

Chapter One

THE PRESENT-DAY PLAYERS

1. FROM ANDERSON TO YOUNT

How well do you know the accomplishments of the present-day players? Let's see how many of the following questions you can answer.

1. _____ Who is the pitcher who struck out a record 20 batters in one game?
2. _____ Who is the player who led the National League in triples his first three years in the majors?
3. _____ Who is the pitcher who holds the major league record of not yielding a home run in 269⅓ innings of pitching?
4. _____ Who is the only active player to have 200 or more hits in a season without batting .300?
5. _____ Who is the pitcher who held Rod Carew to a .100 mark in 1977 when the batting champ hit .388?
6. _____ Who is the only pitcher to win the Cy Young Award while hurling for a last-place club?
7. _____ Who is the player who appeared in a record 243 games before he reached the age of 20?
8. _____ Who is the player who stroked 184 singles, then an American League record, in 1980?
9. _____ Who is the player who ten times hit safely 200 or more times in one season?
10. _____ Who is the National League pitcher who uncorked a record-tying six wild pitches in one game?
11. _____ Who is the player who stole a major league record 38 consecutive times before he was thrown out?
12. _____ Who is the player, in addition to Julio Cruz, who stole an American League record 32 consecutive times before he was thrown out?

3

13. _____ Who is the player who became the first and only player to get caught stealing twice in one inning?

14. _____ Who is the pitcher who hurled a record 168⅓ innings in relief one year in the American League?

15. _____ Who is the pitcher who weaved a record eight shutouts in his rookie year?

16. _____ Who is the player who set a rookie record when he stole 72 bases?

17. _____ Who is the pitcher who led his league in losses a record four consecutive years?

18. _____ Who is the pitcher who lost a record 16 games in relief one year?

19. _____ Who is the player who has poled the most switch-hit homers in National League history?

20. _____ Who is the player whose 42 doubles in 1982 set a National League record for catchers?

21. _____ Who is nicknamed "Hit Man?"

22. _____ Who is the pitcher who tied a National League record for relief hurlers by striking out six consecutive batters?

23. _____ Who is the American League player who set a major league record when he was hit by his 244th pitch in 1987?

24. _____ Who is the pitcher who committed an American League record nine balks in one season?

25. _____ Who is the player who was thrown out stealing a record 42 times in one season?

26. _____ Who is the National Leaguer who won back-to-back RBI titles in 1982–83?

27. _____ Who is the major league manager who has two sons playing for him?

28. _____ From 1979–82 the Dodgers won four consecutive Rookie of the Year awards. Who is the pitcher, now with another team, who won the first?

29. _____ Who is the everyday player who won the fourth?

30. _____ Who registered a National League record 701 official at-bats in his rookie year?

31. _____ Who is the relief pitcher who won an American League record 17 games in one season?

32. _____ Who is the National League third baseman who hit 28 home runs in his rookie year?

33. _____ Who is the Met player who got married at home plate?

34. _____ Who was the former Met pitcher who once won two games in one day for the White Sox?

35. _____ Who is the Phillie who had a club-high .467 batting average in the 1983 playoffs and a club-low .050 in the World Series?

36. _____ Who is the first baseman who was traded to the Pirates and then sent to the Yankees for Jim Spencer and money, but was returned to the Bucs because Commissioner Bowie Kuhn said the deal violated cash restrictions?

37. _____ Who is the player who hit an American League record .349 as a rookie?

38. _____ Who is the pitcher who hurled 22⅓ consecutive no-hit innings, the second longest no-hit string in American League history? (Cy Young hurled 25⅓ consecutive no-hit innings for the 1904 Red Sox.)

39. _____ Who is the player nicknamed the "Human Rain Delay?"

40. _____ Who is the player who once hit for the cycle, getting each hit off a different pitcher?

41. _____ Who is the player who hit an American League record 37 home runs for a catcher?

42. _____ Who is the American League pitcher, recently with the Angels, who has posted five one-hitters?

43. _____ Who is the player who joins two former teammates as the only three members of the same club to hit 40 or more home runs in one season?

44. _____ Who is the Detroit pitcher who in 1983 became the first Tiger pitcher to win 20 games in a season since Joe Coleman did it and the first Bengel hurler to strike out 200 or more batters in a year since Mickey Lolich performed the feat?

45. _____ Who is the right-handed hitter who has connected for more single-season home runs than any other Yankee except Joe DiMaggio?

46. _____ Who is the National Leaguer who holds the all-time American League record for career home runs (333) by a third baseman?

47. _____ Who is the player who hit a club-record 16 home runs at shortstop for the Yankees one year?

48. _____ Who is the catcher who was the youngest player (20) ever to perform for the American League in an All-Star Game?

49. _____ Who is the pitcher whose win broke the National League's 11-year domination in the All-Star Game?

50. _____ Who is the player who has hit the only grand slam in the history of the All-Star Game?

51. _____ Who is the White Sox pitcher who became the youngest Pale Hose hurler to win 20 games since 1913?

52. _____ Who hit the "pine-tar" home run?

53. _____ Who is the relief pitcher who set the major league record for saves (46) in one season?

54. _____ Who holds the DH record for RBIs (133) in a season?

55. _____ Who is the Twin who homered in his first major league at-bat?

56. _____ Who is the reliever who struck out an American League record eight consecutive batters in one game?

57. _____ Who in 1981 became the first American League right-handed batter in 11 years to win the batting title?

58. _____ Who is the Yankee who became the first Bronx Bomber to win the batting title since Mickey Mantle did it in 1956?

59. _____ Who is the pitcher who, before Phil and Joe Niekro, was the only knuckleball thrower in the American League?

60. _____ Who is the Cub player who became the first Bruin since 1911 to surpass 20 homers and 20 steals in the same season?

61. _____ Who is the Expo pitcher who has fired a no-hitter and a one-hitter during his brief major league career?

62. _____ Who is the Gold Glove–Silver Bat winner who shared MVP honors with Willie Stargell in 1979?

63. _____ Who has been the only pitcher to hit two home runs in one game in the 1980s?

64. _____ Who is the pitcher who won both the Comeback of the Year Award and the Cy Young Award in the same season?

65. _____ Who is the player who has won four batting titles but has never started in an All-Star Game?

66. _____ Who is the Brave who was born in West Germany and played Little League baseball in Taiwan?

67. _____ Who is the Red who won three Gold Gloves for his outfield play for another team?

68. _____ Who is the Red pitcher who struck out 701 batters from 1982–84?

69. _____ Who is the player who replaced Pete Rose at third base for the Reds in 1979?

70. _____ Who is the Royal regular who struck out in 11 consecutive official at-bats in 1984?

71. _____ Who is the National League starter who posted a 1.69 ERA in 1981?

72. _____ Who was the 1987 Dodger who had three triples in one game for the Twins against the Rangers in 1980?

73. _____ Who is the pitcher who in 1983 threw a rain-curtailed 4–0 perfect game against the Cardinals?

74. _____ Who is the player who got a record-tying five long hits (two homers and three doubles) in one game?

75. _____ Who is the relief pitcher who set a National League record by striking out 151 batters in one season?

76. _____ Who have been the only pitching brothers to throw no-hitters?

77. _____ Who is the catcher who had only one passed ball in 152 games one year?

78. _____ Who is the second baseman who handled 473 chances in 89 games without making an error in 1982?

79. _____ Who is the Brewer who got a club-high 219 hits in 1980?

80. _____ Who is the manager nicknamed "Captain Hook?"

81. _____ Who is the Tiger who became the first player to have his salary cut—from $280,000 to $250,000 —by an arbitrator?

82. _____ Who is the player who scored 136 runs in 1982, the most in the American League since Ted Williams scored 150 in 1949?

83. _____ Who is the Astro outfielder who has fielded 1.000 in a season?

84. _____ Who is the pitcher who became the first lefty since Mel Parnell to lead the Red Sox in wins in back-to-back years?

85. _____ Who is nicknamed the "Candy Man?"

86. _____ Who is the pitcher who lost a record-tying three games in one World Series?

87. _____ Who is the player who tied a record by rookies when he homered twice in one World Series game?

88. _____ Who is the only player, in addition to Babe Ruth, Johnny Mize, and Larry Parrish to hit three home runs in a game in each league?

89. _____ Who is the one-time Indian who threw a perfect game?

90. _____ Who is the pitcher who broke Sparky Lyle's record when he posted 13 saves in 13 consecutive appearances?

91. _____ Who is the only player in Dodger history to hit at least 30 home runs and steal at least 20 bases in a season? (He's done it twice.)

92. _____ Who is the former White Sox pitcher who set a club record when he reeled off 14 straight wins over a two-year period?

93. _____ Who is the player who became the first graduate of the Royals' Baseball Academy to play in the major leagues?

94. _____ Who is the player who stole a record seven bases in two consecutive games in 1983?

95. _____ Who is the Ranger who has five times hit 20 or more home runs in a season?

96. _____ Who is the former Ranger outfielder who had 24 assists in one season, the most in the league since Stan Spence had 29 for the 1944 Senators?

97. _____ Who has been the most recent Cub to win a batting title?

98. _____ Who is the player who became the first Blue Jay to drive home 100 or more runs in a season?

99. _____ Who is the American League player who drove home 145 runs in 1985?

100. _____ Who is the Blue Jay who once hit seven home runs in a seven-day period?

2. FROM AIKENS TO YOUNT

Repeat the feat.

1. _____ Who is the Blue Jay pitcher who got a win by forfeit when Baltimore refused to continue the game because of field conditions in 1977?

2. _____ Who is the Angel slugger who hit three home runs in a game twice in one week?

3. _____ Who is the Angel who is the son of a former big-league infielder by the same name?

4. _____ Who is the player who became the youngest Pale Hose performer in history to drive in 100 runs (105) in a season?

5. _____ Who is the White Sox pitcher who led the league in strikeouts (209) with another team?

6. _____ Who is the manager who in 1983 got fired while he was the skipper of a first-place club and then assumed the reins of a last-place team in the same season?

7. _____ Who is the manager who has skippered five different teams?

8. _____ Who is the manager who once established a record for second basemen by hitting 43 home runs in one season?

9. _____ Who is the manager who homered in his first major league at-bat?

10. _____ Who is the Astro pitcher who three times won 1–0 games in 1981?

11. _____ Who is the pitcher who set a record for rookies when he struck out 276 batters in 1984?

12. _____ Who is the American Leaguer, in addition to Bo Jackson, who struck out a record-tying five times in a nine-inning game?

13. _____ Who is the second baseman who set an American League record at his position when he went 86 games without committing an error?

14. _____ Who is the Tiger outfielder who recorded more than 500 putouts in a season with the White Sox?

15. _____ Who is the other American League outfielder who has recorded 500 putouts in the 1980s?

16. _____ Who is the catcher who, in a 150 or more game season, fielded an American League high .995?

17. _____ Who is the American Leaguer who is one of three players to steal 300 bases before his 25th birthday?

18. _____ Who is the National Leaguer who has performed the same feat?

19. _____ Who is the player who went 0-for-21 in the last five games of the 1979 World Series and 2-for-16 in the first four games of the 1983 World Series?

20. _____ Who is the only present-day player to lead his league in walks and total bases in the same season?

21. _____ Who is the player who has two cousins connected with pro football?

22. _____ Who is the American League catcher who went errorless for 96 consecutive games in 1983?

23. _____ Who is the player who drove home ten runs in one game in his rookie year?

24. _____ Who is the American League catcher, once a National Leaguer, who threw out 50 percent of opposing base runners in 1982–83?

25. _____ Who is the player who has been named the World Series MVP with two different teams?

26. _____ Who wears the number "72," which represents the year in which he won the Rookie of the Year Award?

27. _____ Who is the White Sox player who drove home 100 runs in his rookie season?

28. _____ Who is the manager whose team had the best National League record in 1981 but finished second in both halves of the strike-tainted season?

29. _____ Who is the manager who lost his job after leading his team to a 103-win season?

30. _____ Who is the manager who played in four World Series with the Orioles?

31. _____ Who is the manager who was once traded for a player?

32. _____ Who is the manager who has won pennants with a record-tying three teams?

33. _____ Who is the pitcher who once won four 1–0 decisions in one season for the Rangers?

34. _____ Who is the present-day American League player who once hit three grand slams in one year for the Reds?

35. _____ Who is the pitcher who posted a club-high 52 shutouts for the Dodgers?

36. _____ Who is the manager who has a law degree?

37. _____ Who was the pitcher who struck out a single-season-high 289 batters for the Mets?

38. _____ Who is the Phillie who struck out a club-high 180 times in 1975?

39. _____ Who is the former Phillie pitcher who struck out a club-high 310 batters in one season?

40. _____ Who is the pitcher who twice saved 31 games in a season for the Pirates?

41. _____ Who is the pitcher who registered a National League-high 45 saves for the Cards in 1984?

42. _____ Who is the American League pitcher who also posted 45 saves in a season?

43. _____ Who is the pitcher who struck out 215 batters as a rookie for the Giants in 1975?

44. _____ Who is the skipper who has groomed managers Tony LaRussa, Rene Lachemann, Doug Rader, and Pat Corrales?

45. _____ Who is the pitcher who struck out 209 batters for the 1966 Dodgers?

46. _____ Who is the player, now in the American League, who set a National League record by drawing at least one walk in 15 consecutive games?

47. _____ Who is the player who has sprayed the most two-base hits (51) by a switch-hitter in a season?

48. _____ Who is the player who has bounced into the fewest double plays (1) by an American League switch-hitter in one season?

49. _____ Who is the first baseman who has led his league in most games played a record eight times?

50. _____ Who is the player who has legged out a record-tying 19 triples by a switch-hitter in one season?

51. _____ Who is the third baseman who set a record when he registered 412 assists in one season?

52. _____ Who is the outfielder who has led the American League in errors at his position a record-tying five times?

53. _____ Who is the National League player who tied a loop record in 1984 when he hit seven home runs in six consecutive games and at least one home run in six consecutive contests?

54. _____ Who is the manager who is nicknamed the "White Rat?"

55. _____ Who is the infielder who became the first switch-hitter to drill 100 or more hits from each side of the plate in a season?

56. _____ Who is the other player to get at least 100 hits from each side of the plate in a season?

57. _____ Who is called "Jack the Ripper?"

58. _____ Who is the player who hit 40-plus home runs while leading his league in hits in the same year?

59. _____ Who is the American League player who got at least 20 homers, 20 triples, and 20 doubles in the same season?

60. _____ Who is the player who hit three home runs in a Championship Series game?

61. _____ Who was the pitcher who became the first hurler to win the Cy Young Award without winning 20 games in that season?

62. _____ Who, in addition to Steve Carlton, is the only present-day hurler to be a unanimous choice for the Cy Young Award?

63. _____ Who is the pitcher who won 46 percent of his team's games one year?

64. _____ Who is the player who has struck out more than any other player in the history of baseball?

65. _____ Who is the player who had 662 at-bats in 162 games without stealing a base?

66. _____ Who is the pitcher who has recorded the highest winning percentage for a hurler who has won 20 or more games in a season?

67. _____ Who is the National League relief pitcher who won Fireman of the Year honors with two different teams in the American League?

68. _____ Who is the former Giant who holds the team's club record with 46 doubles in one season?

69. _____ Who is the Yankee who during a six-year period (1978–83) led the club in stealing five times?

70. _____ Who is the player who holds the White Sox single-season stolen base mark?

71. _____ Who is the present-day pitcher who has won the American League ERA title with the lowest numbers?

72. _____ Who is the player who won the Rookie of the Year Award the longest time ago?

73. _____ Who is the pitcher who committed a record 11 balks in one year?

74. _____ Who is the player whose first major league triple scored the winning run of a 1980 World Series game?

75. _____ Who is the player whose three-run homer, off Goose Gossage, wrapped up the 1980 pennant for the Royals?

76. _____ Who is the only player in history to win home run titles with three different teams?

77. _____ Who is nicknamed the "Italian Stallion" (the National League version)?

78. _____ Who is nicknamed the "Italian Stallion" (the American League version)?

79. _____ Who is nicknamed "Rags"?

80. _____ Who is nicknamed "Pudge"?

81. _____ Who is the 1986 pitcher who had the highest single-season winning percentage (.875) of any present-day hurler in the National League?

82. _____ Who is the Met who set a team record for rookies when he hit 26 home runs in his maiden season?

83. _____ Who is the Tiger who tied a major league record by hitting home runs in four consecutive plate appearances?

84. _____ Who is the player who has been the only shortstop to lead his circuit in hits and total bases in the same season?

85. _____ Who is the pitcher who in 1983 threw the first no-hitter for the Yankees since Don Larsen pitched his perfect game in the 1956 World Series?

86. _____ Who is the oldest player in the majors?

87. _____ Who is the catcher who holds club-high home run marks (26 and 37) at his position with two different teams?

88. _____ Who is the player who set a White Sox rookie record when he hit 35 home runs in one season?

89. _____ Who is the only player, in addition to Ty Cobb, who has won three league titles in hits and in triples?

90. _____ Who is nicknamed "Bye-Bye"?

91. _____ Who is the relief pitcher who set a record for rookies when he won 14 games in 1979?

92. _____ Who is the pitcher who threw a Ranger club-record 36 consecutive scoreless innings in 1983?

93. _____ Who is the former Expo who once hit two homers in one inning?

94. _____ Who is the Expo who homered in his first official at-bat?

95. _____ Who is the player who is second to Babe Ruth in leading his league (eight times) in home runs?

96. _____ Who is the player who has won two batting titles with each of two teams?

97. _____ Who is the Yankee who as a rookie for Oakland in 1974 batted .571 in the World Series?

98. _____ Who is the Red who has a .351 average in 15 National League Championship Series games?

99. _____ Who is the player who in 1983 became the only Tiger left-handed batter since Dick Wakefield to amass 200 hits (206) in a season?

100. _____ Who is the player who became the first rookie to lead either league in slugging (.566) percentage?

3. FROM AASE TO YOUMANS

1. _____ Who is the Cub whose 54 stolen bases in 1985 were the most by a Bruin since 1906?
2. _____ Who was the 1987 Cub who was named Rookie of the Year for the Giants in 1973?
3. _____ Who became the first Cubs' catcher in more than 40 years to hit more than 20 home runs in a year?
4. _____ Who is nicknamed "Thunder Pup"?
5. _____ Who is the Cub pitcher who went 16–1 during the stretch drive in 1984?
6. _____ Who broke Bruce Sutter's club career saves record with the Cubs?
7. _____ Who was the 1987 Cub who, in 1975, didn't allow an earned run in his first 28⅔ innings, a major league record for rookies?
8. _____ Who is the Expo backstop who had a .995 fielding percentage as a Met rookie in 1984?
9. _____ Who is the Expo who is called "Gran Gato" or "Big Cat"?
10. _____ Who is the Expo pitcher who was a boyhood friend of Dwight Gooden?
11. _____ Who is the Expo relief pitcher who tied the one-time major-league rookie record with 78 appearances?
12. _____ Who is the Twin reliever who went 94 games without a loss for the Mets in 1980–81?
13. _____ Who is the Expo who once stole 71 bases in 88 games?
14. _____ Who is the Met who hit his tenth grand slam in 1986?
15. _____ Who was the only National League player to hit 20 home runs and steal 20 bases from 1984–87?
16. _____ Who was the only American League player to do the same from 1984–86?
17. _____ Who is the Met who set a club record with at least one RBI in eight straight games?
18. _____ Who became the first pitcher to strike out 200 batters in his first three years?
19. _____ Who is the Met reliever who set a club record for wins out of the bull pen with 14?

20. _____ Who became the winningest Met lefty (18 wins) since Jerry Koosman in 1976?

21. _____ Who is the Met pitcher who didn't allow the Red Sox a run in four World Series appearances?

22. _____ Who earned his third MVP Award in 1986?

23. _____ Who is the Phillie who averaged 15 triples a year during his first three full seasons in the majors?

24. _____ Who is the Phillie relief pitcher who broke Jim Konstanty's single-season save mark for right-handers?

25. _____ Who, in 1985, became only the fourth catcher in 40 years to register 100 assists?

26. _____ Who is the Buc who is nicknamed "Rambo"?

27. _____ Who is the Buc who is the son of a former major leaguer?

28. _____ Who, in 1985, became only the seventh second baseman in major league history to top 100 RBIs?

29. _____ Who is the player whose batting average in 1985 was the highest ever by a National League switch-hitter?

30. _____ Who, in the 1985 National League Championship Series, hit his first left-handed home run in 3,009 pro at-bats?

31. _____ Who stole 110 bases in his rookie year?

32. _____ Who is the Card who set a Giant record with a 26-game hitting streak in 1978?

33. _____ Who is the Card pitcher who picked up three victories in post-season play in 1985?

34. _____ Who is the moundsman who became only the third European-born pitcher to start a World Series game?

35. _____ Who is the Card pitcher who has thrown two no-hitters?

36. _____ Who is the relief pitcher who was named the National League's Rookie of the Year in 1986?

37. _____ Who is the player whose consecutive-game streak of 740 contests was broken in 1986?

38. _____ Who is the Brave who participated in a triple play in only his second major-league game?

39. _____ Who is the Brave who set a personal single-season high for home runs in 1987?

40. _____ Who is the Brave who is a .313 hitter in nine Championship Series games?

41. _____ Who is the Brave relief pitcher who saved 24 games in 1986 after posting just one in 1985?

42. _____ Who is the pitcher who won 17 games in 1985 and lost 18 in 1986?

43. _____ Who averaged 112 RBIs a season for the 1984–86 Reds?

44. _____ Who is the Red who, in his first full season, hit three home runs in a 1986 game?

45. _____ Who is the Red whose 21-game hitting streak in 1984 is the team's longest since Pete Rose's record 44-game string?

46. _____ Who is the third baseman who is closing in on his dad's career total of 206 home runs?

47. _____ Who is the Red catcher who had a .333 batting average for the Phillies in the 1983 World Series?

48. _____ Who is the Red pitcher who, in 1985, reeled off 11 straight wins, the club's most in 30 years?

49. _____ Who is the player who became the first Astro to steal 40 bases since Cesar Cedeno in 1980?

50. _____ Who became only the fourth National League pitcher to whiff 300 batters in a season?

51. _____ Who was unable to hold 4–0 and 3–0 leads in the 1986 National League Championship Series?

52. _____ Who set the Houston record for the most wins by a rookie southpaw?

53. _____ Who is the Houston pitcher who won two games and saved 16 in his last 22 outings of 1986?

54. _____ Who is the Houston pitcher who allowed more than five hits in only two of his last 23 starts in 1986?

55. _____ Who is the Dodger whose All-Star Game average before 1987 was .600?

56. _____ Who is the Dodger who, in 1981, became the Pacific Coast League's first Triple Crown winner since Steve Bilko in 1956?

57. _____ Who was the 1987 Tiger who batted .375 in the 1979 World Series?

58. _____ Who is the Dodger who three times has hit more than 30 home runs in a season?

59. _____ Who struck out a record-tying five consecutive batters in the 1986 All-Star Game?

60. _____ Who is the Dodger pitcher known for his duels with Reggie Jackson in the 1978 World Series?

61. _____ Who played in 1,207 consecutive National League games?

62. _____ Who is the recent-day Padre who played six different positions for the Mets in 1986?

63. _____ Who is the Padre stopper who had 278 career saves entering the 1987 season?

64. _____ Who is the Padre pitcher who didn't allow a run in three 1984 Championship Series outings and just one in 12 World Series innings?

65. _____ Who is the Giant who hit a home run off Nolan Ryan in his first major-league at-bat?

66. _____ Who is called "Hac Man"?

67. _____ Who is the Giant who set a club record with 15 pinch-hits in 1986?

68. _____ Who, in 1986, became the Giants' first 20-game winner since 1973?

69. _____ Who is the Giant relief pitcher who limited left-handed batters to a .115 mark in 1986 and a .185 average in 1985?

70. _____ Who is the first official captain in the Orioles' modern history?

71. _____ Who topped American League shortstops in home runs and RBIs for the fourth straight year in 1986?

72. _____ Who is the Oriole who won a batting title with another club?

73. _____ Who is the Oriole who hit three home runs in one game against the Yankees in 1986?

74. _____ Who was the first Oriole to win the ERA crown and lead the league in victories?

75. _____ Who set the Oriole club record with 34 saves?

76. _____ Who was the 1987 Oriole pitcher who won the Cy Young Award in 1979?

77. _____ Who is the first player to get 200 hits and 100 walks in the same season since Stan Musial in 1953?

78. _____ Who is the player who has four 200-hit seasons and four 39 home runs-plus years?

79. _____ Who is the Red Sox player who established a record with 24 post-season hits?

80. _____ Who is the Twins player who has hit 25 or more home runs in a season for four different American League teams?

81. _____ Who is the Red Sox player who has moved into third place on the team's list of games played?

82. _____ Who won both the MVP and Cy Young awards in 1986?

83. _____ Who is the left-handed pitcher who threw all four of his shutouts at Fenway Park in 1986?

84. _____ Who became the first Indian to hit 20 home runs, steal 20 bases, and drive home 100 runs in the same season?

85. _____ Who is the Indian who collected at least 180 hits in each season from 1984–86?

86. _____ Who is the Indian who set a club record for most homers (17) by a switch-hitter?

87. _____ Who is the Indian who averaged 13 triples a season from 1983–86?

88. _____ Who broke Bobby Bonds's Indian club record for strikeouts (137) in a season?

89. _____ Who is the Indian who, in 1986, hit .326, the highest team mark since Miguel Dilone hit .341 in 1980?

90. _____ Who won his 300th career victory on the final day of the 1985 season?

91. _____ Who is the first Indian pitcher to have at least two seasons of 20 or more saves?

92. _____ Who was the first Indian pitcher to lead the league in complete games since Gaylord Perry did it in 1973?

93. _____ Who was the first Tiger left-handed-hitting home-run king since Ty Cobb in 1909?

94. _____ Who is the Tiger who was the World Series MVP in 1984?

95. _____ Who is the Tiger who was the Rookie of the Year in 1978?

96. _____ Who is the Tiger pitcher who is the major league leader in wins since 1979?

97. _____ Who is the Tiger pitcher who won the Cy Young Award?

98. _____ Who is the Brewer who was the first shortstop to lead the league in slugging percentage and total bases?

99. _____ Who struck out an American League record 186 times in 1987?

100. _____ Who in 1986 became the first Brewer to steal home since 1978?

4. FROM BALBONI TO WITT

Let's finish this chapter off in style.

1. _____ Who in 1986 became the third Brewer pitcher to win 20 games in a season?

2. _____ Who is the 1986 Brewer who is nicknamed "Horse"?

3. _____ Who set a Yankee record with 238 hits in 1986?

4. _____ Who is the Yankee who, except for 1987, has never failed to lead his league in stolen bases?

5. _____ Who is the Yankees' all-time leader in games played at his position?

6. _____ Who, in 1986, drove home 100 runs for the fifth straight year?

7. _____ Who is the Yankee pitcher who was the Rookie of the Year in 1981?

8. _____ Who is the Blue Jay who led American League outfielders with 20 assists in 1986?

9. _____ Who is the Blue Jay who is nicknamed "Shaker"?

10. _____ Who is the Blue Jay who hit a career-high 47 home runs in 1987?

11. _____ Who is the pitcher whose autobiography is titled *Tomorrow I'll Be Perfect*?

12. _____ Who became the first rookie to start in the All-Star Game since fan voting began in 1970?

13. _____ Who is the Angel infielder who hit 20 or more home runs in each season from 1984–86?

14. _____ Who is the Angel who ranks first on the club's all-time RBI list?

15. _____ Who is the first Angel to record three consecutive 30-plus stolen-base seasons?

16. _____ Who is the pitcher whose 18 wins in 1986 were the most by any Angel since Nolan Ryan won 19 in 1977?

17. _____ Who has had a record 21 consecutive seasons of more than 100 strikeouts?

18. _____ Who set a White Sox club record by hitting 20 or more home runs in six consecutive seasons?

19. _____ Who set a White Sox club record for the fewest errors (12) by a shortstop in 1985?

20. _____ Who ranks second to Yogi Berra in career homers by an American League catcher?

21. _____ Who became the first major leaguer to strike out the first seven batters he faced in a game?

22. _____ Who set a White Sox record with 32 saves in 1985?

23. _____ Who is the Royal who in 1986 was honored with his 11th consecutive All-Star selection?

24. _____ Who, in his first three years with the Royals, averaged 31 home runs a season?

25. _____ Who is the Royal switch-hitter who once led the league in hitting?

26. _____ Who is the Royal infielder who hit 22 home runs in both 1985 and 1986?

27. _____ Who is the Twin who had a club record-tying eight four-hit games in 1986?

28. _____ Who is the Twin who hit a career-high 34 home runs in 1987?

29. _____ Who is the Twin whose 108 RBIs in 1986 was the most by a Minnesota player since Larry Hisle plated 119 runners in 1977?

30. _____ Who is the Twin pitcher who holds the American League record of eight seasons with more than 200 strikeouts?

31. _____ Who is the A's player who was the Rookie of the Year in 1986?

32. _____ Who was the 1986 rookie who set the then American League record for strikeouts (185)?

33. _____ Who is the Texas player who became one of the select few to hit three home runs in a game in both leagues?

34. _____ Who is the Ranger pitcher who, in 1986, set a major-league rookie record with 80 appearances?

35. _____ Who became the first pitcher to win a major league game with no previous professional victories since David Clyde did it for Texas in 1973?

Ruth's Shadow

Babe Ruth captured the attention of the nation on October 2, 1932, for on that historic day he allegedly "called his shot."

The Yankees had won the first two games of the World Series before traveling to Chicago's Wrigley Field. The Cub fans and players were riding Ruth unmercifully for criticizing the Bruin players for failing to award former Yankee infielder Mark Koenig a full share of their series cut.

But Ruth relished the attention.

In the first inning Earle Combs reached second on a two-base throwing error by shortstop Billy Jurges. Bruin pitcher Charlie Root, obviously upset, proceeded to walk Joe Sewell, something he did not want to do with Ruth coming to the plate. On a 2–0 count, Ruth cracked a three-run homer.

The third time that Ruth came to the plate, in the fifth inning, the Yankees were leading, 4–3. In the interim, he had misplayed a ball in right field, much to the delight of the Cub supporters. Before Root got a chance to pitch to the Babe in the fifth, Ruth allegedly pointed his bat toward the center-field bleachers, saying, in effect, "This is where the ball is going to land." The stage had been set for one of the most dramatic moments in baseball history.

Ruth deliberately took two strikes, which he dutifully noted by raising first one finger and then a second one after the calls. Then he proceeded to deposit the ball in the exact spot to which he had pointed his bat. Coincidentally, that was the 15th and last home run that Ruth hit in series play.

Lost in the fanfare of that day were the exploits of another Yankee, who hit two home runs, including the game-winner.

Who was this Yankee great who played in the shadow of Ruth?

(Answer appears on page 321.)

Chapter Two

THE HITTERS

5. HOW GOOD IS .300?

Twenty of the following 40 players have won at least one batting title, though they have lifetime averages of less than .300; the other twenty players have lifetime averages of .300 or better, though they have never won a batting title. Put the batting champs in the left-hand column and the .300 hitters in the right-hand column.

Mickey Mantle	Lou Boudreau
Johnny Pesky	Mickey Vernon
Enos Slaughter	Debs Garms
Tommy Davis	Sam Rice
Norm Cash	Heinie Zimmerman
Joe Cronin	Dale Mitchell
Hal Chase	Pete Reiser
George Stirnweiss	Larry Doyle
Carl Yastrzemski	Hank Greenberg
Mel Ott	Ferris Fain
Bill Dickey	Alex Johnson
Pete Runnels	Eddie Collins
Bobby Avila	Phil Cavarretta
Lloyd Waner	Earle Combs
Harry Walker	Carl Furillo
Bob Meusel	Babe Herman
Joe Jackson	Kiki Cuyler
Hack Wilson	Frankie Frisch
Earl Averill	Pie Traynor
Dick Groat	Mickey Cochrane

Batting Champs   .300 Hitters

Batting Champs	.300 Hitters
1. _____	1. _____
2. _____	2. _____
3. _____	3. _____
4. _____	4. _____
5. _____	5. _____
6. _____	6. _____
7. _____	7. _____
8. _____	8. _____
9. _____	9. _____
10. _____	10. _____
11. _____	11. _____
12. _____	12. _____
13. _____	13. _____
14. _____	14. _____
15. _____	15. _____
16. _____	16. _____
17. _____	17. _____
18. _____	18. _____
19. _____	19. _____
20. _____	20. _____

6. WHO DID IT TWICE?

National League

Five of the following ten players have won one National League batting title; the other five have won two. List the one-time winners in the left-hand column and the two-time winners in the right-hand column: Willie Mays, Lefty O'Doul, Tommy Davis, Harry Walker, Dixie Walker, Henry Aaron, Carl Furillo, Jackie Robinson, Ernie Lombardi, and Richie Ashburn.

1. _____   1. _____
2. _____   2. _____
3. _____   3. _____
4. _____   4. _____
5. _____   5. _____

American League

Five of the following ten players have won one American League batting title; the other five have won two. List the one-time winners in the left-hand column and the two-time winners in the right-hand column: George Kell, Al Kaline, Jimmie Foxx, Norm Cash, Luke Appling, Mickey Vernon, Mickey Mantle, Pete Runnels, Ferris Fain, and Harvey Kuenn.

1. _____   1. _____
2. _____   2. _____
3. _____   3. _____
4. _____   4. _____
5. _____   5. _____

7. THE FABULOUS FIFTIES

Ten players have hit a total of 50 or more home runs in one season: Willie Mays, Mickey Mantle, Hank Greenberg, George Foster, Jimmie Foxx, Roger Maris, Johnny Mize, Ralph Kiner, Hack Wilson, and Babe Ruth. The ten of them have done it a total of 17 times. One of them accomplished the feat four times. Four of them achieved it twice. Place them in the order of their single-season rank. Totals, years, and leagues are given as clues.

1. _____ (61) 1961 (AL)
2. _____ (60) 1927 (AL)
3. _____ (59) 1921 (AL)
4. _____ (58) 1932 (AL)
5. _____ (58) 1938 (AL)
6. _____ (56) 1930 (NL)
7. _____ (54) 1920 (AL)
8. _____ (54) 1928 (AL)
9. _____ (54) 1949 (NL)
10. _____ (54) 1961 (AL)
11. _____ (52) 1956 (AL)
12. _____ (52) 1965 (NL)
13. _____ (52) 1977 (NL)
14. _____ (51) 1947 (NL)
15. _____ (51) 1947 (NL)
16. _____ (51) 1955 (NL)
17. _____ (50) 1938 (AL)

8. THE (500) HOME RUN CLUB

There have been 14 players who have hit more than 500 home runs in their careers. See how many of them you can name. Their respective totals are listed in parentheses. Two of them were still active in 1987.

1. _____ (755)
2. _____ (714)
3. _____ (660)
4. _____ (586)
5. _____ (573)
6. _____ (563)*
7. _____ (536)
8. _____ (534)
9. _____ (530)
10. _____ (521)
11. _____ (521)*
12. _____ (512)
13. _____ (512)
14. _____ (511)

*Still active on July 1, 1987

9. THEY HIT FOR POWER AND AVERAGE

National League

Five National League players have won both the home run crown and the batting title in the same year. One of them did it twice. Match the following players with the year(s) in which they performed the feat: Joe Medwick, Johnny Mize, Heinie Zimmerman, Rogers Hornsby (2), and Chuck Klein.

1. _____ (1912)
2. _____ (1922)
3. _____ (1925)
4. _____ (1933)
5. _____ (1937)
6. _____ (1939)

American League

Do the same with the following nine American Leaguers: Ted Williams (3), Lou Gehrig, Nap Lajoie, Mickey Mantle, Babe Ruth, Ty Cobb, Jimmie Foxx, Carl Yastrzemski, and Frank Robinson.

 1. _____ (1901)
 2. _____ (1909)
 3. _____ (1924)
 4. _____ (1933)
 5. _____ (1934)
 6. _____ (1941)
 7. _____ (1942)
 8. _____ (1947)
 9. _____ (1956)
10. _____ (1966)
11. _____ (1967)

10. THE 3000-HIT CLUB

The following 15 players have accumulated 3000 or more major league hits: Al Kaline, Tris Speaker, Carl Yastrzemski, Ty Cobb, Honus Wagner, Roberto Clemente, Eddie Collins, Stan Musial, Hank Aaron, Nap Lajoie, Pete Rose, Paul Waner, Cap Anson, Lou Brock, and Willie Mays. Their respective totals are included. Place the players in their proper order.

1. _____ (4256)
2. _____ (4192)
3. _____ (3771)
4. _____ (3630)
5. _____ (3515)
6. _____ (3430)
7. _____ (3419)
8. _____ (3311)
9. _____ (3283)
10. _____ (3251)
11. _____ (3152)
12. _____ (3041)
13. _____ (3023)
14. _____ (3007)
15. _____ (3000)

11. TRIPLE CROWN WINNERS

Eleven players have won the Triple Crown a total of 13 times: Ted Williams (2), Rogers Hornsby (2), Carl Yastrzemski, Mickey Mantle, Ty Cobb, Frank Robinson, Jimmie Foxx, Joe Medwick, Lou Gehrig, Chuck Klein, and Nap Lajoie. Fit them into the respective years in which they won the select award.

1. _____ (1901)
2. _____ (1909)
3. _____ (1922)
4. _____ (1925)
5. _____ (1933)
6. _____ (1933)
7. _____ (1934)
8. _____ (1937)
9. _____ (1942)
10. _____ (1947)
11. _____ (1956)
12. _____ (1966)
13. _____ (1967)

12. HIGHEST LIFETIME AVERAGE
FOR POSITION

Identify the player, from the three listed at each position, who has hit for the highest lifetime average. At one position two players are tied for the lead.

National League

1B. _____ (.341) Bill Terry, Johnny Mize, or Stan Musial

2B. _____ (.358) Frankie Frisch, Jackie Robinson, or Rogers Hornsby

SS. _____ (.329) Arky Vaughan, Honus Wagner, or Travis Jackson

3B. _____ (.320) Joe Torre, Heinie Zimmerman, or Pie Traynor

OF. _____ (.336) Chuck Klein, Harry Walker, or Riggs Stephenson

OF. _____ (.333) Paul Waner, Babe Herman, or Zack Wheat

OF. _____ (.349) Kiki Cuyler, Stan Musial, or Lefty O'Doul

C. _____ (.310) Eugene Hargrave, Gabby Hartnett, or Roy Campanella

American League

1B. _____ (.340) Lou Gehrig, Jimmie Foxx, or George Sisler

2B. _____ (.339) Nap Lajoie, Charlie Gehringer, or Eddie Collins

SS. _____ (.314) Joe Cronin, Cecil Travis, or Luke Appling

3B. _____ (.307) George Kell, Frank Baker, or Jimmy Collins

OF. _____ (.367) Harry Heilmann, Tris Speaker, or Ty Cobb

OF. _____ (.356) Babe Ruth, Al Simmons, or Joe Jackson

OF. _____ (.344) Joe DiMaggio, Ted Williams,
or Heinie Manush
C. _____ (.320) Mickey Cochrane, Yogi Berra,
or Bill Dickey

13. HIGHEST SINGLE SEASON AVERAGE FOR POSITION

Identify the player, from the three listed at each position, who has hit for the highest average in a single season.

National League

1B. _____ (.401) Bill Terry, Johnny Mize, or Stan Musial

2B. _____ (.424) Frankie Frisch, Jackie Robinson, or Rogers Hornsby

SS. _____ (.385) Arky Vaughan, Honus Wagner, or Travis Jackson

3B. _____ (.372) Joe Torre, Heinie Zimmerman, or Pie Traynor

OF. _____ (.398) Paul Waner, Fred Lindstrom, or Lefty O'Doul

OF. _____ (.393) Stan Musial, Babe Herman, or Roberto Clemente

OF. _____ (.386) Chuck Klein, Zack Wheat, or Harry Walker

C. _____ (.358) Ernie Lombardi, Gabby Hartnett, or Chief Meyers

American League

1B. _____ (.420) Lou Gehrig, Jimmie Foxx, or George Sisler

2B. _____ (.422) Nap Lajoie, Charlie Gehringer, or Eddie Collins

SS. _____ (.388) Joe Cronin, Cecil Travis, or Luke Appling

3B. _____ (.390) George Kell, Frank Baker, or George Brett

OF. _____ (.420) Harry Heilmann, Tris Speaker, or Ty Cobb

OF. _____ (.408) Babe Ruth, Al Simmons, or Joe Jackson

OF. _____ (.406) Sam Crawford, Ted Williams, or Heinie Manush

C. _____ (.362) Mickey Cochrane, Yogi Berra, or Bill Dickey

14. THE YEAR THEY HIT THE HEIGHTS

Take the following ten hitters and match them up with their highest respective season's batting average: Babe Ruth, Jackie Robinson, Stan Musial, Rogers Hornsby, Charlie Keller, Ted Williams, Roberto Clemente, Ty Cobb, Joe DiMaggio, and Mickey Mantle.

1. _____ (.424)   6. _____ (.376)
2. _____ (.420)   7. _____ (.365)
3. _____ (.406)   8. _____ (.357)
4. _____ (.393)   9. _____ (.342)
5. _____ (.381)   10. _____ (.334)

15. MATCHING AVERAGES

Match the following ten players with their corresponding lifetime averages listed below: Rogers Hornsby, Babe Ruth, Honus Wagner, Ty Cobb, Stan Musial, Jimmie Foxx, Tris Speaker, Mickey Cochrane, Mel Ott, and Bill Terry.

1. _____ (.367)   6. _____ (.331)
2. _____ (.358)   7. _____ (.329)
3. _____ (.344)   8. _____ (.325)
4. _____ (.342)   9. _____ (.320)
5. _____ (.341)   10. _____ (.304)

16. ONCE IS NOT ENOUGH

Eight of the following sluggers have hit four home runs in a major league game: Babe Ruth, Lou Gehrig, Rocky Colavito, Hank Aaron, Gil Hodges, Pat Seerey, Mickey Mantle, Jimmie Foxx, Joe Adcock, Mike Schmidt, Willie Mays, Joe DiMaggio, Bob Horner, and Hank Greenberg. Who are they?

1. _____
2. _____
3. _____
4. _____
5. _____
6. _____
7. _____
8. _____

17. NATIONAL LEAGUE HOME RUN KINGS

Match the following National League home run champs with the number of times they have won the crown: Ted Kluszewski, Johnny Mize, Ralph Kiner, Duke Snider, Eddie Mathews, Johnny Bench, Mike Schmidt, and Mel Ott.

1. _____ (8)
2. _____ (7)
3. _____ (6)
4. _____ (4)
5. _____ (2)
6. _____ (2)
7. _____ (1)
8. _____ (1)

18. AMERICAN LEAGUE HOME RUN KINGS

Match the following American League home run champs with the number of times they have won the crown: Roger Maris, Lou Gehrig, Frank Howard, Babe Ruth, Tony Armas, Carl Yastrzemski, Jimmie Foxx, Joe DiMaggio, Jim Rice, Harmon Killebrew, Frank Baker, Hank Greenberg, George Scott, Reggie Jackson, Graig Nettles, Ted Williams, Gorman Thomas, Larry Doby, Mickey Mantle, and Dick Allen.

1. _____ (12)
2. _____ (6)
3. _____ (4)
4. _____ (4)
5. _____ (4)
6. _____ (4)
7. _____ (4)
8. _____ (4)
9. _____ (3)
10. _____ (3)
11. _____ (2)
12. _____ (2)
13. _____ (2)
14. _____ (2)
15. _____ (2)
16. _____ (2)
17. _____ (1)
18. _____ (1)
19. _____ (1)
20. _____ (1)

19. WOULD YOU PINCH-HIT?

Some of the best pinch-hitters in the history of the game are listed with their averages as substitute batters. Were their lifetime averages higher (Yes–No) than their pinch-hitting marks?

1. _____ (.320) Tommy Davis
2. _____ (.312) Frenchy Bordagaray
3. _____ (.307) Frankie Baumholtz
4. _____ (.303) Red Schoendienst
5. _____ (.300) Bob Fothergill
6. _____ (.299) Dave Philley
7. _____ (.297) Manny Mota
8. _____ (.286) Steve Braun
9. _____ (.283) Johnny Mize
10. _____ (.280) Don Mueller
11. _____ (.279) Mickey Vernon
12. _____ (.278) Gene Woodling
13. _____ (.277) Bobby Adams
14. _____ (.277) Ed Kranepool
15. _____ (.276) Jose Morales
16. _____ (.276) Ron Northey
17. _____ (.273) Sam Leslie
18. _____ (.273) Pat Kelly
19. _____ (.273) Debs Garms
20. _____ (.270) Peanuts Lowrey

20. DECADES OF BATTING CHAMPS

Listed below is one batting champ from each decade and the year in which he led the league. All you have to provide is the team for which he did it.

National League

1. _____ (1908) Honus Wagner
2. _____ (1917) Edd Roush
3. _____ (1929) Lefty O'Doul
4. _____ (1938) Ernie Lombardi
5. _____ (1945) Phil Cavarretta
6. _____ (1953) Carl Furillo
7. _____ (1968) Pete Rose
8. _____ (1970) Rico Carty
9. _____ (1982) Al Oliver

American League

1. _____ (1902) Ed Delahanty
2. _____ (1916) Tris Speaker
3. _____ (1923) Harry Heilmann
4. _____ (1936) Luke Appling
5. _____ (1945) George Stirnweiss
6. _____ (1951) Ferris Fain
7. _____ (1962) Pete Runnels
8. _____ (1970) Alex Johnson
9. _____ (1981) Carney Lansford

21. SUB-.320 BATTING LEADERS

Name the five players from the following ten who have won batting titles with averages that were less than .320: George Stirnweiss, Tony Oliva, Roberto Clemente, Rod Carew, Carl Yastrzemski, Ted Williams, Pete Runnels, Frank Robinson, Alex Johnson, and Elmer Flick.

1. _____ (.318) 1972
2. _____ (.316) 1966
3. _____ (.309) 1945
4. _____ (.306) 1905
5. _____ (.301) 1968

22. .390-PLUS RUNNERS-UP

Name the five players from the following ten who have failed to win batting titles with averages that were better than .390: Harry Heilmann, George Sisler, Babe Ruth, Joe Jackson, Ted Williams, Rogers Hornsby, Al Simmons, Ty Cobb, Babe Herman, and Bill Terry.

1. _____ (.408) 1911
2. _____ (.401) 1922
3. _____ (.393) 1923
4. _____ (.393) 1930
5. _____ (.392) 1927

23. STEPPING INTO THE BOX

In front of the 30 players who are listed, mark an "L" (left-handed), "R" (right-handed), or "S" (switch-hitter) for the way in which they hit.

1. _____ Mel Ott
2. _____ Ernie Lombardi
3. _____ Tom Tresh
4. _____ Tony Lazzeri
5. _____ Pete Rose
6. _____ Willard Marshall
7. _____ Jim Gilliam
8. _____ Wally Westlake
9. _____ Jim Gentile
10. _____ Bud Harrelson
11. _____ Granny Hamner
12. _____ Tommy Holmes
13. _____ George McQuinn
14. _____ Hector Lopez
15. _____ Smoky Burgess
16. _____ Wes Covington
17. _____ Phil Masi
18. _____ Sid Gordon
19. _____ Willie Miranda
20. _____ Maury Wills
21. _____ Nellie Fox
22. _____ Jimmie Foxx
23. _____ Red Schoendienst
24. _____ Eddie Waitkus
25. _____ Sam Mele
26. _____ Frankie Frisch
27. _____ Gino Cimoli
28. _____ Jim Rivera
29. _____ Mickey Mantle
30. _____ Roy White

The Shot Heard 'Round the World

Bobby Thomson's game-winning home run in the final playoff game of the 1951 season gave the Giants the most dramatic come-from-behind title in the history of baseball. It also provided trivia buffs with a gold mine of facts and questions.

Sal Maglie started the game for the Giants; Don Newcombe toed the mound for the Dodgers. They hooked up in a classic pitching duel until the eighth inning when the visiting Dodgers scored three runs to take a 4–1 lead. With Maglie departed from the scene and Newcombe mowing down the Giants in the bottom of the eighth, the Dodgers seemed virtually assured of winning their sixth National League pennant. But the Giants, who had fought back from a 13½-game deficit during the regular season, were not about to give up.

Al Dark led off the bottom of the ninth by singling to center. Charlie Dressen, the manager of the Dodgers, made a tactical mistake when he did not tell first baseman Gil Hodges to play behind the runner, for Don Mueller ripped a single to right, sending Dark to third. If Hodges had been playing deep, Mueller would have hit into a double play; and the Dodgers would have cinched the pennant, for Monte Irvin, the following batter, popped out. Whitey Lockman then ripped a double, scoring Dark and sending Mueller to third. Sliding into the base, Mueller broke his ankle and was replaced by pinch-runner Clint Hartung. That brought Thomson up to the plate with a free base at first. Had Dressen chosen to put the potential winning run on base, the Giants would have had to send a rookie up to the plate—Willie Mays.

Instead Dressen decided to change pitchers. He had Carl Erskine and Ralph Branca warming up in the bull pen. Erskine had looked the sharper of the two, but just before bull pen coach Clyde Sukeforth made his recommendation to Dressen, Erskine bounced a curve. That settled the matter: Branca got the call. When Branca walked in from the bull pen, some of the superstitious "faithful" from Flatbush must have got an ominous feeling when they noted the number "13" on the back of the pitcher's uniform. Coincidentally, Branca had 13 wins at the time. He also had 12 losses. After his second pitch to Thomson, which the "Staten Island Scot" hit for the pennant-winning homer, the 13's were balanced, all the way across.

Almost all of baseball's avid followers of the sport know that Branca was the losing pitcher in that fateful game. But I've run across very few baseball aficionados who know who the winning pitcher was. Do you?

(*Answer appears on page 321.*)

Chapter Three

THE PITCHERS

24. FAMOUS HOME RUN PITCHES

Match the following pitchers with the batters to whom they threw historic home run pitches: Don Newcombe, Bob Purkey, Bob Lemon, Ralph Terry, Howie Pollet, Robin Roberts, Ralph Branca, Jack Billingham, Al Downing, and Barney Schultz.

1. _____ He threw the home run pitch to Bill Mazeroski that gave the Pirates the 1960 World Series. The circuit clout gave Pittsburgh a 10–9 win.

2. _____ He threw the game-winning home run pitch to Joe DiMaggio in the top of the tenth inning in the second game of the 1950 World Series. The Yankees won, 2–1.

3. _____ He threw the home run pitch to Bobby Thomson in the final playoff game of the National League's 1951 season. The Giants outlasted the Dodgers, 5–4.

4. _____ He threw the three-run homer to Dick Sisler in the top of the tenth inning of the final game of the 1950 season. The home run gave Robin Roberts the margin of victory, and it gave the Phillies the National League pennant.

5. _____ He threw the pitch that Hank Aaron hit for home run number 714.

6. _____ He threw the pitch that Hank Aaron hit for home run number 715.

7. _____ He threw the tenth-inning home run pitch to Rudy York in the first game of the 1946 World Series. It gave the Red Sox a 3–2 victory.

8. _____ He threw the ninth-inning home run

pitch to Mickey Mantle in the third game of the 1964 World Series. It gave the Yankees a 2–1 victory.

9. _____ He threw the three-run homer to Dusty Rhodes in the bottom of the tenth inning in Game One of the 1954 World Series. The blow gave the Giants a 5–2 victory.

10. _____ He threw the ninth-inning home run pitch to Roger Maris in the third game of the 1961 World Series. The home run gave the Yankees a 3–2 win.

25. THE PITCHING MASTERS

Walter Johnson, Eddie Plank, Tom Seaver, Early Wynn, Cy Young, Lefty Grove, Warren Spahn, Christy Mathewson, Gaylord Perry, and Grover Alexander all won 300 or more games in their careers. Put them in their proper order. Also, identify the three 300-game winners who were still pitching in 1987.

1. _____ (511)
2. _____ (416)
3. _____ (373)
4. _____ (373)
5. _____ (363)
6. _____ (327)
7. _____ (314)
8. _____ (311)
9. _____ (300)
10. _____ (300)
11. _____ (still pitching)
12. _____ (still pitching)
13. _____ (still pitching)

26. THE PERFECT GAME

Ten of the following 20 pitchers have thrown perfect games: Walter Johnson, Tom Seaver, Carl Hubbell, Ernie Shore, Babe Ruth, Jim Hunter, Sal Maglie, Whitey Ford, Jim Bunning, Cy Young, Steve Carlton, Robin Roberts, Bob Feller, Addie Joss, Sandy Koufax, Wes Ferrell, Don Larsen, Charlie Robertson, Mike Witt, and Len Barker. Name them.

1. _____
2. _____
3. _____
4. _____
5. _____
6. _____
7. _____
8. _____
9. _____
10. _____

27. MULTIPLE NO-HITTERS

All of the 25 pitchers who are listed below have hurled no-hit games. Fifteen of them have done it more than once. In fact, one of them has done it five times; one of them, four times; two of them, three times; and 11 of them, twice. Match the pitcher with the number that denotes how many times he performed the feat.

Bobo Holloman	Warren Spahn
Mel Parnell	Sam Jones
Johnny Vander Meer	Milt Pappas
Steve Busby	Bill Singer
Rick Wise	Carl Erskine
Ken Holtzman	Sal Maglie
Don Wilson	Bob Feller
Gaylord Perry	Virgil Trucks
Dean Chance	Allie Reynolds
Sandy Koufax	Jim Maloney
Jim Bunning	Don Larsen
Juan Marichal	Nolan Ryan
Bo Belinsky	

1. _____ (5)		9. _____ (2)
2. _____ (4)		10. _____ (2)
3. _____ (3)		11. _____ (2)
4. _____ (3)		12. _____ (2)
5. _____ (2)		13. _____ (2)
6. _____ (2)		14. _____ (2)
7. _____ (2)		15. _____ (2)
8. _____ (2)		

28. BACK-TO-BACK 20-GAME WINNERS

Match the pitchers with the span of their careers when they recorded consecutive 20-game winning seasons.

1. ____ Tom Seaver		a.	1969–71
2. ____ Dave McNally		b.	1967–72
3. ____ Lefty Grove		c.	1910–19
4. ____ Paul Derringer		d.	1936–39
5. ____ Hal Newhouser		e.	1911–17
6. ____ Red Ruffing		f.	1968–69
7. ____ Warren Spahn		g.	1965–66
8. ____ Bob Feller		h.	1971–72
9. ____ Carl Hubbell		i.	1968–70
10. ____ Bob Lemon		j.	1963–66
11. ____ Denny McLain		k.	1933–37
12. ____ Vic Raschi		l.	1970–73
13. ____ Christy Mathewson		m.	1948–50
14. ____ Grover Cleveland Alexander		n.	1938–40
15. ____ Don Newcombe		o.	1903–14
16. ____ Juan Marichal		p.	1927–33
17. ____ Mike Cuellar		q.	1949–51
18. ____ Bob Gibson		r.	1942–44
19. ____ Walter Johnson		s.	1968–71
20. ____ Robin Roberts		t.	1939–41, 1946–47*
21. ____ Sandy Koufax		u.	1950–55
22. ____ Mort Cooper		v.	1956–61
23. ____ Ferguson Jenkins		w.	1944–46
24. ____ Jim Palmer		x.	1955–56
25. ____ Dizzy Dean		y.	1933–36
26. ____ Tommy John		z.	1979–80

* The pitcher's consecutive string of 20-win seasons was interrupted by the war.

29. THE FLAMETHROWERS

Name the 11 flamethrowers from the following 22 who
have struck out 300 batters at least once in one season:
Nolan Ryan, Tom Seaver, Sandy Koufax, Ferguson Jenkins,
Mickey Lolich, Sam McDowell, Jim Lonborg, Bob Feller,
Steve Carlton, Herb Score, Dwight Gooden, Jim Bunning,
Walter Johnson, Don Drysdale, Bob Gibson, Red Ruffing,
Rube Waddell, Vida Blue, Bob Turley, Carl Erskine, J. R.
Richard, and Mike Scott.

1. _____
2. _____
3. _____
4. _____
5. _____
6. _____
7. _____
8. _____
9. _____
10. _____
11. _____

30. BLUE-CHIP PITCHERS

Ten of the 20 pitchers who are listed below have recorded winning percentages of .600 or better. Who are they?

Whitey Ford	Jim Perry
Ted Lyons	Vic Raschi
Early Wynn	Jim Kaat
Allie Reynolds	Don Drysdale
Jim Palmer	Sal Maglie
Robin Roberts	Dizzy Dean
Gaylord Perry	Sandy Koufax
Mort Cooper	Mickey Lolich
Tom Seaver	Claude Osteen
Waite Hoyt	Lefty Gomez

1. _____
2. _____
3. _____
4. _____
5. _____
6. _____
7. _____
8. _____
9. _____
10. _____

31. 200 TIMES A LOSER

Ten of the 20 pitchers listed below have lost 200 or more major league games. Name them.

Cy Young   Bob Feller
Billy Pierce   Red Ruffing
Christy Mathewson Milt Pappas
Bobo Newsom   Carl Hubbell
Walter Johnson   Paul Derringer
Juan Marichal   Robin Roberts
Mel Harder   Bob Gibson
Warren Spahn   Bob Friend
Grover Alexander   Early Wynn
Lefty Grove   Jim Bunning

1. _____
2. _____
3. _____
4. _____
5. _____
6. _____
7. _____
8. _____
9. _____
10. _____

32. WINDING UP

Mark "L" in the space provided for the pitchers who threw left-handed and "R" for the hurlers who threw right-handed. There are an even number of each contained in the list.

1. _____ Hal Newhouser
2. _____ Vernon Gomez
3. _____ Mike Garcia
4. _____ Eddie Lopat
5. _____ Virgil Trucks
6. _____ Ellis Kinder
7. _____ Billy Pierce
8. _____ Herb Score
9. _____ Bucky Walters
10. _____ Van Lingle Mungo
11. _____ Vic Raschi
12. _____ Johnny Sain
13. _____ Preacher Roe
14. _____ Dave Koslo
15. _____ Billy Loes
16. _____ Ned Garver
17. _____ Billy Hoeft
18. _____ Don Mossi
19. _____ Frank Lary
20. _____ Max Lanier
21. _____ Harry Brecheen
22. _____ Johnny Podres
23. _____ Larry Jansen
24. _____ Lew Burdette
25. _____ Mudcat Grant
26. _____ Vernon Law
27. _____ Mel Parnell
28. _____ Rip Sewell
29. _____ Tommy Byrne
30. _____ Ron Perranoski

The Asterisk Pitcher

The pitcher who threw the best game that has ever been spun lost the decision. If you don't believe me, you can look it up. Or, better still, you could ask Harvey Haddix.

On May 26, 1959, the Pirates' left-hander pitched a perfect game for nine innings against the host Braves. That puts him in the select company of Cy Young, Addie Joss, Ernie Shore, Charlie Robertson, Don Larsen, Jim Bunning, Sandy Koufax, Jim Hunter, Len Barker, and Mike Witt, the only other pitchers who have thrown a nine-inning perfect game in the modern era. But Haddix was not as fortunate as his select peers. Their teams gave them sufficient support to win the games. Haddix's club did not.

So "The Kitten" was forced to prove that he could pitch a game that had never been thrown before. He put the Braves down one, two, three in the tenth; he mowed them down in order in the eleventh; and he sailed through the lineup in sequence in the twelfth. But still his teammates, though they had touched Lew Burdette for 12 hits, could not dent the plate the one time that was needed to give their special southpaw instant immortality.

Inning 13 proved to be unlucky for Haddix. Felix Mantilla, the first batter, reached first when third baseman Don Hoak made a throwing error on an easy ground ball. Eddie Mathews bunted Mantilla into scoring position. Haddix was then forced to intentionally pass Hank Aaron to set up the double play for the slow-running Joe Adcock. But Adcock crossed up the strategy by hitting a three-run homer to right center.

Yet the final score was only 1–0. And Haddix got credit for another out. Technically, he could have been credited with an additional out. If he had, he might have gotten out of the inning without a run being scored.

Can you unravel that strange sequence of circumstances?

(Answer appears on page 321.)

MULTIPLE CHOICE

33. FOUR BASES TO SCORE

1. _____ Who were the Dodger runners when Cookie Lavagetto's game-winning double with two outs in the bottom of the ninth inning broke up Bill Bevens' no-hitter in the 1947 World Series?
   a. Jackie Robinson and Eddie Stanky b. Eddie Miksis and Pete Reiser c. Jackie Robinson and Spider Jorgensen d. Al Gionfriddo and Eddie Miksis

2. _____ Whom did Don Larsen strike out for the final out in his perfect game in the 1956 World Series?
   a. Gil Hodges b. Roy Campanella c. Dale Mitchell d. Carl Furillo

3. _____ Against whom did Willie Mays hit his first major league home run?
   a. Bob Buhl b. Warren Spahn c. Larry Jansen d. Robin Roberts

4. _____ Against whom did Hank Aaron hit his first major league home run?
   a. Curt Simmons b. Vic Raschi c. Lew Burdette d. Don Newcombe

5. _____ Who hit the last home run in the initial Yankee Stadium?
   a. Duke Sims b. Norm Cash c. Carl Yastrzemski d. Bobby Murcer

6. _____ Who hit the first home run in Shea Stadium?
   a. Willie Stargell b. Frank Thomas c. Stan Musial d. Frank Howard

7. _____ Who were the Giant runners when Bobby Thomson hit the playoff home run against the Dodgers in 1951 to decide the pennant?
   a. Don Mueller and Whitey Lockman b. Al Dark and

Don Mueller c. Whitey Lockman and Al Dark d. Clint Hartung and Whitey Lockman

8. _____ Which team was the last all-white club that won the American League pennant?

a. 1947 Yankees b. 1953 Yankees c. 1959 White Sox d. 1965 Twins

9. _____ Who hit .400 in World Series play a record three times?

a. Ty Cobb b. Babe Ruth c. Lou Gehrig d. Eddie Collins

10. _____ Who was the only Yankee who has won two batting titles?

a. Joe DiMaggio b. Mickey Mantle c. Lou Gehrig d. Babe Ruth

11. _____ Who was doubled off first when Sandy Amoros made the game-saving catch on Yogi Berra's fly ball in the seventh inning of the seventh game of the 1955 World Series between the Dodgers and the Yankees?

a. Billy Martin b. Elston Howard c. Gil McDougald d. Hank Bauer

12. _____ Which team holds the American League record of 111 wins in one season?

a. 1946 Red Sox b. 1927 Yankees c. 1959 White Sox d. 1954 Indians

13. _____ Who was the National League player who moved into third place on the all-time pinch-hit list in 1987?

a. Lee Mazzilli b. Greg Gross c. Manny Sanguillen d. Graig Nettles

14. _____ Who was the American League rookie in 1987 who hit five home runs in two consecutive games?

a. Mickey Brantley b. Bob Jackson c. Mark McGwire d. Ellis Burks

15. _____ Which National League team holds the major league record of 116 wins in one season?

a. 1906 Cubs b. 1930 Cardinals c. 1952 Dodgers d. 1976 Reds

16. _____ Which of the following players has not recorded 500 putouts in one season?

a. Joe DiMaggio b. Dom DiMaggio c. Vince DiMaggio d. Richie Ashburn

17. _____ Who is the only player who has won home run titles in both leagues?

a. Frank Robinson b. Sam Crawford c. Hank Greenberg d. Johnny Mize

18. _____ Who is the only player who has won batting titles in both leagues?

a. Lefty O'Doul b. Dixie Walker c. Rogers Hornsby
d. Ed Delahanty

19. _____ Who was the last player who hit more than 50
home runs in one season? .

a. Mickey Mantle b. Roger Maris c. George Foster
d. Willie McCovey

20. _____ Which of these former Yankees did not play in a
World Series with a National League club?

a. Roger Maris b. Bill Skowron c. Hank Borowy d. Vic
Raschi

21. _____ Which of the following players did not win the
RBI title with two teams in the same league?

a. Orlando Cepeda b. Vern Stephens c. Johnny Mize
d. Ralph Kiner

22. _____ Which of the following pitchers did not lose
more games than he won?

a. Bobo Newsom b. Murry Dickson c. Bob Friend
d. Dizzy Trout

23. _____ Whose line drive, which almost provided the
margin of victory, did Bobby Richardson catch for the final
out of the 1962 World Series?

a. Willie McCovey b. Jim Davenport c. Jose Pagan
d. Orlando Cepeda

24. _____ Which of the following pitchers won the first
playoff game in American League history?

a. Denny Galehouse b. Bob Feller c. Gene Bearden
d. Mel Parnell

25. _____ Who was the losing pitcher for the Dodgers on
the day that Don Larsen threw his perfect game in the 1956
World Series?

a. Clem Labine b. Johnny Podres c. Don Newcombe
d. Sal Maglie

26. _____ Which of the following umpires worked his last
game behind the plate on the day that Don Larsen pitched
his perfect game?

a. Jocko Conlan b. Augie Donatelli c. Babe Pinelli
d. George Magerkurth

27. _____ Which one of the following players won back-to-
back American League batting titles in the 1950s?

a. Al Rosen b. Bobby Avila c. Ferris Fain d. Al Kaline

28. _____ Which one of the following players won back-to-
back National League batting titles in the 1960s?

a. Matty Alou b. Dick Groat c. Tommy Davis d. Richie
Ashburn

57

29. _____ Which one of the following shortstops did not win a batting title?

a. Dick Groat b. Lou Boudreau c. Luke Appling d. Luis Aparicio

30. _____ What was the name of the midget whom Bill Veeck sent up to the plate to pinch-hit for the Browns?

a. Frank Gabler b. Ed Gallagher c. Dick Kokos d. Eddie Gaedel

31. _____ Which one of the following first basemen was the only right-handed hitter?

a. Gordy Coleman b. Dick Gernert c. Norm Cash d. Luke Easter

32. _____ Which one of the following catchers never won an MVP Award?

a. Yogi Berra b. Bill Dickey c. Roy Campanella d. Johnny Bench

33. _____ Which one of the following players did not win the MVP Award three times?

a. Joe DiMaggio b. Stan Musial c. Willie Mays d. Roy Campanella

34. _____ Which runner stole home a record two times in World Series play?

a. Bob Meusel b. Ty Cobb c. Lou Brock d. Jackie Robinson

35. _____ Which one of the following teams did not win four world's championships in one decade?

a. 1910 Red Sox b. 1920 Giants c. 1930 Yankees d. 1940 Yankees

36. _____ Who was the last National League batter who hit .400?

a. Rogers Hornsby b. Lefty O'Doul c. Bill Terry d. Arky Vaughan

37. _____ Against whom did Babe Ruth "call his shot" in the 1932 World Series?

a. Lon Warneke b. Guy Bush c. Burleigh Grimes d. Charlie Root

38. _____ Who hit the "homer in the dark" for the Cubs in 1938?

a. Gabby Hartnett b. Billy Herman c. Stan Hack d. Phil Cavarretta

39. _____ Who misplayed two outfield fly balls for the Cubs when the Athletics rallied with ten runs in the seventh inning of the fourth game of the 1929 World Series to win, 10–8?

a. Kiki Cuyler b. Riggs Stephenson c. Cliff Heathcote d. Hack Wilson

40. _____ Which one of the following teams won the most recent pennant?

a. White Sox b. Phillies c. Indians d. Cubs

41. _____ Who has been the only American League player, in addition to Ty Cobb, who twice hit over .400?

a. Joe Jackson b. Nap Lajoie c. George Sisler d. Harry Heilmann

42. _____ Who was the last National League pitcher who won 30 games in a season?

a. Carl Hubbell b. Dizzy Dean c. Robin Roberts d. Sandy Koufax

43. _____ Who compiled the highest career batting average for left-handers in the history of the National League?

a. Lefty O'Doul b. Bill Terry c. Stan Musial d. Paul Waner

44. _____ Who holds the National League record for playing in the most consecutive games (1,209)?

a. Gus Suhr b. Stan Musial c. Billy Williams d. Steve Garvey

45. _____ Whose modern-day mark did Joe DiMaggio surpass when he batted safely in 56 consecutive games?

a. George Sisler b. Heinie Manush c. Ty Cobb d. Al Simmons

46. _____ Which one of Babe Ruth's following teammates was the only Yankee to hit more home runs in one season than the "Sultan of Swat" during the 1920s?

a. Bob Meusel b. Lou Gehrig c. Tony Lazzeri d. Bill Dickey

47. _____ Which pitcher came the closest to duplicating Johnny Vander Meer's feat of hurling consecutive no-hitters?

a. Nolan Ryan b. Sandy Koufax c. Virgil Trucks d. Ewell Blackwell

48. _____ Which one of the following players did not conclude his career with the Mets?

a. Richie Ashburn b. Gil Hodges c. Gene Woodling d. Eddie Yost

49. _____ Which one of the following catchers did not make an error in 117 games during the 1946 season?

a. Buddy Rosar b. Frank Hayes c. Del Rice d. Mickey Owens

50. _____ Which one of the following teams didn't Bucky Harris manage?

a. Phillies b. Tigers c. Senators d. Braves

51. _____ Who has been the only left-handed batter in National League history to hit 50 home runs in a season?

a. Roger Maris b. Johnny Mize c. Mel Ott d. Lou Gehrig

52. _____ Who holds the American League record for shutouts in one season by a left-handed pitcher?

a. Babe Ruth and Ron Guidry b. Lefty Grove c. Whitey Ford d. Mel Parnell

53. _____ Who was the youngest player ever elected to the Hall of Fame?

a. Ted Williams b. Roberto Clemente c. Sandy Koufax d. Dizzy Dean

54. _____ Which one of the following players did not hit two grand slams in one game?

a. Frank Robinson b. Frank Howard c. Tony Cloninger d. Jim Northrup

55. _____ Which one of the following Yankees stole home the most times (10) in the club's history?

a. Lou Gehrig b. Ben Chapman c. Phil Rizzuto d. George Stirnweiss

56. _____ Who holds the American League record for stealing home the most times (7) in one season?

a. Ty Cobb b. Eddie Collins c. Rod Carew d. Bert Campaneris

57. _____ Who holds the National League record for stealing home the most times (7) in one season?

a. Jackie Robinson b. Pete Reiser c. Lou Brock d. Maury Wills

58. _____ Who were the three players on the same team who hit more than 40 home runs each in the same season?

a. Babe Ruth, Lou Gehrig, Bob Meusel b. Hank Aaron, Davy Johnson, Darrell Evans c. Hank Aaron, Eddie Mathews, Wes Covington d. Johnny Mize, Willard Marshall, Walker Cooper

59. _____ Who was the first black coach in the American League?

a. Larry Doby b. Elston Howard c. Minnie Minoso d. Satchel Paige

60. _____ Who was the first black coach in the National League?

a. Ernie Banks b. Joe Black c. Buck O'Neil d. Willie Mays

61. _____ Who started the double play that ended Joe DiMaggio's 56-game hitting streak?

a. Ken Keltner b. Lou Boudreau c. Ray Mack d. Hal Trosky

62. _____ What was the most money that the Yankees ever paid Babe Ruth for a season?

a. $100,000 b. $125,000 c. $75,000 d. $80,000

63. _____ Which pair of players did not tie for a National League home run title?

    a. Ralph Kiner–Johnny Mize b. Ralph Kiner–Hank Sauer c. Willie McCovey–Hank Aaron d. Willie Mays–Hank Aaron

64. _____ Which pair of players did not tie for an American League home run title?

    a. Hank Greenberg–Jimmy Foxx b. Carl Yastrzemski–Harmon Killebrew c. Babe Ruth–Lou Gehrig d. Reggie Jackson–Dick Allen

65. _____ Who hit the first home run in the initial Yankee Stadium?

    a. Babe Ruth b. Wally Pipp c. Bob Meusel d. Joe Dugan

66. _____ Who hit the first home run in the renovated Yankee Stadium?

    a. Dan Ford b. Tony Oliva c. Graig Nettles d. Chris Chambliss

67. _____ Who led the National League in home runs for the most consecutive years (7)?

    a. Chuck Klein b. Mel Ott c. Ralph Kiner d. Hank Aaron

68. _____ Who were the two players who hit five grand slams in one season?

    a. Jim Northrup–Ralph Kiner b. Willie McCovey–Frank Robinson c. Ernie Banks–Jim Gentile d. Harmon Killebrew–Eddie Mathews

69. _____ Who has pitched the most consecutive shutouts (6) in one season?

    a. Bob Gibson b. Sal Maglie c. Walter Johnson d. Don Drysdale

70. _____ Which one of the following pitchers did not strike out 19 batters in one game?

    a. Bob Feller b. Steve Carlton c. Nolan Ryan d. Tom Seaver

71. _____ Who was the first major leaguer who hit .400 in a season?

    a. Ty Cobb b. Nap Lajoie c. Joe Jackson d. George Sisler

72. _____ Who broke Ty Cobb's run of nine straight batting titles in 1916?

    a. Tris Speaker b. George Sisler c. Hal Chase d. Harry Heilmann

73. _____ Who was the only non-Yankee who won a home run title in the 1920s?

    a. Al Simmons b. Goose Goslin c. Ken Williams d. Jimmie Foxx

74. _____ Which one of the following American Leaguers did not win back-to-back batting titles?

a. Ted Williams b. Pete Runnels c. Joe DiMaggio d. Carl Yastrzemski

75. _____ Which one of the following National Leaguers did not win back-to-back batting titles?

a. Pete Rose b. Roberto Clemente c. Stan Musial d. Jackie Robinson

76. _____ Which one of the following pitchers lost a ground ball "in the sun" in a World Series game?

a. Lefty Gomez b. Billy Loes c. Dave Koslo d. Vida Blue

77. _____ With what team did Red Ruffing conclude his career?

a. Red Sox b. Yankees c. Athletics d. White Sox

78. _____ Against whom did Mickey Mantle hit his last World Series home run?

a. Curt Simmons b. Barney Schultz c. Harvey Haddix d. Bob Gibson

79. _____ Which one of the following Cub players was called "Swish"?

a. Stan Hack b. Phil Cavarretta c. Billy Jurges d. Bill Nicholson

80. _____ Which one of the following players had a career which did not span four decades?

a. Stan Musial b. Ted Williams c. Mickey Vernon d. Early Wynn

81. _____ Which one of the following managers did not win a pennant in both leagues?

a. Joe McCarthy b. Bill McKechnie c. Yogi Berra d. Al Dark

82. _____ Which one of the following Red pitchers played more than 200 games at third base?

a. Paul Derringer b. Jim Maloney c. Bob Purkey d. Bucky Walters

83. _____ Which pitcher who won three games in the 1912 World Series later starred in the outfield for another American League team that played in the 1920 autumn classic?

a. Babe Ruth b. Joe Wood c. Duffy Lewis d. Harry Hooper

84. _____ Which former Yankee pitcher switched to the outfield and compiled a .349 lifetime average?

a. Rube Bressler b. Dixie Walker c. Lefty O'Doul d. Babe Ruth

85. _____ Which of the following Yankee players came up to the majors as a pitcher, switched to the outfield, and ended his big league career on the mound?

a. Johnny Lindell b. Cliff Mapes c. Marius Russo d. Ernie Bonham

86. _____ Which pair of the following players comprised a major league battery?

a. Ted Lyons–Buddy Rosar b. Ellis Kinder–Ernie Lombardi c. Allie Reynolds–Bill Dickey d. Rex Barney–Bruce Edwards

87. _____ Which one of the following players had the nickname of "Lucky"?

a. Whitey Lockman b. Jack Lohrke c. Jim Lemon d. Ted Lepcio

88. _____ Who was the player who once hit three home runs in one game off Whitey Ford?

a. Clyde Vollmer b. Dick Gernert c. Pat Seerey d. Jim Lemon

89. _____ Which one of the following one-two punches had the most home runs on the same team?

a. Babe Ruth–Lou Gehrig b. Mickey Mantle–Roger Maris c. Hank Aaron–Eddie Mathews d. Ernie Banks–Ron Santo

90. _____ Which one of the following pitchers took a timeout in World Series play to watch a plane fly overhead?

a. Daffy Dean b. Dizzy Trout c. Lefty Gomez d. Dazzy Vance

91. _____ Which pair of the following brothers competed against each other in World Series play?

a. Dizzy and Daffy Dean b. Jim and Gaylord Perry c. Ken and Clete Boyer d. Matty and Felipe Alou

92. _____ Which one of the following players was not a member of the "Whiz Kids"?

a. Andy Seminick b. Russ Meyer c. Mike Goliat d. Harry Walker

93. _____ Which one of the following pitchers was the only one to lose a World Series game?

a. Jack Coombs b. Herb Pennock c. Lefty Gomez d. Catfish Hunter

94. _____ Who was the only Phillie pitcher before 1980 who won a World Series game?

a. Grover Cleveland Alexander b. Robin Roberts c. Eppa Rixey d. Jim Konstanty

95. _____ Which one of the following players did not "jump" to the Mexican League?

a. Mickey Owen b. Luis Olmo c. Johnny Hopp d. Max Lanier

96. _____ Who made a shoestring catch of an infield fly to save a World Series?

a. Billy Herman b. Billy Johnson c. Billy Martin d. Bobby Avila

97. _____ Which one of the Indians' "Big Four" won a World Series game with another American League team?

a. Bob Feller b. Bob Lemon c. Mike Garcia d. Early Wynn

98. _____ Which one of the following players did not win an American League home run title with a total below 30?

a. Babe Ruth b. Nick Etten c. Vern Stephens d. Reggie Jackson

99. _____ Which one of the following players did not win a National League home run crown with a total below 30?

a. Hack Wilson b. Johnny Mize c. Ralph Kiner d. Mike Schmidt

100. _____ Which one of the following players once hit 54 home runs in a season but did not win the league's home run title?

a. Ralph Kiner b. Willie Mays c. Mickey Mantle d. Hank Greenberg

Exceptions to the Rule

Most umpires know the rule book from cover to cover. But occasionally a situation that is not covered by the rule book takes place. Then the umpires are in trouble.

Take, for example, the uproar that Herman "Germany" Schaefer created with his zany base running in a game between the Senators and the White Sox in 1911. With the score tied and two outs in the ninth inning, the Senators put runners on the corners, Clyde Milan on third and Schaefer on first. That's the moment when Schaefer decided to create confusion.

On the first pitch to a weak batter, Schaefer promptly stole second without a throw from the catcher. On the next pitch he proceeded to steal first, once again without a throw, but this time with a storm of protest from the White Sox bench. What base was Schaefer entitled to? the Sox wanted to know. The umpires thumbed through the rule book, but they failed to find any clause that prevented a runner from stealing any base that he had previously occupied. So, on the following pitch, Schaefer did the predictable: he stole second again. The frustrated catcher finally relented and threw the ball to second base. But Schaefer beat the throw and Milan raced home with the winning run.

Shortly thereafter, an amendment to the rule book was made: no base runner could steal a base out of sequence. The rules makers decided that Schaefer had tried to make a travesty of the game.

Another bizarre base running feat took place in 1963. This time it involved a Met runner, Jimmy Piersall, who was coming to the end of a celebrated—and clownish—career. In the game in which he hit his 100th career homer, he did something which indelibly impressed the event in the minds of all the people who saw it: he ran around the bases backwards.

Once again the umpires pored through the fine print of the rule book. But it was of no avail: there was no rule which prevented a runner from circling the bases backwards after he had hit a home run. Shortly thereafter, however, there was. The rules makers once again concluded that the runner (Piersall) had tried to make a mockery of the game.

So today, batters who hit home runs have to touch the bases in their proper order.

One more ludicrous baseball situation took place in St. Louis in 1951. In a game between the hometown Browns and the Tigers, the always innovative owner of St. Louis, Bill Veeck, staged a scene that baseball fans still laugh about. In the first inning of the second game of a double-header, Zack Taylor, the manager of St. Louis, sent a midget up to the plate to pinch-hit for the leadoff batter, Frank Saucier. The umpires demanded that Taylor put an end to the farce. But Taylor was ready for them, rule book in hand: there was no provision in the baseball guide that prevented the batter with the number ⅛ on his back from taking his turn at the plate. The next day, you can feel safe to assume, there was.

But before the amendment was made, the batter walked on four consecutive pitches before giving way to a pinch-runner. What most probably comes readily to mind is the name of the midget, Eddie Gaedel. He is the subject of an often-asked trivia question. But what might not come so quickly to mind is the name of the pitcher who threw to the smallest target in baseball history, the name of the catcher who gave the lowest target in the history of the game, and the umpire who had the smallest strike zone in the annals of the sport.

Consider yourself to be in the ranks of a select few if you can name two of the three individuals who figured prominently in one of the most bizarre pitcher-batter confrontations that has ever taken place.

(Answer appears on page 321.)

Chapter Five

FROM RUTH TO REGGIE

34. FROM RUTH TO REGGIE

1. _____ Which slugger (1933–47) missed almost six years of playing time because of the Second World War and injuries and still managed to hit 331 career home runs?

2. _____ Which Indian pitcher, who was 15–0 at the time, lost his only game of the year in his last start?

3. _____ Whose line drive in the 1937 All-Star Game broke Dizzy Dean's toe?

4. _____ Which White Sox pitcher lost one of his legs in a hunting accident?

5. _____ Who was the Indian manager whom the players petitioned the Cleveland owners to fire in 1940?

6. _____ Who pitched a no-hitter on the opening day of the 1940 season?

7. _____ Who was the only player to win the Rookie of the Year Award, the Most Valuable Player Award, and the Triple Crown?

8. _____ Whose home run on the final day of the 1945 season won the pennant for the Tigers?

9. _____ Whose home run on the final night of the 1976 season won the pennant for the Yankees?

10. _____ Which pitcher, who was acquired from the Yankees, led the Cubs to the pennant in 1945?

11. _____ Who scored the only run in the first game of the 1948 World Series after Bob Feller "almost" picked him off second base?

12. _____ Who was the manager of the Red Sox in 1948–49 when they lost the pennants on the last day of the season?

13. _____ Who was the last playing manager?

14. _____ Who was the last playing manager who led his team to a pennant?

15. _____ Who was the name star that the Yankees traded to the Indians for Allie Reynolds in 1948?

16. _____ Who was the American League home run king of 1959 who was traded after the season for batting champ Harvey Kuenn?

17. _____ Which former Giant relief specialist, then with the Orioles, threw the pitch that Mickey Mantle hit for his 500th home run?

18. _____ Who invented the "Williams's Shift"?

19. _____ Which slugging American League outfielder broke his elbow in the 1950 All-Star Game?

20. _____ Which Dodger outfielder did Richie Ashburn throw out at the plate in the ninth inning of the last game of the 1950 season to send the Phillies into extra innings and subsequently the World Series?

21. _____ Who threw a no-hitter in his first major league start?

22. _____ Who threw the pitch that Mickey Mantle hit for his 565-foot home run?

23. _____ Which manager did Walter O'Malley fire for demanding a three-year contract?

24. _____ Who was the 20-game season winner and the two-game World Series winner for the Giants in 1954 whom they acquired from the Braves for Bobby Thomson?

25. _____ Who took Bobby Thomson's centerfield position for the Giants?

26. _____ Who took Bobby Thomson's left-field position—when he broke his ankle—for the Milwaukee Braves?

27. _____ Which Indian slugging outfielder–first baseman was afflicted with polio in 1955?

28. _____ Which pitcher did Joe Adcock literally run off the mound in the early 1950s?

29. _____, Dave McNally, Jim Palmer, and Mike Cuellar were 20-game winners for the Orioles in 1971.

30. _____ Who was the one-time "Wildman" for the Yankees who lost the final game of the 1955 World Series to the Dodgers' Johnny Podres, 2–0?

31. _____ Which versatile infielder hit the line drive which struck Herb Score in the eye?

32. _____ Which pitcher, picked up on waivers from the Indians, won 13 games down the stretch, including

a no-hitter against the Phillies, to pitch the Dodgers to the 1956 pennant?

33. _____ Who hit two two-run homers against Don Newcombe in the 1956 World Series finale to lead the Yankees to a 9–0 victory over the Dodgers?

34. _____ Which Yankee infielder was hit in the throat by Bill Virdon's bad-hop ground ball in the 1960 World Series?

35. _____ Which team was the first in history to come back from a 3–1 World Series deficit in games and win the autumn classic?

36. _____ Which team was the most recent to perform the same feat?

37. _____ Who, in addition to Rogers Hornsby and Nap Lajoie, was the only right-handed batter to hit .400?

38. _____ Which Dodger catcher's throwing arm stopped the "Go-Go Sox" in the 1959 World Series?

39. _____ Who lost his job as a result of Bill Mazeroski's seventh-game home run in the 1960 World Series?

40. _____ Who threw the 60th home run ball to Babe Ruth in 1927?

41. _____ Who threw the 61st home run pitch to Roger Maris in 1961?

42. _____ Who was Whitey Ford's "save-ior" in 1961?

43. _____ Which of the Yankee reserve catchers hit four consecutive home runs in 1961?

44. _____ Who was the pitcher who was known as the "Yankee Killer" in the early 1960s?

45. _____ Which Hall of Famer wore the uniforms of all four New York teams: Giants, Dodgers, Yankees, and Mets?

46. _____ Which Yankee infielder was known for his "harmonica playing"?

47. _____ Which Giant pitcher once hit Johnny Roseboro with a bat?

48. _____ Whom did Sandy Koufax team up with in a joint holdout in 1966?

49. _____ Which Dodger outfielder committed three errors in one inning in the 1966 World Series?

50. _____ For whom did the Reds trade Frank Robinson?

51. _____ Who was known as "Bullet Bob"?

52. _____ What position did Jackie Robinson play when he first came up with the Dodgers?

53. _____ Who was the Commissioner of Baseball when Jackie Robinson broke the color barrier?

54. _____ Who was the first black manager?

55. _____ Who lost three fly balls in the sun, in the same World Series game for the Yankees, in 1957?

56. _____ Which Indian third baseman drove home better than 100 runs per season for five consecutive years in the early 1950s?

57. _____ Which Phillie outfielder didn't make an error during a record 266 consecutive games?

58. _____ Who was Babe Ruth's manager during his final major league season with the Boston Braves?

59. _____ Which free agent (Charley Finley style) did the Red Sox pick up in 1967 to help them win the pennant?

60. _____ Who was the last pitcher to win 30 or more games?

61. _____ Which Brave batter was awarded first base in the 1957 World Series when the black polish on the ball proved that he had been hit with the preceding pitch?

62. _____ Which Met batter was awarded first base in the same manner in the 1969 World Series?

63. _____ Which Senator outfielder filed suit against baseball's reserve system in the early 1970s?

64. _____ Who was the most recent player who won the batting title without hitting a home run?

65. _____ Which second-string catcher, at the time, hit four home runs in a World Series?

66. _____ Which manager resigned after leading his team to two world's championships in the 1970s?

67. _____ With what team did Leo Durocher break into the majors in 1928?

68. _____ Which 35-year-old pitcher, who had appeared in only 11 games all season long, surprised the baseball world by striking out a record 13 batters in the A's opening-game win over the Cubs in the 1929 World Series?

69. _____ Which National League team once posted a .315 team batting average but finished last in the standings?

70. _____ Who won seven games and saved four others in World Series play?

71. _____ Whose home run won the first All-Star Game in 1933?

72. _____ What city was the only one to produce two Triple Crown winners in the same year (1933)?

73. _____ Who succeeded John McGraw as manager of the Giants?

74. _____ Which pitching brothers won 49 games in 1934?

75. _____ Whom did Commissioner Kenesaw Mountain Landis remove from the last game of the 1934 World Series in order to insure the player's safety?

76. _____ Who had a career average of .439 for four World Series?

77. _____ Who got the most hits in one season in the National League?

78. _____ Who stole the most bases in one season in the American League?

79. _____ Which pitcher chalked up the best winning percentages for hurlers with less than 200 but more than 100 wins?

80. _____ Who lost more games than any other pitcher in World Series play?

81. _____ Who was the last Yankee player before Don Mattingly to amass 200 hits in a season?

82. _____ Who was the last Dodger player to win a home run title?

83. _____ Who was the last Yankee player to win a home run title?

84. _____ Who was the only American League player who won a batting title while splitting his time with two teams?

85. _____ Who was the only National League player who won a batting title while performing for two different teams?

86. _____ Who made nine hits in an 18-inning game?

87. _____ Which Yankee pitcher ended Mickey Cochrane's career when he felled the Tigers' playing manager with a high, hard one?

88. _____ Who was the last playing manager in the National League who led his team to a pennant?

89. _____ Which slugging Brave outfielder missed the 1948 World Series—he never played in one—because of a broken ankle he sustained in a collision at home plate during the last week of the season?

90. _____ Whom did the Dodgers trade to the Pirates because he "jumped" the team on its tour of Japan after the 1966 world Series?

91. _____ Which famous pitcher had to retire prematurely because of the potentially dire effects which could have been produced by his arthritic elbow?

92. _____ Who was the Commissioner of Baseball who was fired in 1968?

93. _____ Which National League manager, who was a former first baseman, was fired in August of 1938 when his team, the Cubs, was in third place? The Cubs then went on to win the pennant under Gabby Hartnett.

94. _____ Which Yankee catcher holds the major league record of handling 950 consecutive chances without making an error?

95. _____ Which Astro catcher set a major league record when he played 138 consecutive games without making an error?

96. _____ Who recorded the highest lifetime average (.358) in the history of the National League?

97. _____ Who holds the American League mark of 184 RBIs in a season?

98. _____ Which two players walked 148 times in one season to tie for the National League high in that department?

99. _____ Who recorded the most shutouts in one season in the American League?

100. _____ Whose base hit drove home the winning run for the Reds in the 1975 World Series against the Red Sox?

The Mystery Death

Going into the 1940 season, baseball experts would never have believed that the hero of the upcoming World Series would be Jimmie Wilson, for the .284 lifetime hitter had recently settled down to life as a full-time coach with the Reds after donning the "tools of ignorance" for 17 seasons. But fate has been known to throw tricky pitches to a baseball team.

Ernie Lombardi, the team's regular catcher, had won the batting title two years before; he would also win it two years later. Behind him was a .316 lifetime hitter. So there didn't seem to be any need for Wilson's services.

But on August 2 the second-string catcher took his own life in Boston, and in mid-September Lombardi sprained his ankle. So Wilson was rushed back into action.

Down the stretch, "Ace" batted only .234, but he was primed up by World Series time. He handled the serves of two-game winners Bucky Walters and Paul Derringer faultlessly, and he swung a torrid bat, hitting .353 in the six games he played. In addition, the 40-year-old catcher stole the only base of the entire series.

The following season, Wilson went into permanent retirement, Lombardi took over the regular catching chores once again, and the reasons for the substitute catcher's suicide remained a mystery.

The identity of that .316 lifetime hitter is pretty much a mystery, too. Can you solve it?

(Answer appears on page 321.)

Chapter Six

BASEBALL'S DID YOU KNOW

The PHILLIES of 1961 lost a record 23 straight games.

The METS of 1962 lost 120 games, a single-season record.

GAYLORD PERRY was the only pitcher to win the Cy Young Award in both leagues. He won it with the Indians in 1972 and the Padres in 1978.

SATCHEL PAIGE, who was 59 years old when he pitched for Kansas City in 1965, has been the oldest player to perform in the major leagues.

DIOMEDES OLIVO was 41 when he broke in with the 1960 Pirates. Two years later, at 43, he appeared in 62 games and was 5–1.

FRED ODWELL hit only one home run before his nine four-base blows won the title in 1905; afterward, the Red outfielder never hit another major league home run.

STAN MUSIAL, of the top 15 players to ground into career double plays, was the only left-handed batter.

THURMAN MUNSON was the only Yankee to win both the Rookie of the Year Award (1970) and the MVP Award (1976).

DAVE McNALLY and Mike Cuellar of the 1970 Orioles were the last two pitchers from the same team to tie for the league lead in victories with 24.

WILLIE MAYS has been the only player to hit four home runs in one game and three triples in another.

DAL MAXVILL of the 1968 Cards had the most official at-bats (22) without collecting a hit in a World Series.

J. C. MARTIN of the 1965 White Sox committed a record 33 passed balls in one season. Tom Egan of the 1970 Angels and Mike Stanley of the 1987 Rangers let five pitches get by them in one game; Ray Kaat of the 1954 Giants couldn't handle four serves in one inning.

ROGER MARIS, who hit a record 61 home runs in 1961, won only one home run title.

MARTY MARION, the stellar shortstop of the Cards, was the last manager (1953) of the Browns.

MICKEY MANTLE was the first player to hit a home run in the Astrodome. He did it in an exhibition game between the Yankees and the Astros in 1962.

BILL MADLOCK was the last player to win a batting title one year and be traded away the next season. In 1976 Madlock batted .339 to cop the crown while he was a member of the Cubs. The following year, he was traded to the Giants.

ERNIE LOMBARDI set a major league mark by grounding into the most double plays in the National League in five different seasons.

TED LYONS of the 1935 White Sox and Hank Borowy of the 1946 Cubs, both of whom were pitchers, doubled twice in the same inning.

LEFTY O'DOUL, a pitcher with the pennant-winning Yankees in 1922, and Rube Bressler, a pitcher with the pennant-winning Athletics of 1914, both gained fame as outfielders: O'Doul won two batting titles in the National League and hit .349 lifetime; Bressler hit .302 for his career.

SANDY KOUFAX, the youngest player ever to be elected to the Hall of Fame, received the most votes of any electee—344—in the 1972 balloting.

SANDY KOUFAX (1963 and 1965–66), Tom Seaver (1969, 1973, and 1975), and Jim Palmer (1973 and 1975–76) have won the Cy Young Award three times. Steve Carlton, of course, has won it a record four times.

DAVE KOSLO broke the Yankees' nine-game opening-game World Series winning streak in 1951 when he bested Allie Reynolds, 5–1. The last time that the Bronx Bombers had lost the lead game of the fall classic had been in 1936 when Carl Hubbell, also of the Giants, defeated them, 6–1.

GEORGE KELL of the 1945 Athletics went 0-for-10 in a 24-inning game. His lifetime average, though, was .306.

BOB KEEGAN, a 33-year-old rookie with the 1953 White Sox, won 16 games; at age 37 he pitched a no-hitter.

ADDIE JOSS of the 1908 Indians, on the next-to-last day of the season, pitched a perfect game, besting Ed Walsh of the White Sox, 1–0. Walsh pitched a two-hitter.

"SAD" SAM JONES of the Indians, Red Sox, Yankees, Browns, Senators, and White Sox hurled in the American League for a record 22 *consecutive* years.

WALTER JOHNSON of the 1912–19 Senators set a major league record by copping eight consecutive strikeout titles.

JACKIE JENSEN was the only person to be both an MVP in baseball and an All-American in football.

JOE JACKSON, Buck Weaver, Fred McMullin, Claude Williams, Swede Risberg, Happy Felsch, Eddie Cicotte, and Chick Gandil were the eight White Sox players who allegedly were bribed to throw the 1919 World Series.

The INDIANS of 1948 had an infield that averaged 108 RBIs: first baseman Eddie Robinson, 83; second baseman Joe Gordon, 124; shortstop Lou Boudreau, 106; and third baseman Kenny Keltner, 119.

RON HUNT and Joe Christopher of the 1964 Mets became the first regulars for the "Amazin' Ones" to bat .300.

TOM HUGHES, who threw nine-inning no-hitters for the Yankees and the Browns, racked up a 20–3 lifetime record in relief.

FRANK HOWARD of the 1968 Senators was the last player to lead the majors in homers (44) while playing for a last-place club.

ELSTON HOWARD of the Yankees played in the World Series his first four years in the majors. The Yanks won in 1956 and 1958; they lost in 1955 and 1957.

STAN MUSIAL of the 1954 Cards and Nate Colbert of the 1972 Padres each hit a record five home runs in a doubleheader.

ROGERS HORNSBY of the 1922 Cardinals became the first National Leaguer to hit 40 home runs in a season when he hit 42 base-clearing blows.

FRANK HAYES, catcher for the 1945 Indians and Athletics, took part in a record 29 double plays for a backstop.

BURLEIGH GRIMES, winding up his career in 1934 with the Yankees, Pirates, and Cards, was the last of the legal spitball pitchers;* Red Faber of the 1933 White Sox was the last of the legal spitball pitchers in the American League.

BILL GRAY of the 1909 Senators gave up eight walks in one inning.

HANK GOWDY of the Giants and the Braves was the only major leaguer to serve in both World War I and World War II.

FLOYD GIEBELL shut out Bob Feller and the Indians to win the 1940 pennant for the Tigers, but he never won another big-league game. In fact, he won a total of only three.

BOB GIBSON of the Cardinals didn't steal too often, but when he did, he was usually successful: he stole 13 career bases in 17 attempts.

BOB GIBSON lost his first and last World Series games; in between, he won seven straight, a record.

The GIANTS were the first team to use a public address announcer. They did so at the Polo Grounds on August 25, 1929.

LOU GEHRIG began his consecutive game streak by batting for Pee Wee Wanninger the day before he subbed for ailing first baseman Wally Pipp.

FRANK BAUMHOLTZ of the 1952 Cubs was the only batter that Stan Musial of the Cards pitched to in the majors.

STEVE BARBER and Stu Miller of the 1967 Orioles combined to lose a 2–1 no-hitter to the Tigers.

NEAL BALL, shortstop for the 1904 Indians, pulled off the first unassisted triple play in modern major league history.

The ATHLETICS of 1949 executed a record 217 double plays.

The A's and Dodgers of 1974 played in the only All-California World Series. The A's won four of the five games.

* Commissioner Kenesaw Mountain Landis decreed in 1920 that only existing spitball pitchers could continue to wet the ball. Red Faber of the 1933 White Sox was the last American League pitcher to legally dampen the ball; Burleigh Grimes of the 1934 Giants was the last major league pitcher to legally lubricate the ball.

BOB ASPROMONTE was the last Brooklyn Dodger to remain active in the major leagues. He faded from the scene with the Mets in 1971.

CAP ANSON, Al Kaline, Stan Musial, and Mel Ott played a record 22 years with the same teams. Anson spent his entire major league career with the Cubs; Kaline, the Tigers; Musial, the Cardinals; and Ott, the Giants. Ted Lyons played a 21-year career with the White Sox while Luke Appling and Red Faber donned Pale Hose uniforms for 20 years.

MIKE ANDREWS of the 1973 A's was fired by owner Charlie Finley because he made two errors in the twelfth inning of a World Series loss to the Mets. Commissioner Bowie Kuhn forced Finley to reinstate his second baseman.

MERLE ADKINS, pitcher for the 1902 Red Sox, got roughed up for 12 hits in one inning; Reggie Grabowski, chucker for the 1934 Phils, didn't retire the side in the ninth until he had yielded 11 hits.

BABE ADAMS of the 1909 Pirates, Frank Shea of the 1947 Yankees, Joe Black of the 1952 Dodgers, and Bob Walk of the 1980 Phillies were the only rookies who started—and won—the first game of a World Series.

CY YOUNG of the Red Sox, who was 41 when he no-hit the Yankees (Highlanders) in 1908, was the oldest pitcher to throw a no-hit game.

GEORGE SISLER of the 1920 Browns collected a record 257 hits. From 1920–22 he averaged 240 safeties per season.

TRIS SPEAKER was involved in a career-record 135 double plays in his 22-year career as an outfielder for the Red Sox, Indians, Senators, and Athletics.

JIM THORPE, Ernie Nevers, Paddy Driscoll, Ace Parker, and George Halas are football Hall of Famers who once played in the majors.

JIM BUNNING won 19 games a record four times.

MORDECAI "Three Finger" BROWN of the 1909–10 Cubs was the only pitcher to twice lead the league in saves and complete games in the same season.

WILLIE MAYS slammed more than 50 home runs in seasons ten years apart: in 1955, with New York, he ripped 51; in 1965, with San Francisco, he rocketed 52.

WALTER JOHNSON hit a record 206 batters during his 21-year career with the Senators.

ROGERS HORNSBY holds the club-high batting average for three different teams: .424 for the 1924 Cardinals, .387 for the 1928 Braves, and .380 for the 1929 Cubs.

The BRAVES of 1961 hit four home runs in a row in one inning. They were slugged by Eddie Mathews, Hank Aaron, Joe Adcock, and Frank Thomas, respectively.

The BRAVES of 1965 hit four home runs in a row in one inning. They were drilled by Joe Torre, Eddie Mathews, Hank Aaron, and Gene Oliver, respectively.

RON BLOMBERG of the 1973 Yankees became the first designated hitter in baseball history. He walked on five pitches against the Red Sox.

JACK BILLINGHAM of the Reds, in three World Series, turned in the lowest career ERA (0.36) in World Series history. Harry Brecheen of the Cardinals recorded the second lowest mark (0.83), and Babe Ruth of the Red Sox, the third lowest (0.87).

WALLY BERGER of the 1931 Braves was the last flychaser to chalk up four assists in one game.

AUGIE BERGAMO hit .316 for the 1945 Cards but wasn't invited back to the 1946 spring training camp.

AL BENTON, pitcher for the 1941 Tigers, laid down a record two sacrifice bunts in the same inning.

JIM COMMAND of the 1954 Phillies hit a grand slam off the Dodgers' Carl Erskine for his first major-league hit. He got only three more hits in the big time.

TY COBB (1907–15) won a record nine consecutive batting titles; Rogers Hornsby (1920–25) copped a record six consecutive National League crowns. Both Honus Wagner (1906–09) and Rod Carew (1972–75) dominated the batting averages in their respective leagues for four consecutive years.

TY COBB collected 200 or more hits in a season nine times, the American League mark.

EARL CLARK, flychaser for the 1929 Braves, made a league-record 12 putouts in one game.

TOM CHENEY of the 1962 Senators struck out 21 Orioles in a 16-inning game.

TOMMY BYRNE of the 1951 Browns walked 16 batters in a 13-inning game.

PHIL CAVARRETTA of the Cubs set the following records for a player before he reached his twentieth birthday: runs, 120; hits, 234; triples, 14; and runs batted in, 117.

BILL CAUDILL of the 1984 Blue Jays struck out the only three batters he has faced in All-Star competition: Tim Raines, Ryne Sandberg, and Keith Hernandez.

BILL CARRIGAN, manager of the Red Sox, retired after he had led Boston to back-to-back world titles in 1915–16; Dick Williams, skipper of the A's, resigned after he had guided Oakland to back-to-back world championships in 1972–73.

STEVE BUSBY of the 1973–74 Royals was the first and only pitcher to throw no-hitters in each of his first two seasons.

JIM BUNNING was the first pitcher to hurl for both leagues in the All-Star Game, first for the Tigers, later for the Phillies.

DON DRYSDALE of the 1959 Dodgers was the only pitcher to start two All-Star games in one year. He was not involved in the first decision, a 5–4 National League win, but he got tagged for the loss in the second decision, a 5–3 American League triumph.

PATSY DOUGHERTY of the 1903 Red Sox was the first player to homer twice in the same game of a World Series. He performed the feat in Game Two against the Pirates.

"WILD BILL" DONOVAN has been the only pitcher to post 25 or more win seasons in both leagues. He won 25 for the 1901 Dodgers and 25 for the 1907 Tigers.

VINCE DiMAGGIO led the National League in strikeouts four years in a row (1942–45). His total of 389 whiffs, however, pales in comparison to the 609 times that Reggie Jackson went down via the strikeout route during a four-year period.

JOE DiMAGGIO of the 1950 Yankees became the first player to get paid $100,000 for a season.

FRANK HOWARD of the 1968 Senators hit a record ten home runs in six games.

DOM DiMAGGIO, Joe DiMAGGIO, and Vince DiMAGGIO all have the same middle name—Paul.

BILL DICKEY, catcher for the 1931 Yankees, set an American League record by catching 125 consecutive games without committing a passed ball. Al Todd of the 1937 Pirates holds the major league record with 128 passed ball-free games.

BILL DAHLEN of the 1900 Dodgers, Curt Walker of the 1926 Reds, Al Zarilla of the 1946 browns, and Gil Coan of the 1951 Senators all hit two triples in the same inning.

The CUBS of 1906 won a record 116 games, but they lost the World Series to their intercity rivals, the White Sox, in six games.

GAVVY CRAVATH of the 1919 Phillies won the home run crown despite the fact that he had only 214 official at-bats. He hit 12 four-base blows.

DOC CRAMER of the Red Sox, Rip Radcliff of the Browns, and Barney McCosky of the Tigers each stroked 200 hits to tie for the major league lead in 1940.

JIM COONEY of the White Sox and Johnny Neun of the Tigers pulled off unassisted triple plays on successive days. Cooney, shortstop for the Cubs, recorded his on May 30, 1927; Neun, first baseman for the Tigers, executed his the following day.

JOE DiMAGGIO of the 1936 Yankees was the first rookie to play in an All-Star Game. He went hitless in five at-bats and made an error in the field.

ED COLEMAN of the 1936 Browns, who retired after the season, became the first player to pinch-hit safely 20 times in one season.

STEVE GARVEY of the Padres set the all-time errorless game streak at first base with 193 miscue-free games.

TITO FRANCONA hit .363 and slammed 20 home runs for the 1959 Indians, yet over a 13-year career he batted almost 100 points lower, .272, and parked 119 homers, an average of nine per season.

JIMMIE FOXX, Joe DiMAGGIO, Stan Musial, Roy Campanella, Yogi Berra, Mickey Mantle, and Mike Schmidt won MVP awards a record three times.

OSCAR FELSCH, outfielder for the 1919 White Sox, participated in a record 15 double plays in one season.

GAYLORD PERRY of the 1978 Padres was 40 years old when he won the Cy Young Award, making him the oldest player ever to win the coveted crown.

WILLIE MAYS has been the only player to amass 3,000 hits, 600 home runs, and 300 stolen bases.

BOB FELLER pitched a record 12 one-hitters.

DAN DRIESSEN of the 1976 Reds, in the first year that the DH was used in the World Series, hit .357 in his team's sweep of the Yankees.

DAZZY VANCE didn't win his first major league decision until he was 31, but by the time he hung up his spikes in 1935, he registered a career record of 197–140.

WILLIE MAYS and Stan Musial were the only players who appeared in all eight All-Star games—two per year—from 1959–62.

BABE RUTH was the only player to twice hit three home runs in a World Series game. He did it in 1926 and 1928, both times against the Cards.

MIKE RYBA of the Cards and the Red Sox was the only player to both pitch and catch in both leagues.

JOHNNY SAIN of the 1948 Braves was the only pitcher to lead the league in sacrifice hits—16.

HONUS WAGNER, who was 37 when he won the batting crown in 1911, was the oldest National League player to win the batting title.

RAY SCHALK of the 1914–22 White Sox caught four no-hitters.

WILLIARD SCHMIDT of the 1959 Reds and Frank Thomas of the 1962 Mets each got hit with two pitches in the same inning of a game.

RED SCHOENDIENST and Lou Brock have been the only players to collect 200 or more hits in a season which they split between two teams. Schoendienst played for the Giants and the Braves in 1957; Brock, the Cubs and the Cards in 1964.

FERDIE SCHUPP of the 1916 Giants posted an all-time low 0.90 ERA. He pitched in only 140 innings, though, so Bob Gibson of the 1968 Cardinals, who registered a 1.12 mark in 305 innings, is generally considered to own the lowest ERA for one season in the National League.

JIMMY SEBRING of the 1903 Pirates was the first player to hit a home run in the World Series! He homered in the first game of the initial fall classic and got 11 hits in the classic, two short of the all-time record.

ROY SIEVERS and Jimmie Foxx were the only players to hit pinch-hit grand-slam home runs in both leagues. Sievers did it for the 1961 White Sox and the 1963 Phillies; Foxx, for the 1931 Athletics and the 1945 Phillies.

The YANKEES of 1960 lost the World Series to the Pirates in seven games despite recording the highest team batting average (.338) ever.

The YANKEES, paced by Roger Maris's 61 home runs and Mickey Mantle's 54 circuit clouts, hit a record-setting 240 four-base blows in 1961. Maris and Mantle's combined total of 115 home runs by back-to-back sluggers in a lineup broke the former mark of 109, which had been set by Babe Ruth and Lou Gehrig in 1927.

The YANKEES defeated the Tigers, 9–7, in the American League's longest game (24 innings) on June 24, 1962. Jack Reed's home run, the only one that he hit in his career, broke up the game.

EARLY WYNN of the 1950 Indians led the American League with a 3.20 ERA, the highest earned run mark to lead either circuit.

JOE WOOD was the first player to appear in one World Series (1912) as a pitcher and another fall classic (1920) as an outfielder. Wood won three games for the Red Sox and batted .200 for the Indians.

RICK WISE of the 1971 Phils pitched a no-hitter and hit two home runs in a game against the Reds.

VIC WILLIS, who eight times won 20 or more games during a season, lost a major league record 29 games for the 1905 Braves.

The WHITE SOX of 1940 had the same batting average at the end of one game as they had before it. That's because Bob Feller no-hit them in the opening game of the season.

CARL WEILMAN (1913), Don Hoak (1956), Rich Reichardt (1966), Bill Cowan (1971), and Cecil Cooper (1974) all whiffed six times during extra-inning games.

BABE RUTH of the 1920 Yankees hit 54 home runs, 35 more than his runner-up, George Sisler (19), in the American League home run derby.

HAM HYATT (1909–18) of the Pirates, Cardinals, and Giants was the first player to amass 50 hits as a pinch-hitter. Career-wise, he batted safely 57 times in 240 pinch-hitting performances for a .238 average.

CHARLES HICKMAN, a second baseman for the 1905 Senators, Nap Lajoie, a second baseman for the 1915 Athletics, and Dave Brain, a third baseman for the 1906 Braves, all made five errors in a game.

HARRY STEINFELDT of the 1909 Cubs, Bob Meusel of the 1926 Yankees, Ernie Banks of the 1961 Cubs, and Russ Nixon of the 1965 Red Sox all hit three sacrifice flies in one game.

HONUS WAGNER led the National League in batting a record eight times. Rogers Hornsby and Stan Musial won National League batting titles seven times each.

RED ROLFE of the 1939 Yankees scored a record 30 runs in 18 consecutive games.

PIE TRAYNOR was the only regular named to the all-time team to play his entire career with one club. He played with the Pirates from 1920–37.

TRIS SPEAKER of the 1918 Red Sox executed two unassisted double plays in the month of April.

GEORGE UHLE of the Tigers and Indians, who pitched for 17 years, had a .288 lifetime batting average, the highest mark of any pitcher.

DAZZY VANCE of the 1922–28 Dodgers set a National League record when he won seven consecutive strikeout titles.

HONUS WAGNER, Christy Mathewson, Ty Cobb, Walter Johnson, and Babe Ruth, in 1936, became the first five players to be inducted into the Baseball Hall of Fame at Cooperstown, N.Y.

The PIRATES of 1925, Yankees of 1958, Tigers of 1968,

Pirates of 1979, and Royals of 1985 have won the World Series after trailing in games, three to one.

The PIRATES of 1917 hit nine home runs, the all-time low by a National League team.

The PIRATES of 1960 defeated the Yankees in the World Series despite having a pitching staff that recorded an ERA of 7.11.

The REDS of 1935, the host team, defeated the Phillies, 2–1, in the first night game played in the majors.

The RED SOX, who won four world championships in four tries in the same decade, defeated four different National League teams during a seven-year span: the Giants, 1912; the Phillies, 1915; the Dodgers, 1916; and the Cubs, 1918.

PEE WEE REESE of the 1952 Dodgers came to the plate three times in the same inning.

ROBIN ROBERTs' 28 wins for the 1952 Phillies has been the most wins by a National League pitcher since Dizzy Dean won 30 in 1934.

BROOKS ROBINSON hit into four triple plays in his career.

LYNWOOD "SCHOOLBOY" ROWE was the first major leaguer to play for each league in an All-Star Game. In 1936, when he was with the Tigers, he pitched for the American League; in 1947, when he was with the Phillies, he pinch-hit for the National League.

BABE RUTH reached first base safely a record 379 times in one season; Lefty O'Doul reached first base safely a record 334 times in the National League.

BABE RUTH in 1969 was chosen the greatest all-time player by that year's poll; Joe DiMaggio was voted the greatest living player.

JOE DiMAGGIO, who averaged 118 RBIs per season during his 13-year career, won only two titles in that department. In 13 years in the big leagues he averaged just under one RBI per game.

BABE RUTH walked an all-time-high 170 times in 1923.

A Checkered Career

The Giants of John McGraw had much good fortune—
they won ten pennants and three World Series—but they
had great misfortune also: they lost one pennant and three
World Series that they could have won.

In 1908 they were victimized by "Merkle's Boner." On
September 23, in a key game with the Cubs at the Polo
Grounds, Al Bridwell lined a ball to the outfield that chased
Moose McCormick home with the apparent winning run.
But Merkle, who was on first, did not run out the hit to
second. Instead he bolted straight to the clubhouse in center
field, a custom of the time when the winning hit was made
in the bottom of the ninth inning. Johnny Evers, the Cubs'
second baseman, alertly called for the ball; and Hank O'Day,
the umpire who saw the entire play, ruled that Merkle was
out. He also suspended the 1–1 contest because of darkness.
That necessitated a one-game playoff for the pennant. The
Cubs behind Mordecai Brown defeated Christy Mathewson
of the Giants, 4–2.

In 1912 the Giants muffed the World Series. Leading by
one run in the final inning of the eighth-and-decisive game—
the second game had ended in a 6–6 tie—they made two
costly errors, one of commission and one of omission. Fred
Snodgrass dropped Clyde Engle's routine fly ball for a two-
base error, and first baseman Merkle and catcher Chief
Meyers gave Tris Speaker a second life when they permitted
his easy foul pop to drop untouched. Speaker then singled
home the tying run and advanced what proved to be the
winning run to third. Larry Gardner's sacrifice fly clinched
the championship.

In 1917 the Giants made two physical errors and one
mental error in the fourth inning of the sixth-and-final game.
Heinie Zimmerman, the third baseman for the Giants, made
a bad throw on an easy grounder; Dave Robertson, the
right fielder, dropped an easy fly ball; and Bill Rariden, the
catcher, left home plate unattended in a rundown play that
led to the winning run.

In 1924, McGraw's last chance to win a World Series,
"Little Napoleon" saw fate intervene once again. In the
bottom of the 12th, with the score between the Giants and
the host Senators tied at three, Muddy Ruel lifted a high

foul behind the plate, but the Giant catcher tripped over his own mask, and Ruel, given another opportunity, doubled. Earl McNeely's hopper to third hit a pebble and bounced over Fred Lindstrom's head, scoring Ruel with the winning run.

The Giants' receiver was naturally distraught over his inability to handle Ruel's pop fly properly, for he was a veteran who was used to crisis situations. Up until that time he had been the only catcher to be on the winning side of a World Series sweep. When World War I erupted, he was the first major leaguer to volunteer for military service. Later, when World War II broke out, he became the only major leaguer to see service in both wars. And in the 1914 World Series he batted .545, the second highest average in the history of the Autumn Classic.

Who was this player with the checkered career?

(Answer appears on page 321.)

Chapter Seven

BASEBALL'S WHO'S WHO

35. BASEBALL'S WHO'S WHO

1. _____ Who pitched in 65 1–0 games, winning 38 of them and losing 27, even though in 20 of his losses he allowed four or fewer hits?

2. _____ Who batted for a .403 average over a five-year period of time?

3. _____ Who was the only manager before Dick Williams to win pennants with three different teams?

4. _____ Who was the youngest player to win a batting title?

5. _____ Who was the oldest player to win a batting title?

6. _____ Who was the first player to hit safely in 12 consecutive official at-bats?

7. _____ Who was the only other player to duplicate the feat?

8. _____ Who hit .382 in his last year (570 at-bats) in the majors?

9. _____ Who, in addition to Joe Jackson (.408), was the only player to bat .400 without winning the hitting crown?

10. _____ Who posted the most wins (12) in one season without losing a game?

11. _____ Who pitched three doubleheaders in one month and won all six games, none of which lasted more than one hour and fifty minutes?

12. _____ Who hit two game-winning home runs for the Giants against the Yankees in the 1923 series?

13. _____ Who was the only player to win the MVP Award for two teams in the same league?

14. _____ Who was the first infielder to wear glasses?

15. _____ Who was the first catcher to wear glasses?

16. _____ Who was the National League right-hander who led the circuit in strikeouts for four consecutive years (1932–35) but failed to whiff as many as 200 batters in a season?

17. _____ Who recorded the second-lowest career ERA in the World Series?

18. _____ Who won four batting titles in alternate years?

19. _____ Who won back-to-back batting titles three times?

20. _____ Who was the first baseman who teamed with Joe Gordon, Lou Boudreau, and Ken Keltner to give the Indians an infield that averaged 108 RBIs?

21. _____ Who was the one-time Yankee manager who neither hit a home run nor stole a base in eight major league seasons?

22. _____ Who was the one-time Yankee manager who never finished worse than fourth in 24 years as a major league skipper?

23. _____ Who was the pennant-winning manager who needed the most time—10 years—to win his first league title?

24. _____ Who hit a record six pinch-hit home runs in one year?

25. _____ Who hit five pinch-hit home runs in one year to set an American League record?

26. _____ Who was the only National League pitcher to lead his league in winning percentage for three consecutive years?

27. _____ Who was the only American League pitcher to lead his circuit in winning percentage for three consecutive years?

28. _____ Who shut out every team in the National League in three different years?

29. _____ Who was the left-handed slugger in the National League who tied for the home run title three times?

30. _____ Who was the right-handed slugger in the National League who tied for the home run crown three times?

31. _____ Who posted a 6–0 opening day record?

32. _____ Who pitched six opening day shutouts?

33. _____ Who was the only White Sox player to win a batting title?

34. _____ Who threw the pennant-winning home run to Chris Chambliss in 1976?

35. _____ Who was the only pitcher to win back-to-back MVP awards?

36. _____ Who was the pitcher for the 1914 pennant-winning Athletics who recorded a .302 lifetime mark as an outfielder?

37. _____ Who hit 40 or more home runs in the American League eight times, but never reached the 50 mark?

38. _____ Who hit 40 or more home runs in the National League eight times, but failed to hit the 50 mark?

39. _____ Who was the player who led the American League in batting in 1961 with an average of .361, but never before or after reached the .300 level?

40. _____ Who drove home 106 runs in 1969, at the age of 38, to become the oldest player to deliver that many ribbies?

41. _____ Who was the 273-game winner who hit over .300 eight times and pinch-hit safely 58 times?

42. _____ Who was the pitcher who pinch-hit safely 114 times?

43. _____ Who set a major league record by leading his league in ERA percentage nine times?

44. _____ Who was the only player to win the batting and home run titles with two teams in the same league?

45. _____ Who was the first switch-hitter to win a batting crown?

46. _____ Who was the National League relief pitcher from the 1950s and 1960s who recorded 193 career saves?

47. _____ Who was the player who three times won the batting crown and the home run title in the same year?

48. _____ Who finished 750 of 816 contests for a completion percentage of 92?

49. _____ Who was the only National League player to twice get six hits in six at-bats?

50. _____ Who was the only American League player to twice get six hits in six at-bats?

51. _____ Who was the only American League pitcher to win the Cy Young Award three times?

52. _____ Who, in addition to Sandy Koufax,

was the only National League pitcher to win the Cy Young Award three times?

53. _____ Who was the first National League relief pitcher to win the Cy Young Award?

54. _____ Who has won the Cy Young Award four times?

55. _____ Who was the only pitcher to win the Cy Young Award in both leagues?

56. _____ Who was the only American League pitcher to win the Rookie of the Year Award in the 1970s?

57. _____ Who was the only National League infielder who won the Rookie of the Year Award in the 1970s?

58. _____ Who was the last American League hitter to win consecutive batting crowns?

59. _____ Who has been the only player to win both the Rookie of the Year Award and the MVP Award in the same year?

60. _____ Who was the last National League player to win three consecutive batting titles?

61. _____ Who was the last American League player to win at least three consecutive batting titles?

62. _____ Who was the second, and most recent, National League relief pitcher to win the Cy Young Award?

63. _____ Who was the last National League player to win three consecutive home run crowns?

64. _____ Who was the last American League player to win back-to-back MVP awards?

65. _____ Who was the last National League player to win back-to-back MVP awards?

66. _____ Who is the other present-day player who won back-to-back MVP awards in 1980–81?

67. _____ Who has hit for the highest average in the National League since Stan Musial's .376 in 1948?

68. _____ Who strayed 200 or more hits in a record ten seasons?

69. _____ Who is the recent-day Cub pitcher who won 20 or more games in six consecutive seasons?

70. _____ Who was the recent-day pitcher who won 20 or more games with three different teams?

71. _____ Who was the recent-day pitcher who won 20 or more games eight times?

72. _____ Who is the only present-day left-handed pitcher to strike out 300 batters in a season?

73. _____ Who was the former Yankee relief pitcher who led the American League in saves in 1972 and 1976 with 35 and 23, respectively?

74. _____ Who was the most recent pitcher to both win and lose 20 games in the same season?

75. _____ Who was the player who holds the club batting mark lead with two different teams?

76. _____ Who is the recent-day pitcher who struck out more than 200 batters in nine consecutive seasons?

Classic Comebacks

They say that good things come in twos. That goes for no-hitters, too.

There have been four pitchers in the modern era to throw two no-hitters in one season: Johnny Vander Meer (1938), Allie Reynolds (1951), Virgil Trucks (1952), and Nolan Ryan (1973). One of them (Vander Meer) was the only pitcher to throw two no-hitters in successive starts.

Up until 1968, however, no two teams had exchanged no-hitters on successive days. Now it's been accomplished twice. The first time, on September 23, 1968, a Giant pitcher performed the feat against the visiting Cardinals. The following day, a St. Louis right-hander duplicated the feat against San Francisco.

One year later, two teams traded no-hitters on successive days for the second time. On April 30 a strong-armed Cincinnati right-hander set back the Astros. The next day an Astro flamethrower returned the favor.

If you could name just two of the four pitchers who were involved in these classic comebacks, you would be pitching in coveted company, too. Can you?

(Answer appears on page 321.)

Chapter Eight

BASEBALL'S NUMBER GAME

Just how trivial is baseball "trivia"?

Baseball fans, the most record-conscious of all sports followers, feel very strongly that names and numbers are a vital part of the national pastime. So do the players.

The numbers 56, 60, 61, 367, 511, 755, and 2,130 instantaneously draw to the minds of astute baseball fans and players the names of great diamond stars of the past: Joe DiMaggio, Babe Ruth, Roger Maris, Ty Cobb, Cy Young, Hank Aaron, and Lou Gehrig.

Numbers 300 and 3,000 probably hold the most lure for the baseball fan and player. Three hundred represents a batter's season's average and his career mark. It also signifies a pitcher's season's strikeouts and career wins. Three thousand can stand for either career hits by a batter or career strikeouts by a pitcher.

There are other magical numberes in baseball, too. Quite often they affect the longevity of a player's career.

Mickey Mantle, the great Yankee switch-hitter, lengthened his career two years because of the numbers game. In 1966, when he should have retired, Mantle's RBI total dipped to 56. But his batting average of .288 and his home run total of 23 were still respectable. It would have been a good time to bow out, while he was still on top. But he was just four home runs shy of 500. The temptation was simply too great. So he played another year. In 1967 he hit 22 home runs to up his total to 518, just three short of Ted Williams's 521 and 16 light of Jimmy Foxx's 534. So, of course, he played one more year, and he ended up with 536 home runs. Willie Mays's four-base total, the next rung on the home run ladder, was high above Mantle's. So, with no more numbers to catch, he retired.

The numbers game was costly to Mantle, though. His .245 and .237 batting averages during his last two years dragged his lifetime average down from .302 to .298. In Mantle's case a higher home run total was preferable to a higher lifetime batting average.

"It really bothers me that I didn't end up my career with a .300 lifetime average," Mantle says when he is asked about his decision to play those last two years. "I'd like to be remembered as a good hitter. At the time I fooled myself into thinking that I could hit the extra home runs and keep the .300 average. But it didn't work out."

Al Kaline got caught up in the numbers game, too. His situation was similar to Mantle's. He played two extra years in order to wind up in the select 3,000 Hit Club. He made it with a herculean effort in 1974, when he got 146 hits to finish up his career with 3,007. But, in those last two years, he slipped four points, from .301 to .297, in his lifetime average.

Once Kaline reached 3,000 hits, he was faced with another dilemma. He had 399 home runs. Should he play another year in order to end up in another select circle of hitters: the 400 Home Run Club?

"No, I decided not to," Kaline said shortly after his retirement. "It would have been nice to hit 400 home runs. But the toll that would have been exacted from my body by playing another season would have been too much. I had a good career. I'm satisfied with it."

Unlike Mantle, home runs were less important to him than base hits. Yet he is one of only three members of the 3,000 Hit Club who did not finish his career with a .300 lifetime average.

The numbers game was not always as important to the baseball player as it is today, though.

Take the case of Sam Rice, who played the outfield for the Washington Senators from 1915 to 1934. He ended up his career with a lifetime average of .322 and a total of 2,987 hits, just 13 short of the magic 3,000. But Rice, who had hit .293 and collected 98 hits in his final season, elected to retire. Had he been a modern-day performer, he undoubtedly would have played one more year in order to reach the prestigious milestone. Rice's decision to retire, though he didn't know it at the time, cost him baseball immortality. There are not too many modern-day fans who even recognize his name. A mere 13 additional hits would have added luster to his name. The present-day fans would then include him with the greatest hitters of all time.

"We didn't pay too much attention to records in those days," Rice said shortly before his death. "There wasn't so much emphasis put on them at the time. If I had it to do all over again, though, I think I would have hung around for a while. With all of this stress on records today, history has sort of cheated me, you know."

Sam Crawford was another player who looked back and rued the day that he retired. Today he is mostly remembered as an outfielder who played alongside Ty Cobb. But "Wahoo" Sam turned in a .309 lifetime average, led the major leagues in triples with 309, and proved to be the only player who has led both the National and American leagues in home runs.

But he finished his career with 2,964 hits. He also could have played an extra year, as so many modern baseball players will do, and made the 3,000 Hit Club. Then perhaps he would have moved out of Cobb's shadow. But one hit shy of 3,000 is as distant as 1,000 short of the mark. Most baseball buffs know that Roberto Clemente ended up his career with 3,000 hits on the nose. But few people realize that Rice and Crawford missed the mark by a whisker and could have hit it, if they had elected to do so.

Crawford legally deserves the 3,000 Hit Club recognition anyway. In 1899 he got 87 hits with Grand Rapids in the Western League. When the American League was formed in 1900, the National Commission ruled that any player from the Western League who entered either the National or American leagues would be credited with all the hits that he had made in the Western League. But the statistician who compiled Crawford's lifetime average inadvertently overlooked those hits. So he finished his career with 2,964 hits instead of 3,051, to which he is entitled.

Crawford, it seems, was dealt a double twist of fate: he was victimized by the numbers game and the record book.

Lefty O'Doul was also cheated by the numbers game. The two-time batting champ in the National League finished his career with a .349 average. Yet he is not ranked with the top hitters of all time because the baseball rules makers say that he did not play the required ten years in order to qualify for such exalted distinction. Actually, O'Doul played 11 years in the big leagues. But the first four were spent as a pitcher. The record compilers don't count those years.

But the late, irrepressible Irishman did. "I spent 11 years in the big leagues and ended up with a .349 average," he often said to the surprise of unknowing listeners. "That's lifetime average, not a single season's mark. Only Cobb,

Hornsby, and Jackson ever did better. That's pretty good company."

O'Doul was also denied entrance into another elite club—the .400 Hitters—by a single base hit. In 1929 he batted .398, the closest that anyone has come to .400 without hitting it. (Harry Heilmann also hit .398. But in another season, he batted .401.)

"Only eight hitters in the history of baseball ever hit .400," O'Doul said regretfully. "If an official scorer had ruled one of many plays a hit rather than an error, I would have been the ninth."

Babe Ruth didn't miss .400 by too much, either. In 1923 he hit .393 and didn't even win the batting title. (Heilmann did.) When people think of the Babe, they envision the legendary long-ball hitter. But they sometimes forget that he was a .342 lifetime hitter, too. If the Babe had been able to get three more hits in 1923, they would never be able to forget it.

Ten players in the history of the game have hit 50 or more home runs in one season. You can probably name all of them. But can you recall the six players who did not hit 50, but did smack 49? Well, they are Lou Gehrig, Ted Kluszewski, Frank Robinson, Harmon Killebrew, Mark McGwire, and Andre Dawson.

"Close only counts in horseshoes," they say. So these six sluggers have been relegated to a lower echelon of long-ball hitters.

Billy Goodman wound up his major league career with a lifetime average of .300. Minnie Minoso hit .299. Is there a difference? Well, Minoso prevailed upon Chicago White Sox owner Bill Veeck to reactivate him, at the age of 57, in the final month of the 1976 season. In 1980 he returned for two more at-bats. (His lifetime average dropped a point to .298.) You might say that Minoso thought there was a difference.

Thirteen pitchers have won 30 or more games in one season. "Three-Finger" Brown, George Mullin, Ed Cicotte, and Hal Newhouser did not. They won 29. In the record book that looms as one very important win.

Spud Chandler, like Lefty O'Doul, has been footnoted out of the record book. The Yankees' right-hander won 109 games and lost only 43 for a phenomenal winning percentage of .717. That's the best mark of all time for any pitcher who has won 100 or more games. But the rules makers say that a pitcher has to have recorded 200 victories in order to rank with the all-time best. So Whitey Ford (236–106) tops the list with a mark of .690.

Jim Bunning pitched no-hitters in both leagues. He won over 100 games in each league, too. And he also struck out more than 1,000 batters in each league. Overall, he struck out 2,855 batters. Another 145 would have guaranteed him a bust in Cooperstown. He'll probably never make it, though.

Tom Seaver struck out 200 or more batters in nine consecutive years. That's a record. But his personal high of 289 is still far from the top. Eleven pitchers have gone over 300 strikeouts in a season.

Roy Face still thinks about the one decision in 19 which he dropped in 1959. Nineteen and oh? Wouldn't that be something!

Vic Willis of the old Boston Braves might have welcomed one more loss, though. In 1905 he dropped 29 decisions. No one else has ever done that. But 30 losses? That would really single him out!

Early Wynn and Robin Roberts typify the modern-day players' conflict with the numbers game.

Wynn won only one game in 1963. That was his last major league victory. It was also his 300th career win. He got it in relief. That's struggling. With satisfaction, though.

Roberts struggled, too. In vain, though. Eleven years after his last 20-game season, he called it quits, 14 victories short of the coveted 300 Win Club.

Why did those Hall of Famers put so much time and toil into so few victories at the tail end of their careers? They did so because, competitive as baseball players are prone to be, they played the game to the hilt, until their number(s) were up.

To them, it wasn't any trivial matter!

Speaking of trivia, though, I've got a question for you: who were those two players, in addition to Al Kaline, who collected more than 3,000 lifetime hits but failed to finish their careers with an average of .300?

(Answer appears on page 321.)

The Fateful Farewell

In the 1947 World Series, three players—Bill Bevens, Cookie Lavagetto, and Al Gionfriddo—came out of relative obscurity to figure prominently in the seven-game set between the Yankees and the Dodgers. Afterward they slipped back into obscurity. But they are still remembered today for the pivotal parts they played in the 1947 Fall Classic, one of the most dramatic series of all time.

In Game Four, with the Yankees holding a one-contest lead, Bevens, a pitcher with a less than enviable 7–13 record during the regular season, made World Series history.

With one out remaining in the game, Bevens held tenuously to a 2–1 lead. Up to that point, Bevens had neutralized the Dodgers' big bats; he had not allowed a single base hit. That is not to say, however, that he hadn't allowed any base runners. As a matter of fact, he yielded ten of them, all via the base-on-balls route. (And that's a record!) Two of them, plus a sacrifice and an infield out, cost him a run in the fifth inning. But it was the last two walks he granted that cost him World Series immortality.

In the ninth inning he walked Carl Furillo for pass number nine. Furillo gave way to a pinch-runner, who proceeded to steal second base off rookie catcher Yogi Berra. Then with two outs and a base open, Yankee manager Bucky Harris decided to walk pinch-hitter Pete Reiser, who also gave way to a pinch-runner. That set the stage for pinch-hitter Harry Lavagetto, who responded with a double off the right-field wall to break up the no-hitter and, more important, to win the game for the Dodgers.

In Game Six, Al Gionfriddo, who played the role of a super-sub in the Series, prevented the tying run from scoring with one of the most memorable defensive plays in World Series history.

The Yankees, who had won Game Five on Joe DiMaggio's home run off Rex Barney, had high hopes of wrapping up the classic in Game Six. Once again, it was DiMaggio who almost provided them with the impetus. But with the Dodgers leading 8–5 in the sixth inning, Dodger manager Burt Shotton once again went to his bench. He called on Gionfriddo, whom he inserted in left field as a defensive precaution.

Immediately, Gionfriddo justified the move. DiMaggio boomed a 415-foot shot to the bull pen in deep left center field. But Gionfriddo, who had broken with the crack of the bat, made a circus catch to prevent the homer that would have tied the game. The Dodgers then hung on to win, 8–6. But the Yankees came back to win the seventh game (5–2) and the Series (4–3).

One might think that Bevens, Lavagetto, and Gionfriddo got raises the following year. But in fact none of the three ever played another regular-season major league game.

You can earn a bonus, however, if you can identify the pinch-runner for Furillo, the pinch-runner for Reiser, and the left-fielder whom Gionfriddo replaced in the Dodger lineup.

(Answer appears on page 321.)

Chapter Nine

NICKNAMES

36. MATCHING NAMES

Match the following players with their nicknames.

Tommy Henrich	Walter Johnson
Carl Hubbell	Dom DiMaggio
Frankie Frisch	Tris Speaker
Honus Wagner	Ted Williams
Luke Appling	Casey Stengel
Johnny Mize	Vernon Law
Bobby Thomson	Ty Cobb
Allie Reynolds	Babe Ruth
Joe DiMaggio	Lou Gehrig
Paul Waner	Mickey Mantle

1. "Staten Island Scot" _____
2. "Super Chief" _____
3. "Splendid Splinter" _____
4. "Big Cat" _____
5. "Little Professor" _____
6. "Old Professor" _____
7. "Old Reliable" _____
8. "Deacon" _____
9. "Yankee Clipper" _____
10. "Georgia Peach" _____
11. "Flying Dutchman" _____
12. "Grey Eagle" _____
13. "Sultan of Swat" _____
14. "Big Train" _____
15. "Iron Horse" _____
16. "Meal Ticket" _____
17. "Commerce Comet" _____
18. "Old Aches and Pains" _____
19. "Big Poison" _____
20. "Fordham Flash" _____

37. FIRST NAMES

Substitute the players' first names for their nicknames.

Edwin	Elwin
George	Jerome
Harry	Charles
Edward	Joe
James	Johnny
Leon	Leroy
Fred	Enos
Larry	Robert
Paul	Lynwood
Bill	Charles Dillon

1. "Moose" Skowron   _____
2. "Daffy" Dean   _____
3. "Dizzy" Dean   _____
4. "Yogi" Berra   _____
5. "Preacher" Roe   _____
6. "Snuffy" Stirnweiss   _____
7. "Flash" Gordon   _____
8. "Pepper" Martin   _____
9. "Schoolboy" Rowe   _____
10. "Duke" Snider   _____
11. "Casey" Stengel   _____
12. "Dixie" Walker   _____
13. "Peanuts" Lowrey   _____
14. "Satchel" Paige   _____
15. "Country" Slaughter   _____
16. "Chuck" Dressen   _____
17. "Whitey" Ford   _____
18. "Goose" Goslin   _____
19. "Lefty" Grove   _____
20. "Dusty" Rhodes   _____

38. MIDDLE NAMES

Place the following nicknames between the players' first and last names.

"The Whip"   "The Kid"
"Poosh 'Em Up"   "Birdie"
"Pee Wee"   "The Crow"
"Bobo"   "The Barber"
"Three Finger"   "Home Run"
"Puddin' Head"   "The Lip"
"The Dutch Master"   "King Kong"
"The Man"   "Pie"
"The Hat"   "Twinkletoes"
"The Cat"   "Louisiana Lightning"

1. Harry _____ Walker
2. Stan _____ Musial
3. Harry _____ Brecheen
4. Johnny _____ Vander Meer
5. Sal _____ Maglie
6. Ron _____ Guidry
7. Leo _____ Durocher
8. Ewell _____ Blackwell
9. Charlie _____ Keller
10. Willie _____ Jones
11. Frank _____ Crosetti
12. Frank _____ Baker
13. Tony _____ Lazzeri
14. Billy _____ Martin
15. Harold _____ Traynor
16. Louis _____ Newsom
17. George _____ Tebbetts
18. George _____ Selkirk
19. Mordecai _____ Brown
20. Harold _____ Reese

39. LAST NAMES

Match the players' last names with their nicknames and their first names.

Doby	Reiser
Keeler	Murphy
Jones	Hubbell
Feller	Crawford
Jackson	Dugan
Piniella	Cochrane
Houk	Grimm
Medwick	Bottomley
Wood	Turner
Greenberg	Newhouser

1. "Ducky" Joe _____
2. "Wahoo" Sam _____
3. "Shoeless" Joe _____
4. "Smokey" Joe _____
5. "Jumping" Joe _____
6. "Sweet" Lou _____
7. "Hammerin' " Hank _____
8. "Blackjack" Mickey _____
9. "Rapid" Robert _____
10. "Jolly Cholly" _____
11. "Pistol" Pete _____
12. "Sunny" Jim _____
13. "Larrupin' " Larry _____
14. "Prince" Hal _____
15. "Major" Ralph _____
16. "Wee" Willie _____
17. "Fireman" Johnny _____
18. "Milkman" Jim _____
19. "Sad" Sam _____
20. "King" Carl _____

40. MULTIPLE NAMES

Supply the whole name.

1. "Dr. Strangeglove" _____
2. "Daddy Wags" _____
3. "The Say Hey Kid" _____
4. "Charlie Hustle" _____
5. "The Vacuum Cleaner" _____

Supply the first name.

1. "Hondo" Howard _____
2. "Stretch" McCovey _____
3. "Tug" McGraw _____
4. "Killer" Killebrew _____
5. "Hawk" Harrelson _____

Supply the nickname.

1. Walter Williams _____
2. Jim Hunter _____
3. John Powell _____
4. John Odom _____
5. Jim Grant _____

Supply the last name.

1. "Sudden" Sam _____
2. "Gettysburg" Eddie _____
3. "Shake and Bake" _____
4. "Stonewall" Travis _____
5. "Vinegar Bend" _____

The Iron Horse

There is a touch of irony in respect to the manner in which Lou Gehrig broke into the Yankees' lineup and the way in which he departed from it.

When the 1925 season started, Gehrig was the back-up first baseman. The first-string first sacker was a veteran of 12 years, a two-time home run champion, and the American League's leader in triples (19) the previous year. About one-third of the way through the season, though, the first stringer got hit in the head with a pitch, and he suffered from headaches for the remainder of the season. One day he asked manager Joe McCarthy for a game's rest. Lou Gehrig substituted for him and the rest of the story is history: the "Iron Horse" remained in the lineup for a record 2,130 consecutive games. But he died a short two years after he hung up his cleats.

The player whom he replaced lived for 40 years after he departed from the Yankee lineup. Can you name him?

(Answer appears on page 321.)

Chapter Ten

BREAKING THE BARRIERS

41. DID THEY OR DIDN'T THEY?

Mark "T" or "F" for "True" or "False" before each statement.

1. _____ Don Newcombe hit more home runs (7) in one season than any other pitcher in the history of the National League.
2. _____ Roy Campanella hit more home runs (242) than any other catcher in National League history.
3. _____ Elston Howard hit a home run in his first World Series at-bat.
4. _____ Bob Gibson was the first black pitcher to win the Cy Young Award.
5. _____ Two black pitchers have won the Cy Young Award in the same season.
6. _____ Richie Allen has been the only black third baseman to be named Rookie of the Year.
7. _____ Willie Mays has been the only black player to twice hit more than 50 home runs in a season.
8. _____ Bob Gibson once played for the Harlem Globetrotters.
9. _____ Elston Howard was the last Yankee to win the MVP Award.
10. _____ Ralph Garr's nickname is "The Road Runner."
11. _____ Roy Campanella won a record-tying three MVP awards.
12. _____ Willie Mays was the first player to collect more than 3,000 hits and 500 home runs.
13. _____ Frank Robinson was a unanimous choice as the American League's MVP in 1966.
14. _____ Matty and Felipe Alou have been the only brothers to finish one-two in a batting race.

15. _____ Jackie Robinson was the only black player to appear in the 1947 World Series.

16. _____ Bobby Bonds has four times hit more than 30 home runs and stolen more than 40 bases in a season.

17. _____ Reggie Jackson has hit .300 in a season.

18. _____ Don Newcombe was the first black pitcher to win a series game.

19. _____ Larry Doby was the first black player to win the American League's MVP Award.

20. _____ Jackie Robinson was the first black player to win the National League's MVP Award.

21. _____ Hank Aaron, Roberto Clemente, and Lou Brock won the MVP Award.

22. _____ Reggie Jackson, when he hit three home runs in the final game of the 1977 series, delivered the four-base blows against three different pitchers.

23. _____ Willie Mays never won an RBI crown.

24. _____ No black player has ever won the Triple Crown.

25. _____ Don Newcombe lost all four of his pitching decisions in series play.

26. _____ Roy Campanella was the first black to hit a home run in series play.

27. _____ Larry Doby was the first black to hit two home runs in the same series.

28. _____ Hank Aaron was the first black to hit three home runs in a series.

29. _____ Jim Rice hit more home runs in one season than any other Red Sox player.

30. _____ Al Downing was the first black to appear in a World Series game for the Yankees.

31. _____ Willie Mays never batted .300 or hit a home run in series play.

32. _____ J. R. Richard has been the only black to strike out more than 300 batters in a season.

33. _____ Bob Gibson won more consecutive World Series games than any other pitcher.

34. _____ Al Downing was the first black pitcher to win a series game for an American League team.

35. _____ The Dodgers opened the 1966 World Series against the Orioles with six black players in their starting lineup.

36. _____ Bob Gibson was the last pitcher to win three games in a series.

37. _____ Dave Cash has had more at-bats in one season than any other major leaguer.

38. _____ Ferguson Jenkins has won more games than any other black pitcher.

39. _____ Willie McCovey played in four decades of major league ball.

40. _____ Jackie Robinson recorded the highest lifetime average (.311) of any black or hispanic player who finished his career with at least ten years of active service.

41. _____ Curt Flood handled 538 consecutive chances without making an error.

42. _____ Maury Wills ranks number two to Lou Brock in the number of career steals by a National Leaguer.

43. _____ Willie Mays scored the run in the 1962 Series which snapped Whitey Ford's scoreless inning skein at 33⅔ innings.

44. _____ Zoilo Versalles, Rod Carew, and Reggie Jackson have won the MVP Award in the American League.

45. _____ Willie Mays has a higher lifetime batting average than Mickey Mantle.

46. _____ Before Bill Madlock won back-to-back batting titles (1975–76), the last black or hispanic player in the National League to perform the feat was Tommy Davis (1962–63).

47. _____ Jackie Robinson was the last player in the series to execute a steal of home that was not on the front end of a double theft.

48. _____ Dick Allen won home run titles in both leagues.

42. THE TRAILBLAZERS

The following black or hispanic players were the first ones to perform for teams that previously were exclusively white: Larry Doby, Hank Thompson–Willard Brown, Sam Hairston, Bob Trice, Carlos Paula, Valmy Thomas, Jackie Robinson, Curt Roberts, Elston Howard, Hank Thompson–Monte Irvin, Ozzie Virgil, Sam Jethroe, Pumpsie Green, Ernie Banks–Gene Baker, Joe Black, and Tom Alston–Brooks Lawrence. Match the players with their respective teams.

1. _____ Browns
2. _____ Pirates
3. _____ Phillies
4. _____ Yankees
5. _____ Athletics
6. _____ Indians
7. _____ Cubs
8. _____ Reds
9. _____ Red Sox
10. _____ Senators
11. _____ Dodgers
12. _____ Braves
13. _____ Cardinals
14. _____ Giants
15. _____ Tigers
16. _____ White Sox

43. BLACK CLOUTERS

Fifteen black players have won a total of 33 league home run titles (ties count as wins). Match the following players with the number of times they have won the crown: George Foster, Ben Oglivie, Jim Rice, Larry Doby, Hank Aaron, Dick Allen, Jesse Barfield, Willie Mays, Frank Robinson, Reggie Jackson, Willie McCovey, Willie Stargell, Ernie Banks, George Scott, and Andre Dawson.

1. _____ (4)
2. _____ (4)
3. _____ (4)
4. _____ (3)
5. _____ (3)
6. _____ (2)
7. _____ (2)
8. _____ (2)
9. _____ (2)
10. _____ (2)
11. _____ (1)
12. _____ (1)
13. _____ (1)
14. _____ (1)
15. _____ (1)

44. SINGLE-SEASON SLUGGERS

Ten black players hold the single-season high in home runs for their respective club(s). (Three of them are co-holders of a club's mark.) The numbers of home runs and the clubs are provided. The players are not. One of the players holds the top position for two different teams.

1. _____ (52) San Francisco Giants
2. _____ (52) Cincinnati Reds
3. _____ (51) New York Giants *
4. _____ (49) Baltimore Orioles
5. _____ (47) Atlanta Braves **
6. _____ (47) Toronto Blue Jays
7. _____ (39) California Angels
8. _____ (38) San Diego Padres
9. _____ (37) Chicago White Sox ***
10. _____ (37) Houston Astros
11. _____ (32) Montreal Expos

* Johnny Mize is the co-holder of this record.
** Eddie Mathews is the co-holder of this record.
*** Carlton Fisk is the co-holder of this record.

45. NATIONAL LEAGUE
BATTING CHAMPS

Fifteen black or hispanic players have won the National League batting title a total of 25 times: Bill Madlock, Ralph Garr, Al Oliver, Matty Alou, Roberto Clemente, Willie McGee, Jackie Robinson, Billy Williams, Tony Gwynn, Willie Mays, Rico Carty, Tim Raines, Tommy Davis, Dave Parker, and Hank Aaron. Match the players with the years in which they copped the crowns. Two of the players won the title four times. Five of them won it twice.

1. _____ (1949)
2. _____ (1954)
3. _____ (1956)
4. _____ (1959)
5. _____ (1961)
6. _____ (1962)
7. _____ (1963)
8. _____ (1964)
9. _____ (1965)
10. _____ (1966)
11. _____ (1967)
12. _____ (1970)
13. _____ (1972)
14. _____ (1974)
15. _____ (1975)
16. _____ (1976)
17. _____ (1977)
18. _____ (1978)
19. _____ (1981)
20. _____ (1982)
21. _____ (1983)
22. _____ (1984)
23. _____ (1985)
24. _____ (1986)
25. _____ (1987)

46. AMERICAN LEAGUE BATTING CHAMPS

Six black or hispanic players—Alex Johnson, Frank Robinson, Tony Oliva, Rod Carew, Willie Wilson, and Bobby Avila—have won the American League batting title a total of 13 times. Match the players with the years in which they copped the crown(s). One of them did it seven times, one of them did it three times, and three of them did it once.

1. _____ (1954)
2. _____ (1964)
3. _____ (1965)
4. _____ (1966)
5. _____ (1969)
6. _____ (1970)
7. _____ (1971)
8. _____ (1972)
9. _____ (1973)
10. _____ (1974)
11. _____ (1975)
12. _____ (1977)
13. _____ (1978)
14. _____ (1982)

47. ROOKIES OF THE YEAR

Six of the first seven Rookie of the Year awards in the National League went to black players: Sam Jethroe, Jim Gilliam, Don Newcombe, Willie Mays, Joe Black, and Jackie Robinson. Can you place them in their proper order?

1. _____ (1947)
2. _____ (1949)
3. _____ (1950)
4. _____ (1951)
5. _____ (1952)
6. _____ (1953).

48. THE HALL OF FAME

Twenty-two black or hispanic players have been elected to the Hall of Fame. You should be able to name at least ten of them. If you can name 15, though, you're entitled to a little bit of fame for yourself.

1. _____
2. _____
3. _____
4. _____
5. _____
6. _____
7. _____
8. _____
9. _____
10. _____
11. _____
12. _____
13. _____
14. _____
15. _____
16. _____
17. _____
18. _____
19. _____
20. _____
21. _____
22. _____

To Catch a Thief

The final game of the 1926 World Series has gone down in baseball history as one of the most exciting finishes in the annals of the fall classic.

It certainly did not lack drama.

With the visiting Cardinals leading the Yankees 3–2 in the bottom of the sixth, Jesse Haines developed a finger blister while the Yankees loaded the bases with two out. Rogers Hornsby, the manager of St. Louis, decided to replace Haines with Grover Alexander, who had already won two games in the series. Alexander, one of the all-time greats of the hill, had to face Tony Lazzeri, a long-ball-hitting rookie. On the second pitch of the confrontation, Lazzeri almost decisively won the duel: he hit a long line drive to left that tailed a few feet left of the foul pole. Three pitches later, Alexander struck Lazzeri out on a sweeping curveball.

In a groove, Alexander mowed the Yankees down in order in both the seventh and the eighth innings. He had retired nine consecutive batters before he faced Babe Ruth, with two outs, in the ninth. Working cautiously, he proceeded to walk the Babe. But Alex was still not out of danger. He had to face Bob Meusel, who had won the home run crown the year before. On the first pitch to Meusel, however, Ruth pulled the unexpected: he tried to steal second base. But the Cardinals' catcher threw a strike to Hornsby to nail Ruth, who became the first and only base runner to make the last out of a World Series on an attempted steal.

After the series ended, owner Sam Breadon traded manager Hornsby to the Giants and named his catcher the team's manager. Maybe the backstop's final throw of the 1926 World Series had something to do with the owner's decision.

Who was that veteran of 21 seasons who stopped the Yankees in 1926 and led the Cardinals in 1927?

(Answer appears on page 321.)

Chapter Eleven

THE HOT CORNER

49. WHAT'S THE RETIREMENT AGE?

Fifteen familiar names are listed with the dates on which they broke into the majors. You provide the dates, within two years, when they bowed out of the big leagues.

1. _____ (1930) Luke Appling
2. _____ (1953) Ernie Banks
3. _____ (1948) Roy Campanella
4. _____ (1936) Bob Feller
5. _____ (1952) Harvey Haddix
6. _____ (1949) Monte Irvin
7. _____ (1947) Willie Jones
8. _____ (1946) Ralph Kiner
9. _____ (1941) Stan Musial
10. _____ (1926) Mel Ott
11. _____ (1940) Pee Wee Reese
12. _____ (1942) Johnny Sain
13. _____ (1946) Bobby Thomson
14. _____ (1939) Mickey Vernon
15. _____ (1944) Eddie Yost

50. ONE-TOWN MEN

Which ten of the following 20 players performed for the same club throughout their major league careers: Luke Appling, Brooks Robinson, Bill Terry, Stan Hack, Ralph Kiner, Lefty Grove, Joe Cronin, Walter Johnson, Grover Alexander, Mel Ott, Gil Hodges, Johnny Podres, Lew Burdette, Al Kaline, Ted Kluszewski, Ernie Banks, Cecil Travis, Pee Wee Reese, Eddie Mathews, and Dallas Green.

1. _____
2. _____
3. _____
4. _____
5. _____
6. _____
7. _____
8. _____
9. _____
10. _____

51. THE FIRST INNING

There have been 20 new major league franchises since 1953. Can you recall their first respective managers? The following list may give you a clue: Darrell Johnson, Ted Williams, Gene Mauch, Bob Kennedy, Harry Craft, Harry Lavagetto, Roy Hartsfield, Lou Boudreau, Charlie Grimm, Bill Rigney, Mickey Vernon, Casey Stengel, Joe Gordon, Preston Gomez, Dave Bristol, Joe Schultz, Bobby Bragan, Walt Alston, and Jimmy Dykes.

1. _____ (1953) Milwaukee Braves
2. _____ (1954) Baltimore Orioles
3. _____ (1955) Kansas City Athletics
4. _____ (1958) San Francisco Giants
5. _____ (1958) Los Angeles Dodgers
6. _____ (1961) Minnesota Twins
7. _____ (1961) Washington Senators
8. _____ (1961) Los Angeles Angels
9. _____ (1962) Houston Astros
10. _____ (1962) New York Mets
11. _____ (1966) Atlanta Braves
12. _____ (1968) Oakland A's
13. _____ (1969) Kansas City Royals
14. _____ (1969) Seattle Pilots
15. _____ (1969) Montreal Expos
16. _____ (1969) San Diego Padres
17. _____ (1970) Milwaukee Brewers
18. _____ (1972) Texas Rangers
19. _____ (1977) Seattle Mariners
20. _____ (1977) Toronto Blue Jays

52. THE LAST INNING

There have been ten major league franchises that have switched cities. Can you name the last respective managers of the original franchises? The following ten names should give you a start: Walt Alston, Harry Lavagetto, Charlie Grimm, Ted Williams, Joe Schultz, Marty Marion, Luke Appling, Eddie Joost, Bobby Bragan, and Bill Rigney.

1. _____ (1952) Boston Braves
2. _____ (1953) St. Louis Browns
3. _____ (1954) Philadelphia Athletics
4. _____ (1957) New York Giants
5. _____ (1957) Brooklyn Dodgers
6. _____ (1960) Washington Senators
7. _____ (1965) Milwaukee Braves
8. _____ (1967) Kansas City A's
9. _____ (1969) Seattle Pilots
10. _____ (1971) Washington Senators

53. SECONDARY PURSUITS

Match the following former players with the corresponding pursuits that they took up in their post-playing days.

1. _____ Vinegar Bend Mizell
2. _____ Joe Cronin
3. _____ Moe Berg
4. _____ Bobby Brown
5. _____ Billy Sunday
6. _____ George Moriarty
7. _____ Ralph Terry
8. _____ Johnny Berardino
9. _____ Al Schacht
10. _____ Red Rolfe
11. _____ Jim Brosnan
12. _____ Charlie Keller
13. _____ Greasy Neale
14. _____ Jim Thorpe
15. _____ Clark Griffith

a. Umpire
b. Actor
c. Congressman
d. Horse breeder
e. Secret agent
f. Pro football player
g. American League executive
h. Author
i. Pro football coach
j. Heart specialist
k. Golfer
l. Baseball club owner
m. Comedian ("Clown Prince of Baseball")
n. Athletic director of Dartmouth
o. Evangelist

54. MAJOR LEAGUE OWNERS

Some names of major league owners (past and present) are synonymous with the franchises they direct(ed). See how many of the following you can associate.

1.	_____ Connie Mack	a.	Reds
2.	_____ Horace Stoneham	b.	Indians
3.	_____ Dan Topping	c.	Dodgers
4.	_____ Walter O'Malley	d.	Twins
5.	_____ Charles Comiskey	e.	Athletics
6.	_____ Sam Breadon		(Philadelphia)
7.	_____ Tom Yawkey	f.	Tigers
8.	_____ Lou Perini	g.	Cubs
9.	_____ Bob Carpenter	h.	Giants
10.	_____ Bill Veeck	i.	Padres
11.	_____ Walter O. Briggs	j.	Yankees
12.	_____ Clark Griffith	k.	Braves
13.	_____ Bob Short	l.	Mets
14.	_____ William Crosley	m.	Rangers
15.	_____ Charles Finley	n.	Phillies
16.	_____ Phillip K. Wrigley	o.	Cardinals
17.	_____ Mrs. Joan Payson	p.	White Sox
18.	_____ Arthur Krock	q.	Athletics (Oakland)
19.	_____ Calvin Griffith	r.	Angels
20.	_____ Gene Autry	s.	Senators
		t.	Red Sox

55. THE MISSING LINK

Can you supply the third starting outfielder for the respective teams from the list of players that follow: Carl Furillo, Dick Sisler, Yogi Berra, Frank Robinson, Terry Moore, Roy White, Joe Rudi, Sid Gordon, Jackie Jensen, Al Simmons, Earle Combs, Vic Wertz, Don Mueller, Ted Williams, Jimmy Wynn, Reggie Smith, Roger Maris, Al Kaline, Charlie Keller, Cesar Cedeno, Harry Heilmann, Duffy Lewis, Casey Stengel, Lou Piniella, Matty Alou, and Pete Reiser.

1. Mickey Mantle, Roger Maris, and _____ (Yankees, 1961)

2. Joe DiMaggio, Tommy Henrich, and _____ (Yankees, 1941)

3. Stan Musial, Enos Slaughter, and _____ (Cardinals, 1942)

4. Tris Speaker, Harry Hooper, and _____ (Red Sox, 1916)

5. Babe Ruth, Bob Meusel, and _____ (Yankees, 1927)

6. Andy Pafko, Duke Snider, and _____ (Dodgers, 1952)

7. Dom DiMaggio, Al Zarilla, and _____ (Red Sox, 1950)

8. Bobby Bonds, Elliott Maddox, and _____ (Yankees, 1975)

9. Whitey Lockman, Willie Mays, and _____ (Giants, 1954)

10. Roberto Clemente, Willie Stargell, and _____ (Pirates, 1966)

11. Richie Ashburn, Del Ennis, and _____ (Phillies, 1950)

12. Lou Brock, Curt Flood, and _____ (Cardinals, 1968)

13. Ted Williams, Jimmy Piersall, and _____ (Red Sox, 1954)

14. Hoot Evers, Johnny Groth, and _____ (Tigers, 1950)

15. Willard Marshall, Bobby Thomson, and _____ (Giants, 1947)

16. Dixie Walker, Joe Medwick, and _____ (Dodgers, 1941)
17. Mule Haas, Bing Miller, and _____ (Athletics, 1931)
18. Ty Cobb, Heinie Manush, and _____ (Tigers, 1923)
19. Ross Youngs, Irish Meusel, and _____ (Giants, 1922)
20. Paul Blair, Don Buford, and _____ (Orioles, 1970)
21. Carl Yastrzemski, Tony Conigliaro, and _____ (Red Sox, 1970)
22. Willie Norton, Jim Northrup, and _____ (Tigers, 1969)
23. Jim North, Reggie Jackson, and _____ (Athletics, 1973)
24. Bob Watson, Jimmy Wynn, and _____ (Astros, 1973)
25. Bill Buckner, Willie Crawford, and _____ (Dodgers, 1974)

56. WHO PLAYED THIRD?

There have been many outstanding double-play combinations in the history of the major leagues. Twenty-five of the more recognizable ones, since 1940, are listed. Can you recall the third baseman who played in the same infield with them?

1. _____ Mark Belanger to Davy Johnson to Boog Powell (Orioles, 1970)
2. _____ Bert Campaneris to Dick Green to Gene Tenace (A's, 1974)
3. _____ Larry Bowa to Dave Cash to Willie Montanez (Phillies, 1974)
4. _____ Bill Russell to Dave Lopes to Steve Garvey (Dodgers, 1974)
5. _____ Phil Rizzuto to Joe Gordon to Johnny Sturm (Yankees, 1941)
6. _____ Joe Cronin to Bobby Doerr to Jimmie Foxx (Red Sox, 1941)
7. _____ Pee Wee Reese to Billy Herman to Dolph Camilli (Dodgers, 1941)
8. _____ Marty Marion to Red Schoendienst to Stan Musial (Cardinals, 1946)
9. _____ Lou Boudreau to Joe Gordon to Eddie Robinson (Indians, 1948)
10. _____ Eddie Joost to Pete Suder to Ferris Fain (A's, 1949)
11. _____ Vern Stephens to Bobby Doerr to Billy Goodman (Red Sox, 1949)
12. _____ Pee Wee Reese to Jackie Robinson to Gil Hodges (Dodgers, 1952)
13. _____ Granny Hamner to Mike Goliat to Eddie Waitkus (Phillies, 1950)
14. _____ Al Dark to Ed Stanky to Whitey Lockman (Giants, 1951)
15. _____ Phil Rizzuto to Billy Martin to Joe Collins (Yankees, 1952)
16. _____ Ray Boone to Bob Avila to Luke Easter (Indians, 1952)
17. _____ Roy McMillan to Johnny Temple to Ted Kluszewski (Reds, 1954)

18. _____ Johnny Logan to Red Schoendienst to Joe Adcock (Braves, 1958)

19. _____ Dick Groat to Bill Mazeroski to Dick Stuart (Pirates, 1960)

20. _____ Tony Kubek to Bobby Richardson to Bill Skowron (Yankees, 1961)

21. _____ Luis Aparicio to Nellie Fox to Roy Sievers (White Sox, 1961)

22. _____ Dick Groat to Julian Javier to Bill White (Cardinals, 1964)

23. _____ Don Kessinger to Gene Beckert to Ernie Banks (Cubs, 1965)

24. _____ Billy Myers to Lonny Frey to Frank McCormick (Reds, 1940)

25. _____ Pete Runnels to Cass Michaels to Mickey Vernon (Senators, 1951)

57. BROTHER COMBINATIONS

Provide the first name of the other brother who played in the major leagues.

1. _____, Joe, Dom DiMaggio
2. _____, Rick Ferrell
3. _____, Walker Cooper
4. _____, Larry Sherry
5. _____, Jesse Barnes
6. _____, Jerome Dean
7. _____, Gaylord Perry
8. _____, Phil Niekro
9. _____, Stan Coveleski
10. _____, Henry Mathewson
11. _____, Matty, Felipe Alou
12. _____, Johnny O'Brien
13. _____, Joe Torre
14. _____, Tony Conigliaro
15. _____, Clete, Cloyd Boyer
16. _____, Bob Meusel
17. _____, George Dickey
18. _____, Henry Aaron
19. _____, Paul Waner
20. _____, Jose, Tommy Cruz
21. _____, Harry Walker
22. _____, Dick Sisler
23. _____, Marv Throneberry
24. _____, Tom, Tim, Joe, Frank Delahanty
25. _____, Hal Keller

58. NO HANDICAP

During the annals of major league baseball, there have been many players who had to overcome adversity in order to fulfill their lifelong ambitions. Five of them follow: Mordecai Brown, Pete Gray, Red Ruffing, John Hiller, and William Hoy. Match them with the physical impairments that they had.

1. _____ Missing toes
2. _____ Deaf and dumb
3. _____ Missing fingers
4. _____ Missing arm
5. _____ Heart condition

59. BASEBALL TRAGEDIES

Match the following players who died tragically—either during or shortly after their playing careers—with the year in which they passed away: Roberto Clemente, Kenny Hubbs, Harry Agganis, Lou Gehrig, Thurman Munson, Ray Chapman, and Ed Delahanty.

1. _____ (1903)
2. _____ (1920)
3. _____ (1941)
4. _____ (1955)
5. _____ (1964)
6. _____ (1972)
7. _____ (1979)

60. NO UNTOUCHABLES

It's pretty hard to believe that the top three hitters who ever lived—Ty Cobb, Rogers Hornsby, and Joe Jackson— were traded from one team to another. That's been the case of many great players, though. Twenty-five players who ended up their careers with .300 or better lifetime averages are listed with the team with which they first made their name. Name the team to which they were either traded or sold.

1. _____ Ty Cobb (Tigers)
2. _____ Rogers Hornsby (Cardinals)
3. _____ Joe Jackson (Indians)
4. _____ Tris Speaker (Red Sox)
5. _____ Babe Ruth (Red Sox)
6. _____ George Sisler (Browns)
7. _____ Al Simmons (A's)
8. _____ Paul Waner (Pirates)
9. _____ Eddie Collins (A's)
10. _____ Jimmie Foxx (A's))
11. _____ Joe Medwick (Cardinals)
12. _____ Chuck Klein (Phillies)
13. _____ Frank Frisch (Giants)
14. _____ Hank Greenberg (Tigers)
15. _____ Johnny Mize (Cardinals)
16. _____ Mickey Cochrane (A's)
17. _____ Richie Ashburn (Phillies)
18. _____ George Kell (Tigers)
19. _____ Dixie Walker (Dodgers)
20. _____ Ernie Lombardi (Reds)
21. _____ Harvey Kuenn (Tigers)
22. _____ Hank Aaron (Braves)
23. _____ Willie Mays (Giants)
24. _____ Joe Cronin (Senators)
25. _____ Enos Slaughter (Cardinals)

61. WHEN DID THEY COME UP?

1930s–1940s

See if you can match the players that follow with the year in which they first broke into the majors (if you are within one year of the actual season, before or after, count it as a correct answer): Tom Henrich, Warren Spahn, Red Schoendienst, Joe DiMaggio, Eddie Yost, George Kell, Joe Gordon, Stan Musial, Ted Williams, and Dom DiMaggio.

1. _____ (1936)   6. _____ (1941)
2. _____ (1937)   7. _____ (1942)
3. _____ (1938)   8. _____ (1943)
4. _____ (1939)   9. _____ (1944)
5. _____ (1940)   10. _____ (1945)

1940s–1950s

We're in the post-war era now. See how you do with the following ten players (if you are within one year of the actual season, before or after, count it as a correct answer): Whitey Ford, Willie Mays, Yogi Berra, Rocky Colavito, Jackie Robinson, Hank Aaron, Al Kaline, Richie Ashburn, Jerry Coleman, and Eddie Mathews.

1. _____ (1946)   6. _____ (1951)
2. _____ (1947)   7. _____ (1952)
3. _____ (1948)   8. _____ (1953)
4. _____ (1949)   9. _____ (1954)
5. _____ (1950)   10. _____ (1955)

1950s–1960s

We're moving into your wheelhouse now. Take a good cut at the following players (if you are within one year of the actual season, before or after, count it as a correct answer): Mel Stottlemyre, Roger Maris, Ed Kranepool, Frank Robinson, Maury Wills, Pete Rose, Catfish Hunter, Carl Yastrzemski, Juan Marichal, and Ron Fairly.

1. _____ (1956)	6. _____ (1961)
2. _____ (1957)	7. _____ (1962)
3. _____ (1958)	8. _____ (1963)
4. _____ (1959)	9. _____ (1964)
5. _____ (1960)	10. _____ (1965)

1960s–1970s

We're now in the present era. It's a home run contest. The pitches are coming right down the middle. See how you can do with the following offerings (if you are within one year of the actual season, before or after, count it as a correct answer): Fred Lynn, Cesar Cedeno, George Scott, Jim Rice, Rod Carew, Mike Schmidt, Dave Parker, Bobby Bonds, Chris Speier, and Thurman Munson.

1. _____ (1966)	6. _____ (1971)
2. _____ (1967)	7. _____ (1972)
3. _____ (1968)	8. _____ (1973)
4. _____ (1969)	9. _____ (1974)
5. _____ (1970)	10. _____ (1975)

Two Strikes Against Him

Ray Chapman, had he not been hit by an errant pitch by the Yankees' Carl Mays, might have ended up in the Hall of Fame.

A .278 lifetime hitter, the 29-year-old shortstop was just coming into his own right as a batsman, averaging over .300 in three of his last four years. And he was an accomplished base runner, stealing 233 career bases, including 52 in 1917, the most bases that any Indian had ever pilfered in one season until Miguel Dilone swiped 61 in 1980.

But the deuces were stacked against him on August 16, 1920. The number-two batter in the lineup that day, he stroked two hits—both of them doubles—scored two runs and stole two bases. Defensively, he made two assists, two putouts, and two errors. In fact, he was hit with two pitches by Mays. The second one killed him.

His replacement in the lineup, had Chapman not been killed by that ill-fated pitch, might not have ended up in the Hall of Fame. For he very well could have been relegated to years on the bench behind a blossoming star. But Chapman's back-up did go on to play 14 years in the big leagues. He averaged .312 lifetime and batted .300 ten times, including nine times in his first ten years in the majors. The one time that he failed to bat .300, he missed by just one point. But perhaps the most incredible story about this Hall of Famer was his ability to make contact. He averaged only eight strikeouts per season for 14 years. In his last nine seasons he whiffed just five times per year. And in both 1930 and 1932 he fanned only three times, the all-time low for a full-time player.

Who was this one-time Indian–Yankee star who got his best break on the day that Chapman got the worst break of any major league player?

(Answer appears on page 322.)

Chapter Twelve

TOUCHING ALL THE BASES

62. WHOM DID THEY PRECEDE?

See if you can determine whom the following players preceded at their positions in the field.

1. _____ Bill White (Giants)
   a. Nippy Jones b. Steve Bilko c. Joe Torre d. Orlando Cepeda
2. _____ Tony Lazzeri (Yankees)
   a. George Stirnweiss b. Frankie Crosetti c. Joe Gordon d. Jerry Priddy
3. _____ Leo Durocher (Dodgers)
   a. Arky Vaughan b. Pee Wee Reese c. Billy Herman d. Frenchy Bordagaray
4. _____ Eddie Mathews (Braves)
   a. Clete Boyer b. Dennis Menke c. Frank Bolling d. Roy McMillan
5. _____ Bobby Thomson (Giants)
   a. Clint Hartung b. Whitey Lockman c. Willie Mays d. Monte Irvin*
6. _____ Harry Walker (Phillies)
   a. Richie Ashburn b. Del Ennis c. Dick Sisler d. Bill Nicholson
7. _____ Joe DiMaggio (Yankees)
   a. Cliff Mapes b. Mickey Mantle c. Johnny Lindell d. Irv Noren
8. _____ Dom DiMaggio (Red Sox)
   a. Jackie Jensen b. Gene Stephens c. Tommy Umphlett d. Jimmy Piersall

* Position: Center field.

9. _____ Yogi Berra (Yankees)
   a. Elston Howard b. John Blanchard c. Jake Gibbs
   d. Jesse Gonder
10. _____ Del Crandall (Braves)
    a. Joe Torre b. Del Rice c. Stan Lopata d. Bob Uecker

63. WHOM DID THEY SUCCEED?

See if you can figure out whom the following players succeeded at their positions on the field.

1. _____ Babe Dahlgren (Yankees)
   a. Nick Etten b. George McQuinn c. Wally Pipp d. Lou Gehrig
2. _____ Jackie Robinson (Dodgers)
   a. Eddie Miksis b. Eddie Stanky c. Cookie Lavagetto d. Don Zimmer*
3. _____ Chico Carrasquel (White Sox)
   a. Luke Appling b. Cass Michaels c. Don Kolloway d. Willie Miranda
4. _____ Brooks Robinson (Orioles)
   a. Vern Stephens b. Billy Hunter c. George Kell d. Billy Goodman
5. _____ George Selkirk (Yankees)
   a. Ben Chapman b. Earle Combs c. Bob Meusel d. Babe Ruth
6. _____ Carl Yastrzemski (Red Sox)
   a. Ted Williams b. Clyde Vollmer c. Sam Mele d. Al Zarilla
7. _____ Lou Brock (Cardinals)
   a. Enos Slaughter b. Wally Moon c. Stan Musial d. Joe Cunningham
8. _____ Roger Maris (Yankees)
   a. Tommy Henrich b. Hank Bauer c. Norm Siebern d. Harry Simpson
9. _____ John Roseboro (Dodgers)
   a. Roy Campanella b. Bruce Edwards c. Joe Pignatano d. Rube Walker
10. _____ Wes Westrum (Giants)
    a. Ernie Lombardi b. Sal Yvars c. Walker Cooper d. Ray Mueller

* Position: Second base.

64. CHIPS OFF THE OLD BLOCK

The players who are listed below had fathers who preceded them to the major leagues. Name the source of the offspring.

1. _____ Dick Sisler
2. _____ Tom Tresh
3. _____ Mike Hegan
4. _____ Buddy Bell
5. _____ Doug Camilli
6. _____ Hal Lanier
7. _____ Bob Boone
8. _____ Bump Wills
9. _____ Roy Smalley
10. _____ Steve Trout

65. THE GAS HOUSE GANG

In the 1930s the St. Louis Cardinals had a colorful group of players who were known as the Gas House Gang. Match the Gas Housers with the nicknames that they acquired.

1. _____ James Collins   a. Ducky
2. _____ Frankie Frisch   b. Spud
3. _____ Leo Durocher   c. Wild
4. _____ Johnny Martin   d. Rip
5. _____ Joe Medwick   e. Dizzy
6. _____ Enos Slaughter   f. The Fordham Flash
7. _____ Virgil Davis   g. Daffy
8. _____ Jerome Dean   h. The Lip
9. _____ Paul Dean   i. Pepper
10. _____ Bill Hallahan   j. Country

66. THE YEAR OF _____

Fit the phrases listed below to the years to which they apply.

The Whiz Kids
The Amazin' Ones
The Hitless Wonders
Gionfriddo's Gem
Feller's Pick-off (?)
Sandy's Snatch
Maz's Sudden Shot
The Gas House Gang
Larsen's Perfect Game
The M&M Boys
Pesky's Pause
Home Run Baker
Murderers' Row

The Babe Calls His Shot
The Go-Go Sox
The Black Sox
The Wild Hoss of the Osage
Merkle's Boner
Mays's Miracle Catch
Ernie's Snooze
Billy the Kid
Alex's Biggest Strikeout
The Miracle Braves
Mickey's Passed Ball
The Miracle of Coogan's
Bluff

1. _____ (1906)
2. _____ (1908)
3. _____ (1911)
4. _____ (1914)
5. _____ (1919)
6. _____ (1926)
7. _____ (1927)
8. _____ (1931)
9. _____ (1932)
10. _____ (1934)
11. _____ (1939)
12. _____ (1941)
13. _____ (1946)
14. _____ (1947)
15. _____ (1948)
16. _____ (1950)
17. _____ (1951)
18. _____ (1953)
19. _____ (1954)
20. _____ (1955)
21. _____ (1956)
22. _____ (1959)
23. _____ (1960)
24. _____ (1961)
25. _____ (1969)

67. THE MEN AT THE MIKE

Most teams have an announcer who becomes known in his bailiwick as the "voice" of the club. Some of the announcers who are listed in the left-hand column have called the play-by-play with more than one team. But they have made their reputations as the "voice" of one particular club. Match the "voice" with the respective team.

1. _____ Mel Allen   a. Pirates
2. _____ Red Barber   b. Browns
3. _____ Russ Hodges   c. White Sox
4. _____ Lindsey Nelson   d. A's (Oakland)
5. _____ Curt Gowdy   e. Reds
6. _____ By Saam   f. Giants
7. _____ Bob Prince   g. Yankees
8. _____ Vince Scully   h. Tigers
9. _____ Waite Hoyt   i. Dodgers (Brooklyn)
10. _____ Chuck Thompson   j. Red Sox
11. _____ Dizzy Dean   k. Cardinals
12. _____ Jack Brickhouse   l. Orioles
13. _____ Ernie Harwell   m. Dodgers (Los Angeles)
14. _____ Harry Carey   n. Mets
15. _____ Monte Clark   o. Phillies

68. INFIELD INFLATION

The infield of the 1911 Philadelphia Athletics is said to have been worth $100,000; the infield of the 1948 A's is reported to have been valued at $1,000,000. Take the following ten players and place them at their respective positions: Stuffy McInnis, Hank Majeski, Frank Baker, Ferris Fain, Pete Suder, Jack Barry, Eddie Collins, Eddie Joost, Ira Thomas, and Buddy Rosar.

1911 Athletics
1B _____
2B _____
SS _____
3B _____
 C _____

1948 Athletics
1B _____
2B _____
SS _____
3B _____
 C _____

69. PEN NAMES

In the following pairs of names, see if you can distinguish the major league player from the major league writer. Which one was the artist on the diamond?

1. Grantland Rice–Del Rice
2. Dan Parker–Wes Parker
3. Fred Winchell–Walter Winchell
4. Woody Woodward–Stanley Woodward
5. Frank Sullivan–Ed Sullivan
6. Gary Schumacher–Hal Schumacher
7. Dick Williams–Joe Williams
8. Tom Meany–Pat Meany
9. Art Fowler–Gene Fowler
10. Frank Graham–Jack Graham
11. Quentin Reynolds–Carl Reynolds
12. Frank Adams–Babe Adams
13. Bill Dailey–Arthur Dailey
14. Don Gross–Milton Gross
15. Babe Young–Dick Young
16. Red Smith–Hal Smith
17. Babe Twombly–Wells Twombly
18. Earl Lawson–Roxie Lawson
19. Ray Murray–Jim Murray
20. Johnny Powers–Jimmy Powers

70. MATCHING MOGULS

Match the present-day major league moguls in the left-hand column with the big-league teams that they own in the right-hand column.

1. _____ Peter O'Malley
2. _____ Bill Giles
3. _____ Eddie Chiles
4. _____ Tom Monaghan
5. _____ Tribune Co.
6. _____ Bud Selig
7. _____ August Busch, Jr.
8. _____ Charles Bronfman
9. _____ Edward Bennett Williams
10. _____ John Labatt Ltd.
11. _____ Nelson Doubleday,
    Fred Wilpon
12. _____ Joan Kroc
13. _____ Carl Pohlad
14. _____ Jerry Reinsdorf
15. _____ Haywood Sullivan
16. _____ Robert Lurie
17. _____ Richard Jacobs,
    David Jacobs
18. _____ Gene Autry
19. _____ Robert Haas
20. _____ Mac Prine
21. _____ John McMullen
22. _____ Ted Turner
23. _____ Ewing Kauffman
24. _____ George Argyros
25. _____ Marge Schott
26. _____ George Steinbrenner

a. Atlanta
b. Baltimore
c. Boston
d. California
e. Chicago Cubs
f. Chicago
   White Sox
g. Cincinnati
h. Cleveland
i. Detroit
j. Houston
k. Kansas City
l. Los Angeles
m. Milwaukee
n. Minnesota
o. Montreal
p. New York
   Mets
q. New York
   Yankees
r. Oakland
s. Philadelphia
t. Pittsburgh
u. St. Louis
v. San Diego
w. San Francisco
x. Seattle
y. Texas
z. Toronto

71. A STAR IS BORN

Match the players listed with the cities in which they were born.

1. _____ Hank Aaron
2. _____ Johnny Bench
3. _____ Tommy Davis
4. _____ Al Kaline
5. _____ Brooks Robinson
6. _____ Frank Robinson
7. _____ Pete Rose
8. _____ Bob Gibson
9. _____ Jim Hunter
10. _____ Frank McGraw

a. Omaha, Neb.
b. Martinez, Calif.
c. Hertford, N.C.
d. Mobile, Ala.
e. Beaumont, Tex.
f. Oklahoma City, Oklahoma
g. Little Rock, Ark.
h. Cincinnati, Ohio
i. Brookyn, N.Y.
j. Baltimore, Md.

72. THE NATIONAL PASTIME

Baseball truly is the national pastime. Today's players come from every state in the United States except one. They come from large cities, small hamlets, and rural intersects. In the following five quizzes, they come to you in groups of ten. One of the quizzes contains one state that has not produced a present-day major-league player. See how well you can match up the players in the left-hand columns with their places of birth.

Alabama to Georgia

1. _____ Brian Dayett
2. _____ Tim Raines
3. _____ Eddie Murray
4. _____ Don Sutton
5. _____ Jody Davis
6. _____ Don Martin
7. _____ Ron Hassey
8. _____ Kevin McReynolds
9. _____ Goose Gossage
10. _____ Scott Loucks

a. Clio, Ala.
b. Anchorage, Alaska
c. Tuscon, Ariz.
d. Little Rock, Ark.
e. Los Angeles, Calif.
f. Colorado Springs, Colo.
g. New London, Conn.
h. Dover, Del.
i. Sanford, Fla.
j. Gainesville, Ga.

Hawaii to Maryland

1. _____ Rickey Henderson
2. _____ John Shelby
3. _____ Charlie Hough
4. _____ Bob Horner
5. _____ Cal Ripken
6. _____ Don Mattingly
7. _____ Vance Law
8. _____ Bob Stanley
9. _____ Tim Laudner
10. _____ Ron Guidry

a. Honolulu, Hawaii
b. Boise, Idaho
c. Chicago, Ill.
d. Evansville, Ind.
e. Mason City, Iowa
f. Junction City, Kans.
g. Lexington, Ky.
h. Lafayette, La.
i. Portland, Maine
j. Havre de Grace, Md.

Massachusetts to New Jersey

1. _____ Dave Winfield		a. Brockton, Mass.
2. _____ Rick Sutcliffe		b. Detroit, Mich.
3. _____ Wade Boggs		c. St. Paul, Minn.
4. _____ John Lowenstein		d. Jackson, Miss.
5. _____ Rick Cerone		e. Independence, Mo.
6. _____ Frank Tanana		f. Wolf Point, Mont.
7. _____ Charlie Kerfeld		g. Omaha, Neb.
8. _____ Mike Flanagan		h. Carson City, Nev.
9. _____ Steve Balboni		i. Manchester, N. H.
10. _____ Dave Parker		j. Newark, N. J.

New Mexico to South Carolina

1. _____ Willie Randolph		a. Tularosa, N. M.
2. _____ Johnny Ray		b. Brooklyn, N. Y.
3. _____ Steve Ontiveros		c. Goldsboro, N. C.
4. _____ Bruce Sutter		d. Fargo, N. D.
5. _____ Lou Whitaker		e. Dayton, Ohio
6. _____ Davey Lopes		f. Chouteau, Okla.
7. _____ Jerry Narron		g. Pendleton, Ore.
8. _____ Dave Kingman		h. Lancaster, Pa.
9. _____ Mike Schmidt		i. East Providence, R. I.
		j. Holly Hill, S. C.

South Dakota to Wyoming

1. _____ Ron Cey		a. Rapid City, S. D.
2. _____ Dave Collins		b. Memphis, Tenn.
3. _____ Dan Spillner		c. Refugio, Tex.
4. _____ Pat Putnam		d. Bellows Falls, Utah
5. _____ Shane Rawley		e. Bethel, Vt.
6. _____ George Brett		f. Richmond, Va.
7. _____ Bill Madlock		g. Tacoma, Wash.
8. _____ Carlton Fisk		h. Moundsville, W. Va.
9. _____ Johnny Grubb		i. Racine, Wis.
10. _____ Nolan Ryan		j. Casper, Wyo.

73. THE INTERNATIONAL PASTIME

Not all of the major leaguers in the history of baseball have been born on the mainland of the United States. Many of them have come from foreign states, countries, islands, territories, and provinces. See if you can match the players with their place of birth.

1. _____ Sandy Alomar
2. _____ Cesar Cedeno
3. _____ Bert Campaneris
4. _____ Rod Carew
5. _____ Dave Concepcion
6. _____ Irish McIlveen
7. _____ Jorge Orta
8. _____ Ferguson Jenkins
9. _____ Bobby Thomson
10. _____ Moe Drabowsky
11. _____ Elmer Valo
12. _____ Masanori Murakami
13. _____ Reno Bertoia
14. _____ Elrod Hendricks
15. _____ Andre Rodgers
16. _____ Mike Lum
17. _____ Al Campanis
18. _____ Jimmy Austin

a. Otsuki, Japan
b. Swansea, Wales
c. Gatun, Panama
d. Salinas, Puerto Rico
e. Chartham, (Ontario) Canada
f. Ozanna, Poland
g. Mantanzas, Cuba
h. Honolulu, Hawaii
i. Mazatian, Mexico
j. Santo Domingo, Dominican Republic
k. Nassau, Bahamas
l. Kos, Greece
m. Glasgow, Scotland
n. Ribnik, Czechoslovakia
o. St. Vito, Udine, Italy
p. Aragua, Venezuela
q. St. Thomas, Virgin Islands
r. Belfast, Ireland

Where Are The Iron Men?

What's happened to the complete game in World Series play?

Why, in the first World Series (1903) that was ever played, a Pirate strongman pitched five complete games. That's right, it's still a record. But, in that same series, a rubber arm for the Red Sox pitched four complete games. That's the second highest number of complete games that has ever been pitched in one series.

As recently as 1956, though, five different Yankee pitchers threw complete games in consecutive contests. They were Whitey Ford, Tom Sturdivant, Don Larsen, Bob Turley, and Johnny Kucks, respectively. That's a record, too.

They must not make them the way they used to, though. Take the National League, for example. In the 1970s, 61 World Series games were played. But National League pitchers threw only five complete games. (And one of the pitchers hurled full games twice.) That's a complete-game average of 8.2 percent.

During the 1970s, 29 different pitchers in the National League started a game. Some of them did it a number of times. But only four of those 29 pitchers managed to complete a game. That's a pitcher-completion average of 13.8 percent.

National League pitchers began the decade by failing to get a complete game out of the first seven starters. In 1971 two different pitchers completed three games. But from 1972 to Game Two of the 1977 series, Senior Circuit hurlers failed to complete a game in 31 attempts. Two different pitchers completed games for the National League representative in 1977, but Chub Feeney's league got on another streak: in the next 18 games the National League did not get a route-going performance from one of its starters.

If you can name two of the four complete-game pitchers, you're already doing better than the National League hurlers of the 1970s did. If you can name three of them, you can take your turn with Ford, Kucks, *et al*. If you can come up with four of the pitchers, Bill Dinneen of the 1903 Red Sox will have to move over in order to make room for you. And if you can spiel off all four pitchers, including the one pitcher who did it twice, you and Deacon Phillippe of the 1903 Pirates are in a class by yourselves.

(Answer appears on page 322.)

Chapter Thirteen

THE MANAGERS

74. QUICK QUIZZING
THE MANAGERS

I.

From the names listed in the right-hand column, list in order: 1.) the youngest manager ever to begin a season, 2.) the youngest manager ever to finish a season, 3.) the youngest manager ever to win a pennant, 4.) the oldest manager ever to debut as manager, and 5.) the oldest manager ever to win a pennant for the first time.

1. _____ Roger Peckinpaugh
2. _____ Tom Sheehan
3. _____ Burt Shotton
4. _____ Joe Cronin
5. _____ Lou Boudreau

II.

Match the successful managers listed on the right-hand side with the number of pennants and World Series (combined total) they won. The total is contained in parentheses on the left-hand side.

1. _____ (17)   Walter Alston
2. _____ (16)   Casey Stengel
3. _____ (14)   John McGraw
4. _____ (13)   Joe McCarthy
5. _____ (11)   Connie Mack

III.

The men listed on the left-hand side were all playing managers who won at least one pennant. Yet each was traded—while still a player on that team—to another one which, in every case but one, the player continued to manage. Match the playing manager with the trade in which he was connected.

1. _____ Joe Cronin   a. Indians–Red Sox
2. _____ Rogers Hornsby   b. Senators–Tigers
3. _____ Lou Boudreau   c. Cardinals–Giants
4. _____ Bucky Harris   d. Cubs–Yankees
5. _____ Frank Chance   e. Senators–Red Sox

IV.

Match the managers in the right-hand column with their respective all-time winning percentages in the left-hand column.

1. _____ (.614)   Billy Southworth
2. _____ (.593)   Frank Chance
3. _____ (.593)   John McGraw
4. _____ (.589)   Joe McCarthy
5. _____ (.582)   Al Lopez

75. DID THEY OR DIDN'T THEY . . . MANAGE?

When we look back, we sometimes find it hard to sort out fact from fiction in baseball. See if you can zero in on the 20 players who became managers from the following list of 40.

Joe Adcock
Bobby Brown
Joe Gordon
Ken Keltner
Enos Slaughter
Kerby Farrell
Bill Dickey
Bucky Walters
Bobby Wine
Eddie Pellagrini
Walker Cooper
Nippy Jones
Phil Cavarretta
Christy Mathewson
Sid Hudson
Bob Friend
Bobby Thomson
Luke Appling
Eddie Joost
Mickey Vernon

Red Rolfe
Roy Smalley
Duke Snider
Ben Chapman
Jim Landis
Jim Lemon
Jerry Lynch
Freddie Fitzsimmons
Irv Noren
Wally Post
Bob Elliott
Eddie Lopat
Jerry Priddy
Gene Hermanski
Babe Ruth
Johnny Pesky
Jim Hegan
Dick Sisler
Mel McGaha
Eddie Stanky

1. _____
2. _____
3. _____
4. _____
5. _____
6. _____
7. _____
8. _____
9. _____
10. _____

11. _____
12. _____
13. _____
14. _____
15. _____
16. _____
17. _____
18. _____
19. _____
20. _____

76. POST-WAR WORLD SERIES WINNERS

There have been 29 managers who have led their teams to World Series victories in the post-World War II era. Fourteen of them have been National League managers; fifteen of them have been American League skippers. One of them has won titles in both leagues. See how many of them you can name.

National League	American League
1. _____	1. _____
2. _____	2. _____
3. _____	3. _____
4. _____	4. _____
5. _____	5. _____
6. _____	6. _____
7. _____	7. _____
8. _____	8. _____
9. _____	9. _____
10. _____	10. _____
11. _____	11. _____
12. _____	12. _____
13. _____	13. _____
14. _____	14. _____
	15. _____

77. BACK-TO-BACK PENNANT WINNERS

There have been 11 major league managers in the post-World War II era who have led their teams to consecutive pennants. Two of them have done it twice. See if you can place the name with the period.

1. _____ (1949–53)
2. _____ (1952–53)
3. _____ (1955–56)
4. _____ (1955–58)*
5. _____ (1957–58)
6. _____ (1961–63)
7. _____ (1965–66)*
8. _____ (1967–68)
9. _____ (1969–71)
10. _____ (1972–73)
11. _____ (1975–76)
12. _____ (1976–77)
13. _____ (1977–78)

* The second time.

78. MANAGERS IN SEARCH OF A PENNANT

Name the ten managers from the following 20 who never led a team to the pennant: Red Rolfe, Steve O'Neill, Eddie Stanky, Bill Rigney, Al Dark, Birdie Tebbetts, Fred Hutchinson, Al Lopez, Mike Higgins, Bobby Bragan, Danny Murtaugh, Harry Walker, Mel Ott, Sam Mele, Hank Bauer, Fred Haney, Johnny Keane, Gene Mauch, Dick Williams, and Paul Richards.

1. _____
2. _____
3. _____
4. _____
5. _____
6. _____
7. _____
8. _____
9. _____
10. _____

79. YOU'RE HIRED TO BE FIRED

In the left-hand column are listed men who managed 16 different major league clubs. To their right is noted the team that they managed (many of them guided more than one) and the year in which they were succeeded by a manager who started the season with his team. This eliminates interim managers who finished up a season while their owners were looking for full-time field leaders. Some of the managers who are listed were fired, some resigned, and one died. Match them with their successors who are listed in the right-hand column.

1. _____ Joe McCarthy (Yanks, 1947)

2. _____ Yogi Berra (Yanks, 1965)

3. _____ John McGraw (Giants, 1933)

4. _____ Mel Ott (Giants, 1949)*

5. _____ Leo Durocher (Dodgers, 1949)*

6. _____ Charlie Dressen (Dodgers, 1954)

7. _____ Billy Southworth (Cards, 1946)

8. _____ Johnny Keane (Cards, 1965)

9. _____ Eddie Sawyer (Phils, 1961)

10. _____ Danny Murtaugh (Pirates, 1965)

11. _____ Fred Hutchinson (Reds, 1965)

12. _____ Leo Durocher (Cubs, 1973)

13. _____ Birdie Tebbetts (Braves, 1963)

a. Burt Shotton
b. Bill Terry
c. Leo Durocher
d. Dick Sisler
e. Bucky Harris
f. Bobby Bragan
g. Johnny Keane
h. Eddie Dyer
i. Walt Alston
j. Gene Mauch
k. Whitey Lockman
l. Harry Walker
m. Red Schoendienst
n. Earl Weaver
o. Al Lopez
p. Al Dark
q. Kerby Farrell
r. Joe McCarthy
s. Rogers Hornsby
t. Billy Martin

* These managers were involved in two shake-ups by team organizations shortly into the season.

14. _____ Al Lopez
         (Indians, 1957)
15. _____ Mayo Smith
         (Tigers, 1971)
16. _____ Dick Williams
         (A's, 1974)
17. _____ Zack Taylor
         (Browns, 1952)
18. _____ Marty Marion
         (White Sox, 1957)
19. _____ Joe Cronin
         (Red Sox, 1948)
20. _____ Hank Bauer
         (Orioles, 1969)

80. MANAGERIAL HALF TRUTHS

Mark "T" or "F" for "True" or "False" before each statement.

1. _____ Joe Cronin was the last Red Sox manager to direct the Bosox to a World Series victory.

2. _____ Joe Cronin was the last Senator manager to win a pennant.

3. _____ Lou Boudreau was the last Indian manager to win a World Series.

4. _____ Bill Carrigan (1915–16) has been the only Red Sox manager to direct Boston to back-to-back world championships.

5. _____ Del Baker was the first bench manager to guide the Tigers to a pennant (1940).

6. _____ Mickey Cochrane has been the only Tiger manager to guide the Bengals to back-to-back pennants.

7. _____ Bill Rigney was the last Giant manager to lead his charges to a pennant.

8. _____ Bill Dickey never managed the Yankees.

9. _____ Chuck Dressen was the last manager to win back-to-back pennants (1952–53) with the Dodgers.

10. _____ Walter Alston has been the only manager to lead the Dodgers to the world championship.

11. _____ Leo Durocher's tenure as manager of the Dodgers was longer than his reign as boss of the Giants.

12. _____ Charlie Grimm never managed a World Series winner.

13. _____ Frank Chance was the only manager of the Cubs who has won a world championship.

14. _____ Eddie Dyer, Johnny Keane, and Red Schoendienst have led the Cardinals to world titles in the post-World War II era.

15. _____ Frankie Frisch was a retired player when the Cardinals won the pennant and World Series in 1934.

16. _____ Al Lopez won pennants with two different clubs.

17. _____ Fred Haney directed the Braves to their first world title in 1957.

18. _____ Bucky Harris was the only Senator manager to lead his team to two pennants.

19. _____ Bucky Harris was the youngest manager to lead his team to a world title.

20. _____ Gil Hodges had a losing record as a major league manager.

21. _____ Rogers Hornsby never managed in the American League.

22. _____ Ralph Houk won pennants in his first three years as manager of the Yankees.

23. _____ Miller Huggins won more World Series than he lost.

24. _____ Fred Hutchinson never managed a pennant winner.

25. _____ Hughie Jennings of the Tigers (1907–09) was the only manager to lose three consecutive World Series.

26. _____ Fielder Jones of the White Sox was the winning manager in the only intercity World Series in Chicago.

27. _____ Johnny Keane was the last Cardinal manager to lead the Redbirds to the world title.

28. _____ Al Lopez, in his first nine years of managing (1951–59), never brought his teams home worse than second.

29. _____ Connie Mack's teams won nine pennants, but they appeared in only eight World Series.

30. _____ Gene Mauch managed the last pennant winner for the Phillies.

31. _____ Joe McCarthy had a better World Series winning percentage with the Yankees than Casey Stengel.

32. _____ John McGraw lost more World Series than any other team leader.

33. _____ Bill McKechnie was the only Red manager to lead his team to two consecutive pennants.

34. _____ Walter Alston was the only National League manager to lead his team to more than one pennant in the 1960s.

35. _____ Walter Alston's managerial opponent in the 1965 World Series was Sam Mele.

36. _____ Danny Murtaugh was the only Pirate manager to lead his team to the world title.

37. _____ Steve O'Neill was the last Tiger manager to lead the Bengals to the world championship.

38. _____ Wilbert Robinson won more pennants with the Dodgers than Leo Durocher.

39. _____ Billy Martin led two different teams to pennants.

40. _____ Red Schoendienst won more consecutive pennants as manager of the Cardinals than any other Redbird leader.

158

41. _____ Luke Sewell was the only Brown manager to lead his team to a pennant.

42. _____ Bill Virdon managed the Yankees.

43. _____ Mayo Smith's 1968 Tigers were the first team to defeat the Cardinals in the World Series since Joe McCarthy's 1943 Yankees.

44. _____ Billy Southworth won pennants with two different National League teams.

45. _____ Tris Speaker never managed a World Series winner.

46. _____ Earl Weaver has a winning record in World Series play.

47. _____ Bill Terry's managerial opponent in the 1933 Series (Giants–Senators) was Bucky Harris.

48. _____ Hank Bauer led a team to a World Series sweep.

49. _____ Rogers Hornsby won more games than he lost in World Series play.

50. _____ Luke Appling, Ted Lyons, and Jimmy Dykes all managed the White Sox.

The Trivia Tandem

Sometimes we have a tendency to remember events which happened long ago better than those which occurred "only yesterday."

Take the case of Joe DiMaggio and Pete Rose, for example. Both of them manufactured the longest batting streaks in the history of their respective leagues. In 1941 DiMaggio hit safely in 56 consecutive games, which is the major league record; in 1978 Rose batted cleanly in 44 consecutive games, which is the modern-day National League record.

On the nights on which their respective streaks came to a close, they were handcuffed by a starting and a relieving pitcher. Much has been written about the duo of Indian pitchers who halted DiMaggio's streak. Jim Bagby, the son of a former 31-game season winner for the Indians, was the starter; Al Smith, who won 12 of 25 decisions that year, came on in relief.

So far little has been written about the two Brave pitchers who helped to stop Rose's streak. Undoubtedly, in time, they will become a more important trivia tandem. One of them was a rookie at the time; the other one was a journey-man relief pitcher.

I'll be surprised if you can name both of them. Can you?
(Answer appears on page 322.)

Chapter Fourteen

THE ALL-STAR GAME

81. ALL-STAR GAME STANDOUTS

Match the players who are listed below with the All-Star
Game records that they set.

Phil Cavarretta	Tommy Bridges
Roberto Clemente	Terry Moore
Whitey Ford	Ted Williams
Yogi Berra	Stan Musial
Willie Mays	Pete Rose
Satchel Paige	Dave Winfield
Nelson Fox	Rod Carew
Charlie Gehringer	Brooks Robinson
Joe DiMaggio	Pie Traynor
Tony Oliva	Goose Gossage
Willie Jones	Atlee Hammaker
Hank Aaron	Joe Morgan
Luis Aparicio	George Brett
Tommy Bridges	Jim Palmer
Dwight Gooden	Steve Garvey
Mickey Mantle	Don Drysdale
Lefty Gomez	

1. _____ He, like Willie Mays, played on 17
winning teams.
2. _____ He played on 15 losing teams.
3. _____ He pinch-hit ten times.
4. _____ He has been the youngest player.
5. _____ He was the oldest participant.
6. _____ He played five different positions in
total games.
7. _____ He batted .500 in total games.

8. _____ He had the most total at-bats (10) without a hit.
9. _____ He had the most at bats in a game (7) without a hit.
10. _____ He scored four runs in one game.
11. _____ He was the American Leaguer who hit in seven consecutive games.
12. _____ He was the National Leaguer who hit in seven consecutive games.
13. _____ He, like Ted Williams, reached base safely five times in one game.
14. _____ He has hit four doubles in total games.
15. _____ He hit two triples in one game.
16. _____ He struck out four times in one game.
17. _____ He's hit three sacrifice flies in total games.
18. _____ He, like Pete Rose, hit into three double plays.
19. _____ He was the only player to steal home.
20. _____ He got caught stealing twice in one game.
21. _____ He finished six games.
22. _____ He pitched 19⅓ innings in total games.
23. _____ He pitched six innings in one game.
24. _____ He allowed 13 runs in total games.
25. _____ He allowed seven runs in one inning.
26. _____ He allowed seven hits in one game.
27. _____ He granted three home runs in one game.
28. _____ He played ten games at first base.
29. _____ He played 13 games at second base.
30. _____ He played ten games at shortstop.
31. _____ He played 14 games at catcher.
32. _____ He stole six bases in total games.

82. WHO'S WHO?

Identify the player who starred in a particular year.

1. _____ (1933) Who hit the event's first home run?

2. _____ (1934) Who struck out Babe Ruth, Lou Gehrig, Jimmie Foxx, Al Simmons, and Joe Cronin consecutively?

3. _____ (1934) Who was the National Leaguer who homered for the second consecutive year? (In World Series play he didn't hit a home run in 197 official at-bats.)

4. _____ (1935) Who three-hit the National League over a record six innings?

5. _____ (1937) Who was the American League pitcher who won his third decision in five years?

6. _____ (1937) Who was the National Leaguer, the Triple Crown winner that year, who paced the Senior Circuit to victory with four hits?

7. _____ (1937) Who was the Hall of Famer whose injury in this year's game abruptly short-circuited a great career?

8. _____ (1937) Who was the Hall of Famer whose line drive broke the preceding pitcher's toe?

9. _____ (1941) Who was the player whose three-run homer with two outs in the bottom of the ninth lifted the American League to a 7–5 victory?

10. _____ (1941) Who was the first player to hit two home runs in one game?

11. _____ (1942) Who was the National Leaguer who hit the game's first pinch-hit home run?

12. _____ (1943) Who was the National League pitcher who tied Carl Hubbell's mark of six strikeouts in one game?

13. _____ (1943) Who was the DiMaggio who hit a single, a triple, and a home run?

14. _____ (1944) Who was the National League first baseman who became the first player to reach base five times in one game?

15. _____ (1946) Who was the player whose

four hits, including two home runs, and five RBIs led the American League to a 12–0 win?

16. _____ (1946) Who was the pitcher who gave up his first and only eephus ball home run?

17. _____ (1948) Who was the pitcher whose two-run single turned the game in the American League's favor?

18. _____ (1949) Who were the first four blacks to play in the All-Star Game?

19. _____

20. _____

21. _____

22. _____ (1950) Who was the National League second baseman whose 14th-inning home run gave the Senior Circuit a 2–1 victory?

23. _____ (1950) Who was the Hall of Famer who broke his elbow making a great catch off the left-field wall?

24. _____ (1952) Who was the Cub outfielder whose two-run home run gave the National League a 3–2 win in a five-inning game that was shortened by rain?

25. _____ (1953) Who was the great black pitcher who appeared in his only All-Star Game?

26. _____ (1954) Who was the American League third baseman whose two home runs and five RBIs tied a record?

27. _____ (1955) Who was the Hall of Famer whose home run in the bottom of the 12th gave the National League a sudden-death victory?

28. _____ (1956) Who was the third baseman whose great fielding plays and three hits sparked the National League?

29. _____ (1959) Who was the four-time home run champ whose run-tying single got the National League even in the eighth inning?

30. _____ (1959) Who was the four-time home run champ who followed the above with a game-winning triple?

31. _____ (1960) Who was the famous center fielder who got three hits in each of that year's two games?

32. _____ (1963) Who was the player whose 24th All-Star appearance set a record?

33. _____ (1964) Who was the player whose three-run homer in the bottom of the ninth gave the National League a dramatic come-from-behind 7–4 win?

34. _____ (1966) Who was the infield speedster whose tenth-inning single gave the National League a 2–1 win?

35. _____ (1967) Who was the big first baseman whose 15th-inning homer gave the National League a victory in the All-Star Game's longest contest?

36. _____ (1967) Who was the Cub pitcher whose six strikeouts tied the mark set by Hubbell and equaled by Vander Meer?

37. _____ (1969) Who was the National League first baseman who became the fourth player to hit two home runs in one game?

38. _____ (1971) Who hit the tape-measure home run on top of the roof at Tigers Stadium?

39. _____ (1971) Who became the first player to homer for both leagues?

40. _____ (1974) Who was the player, not even listed on the All-Star ballot, who was the game's star?

41. _____ (1975) Who was the long-ball-hitting left-fielder who hit a three-run pinch-hit homer?

42. _____ (1978) Who was the National League first baseman whose single tied the score in the third and whose triple proved to be the game-winner?

43. _____ (1979) Who was the Met outfielder who hit a pinch-hit home run in the eighth to tie the game, and walked with the bases loaded in the ninth to win the game?

44. _____ (1981) Who was the eight-time home run champ whose two-run homer in the eighth inning gave the National League a one-run victory?

45. _____ Who was the National League hurler who pitched in six consecutive games?

46. _____ Who was the American League moundsman who pitched in six consecutive games?

The Black Sox

The 1919–20 Chicago White Sox, referred to in history books as the infamous Black Sox, had a staggering array of talent.

In the season before they were declared ineligible to play professional baseball—for allegedly conspiring to fix the 1919 World Series—Joe Jackson batted .382, Happy Felsch hit .338, and Buck Weaver averaged .333. Moundsmen Claude "Lefty" Williams and Ed Cicotte won 22 and 21 games, respectively. Chick Gandil and Swede Risberg were solid starters, and Fred McMullin was a valuable utility man. It's little wonder that the White Sox, who were the best team in baseball at the time, did not win another pennant, after 1919, for another 40 years. Their roster was razed.

If it were not for the scandal, Jackson, Weaver, and Cicotte would be comfortably enshrined at the Baseball Hall of Fame in Cooperstown, N. Y. Felsch and Williams might be, too.

The notoriety of the trial of the disqualified players, however, detracted from the honorable records of the Sox stalwarts who transcended the alleged temptation and remained unsullied by the scandal.

History books have paid more attention to the barred players than they have to the untainted stars who managed to win their niche in Cooperstown. There were three such players. If you can name two of them, you deserve a special niche of your own.

(Answer appears on page 322.)

Chapter Fifteen

THE CHAMPIONSHIP SERIES

83. FROM BANDO TO WASHINGTON

Match the following players with the Championship Series records that they set: Richie Hebner, Pete Rose, Jay Johnstone, Reggie Jackson, Claudell Washington, George Brett, Jim Palmer, Mickey Rivers, Phil Niekro, Fred Lynn, Paul Blair, Mike Cuellar, Jerry Martin, Chris Chambliss, Paul Popovich, Steve Garvey, Bob Robertson, Bill North, Chet Lemon, and Sal Bando.

1. _____ He was the youngest non-pitcher to play in the Championship Series.
2. _____ He got 11 hits in one series.
3. _____ He went hitless in 31 consecutive at-bats.
4. _____ He appeared in ten series.
5. _____ He was the pinch-hitter who batted for six total bases in one series.
6. _____ He played on seven losing teams.
7. _____ He played in seven series with one team.
8. _____ He was the oldest non-pitcher to play.
9. _____ He hit .386 in total series.
10. _____ He hit .778 in a three-game series.
11. _____ He hit .611 in a five-game series.
12. _____ He went hitless in 13 total series at-bats.
13. _____ He has a .728 total series slugging average.
14. _____ He slugged the ball for a 1.250 average in one series.
15. _____ He had five hits in one game.

16. _____ He got three consecutive pinch-hit base hits.

17. _____ He got six consecutive hits.

18. _____ He was the only pitcher to hit a grand slam.

19. _____ He had the biggest time span (1969–82) between series appearances.

20. _____ He was the only player to decide a 1–0 game with a home run in the American League's favor.

84. FROM BAYLOR TO WYNN

Match the following players with the Championship Series records that they set: Pete Rose, Rusty Staub, Bob Robertson, Don Baylor, Joe Morgan, Jimmy Wynn, Steve Balboni, Cesar Geronimo, Pedro Guerrero, Tony Taylor, Davey Lopes, Reggie Jackson, Hal McRae, Tug McGraw, Bert Blyleven, Phil Niekro, Jim Hunter, Dave Giusti, Jim Palmer, and Bruce Kison.

1. _____ He sports a 4–0 record.
2. _____ He started ten games.
3. _____ He finished nine games.
4. _____ He pitched five complete games.
5. _____ He has been the youngest pitcher to appear.
6. _____ He has been the oldest pitcher to appear.
7. _____ He went down swinging seven consecutive times.
8. _____ He hit two home runs in consecutive innings.
9. _____ He drove home 21 runs in total series.
10. _____ He collected ten RBIs in one series.
11. _____ He grounded into five double plays in total series.
12. _____ He grounded into three double plays in one game.
13. _____ He stole nine bases in total series.
14. _____ He struck out eight times in one series.
15. _____ He walked nine times in one series.
16. _____ He walked 23 times in total series.
17. _____ He was caught stealing six times in total series.
18. _____ He has been the only player to steal home.
19. _____ He played four positions in series play.
20. _____ He hit for 14 total bases in one game.

85. FROM ANDERSON TO WYNN

Match the following players with the Championship Series records that they set: Tug McGraw, Dave Giusti, Jerry Reuss, Ken Holtzman, Dave McNally, Jim Hunter, Eric Show, Steve Carlton, Mike Cuellar, Jim Palmer, Dave Stieb, Nolan Ryan, Tommy John, Earl Weaver, Sparky Anderson, Billy Martin, Steve Garvey, George Brett, Pete Rose, and Gaylord Perry.

1. _____ He managed four different clubs in series play.

2. _____ He managed in six American League series.

3. _____ He managed five winning teams.

4. _____ He allowed four walks in one inning, nine walks in one game, and 13 walks in one series.

5. _____ He struck out seven batters in relief.

6. _____ He struck out 46 batters in total series.

7. _____ He struck out 18 batters in one series.

8. _____ He hit three batsmen and threw four wild pitches in total series.

9. _____ He recorded five saves in total series.

10. _____ He issued 28 walks in total series.

11. _____ He recorded three saves in one series.

12. _____ He allowed five home runs in one series.

13. _____ He lost seven consecutive games.

14. _____ He got touched for 19 hits in one series.

15. _____ He allowed 12 home runs in total series.

16. _____ He pitched 11 consecutive hitless innings in one game.

17. _____ He pitched 19⅓ consecutive scoreless innings in total series.

18. _____ He scored 22 runs in total series.

19. _____ He sprayed 45 hits in total series.

20. _____ He banged six long hits in one series.

86. FROM BANDO TO YASTRZEMSKI

All of the players who are listed below hit .400 or better for an American League team in a Championship Series. Ten of them hit .500 or better. See if you can zero in on the ten .500 hitters. One of them did it twice.

Spike Owen	Frank White
Bob Boone	Chris Chambliss
Wally Joyner	Carlton Fisk
Brooks Robinson	Graig Nettles
Eddie Murray	Thurman Munson
Kirk Gibson	Boog Powell
Carl Yastrzemski	Amos Otis
Fred Lynn	Chris Chambliss*
Reggie Jackson	Brooks Robinson*
Larry Milbourne	Charlie Moore
Rod Carew	Mickey Rivers
Paul Blair	Tony Oliva
Sal Bando	Jerry Mumphrey
Bob Watson	Rick Burleson
Cliff Johnson	George Brett
Cecil Cooper	Hal McRae
Cal Ripken	Reggie Jackson*

* They hit .400 or better twice.

1. _____
2. _____
3. _____
4. _____
5. _____
6. _____
7. _____
8. _____
9. _____
10. _____

87. FROM BAKER TO ZISK

All of the players who are listed below hit .400 or better for a National League team in a Championship Series. Seven of them hit .500 or better. See if you can zero in on the seven .500 hitters.

Darrell Porter	Dave Concepcion*
Jose Cruz	Willie Stargell**
Bob Boone	Pete Rose
Dusty Baker	Derrel Thomas
Mike Schmidt	Bob Robertson
Jay Johnstone	Terry Puhl
Bill Russell	Gary Carter
Steve Garvey	Ozzie Smith*
Phil Garner	Pete Rose**
Bob Tolan	Willie Stargell**
Tony Perez	Richie Zisk
Art Shamsky	Cleon Jones
Orlando Cepeda	Willie McCovey
Dave Concepcion	Dave Cash
Willie Stargell	Terry Landrum
Pete Rose	Gary Matthews
Ozzie Smith	

* They hit .400 or better twice.
** They hit .400 or better three times.

1. _____
2. _____
3. _____
4. _____
5. _____
6. _____
7. _____

88. FROM AARON TO STAUB

Match the following players with the number of Championship Series home runs that they've hit: Greg Luzinski, Rich Hebner, Boog Powell, Pete Rose, Jim Rice, George Brett, Gary Matthews, Willie Stargell, Tony Perez, Steve Garvey, Reggie Jackson, Ron Cey, Graig Nettles, Johnny Bench, Al Oliver, Hank Aaron, Sal Bando, Bill Madlock, Rusty Staub, Bob Robertson, and George Foster.

1. _____ (9)
2. _____ (8)
3. _____ (6)
4. _____ (5)
5. _____ (5)
6. _____ (5)
7. _____ (5)
8. _____ (5)
9. _____ (4)
10. _____ (4)
11. _____ (4)
12. _____ (4)
13. _____ (4)
14. _____ (3)
15. _____ (3)
16. _____ (3)
17. _____ (3)
18. _____ (3)
19. _____ (3)
20. _____ (3)
21. _____ (2)

89. CHAMPIONSHIP SERIES GAME WINNERS

National League

There have been many dramatic hits in Championship Series play. Some of them are referred to below. See if you can identify the players who provided the drama.

1. _____ Who was the Red in Game One of 1970 whose 10th-inning single, which was followed by Lee May's two-run double, broke up a scoreless pitching duel between winner Gary Nolan and Doc Ellis?

2. _____ Who was the Red in Game Three of 1970 whose single in the eighth inning enabled Cincinnati to break a 2–2 tie and sweep the Bucs?

3. _____ Who was the Pirate in Game Three of 1971 whose eighth-inning homer off Juan Marichal snapped a 1–1 tie and gave Bob Johnson a 2–1 win?

4. _____ Who was the Pirate in Game Three of 1972 who homered for the first Pittsburgh run and drove in the tie-breaking counter in the eighth inning to give his team a 3–2 win?

5. _____ Who was the Red in Game One of 1973 whose ninth-inning homer off Tom Seaver gave Cincinnati a 2–1 come-from-behind victory?

6. _____ Who was the Red in Game Four of 1973 whose 12th-inning home run off Met pitcher Harry Parker gave Cincinnati a 2–1 win?

7. _____ Who was the Dodger in Game Three of 1977 whose ninth-inning single capped a three-run rally that lifted Los Angeles over the Phillies, 6–5?

8. _____ Who was the Dodger in Game Four of 1978 whose tenth-inning single, following Garry Maddox's muff of a fly ball, scored Ron Cey with the winning run to give the Dodgers the National League Championship?

9. _____ Who was the Pirate in Game One of 1979 whose three-run homer in the 11th gave Pittsburgh a 5–2 win over the Reds?

10. _____ Who was the Pirate in Game Two of 1979 whose tenth-inning single gave Pittsburgh a 3–2 win?

11. _____ Who was the Phillie in Game Five of

1980 whose tenth-inning double downed Houston, 8–7, and gave Philadelphia its first pennant since 1950?

12. _____ Who was the Expo in Game Three of 1981 whose three-run homer gave Montreal a 4–1 win over the Dodgers?

13. _____ Who was the Dodger in Game Five of 1981 whose homer with two outs in the ninth inning gave Los Angeles a 2–1 win over Montreal and the National League pennant?

14. _____ Who was the Cardinal in Game Two of 1982 whose ninth-inning single gave St. Louis a 4–3 win over Atlanta?

15. _____ Who was the Phillie in Game One of 1983 whose home run gave Steve Carlton a 1–0 win over Jerry Reuss and the Dodgers?

16. _____ Who was the Padre in Game Four of 1984 whose two-run homer in the bottom of the ninth inning gave San Diego a 7–5 win over the Cubs?

17. _____ Who was the Astro in Game One of 1986 whose home run gave Mike Scott a 1–0 victory over Dwight Gooden and the Mets?

18. _____ Who was the Met in Game Three of 1986 whose two-run homer in the ninth inning lifted New York over Houston, 6–5?

19. _____ Who was the Astro in Game Four of 1986 whose two-run homer made the difference in Houston's 3–1 win over the Mets?

20. _____ Who was the Met in Game Five of 1986 whose 12th-inning single gave New York a 2–1 win over Houston?

American League

1. _____ Who was the Oriole in Game One of 1969 whose two-out suicide squeeze bunt in the 12th inning gave Baltimore a 4–3 win over Minnesota?

2. _____ Who was the Oriole in Game Two of 1969 whose pinch-hit single in the bottom of the 11th inning gave Dave McNally a 1–0 win over Minnesota?

3. _____ Who was the Oriole in Game One of 1971 whose two-run double in the seventh inning ignited Baltimore to a 5–3 win over Oakland?

4. _____ Who was the A in Game Five of

175

1972 whose only hit of the series drove home George Hendrick with the winning run of the game, 2–1, and the series.

5. _____ Who was the A in Game Three of 1973 whose home run in the bottom of the 11th inning gave Ken Holtzman a 2–1 win over Mike Cuellar of the Orioles?

6. _____ Who was the Oriole in Game Four of 1973 whose eighth-inning homer gave Baltimore a come-from-behind 5–4 victory over the A's?

7. _____ Who was the A in Game Three of 1974 whose home run provided Vida Blue the edge in a 1–0 win over Jim Palmer of the Orioles?

8. _____ Who was the A in Game Four of 1974 whose double scored the deciding run in the game, 2–1, and the series, 3–1?

9. _____ Who was the Yankee in Game Five of 1976 whose sudden-death homer in the ninth gave the Yankees their first pennant since 1964?

10. _____ Who was the Yankee in Game Three of 1978 whose two-run homer in the eighth inning gave New York a 6–5 win over Kansas City?

11. _____ Who was the Yankee in Game Four of 1978 whose sixth-inning homer gave New York a 2–1 win and the American League pennant?

12. _____ Who was the Oriole in Game One of 1979 whose three-run pinch-hit home run gave Baltimore a 6–3 win over California?

13. _____ Who was the Angel whose looping double in the bottom of the ninth gave California a 4–3 win?

14. _____ Who was the Royal in Game Three of 1980 whose three-run homer powered Kansas City to its first pennant?

15. _____ Who was the Brewer in Game Three of 1982 whose two-run homer proved to be the margin of difference, 5–3, over the Angels?

16. _____ Who was the Brewer in Game Five of 1982 who singled in the tying and winning runs to give Milwaukee its first American League pennant?

17. _____ Who was the Oriole in Game Four of 1983 whose tenth-inning home run was the catalyst in Baltimore's pennant-winning game?

18. _____ Who was the Tiger in Game Two of 1984 whose two-run double in the eleventh inning sparked Detroit to a 5–3 victory?

19. _____ Who was the Angel in Game Four of

176

1986 whose ninth-inning hit into the left-field corner gave California a 4–3 victory and a 3–1 lead in games?

20. _____ Who was the Red Sox player in Game Five of 1986 whose two-run homer in the bottom of the ninth gave Boston a 6–5 victory and prevented California manager Gene Mauch from winning his first pennant?

The Shoe Polish Plays

Everything is not always black and white in baseball. But in the following two instances it was.

In the fourth game of the 1957 World Series, with the Yankees leading the host Braves by the score of 5–4 in the tenth inning, a pinch-hitter came to the plate for Warren Spahn. A pitch from Tommy Byrne to the pinch-hitter was called a ball. But the substitute batter, who claimed that the ball had hit him, retrieved it and showed the enlightened Augie Donatelli a smudge of black shoe polish on the spheroid. Bob Grim relieved Byrne and was greeted with a game-tying double by Johnny Logan and a game-winning homer by Eddie Mathews. So the shoe polish call was a pivotal one.

In the fifth-and-final game of the 1969 World Series, a similar play took place. In the sixth inning one of the host Mets was hit on the foot with a pitch by Dave McNally. Umpire Lou DiMuro called the pitch a ball. The batter protested. Upon inspection of the ball, DiMuro gave the hitter first base: he detected shoe polish on the ball. The shoe polish call once again proved to be pivotal. At the time the Mets were losing 3–0. But Donn Clendenon followed with a two-run homer, and the Mets were back in the game. Al Weis homered in the seventh to tie the game. The Mets went on to score the decisive two runs of a 5–3 series-clinching victory in the eighth on doubles by two Met outfielders and errors by two Oriole infielders.

Both of the players who figured prominently in the shoe polish plays had the same last name. That should give you a solid clue. Who are the two?

(Answer appears on page 322.)

Chapter Sixteen

THE WORLD SERIES

90. WORLD SERIES STANDOUTS

I.

Match the following players with the World Series records that they set: Lou Gehrig, Hank Bauer, Pee Wee Reese and Elston Howard, Yogi Berra, Willie Wilson, Casey Stengel, Pepper Martin, Babe Ruth, Bobby Richardson, and Mickey Mantle.

1. _____ He was on the winning club ten times.
2. _____ He was on the losing team six times.
3. _____ He was a series manager ten times.
4. _____ He hit .625, the all-time high, in one series.
5. _____ He had a career average of .418.
6. _____ He collected 12 RBI in one series.
7. _____ He hit safely in 17 consecutive games.
8. _____ He hit four home runs in four games.
9. _____ He struck out 12 times in one series.
10. _____ He struck out 54 times in series play.

II.

Match the following pitchers with the World Series records they set: Bill Bevens, Whitey Ford, Harry Brecheen, Babe Ruth, Darold Knowles, Don Larsen, Christy Mathewson, Carl Mays, Bob Gibson, and Jim Palmer.

1. _____ He pitched 33⅔ consecutive scoreless innings.
2. _____ He pitched seven games in one series.
3. _____ He pitched three shutouts in one series.

4. _____ He struck out 17 batters in one game.
5. _____ He issued 10 walks in one game.
6. _____ He did not allow a single walk in 26 innings of pitching in one series.
7. _____ He gave up a total of four hits in two consecutive games.
8. _____ He was the youngest pitcher who threw a shutout.
9. _____ He was the first post-World War II pitcher who won three games.
10. _____ He pitched the longest game, 14 innings, which he won.

III.

Match the following teams that have won consecutive World Series with the proper time spans (teams may be used more than once): Yankees, Cubs, Athletics, Giants, Red Sox, and Reds.

1. _____ (1907–08)
2. _____ (1910–11)
3. _____ (1915–16)
4. _____ (1921–22)
5. _____ (1927–28)
6. _____ (1929–30)
7. _____ (1936–39)
8. _____ (1949–53)
9. _____ (1961–62)
10. _____ (1972–74)
11. _____ (1975–76)
12. _____ (1977–78)

IV.

Match the following World Series defensive standouts with the years in which they excelled: Dick Green, Tommie Agee, Willie Mays, Al Gionfriddo, Brooks Robinson, Billy Cox, Bill Virdon, Mickey Mantle, Eddie Mathews, and Sandy Amoros.

1. _____ (1947)
2. _____ (1952)
3. _____ (1954)
4. _____ (1955)

5. _____	(1956)
6. _____	(1957)
7. _____	(1960)
8. _____	(1969)
9. _____	(1970)
10. _____	(1974)

V.

Match the following World Series starting pitchers with the years in which they stood in the sun: Sandy Koufax, Lew Burdette, Mickey Lolich, Harry Brecheen, Johnny Podres, Bob Gibson, Whitey Ford, Bob Turley, Jim Hunter, and Don Larsen.

1. _____	(1946)
2. _____	(1955)
3. _____	(1956)
4. _____	(1957)
5. _____	(1958)
6. _____	(1960)
7. _____	(1963)
8. _____	(1967)
9. _____	(1968)
10. _____	(1972)

91. WORLD SERIES PLAYERS

From the performers listed below, pick out the ones who played in the World Series. The key word is "played."

Richie Ashburn	Vada Pinson
Ernie Banks	Felipe Alou
Ted Williams	Jesus Alou
Al Kaline	Matty Alou
Luke Appling	Gus Bell
Mickey Vernon	Willard Marshall
Nelson Fox	Walker Cooper
Dean Chance	Ray Sadecki
Ralph Kiner	Bob Allison
Richie Allen	Vern Stephens
Harvey Kuenn	Eddie Yost
George Kell	Ferguson Jenkins
Herb Score	Satchel Paige
Hank Sauer	Johnny Callison
Johnny Logan	Buddy Kerr
Ted Kluszewski	Bill White
Ted Lyons	Jeff Heath
Gordy Coleman	Milt Pappas
Ferris Fain	Frank Torre
Gaylord Perry	Hank Majeski

1. _____   11. _____
2. _____   12. _____
3. _____   13. _____
4. _____   14. _____
5. _____   15. _____
6. _____   16. _____
7. _____   17. _____
8. _____   18. _____
9. _____   19. _____
10. _____   20. _____

92. TWO-TEAM WORLD SERIES PLAYERS

From the performers listed below, pick out the ones who played in the World Series with two different teams.

Rocky Nelson	Enos Slaughter
Juan Marichal	Don Hoak
Denny McLain	Ron Fairly
Gino Cimoli	Orlando Cepeda
Rudy York	Maury Wills
Tommy Holmes	Bob Tolan
Willie Horton	Moe Drabowsky
Bill Skowron	Joe Cronin
Roger Maris	Luis Aparicio
Al Dark	Don Gullett
George McQuinn	Dick Groat
Mickey Cochrane	Ron Perranoski
Julian Javier	Claude Osteen
Rusty Staub	Frank Robinson
Jim Lonborg	Willie Davis
Reggie Smith	Camilo Pascual
Joe Gordon	Tony Oliva
Curt Simmons	Mike Garcia
Tommy Davis	Ken Boyer
Johnny Sain	Curt Flood

1. _____	11. _____
2. _____	12. _____
3. _____	13. _____
4. _____	14. _____
5. _____	15. _____
6. _____	16. _____
7. _____	17. _____
8. _____	18. _____
9. _____	19. _____
10. _____	20. _____

93. MOUND CLASSICS

Below you will find the matchups and years in which pitchers have engaged in 1–0 mound duels since 1946. Name the pitcher who won their duels.

1. _____ Bob Feller vs. Johnny Sain (1948)
2. _____ Don Newcombe vs. Allie Reynolds (1949)
3. _____ Preacher Roe vs. Vic Raschi (1949)
4. _____ Vic Raschi vs. Jim Konstanty (1950)
5. _____ Bob Turley vs. Clem Labine (1956)
6. _____ Whitey Ford vs. Lew Burdette (1957)
7. _____ Bob Shaw, Billy Pierce, and Dick Donovan vs. Sandy Koufax (1959)
8. _____ Ralph Terry vs. Jack Sanford (1962)
9. _____ Jim Bouton vs. Don Drysdale (1963)
10. _____ Claude Osteen vs. Wally Bunker (1966)
11. _____ Don Drysdale vs. Dave McNally (1966)
12. _____ Jack Billingham and Clay Carroll vs. John Odom (1972)
13. _____ Bruce Hurst vs. Ron Darling (1986)

94. SEVENTH-GAME WINNERS

From the following pairs of seventh-game starting pitchers since the end of World War II, pick the 12 moundsmen who have been credited with wins. One of the 12 pitchers picked up two victories.

1. _____ (1946) Boo Ferriss (Red Sox) vs. Murry Dickson (Cardinals)

2. _____ (1947) Hal Gregg (Dodgers) vs. Frank Shea (Yankees)

3. _____ (1952) Ed Lopat (Yankees) vs. Joe Black (Dodgers)

4. _____ (1953) Carl Erskine (Dodgers) vs. Whitey Ford (Yankees)

5. _____ (1955) Johnny Podres (Dodgers) vs. Tommy Byrne (Yankees)

6. _____ (1956) Johnny Kucks (Yankees) vs. Don Newcombe (Dodgers)

7. _____ (1957) Lew Burdette (Braves) vs. Don Larsen (Yankees)

8. _____ (1958) Don Larsen (Yankees) vs. Lew Burdette (Braves)

9. _____ (1960) Bob Turley (Yankees) vs. Vernon Law (Pirates)

10. _____ (1962) Ralph Terry (Yankees) vs. Jack Sanford (Giants)

11. _____ (1964) Mel Stottlemyre (Yankees) vs. Bob Gibson (Cards)

12. _____ (1967) Bob Gibson (Cards) vs. Jim Lonborg (Red Sox)

13. _____ (1968) Mickey Lolich (Tigers) vs. Bob Gibson (Cards)

14. _____ (1971) Steve Blass (Pirates) vs. Dave McNally (Orioles)

15. _____ (1972) John Odom (A's) vs. Jack Billingham (Reds)

16. _____ (1973) Jon Matlack (Mets) vs. Ken Holtzman (A's)

17. _____ (1975) Don Gullett (Reds) vs. Bill Lee (Red Sox)

18. _____ (1979) Jim Bibby (Pirates) vs. Scott McGregor (Orioles)

19. _____ (1982) Pete Vuckovich (Brewers) vs. Joaquin Andujar (Cards)

20. _____ (1985) John Tudor (Cards) vs. Bret Saberhagen (Royals)

21. _____ (1986) Bruce Hurst (Red Sox) vs. Ron Darling (Mets)

22. _____ (1987) Joe Magrane (Cards) vs. Frank Viola (Twins)

95. WORLD SERIES SHORTS

Three-Game Winners

The last five pitchers who won three games in a World Series were Lew Burdette, Stan Coveleski, Harry Brecheen, Mickey Lolich, and Bob Gibson. Put them in their proper order.

1. _____ (1920)
2. _____ (1946)
3. _____ (1957)
4. _____ (1967)
5. _____ (1968)

Home Run Hitters

Match the following players with the number of series homers they hit: Duke Snider, Mickey Mantle, Babe Ruth, Lou Gehrig, and Yogi Berra.

1. _____ (18)
2. _____ (15)
3. _____ (12)
4. _____ (11)
5. _____ (10)

Individual Records

Match the following players with the World Series records they set: Whitey Ford, Christy Mathewson, Lefty Gomez, Lefty Grove, and Bob Gibson.

1. _____ Fewest number of chances accepted (0), series (26 innings)
2. _____ Most career wins (10)
3. _____ Most strikeouts per nine innings (10.22)
4. _____ Most career shutouts (4)
5. _____ Best career-winning percentage (1.000), six decisions

Career Records

Match the following players with the career World Series records they set: Yogi Berra, Bobby Richardson, Frank Isbell, Dusty Rhodes, and Eddie Collins and Lou Brock.

1. _____ Tied for stolen base leadership (14)
2. _____ Most games (75)
3. _____ Most runs batted in (7) consecutive times at bat
4. _____ Most two-base hits (4), one game
5. _____ Most consecutive games played (30)

96. FOUR HOMERS IN ONE SERIES

Reggie Jackson, of course, hit five home runs in the 1977 World Series. But there have been six players who hit four home runs in a series. One of them did it twice. Out of the following players pick the ones who accomplished the feat: Mickey Mantle, Willie Mays, Lou Gehrig, Gene Tenace, Roy Campanella, Joe DiMaggio, Babe Ruth, Duke Snider, Johnny Bench, Hank Bauer, and Willie Aikens. Also, see if you can put them in their proper time spans. And remember, one of them did it twice.

1. _____ (1926)
2. _____ (1928)
3. _____ (1952)
4. _____ (1955)
5. _____ (1958)
6. _____ (1972)
7. _____ (1980)

97. WORLD SERIES CHRONOLOGY

There have been 84 World Series. The autumn classic began in 1903 and has been played every year with the exception of 1905, when the Giants refused to play the Red Sox, winners of the first series. I'm going to give you one question for each series, presented in sequence. Let's see how you know the World Series—from start to finish.

1. _____ Who hit the first home run?
2. _____ Who has been the only pitcher to spin three shutouts in the same series?
3. _____ Who struck out a record 12 batters in the intercity series between the White Sox and Cubs in 1906?
4. _____ Who was the other member of the Tinker to Evers to Chance infield who hit .471 in 1907?
5. _____ Who was the Cub pitcher, in addition to Three Finger Brown, who won two games in 1908?
6. _____ Who has been the only rookie pitcher to win three games in one series?
7. _____ Who managed to win all three of his decisions in 1910 despite the fact that he yielded 23 hits and 14 free passes?
8. _____ Who hit home runs in consecutive games for the Athletics in 1911?
9. _____ Who won three games for the Red Sox in 1912?
10. _____ Who was the only substitute whom the Athletics used in 1913?
11. _____ Who was the member of the Tinker to Evers to Chance infield who hit .438 for the winning Braves in 1914?
12. _____ Who was the Red Sox pitcher who won two games and batted .500 in 1915?
13. _____ Who strung together the most consecutive scoreless innings in one game?
14. _____ Who was the White Sox pitcher who won three games in 1917?
15. _____ Who was the Cub second baseman who became the last out of the third game in 1918 when he unsuccessfully tried to steal home?

16. _____ Who was the untainted member of the 1919 Black Sox who won both of his decisions?

17. _____ Who hit the first grand slam?

18. _____ Who did not allow an earned run in 27 innings of pitching, but lost the final game of 1921 on an error?

19. _____ Who was the first pitcher to win the final game of two consecutive series?

20. _____ Who was the first player to hit three home runs in the same series?

21. _____ Who hit the bad-hop single that gave the Senators their first and only world championship?

22. _____ Who was the first pitcher to win the seventh game of one world series (1924) and lose the seventh game of the following post-season get-together?

23. _____ Who, in addition to Grover Alexander, won two games for the Cardinals in 1926?

24. _____ Who hit the only two home runs of the 1927 classic?

25. _____ Who was deprived of a "quick-pitch" strikeout of Babe Ruth in 1928?

26. _____ Who was the Athletic outfielder who, in addition to Jimmie Foxx and Mule Haas, hit two home runs in 1929?

27. _____ Who was the 46-year-old pitcher who appeared in the 1930 series?

28. _____ Who "peppered" 12 hits and swiped five bases in 1931?

29. _____ Who was the Yankee player who, in addition to Babe Ruth and Lou Gehrig, hit two home runs in one game in 1932?

30. _____ Who hit the home run in the tenth inning that won the 1933 finale?

31. _____ Who, in 1934, played on his second world championship team with one club in the 1930s after performing on two world title clubs with another team in the 1920s?

32. _____ Who was the veteran outfielder whose single in 1935 gave the Tigers their first world championship?

33. _____ Who was the Giant pitcher who stopped the Yankees' 12-game win streak in 1936?

34. _____ Who was the 20-game winner for the Giants in 1937 who lost both of his series decisions?

35. _____ Who won two games during the Yankees' four-game sweep in 1938?

36. _____ Who won his fourth and final game (1939) without a defeat in series play?

37. _____ Who won both of his decisions, weaved a 1.50 ERA, and hit a home run in 1940?

38. _____ Who was the Dodger pitcher in 1941 who broke the Yankees' ten-game winning streak?

39. _____ Who hit a two-run homer in the final game of 1942 to give the Cardinals the world title?

40. _____ Who allowed only one run in 18 innings of pitching as the Yankees scored a turnabout five-game win over the Cardinals in 1943?

41. _____ Who was the Cardinal pitcher who lost a two-hitter to the Browns in 1944?

42. _____ Who was the starting pitcher who did not retire a single Tiger batter in Game Seven of 1945?

43. _____ Who scored the decisive run of 1946 by racing from first to home on a single?

44. _____ Who was the Dodger pitcher who finished a record six games against the Yankees in 1947?

45. _____ Who was the Indian pitcher who suffered both of his team's reversals in 1948?

46. _____ Who hit the ninth-inning home run that scored the only run in a classic duel between Allie Reynolds and Don Newcombe in the 1949 opener?

47. _____ Who was the 21-year-old rookie pitcher who won the final game in 1950?

48. _____ Who made the sliding catch that ended the 1951 series on a victorious note for the Yankees?

49. _____ Who was the Yankee part-time player who hit a record three home runs in three consecutive games in 1952?

50. _____ Who was the Dodger pitcher who struck out a record 14 batters in one game?

51. _____ Who was the Indian slugger who hit the 450-foot fly ball that Willie Mays ran down in Game One of 1954?

52. _____ Who was the Dodger slugger who drove home both runs in Johnny Podres' 2–0 win over Tommy Byrne in Game Seven of 1955?

53. _____ Who was the 40-year-old outfielder whose three-run game-winning homer (Game Three) turned the series around for the Yankees in 1956?

54. _____ Who was the Brave pitcher of 1957 who won three games?

55. _____ Who won two of the last three games—and saved the other one—in 1958?

56. _____ Who was the former Rose Bowl performer who set a record by hitting two pinch-hit homers for the Dodgers in 1959?

57. _____ Who was the Pirate pitcher who saved three games in a winning cause in 1960?

58. _____ Who was the Yankee pitcher who won two games for the second consecutive year in 1961?

59. _____ Who was the former Yankee celebrity who defeated the Pinstripers in his only decision in 1962?

60. _____ Who was the Yankee pinch-hitter whom Sandy Koufax fanned for his record 15th strikeout in 1963?

61. _____ Who was the last runner to steal home?

62. _____ Who (in addition to Sandy Koufax, who threw two shutouts) pitched a whitewash for the Dodgers in 1965?

63. _____ Who was the only Oriole pitcher who did not complete a game in 1966?

64. _____ Who was the only Cardinal pitcher to throw three consecutive complete-game wins in a series?

65. _____ Who picked two runners off first base in the sixth inning of the final game in 1968?

66. _____ Who was the light-hitting infielder for the Mets who batted .455 in 1969?

67. _____ Who was the Oriole player who excelled on offense and defense in 1970?

68. _____ Who was the Pirate player who extended his batting streak to 14 games in 1971?

69. _____ Who was the Oakland starter who picked up his second win of the series in relief in Game Seven of 1972?

70. _____ Who outpitched Jon Matlack in both the first and last game of 1973?

71. _____ Who, in addition to Catfish Hunter, won two games for the A's in 1974?

72. _____ Who was the Red slugger who hit three home runs in 1975?

73. _____ Who was the Red slugger who batted .533 during his team's sweep of the Yankees in 1976?

74. _____ Who was the Yankee batter who extended his consecutive-game hitting streak to ten in 1977?

75. _____ Who was the Yankee fill-in infielder who batted .438 in 1978?

76. _____ Who, in addition to Willie Stargell, collected 12 hits for the Pirates in 1979?

77. _____ Who was the Phillie pitcher who won Game Five and saved Game Six in 1980?

78. _____ Who, in addition to Pedro Guerrero, hit an eighth-inning home run in Game Five of 1981 to give Jerry Reuss and the Dodgers a 2–1 win?

79. _____ Who was the Brewer who got 12 hits in 1982?

80. _____ Who was the Oriole slugger who came out of a slump to hit two home runs in the series-clinching game of 1983?

81. _____ Who was the Tiger who hit two home runs in the series-clinching game of 1984?

82. _____ Who was the second-year Royal pitcher who was 2–0 in 1985?

83. _____ Who was the 1986 MVP whom the winning team didn't sign for 1987?

84. _____ Who was the pitcher who won the first and seventh games for the Twins in 1987?

98. WORLD SERIES MULTIPLE CHOICE

1. _____ Who was eligible to play in 37 games but appeared in only one?
   a. Gus Niarhos b. Jake Gibbs c. Charlie Silvera d. Stan Lopata

2. _____ Who was eligible to play in 23 games but didn't appear in one of them?
   a. Dick Williams b. Arndt Jorgens c. Bruce Edwards d. Mike Hegan

3. _____ Who played on four world championship teams his first four years in the majors?
   a. Jackie Robinson b. Reggie Jackson c. Charlie Keller d. Joe DiMaggio

4. _____ Who was the infielder who played in his first and in his second series 14 years apart?
   a. Billy Herman b. Stan Hack c. Rabbit Maranville d. Johnny Evers

5. _____ Who was the pitcher who played in his first and in his last series 17 years apart?
   a. Walter Johnson b. Jim Kaat c. Grover Alexander d. Eppa Rixey

6. _____ Who was the outfielder who played in his first and in his last series 22 years apart?
   a. Sam Crawford b. Al Kaline c. Willie Mays d. Mickey Mantle

7. _____ Who was the pitcher who played in his first and in his last series 18 years apart?
   a. Burleigh Grimes b. Christy Mathewson c. Joe Bush d. Herb Pennock

8. _____ Who was the pitcher who played the most years in the majors before appearing in his first series?
   a. Joe Niekro b. Steve Carlton c. Ted Lyons d. Early Wynn

9. _____ Who was the oldest regular-day player to appear in the series?
   a. Enos Slaughter b. Johnny Hopp c. Johnny Mize d. Pete Rose

10. _____ Who pinch-hit in ten games?
   a. Bobby Brown b. Johnny Blanchard c. Dusty Rhodes d. Gino Cimoli

11. _____ Who pinch-ran in nine games?
   a. Herb Washington b. Allan Lewis c. Bill North d. Sam Jethroe
12. _____ Who twice got four hits in a game?
   a. Pete Rose b. Lou Brock c. Robin Yount d. Paul Molitor
13. _____ Who went hitless in 31 consecutive at-bats?
   a. Mark Belanger b. Marv Owen c. Julian Javier d. Dal Maxvill
14. _____ Who hit ten doubles in total series?
   a. Mickey Mantle b. Joe Medwick c. Frank Frisch d. Pee Wee Reese
15. _____ Who hit six doubles in one series?
   a. Pete Fox b. Nellie Fox c. Frank Isbell d. Pete Rose
16. _____ Who was the rookie who hit three home runs in his first series?
   a. Tony Kubek b. Willie Aikens c. Amos Otis d. Charlie Keller
17. _____ Who twice hit four home runs in a series?
   a. Hank Bauer b. Duke Snider c. Gene Tenace d. Roberto Clemente
18. _____ Who hit seven home runs in two consecutive series?
   a. Babe Ruth b. Reggie Jackson c. Lou Gehrig d. Mickey Mantle
19. _____ Who hit nine home runs in three consecutive series?
   a. Mickey Mantle b. Roger Maris c. Reggie Jackson d. Babe Ruth
20. _____ Who got the most long hits in one game?
   a. Reggie Jackson b. Frank Isbell c. Yogi Berra d. Babe Ruth
21. _____ Who drove home six runs in one game?
   a. Bobby Richardson b. Monte Irvin c. Gil Hodges d. Hank Aaron
22. _____ Who was hit by pitches three times in one series?
   a. Minnie Minoso b. Ron Hunt c. Don Baylor d. Max Carey
23. _____ Who grounded into five double plays in one series?
   a. Willie Mays b. Irv Noren c. Joe DiMaggio d. Gil McDougald
24. _____ Who was caught stealing nine times in total series?
   a. Ty Cobb b. Pee Wee Reese c. Frank Schulte d. Willie Randolph
25. _____ Who pitched consecutive games in consecutive series?

a. Deacon Phillippe b. George Earnshaw c. Lefty Grove
d. Ed Reulbach

26. _____ Who was the relief pitcher who appeared in 16
games in total series?

a. Johnny Murphy b. Wilcy Moore c. Rollie Fingers
d. Hugh Casey

27. _____ Who was the relief pitcher who appeared in six
different series?

a. Joe Page b. Bob Kuzava c. Elroy Face d. Johnny
Murphy

28. _____ Who won seven consecutive games?

a. Bob Gibson b. Red Ruffing c. Lefty Gomez d. Herb
Pennock

29. _____ Who pitched four consecutive opening games?

a. Allie Reynolds b. Whitey Ford c. Red Ruffing d. Carl
Hubbell

30. _____ Who was the pitcher who was on the losing end
of three shutouts, including two 1–0 scores?

a. Vic Raschi b. Preacher Roe c. Bob Turley d. Eddie
Plank

31. _____ Who pitched a 12-inning game without issuing a
base on balls?

a. Whitey Ford b. Schoolboy Rowe c. Dizzy Dean
d. Tommy Bridges

32. _____ Who, in a nine-inning game, struck out 11 batters but lost, 1–0?

a. Don Newcombe b. Bob Turley c. Tom Seaver d. Bob
Feller

33. _____ Who, in a ten-inning game, struck out 11 batters
but lost, 1–0?

a. Carl Hubbell b. Bob Turley c. Ewell Blackwell d. Lefty
Grove

34. _____ Who, in a 12-inning game, struck out 12 batters
but lost?

a. Rube Waddell b. Christy Mathewson c. Chief Bender
d. Walter Johnson

35. _____ Who was the first baseman who didn't make an
error in 31 consecutive games?

a. Gil Hodges b. Bill Skowron c. Bill Terry d. Hank
Greenberg

36. _____ Who played in seven series at second base?

a. Frank Frisch b. Joe Gordon c. Jackie Robinson d.
Eddie Stanky

37. _____ Who was the second baseman who didn't make
an error in 23 consecutive games?

a. Junior Gilliam b. Red Schoendienst c. Tony Lazzeri d. Billy Martin

38. _____ Who played in six series at third base?
   a. Pepper Martin b. Red Rolfe c. Billy Cox d. Sal Bando

39. _____ Who was the third baseman who didn't make an error in 22 consecutive games?
   a. Graig Nettles b. Ron Cey c. Pete Rose d. Brooks Robinson

40. _____ Who was the shortstop who didn't make an error in 21 consecutive games?
   a. Leo Durocher b. Marty Marion c. Pee Wee Reese d. Phil Rizzuto

41. _____ Who played in 12 series as an outfielder?
   a. Casey Stengel b. Joe DiMaggio c. Babe Ruth d. Mickey Mantle

42. _____ Who was the catcher who didn't make an error in 30 consecutive games?
   a. Roy Campanella b. Yogi Berra c. Walker Cooper d. Bill Dickey

43. _____ Who was the pitcher who didn't make an error in 18 consecutive games?
   a. Carl Hubbell b. Sandy Koufax c. Don Drysdale d. Whitey Ford

44. _____ Who was the youngest manager of a series winner?
   a. Lou Boudreau b. Bucky Harris c. Joe Cronin d. Mickey Cochrane

45. _____ Who was the youngest manager of a series club?
   a. Joe Cronin b. Roger Peckinpaugh c. Frank Frisch d. Lou Boudreau

46. _____ Who was the manager who lost 28 series games?
   a. Connie Mack b. Leo Durocher c. John McGraw d. Bill Terry

47. _____ Who was the manager who won 37 series games?
   a. Casey Stengel b. Joe McCarthy c. Walter Alston d. Connie Mack

48. _____ Who managed in the series with three different teams from the same league?
   a. Sparky Anderson b. Dick Williams c. Bill McKechnie d. Alvin Dark

49. _____ Who appeared in 15 series as a coach?
   a. Jimmy Dykes b. Art Fletcher c. Frank Crosetti d. Chuck Dressen

50. _____ Who appeared in 18 series as an umpire?
   a. Shag Crawford b. Bill Klem c. Tom Connolly d. Bill McKinley

99. WORLD SERIES CLUES
WHO'S WHO

1. _____ Who pitched a record ten complete games in World Series play?
   a. He won five and lost five.
   b. He pitched 27 consecutive scoreless innings in one series.

2. _____ Who was the Yankee pitcher from the 1930s and 1940s who won seven of nine decisions in series action?
   a. He twice led the American League in losses.
   b. He won 20 or more games four straight years.

3. _____ Who was the Yankee pitcher from the 1920s and 1930s who won five of five decisions in series play?
   a. He got three saves, too.
   b. He won 240 career games.

4. _____ Who was the Yankee pitcher from the 1940s and 1950s who won seven of nine decisions in World Series play?
   a. He picked up four saves, too.
   b. In 1953, his last series, he saved Game Six and he won Game Seven in relief.

5. _____ Who picked up a record six series saves?
   a. He picked them up in three consecutive series.
   b. In those three series he pitched in a total of 16 games.

6. _____ Who struck out a record 11 batters in relief in one series game?
   a. He did it for the Orioles . . .
   b. . . . against the Dodgers.

7. _____ Who was picked off base twice in the same series game?
   a. He played with the 1918 Cubs at the time.
   b. He once played with two different teams on the same day.

8. _____ Who was the pitcher who walked a record two times with the bases loaded in the same series game?
   a. Eight times he won 20 or more games.
   b. He won three Cy Young awards.

9. _____ Who hit a double and a triple in the same inning of a series game?
   a. He did it for the 1921 Giants.
   b. He hit .300 in nine of his ten seasons.

10. _____ Who was the player who ripped five consecutive extra-base hits in series action?
   a. He got 25 hits in two consecutive series.
   b. He stole seven bases in each of those series, too.

11. _____ Who was the player for the Giants who got all three of his team's hits in a 1923 series game against the Yankees?
   a. He batted .310 lifetime, one point higher than his brother.
   b. He and his brother played against each other in three World Series.

12. _____ Who allowed a record eight home runs in series play?
   a. He pitched in four series from 1920–32.
   b. He pitched for the Dodgers, Cards, and Cubs.

13. _____ Who got a record five hits in one series game?
   a. He got 11 hits in the entire series.
   b. He did it in 1982.

14. _____ Who was the pitcher who allowed three home runs in the same inning?
   a. He pitched for the 1967 Cards.
   b. Two years later he was out of baseball.

15. _____ Who was the outfielder who started two double plays in the same series game?
   a. He did it for the 1919 Reds.
   b. A Hall of Famer, he hit .323 lifetime.

16. _____ Who was the youngest player ever to appear in a series?
   a. He was 18.
   b. In that series he got four hits in one game against Walter Johnson.

17. _____ Who played in 50 games and never hit a homer?
   a. He appeared for the Giants and the Cards.
   b. He hit two home runs in All-Star games.

18. _____ Who, in addition to Bob Gibson, has been the only pitcher to hit two home runs in series play?
   a. He won four of six series decisions . . .
   b. . . . for the Orioles.

19. _____ Who hit three home runs in each of back-to-back series?
   a. He played for the 1924–25 Senators.
   b. He batted .316 lifetime and .287 in five series with the Senators and the Tigers.

20. _____ Who threw out ten runners in one series?
   a. He did it for the 1919 White Sox.
   b. He's in the Hall of Fame.

21. _____ Who pitched the longest complete-game loss in series history?
   a. In two series he had an 0.89 ERA.
   b. His initials are S.S.

22. _____ Who hit two home runs in one game and two triples in another?
   a. He did it in the first series for the winning Red Sox.
   b. Two years later he played with the winning White Sox.

23. _____ Who was the player who was fired after a series because he struck out nine times?
   a. The series took place in 1909.
   b. He played for the Pirates, who defeated the Tigers.

24. _____ Who was the three-game winner for the White Sox who tried to steal third with the base already occupied?
   a. He did it in 1917.
   b. He won 254 major league games.

25. _____ Who retired the last 21 batters of a game in order?
   a. He did it in 1926.
   b. He was 39 at the time.

26. _____ Who, in the 1920s, struck out ten batters in a relief appearance?
   a. His brother pitched on the same team.
   b. They won 214 major league games between them.

27. _____ Walter Johnson pitched 21 years with one club. So did one other American League pitcher. Who was he?
   a. He never played in a World Series.
   b. Yet he won 260 career games.

28. _____ Who was traded after he player-managed his team to the world title?
   a. He won batting titles with two different teams.
   b. He was a second baseman.

29. _____ Who made the "$30,000 Muff?"
   a. He did it while playing with the 1912 Giants.

b. Later in that inning, he made one of the greatest catches in series history.

30. _____ Who has been the only Tiger manager in 76 years to lead his team into the series in back-to-back years?

a. He was a .320 lifetime hitter.

b. He played in five series in seven years.

31. _____ Who was the Cardinal pitcher who lost a two-hitter?

a. George McQuinn's two-run homer was the key hit.

b. He bounced back to win Game Five, 2–0.

32. _____ Who has been the only Red manager to win back-to-back world titles?

a. He played just one season in the majors.

b. With the 1959 Phillies.

33. _____ Who was the youngest pitcher ever to hurl in the series?

a. He was 19 at the time.

b. He has a famous brother who is still playing.

34. _____ Who missed the opening assignment of a series because it fell on a Jewish religious holiday?

a. He had a .655 lifetime winning percentage.

b. He had an .097 lifetime batting average.

35. _____ Who hit for the highest series average (.391) in 20 or more games?

a. He got a record-tying 13 hits in one series.

b. He played on two world title teams in the 1960s.

36. _____ Who was the pitcher who hit important doubles in the opening games of the 1973 and 1974 series?

a. He won four series games for Oakland.

b. He once hit a series home run.

37. _____ Who got a record six consecutive hits in the 1924 World Series?

a. He hit seven home runs in three series.

b. He got the series-winning hit for the Tigers in 1935.

38. _____ Who got seven consecutive hits in back-to-back series?

a. He was a catcher.

b. He was a Rookie of the Year and an MVP.

39. _____ Who batted in six runs in one series as a pinch-hitter?

a. He did it in the 1950s.

b. He helped his team to a four-game sweep.

40. _____ Who was the National Leaguer who hit the most homers in series play?
   a. He hit 11.
   b. He twice hit four homers in a series.

41. _____ Who pitched a one-hitter for the Cubs in 1906?
   a. He won 181 games.
   b. He was called "Big Ed."

42. _____ Who was the American League player who hit safely in 15 of the 16 games in which he played?
   a. He hit better than .300 and drove home 100 or more runs in three consecutive years.
   b. He once hit .529 in a series.

43. _____ Who was the infielder in the 1920s who cost two different teams world titles because of errors in seventh games?
   a. He managed the Yankees before he cost them the 1921 title.
   b. He was the MVP in one of those years (1925).

44. _____ Who won three pennants and two world titles in his first three years of managing?
   a. He was a catcher who hit .272 lifetime.
   b. He moved into the front office after his three straight successes.

45. _____ Who has been the only pitcher, in addition to Don Drysdale, to both win and lose 1–0 decisions in series play?
   a. He beat Jim Konstanty.
   b. He lost to Preacher Roe.

46. _____ Who was the most recent pitcher to win the final game of back-to-back series?
   a. The years were 1952–53.
   b. He starred as a starter and as a reliever.

47. _____ Who was the Yankee pitcher who picked up saves in the final game of the back-to-back series?
   a. The years were 1951–52.
   b. They called him "Sarge."

48. _____ Who lost a record two 1–0 games?
   a. He did it in 1905 and 1914.
   b. He won over 300 career games.

49. _____ Who picked off two runners in the sixth inning of the seventh game in 1968?
   a. He picked off Lou Brock and Curt Flood.
   b. He won three games in that series.

50. _____ Who was the first pitcher to win the seventh game of one series and lose the seventh game of the following series?

    a. He won the seventh game in 1924.

    b. He was 1–2 the year that his team won and 2–1 the season that his club lost.

51. _____ Who was the first pitcher to win the final game of two consecutive series?

    a. He did it in 1921 and 1922.

    b. He split eight decisions in series play for the Giants.

52. _____ Who pitched a one-hitter for the Cubs in 1945?

    a. He won 162 games.

    b. Rudy York got the hit.

53. _____ Who was intentionally passed in his only series at-bat?

    a. He played for the 1962 Giants at the time.

    b. He came up with the 1951 Browns.

54. _____ Who was the player who, after getting 11 hits in the 1951 World Series, was pinch-hit for three times in the 1954 classic?

    a. He got four hits and stole home in Game One of 1951.

    b. Dusty Rhodes pinch-hit for him.

55. _____ Who was the catcher whose passed ball cost his team a big victory in 1941?

    a. The pitcher was Hugh Casey.

    b. He later jumped to the Mexican Leagues.

56. _____ Who tagged Don Newcombe for three homers and eight RBIs in the same series?

    a. He did it in 1956.

    b. Two of the shots were two-run blasts in the final game.

57. _____ Who won the last game of the 1927 series as a starter and the last game of the 1932 series as a reliever?

    a. He won 13 games in relief in 1927.

    b. He also saved 13 games that season.

58. _____ Who was the pitcher who threw a one-hitter for the Yankees in 1947?

    a. He lost.

    b. He never started another major league game.

59. _____ Who was the only pitcher, in addition to Carl Hubbell, to beat the Yankees in the 1930s?

    a. He did it for the Giants in 1936.

    b. He was called "Prince Hal."

60. _____ Who was the Yankee pitcher who struck out a record five times in one World Series game?

    a. In 1928 he had a league-high 24 wins.

    b. He later became an umpire.

61. _____ Who batted into five outs in two consecutive at-bats in a World Series game?

    a. He hit into a triple play the first time.

    b. He hit into a double play the second time.

62. _____ Who pitched a one-hitter for the Red Sox in 1967?

    a. Julian Javier got the hit.

    b. A skiing accident didn't help his future.

63. _____ Who was the catcher off whom Pepper Martin stole seven bases in two series?

    a. He played in five series with two teams.

    b. He player-managed a team to a world title.

64. _____ Who, in the 1920s, won the sixth and seventh games of a series?

    a. He did it for the 1925 Pirates.

    b. He twice won 20 games for the Pirates.

65. _____ Who was the .257 regular-season hitter in 1953 who batted .500 in the series and delivered a record 12 hits for a six-game clash?

    a. He batted .257 lifetime, too.

    b. In five series, however, he hit .333.

66. _____ Who got picked off second base for the final out of a series?

    a. The year was 1942.

    b. The catcher was Walker Cooper.

67. _____ Who set a record when he struck out the first five batters to face him in a starting assignment?

    a. He was the MVP in 1942.

    b. He won more than 20 games three years in a row.

68. _____ Who was the Oriole short-inning man who did not allow a run in three consecutive series?

    a. He won ten games in relief in 1970.

    b. Despite an 0.00 ERA, he lost his only decision in post-season play.

69. _____ Who was the first pitcher to hit a home run in series play?

    a. He did it for the 1920 Indians.

    b. He won 31 games that year.

70. _____ Who was the National League pitcher who allowed only one run in 25 ⅓ innings of pitching in series play?

a. He did it in the 1970s . . .
b. . . . for the Reds.

71. _____ Who was the Pirate star who was benched by manager Donie Bush in the 1927 series?
a. He hit .321 over 18 years.
b. He got the series-winning hit in 1925 for the Pirates.

72. _____ Who was the 40-year-old player who hit a game-winning home run in 1956?
a. He played on two world championship clubs in St. Louis.
b. He played on two world championship clubs in New York.

73. _____ Who hit the single that scored Enos Slaughter from first base for the winning run in the 1946 series?
a. He won a batting title.
b. His brother won one, too.

74. _____ Who became the first player to hit two home runs in two different games in the same series?
a. He hit .400 in the 1980 World Series.
b. He was named after Willie Mays.

75. _____ Who was the only National League pitcher to throw two complete-game wins in the 1970s?
a. He did it for the Pirates.
b. Mysteriously, his career came to an end because, a one-time location pitcher, he couldn't throw strikes anymore.

76. _____ Who pitched the opening game of back-to-back series for reverse teams?
a. He defeated the Yankees in 1976.
b. He lost to the Dodgers in 1977.

77. _____ Who, on his special night, got four hits, including a home run?
a. The year was 1973.
b. He ended up his career as a deluxe pinch-hitter.

78. _____ Who was the only pitcher to hit a grand slam in the series?
a. He won 20 or more games four years in a row.
b. He hit two home runs in World Series play.

79. _____ Who was the Yankee third baseman who repeatedly bailed out Ron Guidry in Game Three of the 1978 series with defensive gems?
a. He hit more home runs than any other third baseman in American League history.
b. They called him "Puff."

80. _____ Who was the Red Sox outfielder who dove into the right-field seats to rob Joe Morgan of a home run in 1975 and then doubled off Ken Griffey trying to return to first base after the catch?

    a. He has a strong throwing arm.

    b. He hits the long ball.

81. _____ Who, in Game Three of 1969, made two sensational catches—on balls hit by Elrod Hendricks and Paul Blair—that rank with the classic catches of series past?

    a. He also homered in that game.

    b. He came to the Mets from the White Sox.

82. _____ Who was the Tiger left fielder whose perfect throw cut down Lou Brock, trying to score, in the key play of Game Five in 1968?

    a. He played 18 years in the majors.

    b. He hit 325 career homers.

83. _____ Who was the third baseman whose diving backhand stab of Zoilo Versalles' smash down the third-base line, and subsequent tag of third for the inning-ending force, took Sandy Koufax out of his only jam in his 2–0 seventh-game victory over the Twins in 1965?

    a. He pushed Jackie Robinson out of his second-base job.

    b. He died while he was a coach with the Dodgers.

84. _____ Who was the outfielder whose outstanding running backhand stop of Willie Mays's double prevented Matty Alou from scoring and enabled the Yankees' Ralph Terry to preserve a 1–0 lead for the world title?

    a. He came up with Cleveland.

    b. He bowed out with St. Louis.

85. _____ Who was the infielder—noted for his good glove—whose three errors paved the way for the Pirates in 1979?

    a. He took Brooks Robinson's place at third.

    b. He moved on to the Angels.

86. _____ Who was the Yankee first baseman who lost a crucial throw from third baseman Clete Boyer because of the glare of the shirt-sleeves in the third-base boxes?

    a. He replaced Bill Skowron.

    b. The following year, he hit a grand slam home run against the Cardinals.

87. _____ Who was the Cardinal outfielder who, first, lost Jim Northrup's fly ball in the sun and, second,

slipped as the ball sailed by him for the game-winning triple in Game Seven of 1968?

   a. He was a great defensive outfielder.

   b. He tested baseball's reserve clause.

88. _____ Who stole six bases in a five-game series?

   a. He played with the 1907 Cubs.

   b. He was called "The Human Mosquito."

89. _____ Who was the player whose pinch-hit single in the 14th inning drove home the winning run in the classic's longest game?

   a. He did it for the Red Sox . . .

   b. . . . giving Babe Ruth the win.

90. _____ Who was the youngest pitcher to throw a complete-game win?

   a. He was 20 when he did it for the Athletics.

   b. His nickname was "Bullet Joe."

91. _____ Who pitched back-to-back complete games twice in the same series?

   a. He won three games and lost two.

   b. He pitched five complete games.

92. _____ Who was the three-game winner who allowed seven hits in one inning?

   a. He won 34 games that year.

   b. He was the roommate of Tris Speaker's during all of his 14 years in the majors.

93. _____ Who won five games and posted a .333 batting average in series play?

   a. He once won 31 games in a season.

   b. They called him "Colby Jack."

94. _____ Who was the first pitcher to lose three games in a series?

   a. He pitched for the 1919 White Sox.

   b. He was banned from baseball for allegedly conspiring to lose games.

95. _____ Who pinch-hit three times in a World Series and walked each time?

   a. He did it for the Senators . . .

   b. . . . in 1924.

96. _____ Who played on five losing teams in five tries?

   a. He caused a 1908 playoff in the National League.

   b. He has gone down in baseball's history as the sport's perennial "Sad Sack."

97. _____ Who was the player who hit two home runs in the 1924 series, despite the fact that he hit only 9 in 12 major league seasons?

a. He was a young manager.

b. He ended up an old manager.

98. _____ Who retired the first 22 batters in order?

a. He was 5–0 in series play.

b. He pitched in series 18 years apart.

99. _____ Who was the first player to hit a pinch-hit home run in series play?

a. He hit a total of 12 homers in series play.

b. He, like Frankie Frisch, hit ten doubles.

100. _____ Who was the Cardinal rookie who made four hits in one series game?

a. He grew up with Yogi Berra.

b. He later became a famous announcer.

The Shutout Series

If you don't believe that there was a dead ball era, you should glance at the statistics of the 1905–07 World Series, and then zero in on the records of the first of those classics.

In 16 games during the 1905–07 time span, there was not one home run hit in post-season play. To say that the pitchers dominated the hitters is to underscore the obvious.

Take the 1905 series, for example. The victorious Giants allowed the formidable Athletics just three runs in 45 innings of play. And none of the runs was earned. Christy Mathewson, the ace of John McGraw's staff, pitched a record three shutouts against Connie Mack's vaunted heroes. "Bix Six" was so completely in control that he allowed just 14 hits and a walk in 27 innings of pitching.

Joe McGinnity, also of the Giants, was almost as good as his celebrated teammate. He pitched a shutout, allowed only ten hits in 17 innings of pitching—a 22-game winner hurled one inning of relief in the "Iron Man's" first outing—and posted an 0.00 ERA. But his record was not perfect—he split his two decisions. In Game Two he was victimized by his defense, which allowed three unearned runs, and by his pitching opponent, who threw a four-hit shutout. (All five games ended in shutouts.)

Who was that Giant relief pitcher who later hurled a no-hitter for nine innings in the opening game of 1909—he lost the game in 13 innings, 3–0— and who was the Athletic shutout pitcher who went on to set a record by pitching nine consecutive complete games in World Series play?

(Answer appears on page 322.)

Chapter Seventeen

MAJOR LEAGUE CLUBS

CHICAGO CUBS

Infielders

True or False.

1. _____ Frank Chance, Charlie Grimm, and Phil Cavarretta ended their careers with lifetime batting averages in the .290s.

2. _____ Rogers Hornsby hit a club-high .380 in 1929.

3. _____ Ernie Banks played more games at shortstop than he did at first base.

4. _____ Heinie Zimmerman was the third baseman in the Tinker-to-Evers-to-Chance infield.

5. _____ Billy Herman compiled a lifetime average of .300 or better.

6. _____ Bill Madlock was the only Cub to win two batting titles.

Outfielders

Fill in the blanks.

7. _____ Who was the Bruin who won four home run crowns?

8. _____ Who is the present-day player who is nicknamed "Sarge"?

9. _____ Who won back-to-back home run titles in 1943–44?

10. _____ Who was the .320 lifetime hitter—he played two and one-half seasons with the Cubs—who ended his career with 300 home runs?

11. _____ Who was the Cub outfielder who played in 1,117 consecutive games to set a then-National League record?

12. _____ Who was the one-time Cub—he batted .285 lifetime with 213 career home runs—who played in World Series with the Cubs, Dodgers, and Braves?

Catchers

Matching.

13. _____ Johnny Kling   a. He managed the Cubs and the Tigers.
14. _____ Gabby Hartnett   b. He managed the Braves.
15. _____ Bob Scheffing   c. He player-managed the Cubs to a pennant.

Pitchers

Multiple Choice.

16. _____ Who was the pitcher against whom Babe Ruth "called his shot" in the 1932 World Series?
    a. Charlie Root b. Pat Malone c. Hippo Vaughn d. Guy Bush.

17. _____ Name the 176-game winner who was called the "Mississippi Mudcat."
    a. Bill Lee b. Guy Bush c. Hooks Wyse d. Lon Warneke

18. _____ Who was the losing pitcher—Fred Toney of the Reds was the winner—in the only nine-inning double no-hit game in major league history?
    a. Grover Alexander b. Hank Borowy c. Larry French d. Hippo Vaughn

19. _____ A winner of 162 major league games, he picked up a victory and a save in the 1945 World Series.
    a. Hank Borowy b. Lon Warneke c. Claude Passeau d. Charlie Root

20. _____ Who was the three-time 20-game winner who later became an umpire?
    a. Pat Malone b. Guy Bush c. Lon Warneke d. Bill Lee

21. _____ Who was the Cub pitcher who won 20 or more games in each of his first six full seasons in the majors?
    a. Ferguson Jenkins b. Ed Reulbach c. Mordecai Brown d. Johnny Schmitz

22. _____ Name the five-time 20-game winner who turned in the best single-season ERA (1.04) in National League history.

a. Ferguson Jenkins b. Grover Alexander c. Bob Rush
d. Mordecai Brown

23. _____ A 21-game winner for the Yankees and the Cubs in 1945, he split four World Series decisions that year.

a. Lon Warneke b. Claude Passeau c. Hank Borowy
d. Johnny Schmitz

24. _____ This 300-plus winner led the league in 1920, with the Cubs, in wins (27) and ERA (1.91).

a. Mordecai Brown b. Grover Alexander c. Guy Bush
d. Charlie Root

25. _____ The only National League pitcher to lead the loop in winning percentage for three consecutive seasons, he was the only pitcher to throw shutouts in both ends of a doubleheader.

a. Grover Alexander b. Ed Reulbach c. Pat Malone
d. Larry French

MONTREAL EXPOS

Infielders

Matching.

1. _____ Ron Fairly
2. _____ Dave Cash
3. _____ Ron Hunt
4. _____ Maury Wills
5. _____ Bob Bailey
6. _____ Larry Parrish

a. In 1971 he was hit by pitches a record 50 times.

b. A former Expo infielder, he's hit well over 200 career home runs.

c. He came up with the Pirates; he bowed out with the Red Sox. In between, he averaged 21 homers a year over a five-year span for the Expos.

d. In the three years before he joined the Expos, he led the league in at-bats with an average of 685 per season.

e. In his only season with the Expos, he led the team in stolen bases.

f. This veteran of 21 years—and four World Series—averaged 15 home runs a year in his five seasons with the Expos.

Outfielders

Multiple Choice.

7. _____ Who hit a single-season-high .334 for the Expos?
a. Ken Singleton b. Tim Raines c. Mack Jones d. Manny Mota

8. _____ Name the Expo who drove home 123 runs in one season.
a. Boots Day b. Tim Wallach c. Rusty Staub d. Larry Parrish

9. _____ Who was the outfielder with the strong arm who averaged 24 home runs a year from 1977–79?
a. Ellis Valentine b. Warren Cromartie c. Andre Dawson d. Rico Carty

10. _____ Who is the present-day outfielder who has played for eight teams and, from 1983–86, four clubs?
   a. Dave Collins b. Mitch Webster c. George Wright d. Gary Ward

11. _____ Who was the Expo who set a record when he pinch-hit safely 25 times in 1977?
   a. Jerry White b. Warren Cromartie c. Sam Mejias d. Jose Morales

12. _____ Who, in 1971, hit a then-club-high .311, drove home 97 runs, and moved to the Mets in 1972?
   a. Manny Mota b. Rico Carty c. Rusty Staub d. Tommy Davis

Catchers

True or False.

13. _____ Barry Foote was the first-string catcher for the Expos before Gary Carter took over full-time in 1977.

14. _____ Tim McCarver played at least two full seasons with Montreal.

15. _____ Gary Carter tied a record with five home runs in two consecutive games.

Pitchers

Fill in the blanks.

16. _____ Who won the most games (20) in one season for Montreal?

17. _____ Who was the pitcher who struck out the most batters (251) in one season for the Expos?

18. _____ Name the starting pitcher whom the Expos traded to the Reds for Tony Perez.

19. _____ Who was the only relief pitcher, in addition to Goose Gossage, to register at least 20 saves a season from 1982–86?

20. _____ Who was the relief pitcher who led the loop in appearances for two consecutive years before he set records for games by a fireman with the Dodgers and the Twins?

21. _____ Who was the Rookie of the Year in 1979?

22. _____ Who pitched two no-hitters for the Expos?

23. _____ Who no-hit the Giants in 1981?

24. _____ Who was the 158-game winner who two times led the National League in losses?

25. _____ Who, along with Ken Singleton, was traded to the Orioles, where he won 20 games in his only year with Baltimore, for Dave McNally and Rich Coggins?

NEW YORK METS

Infielders

True or False.

1. _____ Gil Hodges ended his career with the Mets.
2. _____ Ron Hunt hit a key home run for the Mets in the final game of the 1969 World Series.
3. _____ Bud Harrelson hit .250 or over lifetime.
4. _____ Wayne Garrett came to the Mets in the deal for Nolan Ryan.
5. _____ Ed Kranepool was a lifetime Met.
6. _____ Donn Clendenon hit three home runs in the 1969 World Series.

Outfielders

Fill in the blanks.

7. _____ Who, in addition to Gary Carter, drove home a club-high 105 runs one year?
8. _____ Who stroked a club-high 39 homers in a season?
9. _____ Who hit a team-high .340 one year?
10. _____ Who was the former "Whiz Kid"— he hit .308 lifetime—who ended his career with the Mets?
11. _____ Who is the Met who averaged 27 home runs per year in his first four years in the majors?
12. _____ Who hit two home runs to defeat Steve Carlton in a game in which the Card lefty struck out a then-record 19 batters?

Catchers

Matching.

13. _____ Yogi Berra   a. He was born in St. Louis.
14. _____ Jerry Grote   b. He was born in San Antonio.
15. _____ John Stearns
                             c. He was born in San Francisco.

Multiple Choice.

16. _____ Who holds the club record for season wins (25) and strikeouts (289)?

a. Jerry Koosman b. Nolan Ryan c. Tom Seaver d. Jon Matlack.

17. _____ Who was the pitcher who gave up Roberto Clemente's 3,000th—and final—hit?

a. Jon Matlack b. Tug McGraw c. Danny Frisella d. Gary Gentry

18. _____ Who was the pitcher who coined the expression "You gotta believe"?

a. Tom Seaver b. Bob Apodaca c. Tug McGraw d. Jerry Koosman

19. _____ Which one of the following pitchers won four of his 363 wins with the Mets?

a. Mickey Lolich b. Warren Spahn c. Juan Marichal d. Early Wynn

20. _____ The pitcher who threw the historic 61st home run pitch to Roger Maris in 1961, he later lost 20 games for the 1964 Mets.

a. Tracy Stallard b. Bill Monbouquette c. Dick Schwall d. Mike Fornieles

21. _____ Who became the first pitcher to go 3–0 in a championship series?

a. Tug McGraw b. Jesse Orosco c. Nolan Ryan d. Dwight Gooden

22. _____ Who has posted the most wins (14) in one season out of the Met bull pen?

a. Tug McGraw b. Jesse Orosco c. Roger McDowell d. Doug Sisk

23. _____ Twice a 20-game loser for the Mets, he split four World Series decisions with three different teams.

a. Jack Fisher b. Roger Craig c. Al Jackson d. Pedro Ramos

24. _____ Which one of the following pitchers is 3–0 in World Series play?

a. Jon Matlack b. Tom Seaver c. Gary Gentry d. Jerry Koosman

25. _____ Who became the first pitcher to fan 200 batters in his first three seasons in the majors?

a. Dwight Gooden b. Nolan Ryan c. Tom Seaver d. Jerry Koosman

PHILADELPHIA PHILLIES

Infielders

True or False.

1. _____ Dolph Camilli won a home run title with the Phillies.

2. _____ Dave Cash registered more official at-bats (699) in one season than any other National League player.

3. _____ Larry Bowa hit .300 in a season.

4. _____ Mike Schmidt has led the National League in home runs a loop-high eight times.

5. _____ Emil Verban was the "Whiz Kid" second baseman in 1950.

6. _____ Willie Jones hit more home runs in a season than Dick Allen did.

Outfielders

Fill in the blanks.

7. _____ Who hit .400 three times with the Phillies?

8. _____ Who was the Phillie slugger who two times led the National League in home runs three years in a row?

9. _____ Who didn't win the RBI title despite the fact that he drove home 170 runs?

10. _____ Name the Phillie who hit a league-leading .398 one year?

11. _____ Whose tenth-inning home run on the last day of the 1950 season won the pennant for the Phillies?

12. _____ A .308 lifetime hitter, he won two batting titles with the Phillies in the 1950s.

Catchers

Matching.

13. _____ Curt Davis
14. _____ Andy Seminick
15. _____ Tim McCarver

a. He was Steve Carlton's favorite receiver.
b. He was the "Whiz Kids'" receiver?
c. He hit .333 career-wise for the Phillies, .308 overall.

Pitchers

Multiple Choice.

16. _____ Who was the pitcher who won a record 28 games in his rookie year?

    a. Grover Alexander b. Harry Coveleski c. Eppa Rixey d. Bucky Walters

17. _____ Name the 500-plus home run hitter who ended his career with the Phillies as a pitcher.

    a. Babe Ruth b. Ernie Banks c. Eddie Mathews d. Jimmie Foxx

18. _____ "The Giant Killer," he defeated New York five times in one week.

    a. Cal McLish b. Chris Short c. Harry Coveleski d. Art Mahaffey

19. _____ Who was the first relief pitcher to win the MVP Award?

    a. Mike Marshall b. Jim Konstanty c. Tug McGraw d. Joe Black

20. _____ Excluding Warren Spahn and Steve Carlton, he won more games than any other National League left-hander.

    a. Eppa Rixey b. Curt Simmons c. Chris Short d. Jim Kaat

21. _____ Who was the Phillie pitcher who threw a career-record 502 home runs?

    a. Steve Carlton b. Bucky Walters c. Jim Bunning d. Robin Roberts

22. _____ An American League transplant, he notched the 250th win of his 283-win career with the Phils.

    a. Jim Bunning b. Mickey Lolich c. Jim Kaat d. Jim Lonborg

23. _____ Who was the pitcher who threw a perfect game for the Phils?

    a. Jim Bunning b. Schoolboy Rowe c. Jim Lonborg d. Curt Simmons

220

24. _____ Who was the pitcher who led the league in wins
(27) one year and losses (20) the following season?
   a. Grover Alexander b. Steve Carlton c. Jim Lonborg
   d. Curt Simmons
25. _____ Which one of the following pitchers was a Cy
Young Award winner?
   a. Jim Lonborg b. Robin Roberts c. Jim Bunning d. Jim
   Kaat

PITTSBURGH PIRATES

Infielders

Fill in the blanks.

1. _____ Who was the first baseman who set a record when he drilled home runs in eight straight games?

2. _____ Who was the second baseman who hit two game-winning home runs in the 1960 World Series?

3. _____ Who was the Pirate shortstop who hit a club-high .385 in 1935?

4. _____ Who was the .320 lifetime hitter whom many experts consider to be the best all-round third baseman ever to play the game?

5. _____ A four-time home run champ in the American League, he finished his career in 1947 when he hit 25 home runs for the Pirates. Who was he?

6. _____ Name the infielder who won batting titles a National League-high eight times.

Outfielders

Matching.

7. _____ Tommy Leach
8. _____ Max Carey
9. _____ Paul Waner
10. _____ Jerry Lynch
11. _____ Roberto Clemente
12. _____ Lloyd Waner

a. He led the National League in stolen bases ten times.

b. A .317 lifetime hitter, he won four batting titles.

c. He set a then-record by hitting 18 pinch-hit career homers.

d. A .333 lifetime hitter, he won three batting crowns.

e. He collected over 200 hits in each of his first three years in the majors.

f. In 1902 he won the home run crown with six home runs, the lowest figure in history.

Catchers

Multiple Choice.
13. _____ He caught in the 1909 World Series.
a. George Gibson b. Al Lopez c. Earl Smith d. Johnny Gooch
14. _____ He caught in the 1925 and the 1927 World Series.
a. Al Lopez b. George Gibson c. Earl Smith d. Hal Smith
15. _____ He caught in the 1960 World Series.
a. Manny Sanguillen b. Johnny Gooch c. Earl Smith d. Smoky Burgess

Pitchers

True or False.
16. _____ Rip Sewell (143–97) was known primarily for his knuckleball.
17. _____ Bob Friend had a winning major league record.
18. _____ Roy Face was the first reliever to pick up three saves in the same series.
19. _____ Vernon Law was the winning pitcher in the seventh game of the 1960 World Series.
20. _____ Murry Dickson led the National League in losses more times than any other Senior Circuit hurler.
21. _____ Steve Blass led his league in winning percentage one year.
22. _____ Deacon Phillippe had the most decisions in one World Series.
23. _____ Howie Camnitz registered more career wins than Sam Leever did.
24. _____ Wilbur Cooper recorded more lifetime victories than Babe Adams did.
25. _____ Larry French (197–171) never won 20 games in a season.

ST. LOUIS CARDINALS

Infielders

Multiple Choice.

1. _____ Which one of the following first basemen won one home run title, two RBI crowns, and hit over .300 in nine of his first ten years in the majors?
   a. Jim Bottomley b. Rip Collins c. Johnny Mize d. Stan Musial

2. _____ Which one of the following second basemen hit .400 three times?
   a. Frankie Frisch b. Red Schoendienst c. Emil Verban d. Rogers Hornsby

3. _____ Identify the shortstop whom they called "The Ground Hog."
   a. Specs Toporcer b. Marty Marion c. Leo Durocher d. Dick Groat

4. _____ Which one of the following players hit a grand slam home run in a World Series game?
   a. Pepper Martin b. Whitey Kurowski c. Ken Boyer d. Joe Torre

5. _____ Select the player from the following first basemen who performed for the 1934 "Gashouse Gang."
   a. Rip Collins b. Johnny Hopp c. Johnny Mize d. Stan Musial

6. _____ Who, among the following players, hit a home run that won an All-Star Game?
   a. Bill White b. Red Schoendienst c. Dick Groat d. Joe Torre

Outfielders

True or False.

7. _____ Stan Musial was the last National League player to win three consecutive batting titles.

8. _____ Joe Medwick won a Triple Crown.

9. _____ Enos Slaughter retired with a lifetime average that was under .300.

10. _____ Lou Brock broke Ty Cobb's stolen base record (96 thefts) when he stole 118 bases in 1974.

11. _____ Terry Moore played center field, between left fielder Stan Musial and right fielder Enos Slaughter, in the early 1940s.

12. _____ Chick Hafey, Joe Medwick, Harry Walker, and Curt Flood won batting titles.

Catchers

Fill in the blanks.

13. _____ Who was the catcher who threw out Babe Ruth, in an attempted steal, to end the 1926 World Series?

14. _____ Name the receiver who played in three consecutive World Series for the Cardinals.

15. _____ Who was the rookie receiver who stroked four hits in a game in the 1946 World Series?

Pitchers

Matching.

16. _____ Jesse Haines
17. _____ Grover Alexander
18. _____ Burleigh Grimes
19. _____ Dizzy Dean
20. _____ Mort Cooper
21. _____ Max Lanier
22. _____ Harry Brecheen
23. _____ Bob Gibson
24. _____ Steve Carlton
25. _____ Johnny Beazley

a. Nine times he struck out more than 200 batters in a season, and he pitched 13 shutouts in one year.

b. In five full seasons with the Cardinals, he averaged 24 victories a season.

c. He picked up three wins, one of them coming in relief, in a series.

d. With another team he won 30 or more games three straight years.

e. He, like Grover Alexander, won two games against the Yankees in 1926.

f. He missed the 1947–48 seasons because he was banned from baseball for "jumping" to the Mexican Leagues in 1946.

g. He won only 31 career contests, but he copped 21 of them, in addition to two series victories, in 1942.

h. In 1942 he led the league in ERA (1.78) and shutouts (10).

i. At the age of 38, he won two World Series games for the Cardinals.

j. He struck out 19 batters in a 10-inning game, but lost.

ATLANTA BRAVES

Infielders

Multiple Choice.

1. _____ Whom did they call "The Baby Bull"?
   a. Felipe Alou b. Deron Johnson c. Tito Francona d. Orlando Cepeda

2. _____ Identify the player who hit more home runs (43) in one season than any other second baseman in the history of the game.
   a. Milt Bolling b. Felix Millan c. Bob Aspromonte d. Davy Johnson

3. _____ Who is the Brave infielder who with another team led the league in fielding at two different positions?
   a. Dennis Menke b. Ken Oberkfell c. Marty Perez d. Glenn Hubbard

4. _____ Which one of the following third basemen played in five World Series?
   a. Clete Boyer b. Eddie Mathews c. Darrell Evans d. Dennis Menke

5. _____ Who was the Brave who hit a season-high 47 homers and a season-high 135 RBIs?
   a. Orlando Cepeda b. Eddie Mathews c. Deron Johnson d. Willie Montanez

6. _____ Who is the first baseman who once hit 30 home runs in a season for the Phillies and, in a brief stint with the Braves, hit .321 in 1976 and 20 home runs in 1977?
   a. Darrell Evans b. Darrel Chaney c. Willie Montanez d. Jerry Royster

Outfielders

True or False.

7. _____ Mike Lum was the only batter ever to pinch-hit for Hank Aaron.

8. _____ Hank Aaron hit more home runs in Atlanta than he did in Milwaukee.

9. _____ Felipe Alou was called "The Road Runner."

10. _____ Dale Murphy has been the youngest back-to-back MVP winner in National League history.

227

11. _____ Rico Carty put big numbers on the board (.330 batting average and 22 home runs) as a rookie.
12. _____ Ken Griffey played on back-to-back World Series winners.

Catchers

Fill in the blanks.
13. _____ Name the catcher who hit .315 with 36 home runs and 101 RBIs in 1966.
14. _____ Who was the rookie catcher who hit 33 home runs in 1971?
15. _____ Who is the catcher who hit home runs in five consecutive games?

Pitchers

Matching.

16. _____ Tony Cloninger
17. _____ Phil Niekro
18. _____ Gene Garber
19. _____ Milt Pappas
20. _____ Hoyt Wilhelm
21. _____ Denny McLain
22. _____ Andy Messersmith
23. _____ Rick Mahler
24. _____ David Palmer
25. _____ Joe Niekro

a. He pitched a five-inning rain-abbreviated perfect game.
b. He drove home nine runs in one game.
c. He was the only 200-game winner who never won 20 games in a season.
d. He led the league in wins (21) and losses (20) in the same year.
e. He has more than 200 career saves.
f. His 7–0 start in 1985 was among the best in Braves' history.
g. He played out his option and signed with the Braves in an historic free agent deal.
h. The last 30-game winner in the majors, he ended up his career in Atlanta.
i. He won 20 games in back-to-back years for another club.
j. He played with nine major league teams.

CINCINNATI REDS

Infielders

Matching.

1. _____ Ted Kluszewski
2. _____ Joe Morgan
3. _____ Lonny Frey
4. _____ Pete Rose
5. _____ Frank McCormick
6. _____ Connie Ryan

a. He succeeded Eddie Stanky as manager of the Rangers.

b. He won the MVP Award in 1940.

c. He won back-to-back MVP titles.

d. He got five hits in a game a National League record-tying nine times.

e. He played second base for the pennant-winning clubs of 1939–40.

f. He averaged 43 home runs a year for a four-year span.

Outfielders

Multiple Choice.

7. _____ Who was the player who made a bigger name for himself in professional football than he did in professional baseball?

   a. Harry Craft b. Ival Goodman c. Greasy Neale d. Wally Berger

8. _____ Which one of the following players has led the National League in RBIs?

   a. Cesar Geronimo b. George Foster c. Vada Pinson d. Ken Griffey

9. _____ In one season he hit .377, the club high.

   a. Cy Seymour b. Frank Robinson c. Edd Roush d. Curt Walker

10. _____ An ineffective pitcher for the Athletics, he switched to the outfield with the Reds and posted a .301 lifetime batting average, which included a .351 mark over a three-year period (1924–26).

230

a. Rube Bressler b. Curt Walker c. Ival Goodman d. Harry Craft

11. _____ Name the .323 lifetime hitter who won two batting titles.

a. Frank Robinson b. Vada Pinson c. Edd Roush d. Cy Seymour

12. _____ Who was the Red MVP winner who posted a .294 lifetime average and slugged 586 home runs?

a. Edd Roush b. Wally Berger c. Vada Pinson d. Frank Robinson

Catchers

True or False.

13. _____ Johnny Bench has won more than one home run crown.

14. _____ Bubbles Hargrave was one of two catchers to win the batting title.

15. _____ Ernie Lombardi had a lifetime batting average of .300 or better.

Pitchers

Fill in the blanks.

16. _____ Who was the only pitcher to throw consecutive no-hitters?

17. _____ The youngest player ever to appear in a major league game, he led the National League in shutouts (5) in 1955.

18. _____ Who was the two-time 20-game winner who struck out more than 200 batters four years in a row?

19. _____ Name the 198-game winner who began his major league career as a third baseman.

20. _____ A one-time 27-game loser, he reeled off three straight 20-game winning seasons for the 1938–40 Reds.

21. _____ Called "The Whip," he led the league in wins (22), complete games (23), and strikeouts (193) in 1947.

22. _____ Who was the 1985 starter who became the first rookie 20-game winner in the majors since the Yankees' Bob Grim in 1954?

23. _____ In the 1972 World Series he, with relief aid from Clay Carroll in the ninth inning, pitched the Reds to their only 1–0 win in post-season play.

24. _____ Who was the first Little League product to pitch in the major leagues?

25. _____ Who is the Red relief specialist who notched 29 saves in 1986?

HOUSTON ASTROS

Infielders

Fill in the blanks.

1. _____ Who was the first baseman—the American League's RBI champ in 1976—who averaged 27 home runs per year during his three-year stay in Houston?

2. _____ Who was the .288 lifetime hitter who finished his career with the Astros after setting a record of appearing at the plate 600 or more times for 12 consecutive years in the American League?

3. _____ Who, going into the 1987 season, was the Astros' all-time leader with 70 pinch-hits?

4. _____ Who was the Astro third baseman who three times hit more than 20 home runs in a season?

5. _____ Who was the former first baseman with the Astros who wrote a confessional best seller, *Joe, You Coulda Made Us Proud*?

6. _____ Who was the Houston rookie second baseman (1965) who reached double figures in doubles (22), triples (12), and home runs (14)?

Outfielders

Matching.

7. _____ Cesar Cedeno
8. _____ Rusty Staub
9. _____ Jimmy Wynn
10. _____ Jose Cruz
11. _____ Terry Puhl
12. _____ Greg Gross

a. He was the .314 hitter who was named National League Rookie Player of the Year by *The Sporting News* in 1974.

b. He tied a record when he didn't make one error in a 157-game season.

c. He hit a homer in his first game with the Astros and has topped .300 six times with them.

d. He stole 61 bases, a club record, one year.

e. He hit .333, the club high, one season.

f. He clubbed 37 home runs, the team top, one year.

Catchers

Multiple Choice.

13. _____ This veteran of 16 campaigns played in two Word Series with both the Mets and the Dodgers, but he played his first two years in the majors with the Astros.

a. Jerry Grote b. Ed Herrman c. John Bateman d. Johnny Edwards

14. _____ A long-ball hitter with defensive liabilities, he was traded to the Yankees during the 1977 season.

a. Joe Ferguson b. Cliff Johnson c. Ed Herrman d. John Bateman

15. _____ Name the catcher who was traded for Larry Dierker.

a. Cliff Johnson b. Jerry Grote c. Ed Herrman d. Joe Ferguson

True or False.

16. _____ Joe Niekro is the Astros' all-time single-season winner.

17. _____ Don Wilson pitched two no-hitters for the Astros.

18. _____ Mike Cuellar came up to the majors with Houston.

19. _____ Larry Dierker had a 20-win season with the Astros.

20. _____ Dave Smith established club save records for single season (33) and career (100) recently.

21. _____ Jim Bouton finished his career with the Astros.

22. _____ Nolan Ryan established a modern mark when he struck out the first eight batters in a game.

23. _____ Bob Knepper's 17 wins in 1986 is the all-time high for an Astro lefty.

24. _____ Bo Belinsky pitched a no-hitter for Houston.

25. _____ Mike Scott's 306 strikeouts in 1986 is the all-time high for the Astros.

LOS ANGELES DODGERS

Infielders

Matching.

1. _____ Steve Garvey
2. _____ Charlie Neal
3. _____ Maury Wills
4. _____ Ron Cey
5. _____ Gil Hodges
6. _____ Davey Lopes

a. He drove home 100 or more runs for seven consecutive years.
b. He stole 11 bases in the World Series.
c. He hit four home runs in a Championship Series.
d. He hit .370 in the 1959 World Series.
e. He's hit more than 300 home runs.
f. He won the stolen base title six consecutive years.

Outfielders

Multiple Choice.

7. _____ Who was called "The Reading Rifle"?
   a. Manny Mota b. Carl Furillo c. Dick Allen d. Rick Monday

8. _____ Who was the Dodger who hit two pinch-hit home runs in the 1959 World Series?
   a. Chuck Essegian b. Ron Fairly c. Jimmy Wynn d. Gino Cimoli

9. _____ Name the Dodger who hit 407 lifetime home runs.
   a. Duke Snider b. Wally Moon c. Frank Howard d. Tommy Davis

10. _____ Who's hit more than 30 home runs three times?
   a. Mike Marshall b. Dusty Baker c. Pedro Guerrero d. Ken Landreaux

11. _____ A seven-year member of the Dodgers, he hit better than 40 home runs three straight years for another club.
   a. Frank Howard b. Jimmy Wynn c. Tommy Davis d. Dick Allen

236

12. _____ Winner of back-to-back batting titles, he drove home a club-high 153 runs in one season.
a. Tommy Davis b. Duke Snider c. Frank Howard d. Jimmy Wynn

Catchers

True or False.
13. _____ Johnny Roseboro spent his entire career with the Dodgers.
14. _____ Steve Yeager and John Ferguson both had lifetime batting averages that were above .250.
15. _____ Jeff Torborg hit higher than .250 in his career.

Pitchers

Fill in the blanks.
16. _____ From 1959–65 he struck out more than 200 batters six of seven times.
17. _____ Who tied Carl Hubbell's record in the All-Star Game when he struck out five consecutive American League batters?
18. _____ Who threw the 715th home run pitch to Hank Aaron?
19. _____ Who in a recent year chalked up an 11–0 record at Dodger Stadium?
20. _____ Who posted a record 21 consecutive seasons of more than 100 strikeouts?
21. _____ Who did the Dodgers get from the White Sox for Dick Allen?
22. _____ Name the 148-game winner who won his last four World Series decisions, including a seventh-game clincher.
23. _____ Who was the 16–3 relief pitcher who led the National League in winning percentage (.842) and games (69) in 1963 while he saved 21 contests?
24. _____ Who was the Dodger reliever who was nicknamed "The Vulture"?
25. _____ Who was the Dodger lefty, a two-time 20-game winner, who ended his career with 196 wins and 195 losses?

SAN DIEGO PADRES

Infielders

True or False.

1. _____ Nate Colbert hit more home runs in one season than any other Padre.

2. _____ Alan Wiggins stole a club-high 70 bases.

3. _____ Garry Templeton receives few bases on balls.

4. _____ Graig Nettles, in back-to-back seasons in which he played 150 or more games, failed to hit a triple.

5. _____ Steve Garvey has hit more than 300 career homers.

6. _____ Kevin Mitchell, who took Graig Nettles's position at third base, is the son of a former basketball teammate of Nettles's at San Diego State.

Outfielders

Fill in the blanks.

7. _____ Who led the league in hits in both 1984 and 1986?

8. _____ Who was selected by the Atlanta Hawks in the NBA draft, the Utah Stars in the ABA draft, and the Minnesota Vikings in the NFL draft?

9. _____ Nicknamed "Downtown," he twice hit 20 or more home runs in a season for the Padres. What's his real name?

10. _____ Who was the long-ball hitter who tied a record by playing on four different teams in the same year?

11. _____ Who is the current player who averaged 20 home runs per season in his first three years in the majors?

12. _____ Who was the 1975–76 outfielder who played for the Cardinals in the 1967–68 World Series and the Reds in the 1970 and 1972 fall classics?

Catchers

Matching.

13. _____ Gene Tenace
14. _____ Fred Kendall
15. _____ Terry Kennedy

a. He was part of a package deal for George Hendrick.
b. He is the son of a former major leaguer.
c. He averaged 17 home runs a year for the Padres in four seasons.

Pitchers

Multiple Choice.

16. _____ He won the Cy Young Award.
   a. Randy Jones b. Ed Whitson c. Rick Wise d. John Montefusco

17. _____ He won Cy Young awards in both leagues.
   a. Rollie Fingers b. LaMarr Hoyt c. Randy Jones d. Gaylord Perry

18. _____ Identify the Padre pitcher who struck out a club-record 231 batters in one season.
   a. Butch Metzger b. Johnny Podres c. Clay Kirby d. Steven Arlen

19. _____ Who was the winner over the Yankees in the 1976 World Series who was 13–30 in his short stay with the Padres?
   a. Butch Metzger b. Dave Roberts c. Fred Norman d. Clay Kirby

20. _____ Who was the pitcher whose 12 consecutive victories at the start of his career are a record?
   a. Bruce Metzger b. Pat Dobson c. Rich Folkers d. Johnny Podres

21. _____ Who is the pitcher who was suspended in 1986 for criticizing the owner's product?
   a. Ed Whitson b. Eric Show c. Goose Gossage d. Dave Dravecky

22. _____ Who was the winner of 148 career games and four World Series starts who finished his career by posting a 5–6 record with the Padres?
   a. Don Larsen b. Mudcat Grant c. Johnny Podres d. Jim Bouton

23. _____ Who was the Cy Young Award winner in the

American League who was released by the Padres before the 1987 season?

a. Joe Niekro b. Goose Gossage c. LaMarr Hoyt d. Rollie Fingers

24. _____ Who led the league in saves in back-to-back years?

a. Bob Shirley b. Tim Lollar c. Rollie Fingers d. Goose Gossage

25. _____ Who was the two-game winner for the Brewers in the 1982 World Series who pitched his first three years with the Padres?

a. Rollie Fingers b. Tim Lollar c. Mike Caldwell d. Joe Niekro

SAN FRANCISCO GIANTS

Infielders

Multiple Choice.

1. _____ Who was the slugger who tied Ted Williams for tenth place on the all-time home run list?
   a. Orlando Cepeda b. Willie McCovey c. Willie Montanez d. Dave Kingman

2. _____ Which one of the following players hit a grand slam in World Series play?
   a. Chuck Hiller b. Don Blasingame c. Ron Hunt d. Hal Lanier

3. _____ Which one of the following players was the first San Francisco Giant shortstop?
   a. Chris Speier b. Tito Fuentes c. Jose Pagan d. Daryl Spencer

4. _____ Who tied a league record when he drove home six runs in one inning?
   a. Jim Davenport b. Bill Madlock c. Jim Ray Hart d. Darrell Evans

5. _____ Which one of the following hit .300 for three different teams?
   a. Willie McCovey b. Orlando Cepeda c. Darrell Evans d. Jose Pagan

6. _____ In three consecutive years he hit .300 in three different cities.
   a. Willie Montanez b. Jim Ray Hart c. Ron Hunt d. Tito Fuentes

Outfielders

True or False.

7. _____ Willie Kirkland hit the first home run at Candlestick Park.

8. _____ Dave Kingman struck out more times (189) in one season than any other player in the history of the game.

9. _____ Willie Mays hit more home runs in one season in New York than he did in San Francisco.

10. _____ Bobby Murcer was traded to the Giants in a deal for Bobby Bonds.

11. _____ Harvey Kuenn won a batting title with the Giants.
12. _____ All three Alou brothers—Matty, Felipe, and Jesus—once played in the same outfield at the same time.

Catchers

Fill in the blanks.
13. _____ Who was the Giant catcher who hit 27 home runs one year?
14. _____ Name the former Red backstop who hit 17 and 21 home runs in his two full seasons with the Giants?
15. _____ Who is the present-day catcher who topped National League receivers with a .995 fielding percentage in 1986?

Pitchers

Matching.
16. _____ John Montefusco
17. _____ Gaylord Perry
18. _____ Juan Marichal
19. _____ Stu Miller
20. _____ Jack Sanford
21. _____ Billy Loes
22. _____ Don Larsen
23. _____ Ruben Gomez
24. _____ Billy O'Dell
25. _____ Billy Pierce

a. A former Yankee, he beat the Bombers in the 1962 World Series.

b. He won a club-record 16 consecutive games in 1962.

c. He pitched the last Giant no-hitter.

d. Joe Adcock "ran him off" the mound one day.

e. He pitched two of his four 20-game-win seasons with the Giants.

f. He was a uniformed witness on the days Gil Hodges, Joe Adcock, Rocky Colavito, and Willie Mays hit four home runs in a game.

g. He won 20 or more games six times in a seven-year period of time.

h. In 1961 he led the league's relief pitchers in wins (14), winning percentage (.737), and saves (17).

i. A 19-game winner for the pennant-winning 1962 club, he led the league's relief pitchers in wins in both 1964 and 1965.

j. Two times a 20-game winner in the American League, he helped the Giants win the 1962 pennant by posting a 16–6 record.

BALTIMORE ORIOLES

Infielders

Fill in the blanks.

1. _____ From 1960–62 this slugging first baseman hit 100 home runs, including a career-high 46 in 1961.

2. _____ Name the second baseman who hit .280 or better for three consecutive pennant winners.

3. _____ Who was the infielder who set a club record when he stole 57 bases in 1964?

4. _____ In 1969 he hit .500 in the league Championship Series, and in 1970 he hit .583; in 1970 he hit .429 in the World Series, and in 1971 he hit .318.

5. _____ A consistent Gold Glove winner, he turned in an American League record lifetime fielding average of .977 at his position.

6. _____ Three times an RBI champ, this long-ball-hitting right-handed hitter (247 career homers) was the first starting third baseman with the Orioles.

Outfielders

Matching.

7. _____ Bob Nieman
8. _____ Dick Williams
9. _____ Paul Blair
10. _____ Frank Robinson
11. _____ Gene Woodling
12. _____ Ken Singleton

a. A .284 lifetime hitter, "Young Reliable" played on five world championship teams.

b. In 1958 he hit .325, which remained the Orioles' all-time batting high for one season until 1977.

c. He hit 49 home runs in one season, the club's all-time high.

d. A journeyman outfielder with a .260 lifetime average, he later managed three different teams to four pennants and two world titles.

e. He presently holds the club's all-time single-season (.328) batting high.

f. Considered the best defensive outfielder in the American League during his time, he turned slugger in the 1970 World Series, ripping the Red pitching staff for a .474 average.

Catchers

Multiple Choice.

13. _____ Which one of the following Oriole receivers had a couple of on-field run-ins with Billy Martin?

    a. Hal Smith b. Clint Courtney c. John Orsino d. Dick Brown

14. _____ A .255 lifetime hitter, he later emerged as one of the premiere batting instructors in the game.

    a. Charlie Lau b. Gus Triandos c. Hal Smith d. Dick Brown

15. _____ Who was the power-hitting backstop (167 home runs) whose career began to decline when Hoyt Wilhelm brought his knuckleball to Baltimore?

a. John Orsino b. Dick Brown c. Gus Triandos d. Hal Smith

Pitchers

True or False.

16. _____ Both Mike Cuellar and Dave McNally won 24 games, the club high, in one season.

17. _____ Jim Palmer holds the strikeout mark with 202 in a season.

18. _____ Wally Bunker was the youngest pitcher to hurl a shutout in World Series play.

19. _____ Chuck Estrada was traded to Cincinnati in the controversial deal for Frank Robinson.

20. _____ Stu Miller threw the pitch that Mickey Mantle hit for his 500th home run.

21. _____ Don Larsen won 21 games in his only season with the Orioles.

22. _____ Mike Flanagan won a Cy Young Award.

23. _____ Jim Palmer, Wally Bunker, and Dave McNally tossed shutouts against the Dodgers in the 1966 World Series.

24. _____ Hoyt Wilhelm, in a rare start, pitched a no-hitter against the Yankees in 1958.

25. _____ Robin Roberts had a losing record with the Orioles.

BOSTON RED SOX

Infielders

Matching.

1. _____ Billy Goodman
2. _____ Pete Runnels
3. _____ Vern Stephens
4. _____ Rico Petrocelli
5. _____ Jimmy Collins
6. _____ Pinky Higgins

a. He managed the Sox for eight seasons.
b. A .294 lifetime hitter, he managed Boston to its first pennant and series victory.
c. A batting champ, he ended his career with a *.300* lifetime average.
d. From 1969–71 he averaged almost 33 home runs per season.
e. He won batting titles two years apart.
f. A two-time RBI champ with Boston, he won another crown before coming to the Sox.

Outfielders

Multiple Choice.

7. _____ Though this .306 lifetime hitter played only seven years in the big time, he set a major league record when he rocked 67 doubles in one season.

a. Duffy Lewis b. Ben Chapman c. Harry Hooper d. Earl Webb

8. _____ He was the only player ever to pinch-hit for Ted Williams.

a. Gene Stephens b Carroll Hardy c. Sam Mele d. Al Zarilla

9. _____ He holds the club's stolen base record for one season.

a. Dom DiMaggio b. Tris Speaker c. Tommy Harper d. Reggie Smith

10. _____ In the same year that he led the league in stolen

bases (22), he rapped into 32 double plays, a major league record at that time.

    a. Jackie Jensen b. Clyde Vollmer c. Fred Lynn d. Ken Harrelson

11. _____ Hollywood made a movie, *Fear Strikes Out,* about a segment of his life.

    a. Jimmie Foxx b. Hoot Evers c. Ted Williams d. Jimmy Piersall

12. _____ He won three batting titles with a combined mark of .315 for those years.

    a. Dale Alexander b. Carl Yastrzemski c. Elmer Flick d. Ted Williams

Catchers

True or False.

13. _____ Bill Carrigan, who hit .257 during a ten-year career with the Red Sox, later managed Boston to back-to-back world titles.

14. _____ Rick Ferrell handled the pitching serves of his brother, Wes, with the Red Sox.

15. _____ Birdie Tebbetts was the starting catcher on the great Red Sox teams of the late 1940s.

Pitchers

Fill in the blanks.

16. _____ Which Red Sox pitcher threw the first perfect game of the modern era?

17. _____ Who won two games, including a one-hitter, in the 1967 World Series?

18. _____ Son of a Hall of Famer, he pitched for Boston from 1956–59. Who was he?

19. _____ Name the relief pitcher who led the American League bull pen specialists in wins in each of his first three years in the majors (1962–64) and who struck out more batters than he pitched innings in each of those seasons.

20. _____ Who was the pitcher who lost the playoff game, between the Indians and the Red Sox, that decided the 1948 pennant?

21. _____ Who set the league record for shut-outs by southpaws (9) in one season?

22. _____ Name the pitcher who won his 300th—and final—game with the Red Sox.

23. _____ A two-time 20-game loser with the Red Sox, he went on to win seven World Series games with another American League team. Who was he?

24. _____ Who was the pitcher who, including the regular season and series, won 37 games and lost six in 1912?

25. _____ Who was the pitcher who came on in relief, with a runner who had walked on first base with no one out in the first inning, and proceeded to pitch a perfect game?

CLEVELAND INDIANS

Infielders

Fill in the blanks.

1. _____ Who was the first baseman who drove home 162 runs, a club record, in one season?

2. _____ Who was the second baseman who made an unassisted triple play in the 1920 World Series?

3. _____ When Lou Boudreau was traded to the Red Sox, who took his place at shortstop?

4. _____ Name the third baseman who made two great defensive plays against Joe DiMaggio on the night "The Yankee Clipper's" 56-game batting streak was broken.

5. _____ Can you name the last Indian who won a batting title?

6. _____ Who was the batter who hit the ball that Willie Mays ran down in the 1954 World Series?

Outfielders

Matching.

7. ____ Elmer Flick
8. ____ Joe Jackson
9. ____ Tris Speaker
10. ____ Earl Averill
11. ____ Jeff Heath
12. ____ Larry Doby

a. He was the first black player to compete in the American League.

b. He won a batting title with a .306 average.

c. He never won a batting title, even though he hit .408 in one season and .356 lifetime.

d. He hit at least one home run in every major league park that was in use during his career.

e. He stopped Ty Cobb's string of nine consecutive batting titles when he led the league with a .386 average in 1916.

f. He had a son who played in the big leagues.

Catchers

Multiple Choice.
13. _____ Who caught Bob Feller when "Rapid Robert" no-hit the Yankees, 1–0, in 1946, and provided the only run in the game with a home run?

    a. Buddy Rosar b. Frank Hayes c. Rollie Hemsley d. Jim Hegan

14. _____ Name the catcher who handled six different 20-game winners during his career with the Tribe.

    a. Steve O'Neill b. Luke Sewell c. Jim Hegan d. Johnny Romano

15. _____ Which one of the following catchers had the highest lifetime average?

    a. Buddy Rosar b. Luke Sewell c. Jim Hegan d. Russ Nixon

Pitchers

True or False.
16. _____ Jim Bagby won more games in one season than any other Indian pitcher.

17. _____ Herb Score never won 20 games in a season.

18. _____ Johnny Allen won 15 of 16 decisions in 1937 to set an American League mark (.938) for winning percentage in one season.

19. _____ The two pitchers who joined forces to halt Joe DiMaggio's 56-game hitting streak were Jim Bagby and Al Smith.

20. _____ Bob Feller, Bob Lemon, Early Wynn, and Mike Garcia all won 20 or more games in the same season.

21. _____ Gene Bearden, who pitched Cleveland to a pennant and a World Series crown in 1948 when he posted a record of 20–7, never before or after registered a winning record.

22. _____ Bob Feller pitched more no-hitters than any other right-handed pitcher.

23. _____ Both Jim and Gaylord Perry turned in 20-win seasons with the Tribe.

24. _____ Wes Ferrell had more consecutive 20-win seasons than did Bob Feller, Bob Lemon, or Early Wynn.

25. _____ Early Wynn finished his career with the Indians.

DETROIT TIGERS

Infielders

Multiple Choice.

1. _____ One year he drove home 183 runs, the club high; the following season, he clubbed 58 home runs, the team high.
   a. Norm Cash b. Hank Greenberg c. Walt Dropo d. George Burns

2. _____ He was the last Tiger to win a batting title.
   a. George Kell b. Harvey Kuenn c. Al Kaline d. Norm Cash

3. _____ Which one of the following players has been one of only two players who competed in every game of a 154-game schedule without hitting into a double play?
   a. Dick McAuliffe b. Lu Blue c. Tom Tresh d. George Kell

4. _____ Who was the only third baseman, in addition to George Brett and Carney Lansford, to win a batting title?
   a. Marv Owen b. Ray Boone c. Eddie Yost d. George Kell

5. _____ Name the league's batting titlist (1959) who was traded after the season for the league's home run hitter.
   a. Charlie Gehringer b. Harvey Kuenn c. Al Kaline d. Norm Cash

6. _____ The Tigers won 18 of their 23 batting titles before one of their infielders won the coveted award. Who was that 1937 standout?
   a. Harvey Kuenn b. George Kell c. Charlie Gehringer d. Hank Greenberg

Outfielders

True or False.

7. _____ Sam Crawford was the only modern-day player to lead the National League and the American League in both triples and home runs.

8. _____ Ty Cobb and Harry Heilmann have been the only teammates to hit .400.

9. _____ Al Kaline compiled a .300 lifetime average.

252

10. _____ In the seventh inning of the seventh game of the 1968 World Series, Rocky Colavito got the key triple that broke up a pitching duel between Mickey Lolich and Bob Gibson and paced the Bengals to a 4–1 victory.

11. _____ Hoot Evers, Johnny Groth, and Vic Wertz, outfielders for the Tigers, all hit .300 or better in the same season.

12. _____ Ty Cobb was the youngest player to win a major league batting title.

Catchers

Fill in the blanks.

13. _____ Who set a record when he hit 18 home runs in one month?

14. _____ Who was the playing manager who compiled a lifetime batting average of .320?

15. _____ Who was the starting receiver for the Tigers' 1968 world champions?

Matching.

16. _____ Mark Fidrych
17. _____ Denny McLain
18. _____ Mickey Lolich
19. _____ Jim Bunning
20. _____ Frank Lary
21. _____ Bob Cain
22. _____ Virgil Trucks
23. _____ Hal Newhouser
24. _____ Schoolboy Rowe
25. _____ George Mullin

a. He was the pitcher who tried to keep the ball low to Bill Veeck's midget, Eddie Gaedel.

b. He tied an American League record by winning 16 consecutive decisions.

c. He was the only modern-day pitcher to lose 20 games with a pennant winner.

d. He was the only Tiger pitcher to win the Rookie of the Year Award.

e. He was known as "The Yankee Killer."

f. He won Cy Young awards in back-to-back seasons.

g. He was the only Tiger pitcher to strike out 300 or more batters in a season.

h. Two of the five games he won in one season were no-hitters.

i. He won more than 100 games in each league, and he struck out more than 1,000 batters in each loop.

j. He led the league in wins three straight years.

MILWAUKEE BREWERS

Infielders

True or False.

1. _____ George Scott led the American League in home runs one year.

2. _____ Jim Gantner has more than 1,000 career hits.

3. _____ Robin Yount has more than 2,000 hits.

4. _____ Paul Molitor holds the team record for most steals (45) in a season.

5. _____ Cecil Cooper is the team leader in season batting average and RBIs.

6. _____ Don Money never hit more than 20 home runs in a season for the Brewers.

Outfielders

Fill in the blanks.

7. _____ Who was the Hall of Famer who played the last two years of his 23-year record-studded career with the Brewers?

8. _____ Who is the player who hit 33 home runs in his rookie season?

9. _____ Who hit a season-high 45 homers in 1979?

10. _____ Who was the infielder-outfielder, known more for his base-stealing exploits than his power, who blasted 31 home runs in 1970, the first year of the franchise?

11. _____ Who tied Reggie Jackson for the home run lead in 1980?

12. _____ Who tied Reggie Jackson for the home run lead in 1982?

Catchers

Matching.

13. _____ Darrell Porter
14. _____ Ellie Rodriguez
15. _____ Charlie Moore

a. His best batting average with Milwaukee was .285.
b. His best mark with the Brewers was .254.
c. His best season with Milwaukee was .301.

Pitchers

Multiple Choice.

16. _____ Who won a club-high 22 games in 1978?
a. Jim Slaton b. Ken Sanders c. Mike Caldwell d. Jim Lonborg

17. _____ Who leads the Brewer moundsmen with 207 strikeouts in a season?
a. Ken Brett b. Billy Champion c. Bill Travers d. Ted Higuera

18. _____ Who was the former bonus baby who lost 18 games in 1970?
a. Lew Krausse b. Gene Brabender c. Skip Lockwood d. John O'Donoghue

19. _____ Who was the Milwaukee pitcher who was killed in an Arizona dune buggy crash on January 1, 1976?
a. Danny Frisella b. Milt Tracy c. Dan Story d. Jim Clancy

20. _____ Name the former Cy Young Award winner who was 14–12 in his only season with the Brewers?
a. Chris Short b. Jim Lonborg c. Bill Parsons d. Al Downing

21. _____ Who won 20 games in his rookie season?
a. Ted Higuera b. Mike Caldwell c. Moose Haas d. Jim Slaton

22. _____ Who won the MVP Award?
a. Mike Caldwell b. Rollie Fingers c. Pete Vuckovich d. Pete Ladd

23. _____ Who won the Cy Young Award?
a. Don Sutton b. Mike Caldwell c. Pete Vuckovich d. Moose Haas

24. _____ Who is the present-day 300-game winner who once pitched for the Brewers?

a. Phil Niekro b. Tom Seaver c. Steve Carlton d. Don Sutton

25. _____ Who was the former All-Star Game pitcher who chalked up a career-high 16 saves in 1986?

a. Mark Clear b. Juan Nieves c. Dan Plesac d. Bill Wegman

NEW YORK YANKEES

Infielders

Fill in the blanks.

1. _____ Who was the first baseman who replaced Lou Gehrig in the lineup after "The Iron Horse" ended his string of 2,130 consecutive games?

2. _____ Who was the second baseman whose twelfth hit of the 1953 World Series scored Hank Bauer with the winning run in the ninth inning of the sixth and decisive game?

3. _____ Name the shortstop who was given his release on Old Timers' Day in 1956.

4. _____ Who was the Yankee third baseman who won four home run titles with another team?

5. _____ Who was the infielder whose only two hits in a World Series were home runs?

6. _____ Who was the first baseman who hit .293 and banged eight home runs in eight series?

Outfielders

Matching.

7. _____ Joe DiMaggio
8. _____ Hank Bauer
9. _____ Roger Maris
10. _____ Elston Howard
11. _____ Tommy Henrich
12. _____ Babe Ruth

a. He came to the Yankees in a trade with Kansas City.

b. Primarily a catcher, he also played the outfield and first base in the series.

c. He won two home run titles.

d. He was called "Old Reliable."

e. He got a second chance, after a quick pitch, and hit a home run.

f. He drove home all four of his team's runs in a series win.

Catchers

Multiple Choice.

13. _____ One year he hit .362, the all-time high for catchers.
   a. Bill Dickey b. Yogi Berra c. Thurman Munson d. Elston Howard

14. _____ He hit two two-run home runs in the seventh game of a World Series win.
   a. Wally Schang b. Bill Dickey c. Yogi Berra d. Aaron Robinson

15. _____ He hit .373, the third all-time best, in series play.
   a. Ralph Houk b. Yogi Berra c. Bill Dickey d. Thurman Munson

Pitchers

True or False.

16. _____ Bill Bevens, after he lost both a no-hitter and the game on the last pitch of a 1947 series game, never again won an outing in the major leagues.

17. _____ Don Larsen struck out Duke Snider for the last out of his perfect game in the 1956 World Series.

18. _____ Johnny Sain saved the last game in both the 1951 and the 1952 World Series.

19. _____ Whitey Ford both won and lost more games than any other pitcher in series competition.

20. _____ Red Ruffing hit more home runs than any other major league pitcher.

21. _____ Herb Pennock and Lefty Gomez won a combined total of 11 games without dropping a decision in series play.

22. _____ Allie Reynolds pitched more no-hitters than any other Yankee hurler.

23. _____ Before 1977, Jim Bouton was the last Yankee pitcher to win a World Series game.

24. _____ Joe Page, Johnny Murphy, Luis Arroyo, and Lindy McDaniel were relief pitchers, in the presented order, for the Yankees.

25. _____ Spud Chandler and Sparky Lyle both won MVP awards.

TORONTO BLUE JAYS

Infielders

Matching.

1. _____ Tony Fernandez
2. _____ Willie Upshaw
3. _____ Damaso Garcia
4. _____ Alfredo Griffin
5. _____ John Mayberry
6. _____ Danny Ainge

a. A Brigham Young graduate, he's played major league baseball and NBA basketball.

b. In his four years in Toronto, he averaged over 22 home runs a season.

c. He was the first player in Blue Jay history to surpass 200 hits (213) in a season.

d. He hit 27 home runs and drove home 104 runs in 1983.

e. He was the co-winner of the Rookie of the Year Award in 1979.

f. He stole a club-high 54 bases in 1982.

Outfielders

Multiple Choice.

7. _____ Who hit a then club-high .315 in 1983?
a. Jesse Barfield b. George Bell c. Lloyd Moseby d. Dave Collins

8. _____ Who hit a club-high 47 home runs in one year?
a. John Mayberry b. Ron Fairly c. Rico Carty d. George Bell

9. _____ Who drove home a club-record 134 runs one year?
a. Rico Carty b. George Bell c. Jesse Barfield d. John Mayberry

10. _____ Who was the one-time Blue Jay who struck out three out of three times for the Yankees in a World Series?
a. Bob Bailor b. Otto Velez c. Barry Bonnell d. Al Woods

11. _____ Who in one of his two seasons with Toronto hit .308 and hit a league-high 15 triples?

a. Dave Collins b. Al Woods c. Barry Bonnell d. Tommy Hutton

12. _____ Who at age 39—in his only season with Toronto—batted .279, hit 19 home runs, and drove home 64 runs?

a. Rico Carty b. Tommy Hutton c. Ron Fairly d. Bob Bailor

Catchers

True or False.

13. _____ Alan Ashby was the first full-time catcher of the Blue Jays.

14. _____ Rick Cerone, among others, was traded by the Blue Jays to the Yankees for Chris Chambliss, among others, who never played a game for Toronto.

15. _____ Ernie Whitt has hit 20 home runs in a season.

Pitchers

Fill in the blanks.

16. _____ Who was the former Blue Jay who won a club-high 17 games twice?

17. _____ Who is the pitcher who struck out a club-high 198 batters in one season?

18. _____ Who became the first starting left-handed pitcher to win for the Blue Jays since Paul Mirabella in 1980?

19. _____ Who, with a glittering 1.72 ERA, fell five innings short of qualifying for the American League title one year?

20. _____ Who led Toronto in saves in his first three seasons with the club?

21. _____ Who became the first Toronto pitcher to go over 100 career wins?

22. _____ Who was the 1982 Cy Young Award winner who was 7–7 in his only season with the Blue Jays?

23. _____ Who was the Blue Jay reliever who, with a National League team, won a league-high 15 games out of the bull pen one year and then turned around and lost a league-high nine games the following season?

24. _____ Who was the one-time no-hit pitcher

261

with the Dodgers who finished up with the Blue Jays in
1977, their maiden season?

25. _____ Who was the Blue Jays' "big" winner
in their initial season?

CALIFORNIA ANGELS

Infielders

Multiple Choice.

1. _____ Which one of the following first basemen did not perform for the Angels?
   a. Steve Bilko b. Ted Kluszewski c. Vic Power d. Dick Stuart

2. _____ Which one of the following second basemen did not perform for the Angels?
   a. Rocky Bridges b. Jerry Adair c. Bobby Knoop d. Sandy Alomar

3. _____ Which one of the following shortstops did not compete for the Angels?
   a. Freddie Patek b. Jim Fregosi c. Joe Koppe d. Leo Cardenas

4. _____ Which one of the following third basemen did not suit up for the Angels?
   a. Joe Foy b. Eddie Yost c. Aurelio Rodriguez d. Ken McMullen

5. _____ Which one of the following infielders did not appear on the roster of the Angels?
   a. Lee Thomas b. Joe Adcock c. Bob Oliver d. Pete Runnels

6. _____ Which one of the following infielders did not take the field for the Angels?
   a. Norm Siebern b. Jerry Remy c. Dick Green d. Rick Burleson

Outfielders

True or False.

7. _____ Leon Wagner hit more home runs (37) in one season than any other Angel.

8. _____ Bobby Bonds stole more bases in one season than any other Angel.

9. _____ Alex Johnson hit for the highest Angel average in one season.

10. _____ Joe Rudi, Don Baylor, and Bobby Bonds were all free agents when the Angels signed them.

11. _____ Frank Robinson hit 30 home runs in one season for the Angels.

12. _____ Brian Downing holds the American League record for most consecutive errorless (244) games.

Catchers

Fill in the blanks.

13. _____ Name the Angel catcher who is the son of a former big leaguer.

14. _____ Name the Angel receiver who was California's starting catcher for the most seasons.

15. _____ Name the Angel backstop who later managed Cleveland to three sixth-place finishes.

Pitchers

Matching.

16. _____ Dean Chance
17. _____ Bo Belinski
18. _____ Don Sutton
19. _____ Andy Messersmith
20. _____ Clyde Wright
21. _____ Nolan Ryan
22. _____ Frank Tanana
23. _____ Bill Singer
24. _____ Rudy May
25. _____ George Brunet

a. He won 22 in 1970 for the Angels; he lost 20 in 1974 for the Twins.

b. He pitched four no-hitters for the Angels.

c. He was the first Angel pitcher to win 20 games in a season.

d. He was the first Angel pitcher to throw a no-hitter.

e. After spending the majority of his first 11 years with the Angels, he started for the Yankees in the historic opening of the new stadium in 1976.

f. Before excelling for the Dodgers, he spent four years with the Angels, winning 20 games in 1971.

g. He won 20 games for the Dodgers in 1969 before he equaled that total for the Angels in 1973.

h. He started his 700th game, the second all-time high, for the Angels in 1986.

i. Twice this lefty flame-thrower has struck out more than 250 batters in a season.

j. Twice he led the American League in losses.

CHICAGO WHITE SOX

Infielders

Matching.

1. _____ Dick Allen		a. He played the most consecutive major league games (98) without striking out.
2. _____ Eddie Collins		
3. _____ Luke Appling		
4. _____ Bill Melton		b. He played on four world championship teams.
5. _____ Nelson Fox		
6. _____ Buck Weaver		c. He batted .333 in his last big-league season.

d. He had a career slugging average of .534.

e. He was the first Pale Hose player to win a home run title.

f. One year he hit only six home runs but drove home 128 runs.

Outfielders

Multiple Choice.

7. _____ He never hit less than .300 in his entire career.
   a. Rip Radcliff b. Wally Moses c. Bibbs Fall d. Joe Jackson

8. _____ He set the then-American League record for strikeouts (175) in one season.
   a. Gus Zernial b. Smead Jolley c. Dave Nicholson d. Larry Doby

9. _____ Once part of a famous outfield, he finished his career with the White Sox, batting .302 over his last five seasons.
   a. Happy Felsch b. Harry Hooper c. Mule Haas d. Minnie Minoso

10. _____ Which one of the following outfield trios had ballhawks who each hit .300 or better in the same season?
   a. Dixie Walker, Mike Kreevich, and Rip Radcliff b. Mule Haas, Al Simmons, and Rip Radcliff c. Smead

Jolley, Red Barnes, and Carl Reynolds d. Nemo Leibold, Happy Felsch, and Joe Jackson

11. _____ Which one of the following White Sox outfielders copped the batting crown with another team?

a. Bob Fothergill b. Taft Wright c. Wally Moses d. Ralph Garr

12. _____ Which one of the following players was hit by more pitches than any other American League player before Don Baylor?

a. Al Simmons b. Minnie Minoso c. Johnny Mostil d. Jim Landis

Catchers

True or False.

13. _____ Ray Schalk	a.	He became a double agent after his baseball career.
14. _____ Moe Berg	b.	He called the signals for four pitchers who won 20 or more games in the same season.
15. _____ Mike Tresh	c.	He was the father of a son who hit four World Series home runs.

Pitchers

Fill in the blanks.

16. _____ Who was the White Sox pitcher who threw a perfect game?

17. _____ Who holds the club record for wins (40) and strikeouts (269)?

18. _____ Name the pitcher who won 260 games in 21 years, all with the White Sox.

19. _____ Can you recall the promising young hurler who lost a leg in a 1938 hunting accident?

20. _____ A 21-game winner for the 1920 White Sox, he was a holdout for the entire 1922 season and a suspended player for the following three years. Who was he?

21. _____ Who was the Black Sox pitcher who lost all three of his decisions in the tainted 1919 World Series?

22. _____ Who is the recent-day pitcher who both won and lost 20 games in the same season?

23. _____ Who was the 200-game winner who used to hook up with Whitey Ford in some classic pitching duels in the 1950s?

24. _____ Who won three games in a World Series?

25. _____ Who was the "steady" White Sox pitcher who later played on five consecutive world championship teams with the Yankees?

KANSAS CITY ROYALS

Infielders

Multiple Choice.

1. _____ Name the first baseman who holds the season club high in home runs.
   a. Bob Oliver b. John Mayberry c. Steve Balboni d. Tommy Davis

2. _____ Who has been the only second baseman in American League history to win seven Gold Gloves?
   a. Frank White b. Cookie Rojas c. Jackie Hernandez d. Jerry Adair

3. _____ In nine seasons at shortstop for the Royals, he averaged 37 steals.
   a. Jackie Hernandez b. Freddie Patek c. Bobby Knoop d. U. L. Washington

4. _____ Who became the sixth player to collect 20 or more doubles, triples, and home runs in the same season?
   a. Frank White b. John Mayberry c. Willie Aikens d. George Brett

5. _____ Who set the record for at least one strikeout in 13 consecutive games?
   a. John Mayberry b. Frank White c. Cookie Rojas d. Steve Balboni

6. _____ Who hit a record two home runs in each of two World Series games in 1980?
   a. Willie Aikens b. John Mayberry c. George Brett d. Frank White

Outfielders

True or False.

7. _____ Lou Piniella won the Rookie of the Year Award.

8. _____ Amos Otis drove home more runs (133) in one season than any other Royal player.

9. _____ Willie Wilson hits a high percentage of inside-the-park home runs.

10. _____ Hal McRae won a batting title.

11. _____ Amos Otis hit three home runs in a World Series.

12. _____ None of the present-day Royal outfielders' fathers played in the major leagues.

Catchers

Fill in the blanks.
13. _____ Who was the recent-day catcher who led the American League with a .995 fielding percentage?
14. _____ Who had a career-high .291 batting average, 20 home runs, and 112 RBIs in 1979?
15. _____ Who stole a record 36 bases for catchers in 1982?

Pitchers

Matching.

16. _____ Steve Busby
17. _____ Mark Littell
18. _____ Larry Gura
19. _____ Dennis Leonard
20. _____ Paul Splittorff
21. _____ Bret Saberhagen
22. _____ Mark Gubicza
23. _____ Dan Quisenberry
24. _____ Jim Colborn
25. _____ Dick Drago

a. He averaged five wins a year during the early years of the franchise.
b. He pitched two no-hitters.
c. He struck out a club-high 244 batters in one year.
d. He was the youngest recipient of the World Series MVP Award.
e. The Yankees traded him for Fran Healy.
f. He threw the pitch that Chris Chambliss hit for the playoff-deciding homerun in 1976.
g. He won two games and lost none in the three Championship Series from 1976–78.
h. He logged the highest number of saves (212) from 1980 through 1985.
i. A 20-game winner with the Brewers, he pitched a no-hitter in his only full season with the Royals.
j. In 1986 this double-figure winner in his first three major league seasons won nine of his last ten, including his last five.

MINNESOTA TWINS

Infielders

Matching.

1. _____ Rod Carew
2. _____ Gary Gaetti
3. _____ Zoilo Versalles
4. _____ Harmon Killebrew
5. _____ Bob Allison
6. _____ Billy Martin

a. He won six home run titles.

b. He hit two home runs on the opening day of the season.

c. Four times he got 200 hits, including a career-high 239 in 1977.

d. From 1963–65 he led the league in triples.

e. A veteran of four world championship teams, he finished his career with the Twins, a team he later managed to a division title.

f. He was the only American League player to win the Rookie of the Year Award and the three-base crown in the same year.

Outfielders

Multiple Choice.

7. _____ From 1956–58 he led the league in strikeouts.

a. Jimmy Hall b. Don Mincher c. Bob Allison d. Jim Lemon

8. _____ Who is the recent-day Twin who collected 223 hits in a season?

a. Kirby Puckett b. Tom Brunansky c. Mickey Hatcher d. Gary Ward

9. _____ He hit 20 home runs in 1976, including an historic one at Yankee Stadium.

a. Steve Braun b. Lyman Bostock c. Larry Hisle d. Dan Ford

272

10. _____ He made a great sliding catch against the Dodgers in the 1965 World Series.
a. Sandy Valdespino b. Ted Uhlaender c. Bob Allison d. Bill Tuttle
11. _____ Who was the player who hit 33 circuit clouts in 1963, the all-time high for a Twin lefty before Ken Hrbek?
a. Jimmy Hall b. Lenny Green c. Ted Uhlaender d. Tony Oliva
12. _____ From 1959–64 he averaged 119 RBIs per year.
a. Tony Oliva b. Harmon Killebrew c. Bob Allison d. Cesar Tovar

Catchers

True or False.
13. _____ Butch Wynegar made the All-Star team in his rookie year.
14. _____ Johnny Roseboro had a higher lifetime batting average than Earl Battey did.
15. _____ In their most productive long-ball seasons, Roseboro hit more home runs than Battey did.

Pitchers

Fill in the blanks.
16. _____ Who was the Twin pitcher who won more games in one season than any other Minnesota hurler?
17. _____ Name the pitcher who struck out 258 batters, the club high, in one season.
18. _____ Can you recall the pitcher whom Billy Martin "punched out" in 1969?
19. _____ Which of the Perry brothers enjoyed 20-win seasons in 1969–70 for the Twins?
20. _____ Who was the first Minnesota pitcher to register back-to-back 20-win seasons?
21. _____ Who was the pitcher who won two games in the 1965 World Series?
22. _____ Name the pitcher who was a 20-game winner with the Angels before he was a 20-game winner with the Twins.
23. _____ Who was the Twin relief pitcher who starred with the Dodgers before he led the American League in saves in 1969 (31) and 1970 (34)?

24. _____ Who was the relief pitcher who bounced from club to club before he averaged 18 saves a year for the 1965–68 Twins?

25. _____ Who was the only Twin pitcher to lose 20 games in a season?

OAKLAND A'S

Infielders

Fill in the blanks.

1. _____ Who played in four World Series, on four championship teams, with two different teams?

2. _____ Who hit two home runs in his first major league game?

3. _____ Who, in 1986, played in 162 games for the second straight year, batted .285, and stole 33 bases?

4. _____ Who was the Oakland infielder of the 1970s who ended his career with 242 home runs?

5. _____ Who was traded to the A's when the Red Sox had to make room for the emerging Wade Boggs?

6. _____ Who was one of the two major leaguers who has played all nine positions in a game?

Outfielders

Matching.

7. _____ Tony Armas

8. _____ Rick Monday

9. _____ Dave Kingman

10. _____ Bill North

11. _____ Gonzalo Marquez

12. _____ Herb Washington

a. He was the A's designated runner in the 1974 World Series.

b. He tied for a home run title.

c. Three times he pinch-hit singles in the 1972 World Series.

d. The 1976 stolen base champ, he averaged 53 thefts per season in his first four years in the majors.

e. In 1986 he hit over 30 home runs for the third straight year; the following year, he was out of baseball.

f. He was the first player to be selected in the free agent draft.

Catchers

Multiple Choice.

13. _____ Who was the only player to be traded for a manager?

    a. Dave Duncan b. Gene Tenace c. Ray Fosse d. Manny Sanguillen

14. _____ Which one of the following catchers compiled the highest single-season average with the A's?

    a. Dave Duncan b. Ray Fosse c. Phil Roof d. Frank Fernandez

15. _____ Which one of the following catchers hit the most home runs in one season?

    a. Dave Duncan b. Ray Fosse c. Phil Roof d. Frank Fernandez

Pitchers

True or False.

16. _____ Catfish Hunter was the last pitcher to throw a perfect game.

17. _____ Vida Blue was the youngest player to win the MVP Award.

18. _____ Catfish Hunter won all of his four World Series decisions with the A's.

19. _____ Jay Howell has recorded 29 saves in a season.

20. _____ Ken Holtzman never won 20 games for the A's.

21. _____ Holtzman matched Hunter's total of four World Series wins with Oakland.

22. _____ Vida Blue has won the most games in one season for the A's.

23. _____ Blue never won a World Series game.

24. _____ Rollie Fingers has been the only pitcher to hurl in all seven games of a World Series.

25. _____ Fingers has recorded the most saves by any pitcher in series history.

SEATTLE MARINERS

Infielders

True or False.

1. _____ Ken Phelps was the Mariners' starting first baseman until he broke a bone in his hand.

2. _____ If a player is batting very low, an announcer may say he's under the (Mario) "Mendoza Line."

3. _____ Rey Quinones went to the Mariners in a deal for Jerry Remy.

4. _____ Julio Cruz tied an American League record for most consecutive stolen bases (32) without being caught stealing.

5. _____ Al Davis's 116 RBIs in 1984 were the most ever by a rookie.

6. _____ Jim Presley is a good contact hitter.

Outfielders

Fill in the blanks.

7. _____ Who is the present-day player who went his first 398 major league at-bats without hitting a home run?

8. _____ Who hit a club-high 32 home runs in 1985?

9. _____ Who hit a club-high .326 in 1981?

10. _____ Who was the rookie with 25 home runs whom the Mariners traded after the 1986 season?

11. _____ Who was the slugger with 325 career home runs who hit 29 circuit clouts for the Mariners in 1979?

12. _____ Who is the former Mariner who shined in post-season play for the 1986 Red Sox?

Catchers

Matching.

13. _____ Jerry Narron
14. _____ Jim Essian
15. _____ Bob Kearney

   a. He led American League catchers in total chances (897) in 1984.
   b. He became the Yankees' catcher after Thurman Munson's tragic death.
   c. A veteran of six major league clubs, he batted .275 in his only year in Seattle.

Pitchers

Multiple Choice.

16. _____ Who struck out a club-high 262 batters in one season?
   a. Mark Langston b. Mike Moore c. Pete Ladd d. Mike Morgan

17. _____ Who won a club-record 19 games in one season?
   a. Mike Morgan b. Bill Swift c. Mark Langston d. Mike Moore

18. _____ Who struck out a record 20 Mariner batters in 1986?
   a. Bert Blyleven b. Bret Saberhagen c. Ron Guidry d. Roger Clemens

19. _____ Who was the former Mariner pitcher who was once suspended for "doctoring" a baseball?
   a. Rick Honeycutt b. Jim Colborn c. Gaylord Perry d. Bill Caudill

20. _____ Who was the Mariner pitcher who led the league in strikeouts (209) in 1982?
   a. Gaylord Perry b. Floyd Bannister c. Dick Drago d. Jim Colborn

21. _____ Who was the former Mariner moundsman who won a Championship Series game and a World Series game with another club?
   a. Jim Beattie b. Ken Clay c. Shane Rawley d. Jim Colborn

22. _____ Who won his 300th game with the Mariners?
   a. Don Sutton b. Tom Seaver c. Phil Niekro d. Gaylord Perry

23. _____ Who established a major league record for most games (78) by a pitcher in his rookie season?
    a. Matt Young b. Bill Caudill c. Ed Vande Berg d. Dick Drago
24. _____ Who racked up 102 saves from 1982–85?
    a. Matt Young b. Bill Caudill c. Ed Vande Berg d. Dick Drago
25. _____ Who was traded to the Yankees for Gene Nelson, Bill Caudill, and a player to be named later?
    a. Jim Beattie b. Mike Kekich c. Shane Rawley d. Bill Caudill

TEXAS RANGERS

Infielders

Matching.

1. _____ Pete O'Brien
2. _____ Lenny Randle
3. _____ Buddy Bell
4. _____ Bump Wills
5. _____ Scott Fletcher
6. _____ Toby Harrah

a. He stole a club-record 52 bases in one season.
b. He hit a club-high 23 home runs by a left-handed hitter.
c. After failing to hit over .256 in five seasons with the White Sox, he moved to Texas in 1986 and led the Rangers with a .300 average.
d. He was traded after a one-sided fight with former manager Frank Lucchesi.
e. A shortstop, he hit 27 home runs one year.
f. This third baseman averaged .302 for the six full seasons he played in Texas.

Outfielders

Multiple Choice.

7. _____ Name the player who set the club record for home runs in one season.
   a. Rico Carty b. Larry Parrish c. Gary Ward d. Frank Howard.

8. _____ Name the rookie who hit 30 home runs in 1986.
   a. Pete Incaviglia b. Al Oliver c. Frank Howard d. Rico Carty

9. _____ Who was the outfielder who, after playing in three consecutive World Series, became expendable and was traded to Texas?
   a. Rico Carty b. Tom Grieve c. Mickey Rivers d. Willie Horton

10. _____ Which one of the following Texas players hit .300 lifetime?
   a. Al Oliver b. Elliot Maddox c. Ken Henderson d. Larry Bittner

11. _____ Who is the present-day player who, going into the 1987 season, had three times hit more than 20 home runs in a season for the Rangers?
   a. Oddibee McDowell b. Pete Incaviglia c. Toby Harrah d. Larry Parrish

12. _____ Name the player who hit 262 home runs before he joined the Rangers as a designated hitter.
   a. Al Oliver b. Frank Howard c. Ken Henderson d. Willie Horton

Catchers

True or False.

13. _____ Dick Billings was the Rangers' initial catcher in their franchise history.

14. _____ John Ellis hit 20 or more home runs in a season for Texas.

15. _____ Darrell Porter played on pennant-winning teams on two clubs outside of Texas.

Pitchers

Fill in the blanks.

16. _____ Who won 25 games, the club's all-time high, in one season?

17. _____ Who struck out 233 batters, the team's all-time high, in one year?

18. _____ Who was the former Texas mounds-man who started the first game of the 1976 World Series?

19. _____ Who is the former Texas hurler who was just 23–23 with the Rangers despite the fact that he has won well over 200 games?

20. _____ Name the one-time 19-game winner who was traded to Cleveland in the Gaylord Perry deal.

21. _____ Who is the 39-year-old pitcher who won a career-high 18 games in 1987?

22. _____ Who was the former Ranger pitcher who started World Series games for the Pirates and the Yankees?

23. _____ Who in 1985 led all American League relievers with 111 strikeouts?

24. _____ Who is the relief pitcher who set a record for rookies when he appeared in 80 games?

25. _____ Bert Blyleven pitched a no-hitter for the Rangers in 1977. Who pitched the first—and only other—no-hitter for Texas?

A Man for All Seasons

A baseball executive who never played in the major leagues had the Midas touch when it came to getting the most out of ballplayers; undoubtedly he "touched," either directly or indirectly, every era that we've covered in this book.

In the late 1890s he discovered Honus Wagner, who later won eight batting championships for the Pirates. In 1903 and 1904 he managed the Tigers to second-division finishes. But he put together the machinery that later (1907–09) produced three straight pennants. In 1918 he took over the managerial duties of the Red Sox, and he led them to a pennant and world title. But more important, in the same year he switched Babe Ruth from a regular-turn pitcher to an everyday first baseman–outfielder.

This baseball administrator managed the Red Sox through 1920. In the interim between 1918 and 1920, he had seen a pattern beginning to take shape. Red Sox owner Harry Frazee, who was in financial trouble, was unloading pennant-winning ballplayers to the Yankees. So when Yankee owner Jake Ruppert offered him the general manager's job in New York, he moved to the Bronx.

In 1921, his first year in New York, the Yankees won their first pennant. In his additional 24 years in the Yankee G.M. job, the Bronx Bombers won 13 pennants and 10 world championships. The pride that he helped to build in the pinstripe uniform has carried over to the present time; the Yankees have gone on to win 19 additional pennants and 12 world titles.

If you can name this "man for all seasons," you most probably have "touched" all of the bases in this book. Who was he?

(Answer appears on page 322.)

Chapter Eighteen

THE RECORD BOOK

This chapter is divided into three parts. The first section deals only with American League records. The second section deals only with National League marks. (In some cases, where players from both leagues share a major league record, statements about each player may appear under their respective league.) The third section deals only with major league marks. Let's see how many of the record-holders you can call to mind.

100. AMERICAN LEAGUE RECORDS

1. _____ Who compiled the highest average (.422) in one season?
   a. George Sisler b. Napoleon Lajoie c. Harry Heilmann d. Ty Cobb

2. _____ Who collected 107 pinch-hits in his career?
   a. Dave Philley b. Johnny Mize c. Gates Brown d. Bobby Brown

3. _____ Who had one or more hits in 135 games one year?
   a. Johnny Pesky b. George Brett c. Rod Carew d. Wade Boggs

4. _____ Who was the right-handed batter who had 200 or more hits in five consecutive years?
   a. Joe DiMaggio b. Jimmie Foxx c. Al Simmons d. Hank Greenberg

5. _____ Who was the left-handed batter who had 200 or more hits in five consecutive seasons?

a. Charlie Gehringer b. George Sisler c. Joe Jackson d. Lou Gehrig

6. _____ Who hit for the cycle three times?
a. Bob Meusel b. Nellie Fox c. Larry Doby d. Harvey Kuenn

7. _____ Who got seven consecutive pinch-hits?
a. Dave Philley b. Merv Rettenmund c. Sam Leslie d. Bill Stein

8. _____ Who collected 187 singles in one season?
a. Willie Wilson b. Ty Cobb c. Wade Boggs d. George Sisler

9. _____ Who was the right-handed batter who hit 64 doubles in one season?
a. Hank Greenberg b. Luke Appling c. George Burns d. Vern Stephens

10. _____ Who was the right-handed batter who hit 573 career home runs?
a. Frank Robinson b. Harmon Killebrew c. Hank Greenberg d. Jimmie Foxx

11. _____ Who hit 16 career pinch-hit home runs?
a. Cliff Johnson b. Gates Brown c. Johnny Mize d. Merv Rettenmund

12. _____ Who was the rookie who hit 49 home runs?
a. Mark McGwire b. Joe DiMaggio c. Ted Williams d. Roy Sievers

13. _____ Who was the left-handed batter who hit four consecutive home runs in a nine-inning game?
a. Jim Gentile b. Norm Cash c. Luke Easter d. Lou Gehrig

14. _____ Who was the right-handed batter who hit four consecutive home runs in a nine-inning game?
a. Hank Greenberg b. Pat Seerey c. Clyde Vollmer d. Rocky Colavito

15. _____ Who, in addition to Bob Nieman, hit two home runs in his first major league game?
a. Cesar Tovar b. Bert Campaneris c. Hal McRae d. Gorman Thomas

16. _____ Who hit five home runs, out of five hits, in five games?
a. Bob Meusel b. Ken Williams c. Gus Zernial d. Dick Wakefield

17. _____ Who was the Twin who three times hit pinch-hit grand slams in his career?
a. Rich Reese b. Jimmy Hall c. Bob Allison d. Jim Lemon

18. _____ Who totaled 400 bases five times in his career?

   a. Jimmie Foxx b. Babe Ruth c. Lou Gehrig d. Joe DiMaggio

19. _____ Who had five long hits in one game?

   a. Ted Williams b. Jim Rice c. Lou Boudreau d. Fred Lynn

20. _____ Who was the right-handed batter who drove home 183 runs in one season?

   a. Hank Greenberg b. Al Simmons c. Joe DiMaggio d. Frank Howard

21. _____ Who was the catcher who drove home 133 runs one year?

   a. Yogi Berra b. Gus Triandos c. Carlton Fisk d. Bill Dickey

22. _____ Who drove home at least one run in 13 consecutive games?

   a. Cass Michaels b. George Kell c. Dale Mitchell d. Taft Wright

23. _____ Who drove home 11 runs in one game?

   a. Earl Averill b. Hal Trosky c. Tony Lazzeri d. Ben Chapman

24. _____ Who walked seven consecutive times?

   a. Eddie Yost b. Billy Rogell c. Jimmy Dykes d. Lou Gehrig

25. _____ Who drew 33 intentional walks one year?

   a. Jimmie Foxx b. Ted Williams c. Harmon Killebrew d. Roger Maris

26. _____ Who hit 17 sacrifice flies in 1971?

   a. Roy White b. Frank Robinson c. Reggie Jackson d. Brooks Robinson

27. _____ Who is the pitcher who started 33 games one year but didn't finish one of them?

   a. Frank Tanana b. Wilbur Wood c. Milt Wilcox d. Ed Whitson

28. _____ Who was the pitcher who finished up a game with 17 innings of relief?

   a. Schoolboy Rowe b. Ed Rommel c. Ed Walsh d. George Pipgras

29. _____ Who won 24 games in his rookie season?

   a. Bob Grim b. Edgar Summers c. Carl Mays d. Urban Shocker

30. _____ Who was the Indian pitcher who won 17 consecutive games?

   a. Bob Feller b. Early Wynn c. Bob Lemon d. Johnny Allen

31. _____ Who was the Oriole pitcher who won 17 consecutive games?

a. Mike Cuellar b. Mike Flanagan c. Jim Palmer d. Dave McNally

32. _____ Who was the starting pitcher who won nine consecutive games at the start of his career?

a. Whitey Ford b. Ned Garver c. Ellis Kinder d. Hal Newhouser

33. _____ Who was the Yankee pitcher who won 23 consecutive games from the Athletics?

a. Bob Shawkey b. Joe Bush c. Waite Hoyt d. Carl Mays

34. _____ Who was the Yankee relief pitcher who won 12 consecutive games one season?

a. Joe Page b. Bob Grim c. Luis Arroyo d. Ron Davis

35. _____ Who was the Yankee who won 12 consecutive games in his rookie season?

a. Atley Donald b. Spud Chandler c. Bump Hadley d. Monte Pearson

36. _____ Who won 15 consecutive games at the end of the season?

a. Schoolboy Rowe b. Ted Lyons c. Alvin Crowder d. Tommy Bridges

37. _____ Who was the Senator pitcher who lost 19 consecutive games?

a. Bob Groom b. Bob Porterfield c. Sid Hudson d. Walt Masterson

38. _____ Who was the Athletic pitcher who lost 19 consecutive games?

a. Carl Scheib b. Lou Brissie c. John Nabors d. Alex Kellner

39. _____ Who was the two-time batting champ who, as a pitcher, allowed 13 runs in one inning?

a. Lefty O'Doul b. Jimmie Foxx c. Pete Runnels d. Luke Appling

40. _____ Who led the league in lowest ERA four consecutive years?

a. Whitey Ford b. Lefty Grove c. Hal Newhouser d. Bob Feller

41. _____ Who pitched five consecutive shutouts?

a. Jack Chesbro b. Ed Walsh c. Cy Young d. Doc White

42. _____ Who pitched an 18-inning 1–0 shutout?

a. George Earnshaw b. Walter Johnson c. Lefty Grove d. Stan Coveleski

43. _____ Who retired 33 consecutive batters one year?

a. Mike Caldwell b. Larry Gura c. Steve Busby d. Mike Boddicker

44. _____ Who allowed 374 career home runs?

a. Mike Torrez b. Bert Blyleven c. Jim Hunter d. Dizzy Trout

45. _____ Who was the left-handed pitcher who struck out 2,679 batters?

a. Mickey Lolich b. Hal Newhouser c. Whitey Ford d. Lefty Grove

46. _____ Who was the rookie left-hander who struck out 245 batters in a season?

a. Mel Parnel b. Herb Score c. Billy Pierce d. Ron Guidry

47. _____ Who is the present-day left-hander who struck out 18 batters in a game?

a. Frank Tanana b. Ted Higuera c. Bruce Hurst d. Ron Guidry

48. _____ Who struck out 18 batters in one game but lost?

a. Nolan Ryan b. Bob Feller c. Bob Turley d. Luis Tiant

49. _____ Who, in a rare relief assignment, struck out 14 batters in one game?

a. Denny McLain b. Sam McDowell c. Luis Tiant d. Mel Stottlemyre

50. _____ Who was the left-handed pitcher who threw 45 consecutive scoreless innings?

a. Doc White b. Walter Johnson c. Lefty Gomez d. Lefty Grove

101. NATIONAL LEAGUE RECORDS

1. _____ Who had a slugging average of .756 one year?
   a. Chuck Klein b. Hack Wilson c. Rogers Hornsby d. Joe Medwick

2. _____ Who had one or more hits in 135 games one year?
   a. Paul Waner b. Pete Rose c. Chuck Klein d. Honus Wagner

3. _____ Who had 200 or more hits for five consecutive years?
   a. Pete Rose b. Chuck Klein c. Paul Waner d. Lloyd Waner

4. _____ Who twice had six hits in six at-bats?
   a. Stan Musial b. Jim Bottomley c. Bill Terry d. Lefty O'Doul

5. _____ Who had 14 hits in two consecutive double-headers?
   a. Bill White b. Enos Slaughter c. Terry Moore d. Marty Marion

6. _____ Who hit for the cycle three times?
   a. Stan Musial b. Pete Reiser c. Roberto Clemente d. Babe Herman

7. _____ Who led the league in doubles eight times?
   a. Honus Wagner b. Pete Rose c. Stan Musial d. Paul Waner

8. _____ Who was the left-handed batter who hit 521 career homers?
   a. Duke Snider b. Willie McCovey c. Mel Ott d. Willie Stargell

9. _____ Who hit 18 career pinch-hit homers?
   a. Gus Bell b. Red Schoendienst c. Jerry Lynch d. Rusty Staub

10. _____ Who was the switch-hitter who banged 36 home runs in one season?
    a. Ted Simmons b. Howard Johnson c. Reggie Smith d. Pete Rose

11. _____ Who was the pitcher who twice hit seven home runs in a season?
    a. Don Newcombe b. Warren Spahn c. Don Drysdale d. Ken Brett

12. _____ Who hit 34 home runs at his home grounds one year?

a. Ted Kluszewski b. Mel Ott c. Eddie Mathews d. Ralph Kiner

13. _____ Who hit 30 or more home runs for nine consecutive years?
   a. Hank Aaron b. Eddie Mathews c. Willie McCovey d. Willie Mays

14. _____ Who hit 101 home runs in back-to-back seasons?
   a. Johnny Mize b. Willie Mays c. Hack Wilson d. Ralph Kiner

15. _____ Who was the left-handed batter who hit 96 home runs in back-to-back seasons?
   a. Mel Ott b. Willie McCovey c. Ted Kluszewski d. Eddie Mathews

16. _____ Who hit 17 home runs in one month?
   a. Willie McCovey b. Ernie Banks c. Willie Mays d. Johnny Mize

17. _____ Who was the one-time Cardinal who hit five home runs in a doubleheader?
   a. Johnny Mize b. Rogers Hornsby c. Stan Musial d. Joe Cunningham

18. _____ Who was the Padre who hit five home runs in a doubleheader?
   a. Nate Colbert b. Willie McCovey c. Graig Nettles d. Steve Garvey

19. _____ Who was the Expo who hit pinch-hit homers in both ends of a doubleheader?
   a. Harold Breeden b. Andre Dawson c. Ellis Valentine d. Larry Parrish

20. _____ Who five times hit three home runs in a Senior Circuit game?
   a. Joe Morgan b. Ernie Banks c. Johnny Mize d. Bill Nicholson

21. _____ Who was the pitcher who three times hit two home runs in a game?
   a. Steve Carlton b. Don Newcombe c. Rick Wise d. Tony Cloninger

22. _____ Who hit for 450 total bases in one season?
   a. Hack Wilson b. Mel Ott c. Hank Aaron d. Rogers Hornsby

23. _____ Who three times had more than 400 total bases in a season?
   a. Stan Musial b. Hank Aaron c. Chuck Klein d. Bill Terry

24. _____ Who had 25 total bases in two consecutive games?

a. George Foster b. Dave Kingman c. Joe Adcock d. Tony Perez

25. _____ Who was the Pirate who hit four or more long hits in a game four times?
   a. Willie Stargell b. Ralph Kiner c. Roberto Clemente d. Bob Robertson

26. _____ Who walked 1,799 times?
   a. Jimmy Wynn b. Eddie Stanky c. Joe Morgan d. Richie Ashburn

27. _____ Who walked 100 times in his rookie year?
   a. Maury Wills b. Jim Gilliam c. Richie Ashburn d. Willie McCovey

28. _____ Who was walked seven consecutive times?
   a. Ralph Kiner b. Willie Mays c. Johnny Mize d. Mel Ott

29. _____ Who was the right-handed all-fields hitter who walked seven consecutive times?
   a. Eddie Stanky b. Al Dark c. Harvey Kuenn d. Dick Groat

30. _____ Who was the Brave who walked at least once in 15 consecutive games?
   a. Joe Adcock b. Darrell Evans c. Hank Aaron d. Billy Bruton

31. _____ Who struck out 1,936 times during his career?
   a. Bobby Bonds b. Dave Kingman c. Willie Stargell d. Vince DiMaggio

32. _____ Who struck out only 173 times in 18 years?
   a. Tommy Holmes b. Paul Waner c. Pete Reiser d. Lloyd Waner

33. _____ Who was the pitcher who struck out 62 times in a season?
   a. Jerry Koosman b. Bob Buhl c. Sandy Koufax d. Russ Meyer

34. _____ Who grounded into 30 double plays in one year?
   a. Joe Medwick b. Ernie Lombardi c. Roy Campanella d. Walker Cooper

35. _____ Who stole home 33 times during his career?
   a. Pete Reiser b. Jackie Robinson c. Max Carey d. Pee Wee Reese

36. _____ Who got caught stealing 36 times in one year?
   a. Maury Wills b. Ron LeFlore c. Miller Huggins d. Tim Raines

37. _____ Who pitched 434 innings one year?
   a. Christy Mathewson b. Grover Alexander c. Joe McGinnity d. Dazzy Vance

38. _____ Who was the 22-game winner for the Dodgers who had an .880 winning percentage one year?

    a. Whit Wyatt b. Carl Erskine c. Preacher Roe d. Don Newcombe

39. _____ Who was the Giant pitcher who won six opening-day games?

    a. Juan Marichal b. Carl Hubbell c. Sal Maglie d. Christy Mathewson

40. _____ Who pitched 90 career shutouts?

    a. Warren Spahn b. Grover Alexander c. Christy Mathewson d. Bob Gibson

41. _____ Who was the pitcher who lost 13 1–0 games?

    a. Burleigh Grimes b. Lee Meadows c. Bill Hallahan d. Bill Lee

42. _____ Who pitched 21 consecutive hitless innings one year?

    a. Don Drysdale b. Sal Maglie c. Johnny Vander Meer d. Ewell Blackwell

43. _____ Who allowed nine career grand slams?

    a. Jerry Reuss b. Don Sutton c. Robin Roberts d. Steve Carlton

44. _____ Who was the Cardinal pitcher who allowed nine walks in a shutout game?

    a. Wilmer Mizell b. Dizzy Dean c. Howie Pollet d. Harry Brecheen

45. _____ Who was the right-hander who struck out 313 batters in one season?

    a. Tom Seaver b. J. R. Richard c. Dizzy Dean d. Don Drysdale

46. _____ Who is the present-day pitcher, in addition to Nolan Ryan, who struck out 18 batters in one game?

    a. Bill Gullickson b. Fernando Valenzuela c. Dwight Gooden d. Mike Scott

47. _____ Who was the left-handed pitcher who struck out 15 batters in his first game?

    a. Steve Carlton b. Fernando Valenzuela c. Karl Spooner d. Tommy John

48. _____ Who was the right-handed pitcher who struck out 15 batters in his first major-league game?

    a. Dizzy Dean b. Tom Seaver c. Bob Gibson d. J. R. Richard

49. _____ Who hit 154 batters during his career?

    a. Bobo Newsom b. Steve Carlton c. Don Drysdale d. Sam Jones

50. _____ Who was the catcher who fielded .992 over a 14-year career?

   a. Johnny Edwards b. Roy Campanella c. Johnny Bench
   d. Gabby Hartnett

102. MAJOR LEAGUE RECORDS

1. _____ Who played the most games in one season?
   a. Pete Rose b. Maury Wills c. Bobby Richardson d. Rickey Henderson
2. _____ Who was the left-handed batter who hit for the highest single-season batting average?
   a. Bill Terry b. Ted Williams c. George Sisler d. Joe Jackson
3. _____ Who hit for the highest single-season average as a switch-hitter?
   a. Jimmy Collins b. Eddie Murray c. Pete Rose d. Mickey Mantle
4. _____ Who scored one or more runs in 18 consecutive games?
   a. Red Rolfe b. Nellie Fox c. Bobby Richardson d. Red Schoendienst
5. _____ Who was the right-handed batter who got 253 hits in one season?
   a. Rogers Hornsby b. Jimmie Foxx c. Heinie Manush d. Al Simmons
6. _____ Who had seven hits in a nine-inning game?
   a. Bill Mazeroski b. Johnny Ray c. Willie Randolph d. Rennie Stennett
7. _____ Who had five hits in his first major-league game?
   a. Cecil Travis b. Joe Cronin c. Casey Stengel d. Bob Nieman
8. _____ Who hit for the cycle in both leagues?
   a. Frank Robinson b. Bob Watson c. Nellie Fox d. Davey Lopes
9. _____ Who got three hits in one inning?
   a. Sammy White b. Gene Stephens c. Pee Wee Reese d. Stan Musial
10. _____ Who got two hits in one inning in his first major-league game?
    a. Bob Nieman b. Bert Campaneris c. Billy Martin d. Junior Gilliam
11. _____ Who reached base 16 consecutive times?
    a. George Brett b. Ted Williams c. Eddie Yost d. Garry Templeton
12. _____ Who got nine consecutive pinch-hits?

a. Dave Philley b. Rusty Staub c. Del Unser d. Davy Johnson

13. _____ Who was the pitcher who had eight hits in two consecutive games?
   a. George Earnshaw b. Wes Ferrell c. Red Ruffing d. Don Newcombe

14. _____ Who sprayed 198 singles in one season?
   a. Willie Wilson b. Wade Boggs c. Lloyd Waner d. Nelson Fox

15. _____ Who hit six doubles in a doubleheader?
   a. Pete Rose b. Stan Musial c. Tris Speaker d. Hank Majeski

16. _____ Who hit 36 triples in one season?
   a. Sam Crawford b. J. Owen Wilson c. Joe Jackson d. Earle Combs

17. _____ Who two times hit three triples in one game in one season?
   a. Kiki Cuyler b. George Stirnweiss c. Dave Brain d. Ty Cobb

18. _____ Who hit 20 pinch-hit home runs?
   a. Johnny Mize b. Rusty Staub c. Bob Cerv d. Cliff Johnson

19. _____ Who hit 30 or more home runs for 12 consecutive years?
   a. Hank Aaron b. Harmon Killebrew c. Babe Ruth d. Jimmie Foxx

20. _____ Who hit 20 or more home runs for 20 consecutive years?
   a. Frank Robinson b. Hank Aaron c. Ted Williams d. Jimmie Foxx

21. _____ Who hit 114 home runs in back-to-back years?
   a. Babe Ruth b. Hank Aaron c. Willie Mays d. Ralph Kiner

22. _____ Who was the pitcher who hit three home runs in a game?
   a. Tony Cloninger b. Rick Wise c. Red Ruffing d. Jim Tobin

23. _____ Who was the pitcher who five times hit two home runs in a game?
   a. Bob Lemon b. Wes Ferrell c. Don Newcombe d. Don Drysdale

24. _____ Who was the part-time player who hit four consecutive home runs in three consecutive games?
   a. George Shuba b. Gino Cimoli c. John Blanchard d. Chuck Essegian

25. _____ Who was the pitcher who hit home runs in four consecutive games?
   a. Warren Spahn b. Red Lucas c. Walter Johnson d. Ken Brett

26. _____ Who got six home runs, out of six hits, in six consecutive games?
   a. Mike Schmidt b. Del Ennis c. Frank Hurst d. Willie Jones

27. _____ Who hit three home runs in his first two major league games?
   a. Buddy Hassett b. Dolph Camilli c. Joe Cunningham d. Jim Tobin

28. _____ Who hit a grand slam in his first major league game?
   a. Bobby Bonds b. Bobby Murcer c. Dwayne Murphy d. Tony Armas

29. _____ Who had 17 total bases in an extra-inning game?
   a. Willie Mays b. Rudy York c. Mike Schmidt d. Rocky Colavito

30. _____ Who was the Indian who had seven consecutive long hits?
   a. Elmer Smith b. Larry Doby c. Al Rosen d. Andre Thornton

31. _____ Who was the White Sox who had seven consecutive long hits?
   a. Richie Allen b. Earl Sheely c. Bill Melton d. Sherman Lollar

32. _____ Who had one or more long hits in 14 consecutive games?
   a. Walker Cooper b. Johnny Mize c. Sid Gordon d. Paul Waner

33. _____ Who drove home at least one run in 17 consecutive games?
   a. Ray Grimes b. George Stirnweiss c. Taft Wright d. Elmer Valo

34. _____ Who was the right-handed hitter who walked 151 times in a season?
   a. Jimmy Wynn b. Eddie Stanky c. Eddie Yost d. Jimmie Foxx

35. _____ Who was the Tiger who walked at least once in 18 consecutive games?
   a. Roy Cullenbine b. Harvey Kuenn c. Charlie Gehringer d. Jake Woods

36. _____ Who struck out only 113 times in a 14-year career?

a. Luke Appling b. Richie Ashburn c. Earle Combs
d. Joe Sewell

37. _____ Who had 67 sacrifices in one season?
a. Ray Chapman b. Phil Rizzuto c. Nellie Fox d. Eddie
Yost

38. _____ Who hit 114 sacrifice flies in his career?
a. Gil Hodges b. Brooks Robinson c. Frank Robinson
d. Willie McCovey

39. _____ Who hit 19 sacrifice flies in 1954?
a. Joe Adcock b. Gil Hodges c. Andy Pafko d. Eddie
Mathews

40. _____ Who pitched for 25 years?
a. Gaylord Perry b. Phil Niekro c. Grover Alexander
d. Jim Kaat

41. _____ Who started 37 games in a season but didn't
complete one of them?
a. Steve Bedrosian b. Bob Buhl c. Vern Bickford d. Joe
Cowley

42. _____ Who pitched in 13 consecutive games?
a. Mike Marshall b. Rollie Fingers c. Bruce Sutter
d. Goose Gossage

43. _____ Who pitched 39 consecutive complete games in
one year?
a. Ed Walsh b. Jack Chesbro c. Joe McGinnity d. Jack
Taylor

44. _____ Who pitched 464 innings in one season?
a. Vic Willis b. Ed Walsh c. Joe McGinnity d. Jack
Chesbro

45. _____ Who registered 341 career saves?
a. Sparky Lyle b. Elroy Face c. Bruce Sutter d. Rollie
Fingers

46. _____ Who, at the start of his career, pitched 22 consecutive scoreless innings?
a. Hank Borowy b. Dave Ferris c. Tex Hughson d. Howie
Pollett

47. _____ Who allowed 11 walks in a shutout win?
a. Wilmer Mizell b. Lefty Gomez c. Spud Chandler
d. Mario Russo

48. _____ Who pitched 21 consecutive scoreless innings in
one game?
a. Leon Cadore b. Carl Hubbell c. Walter Johnson d. Joe
Oeschger

49. _____ Who pitched a 21-inning game without allowing
a walk?

a. Stan Coveleski b. Babe Adams c. Carl Mays d. Jim Hunter

50. _____ Who struck out seven consecutive batters in his first major league game?

a. Mort Cooper b. Ron Davis c. Sammy Stewart d. Nolan Ryan

Three Men on Third

Babe Herman looked like a knightly champion when he stepped into the batter's box—he hit .393 in 1930 and he batted .324 lifetime—but when he played the outfield or ran the bases, he seemed to develop some chinks in his armor.

Fly balls, the stories go, used to either bounce off his head or carom off his shoulders with great regularity. Some baseball observers have said that his glove was a mere ornament on his hand.

His base running didn't help the Brooklyn franchise lose its nickname of "Bums," either. Take the case of the day in 1926, for example, when the Dodgers hosted the Braves. The bases were full of Dodgers when Herman, a rookie at the time, advanced mightily to the plate. Hank DeBerry led off third, Dazzy Vance danced off second, and Chick Fewster leaned off first.

Herman did not disappoint them. He rocketed a ball high off the right-field wall. DeBerry scored easily. Vance could have, too, but he changed his mind after taking a wide turn around third. He retreated to third base where he met Fewster sliding into the "hot corner." In the meantime, Herman got a good start out of the box. He put his head down and raced around the bases with reckless abandon. Sliding into third, with what he thought was a sure triple, he was perplexed to bump into his two teammates. You might call the Dodgers' base running, in that instance, a "comedy of errors," or you might label Herman's aggressive dash an example of a "rookie's mistake."

But the third baseman was confused, too. He knew that two of the runners didn't belong there, but he didn't know which two runners were trespassing. So he did the obvious: he tagged all three of the runners. And the umpire called two of them out. But which two? Who, do you think, had the right to be there?

(Answer appears on page 322.)

Chapter Nineteen

THE HALL OF FAME

103. CLUES TO COOPERSTOWN

From Barrow to Youngs

Match the following 50 Hall of Famers with the descriptions that follow.

Jackie Robinson	Josh Gibson
Zack Wheat	Ed Barrow
Herb Pennock	Eppa Rixey
Carl Hubbell	Fred Clarke
John McGraw	Jesse Haines
Bob Lemon	Babe Ruth
Bill Dickey	Ross Youngs
Hank Greenberg	Johnny Evers
Dazzy Vance	Satchel Paige
Al Simmons	Chick Hafey
Bill Terry	Edd Roush
Mel Ott	Goose Goslin
Branch Rickey	Max Carey
Heinie Manush	Frankie Frisch
Frank Baker	Lefty Gomez
Jimmy Collins	Sam Rice
Dave Bancroft	George Sisler
Red Faber	Monte Irvin
Bob Feller	Pie Traynor
Harry Hooper	Ray Schalk
Cool Papa Bell	Lou Boudreau
Nap Lajoie	Rabbit Maranville
Joe Cronin	Charlie Gehringer
Lou Gehrig	George Kelly
Ted Lyons	Robin Roberts

1. _____ This celebrated National League screwball artist won 253 major league games (24 in succession), pitched a 1–0 18-inning win against the Cardinals in 1933 (it wrapped up the pennant), and gained baseball immortality in the 1934 All-Star Game when he struck out Babe Ruth, Lou Gehrig, Jimmie Foxx, Al Simmons, and Joe Cronin in succession.

2. _____ This slugging American League first baseman scored more than 100 runs in 13 consecutive seasons, batted in more than 100 runs in 13 consecutive seasons, and played in every one of his team's games for 13 consecutive seasons while, at one time or another, leading the league in almost every conceivable batting title.

3. _____ The third best winning percentage (.671) pitcher of all time, he also won 12 league home run titles.

4. _____ Part of a double-play trio immortalized in a famous poem, he had the good judgment to retrieve Al Bridwell's apparent hit and touch second base to force Fred Merkle on a play that pushed the Giants into a one-game playoff that they lost to the Cubs in 1908.

5. _____ A six-time home run champion, he hit more National League round-trippers with one team than any other left-handed batter.

6. _____ This American League outfielder, who won two batting titles (1930–31) and hit .334 lifetime, batted better than .380 four times, and hit better than .300 for four American League teams.

7. _____ Though he never played in a World Series, he twice hit over .400, sported a .340 lifetime average, hit safely a record 257 times in one season, earned the reputation of being the best defensive first baseman of his time, and produced two sons who played in the majors.

8. _____ The last National Leaguer to hit over .400, he has been the Giants' most successful manager since John McGraw: he led New York to three pennants and one world title.

9. _____ A four-time home run champion who lost four peak years to the military service, he was discharged in mid-season of 1945, just in time to lead his team to pennant and World Series victories.

10. _____ Winner of 286 major league games, he claims that his most satisfying victory was his pennant-clinching decision against the Dodgers in 1950.

11. _____ One of the most exciting base runners of all time, he led the Dodgers to six pennants and one

World Series victory between 1947–56; however, his greatest contribution came in 1949 when he was named the MVP for leading the league in batting (.342) and stolen bases (37). In that same year he drove home 124 runs and he scored 122 runs.

12. _____ Though he never won a World Series game, he did win 266 lifetime contests, hurled three no-hitters, and pitched 12 one-hitters in his 18-year major league career.

13. _____ In a 22-year career divided between the Phillies and the Reds, he won 266 games, the most victories by a National League southpaw until Warren Spahn recorded 363 triumphs.

14. _____ A pennant-winning manager in his first year, he was sold two years later, by Clark Griffith (his father-in-law), to the Red Sox for $250,000.

15. _____ Untainted catcher for the infamous Black Sox of 1919, he led American League receivers in putouts for nine years; fielding, eight years; and he caught over 100 games a season for 11 consecutive years.

16. _____ One of the four men who have won four consecutive home run titles, he starred in the infield for the Athletics (1908–14) and the Yankees (1916–22).

17. _____ One of the best defensive catchers who ever played the game, one of the best average-hitting catchers who ever played the game (.313), one of the best home run-hitting catchers who ever played the game (202), he played on eight world championship clubs.

18. _____ Shortstop for the "Miracle Braves," he played with five National League teams over a 23-year span, during which time he established the major league shortstop record for putouts (5,139), and placed second in assists (7,354) and total chances (13,124).

19. _____ A three-time 20-game winner, he set a National League record when he led the loop in strikeouts for seven consecutive years.

20. _____ In 21 years of pitching in the American League, his team finished in the first division only five times (its highest finish was third); however this durable right hander won 260 games, a club record.

21. _____ Possessor of a 29-game batting streak, he played 18 years in the Dodgers' outfield while posting a .317 career batting mark and winning the 1918 batting championship with a .335 batting average.

22. _____ This Pirate outfielder, who stole 738

lifetime bases, led the National League in thefts for ten years. In 1922 he stole successfully 51 out of 53 times.

23. _____ A great defensive outfielder with the Reds and Giants (1916–31), he was also an accomplished batter, hitting .323 lifetime and winning batting championships in 1917 and 1919.

24. _____ He played in more games, registered more at-bats, scored more runs, collected more hits, slashed more doubles, slammed more triples, ran more total bases, and batted in more runs than any other Senator player.

25. _____ Second on the Tigers to Ty Cobb in games played, at-bats, runs, hits, doubles, and total bases, he starred in the 1934–35 World Series and won the batting championship in 1937.

26. _____ Though he led the league in only one offensive department (triples, 19, in 1923), he batted .320 lifetime and gained baseball's admiration as the greatest defensive third baseman in National League history.

27. _____ A 240-game winner for the Athletics, Red Sox, and Yankees, he excelled in World Series play with a spotless 5–0 record. He also saved three games in series competition.

28. _____ A .316 lifetime hitter, and manager of "The Gashouse Gang" that won the pennant and series in 1934, he was traded to the Cardinals for Rogers Hornsby.

29. _____ Considered by many to be the greatest third baseman ever to play the game, he revolutionized the style of third base play while compiling a .294 lifetime average and managing the Red Sox to back-to-back pennants in 1903–04.

30. _____ The first successful "boy manager"— he won consecutive pennants from 1901–3 and in 1909—he played 15 years in the Pirates' outfield while recording a .312 lifetime average.

31. _____ A .334-hitting third baseman, he gained greater fame when he led his charges to ten pennants and three World Series victories.

32. _____ Winner of batting championships in 1901, 1903, and 1904, he once hit .422 for the Athletics, the highest single-season batting average in American League history.

33. _____ This .322 lifetime hitter for the Giants batted .300 in nine of his ten years in the majors while leading New York to five pennants and two world titles. At the age of 30, he died of a kidney ailment.

34. _____ Winner of 254 games, he was one of

the four White Sox pitchers who won 20 games in 1920. During 15 of his 20 seasons in the majors, his team finished in the second division. He was also the last of the legal spitball pitchers in the American League.

35. _____ He played on five pennant winners with the Senators and the Tigers while compiling a .316 lifetime average. In 1928 he won the batting title with a .379 mark. Eleven times he drove home 100 runs.

36. _____ Though he did not get to the majors until he was 30, this outfielder for the Giants won an RBI title and finished his career with a .293 mark. In the 1951 series he batted .458 and stole home once.

37. _____ First baseman for the Giants, Reds, and Dodgers (1915–32), he batted .297. He once hit three home runs in three consecutive innings. At another time he banged seven home runs in six games.

38. _____ The oldest rookie in the history of the game (42), he posted a 6–1 record in 1948 to help the Indians win the pennant. At the age of 59, he pitched his last game for the Athletics. Dizzy Dean called him the greatest pitcher he had ever seen.

39. _____ This American League left-hander was 6–0 in World Series play and 3–1 in all-star action. He was also a four-time 20-game winner with an overall record of 189–102.

40. _____ The last player-manager who led his team to a pennant and World Series victory, he owns a .295 lifetime average. He had his greatest year in 1948 when he hit .355, got four hits in the playoff game, and won the Most Valuable Player award.

41. _____ He recorded a .317 lifetime average despite poor eyesight. For six consecutive years he batted better than .329. In 1929 the flyhawk, who played with both the Cardinals and the Reds, hit safely ten consecutive times to tie a league record.

42. _____ They called him "Beauty," because in his time he was considered a shortstop without peer. In 1922 he set a record when he handled 984 chances at shortstop for the Giants. He averaged 5.97 chances a game during his major league career.

43. _____ Considered the best defensive outfielder, next to Tris Speaker, during his time, he was responsible for talking Ed Barrow into converting Babe Ruth into an outfielder. Along with Speaker and Duffy Lewis, he played in one of the most famous outfields of all time. A

304

great World Series performer, he turned in his best season's batting marks in 1921 and 1924 with the White Sox.

44. _____ He didn't come up to the majors until he was 27, but he won 210 games before he pitched his last major league ball at the age of 44. In the 1926 World Series he beat the Yankees twice.

45. _____ He was likened to Willie Keeler with the bat, Tris Speaker in the field, and Ty Cobb on the bases. Yet this all-round performer never got a chance to show his skills in the majors. He was limited to 29 summers of Negro ball and 21 winters of off-season play.

46. _____ He won four batting titles and hit almost 800 home runs in the Negro leagues. Twice he hit more than 70 home runs in a season. He died at the age of 35, the year Jackie Robinson was admitted to the major leagues.

47. _____ A player, manager, and general manager, "The Mahatma" reached greatness in the game as an innovative administrator. He established the first farm system with the Cardinals, broke the color line when he signed Jackie Robinson, and created dynasties in St. Louis and Brooklyn.

48. _____ The manager of the 1918 Red Sox world championship team, he is more singularly remembered for having discovered Honus Wagner, converting Babe Ruth into an outfielder, and establishing a dynasty as general manager of the Yankees.

49. _____ Winner of two games in the 1948 World Series and loser of two games in the 1954 World Series, he started out as a third baseman and ended up winning 207 major league games.

50. _____ A .330 lifetime hitter, he won one batting title (Tigers), collected 200 hits four times, and batted .300 for four major league clubs.

From Aaron to Kell

Match the following 47 Hall of Famers with the descriptions that follow.

Hank Aaron	Ed Delahanty
Grover Alexander	Joe DiMaggio
Luis Aparicio	Don Drysdale
Luke Appling	Rick Ferrell
Earl Averill	Elmer Flick
Ernie Banks	Chief Bender

Yogi Berra	Whitey Ford
Jim Bottomly	Jimmie Foxx
Mordecai Brown	Willie McCovey
Jesse Burkett	Burleigh Grimes
Roy Campanella	Lefty Grove
Frank Chance	Gabby Hartnett
Jack Chesbro	Harry Heilmann
Roberto Clemente	Billy Herman
Ty Cobb	Rogers Hornsby
Mickey Cochrane	Waite Hoyt
Eddie Collins	Jim Hunter
Earle Combs	Travis Jackson
Stan Coveleski	Hugh Jennings
Sam Crawford	Walter Johnson
Kiki Cuyler	Addie Joss
Ray Dandridge	Al Kaline
Dizzy Dean	Willie Keeler
	George Kell

1. _____ A winner of 239 games during the regular season and five games in World Series play, he won 20 or more games six consecutive years (1906–11), posted an ERA of 1.04 in 1906—the lowest mark for any pitcher with more than 250 innings of pitching—and he didn't allow an earned run in the 1907–08 series.

2. _____ In 1941 he won his 300th—and last—game with the Boston Red Sox.

3. _____ A multi-time batting champ, he once batted .360 over an eight-year span (1920–27) without winning a crown.

4. _____ A four-time batting champ, he hit safely in 14 consecutive World Series games, and he finished his career with *3,000* hits.

5. _____ He once hit 50 home runs in a season, but he didn't win the home run crown; he finished his regular-season career with a .609 slugging average, and he finished his World Series career with a .609 slugging average.

6. _____ A lifetime .321 hitter, he played in three World Series with the Pirates and the Cubs, and in his best overall year (1925), he batted .357, hit a league-leading 26 triples, scored a league-leading 144 runs, and stole 41 bases.

7. _____ A .281 lifetime hitter, he caught 1,805 games over an 18-year career with three American League teams, some of which were spent handling the pitches of a brother who six times won 20 games.

306

8. _____ The Cubs have not won a World Series since this .297 career hitter led them to back-to-back crowns (1907–08) as their player-manager.

9. _____ Third on the all-time hit list (3,771), he also won four home run crowns, three of the times with the number of four-base blows he hit corresponding to the number (44) he wore on his back.

10. _____ A three-time winner of the home run crown, he hit more home runs than any other left-handed batter in National League history.

11. _____ He ranks first in World Series games, at-bats, hits, and doubles; second in runs and runs batted in; and third in home runs and walks.

12. _____ A .304 lifetime hitter, he got a career-high 227 hits in 1935, and played in four World Series with the Cubs and Dogers at three-year intervals (1932–35–38–41).

13. _____ A 300-game winner, he posted ERAs below 2.00 for six consecutive years (1915–20).

14. _____ His lifetime ERA was 1.88, the second all-time low, but unfortunately he died young, at the age of 31.

15. _____ In the 1921 World Series he didn't allow an earned run in 27 innings of pitching, but he won only two of three decisions, losing the final game, 1-0, on an error by Roger Peckinpaugh.

16. _____ A 236-game lifetime winner, he posted the best all-time winning percentage (.690) in modern-day ball.

17. _____ A 210-game lifetime winner, he failed to complete a game in World Series play only one out of ten times, the last time, after completing a record nine games in a row.

18. _____ In 1904 this old Highlander started 51 games, finished 48 contests, and won 41 games, all-time bests.

19. _____ A five-time 20-game winner, he won three games for the Indians in the 1920 World Series, and lost two games for the Senators in the 1925 post-season classic.

20. _____ The second all-time winner with 416 victories, he won the last game of the 1924 World Series, and lost the curtain-caller the following year.

21. _____ He didn't pitch his first full season in the National League until he was 30 years old, yet he went on to win 270 major league games.

22. _____ He was the last National League pitcher (1934) to win 30 games in a season.

23. _____ From 1962–65 he had 40 or more starts every year, and he pitched over 300 innings in each of those seasons.

24. _____ A .341 liftime hitter, he three times batted .400 in the 1890s before leading the league with a .382 mark for the 1901 Cards.

25. _____ A catcher in the National League for 20 years, he hit 236 career homers, high at his position until Roy Campanella ended up with 242.

26. _____ He was the only player to win batting titles in both leagues, hitting .408 for the 1899 Phillies and .376 for the 1902 Senators.

27. _____ This catcher four times hit more than 30 home runs in a season, and in 1953 he drove home a league-leading 142 RBIs.

28. _____ He led the American League in stolen bases his first nine years (1956–64) in the circuit.

29. _____ He won batting titles in 1936 and 1943, the only ones that a player on his team has won.

30. _____ He hit .333 lifetime but never won a batting crown.

31. _____ Four times he hit more than 20 triples in a season, and twice—once in each league—he won the home run crown.

32. _____ In the 11 full seasons that this .318 career hitter played in the majors, he averaged 104 RBIs a year.

33. _____ A .320 lifetime hitter, he played in five World Series, four of them in the 1930s, and player-managed a team to back-to-back penants.

34. _____ From 1924 to 1929 this .310 lifetime hitter—who had seasons of most hits, doubles, triples, home runs, and RBIs—averaged 126 runs batted in a year.

35. _____ A middle infielder, he averaged 44 home runs a year from 1957–60.

36. _____ Until Don Mattingly eclipsed it, he held the Yankee team record of 231 hits in a season.

37. _____ Eight years in a row this .345 lifetime hitter collected more than 200 hits.

38. _____ He finished his career one home run shy of 400.

39. _____ This .315 lifetime hitter once (1905) won a batting title with a mark of .306.

40. _____ A second baseman, he hit 301 career homers.

41. _____ This .325 lifetime hitter, in his first

308

five years in the majors, averaged better than one RBI for every game he played.

42. _____ This .312 lifetime hitter became the first manager to lead his team to three consecutive penants (1907–09); he was also the first of only two skippers to lead his club to three consecutive World Series defeats.

43. _____ A .306 lifetime batter, this infielder hit better than .300 eight straight years and won the batting title in 1949.

44. _____ A defensive standout, this middle infielder played his entire career with one club and posted a .291 lifetime average.

45. _____ In 1921 he won the batting title, outhitting his manager by five points.

46. _____ People who saw him play say that Brooks Robinson couldn't match his defensive skills at third base, but unfortunately he didn't get the opportunity to showcase them in the big leagues.

47. _____ In World Series play he won four-of-four decisions for a West Coast team and one-of-three for an East Coast club.

From Killebrew to Wynn

Match the following 46 Hall of Famers with the descriptions that follow.

Harmon Killebrew	Tris Speaker
Ralph Kiner	Joe Tinker
Chuck Klein	Rube Waddell
Sandy Koufax	Honus Wagner
Fred Lindstrom	Bobby Wallace
Mickey Mantle	Ed Walsh
Juan Marichal	Lloyd Waner
Rube Marquard	Paul Waner
Eddie Mathews	Ted Williams
Christy Mathewson	Hack Wilson
Willie Mays	Billy Williams
Joe McGinnity	Early Wynn
Joe Medwick	Walter Alston
Johnny Mize	Charles Comiskey
Stan Musial	Clark Griffith
Eddie Plank	Bucky Harris
Pee Wee Reese	Miller Huggins

Brooks Robinson   Al Lopez
Frank Robinson   Connie Mack
Red Ruffing   Joe McCarthy
Joe Sewell   Bill McKechnie
Duke Snider   Wilbert Robinson
Warren Spahn   Casey Stengel

1. _____ In back-to-back years (1903–04) he pitched more than 400 innings in each season.

2. _____ In his last five years (1962–66) he posted ERAs under 2.00.

3. _____ He finished his career with *300* victories.

4. _____ This 201-game winner pitched in five World Series with the Giants and Dodgers, winning two games and losing five.

5. _____ Six times he won more than 20 games in a season for the Giants.

6. _____ He held the American League strikeout record for one season (349) until Nolan Ryan broke it.

7. _____ Four times—three times in a row—he won 30 or more games in a season.

8. _____ Eight times he won 20 or more games for Connie Mack.

9. _____ The most games he won in a season was 23, but he won 20 or more games in a year a record 13 times.

10. _____ He won six consecutive games in World Series play.

11. _____ He hit more than 500 career homers, including 40 or more in his second, third, and fourth years in the majors.

12. _____ In his first five full seasons in the majors (1929–33) he won four home run crowns.

13. _____ He led the National League in home runs in back-to-back years with two clubs.

14. _____ He played on five consecutive World Series losers before he played on a winning team.

15. _____ A .324 lifetime batter, he led the National League in doubles and RBIs from 1936–38.

16. _____ He hit .365 one year (1957) but finished second to Ted Williams in the batting race.

17. _____ He hit more right-handed home runs (586) than any other player except Willie Mays and Hank Aaron.

18. _____ He averaged 37 home runs a season in his ten-year career.

19. _____ A .333 lifetime hitter, he won batting crowns in 1927, 1934, and 1936.

20. _____ At age 18 he got four hits in a World Series game against Walter Johnson.

21. _____ After the Giants traded him to the Cubs, he promptly proved that his former team had made a mistake by winning three home run titles in his first three years in the Windy City.

22. _____ In the four years that he won home run crowns he averaged 50 circuit clouts a season.

23. _____ From 1953–57 he hit 40 or more home runs in each season.

24. _____ Eight times he hit more than 40 home runs in a season but never hit 50.

25. _____ He broke into Cleveland's lineup after Ray Chapman was killed by a Carl Mays pitch.

26. _____ At the age of 37 this .344 lifetime hitter batted .389.

27. _____ A .329 lifetime batter, he had a career average that was higher than any other player at his position.

28. _____ This .331 lifetime hitter player in four World Series (1942–46) in a five-year period of time.

29. _____ This .316 lifetime batter collected more than 200 hits in four of his first five years in the majors.

30. _____ In his first two league Championship Series (1969–70), this .267 lifetime batter hit .500 and .583.

31. _____ A .344 lifetime hitter, he won a batting title at the age of 40.

32. _____ A .263 lifetime hitter, he played in consecutive World Series from 1906–08.

33. _____ A one-time 40-game winner, he posted the lowest career ERA (1.82) of all time.

34. _____ This super defensive shortstop played 25 years, most of them with the Browns; he was called "Rhody."

35. _____ He won back-to-back pennants with Cincinnati.

36. _____ He won two pennants and finished a runner-up ten times.

37. _____ He won World Series on both coasts, one in the East and three in the West.

38. _____ He won World Series 23 years apart.

39. _____ In 24 years of managing he won nine pennants—one in the National League and eight in the

American League—and never finished lower than fourth in the standings.

40. _____ Called "The Tall Tactician," he finished first nine times, but ended up last 17 times.

41. _____ A one-time coach for John McGraw, with whom he played with the Orioles, he later managed Brooklyn to two pennants.

42. _____ Called "The Old Roman," he once managed St. Louis to four straight pennants; he was later the owner of the White Sox during the Black Sox scandal.

43. _____ No stranger to highs and lows, he won ten pennants but finished up his managerial career with four consecutive tenth-place finishers.

44. _____ Called "The Old Fox," he managed just one winner in 20 years, but he also became an owner who presided over three pennant winners and one World Series champ.

45. _____ Called "The Mighty Mite," he twice led one team to three consecutive pennants.

46. _____ Thirteen years in a row he hit 20 or more round-trippers—he slugged 426 lifetime—but he never won a home run crown.

What Have you Done Lately?

Career-wise, Dusty Rhodes was a less-than-mediocre pinch-hitter, but for one season, 1954, he was probably the best clutch-hitting pinch-hitter in baseball history.

In 1954, the year the Giants won the pennant and swept the Indians in the World Series, Rhodes seemed to come through almost every time he stepped to the plate with men on base in a clutch situation. Actually, he made 15 hits in 45 at bats, in pinch-hitting situations, for a .333 average. Overall, he batted .341 and he belted 15 home runs.

In the World Series that year, he made four hits in six plate appearances. Pinch-hitting, he batted safely all three times he stepped to the plate. All three pinch-hits were timely. In Game One he hit a three-run homer in the bottom of the tenth to provide the winning margin in a 5–2 contest. In Game Two his pinch-hit single tied the score at 1–1. Inserted in left field, he proceeded to hit a long home run en route to a Giant 3–1 win. In Game Three he delivered a pinch-hit single with the bases loaded to score the runs that turned out to be the tying and winning counters.

But after that season his star faded. Four years later, he was out of the big leagues. His seven-year pinch-hitting average was an anemic .212.

Another irony of Rhodes's 1954 performance was that in each one of his pinch-hitting appearances he batted for a Giant star—now a Hall of Famer—who in the 1951 World Series clubbed the ball for a .458 mark and stole home in the opening game.

Who was that Giant superstar of 1951—he got seven hits in the first two games—who bowed in favor of the Giant superstar of 1954?

(Answer appears on page 322.)

Chapter Twenty

RETIRED UNIFORM NUMBERS

NATIONAL LEAGUE

We'll give you the teams, the number of "numbers" they've retired, and the players' uniform numbers. You identify the players.

Atlanta (4)

1. _____ (21)
2. _____ (35)
3. _____ (41)
4. _____ (44)

Chicago (2)

1. _____ (14)
2. _____ (26)

Cincinnati (2)

1. _____ (1)
2. _____ (5)

Houston (2)

1. _____ (22)
2. _____ (40)

Los Angeles (8)

1. _____ (1)
2. _____ (4)
3. _____ (19)
4. _____ (24)
5. _____ (32)
6. _____ (39)
7. _____ (42)
8. _____ (56)

New York (2)

1. _____ (14)
2. _____ (37)

Philadelphia (2)

1. _____ (1)
2. _____ (36)

Pittsburgh (8)

1. _____ (1)
2. _____ (4)
3. _____ (8)
4. _____ (9)
5. _____ (20)
6. _____ (21)
7. _____ (33)
8. _____ (40)

St. Louis (5)   San Francisco (5)

1. _____ (6)   1. _____ (4)
2. _____ (14)   2. _____ (11)
3. _____ (17)   3. _____ (24)
4. _____ (20)   4. _____ (27)
5. _____ (45)   5. _____ (44)

AMERICAN LEAGUE

Baltimore (3)

1. _____ (4)
2. _____ (5)
3. _____ (20)

Boston (2)

1. _____ (4)
2. _____ (9)

California (1)

1. _____ (26)

Chicago (5)

1. _____ (2)
2. _____ (4)
3. _____ (9)
4. _____ (11)
5. _____ (19)

Cleveland (3)

1. _____ (3)
2. _____ (5)
3. _____ (19)

Detroit (3)

1. _____ (2)
2. _____ (5)
3. _____ (6)

Milwaukee (1)

1. _____ (44)

Minnesota (2)

1. _____ (3)
2. _____ (29)

New York (10)

1. _____ (3)
2. _____ (4)
3. _____ (5)
4. _____ (7)
5. _____ (8)
6. _____ (8)
7. _____ (9)
8. _____ (15)
9. _____ (16)
10. _____ (32)
11. _____ (37)

Moe the Pro

Moe Drabowsky was just a .426 winning percentage pitcher during his 17-year career but he was a 1.000 winning percentage moundsman in the 1966 fall classic, his only World Series appearance.

In Game One of the Orioles' four-game sweep of the Dodgers, Bird manager Hank Bauer summoned Drabowsky to relieve starter Dave McNally in the third inning with Baltimore clinging tenuously to a 4–2 lead. Drabowsky was superb. He pitched six and two thirds innings of shutout ball en route to the Orioles' 5–2 win. But it was the manner in which Drabowsky stifled the Dodgers that raised the eyebrows of veteran World Series observers. He allowed just one hit, issued two free passes, and struck out *11* batters, a fall classic record for pitchers in relief.

Drabowsky's pitching performance turned out to be the catalyst that the Birds' staff needed. In Game Two, Jim Palmer blanked Los Angeles, 9–0; in Game Three, Wally Bunker zipped the Dodgers, 1–0; and in Game Four, Dave McNally whitewashed manager Walter Alston's men, 1–0. In the last 33⅔ innings of the 1966 Series, Baltimore's staff did not allow the Dodgers a single run.

At one point in Game One, Drabowsky fanned six consecutive Los Angeles batters, another record for relief pitchers in World Series play.

A Cincinnati pitcher of 1919 recorded six consecutive outs via the strikeout route, but he permitted White Sox batters to reach base during the skein. A Giant pitcher topped that performance in 1921 when he got seven consecutive outs in strikeout fashion, but he permitted three Yankee batters to walk during the intervening time.

Can you name either the Red or the Giant pitcher who recorded a World Series first? If you can name both of them you will be a 1.000 winning percentage pitcher—just like Moe Drabowsky!

(Answer appears on page 322.)

ANSWERS SECTION

Introduction: Warren Sandell, who according to *The New York Times* "had a propensity to throw home-run pitches," never made it to the major leagues.

Ruth's Shadow: Lou Gehrig

The Shot Heard 'Round the World: Larry Jansen

The Asterisk Pitcher: Hank Aaron, the runner on first base, thought that Joe Adcock's game-winning hit had remained in play; so, when he saw Felix Mantilla racing toward home, he assumed that the one run would automatically bring the game to an end. Consequently, shortly after rounding second base, he stopped and headed for the dugout. Adcock, who had not noticed Aaron's error in judgment, naturally passed his teammate. Since the hitter had illegally passed the base runner, he was ruled out by the umpire. Aaron, on the other hand, could have been called out for illegally running the base paths. If both runners had been called out before Mantilla crossed home plate, no run would count because the third out would have been recorded before the winning run scored. But Mantilla did score and the Braves did win.

And Harvey Haddix has become an asterisk!

Exceptions to the Rule: Bob Cain, pitcher; Bob Swift, catcher; and Bill Stewart, umpire

The Mystery Death: Willard Hershberger

A Checkered Career: Hank Gowdy

Classic Comebacks: Gaylord Perry (Giants) and Ray Washburn (Cardinals); Jim Maloney (Reds) and Don Wilson (Astros)

Baseball's Number Game: Lou Brock (.293) and Carl Yastrzemski (.285)

The Fateful Farewell: Al Gionfriddo was Furillo's pinch-runner, Eddie Miksis was Reiser's, and Eddie Miksis was the fielder.

The Iron Horse: Wally Pipp

To Catch a Thief: Bob O'Farrell

Two Strikes Against Him: Joe Sewell

Where Are the Iron Men: The pitchers are Steve Blass and Nelson Briles of the 1971 Pirates and Burt Hooton and Don Sutton of the 1977 Dodgers. Blass recorded the two complete games.

The Trivia Tandem: Larry McWilliams (starter) and Gene Garber (reliever)

The Black Sox: Ray Schalk, catcher; Eddie Collins, second baseman; and Red Faber, pitcher

The Shoe Polish Plays: Nippy Jones and Cleon Jones

The Shutout Series: Red Ames (Giants) and Chief Bender (Athletics)

A Man for All Seasons: Ed Barrow

Three Men on Third: Dazzy Vance, since there was no force, had rightful possession of the bag. Chick Fewster and Babe Herman, who were the trespassers, were declared out. Since that day, whenever someone says, "The Dodgers have three men on base," a listener with a keen sense of wit will invariably say, "Which one?"

What Have You Done Lately: Monte Irvin

Moe the Pro: Hod Eller (Reds) and Jesse Barnes (Giants)

Chapter One Answers

1. From Anderson to Yount

1. Roger Clemens (1986)
2. Garry Templeton (1977–79 Cards)
3. Greg Minton (1978–82 Giants)
4. Buddy Bell (.299 for the 1979 Rangers)
5. Ron Guidry (Yankees)
6. Steve Carlton (1972 Phillies)
7. Robin Yount (Brewers)
8. Willie Wilson (Royals)
9. Pete Rose
10. Bill Gullickson (1982 Expos)
11. Davey Lopes (1975 Dodgers)
12. Willie Wilson
13. Don Baylor (1974 Orioles)
14. Bob Stanley (1982 Red Sox)
15. Fernando Valenzuela (1981 Dodgers)
16. Juan Samuel (1984 Phillies)
17. Phil Niekro (1977–80 Braves)
18. Gene Garber (1979 Braves)
19. Ted Simmons (180 at the beginning of 1988)
20. Terry Kennedy (Padres)
21. Mike Easler
22. Bruce Sutter (1977 Cubs)
23. Don Baylor
24. Frank Tanana (1978 Angels)
25. Rickey Henderson (1982 A's)
26. Dale Murphy (Braves)
27. Cal Ripken, Sr.
28. Rick Sutcliffe
29. Steve Sax
30. Juan Samuel (1983 Phillies)
31. Bill Campbell (1976 Twins)
32. Tim Wallach (1982 Expos)
33. Mookie Wilson (Jackson, Miss., in 1978)
34. Tom Seaver (1985)
35. Mike Schmidt
36. Jason Thompson
37. Wade Boggs (1982 Red Sox)
38. Dennis Eckersley (1981 Red Sox)
39. Mike Hargrove
40. Andre Thornton (1978 Indians)
41. Carlton Fisk (1985 White Sox)
42. Don Sutton
43. Darrell Evans (1973 Braves)
44. Jack Morris (20 and 232)
45. Dave Winfield (37)
46. Graig Nettles
47. Roy Smalley (1982)
48. Butch Wynegar (1976 Twins)

49. Dave Stieb (1983 Blue Jays)
50. Fred Lynn (1983)
51. Richard Dotson (He was 24 when he won 22 in 1983)
52. George Brett (1983 Royals)
53. Dave Righetti (1986 Yankees)
54. Hal McRae (1982 Royals)
55. Gary Gaetti (1981)
56. Ron Davis (1981 Yankees)
57. Carney Lansford (Red Sox)
58. Don Mattingly (1984)
59. Charlie Hough (Rangers)
60. Leon Durham (1982)
61. Charlie Lea
62. Keith Hernandez
63. Walt Terrell (1983 Mets)
64. John Denny (1983 Phillies)
65. Bill Madlock
66. Glenn Hubbard
67. Dave Parker (Pirates)
68. Mario Soto
69. Ray Knight
70. Steve Balboni
71. Nolan Ryan
72. Ken Landreaux
73. David Palmer (Expos)
74. Steve Garvey (1977 Dodgers)
75. Goose Gossage (1977 Pirates)
76. Bob and Ken Forsch
77. Gary Carter (1978 Expos)
78. Manny Trillo (Phillies)
79. Cecil Cooper
80. Sparky Anderson
81. Aurelio Lopez
82. Paul Molitor (Brewers)
83. Terry Puhl (1979)
84. John Tudor (1982–83)
85. John Candelaria
86. George Frazier (1981 Yankees)
87. Willie McGee (1982 Cards)
88. Claudell Washington (1979 White Sox, 1980 Mets)
89. Len Barker (1981)
90. Steve Bedrosian (1987 Phillies)
91. Pedro Guerrero (1981–82)
92. LaMarr Hoyt (1981–82)
93. Frank White
94. Rickey Henderson (A's)
95. Larry Parrish
96. Gary Ward (1983)
97. Bill Buckner (1980)
98. Willie Upshaw (104 in 1983)
99. Don Mattingly
100. Jesse Barfield

2. From Aikens to Yount

1. Jim Clancy
2. Doug DeCinces (1982)
3. Dick Schofield, Jr.
4. Harold Baines (He was 23 in 1982.)
5. Floyd Bannister (1982 Mariners)

6. Pat Corrales (Phillies–Indians)
7. John McNamara (Padres, A's, Reds, Angels, and Red Sox)
8. Davy Johnson (1973 Braves)
9. Chuck Tanner (1955 Braves)
10. Bob Knepper
11. Dwight Gooden (Mets)
12. Rick Manning (1977 Indians)
13. Rich Dauer (1978 Orioles)
14. Chet Lemon (1977)
15. Dwayne Murphy (1980 A's)
16. Jim Sundberg (1979 Rangers)
17. Rickey Henderson
18. Tim Raines
19. Eddie Murray (Orioles)
20. Dwight Evans (1981 Red Sox)
21. Willie Upshaw (Gene and Marvin Upshaw)
22. Ernie Whitt (Blue Jays)
23. Fred Lynn (1975 Red Sox)
24. Bob Boone (Angels)
25. Reggie Jackson (1973 A's, 1977 Yankees)
26. Carlton Fisk (White Sox)
27. Ron Kittle (1983)
28. John McNamara (Reds)
29. Dick Howser (1980 Yankees)
30. Davy Johnson
31. Chuck Tanner (for Manny Sanguillen)
32. Dick Williams (1967 Red Sox, 1972–73 A's, 1984 Padres)
33. Bert Blyleven (1977)
34. Ray Knight
35. Don Sutton
36. Tony LaRussa
37. Tom Seaver (1971)
38. Mike Schmidt
39. Steve Carlton (1972)
40. Kent Tekulve (1978–79)
41. Bruce Sutter
42. Dan Quisenberry (1983)
43. John Montefusco
44. John McNamara
45. Don Sutton
46. Darrell Evans (1976 Braves)
47. Pete Rose (1978 Reds)
48. Willie Wilson (1979 Royals)
49. Steve Garvey
50. Garry Templeton (1979 Cards)
51. Graig Nettles (1971 Indians)
52. Reggie Jackson
53. Graig Nettles (Padres)
54. Whitey Herzog
55. Garry Templeton (1979 Cards)
56. Willie Wilson (1980 Royals)
57. Jack Clark
58. Jim Rice (46 home runs, 213 hits in 1978)
59. George Brett (1979 Royals)
60. George Brett (1978)
61. Tom Seaver (1973 Mets)
62. Ron Guidry (1978 Yankees)
63. Steve Carlton (1972 Phillies)
64. Reggie Jackson

65. Pete Rose (1975 Reds)
66. Ron Guidry (.893 for the 1978 Yankees)
67. Goose Gossage (1975 White Sox, 1978 Yankees)
68. Jack Clark (1978)
69. Willie Randolph
70. Rudy Law (77 in 1983)
71. Ron Guidry (1.74 for the 1978 Yankees)
72. Pete Rose (1963 Reds)
73. Steve Carlton (1979 Phillies)
74. Willie Aikens (Royals)
75. George Brett
76. Reggie Jackson (1973, 1975 A's; 1980 Yankees; and 1982 Angels)
77. Lee Mazzilli
78. Rick Cerone
79. Dave Righetti
80. Carlton Fisk
81. Tom Seaver (1981 Reds)
82. Darryl Strawberry (1983)
83. Larry Herndon
84. Robin Yount (1982 Brewers)
85. Dave Righetti
86. Phil Niekro (At the start of the 1987 season, he was 48.)
87. Carlton Fisk (Red Sox and White Sox)
88. Ron Kittle (1983)
89. George Brett
90. Steve Balboni
91. Ron Davis (Yankees)
92. Charlie Hough
93. Andre Dawson (against the 1978 Braves)
94. Tim Wallach (1980)
95. Mike Schmidt
96. Bill Madlock (Cubs and Pirates)
97. Claudell Washington
98. Dave Concepcion
99. Lou Whitaker
100. Fred Lynn (1975 Red Sox)

3. From Aase to Youmans

1. Ryne Sandberg
2. Gary Matthews
3. Jody Davis (1983)
4. Shawon Dunston
5. Rick Sutcliffe
6. Lee Smith
7. Dennis Eckersley
8. Mike Fitzgerald
9. Andres Galarraga
10. Floyd Youmans
11. Tim Burke (1985)
12. Jeff Reardon
13. Tim Raines (1981)
14. Gary Carter
15. Darryl Strawberry
16. Kirk Gibson
17. Keith Hernandez (1986)
18. Dwight Gooden (1984–86)
19. Roger McDowell (1986)
20. Bob Ojeda (1986)
21. Jesse Orosco
22. Mike Schmidt
23. Juan Samuel (1984–86)
24. Steve Bedrosian (40 in 1987)
25. Tony Peña
26. Mike Diaz

27. Barry Bonds
28. Tommy Herr
29. Willie McGee (.353 for 1985 Cards)
30. Ozzie Smith
31. Vince Coleman (1985)
32. Jack Clark
33. John Tudor
34. Danny Cox (1985 Cards)
35. Bob Forsch
36. Todd Worrell (Cards)
37. Dale Murphy
38. Glen Hubbard (1978)
39. Ozzie Virgil (27)
40. Ken Griffey
41. Gene Garber
42. Rick Mahler
43. Dave Parker
44. Eric Davis
45. Ron Oester
46. Buddy Bell (194)
47. Bo Diaz
48. John Franco
49. Bill Doran (1986)
50. Mike Scott (1986)
51. Bob Knepper
52. Jim Deshaies (12 in 1986)
53. Dave Smith
54. Nolan Ryan
55. Steve Sax
56. Mike Marshall
57. Bill Madlock
58. Pedro Guerrero
59. Fernando Valenzuela
60. Bob Welch
61. Steve Garvey
62. Kevin Mitchell
63. Goose Gossage
64. Andy Hawkins

65. Will Clark (1986)
66. Jeff Leonard
67. Candy Maldonado
68. Mike Krukow
69. Mark Davis
70. Eddie Murray
71. Cal Ripken
72. Fred Lynn (1979 Red Sox)
73. Lee Lacy
74. Mike Boddicker (1984)
75. Don Aase (1986)
76. Mike Flanagan
77. Wade Boggs
78. Jim Rice
79. Marty Barrett (1986)
80. Don Baylor (Orioles, Angels, Yankees, and Red Sox)
81. Dwight Evans
82. Roger Clemens
83. Bruce Hurst
84. Joe Carter (1986)
85. Julio Franco
86. Tony Bernazard
87. Brett Butler
88. Brook Jacoby
89. Pat Tabler
90. Phil Niekro
91. Ernie Camacho
92. Tom Candiotti
93. Darrell Evans (1985)
94. Alan Trammell
95. Lou Whitaker
96. Jack Morris
97. Willie Hernandez (1984)
98. Robin Yount
99. Rob Deer
100. Paul Molitor

4. From Balboni to Witt

1. Ted Higuera
2. Mark Clear
3. Don Mattingly
4. Rickey Henderson
5. Willie Randolph
6. Dave Winfield
7. Dave Righetti
8. Jesse Barfield
9. Lloyd Moseby
10. George Bell
11. Dave Stieb
12. Wally Joyner (1986)
13. Doug DeCinces
14. Brian Downing
15. Gary Pettis (1984–86)
16. Mike Witt
17. Don Sutton
18. Harold Baines (1982–87)
19. Ossie Guillen
20. Carlton Fisk
21. Joe Cowley (1986)
22. Bob James
23. George Brett
24. Steve Balboni
25. Willie Wilson (1982)
26. Frank White
27. Kirby Puckett
28. Kent Hrbek
29. Gary Gaetti
30. Bert Blyleven
31. Jose Canseco
32. Pete Incaviglia
33. Larry Parrish
34. Mitch Williams
35. Bobby Witt

Chapter Two Answers

5. How Good Is .300?

Batting Champs

1. Mickey Mantle (.298)
2. Tommy Davis (.294)
3. Norm Cash (.271)
4. Hal Chase (.291)
5. George Stirnweiss (.268)
6. Carl Yastrzemski (.285)
7. Pete Runnels (.291)
8. Bobby Avila (.281)
9. Harry Walker (.296)
10. Dick Groat (.286)
11. Lou Boudreau (.295)
12. Mickey Vernon (.286)
13. Debs Garms (.293)
14. Heinie Zimmerman (.295)
15. Pete Reiser (.295)
16. Larry Doyle (.290)
17. Ferris Fain (.290)
18. Alex Johnson (.288)
19. Phil Cavarretta (.293)
20. Carl Furillo (.299)

.300 Hitters

1. Johnny Pesky (.307)
2. Enos Slaughter (.300)
3. Joe Cronin (.302)
4. Mel Ott (.304)
5. Bill Dickey (.313)
6. Lloyd Waner (.316)
7. Bob Meusel (.309)
8. Joe Jackson (.356)
9. Hack Wilson (.307)
10. Earl Averill (.318)
11. Sam Rice (.322)
12. Dale Mitchell (.312)
13. Hank Greenberg (.313)
14. Eddie Collins (.333)
15. Earle Combs (.325)
16. Babe Herman (.324)
17. Kiki Cuyler (.321)
18. Frankie Frisch (.316)
19. Pie Traynor (.320)
20. Mickey Cochrane (.320)

6. Who Did It Twice?

National League

1. Willie Mays
2. Harry Walker
3. Dixie Walker
4. Carl Furillo
5. Jackie Robinson

1. Lefty O'Doul
2. Tommy Davis
3. Henry Aaron
4. Ernie Lombardi
5. Richie Ashburn

American League

1. George Kell
2. Al Kaline
3. Norm Cash
4. Mickey Mantle
5. Harvey Kuenn

1. Jimmie Foxx
2. Luke Appling
3. Mickey Vernon
4. Pete Runnels
5. Ferris Fain

7. The Fabulous Fifties

1. Roger Maris
2. Babe Ruth
3. Babe Ruth
4. Jimmie Foxx
5. Hank Greenberg
6. Hack Wilson
7. Babe Ruth
8. Babe Ruth
9. Ralph Kiner

10. Mickey Mantle
11. Mickey Mantle
12. Willie Mays
13. George Foster
14. Both answers can be
15. Johnny Mize or Ralph Kiner
16. Willie Mays
17. Jimmie Foxx

8. The (500) Home Run Club

1. Hank Aaron
2. Babe Ruth
3. Willie Mays
4. Frank Robinson
5. Harmon Killebrew
6. Reggie Jackson
7. Mickey Mantle
8. Jimmie Foxx

9. Mike Schmidt
10. Both 10–11 can be Ted
11. Williams or Willie McCovey
12. Both 12–13 can be
13. Eddie Mathews or Ernie Banks
14. Mel Ott

9. They Hit for Power and Average

National League

1. Heinie Zimmerman
2. Rogers Hornsby
3. Rogers Hornsby
4. Chuck Klein
5. Joe Medwick
6. Johnny Mize

American League

1. Nap Lajoie
2. Ty Cobb
3. Babe Ruth
4. Jimmie Foxx
5. Lou Gehrig
6. Ted Williams
7. Ted Williams

8. Ted Williams
9. Mickey Mantle

10. Frank Robinson
11. Carl Yastrzemski

10. The 3000-Hit Club

1. Pete Rose
2. Ty Cobb
3. Hank Aaron
4. Stan Musial
5. Tris Speaker
6. Honus Wagner
7. Carl Yastrzemski
8. Eddie Collins

9. Willie Mays
10. Nap Lajoie
11. Paul Waner
12. Cap Anson
13. Lou Brock
14. Al Kaline
15. Roberto Clemente

11. Triple Crown Winners

1. Nap Lajoie
2. Ty Cobb
3. Rogers Hornsby
4. Rogers Hornsby
5. Chuck Klein or Jimmie Foxx
6. Chuck Klein or Jimmie Foxx

7. Lou Gehrig
8. Joe Medwick
9. Ted Williams
10. Ted Williams
11. Mickey Mantle
12. Frank Robinson
13. Carl Yastrzemski

12. Highest Lifetime Average for Position

National League

1. Bill Terry
2. Rogers Hornsby
3. Honus Wagner
4. Pie Traynor
5. Riggs Stephenson
6. Paul Waner
7. Lefty O'Doul
8. Eugene Hargrave

American League

1. Lou Gehrig and George Sisler
2. Nap Lajoie
3. Cecil Travis
4. Frank Baker
5. Ty Cobb
6. Joe Jackson
7. Ted Williams
8. Mickey Cochrane

13. Highest Single Season Average for Position

National League

1. Bill Terry
2. Rogers Hornsby
3. Arky Vaughan
4. Heinie Zimmerman
5. Lefty O'Doul
6. Babe Herman
7. Chuck Klein
8. Chief Meyers

American League

1. George Sisler
2. Nap Lajoie
3. Luke Appling
4. George Brett
5. Ty Cobb
6. Joe Jackson
7. Ted Williams
8. Bill Dickey

14. The Year They Hit the Heights

1. Rogers Hornsby
2. Ty Cobb
3. Ted Williams
4. Babe Ruth
5. Joe DiMaggio
6. Stan Musial
7. Mickey Mantle
8. Roberto Clemente
9. Jackie Robinson
10. Charlie Keller

15. Matching Averages

1. Ty Cobb
2. Rogers Hornsby
3. Tris Speaker
4. Babe Ruth
5. Bill Terry
6. Stan Musial
7. Honus Wagner
8. Jimmie Foxx
9. Mickey Cochrane
10. Mel Ott

16. Once Is Not Enough

1. Lou Gehrig
2. Rocky Colavito
3. Gil Hodges
4. Pat Seerey
5. Joe Adcock
6. Mike Schmidt
7. Willie Mays
8. Bob Horner

17. National League Home Run Kings

1. Mike Schmidt
2. Ralph Kiner
3. Mel Ott
4. Johnny Mize
5. Eddie Mathews or
   Johnny Bench

6. Eddie Mathews or
   Johnny Bench
7. Ted Kluszewski or
   Duke Snider

8. Ted Kluszewski or
   Duke Snider

18. American League Home Run Kings

1. Babe Ruth
2. Harmon Killebrew
3–8. Any combination of
   Jimmie Foxx, Frank
   Baker, Hank Green-
   berg, Reggie Jack-
   son, Ted Williams
   and Mickey Mantle
9–10. Either Lou Gehrig
   or Jim Rice

11–16. Any combination
   of Frank Howard,
   Tony Armas, Joe
   DiMaggio, Gorman
   Thomas, Larry
   Doby, and Dick
   Allen
17–20. Any combination of
   Roger Maris, George
   Scott, Graig Nettles,
   and Carl Yastrzemski

19. Would You Pinch-Hit?

1. No (.294)
2. No (.283)
3. No (.290)
4. No (.289)
5. Yes (.326)
6. No (.270)
7. Yes (.304)
8. No (.272)
9. Yes (.312)
10. Yes (.296)

11. Yes (.286)
12. Yes (.284)
13. No (.269)
14. No (.261)
15. Yes (.287)
16. Same (.276)
17. Yes (.304)
18. No (.264)
19. Yes (.293)
20. Yes (.273)

20. Decades of Batting Champs

National League

1. Pirates
2. Reds
3. Phillies
4. Reds

5. Cubs
6. Dodgers
7. Reds
8. Braves
9. Expos

1. Senators
2. Indians
3. Tigers
4. White Sox
5. Yankees

6. Athletics
7. Red Sox
8. Angels
9. Red Sox

21. Sub-.320 Batting Leaders

1. Rod Carew
2. Frank Robinson
3. George Stirnweiss

4. Elmer Flick
5. Carl Yastrzemski

22. .390-Plus Runners-up

1. Joe Jackson
2. Ty Cobb
3. Babe Ruth

4. Babe Herman
5. Al Simmons

23. Stepping into the Box

1. L
2. R
3. S
4. R
5. S
6. L
7. S
8. R
9. L
10. S
11. R
12. L
13. L
14. R
15. L

16. L
17. R
18. R
19. S
20. S
21. L
22. R
23. S
24. L
25. R
26. S
27. R
28. L
29. S
30. S

24. Famous Home Run Pitches

1. Ralph Terry
2. Robin Roberts
3. Ralph Branca
4. Don Newcombe
5. Jack Billingham
6. Al Downing
7. Howie Pollet
8. Barney Schultz
9. Bob Lemon
10. Bob Purkey

25. The Pitching Masters

1. Cy Young
2. Walter Johnson
3. Christy Mathewson or Grover Alexander
4. Grover Alexander or Christy Mathewson
5. Warren Spahn
6. Eddie Plank
7. Gaylord Perry
8. Tom Seaver
9. Lefty Grove or Early Wynn
10. Lefty Grove or Early Wynn
11–13. Any combination of Steve Carlton, Phil Niekro, or Don Sutton

26. The Perfect Game

1. Ernie Shore
2. Jim Hunter
3. Jim Bunning
4. Cy Young
5. Addie Joss
6. Sandy Koufax
7. Don Larsen
8. Charlie Robertson
9. Mike Witt
10. Len Barker

27. Multiple No-Hitters

1. Nolan Ryan
2. Sandy Koufax
3. Bob Feller or Jim Maloney
4. Bob Feller or Jim Maloney
5–15. Any combination of the following: Johnny Vander Meer, Steve Busby, Ken Holtzman, Don Wilson, Dean Chance, Jim Bunning, Warren Spahn, Sam Jones, Carl Erskine, Allie Reynolds, Virgil Trucks

28. Back-to-Back 20-Game Winners

1. h
2. s
3. p
4. n
5. w
6. d
7. v
8. t
9. k
10. m
11. f
12. q
13. o
14. e
15. x
16. j
17. a
18. i
19. c
20. u
21. g
22. r
23. b
24. l
25. y
26. z

29. The Flamethrowers

1. Nolan Ryan
2. Sandy Koufax
3. Mickey Lolich
4. Sam McDowell
5. Bob Feller
6. Steve Carlton
7. Walter Johnson
8. Rube Waddell
9. Vida Blue
10. J. R. Richard
11. Mike Scott

30. Blue-Chip Pitchers

1. Whitey Ford (.690)
2. Allie Reynolds (.630)
3. Jim Palmer (.638)
4. Mort Cooper (.631)
5. Tom Seaver (.603)
6. Vic Raschi (.667)
7. Sal Maglie (.657)
8. Dizzy Dean (.644)
9. Sandy Koufax (.655)
10. Lefty Gomez (.649)

31. 200 Times a Loser

1. Cy Young
2. Bobo Newsom
3. Walter Johnson
4. Warren Spahn
5. Grover Alexander
6. Red Ruffing
7. Paul Derringer
8. Robin Roberts
9. Bob Friend
10. Early Wynn

32. Winding Up

1. L
2. L
3. R
4. L
5. R
6. R
7. L
8. L
9. R
10. R
11. R
12. R
13. L
14. L
15. R
16. R
17. L
18. L
19. R
20. L
21. L
22. L
23. R
24. R
25. R
26. R
27. L
28. R
29. L
30. L

Chapter Four Answers

33. Four Bases to Score

1. d
2. c
3. b
4. b
5. a
6. a
7. d
8. b
9. d (1910, 1913, and 1917)
10. a (1939–40)
11. c
12. d
13. b (117)
14. c
15. a
16. a
17. b (1901, Reds; 1908 and 1914, Tigers)
18. d (.410 with 1899 Phillies and .376 with 1902 Senators)
19. c (52 in 1977)
20. d
21. d
22. d (170–161)
23. a
24. c (for the 1948 Indians)
25. d
26. c
27. c (1951–52)
28. c (1962–63)
29. d
30. d
31. b
32. b

33. c
34. a
35. b
36. c (.401 in 1930)
37. d
38. a
39. d
40. b (1983)
41. c (.407 in 1920 and .420 in 1922)
42. b (30–7 in 1934)
43. a (.349)
44. d
45. a (41)
46. a (33–25 in 1925)
47. d (1947) He was two outs short of duplicating the feat.
48. d
49. a
50. d
51. b (51 in 1947)
52. a (9)
53. c (36)
54. b
55. a
56. c
57. b
58. b (1973)
59. b
60. c
61. b
62. d
63. d
64. d
65. a (1923)
66. a (1976)

67. c (1946–52)
68. c
69. d ((1968)
70. a
71. b (.422 in 1901)
72. a
73. c (1922)
74. b
75. d
76. b
77. d (1947)
78. d (1964)
79. d
80. a
81. b
82. d
83. b (Indians)

84. c
85. a
86. d
87. b
88. d
89. c (1226)
90. c
91. c (1964)
92. d
93. d (Hunter was 5–3 in series play.)
94. a (1915)
95. c
96. c (1952)
97. d (1959, with the White Sox)
98. d
99. d
100. c (1961)

Chapter Five Answers

34. From Ruth to Reggie

1. Hank Greenberg
2. Johnny Allen (1937)
3. Earl Averill
4. Monty Stratton (1938)
5. Ossie Vitt
6. Bob Feller
7. Frank Robinson
8. Hank Greenberg
9. Chris Chambliss
10. Hank Borowy
11. Phil Masi
12. Joe McCarthy
13. Don Kessinger (1979 White Sox)
14. Lou Boudreau (Cleveland, 1948)
15. Joe Gordon
16. Rocky Colavito
17. Stu Miller
18. Lou Boudreau
19. Ted Williams
20. Cal Abrams
21. Bobo Holloman (Browns, 1953)
22. Chuck Stobbs
23. Chuck Dressen
24. Johnny Antonelli
25. Willie Mays
26. Hank Aaron
27. Vic Wertz
28. Ruben Gomez
29. Pat Dobson
30. Tommy Byrne
31. Gil McDougald
32. Sal Maglie
33. Yogi Berra
34. Tony Kubek
35. Pirates (1925)
36. Royals (1985)
37. Harry Heilmann (.403 in 1923)
38. Johnny Roseboro
39. Casey Stengel
40. Tom Zachary
41. Tracy Stallard
42. Luis Arroyo
43. Johnny Blanchard
44. Frank Lary
45. Casey Stengel
46. Phil Linz
47. Juan Marichal
48. Don Drysdale
49. Willie Davis
50. Milt Pappas
51. Bob Turley
52. First Base
53. Happy Chandler
54. Frank Robinson
55. Norm Siebern
56. Al Rosen
57. Don Demeter
58. Bill McKechnie
59. Ken Harrelson
60. Denny McLain (31–6 in 1968)
61. Nippy Jones
62. Cleon Jones
63. Curt Flood
64. Rod Carew (1972)
65. Gene Tenace (1972)
66. Dick Williams
67. Yankees
68. Howard Ehmke
69. Phillies (1930)
70. Allie Reynolds
71. Babe Ruth

72. Philadelphia (Jimmie Foxx, A's; Chuck Klein, Phillies)
73. Bill Terry
74. Jerome and Paul Dean
75. Joe Medwick
76. Bobby Brown (1947, 1949–51)
77. Lefty O'Doul (254, 1929) and Bill Terry (254, 1930)
78. Rickey Henderson (130 in 1982)
79. Spud Chandler (.717)
80. Whitey Ford (8)
81. Bobby Richardson (209, 1962)
82. Duke Snider (1956)
83. Reggie Jackson (1980 Yankees)
84. David Dale Alexander (1932, Tigers and Red Sox)
85. Harry Walker (1947, Cardinals and Phillies)
86. Johnny Burnett (1932 Indians)
87. Bump Hadley (1937)
88. Leo Durocher (1941)
89. Jeff Heath
90. Maury Wills
91. Sandy Koufax (1966)
92. Bill Eckert
93. Charlie Grimm
94. Yogi Berra
95. Johnny Edwards
96. Rogers Hornsby
97. Lou Gehrig (1931)
98. Eddie Stanky (1945) and Jimmy Wynn (1969)
99. Jack Coombs (13, 1910 Athletics)
100. Joe Morgan

35. Baseball's Who's Who

1. Walter Johnson
2. Rogers Hornsby (1921–25)
3. Bill McKechnie (Pirates, 1925; Cardinals, 1928; and Reds, 1939–40)
4. Al Kaline of the Tigers, who was 20 in 1955
5. Ted Williams of the Red Sox, who was 40 in 1958
6. Mike Higgins of the 1938 Red Sox
7. Walt Dropo of the 1952 Tigers
8. Joe Jackson (1920)
9. Ty Cobb, whose .401 for the Tigers in 1922 finished second to George Sisler's .420
10. Tom Zachary of the 1929 Yankees
11. "Iron Man" Joe McGinnity of the 1903 Giants
12. Casey Stengel
13. Jimmie Foxx (A's, 1932–33; and Red Sox, 1938)
14. George "Specs" Toporcer of the 1921 Cardinals
15. Clint Courtney of the 1951 Yankees
16. Dizzy Dean
17. Harry Brecheen (0.83) of the Cardinals
18. Harry Heilmann of the 1921, 1923, 1925, and 1927 Tigers
19. Ted Williams of the 1941–42, 1947–48, and 1957–58 Red Sox
20. Eddie Robinson (1948)
21. Ralph Houk
22. Joe McCarthy
23. Casey Stengel
24. Johnny Frederick of the 1932 Dodgers
25. Joe Cronin of the 1943 Red Sox
26. Ed Reulbach of the 1906–08 Cubs
27. Lefty Grove of the 1929–31 Athletics
28. Grover Alexander
29. Mel Ott of the 1932, 1934, and 1937 Giants
30. Ralph Kiner of the 1947–48, and 1952 Pirates
31. Wes Ferrell
32. Walter Johnson
33. Luke Appling (1936 and 1943)
34. Mark Littell
35. Hal Newhouser (1944–45)
36. Rube Bressler
37. Harmon Killebrew
38. Hank Aaron
39. Norm Cash
40. Ernie Banks
41. Red Ruffing
42. Red Lucas

43. Lefty Grove
44. Jimmie Foxx: batting, 1933 (Athletics) and 1938 (Red Sox); home runs, 1932–33, 1935 (Athletics) and 1939 (Red Sox).
45. Mickey Mantle (1956)
46. Roy Face
47. Ted Williams (1941–42 and 1947)
48. Cy Young
49. Jim Bottomley
50. Roger Cramer
51. Jim Palmer of the 1973, 1975–76 Orioles
52. Tom Seaver of the 1969, 1973, 1975 Mets
53. Mike Marshall of the 1974 Dodgers
54. Steve Carlton of the 1972, 1977, 1980, and 1982 Phillies
55. Gaylord Perry (Indians, 1972; Padres, 1978)
56. Mark Fidrych of the 1976 Tigers
57. Bob Horner of the 1978 Braves
58. Wade Boggs of the 1985–87 Red Sox
59. Fred Lynn of the 1975 Red Sox
60. Stan Musial of the 1950–52 Cardinals
61. Wade Boggs
62. Bruce Sutter (1979)
63. Mike Schmidt of the 1974–76 Phillies
64. Roger Maris of the 1960–61 Yankees
65. Dale Murphy of the 1982–83 Braves
66. Mike Schmidt
67. Tony Gwynn, who hit .370 for the Padres in 1987
68. Pete Rose
69. Ferguson Jenkins (1967–72)
70. Gaylord Perry of the Giants, Indians, and Padres
71. Jim Palmer of the Orioles
72. Steve Carlton (310) of the 1972 Phillies
73. Sparky Lyle
74. Phil Niekro (21–20) of the 1979 Braves
75. Rod Carew (.388 with the Twins and .339 with the Angels)
76. Tom Seaver of the 1968–76 Mets

36. Matching Names

1. Bobby Thomson
2. Allie Reynolds
3. Ted Williams
4. Johnny Mize
5. Dom DiMaggio
6. Casey Stengel
7. Tommy Henrich
8. Vernon Law
9. Joe DiMaggio
10. Ty Cobb
11. Honus Wagner
12. Tris Speaker
13. Babe Ruth
14. Walter Johnson
15. Lou Gehrig
16. Carl Hubbell
17. Mickey Mantle
18. Luke Appling
19. Paul Waner
20. Frankie Frisch

37. First Names

1. Bill
2. Paul
3. Jerome
4. Larry
5. Elwin
6. George
7. Joe
8. Johnny
9. Lynwood
10. Edwin
11. Charles Dillon
12. Fred
13. Harry
14. Leroy
15. Enos
16. Charles
17. Edward
18. Leon
19. Robert
20. James

38. Middle Names

1. "The Hat"
2. "The Man"
3. "The Cat"
4. "The Dutch Master"
5. "The Barber"
6. "Louisiana Lightning"
7. "The Lip"
8. "The Whip"
9. "King Kong"
10. "Puddin' Head"
11. "The Crow"
12. "Home Run"
13. "Poosh 'Em Up"
14. "The Kid"
15. "Pie"
16. "Bobo"
17. "Birdie"
18. "Twinkletoes"
19. "Three Finger"
20. "Pee Wee"

39. Last Names

1. Medwick
2. Crawford
3. Jackson
4. Wood
5. Dugan
6. Piniella
7. Greenberg
8. Cochrane
9. Feller
10. Grimm
11. Reiser
12. Bottomley
13. Doby
14. Newhouser
15. Houk
16. Keeler
17. Murphy
18. Turner
19. Jones
20. Hubbell

40. Multiple Names

1. Dick Stuart
2. Leon Wagner
3. Willie Mays
4. Pete Rose
5. Brooks Robinson

1. "No-Neck"
2. "Catfish"
3. "Boog"
4. "Blue Moon"
5. "Mudcat"

1. Frank
2. Willie
3. Frank
4. Harmon
5. Ken

1. McDowell
2. Plank
3. McBride
4. Jackson
5. Mizell

41. Did They or Didn't They?

1. False (Don Drysdale hit seven twice.)
2. False (Johnny Bench)
3. True (1955)
4. False (Don Newcombe, 1956)
5. True (Ferguson Jenkins, Cubs, and Vida Blue, A's, in 1971)
6. True
7. True (51 in 1955 and 52 in 1965)
8. True
9. False (Don Mattingly, 1985)
10. True
11. True (1951, 1953, and 1955)
12. False (Hank Aaron)
13. True
14. True (1966)
15. False (Dan Bankhead did, too.)
16. True (1969, 1973, 1977–78)
17. True (.300 for 1980 Yankees)
18. False (Joe Black, 1952)
19. False (Elston Howard, 1963)
20. True (1949)
21. False (Lou Brock did not.)
22. True (Burt Hooton, Elias Sosa, and Charlie Hough)
23. True
24. False (Frank Robinson, 1966)
25. True
26. False (Larry Doby, 1948)
27. False (Jim Gilliam, 1953)
28. True (1957)
29. False (Jimmie Foxx, 50 in 1938)
30. False (Marshall Bridges, 1962)
31. True
32. False (Vida Blue, 301 in 1971)
33. True (7)
34. False (Mudcat Grant, 1965)
35. True (Maury Wills, Jim Gilliam, John Roseboro, Tommy Davis, Willie Davis, and Lou Johnson)
36. False (Mickey Lolich, 1968)
37. False (Willie Wilson, 705 in 1980)
38. True (284)
39. True (the 1950s, 1960s, 1970s, and 1980s)
40. False (Rod Carew, .328)
41. True (1965–67)
42. False (Max Carey had 738; Wills, 586.)
43. True
44. True
45. True (.302–.298)
46. False (Roberto Clemente, 1964–65)
47. True (1955)
48. False (He won two AL titles, 1972 and 1974.)

42. The Trailblazers

1. Thompson–Brown
2. Roberts
3. Thomas
4. Howard
5. Trice
6. Doby
7. Banks–Baker
8. Black
9. Green
10. Paula
11. Robinson
12. Jethroe
13. Alston–Lawrence
14. Thompson–Irvin
15. Virgil
16. Hairston

43. Black Clouters

1–3. Willie Mays, Hank Aaron, or Reggie Jackson
4. Willie McCovey or Jim Rice
5. Jim Rice or Willie McCovey
6–10. Any combination of Larry Doby, Dick Allen, Willie Stargell, Ernie Banks, or George Foster
11–15. Any combination of Frank Robinson, George Scott, Ben Oglivie, Jesse Barfield, or Andre Dawson

44. Single-Season Sluggers

1. Willie Mays
2. George Foster
3. Willie Mays
4. Frank Robinson
5. Hank Aaron
6. George Bell
7. Reggie Jackson
8. Nate Colbert
9. Dick Allen
10. Jimmy Wynn
11. Andre Dawson

45. National League Batting Champs

1. Robinson
2. Mays
3. Aaron
4. Aaron
5. Clemente
6. Davis
7. Davis
8. Clemente
9. Clemente
10. Alou
11. Clemente
12. Carty
13. Williams
14. Garr
15. Madlock
16. Madlock

17. Parker
18. Parker
19. Madlock
20. Oliver

21. Madlock
22. Gwynn
23. McGee
24. Raines
25. Gwynn

46. American League Batting Champs

1. Avila
2. Oliva
3. Oliva
4. Robinson
5. Carew
6. Johnson
7. Oliva

8. Carew
9. Carew
10. Carew
11. Carew
12. Carew
13. Carew
14. Wilson

47. Rookies of the Year

1. Robinson
2. Newcombe
3. Jethroe

4. Mays
5. Black
6. Gilliam

48. The Hall of Fame

1–22. Any combination of
the following
players:
Jackie Robinson
Roy Campanella
Satchel Paige
Buck Leonard
Josh Gibson
Cool Papa Bell
Roberto Clemente
Monte Irvin
Judy Johnson
Ernie Banks

John "Pop" Lloyd
Martin Dihigo
Willie Mays
Oscar Charleston
Hank Aaron
Lou Brock
Bob Gibson
Juan Marichal
Frank Robinson
Willie McCovey
Ray Dandridge
Billy Williams

49. What's the Retirement Age?

1. 1950
2. 1971
3. 1957
4. 1956
5. 1965
6. 1956
7. 1961
8. 1955
9. 1963
10. 1947
11. 1958
12. 1955
13. 1960
14. 1960
15. 1962

50. One-Town Men

1. Luke Appling
2. Brooks Robinson
3. Bill Terry
4. Stan Hack
5. Walter Johnson
6. Mel Ott
7. Al Kaline
8. Ernie Banks
9. Cecil Travis
10. Pee Wee Reese

51. The First Inning

1. Charlie Grimm
2. Jimmy Dykes
3. Lou Boudreau
4. Bill Rigney
5. Walter Alston
6. Harry Lavagetto
7. Mickey Vernon
8. Bill Rigney
9. Harry Craft
10. Casey Stengel
11. Bobby Bragan
12. Bob Kennedy
13. Joe Gordon
14. Joe Schultz
15. Gene Mauch
16. Preston Gomez
17. Dave Bristol
18. Ted Williams
19. Darrell Johnson
20. Roy Hartsfield

52. The Last Inning

1. Charlie Grimm
2. Marty Marion
3. Eddie Joost
4. Bill Rigney
5. Walter Alston
6. Harry Lavagetto
7. Bobby Bragan
8. Luke Appling
9. Joe Schultz
10. Ted Williams

53. Secondary Pursuits

1. c
2. g
3. e
4. j
5. o
6. a
7. k
8. b
9. m
10. n
11. h
12. d
13. i
14. f
15. l

54. Major League Owners

1. e
2. h
3. j
4. c
5. p
6. o
7. t
8. k
9. n
10. b
11. f
12. s
13. m
14. a
15. q
16. g
17. l
18. i
19. d
20. r

55. The Missing Link

1. Yogi Berra
2. Charlie Keller
3. Terry Moore
4. Duffy Lewis
5. Earle Combs
6. Carl Furillo
7. Ted Williams
8. Lou Piniella
9. Don Mueller
10. Matty Alou
11. Dick Sisler
12. Roger Maris
13. Jackie Jensen
14. Vic Wertz
15. Sid Gordon
16. Pete Reiser

17. Al Simmons
18. Harry Heilmann
19. Casey Stengel
20. Frank Robinson
21. Reggie Smith

22. Al Kaline
23. Joe Rudi
24. Cesar Cedeno
25. Jimmy Wynn

56. Who Played Third?

1. Brooks Robinson
2. Sal Bando
3. Mike Schmidt
4. Ron Cey
5. Red Rolfe
6. Jim Tabor
7. Harry Lavagetto
8. Whitey Kurowski
9. Ken Keltner
10. Hank Majeski
11. Johnny Pesky
12. Billy Cox
13. Willie Jones

14. Hank Thompson
15. Gil McDougald
16. Al Rosen
17. Bobby Adams
18. Eddie Mathews
19. Don Hoak
20. Clete Boyer
21. Al Smith
22. Ken Boyer
23. Ron Santo
24. Billy Werber
25. Eddie Yost

57. Brother Combinations

1. Vince
2. Wes
3. Mort
4. Norm
5. Virgil
6. Paul
7. Jim
8. Joe
9. Harry
10. Christy
11. Jesus
12. Eddie
13. Frank

14. Billy
15. Ken
16. Emil
17. Bill
18. Tommie
19. Lloyd
20. Hector
21. Fred
22. Dave
23. Faye
24. Ed
25. Charlie

58. No Handicap

1. Red Ruffing
2. William "Dummy" Hoy
3. Mordecai "Three Finger" Brown
4. Pete Gray
5. John Hiller

59. Baseball Tragedies

1. Ed Delahanty
2. Ray Chapman
3. Lou Gehrig
4. Harry Agganis
5. Kenny Hubbs
6. Roberto Clemente
7. Thurman Munson

60. No Untouchables

1. Athletics
2. Giants
3. White Sox
4. Indians
5. Yankees
6. Senators
7. White Sox
8. Dodgers
9. White Sox
10. Red Sox
11. Dodgers
12. Cubs
13. Cardinals
14. Pirates
15. Giants
16. Tigers
17. Cubs
18. Red Sox
19. Pirates
20. Braves
21. Indians
22. Brewers
23. Mets
24. Red Sox
25. Yankees

61. When Did They Come Up?

1930s–1940s

1. Joe DiMaggio
2. Tommy Henrich
3. Joe Gordon
4. Ted Williams
5. Dom DiMaggio
6. Stan Musial
7. Warren Spahn
8. George Kell
9. Eddie Yost
10. Red Shoendienst

1940s–1950s

1. Yogi Berra
2. Jackie Robinson
3. Richie Ashburn
4. Jerry Coleman
5. Whitey Ford
6. Willie Mays
7. Eddie Mathews
8. Al Kaline
9. Hank Aaron
10. Rocky Colavito

1950s–1960s

1. Frank Robinson
2. Roger Maris
3. Ron Fairly
4. Maury Wills
5. Juan Marichal
6. Carl Yastrzemski
7. Ed Kranepool
8. Pete Rose
9. Mel Stottlemyre
10. Catfish Hunter

1960s–1970s

1. George Scott
2. Rod Carew
3. Bobby Bonds
4. Thurman Munson
5. Cesar Cedeno
6. Chris Speier
7. Mike Schmidt
8. Dave Parker
9. Jim Rice
10. Fred Lynn

Chapter Twelve Answers

62. Whom Did They Precede?

1. d	6. a
2. c	7. b
3. b	8. d
4. a	9. a
5. c	10. a

63. Whom Did They Succeed?

1. d	6. a
2. b	7. c
3. a	8. b
4. c	9. a
5. d	10. c

64. Chips off the Old Block

1. George Sisler	6. Max Lanier
2. Mike Tresh	7. Ray Boone
3. Jim Hegan	8. Maury Wills
4. Gus Bell	9. Roy Smalley
5. Dolph Camilli	10. Paul "Dizzy" Trout

65. The Gas House Gang

1. d	6. j
2. f	7. b
3. h	8. e
4. i	9. g
5. a	10. c

66. The Year of _____

1. The Hitless Wonders	3. Home Run Baker
2. Merkle's Boner	4. The Miracle Braves

5. The Black Sox
6. Alex's Biggest Strikeout
7. Murderers' Row
8. The Wild Hoss of the Osage
9. The Babe Calls His Shot
10. The Gas House Gang
11. Ernie's Snooze
12. Mickey's Passed Ball
13. Pesky's Pause
14. Gionfriddo's Gem
15. Feller's Pick-off (?)
16. The Whiz Kids
17. The Miracle of Coogan's Bluff
18. Billy the Kid
19. Mays' Miracle Catch
20. Sandy's Snatch
21. Larsen's Perfect Game
22. The Go-Go Sox
23. Maz's Sudden Shot
24. The M&M Boys
25. The Amazin' Ones

67. The Men at the Mike

1. g
2. i
3. f
4. n
5. j
6. o
7. a
8. m
9. e
10. l
11. b
12. c
13. h
14. k
15. d

68. Infield Inflation

1. Stuffy McInnis
2. Eddie Collins
3. Jack Barry
4. Frank Baker
5. Ira Thomas

1. Ferris Fain
2. Pete Suder
3. Eddie Joost
4. Hank Majeski
5. Buddy Rosar

69. Pen Names

1. Del Rice
2. Wes Parker
3. Fred Winchell
4. Woody Woodward
5. Frank Sullivan
6. Hal Schumacher
7. Dick Williams
8. Pat Meany
9. Art Fowler
10. Jack Graham
11. Carl Reynolds
12. Babe Adams
13. Bill Dailey
14. Don Gross
15. Babe Young
16. Hal Smith

17. Babe Twombly
18. Roxie Lawson
19. Ray Murray
20. Johnny Powers

70. Matching Moguls

1. l
2. s
3. y
4. i
5. e
6. m
7. u
8. o
9. b
10. z
11. p
12. v
13. n
14. t
15. c
16. w
17. h
18. d
19. r
20. t
21. j
22. a
23. k
24. x
25. g
26. q

71. A Star Is Born

1. d
2. f
3. i
4. j
5. g
6. e
7. h
8. a
9. c
10. b

72. The National Pastime

Alabama to Georgia

1. g
2. i
3. e
4. a
5. j
6. h
7. c
8. d
9. f
10. b

Hawaii to Maryland

1. c
2. g
3. a
4. f

5. j	8. i
6. d	9. e
7. b	10. h

Massachusetts to New Jersey

1. c	6. b
2. e	7. h
3. g	8. i
4. f	9. a
5. j	10. d

New Mexico to South Carolina

1. j	5. b
2. f	6. i
3. a	7. c
4. h	8. g
	9. e

South Dakota to Wyoming

1. g	6. h
2. a	7. b
3. j	8. d
4. e	9. f
5. i	10. c

73. The International Pastime

1. d	10. f
2. j	11. n
3. g	12. a
4. c	13. o
5. p	14. q
6. r	15. k
7. i	16. h
8. e	17. l
9. m	18. b

74. Quick Quizzing the Managers

I.

1. Lou Boudreau (24)
2. Roger Peckinpaugh (23)
3. Joe Cronin (26)
4. Tom Sheehan (66)
5. Burt Shotton (62)

III.

1. e
2. c
3. a
4. b
5. d

II.

1. Casey Stengel
2. Joe McCarthy
3. Connie Mack
4. John McGraw
5. Walter Alston

IV.

1. Joe McCarthy
2. Frank Chance or Billy Southworth
3. Frank Chance or Billy Southworth
4. John McGraw
5. Al Lopez

75. Did They or Didn't They . . . Manage?

1. Joe Adcock
2. Joe Gordon
3. Kerby Farrell
4. Bill Dickey
5. Bucky Walters
6. Phil Cavarretta
7. Christy Mathewson
8. Luke Appling
9. Eddie Joost
10. Mickey Vernon
11. Red Rolfe
12. Ben Chapman
13. Jim Lemon
14. Freddie Fitzsimmons
15. Bob Elliott
16. Eddie Lopat
17. Johnny Pesky
18. Dick Sisler
19. Mel McGaha
20. Eddie Stanky

76. Post-War World Series Winners

National League	*American League*
1. Eddie Dyer	1. Bucky Harris
2. Leo Durocher	2. Lou Boudreau
3. Walter Alston	3. Casey Stengel
4. Fred Haney	4. Ralph Houk
5. Danny Murtaugh	5. Hank Bauer
6. Johnny Keane	6. Mayo Smith
7. Red Schoendienst	7. Earl Weaver
8. Gil Hodges	8. Dick Williams
9. Sparky Anderson	9. Al Dark
10. Chuck Tanner	10. Billy Martin
11. Dallas Green	11. Bob Lemon
12. Tom Lasorda	12. Joe Altobelli
13. Whitey Herzog	13. Sparky Anderson
14. Davy Johnson	14. Dick Howser
	15. Tom Kelly

77. Back-to-Back Pennant Winners

1. Casey Stengel
2. Chuck Dressen
3. Walter Alston
4. Casey Stengel
5. Fred Haney
6. Ralph Houk
7. Walter Alston
8. Red Schoendienst
9. Earl Weaver
10. Dick Williams
11. Sparky Anderson
12. Billy Martin
13. Tom Lasorda

78. Managers in Search of a Pennant

1. Red Rolfe
2. Eddie Stanky
3. Bill Rigney
4. Birdie Tebbetts
5. Mike Higgins
6. Bobby Bragan
7. Harry Walker
8. Mel Ott
9. Gene Mauch
10. Paul Richards

79. You're Hired to Be Fired

1. e
2. g
3. b
4. c
5. a
6. i

7. h
8. m
9. j
10. l
11. d
12. k
13. f
14. q
15. t
16. p
17. s
18. o
19. r
20. n

80. Managerial Half Truths

1. F (Ed Barrow, 1918)
2. T (1933)
3. T (1948)
4. T
5. T
6. F (Hughie Jennings, 1907–09, too)
7. F (Al Dark, 1962)
8. F (1946, as an interim skipper)
9. F (Tom Lasorda, 1977–78)
10. F (Tommy Lasorda, 1981 also)
11. T (8½ years to 7½ years)
12. T
13. T (1907–08)
14. T
15. F (He was the playing manager.)
16. T (1954 Indians and 1959 White Sox)
17. F (George Stallings, 1914)
18. T (1924–25)
19. T (27)
20. T (660–754)
21. F (Browns, 1933–37 and 1952)
22. T (1961–63)
23. F (3–3)
24. F (1961 Reds)
25. F (John McGraw of the 1911–13 Giants also)
26. T (1906)
27. F (Whitey Herzog, 1982)
28. T
29. T (In 1902, when he won a pennant, the World Series had not yet been established.)
30. F (Paul Owens, 1983)
31. T (.875–.700)
32. T (6)
33. F (Sparky Anderson did it, too.)
34. F (Red Schoendienst, in 1967–68, did it also.)
35. T
36. F (Fred Clarke, 1909; Bill McKechnie, 1925; and Chuck Tanner, 1979)
37. F (Mayo Smith, 1968)
38. T (2–1)
39. F (1976–77 Yankees)
40. F (Billy Southworth, 1942–44)
41. T (1944)
42. T (1974–75)
43. T
44. T (Cardinals, 1942–44; Braves, 1948)
45. F (1920 Indians)
46. F (1–3)
47. F (Joe Cronin)
48. T (1966 Orioles)
49. T (He was 4–3 in 1926, his only series as a manager.)
50. F (Appling did not.)

81. All-Star Standouts

1. Hank Aaron
2. Brooks Robinson
3. Stan Musial
4. Dwight Gooden (19 years, seven months, 24 days)
5. Satchel Paige (47 years, seven days)
6. Pete Rose (first, second, third, left and right field)
7. Charlie Gehringer
8. Terry Moore
9. Willie Jones
10. Ted Williams
11. Mickey Mantle
12. Joe Morgan
13. Phil Cavarretta
14. Dave Winfield
15. Rod Carew
16. Roberto Clemente
17. George Brett
18. Joe DiMaggio
19. Pie Traynor
20. Tony Oliva
21. Goose Gossage
22. Don Drysdale
23. Lefty Gomez
24. Whitey Ford
25. Atlee Hammaker
26. Tommy Bridges
27. Jim Palmer
28. Steve Garvey
29. Nelson Fox
30. Luis Aparicio
31. Yogi Berra
32. Willie Mays

82. Who's Who

1. Babe Ruth
2. Carl Hubbell
3. Frankie Frisch
4. Lefty Gomez
5. Lefty Gomez
6. Joe Medwick
7. Dizzy Dean
8. Earl Averill
9. Ted Williams
10. Arky Vaughan
11. Mickey Owen
12. Johnny Vander Meer
13. Vince DiMaggio
14. Phil Cavarretta
15. Ted Williams
16. Rip Sewell
17. Vic Raschi
18. Jackie Robinson
19. Roy Campanella
20. Don Newcombe
21. Larry Doby
22. Red Schoendienst
23. Ted Williams
24. Hank Sauer
25. Satchel Paige
26. Al Rosen
27. Stan Musial
28. Ken Boyer
29. Hank Aaron
30. Willie Mays

31. Willie Mays
32. Stan Musial
33. Johnny Callison
34. Maury Wills
35. Tony Perez
36. Ferguson Jenkins
37. Willie McCovey
38. Reggie Jackson
39. Frank Robinson
40. Steve Garvey
41. Carl Yastrzemski
42. Steve Garvey
43. Lee Mazzilli
44. Mike Schmidt
45. Ewell Blackwell
46. Early Wynn

83. From Bando to Washington

1. Claudell Washington (20 years, one month, and five days)
2. Chris Chambliss (1976 Yankees)
3. Bill North (1974–75 A's, 1978 Dodgers)
4. Reggie Jackson
5. Jerry Martin (1978 Phillies)
6. Richie Hebner
7. Jim Palmer (Orioles)
8. Pete Rose (42 years, five months, 24 days)
9. Mickey Rivers (1976–78 Yankees)
10. Jay Johnstone (1976 Phillies)
11. Fred Lynn (1982 Angels)
12. Chet Lemon
13. George Brett
14. Bob Robertson (1971 Pirates)
15. Paul Blair (1969 Orioles)
16. Paul Popovich (1974 Pirates)
17. Steve Garvey (1977 Dodgers)
18. Mike Cuellar (1970 Orioles)
19. Phil Niekro
20. Sal Bando (1974 A's)

84. From Baylor to Wynn

1. Bruce Kison
2. Jim Hunter
3. Dave Giusti
4. Jim Palmer
5. Bert Blyleven (19 years, five months, 29 days)
6. Phil Niekro (43 years, six months, eight days)
7. Cesar Geronimo (1975 Reds)
8. Rusty Staub (1973 Mets)
9. George Brett
10. Don Baylor (1982 Angels)
11. Pedro Guerrero
12. Tony Taylor (1972 Tigers)
13. Davey Lopes
14. Steve Balboni (1985 Royals)
15. Jimmy Wynn (1974 Dodgers)
16. Joe Morgan
17. Hal McRae
18. Reggie Jackson (1972 A's)
19. Pete Rose (right field, left field, third base, first base)
20. Bob Robertson (1971 Pirates)

85. From Anderson to Wynn

1. Billy Martin (1970 Twins, 1972 Tigers, 1976–77 Yankees, 1981 A's)
2. Earl Weaver
3. Sparky Anderson (1970, 1972, 1975–76 Reds; 1984 Tigers)
4. Mike Cuellar (1974 Orioles)
5. Nolan Ryan (1969 Mets)
6. Jim Palmer
7. Dave Stieb (1985 Blue Jays)
8. Tommy John
9. Tug McGraw
10. Steve Carlton
11. Dave Giusti (1971 Pirates)
12. Eric Show (1984 Padres)
13. Jerry Reuss
14. Gaylord Perry (1971 Giants)
15. Jim Hunter
16. Dave McNally (1969 Orioles)
17. Ken Holtzman (1973–75 A's)
18. George Brett
19. Pete Rose
20. Steve Garvey (1978 Dodgers)

86. From Bando to Yastrzemski

1. Fred Lynn (.611 for the 1982 Angels)
2. Brooks Robinson (.583 for the 1970 Orioles)
3. Frank White (.545 for the 1980 Royals)
4. Chris Chambliss (.524 for the 1976 Yankees)
5. Brooks Robinson (.500 for the 1969 Orioles)
6. Tony Oliva (.500 for the 1970 Twins)
7. Sal Bando (.500 for the 1975 A's)
8. Bob Watson (.500 for the 1980 Yankees)
9. Graig Nettles (.500 for the 1981 Yankees)
10. Jerry Mumphrey (.500 for the 1981 Yankees)

87. From Baker to Zisk

1. Jay Johnstone (.778 for the 1976 Phillies)
2. Darrell Porter (.556 for the 1982 Cardinals)
3. Ozzie Smith (.556 for the 1982 Cardinals)
4. Art Shamsky (.538 for the 1969 Mets)
5. Terry Puhl (.526 for the 1980 Astros)
6. Willie Stargell (.500 for the 1970 Pirates)
7. Richie Zisk (.500 for the 1975 Pirates)

88. From Aaron to Staub

1. George Brett
2. Steve Garvey
3. Reggie Jackson
4–8. Any combination of the following: Sal Bando, Graig Nettles, Gary Matthews, Greg Luzinski, and Johnny Bench
9–13. Any combination of the following: Boog Powell, Bill Madlock, Bob Robertson, Ron Cey, and Willie Stargell
14–20. Any combination of the following: Hank Aaron, Rusty Staub, George Foster, Al Oliver, Tony Perez, Pete Rose, and Richie Hebner
21. Jim Rice

89. Championship Series Game Winners

National League

1. Pete Rose
2. Bob Tolan
3. Richie Hebner
4. Manny Sanguillen
5. Johnny Bench
6. Pete Rose
7. Bill Russell
8. Bill Russell
9. Willie Stargell
10. Dave Parker
11. Garry Maddox
12. Jerry White
13. Rick Monday
14. Ken Oberkfell
15. Mike Schmidt
16. Steve Garvey
17. Glenn Davis
18. Lenny Dykstra
19. Alan Ashby
20. Gary Carter

American League

1. Paul Blair
2. Curt Motton
3. Paul Blair
4. Gene Tenace
5. Bert Campaneris
6. Bobby Grich
7. Sal Bando
8. Reggie Jackson
9. Chris Chambliss
10. Thurman Munson
11. Roy White
12. John Lowenstein
13. Larry Harlow
14. George Brett
15. Paul Molitor
16. Cecil Cooper
17. Tito Landrum
18. Johnny Grubb
19. Bobby Grich
20. Dave Henderson

Chapter Sixteen Answers

90. World Series Standouts

I.

1. Yogi Berra
2. Pee Wee Reese, Elston Howard
3. Casey Stengel
4. Babe Ruth (1928)
5. Pepper Martin
6. Bobby Richardson
7. Hank Bauer
8. Lou Gehrig (1928)
9. Willie Wilson
10. Mickey Mantle

6. Athletics
7. Yankees
8. Yankees
9. Yankees
10. A's
11. Reds
12. Yankees

II.

1. Whitey Ford
2. Darold Knowles
3. Christy Mathewson
4. Bob Gibson
5. Bill Bevens
6. Carl Mays
7. Jim Lonborg (1967)
8. Jim Palmer (20)
9. Harry Brecheen
10. Babe Ruth

IV.

1. Al Gionfriddo
2. Billy Cox
3. Willie Mays
4. Sandy Amoros
5. Mickey Mantle
6. Eddie Mathews
7. Bill Virdon
8. Tommie Agee
9. Brooks Robinson
10. Dick Green

III.

1. Cubs
2. Athletics
3. Red Sox
4. Giants
5. Yankees

V.

1. Harry Brecheen
2. Johnny Podres
3. Don Larsen
4. Lew Burdette
5. Bob Turley
6. Whitey Ford
7. Sandy Koufax
8. Bob Gibson
9. Mickey Lolich
10. Jim Hunter

91. World Series Players

1. Richie Ashburn
2. Ted Williams
3. Al Kaline
4. Nelson Fox
5. Harvey Kuenn
6. Johnny Logan
7. Ted Kluszewski
8. Gordy Coleman
9. Vada Pinson
10. Felipe Alou
11. Matty Alou
12. Gus Bell
13. Walker Cooper
14. Ray Sadecki
15. Bob Allison
16. Vern Stephens
17. Satchel Paige
18. Bill White
19. Frank Torre
20. Hank Majeski

92. Two-Team World Series Players

1. Rocky Nelson (Dodgers, 1952; Pirates, 1960)
2. Gino Cimoli (Dodgers, 1956; Pirates, 1960)
3. Rudy York (Tigers, 1940, 1945; Red Sox, 1946)
4. Tommy Holmes (Braves, 1948; Dodgers, 1952)
5. Bill Skowron (Yankees, 1955–58, 1961–62; Dodgers, 1963)
6. Roger Maris (Yankees, 1960–64; Cardinals, 1967–68)
7. Al Dark (Braves, 1948; Giants, 1951 and 1954)
8. George McQuinn (Browns, 1944; Yankees, 1947)
9. Mickey Cochrane (Athletics, 1929–31; Tigers, 1934–35)
10. Reggie Smith (Red Sox, 1967; Dodgers, 1977–78)
11. Joe Gordon (Yankees, 1938–39, 1941–43; Indians, 1948)
12. Johnny Sain (Braves, 1948; Yankees, 1951–53)
13. Enos Slaughter (Cardinals, 1942, 1946; Yankees, 1956–58)
14. Don Hoak (Dodgers, 1955; Pirates, 1960)
15. Orlando Cepeda (Giants, 1962; Cardinals, 1967–68)
16. Bob Tolan (Cardinals, 1967–68; Reds, 1970, 1972)
17. Luis Aparicio (White Sox, 1959; Orioles, 1966)
18. Don Gullett (Reds, 1970, 1972, 1975–76; Yankees, 1977)
19. Dick Groat (Pirates, 1960; Cardinals, 1964)
20. Frank Robinson (Reds, 1961; Orioles, 1966, 1969–71)

93. Mound Classics

1. Johnny Sain
2. Allie Reynolds
3. Preacher Roe
4. Vic Raschi
5. Clem Labine
6. Lew Burdette
7. Bob Shaw, Billy Pierce, and Dick Donovan
8. Ralph Terry
9. Don Drysdale
10. Wally Bunker
11. Dave McNally
12. Jack Billingham and Clay Carroll
13. Bruce Hurst

94. Seventh-Game Winners

1. Johnny Podres
2. Johnny Kucks
3. Lew Burdette
4. Ralph Terry
5. Bob Gibson
6. Bob Gibson
7. Mickey Lolich
8. Steve Blass
9. Ken Holtzman
10. Joaquin Adujar
11. Bret Saberhagen
12. Frank Viola

95. World Series Shorts

Three-Game Winners

1. Stan Coveleski
2. Harry Brecheen
3. Lew Burdette
4. Bob Gibson
5. Mickey Lolich

Individual Records

1. Lefty Grove
2. Whitey Ford
3. Bob Gibson
4. Christy Mathewson
5. Lefty Gomez

Home Run Hitters

1. Mickey Mantle
2. Babe Ruth
3. Yogi Berra
4. Duke Snider
5. Lou Gehrig

Career Records

1. Eddie Collins, Lou Brock
2. Yogi Berra
3. Dusty Rhodes
4. Frank Isbell
5. Bobby Richardson

96. Four Homers in One Series

1. Babe Ruth
2. Lou Gehrig
3. Duke Snider
4. Duke Snider
5. Hank Bauer
6. Gene Tenace
7. Willie Aikens

97. World Series Chronology

1. Jimmy Sebring (Pirates)
2. Christy Mathewson
3. Ed Walsh (White Sox)
4. Harry Steinfeldt
5. Orval Overall
6. Babe Adams
7. Jack Coombs (Athletics)
8. Frank Baker
9. Joe Wood
10. Jack Lapp
11. Johnny Evers
12. George "Rube" Foster
13. Babe Ruth (13⅓)
14. Red Faber
15. Charlie Pick
16. Dickie Kerr
17. Elmer Smith (Indians)
18. Waite Hoyt (Yankees)
19. Art Nehf
20. Babe Ruth (1923 Yankees)
21. Earl McNeely
22. Walter Johnson
23. Jesse Haines
24. Babe Ruth
25. Bill Sherdel
26. Al Simmons
27. Jack Quinn
28. Pepper Martin
29. Tony Lazzeri
30. Mel Ott
31. Frankie Frisch
32. Goose Goslin
33. Carl Hubbell
34. Cliff Melton
35. Red Ruffing
36. Monte Pearson
37. Bucky Walters
38. Whit Wyatt
39. Whitey Kurowski
40. Spud Chandler
41. Mort Cooper
42. Hank Borowy
43. Enos Slaughter
44. Hugh Casey
45. Bob Feller
46. Tommy Henrich
47. Whitey Ford
48. Hank Bauer
49. Johnny Mize
50. Carl Erskine
51. Vic Wertz
52. Gil Hodges
53. Enos Slaughter
54. Lew Burdette
55. Bob Turley
56. Chuck Essegian
57. Roy Face
58. Whitey Ford
59. Don Larsen
60. Harry Bright
61. Tim McCarver (1964 Cardinals)
62. Claude Osteen
63. Dave McNally (Game One)
64. Bob Gibson
65. Mickey Lolich
66. Al Weis
67. Brooks Robinson

68. Roberto Clemente	76. Phil Garner
69. Jim Hunter	77. Tug McGraw
70. Ken Holtzman	78. Steve Yeager
71. Ken Holtzman	79. Robin Yount
72. Tony Perez	80. Eddie Murray
73. Johnny Bench	81. Kirk Gibson
74. Thurman Munson	82. Bret Saberhagen
75. Brian Doyle	83. Ray Knight
	84. Frank Viola

98. World Series Multiple Choice

1. c (Yankees)
2. b (Yankees)
3. d (1936–39 Yankees)
4. c (1914 Braves–1928 Cards)
5. b (1965 Twins–1982 Cards)
6. c (1951 Giants–1973 Mets)
7. d (1914 Athletics–1932 Yankees)
8. a (19 years before the 1987 series)
9. d (44 with 1983 Phillies)
10. b (1960–62, 1964 Yankees)
11. b (1972–73 A's)
12. c (1982 Brewers)
13. b (1934–35 Tigers)
14. c (Giants and Cards)
15. a (1934 Tigers)
16. d (1939 Yankees)
17. b (1952, 1955 Dodgers)
18. b (1977–78 Yankees)
19. d (1926–28 Yankees)
20. b (1906 Tigers: four doubles)
21. a (1960 Yankees)
22. d (1925 Pirates)
23. b (1955 Yankees)

24. c (1906–08, 1910 Cubs)
25. b (1929–30 Athletics)
26. c (1972–74 A's)
27. d (1936–39, 1941, 1943 Yankees)
28. a (1964, 1967–68 Cards)
29. b (1955–58 Yankees)
30. d (1905, 1914 Athletics)
31. b (1934 Tigers)
32. a (1949 Dodgers)
33. b (1956 Yankees)
34. d (1924 Senators)
35. b (Yankees)
36. a (Giants and Cards)
37. d (Yankees)
38. b (Yankees)
39. b (Dodgers)
40. d (Yankees)
41. d (Yankees)
42. b (Yankees)
43. d (Yankees)
44. b (27 for the 1924 Senators)
45. a (26 for the 1933 Senators)
46. c (Giants)
47. a (Yankees)
48. c (1925 Pirates, 1928 Cards, 1939–40 Reds)
49. c (Yankees)
50. b

99. World Series Clues Who's Who

1. Christy Mathewson
2. Red Ruffing
3. Herb Pennock
4. Allie Reynolds
5. Rollie Fingers (1972–74 A's)
6. Moe Drabowski (1966)
7. Max Flack
8. Jim Palmer (1971 Orioles)
9. Ross Youngs
10. Lou Brock (1968 Cards)
11. Emil "Irish" Meusel
12. Burleigh Grimes
13. Paul Molitor
14. Dick Hughes
15. Edd Roush
16. Fred Lindstrom (1924 Giants)
17. Frankie Frisch
18. Dave McNally
19. Goose Goslin
20. Ray Schalk
21. Sherry Smith (Dodgers)
22. Patsy Dougherty (1903)
23. Bill Abstein
24. Red Faber
25. Grove Alexander (Cards)
26. Jesse Barnes
27. Ted Lyons (White Sox)
28. Rogers Hornsby (1926 Cards)
29. Fred Snodgrass
30. Mickey Cochrane (1934–35 Tigers)
31. Mort Cooper (1944)
32. Sparky Anderson (1975–76 Reds)
33. Ken Brett (1967 Red Sox)
34. Sandy Koufax (1965 Dodgers)
35. Lou Brock (Cards)
36. Ken Holtzman
37. Goose Goslin (Senators)
38. Thurman Munson (Yankees)
39. Dusty Rhodes (1954 Giants)
40. Duke Snider (Dodgers)
41. Ed Reulbach
42. Thurman Munson
43. Roger Peckinpaugh
44. Ralph Houk (1961–63 Yankees)
45. Vic Raschi (1949–50 Yankees)
46. Allie Reynolds (Yankees)
47. Bob Kuzava
48. Eddie Plank (Athletics)
49. Mickey Lolich (Tigers)
50. Walter Johnson (Senators)
51. Art Nehf
52. Claude Passeau
53. Bob Nieman
54. Monte Irvin (Giants)
55. Mickey Owen (Dodgers)
56. Yogi Berra (Yankees)
57. Wilcy Moore (Yankees)
58. Bill Bevens
59. Hal Schumacher
60. George Pipgras
61. Clarence Mitchell (1920 Dodgers)
62. Jim Lonborg
63. Mickey Cochrane
64. Ray Kremer

65. Billy Martin (Yankees)
66. Joe Gordon (Yankees)
67. Mort Cooper (Cards)
68. Dick Hall
69. Jim Bagby
70. Jack Billingham
71. Kiki Cuyler
72. Enos Slaughter
73. Harry Walker (Cards)
74. Willie Aikens (Royals)
75. Steve Blass
76. Don Gullett
77. Rusty Staub (Mets)
78. Dave McNally (Orioles)
79. Graig Nettles
80. Dwight Evans
81. Tommie Agee
82. Willie Horton
83. Jim Gilliam
84. Roger Maris (1962 Yankees)
85. Doug DeCinces (Orioles)
86. Joe Pepitone (1963 Yankees)
87. Curt Flood
88. Jimmy Slagle
89. Del Gainor (1916)
90. Joe Bush (1913)
91. Deacon Phillippe (1903 Pirates)
92. Joe Wood (1912 Red Sox)
93. Jack Coombs (Athletics)
94. Claude "Lefty" Williams
95. Benny Tate
96. Fred Merkle (Giants, Dodgers, Cubs)
97. Bucky Harris (Senators)
98. Herb Pennock (1927 Yankees)
99. Yogi Berra
100. Joe Garagiola (Cards)

Chapter Seventeen Answers

Chicago Cubs Infielders

1. True (Chance, .296; Cavarretta, .293; and Grimm, .290)
2. True
3. False (1,125–1,259)
4. False (Harry Steinfeldt)
5. True (.304)
6. True (1975–76)
7. Hack Wilson
8. Gary Matthews
9. Bill "Swish" Nicholson
10. Chuck Klein
11. Billy Williams
12. Andy Pafko
13. b
14. c
15. a
16. a
17. b
18. d (1917)
19. c
20. c
21. a (1967–72)
22. d (1906)
23. c
24. b
25. b (1906–08)

Montreal Expos

1. f (1970–74)
2. d (1974–76)
3. a
4. e (1969)
5. c (1970–74)
6. b
7. b (1986)
8. b (1987)
9. a
10. a
11. d
12. c
13. True
14. False (less than one season)
15. True (1985)
16. Ross Grimsley (20 in 1978)
17. Bill Stoneman (1971)
18. Woodie Fryman
19. Jeff Reardon
20. Mike Marshall (1972–73)
21. Carl Morton
22. Bill Stoneman (1969 and 1972)
23. Charlie Lea
24. Steve Rogers
25. Mike Torrez (1974)

New York Mets

1. True (1963)
2. False (Al Weis)
3. False (.238)
4. False (Jim Fregosi did.)
5. True (1962–79)
6. True
7. Rusty Staub (1975)
8. Darryl Strawberry (1987)
9. Cleon Jones (1969)
10. Richie Ashburn
11. Darryl Strawberry (1983–86)
12. Ron Swoboda
13. a
14. b
15. c
16. c (1969 and 1971)
17. a (1972)
18. c
19. b (1965)
20. a
21. b (1986)
22. c (1986)
23. b
24. d
25. a (1984–86)

Philadelphia Phillies

1. False (He did it with the 1941 Dodgers.)
2. False (Juan Samuel had 701 official at-bats in his rookie 1984 season.)
3. True (.305 in 1975)
4. True
5. False (Mike Goliat)
6. False (25–37)
7. Ed Delahanty (all in the 1890s)
8. Gavvy Cravath (1913–15, 1917–19)
9. Chuck Klein (Hack Wilson had a record 190 RBIs that year.)
10. Lefty O'Doul (1929)
11. Dick Sisler
12. Richie Ashburn (1955 and 1958)
13. c
14. b
15. a
16. a (1911)
17. d (1945)
18. c (1909)
19. b (1950)
20. a (266)
21. d
22. c
23. a (1964)
24. b (1972–73)
25. a (1967)

Pittsburgh Pirates

1. Dale Long (1956)
2. Bill Mazeroski
3. Arky Vaughan
4. Pie Traynor
5. Hank Greenberg
6. Honus Wagner
7. f
8. a
9. d
10. c
11. b
12. e
13. a
14. c
15. d
16. False (eephus pitch)
17. False (197–230)
18. True (1960)
19. False (Harvey Haddix)
20. False (Phil Niekro, 1977–80 Braves)
21. True (.750 in 1968)
22. True (3–2 in 1903)
23. False (132–195)
24. True (216–194)
25. True

St. Louis Cardinals

1. a
2. d
3. b
4. c (1964)
5. a
6. b (1950)
7. True (1950–52)
8. True (1937)
9. False (.300)
10. False (Maury Wills stole 104 bases in 1962.)
11. True
12. False (Flood didn't.)
13. Bob O'Farrell
14. Walker Cooper (1942–44)
15. Joe Garagiola (1946)
16. e
17. d
18. i (1931)
19. b (1933–36)
20. h
21. f
22. c (1946)
23. a (The shutouts came in 1968.)
24. j
25. g

Atlanta Braves

1. d
2. d (1973)
3. b (Cardinals)
4. a (1960–64 Yankees)
5. b (1953; Hank Aaron also hit 47 homers in 1971.)
6. c
7. True
8. False (335–398)
9. False (Ralph Garr)
10. True (26–27 in 1982–83)
11. True (1964)
12. True (1975–76 Reds)
13. Joe Torre
14. Earl Williams
15. Ozzie Virgil (1987)
16. b
17. d (1979)
18. e
19. c (209)
20. j
21. h
22. g
23. f
24. a
25. i (Houston, 1979–80)

Cincinnati Reds

1. f (1953–56)
2. c (1975–76)
3. e
4. d
5. b
6. a
7. c
8. b (1976–77)
9. a (1905)
10. a
11. c (1917 and 1919)
12. d
13. True (1970 and 1972)
14. True (1926)
15. True (.306)
16. Johnny Vander Meer
17. Joe Nuxhall
18. Jim Maloney
19. Bucky Walters
20. Paul Derringer
21. Ewell Blackwell
22. Tom Browning
23. Jack Billingham
24. Joey Jay
25. John Franco

Houston Astros

1. Lee May (1972–74)
2. Nellie Fox
3. Denny Walling
4. Doug Rader
5. Joe Pepitone
6. Joe Morgan
7. d (1977)
8. e (1967)
9. f (1967)
10. c
11. b (1979)
12. a
13. a (1963–64)
14. b
15. d (1976)
16. True (21 in 1979)
17. True (1967 and 1969)
18. False (Reds)
19. True (1969)
20. True
21. False (1978 Braves)
22. False (Jim Deshaies did it.)
23. True
24. False (He pitched one for the Angels.)
25. False (J. R. Richard struck out 313 in 1979.)

Los Angeles Dodgers

1. c (1978)
2. d
3. f (1960–65)
4. e
5. a (1949–55)
6. b
7. b
8. a
9. a
10. c (1982–83, 1985)
11. a (1968–70 Senators)
12. a (1962)
13. False (He ended his career with the Twins.)
14. False (Ferguson, .240; Yeager, .229)
15. False (His highest season average was 240; his career mark was .214.)
16. Don Drysdale
17. Fernando Valenzuela
18. Al Downing
19. Orel Hershiser (1985)
20. Don Sutton
21. Tommy John
22. Johnny Podres
23. Ron Perranoski
24. Phil Regan
25. Claude Osteen

San Diego Padres

1. True (38 in 1970)
2. True (1984)
3. False (He led league in intentional passes in 1984 and tied for league lead in 1985.)
4. True (1972 and 1973)
5. False
6. True
7. Tony Gwynn
8. Dave Winfield
9. Ollie Brown
10. Dave Kingman (1977)
11. Kevin McReynolds (1984–86)
12. Bob Tolan
13. c
14. a
15. b
16. a (1976)
17. d (1972 Indians, 1978 Padres)
18. c (1971)
19. c
20. a (1974–76)
21. c
22. c
23. c
24. c (1977–78)
25. c

San Francisco Giants

1. b
2. a (1962)
3. d
4. c
5. b (Giants, Cardinals, and Braves)
6. a (1974–76 in Philadelphia, San Francisco, and Atlanta)
7. True
8. False (Bobby Bonds did it in 1970.)
9. False (51–52)
10. True (before the 1975 season)
11. False (He won one with the Tigers.)
12. True (1963)
13. Tom Haller (1966)
14. Ed Bailey (1962–63)
15. Bob Brenly
16. c (1976)
17. e
18. g (1963–69)
19. h
20. b
21. f
22. a
23. d
24. i
25. j

Baltimore Orioles

1. Jim Gentile
2. Davy Johnson
3. Luis Aparicio
4. Brooks Robinson
5. Mark Belanger
6. Vern Stephens
7. b
8. d (Red Sox, A's, and Padres)
9. f
10. c
11. a
12. e (1977)
13. b
14. a
15. c
16. False (Steve Stone, 25 in 1980)
17. False (Dave McNally)
18. False (Jim Palmer, 20)
19. False (Milt Pappas)
20. True
21. False (He lost 21.)
22. True (1979)
23. True
24. True
25. False (42–36)

Boston Red Sox

1. c
2. e (1960 and 1962)
3. f (the 1944 Browns)
4. d
5. b (1903)
6. a (1955–62)
7. d
8. b
9. c (54)
10. a
11. d
12. b
13. True (1915–16)
14. True
15. True
16. Cy Young (1904)
17. Jim Lonborg
18. Dave Sisler
19. Dick Radatz
20. Denny Galehouse
21. Babe Ruth (1916)
22. Lefty Grove (1941)
23. Red Ruffing
24. Joe Wood
25. Ernie Shore

Cleveland Indians

1. Hal Trosky (1936)
2. Bill Wambsganss
3. Ray Boone
4. Kenny Keltner
5. Bobby Avila (.341 in 1954)
6. Vic Wertz
7. b (in 1905)
8. c
9. e
10. f (Earl Averill, Jr.)
11. d
12. a (1948)
13. b
14. c (Bob Feller, Bob Lemon, Gene Bearden, Mike Garcia, Early Wynn, and Herb Score)
15. d (Russ Nixon, .268; Buddy Rosar, .261; Luke Sewell, .259; and Jim Hegan, .228)
16. True (31 in 1920)
17. False (20–9 in 1956)
18. True
19. True
20. False
21. True
22. False (Nolan Ryan, 5; Feller and Jim Maloney, 3)
23. False (Jim didn't.)
24. True (from 1929–32)
25. True

Detroit Tigers

1. b (1937–38)
2. d (.361 in 1961)
3. a
4. d (.343 in 1949)
5. b (for Cleveland's Rocky Colavito)
6. c
7. True
8. True
9. False (.297)
10. False (Jim Northrup hit the ball.)
11. True (1950)
12. False (Al Kaline, 20)
13. Rudy York (1937)
14. Mickey Cochrane
15. Bill Freehan
16. d (1976)
17. f (1968–69)
18. g (308 in 1971)
19. i
20. e
21. a
22. h (1952)
23. j (1944–46)
24. b (1934)
25. c (He was 21–20 in 1907.)

Milwaukee Brewers

1. True (1975)
2. True
3. True
4. True (1987)
5. False (Paul Molitor hit .353 in 1987.)
6. False (25 in 1977)
7. Hank Aaron (1975–76)
8. Rob Deer (1986)
9. Gorman Thomas
10. Tommy Harper
11. Ben Oglivie
12. Gorman Thomas
13. b
14. a
15. c
16. c
17. d (1986)
18. a
19. a
20. b
21. a
22. b (1981)
23. c (1982)
24. d (1982–84)
25. a

New York Yankees

1. Babe Dahlgren (1939)
2. Billy Martin
3. Phil Rizzuto
4. Frank Baker (1911–14)
5. Aaron Ward (1922)
6. Bill Skowron
7. c (1937 and 1948)
8. f (1958)
9. a
10. b
11. d
12. e
13. a (1936)
14. c (1956)
15. d
16. True
17. False (Dale Mitchell)
18. False (Bob Kuzava)
19. True (10 and 8)
20. False (Wes Ferrell)
21. True
22. True (2)
23. True (1964)
24. False (Reverse Page and Murphy.)
25. False (Lyle didn't.)

Toronto Blue Jays

1. c (1986)
2. d
3. f
4. e
5. b (1978–81)
6. a (Blue Jays and Celtics)
7. c
8. d (1987)
9. b (1987)
10. b (1976)
11. a (1984)
12. c (1977)
13. True (1977)
14. True (1979)
15. False (19 was his high.)
16. Doyle Alexander (1984–85)
17. Dave Stieb (1984)
18. Jimmy Key (1985)
19. Mark Eichhorn (1986)
20. Tom Henke (1985–87)
21. Jim Clancy (1986)
22. Pete Vuckovich (1977)
23. Dale Murray (1975–76 Expos)
24. Bill Singer (1970)
25. Dave Lemanczyk (13–16)

California Angels

1. d
2. b
3. a
4. a
5. d
6. c
7. False (Reggie Jackson, 39 in 1982)
8. False (Mickey Rivers, 70 in 1975)
9. False (Rod Carew, .339 in 1983)
10. False (Bonds was traded to the Angels by the Yankees.)
11. True (1973)
12. True
13. Bob Boone
14. Bob Rodgers (8 years)
15. Jeff Torborg
16. c (1964)
17. d (1962)
18. h (1963)
19. f
20. a
21. b
22. i
23. g
24. e
25. j (1967–68)

Chicago White Sox

1. d
2. b
3. f (1936)
4. e (with 33 homers in 1971)
5. a
6. c (After the 1920 season he was barred from baseball along with the other "Black Sox" players.)
7. d
8. c (1963)
9. b (1921–25)
10. a (1937)
11. d (.353 in 1974 with the Braves)
12. b (188)
13. b (In 1920 Red Faber won 23 games; Claude Williams, 22; Ed Cicotte and Dickie Kerr, 21.)
14. a
15. c (Tom)
16. Charlie Robertson (1922)
17. Ed Walsh (1908)
18. Ted Lyons
19. Monty Stratton
20. Dickie Kerr
21. Claude Williams
22. Wilbur Wood (He was 24–20 in 1973.)
23. Billy Pierce
24. Red Faber (1917)
25. Ed Lopat (1949–53)

Kansas City Royals

1. c (36 in 1985)
2. a
3. b (1971–79)
4. d (1979)
5. d (1986)
6. a
7. True (1969)
8. False (Hal McRae, 1982)
9. True (Thirteen of his first 21 were within the playing confines.)
10. False
11. True (1980)
12. False (Danny Tartabull's father, Jose, did.)
13. Jim Sundberg (1986)
14. Darrell Porter
15. John Wathan
16. b
17. f
18. e
19. c (1977)
20. g
21. d (21 in 1985)
22. j
23. h
24. i (1977)
25. a (1969–74)

Minnesota Twins

1. c
2. b (1982)
3. d
4. a
5. f
6. e
7. d
8. a (1986)
9. d
10. c
11. a
12. b
13. True
14. False (Roseboro, .249; Battey, .270)
15. True (33–26)
16. Jim Kaat (25 in 1966)
17. Bert Blyleven (258 in 1973)
18. Dave Boswell
19. Jim Perry
20. Camilo Pascual (1962–63)
21. Mudcat Grant
22. Dean Chance
23. Ron Perranosky
24. Alan Worthington
25. Pedro Ramos (1961)

Oakland A's

1. Gene Tenace (1972–74 A's, 1982 Cards)
2. Bert Campaneris (1964 Kansas City Athletics)
3. Alfredo Griffin
4. Sal Bando
5. Carney Lansford
6. Bert Campaneris (1965)
7. b (1981)
8. f (1965)
9. e
10. d
11. c
12. a
13. d
14. b (.256)
15. a (19)
16. False
17. True (22)
18. True
19. True (1985)
20. False (He won 21 in 1973.)
21. True (4–1)
22. False (Hunter, 25; Blue, 24)
23. True (0–3)
24. False (Darold Knowles)
25. True (6)

Seattle Mariners

1. True
2. True
3. False (Spike Owen)
4. True (1984)
5. False (Ted Williams, 145 in 1939)
6. False (He struck out a club-record 172 times in 1986.)
7. Phil Bradley
8. Gorman Thomas
9. Tom Paciorek
10. Danny Tartabull
11. Willie Horton
12. Dave Henderson
13. b
14. c
15. a
16. a (1987)
17. c (1987)
18. d
19. a
20. b
21. a (1978 Yankees)
22. d (1982)
23. c (1982)
24. b
25. c

Texas Rangers

1. b (1986)
2. d
3. f (1979–84)
4. a (1978)
5. c
6. e
7. b (32 in 1987)
8. a
9. c
10. a (.305)
11. d
12. d
13. True
14. False
15. True (1980 Royals and 1982 Cardinals)
16. Ferguson Jenkins (1974)
17. Gaylord Perry (1975)
18. Doyle Alexander (Yankees)
19. Bert Blyleven
20. Jim Bibby
21. Charlie Hough
22. Dock Ellis (Pirates, 1971; Yankees, 1976)
23. Greg Harris
24. Mitch Williams (1986)
25. Jim Bibby (1973)

Chapter Eighteen Answers

100. American League Records

1. b (1901 Athletics)
2. c (Tigers)
3. d (1985 Red Sox)
4. c (1929–33 Athletics–White Sox)
5. a (1933–37 Tigers)
6. a (Yankees)
7. d (1981 Rangers)
8. c (1985 Red Sox)
9. c (1926 Indians)
10. b (Senators–Twins–Royals)
11. b
12. a (1987 A's)
13. d (1932 Yankees)
14. d (1959 Indians)
15. b (1964 Athletics)
16. b (1922 Browns)
17. a
18. c
19. c (1946 Indians)
20. a (1937 Tigers)
21. d (1937 Yankees)
22. d (1941 White Sox)
23. c (1936 Yankees)
24. b (1938 Tigers)
25. b (1957 Red Sox)
26. a (Yankees)
27. c (1984 Tigers)
28. b (1932 Athletics)
29. b (1908 Tigers)
30. d (1936–37)
31. d (1968–69)
32. a (1950 Yankees)
33. d (1918–23)
34. c (1961)
35. a (1939)
36. c (1932 Senators)
37. a (1909)
38. c (1916)
39. a (1923 Red Sox)
40. b (1929–32 Athletics)
41. d (1904 White Sox)
42. b (1918 Senators)
43. c (1974 Royals)
44. c (A's–Yankees)
45. a (Tigers)
46. b (1955 Indians)
47. d (1978)
48. b (1938 Indians)
49. a (1965 Tigers)
50. a (1904 White Sox)

101. National League Records

1. c (1925 Cards)
2. c (1930 Phillies)
3. b (1929–33 Phillies)
4. b (1924, 1931 Cards)
5. a (1961 Cards)
6. d (Dodgers and Cubs)
7. a
8. b (Giants and Padres)
9. c (Reds and Pirates)
10. b (1987 Mets)
11. c (1958, 1965 Dodgers)
12. a (1954 Reds)
13. b (1953–61 Braves)
14. d (1949–50 Pirates)
15. c (1954–55 Reds)
16. c (Giants: August 1965)

17. c (1954)
18. a (1972)
19. a (1973)
20. c
21. b (Dodgers)
22. d (1922 Cards)
23. c (Phillies)
24. c (1954 Braves)
25. a (Pirates)
26. c
27. b (1953 Dodgers)
28. d (1943 Giants)
29. a (1950 Giants)
30. b (1976)
31. c
32. d
33. a (1968 Mets)

34. b (1938 Reds)
35. c (Pirates–Dodgers)
36. c (1914 Cards)
37. c (1903 Giants)
38. c (1951)
39. a
40. b
41. b (Cards-Phils-Pirates)
42. c (1938 Reds)
43. a
44. a (1958 Cards)
45. b (1979 Astros)
46. a (1980 Expos)
47. c (1954 Dodgers)
48. c (1971 Astros)
49. c
50. a

102. Major League Records

1. b (165 for the Dodgers in 1962)
2. c (.420 for the Browns in 1922)
3. d (.365 for the Yankees in 1957)
4. a (1939 Yankees)
5. d (1925 Athletics)
6. d (1975 Pirates)
7. a (1933 Senators)
8. b (Astros-Red Sox)
9. b (1953 Red Sox)
10. c (1950 Yankees)
11. b (1957 Red Sox)
12. a (1958–59 Phillies)
13. a (1931 Athletics)
14. c (1927 Pirates)
15. d (1948 Athletics)
16. d (1912 Pirates)
17. c
18. d
19. d (Athletics–Red Sox)
20. b (Braves)
21. a (1927–28 Yankees)
22. d (1942 Braves)
23. b (Indians–Red Sox)
24. c (1961 Yankees)

25. d (1973 Phillies)
26. c (1929 Phillies)
27. c (1954 Cards)
28. a (1968 Giants)
29. c (1976 Phillies)
30. a (1921)
31. b (1926)
32. d (1927 Pirates)
33. a (1922 Cubs)
34. c (1956 Senators)
35. a (1947)
36. d (Indians–Yankees)
37. a (1917 Indians)
38. b (Orioles)
39. b (Dodgers)
40. d
41. a (1985 Braves)
42. a (1974 Dodgers)
43. d (1904 Browns)
44. b (1908 White Sox)
45. d (A's, Padres, Brewers)
46. b (1945 Red Sox)
47. b (1941 Yankees)
48. d (1920 Braves)
49. b (1914 Pirates)
50. c (1978 Orioles)

Chapter Nineteen Answers

103. Clues to Cooperstown

I. From Barrow to Youngs

1. Carl Hubbell
2. Lou Gehrig
3. Babe Ruth
4. Johnny Evers
5. Mel Ott
6. Al Simmons
7. George Sisler
8. Bill Terry
9. Hank Greenberg
10. Robin Roberts
11. Jackie Robinson
12. Bob Feller
13. Eppa Rixey
14. Joe Cronin
15. Ray Schalk
16. Frank Baker
17. Bill Dickey
18. Rabbit Maranville
19. Dazzy Vance
20. Ted Lyons
21. Zack Wheat
22. Max Carey
23. Edd Roush
24. Sam Rice
25. Charlie Gehringer
26. Pie Traynor
27. Herb Pennock
28. Frankie Frisch
29. Jimmy Collins
30. Fred Clarke
31. John McGraw
32. Nap Lajoie
33. Ross Youngs
34. Red Faber
35. Goose Goslin
36. Monte Irvin
37. George Kelly
38. Satchel Paige
39. Lefty Gomez
40. Lou Boudreau
41. Chick Hafey
42. Dave Bancroft
43. Harry Hooper
44. Jesse Haines
45. Cool Papa Bell
46. Josh Gibson
47. Branch Rickey
48. Ed Barrow
49. Bob Lemon
50. Heinie Manush

From Aaron To Kell

1. Modercai "Three Finger" Brown
2. Lefty Grove
3. Ty Cobb
4. Roberto Clemente
5. Jimmie Foxx
6. Kiki Cuyler
7. Rick Ferrell
8. Frank Chance
9. Hank Aaron
10. Willie McCovey
11. Yogi Berra
12. Billy Herman
13. Grover Alexander
14. Addie Joss
15. Waite Hoyt

388

16. Whitey Ford
17. Chief Bender
18. Jack Chesbro
19. Stan Coveleski
20. Walter Johnson
21. Burleigh Grimes
22. Dizzy Dean (1934 Cards)
23. Don Drysdale
24. Jesse Burkett
25. Gabby Hartnett
26. Ed Delahanty
27. Roy Campanella
28. Luis Aparicio
29. Luke Appling (White Sox)
30. Eddie Collins
31. Sam Crawford

32. Earl Averill
33. Mickey Cochrane
34. Jim Bottomley
35. Ernie Banks
36. Earle Combs (1927)
37. Willie Keeler
38. Al Kaline
39. Elmer Flick
40. Rogers Hornsby
41. Joe DiMaggio
42. Hughie Jennings (Tigers)
43. George Kell
44. Travis Jackson (Giants)
45. Harry Heilmann
46. Ray Dandridge
47. Jim Hunter

From Killebrew to Wynn

1. Joe McGinnity
2. Sandy Koufax
3. Early Wynn
4. Rube Marquard
5. Juan Marichal
6. Rube Waddell
7. Christy Mathewson
8. Eddie Plank
9. Warren Spahn
10. Red Ruffing
11. Eddie Mathews
12. Chuck Klein
13. Johnny Mize (1939–40 Cards and 1948–49 Giants)
14. Pee Wee Reese
15. Joe Medwick
16. Mickey Mantle
17. Frank Robinson
18. Ralph Kiner
19. Paul Waner
20. Fred Lindstrom
21. Hack Wilson
22. Willie Mays
23. Duke Snider

24. Harmon Killebrew
25. Joe Sewell
26. Tris Speaker
27. Honus Wagner
28. Stan Musial
29. Lloyd Waner
30. Brooks Robinson
31. Ted Williams
32. Joe Tinker
33. Ed Walsh
34. Bobby Wallace
35. Bill McKechnie
36. Al Lopez
37. Walter Alston
38. Bucky Harris
39. Joe McCarthy
40. Connie Mack
41. Wilbert Robinson
42. Charles Comiskey
43. Casey Stengel
44. Clark Griffith
45. Miller Huggins (Yankees, 1921–23 and 1926–28)
46. Billy Williams

Chapter Twenty Answers

National League

Atlanta

1. Warren Spahn
2. Phil Niekro
3. Eddie Mathews
4. Hank Aaron

Chicago

1. Ernie Banks
2. Billy Williams

Cincinnati

1. Fred Hutchinson
2. Johnny Bench

Houston

1. Jim Umbricht
2. Don Wilson

Los Angeles

1. Pee Wee Reese
2. Duke Snider
3. Jim Gilliam
4. Walter Alston
5. Sandy Koufax
6. Roy Campanella
7. Jackie Robinson
8. Don Drysdale

New York

1. Gil Hodges
2. Casey Stengel

Philadelphia

1. Richie Ashburn
2. Robin Roberts

Pittsburgh

1. Billy Meyer
2. Ralph Kiner
3. Willie Stargell
4. Bill Mazeroski
5. Pie Traynor
6. Roberto Clemente
7. Honus Wagner
8. Danny Murtaugh

St. Louis

1. Stan Musial
2. Ken Boyer
3. Dizzy Dean
4. Lou Brock
5. Bob Gibson

San Francisco

1. Mel Ott
2. Carl Hubbell
3. Willie Mays
4. Juan Marichal
5. Willie McCovey

American League

Baltimore

1. Earl Weaver
2. Brooks Robinson
3. Frank Robinson

Boston

1. Joe Cronin
2. Ted Williams

California

1. Gene Autry

Chicago

1. Nellie Fox
2. Luke Appling
3. Minnie Minoso
4. Luis Aparicio

Cleveland

1. Earl Averill
2. Lou Boudreau
3. Bob Feller

Detroit

1. Charlie Gehringer
2. Hank Greenberg
3. Al Kaline

Milwaukee

1. Hank Aaron

Minnesota

1. Harmon Killebrew
2. Rod Carew

New York

1. Babe Ruth
2. Lou Gehrig
3. Joe DiMaggio
4. Mickey Mantle
5. Bill Dickey
6. Yogi Berra
7. Roger Maris
8. Thurman Munson
9. Whitey Ford
10. Elston Howard
11. Casey Stengel

About the Author

Dom Forker has written seven books, six of which are on baseball. The subjects include *Almost Everything You've Ever Wanted to Know about Baseball* and a series of quiz books. A former college pitcher and a coach at almost every level of amateur play, the author teaches English and creative writing at Delaware Valley Regional High School in Frenchtown, N.J. He is currently at work on a book about the 1949–53 Yankees and a book of poetry on the history of the World Series. He is married and has three sons: Tim, a Met fan; Geoff, a Phillie fan; and Ted, a Yankee fan.